Geoplanet

Geography for Junior Certificate

Liam Ashe · Kieran McCarthy

The Educational Company of Ireland

First published 2016
The Educational Company of Ireland
Ballymount Road
Walkinstown
Dublin 12
www.edco.ie

A member of the Smurfit Kappa Group plc
© Liam Ashe and Kieran McCarthy, 2016

All rights reserved. No part of this publication may be reproduced, stored in a retrieval system, or transmitted in any form or by any means, electronic, mechanical, photocopying, recording or otherwise, without either the prior permission of the Publisher or a licence permitting restricted copying in Ireland issued by the Irish Copyright Licensing Agency, 63 Patrick Street, Dún Laoghaire, Co Dublin.

ISBN: 978-1-84536-689-6

Editor: Simon Coury
Design: Identikit Design Consultants
Layout: Compuscript
Cover Design: Identikit Design Consultants, redrattledesign.com
Illustration: Compuscript, Dusan Pavlic, Q2A Media Services Pvt. Ltd.
Cover Photography: Alamy, Shutterstock

Ordnance Survey maps and aerial photographs
Ordnance Survey Ireland Permit No. 9055
© Ordnance Survey Ireland/Government of Ireland

The authors wish to acknowledge their debt to Simon Coury and to the staff of The Educational Company of Ireland.

While every care has been taken to trace and acknowledge copyright, the publishers tender their apologies for any accidental infringement where copyright has proved untraceable. They would be pleased to come to a suitable arrangement with the rightful owner in each case.

Web references in this book are intended as a guide only. At the time of going to press, all web addresses were active and contained information relevant to the topics in this book. However, The Educational Company of Ireland and the authors do not accept responsibility for the views or information contained on these websites. Content and addresses may change beyond our control and pupils should be supervised when investigating websites.

Foreword

Geoplanet is the successor to the very popular *New Geo*, and has been written by the same two highly experienced teachers and authors. It is designed to meet the needs of the Junior Certificate Geography syllabus at both Higher and Ordinary Levels.

Great care has been taken to ensure that the **language level** is appropriate to Junior Certificate Geography students. **Bullet points** and **bold typeface** are used to highlight key terms and ideas.

Geoplanet is lavishly illustrated with **maps**, **graphs**, **diagrams** and up-to-date **tables**. Particular attention has been paid to the choice of **photographs** to advance pupils' understanding of the syllabus. A range of **cartoons**, many of them original, is also included.

All information and examples are up to date at the time of going to press. The text includes several **case studies** that take account of recent developments in the world of Geography. There is a comprehensive range of the new **Ordnance Survey Ireland (OSI) maps** and the new legend, along with complementary **aerial photographs**.

- Each chapter begins with brief **learning outcomes** for that chapter. **Keywords** are listed at the beginning of each section. The text also includes **Geo fact**, **Link** and **Definition** boxes throughout.

- **Activity** boxes are used to prompt questions throughout the book. Four icons indicate the different activities involved.

Discussion **Thinking** **Skills** **Research**

- **Revision questions** are contained at the end of each section. Each chapter ends with a **summary chart**. The textbook also includes a broad range of questions from recent Junior Certificate **examination papers**.

- *Geoplanet* is presented as a package of a textbook and a free workbook. Teachers who use the textbook will be provided with a free Teacher's Resource Book and digital resources (see page iv).

Digital resources

The *Geoplanet* digital resources will enhance classroom learning by encouraging student participation and engagement. The resources are integrated with the student textbook and will complement the material contained in the Teacher's Resource Book.

To provide guidance for the integration of digital resources in the classroom, animations, videos and PowerPoints are referenced in the student textbook using the following icons:

Animations bring key diagrams from the textbook to life and reinforce the topic at hand.

A series of stimulating videos, covering a variety of different topics, allows students to observe Geography in action.

PowerPoint presentations provide a summary of every chapter of the student textbook, highlighting key themes and topics.

Teachers can access the animations, videos and PowerPoints, as well as useful template documents and weblinks, online at **www.edcodigital.ie**.

Contents

Section 1 Physical Geography

Chapter 1 Our Restless Earth — 2

- 1.1 The structure of the Earth — 2
- 1.2 Plate tectonics — 3
- 1.3 Fold mountains — 7
- 1.4 Volcanic activity — 9
  - **Case study** · Iceland: a volcanic island — 10
  - **Case study** · Mount St Helens — 12
- 1.5 Earthquakes — 13
  - **Case study** · Nepal earthquake (2015) — 14
  - **Case study** · Tsunami in Japan (2011) — 16

Chapter 2 Rocks — 19

- 2.1 What is rock? — 19
- 2.2 Igneous rocks — 20
- 2.3 Sedimentary rocks — 22
- 2.4 Metamorphic rocks — 23
- 2.5 Common rocks in Ireland — 25
- 2.6 Resources from the Earth — 25
  - **Case study** · Quarrying — 26
  - **Case study** · Natural gas production in Ireland — 27

Chapter 3 Weathering and Mass Movement — 30

- 3.1 Denudation: an introduction — 30
- 3.2 Mechanical weathering — 31
- 3.3 Chemical weathering — 32
  - **Case study** · The Burren National Park — 36
- 3.4 Mass movement — 37
  - **Case study** · Lahar: the volcano of Nevado del Ruiz — 40

v

Contents

Chapter 4 Agents of Erosion — 44

- 4.1 Rivers: shapers of our land — 45
- 4.2 River landforms — 47
- 4.3 Rivers and people — 53
  - **Case study** · The River Shannon — 54
- 4.4 Sea: the destroyer — 57
- 4.5 Sea: the builder — 60
- 4.6 People and the sea — 64
  - **Case study** · Rosslare — 65
- 4.7 Glaciation: the work of erosion — 67
- 4.8 Glaciation: the work of deposition — 71
- 4.9 Glaciation and people — 74
  - **Case study** · Wicklow: the effects of glaciation — 74

Chapter 5 The Restless Atmosphere — 78

- 5.1 The atmosphere — 78
- 5.2 The heat machine — 79
- 5.3 Wind: the atmosphere on the move — 82
- 5.4 Ocean currents — 85
  - **Case study** · Currents of the North Atlantic — 86
- 5.5 Air masses and weather systems — 88
- 5.6 Water in the atmosphere — 93
- 5.7 Weather — 97
- 5.8 The greenhouse effect and global warming — 104

Chapter 6 Climates and Natural Regions — 111

- 6.1 Introducing climate — 111
- 6.2 Natural regions and world climates — 115
- 6.3 Hot climates of the world — 116
- 6.4 Temperate climates of the world — 121
  - **Case study** · Ireland and its cool temperate oceanic climate — 122
- 6.5 Cold climates of the world — 126

Chapter 7 Soils — 133

- 7.1 What is soil? — 133
- 7.2 Soils of Ireland — 138
- 7.3 A world soil: tropical red soil — 140
- 7.4 Natural vegetation and soil — 141

Section 2 Maps and Photographs

Chapter 8 Maps and Photographs — 146

- **8.1** Ordnance Survey maps — 146
- **8.2** Reading the physical landscape — 162
- **8.3** Reading the human landscape — 163
  - **Case study** · Location of Ballina — 169
  - **Case study** · Urban functions of Drogheda — 171
- **8.4** Aerial photographs — 181
- **8.5** Rural settlement and land use — 186
- **8.6** Urban settlement and land use — 187
- **8.7** Comparing maps and photographs — 196
- **Maps**
  - Ireland — 212
  - Europe — 214
  - World — 216

Section 3 Social Geography

Chapter 9 Population: Distribution, Diversity and Change — 222

- **9.1** Population growth — 222
- **9.2** Factors that affect the rate of population change — 225
- **9.3** Future rates of population increase — 230
- **9.4** Population pyramids — 232
- **9.5** Variations in population distribution and density — 234
- **9.6** Low population densities — 243
- **9.7** High population densities — 247
- **9.8** Global patterns: the North/South divide — 251
- **9.9** People on the move — 255
  - **Case studies** · Nicola and Stanislaw — 259
  - **Case study** · 1 The plantation of Ulster — 260
  - **Case study** · 2 European colonisation of South America — 261

Contents

Chapter 10 Settlement — 266

10.1	Early settlers in Ireland	266
10.2	Nucleated settlements	270
10.3	Resources, terrain and the distribution of settlements	274
10.4	Settlement in the new polders of the Netherlands	277
10.5	Functions of nucleated settlements	279
	Case study · Settlement in an Irish river basin: the Shannon basin	281
	Case study · Limerick City: a multi-functional urban centre	282
	Case study · Köln (Cologne)	285
10.6	Change in the function of settlements	286
	Case study · 1 Trim: change in function over time	287
	Case study · 2 Navan: where mining has become important	288
	Case study · 3 Leixlip becomes a manufacturing centre	290
10.7	Communication links	291
	Case study · The Irish road network	292
	Case study · EU airports	294
	Case study · Transport on the River Rhine	297

Chapter 11 Urbanisation — 301

11.1	Changing patterns in where we live: cities	301
11.2	Cities: functional zones	304
	Case study · Paris	306
11.3	Land values and land use in cities	308
11.4	Residential accommodation in Irish cities	310
11.5	Commuting to work in cities	312
11.6	Urban problems	315
11.7	Urban improvements	318
	Case study · Urban renewal: Killarney Court, Killarney St, Dublin	319
	Case study · Urban redevelopment: Grand Canal Dock	320
	Case study · New towns: Tallaght	321
11.8	Urbanisation in the developing world	323
	Case study · Kolkata: a city of contrasts	324
	Case study · São Paulo	326

Section 4 Economic Geography

Chapter 12 Primary Economic Activities — 332

- 12.1 The Earth as a resource — 332
- 12.2 Water as a resource — 335
  - **Case study** · Water supply for the Dublin region — 336
  - **Case study** · Irrigation in the Nile valley, Egypt — 338
  - **Case study** · Irrigation in the south of France — 340
- 12.3 Oil: a finite resource — 341
  - **Case study** · Saudia Arabia: an oil-producing country — 342
  - **Case study** · The search for oil in Irish waters — 344
- 12.4 The exploitation of Ireland's peatlands — 346
- 12.5 Fishing — 349
- 12.6 Farming — 353
  - **Case study** · A mixed farm — 354

Chapter 13 Secondary Economic Activities — 359

- 13.1 Turning resources into products — 359
  - **Case study** · 1 Nutricia Infant Nutrition Ltd — 360
  - **Case study** · 2 Intel Ireland — 361
- 13.2 Factory location — 362
  - **Case study** · Intel Ireland, Leixlip – a light industry — 363
  - **Case study** · RUSAL Aughinish – a heavy industry — 366
- 13.3 Footloose industry — 369
- 13.4 Industrial location: change over time — 371
- 13.5 The role of women in industry — 374
- 13.6 Manufacturing on a world scale — 378
- 13.7 The impact of industrial activity on the environment — 380
- 13.8 Conflicts of interest — 383
  - **Case study** · 1 The wind turbine controversy in Ireland — 383
  - **Case study** · 2 Incineration in Poolbeg, Dublin Bay — 384

Chapter 14 Tertiary Economic Activities　　387

14.1	Services	387
14.2	Tourism	389
14.3	Tourism in Europe	393
	Case study · Tourism in Spain	394
14.4	Tourism and transport links	397
14.5	The impact of tourism	399

Chapter 15 Economic Inequality　　404

15.1	The Earth's resources: who benefits?	404
15.2	Exploitation of poor countries by wealthy countries	407
	Case study · The story of coffee	410
15.3	Aid to the South	412
	Case study · Emergency aid: the Ebola outbreak in West Africa	417
15.4	Factors that hinder economic development	418
	Case study · South Sudan	418
15.5	Economic inequalities within the EU	420
	Case study · Economic inequalities in Italy	422
15.6	Ending economic inequality	424

Glossary	429
Index	433
Acknowledgements	438

Section 1
Physical Geography

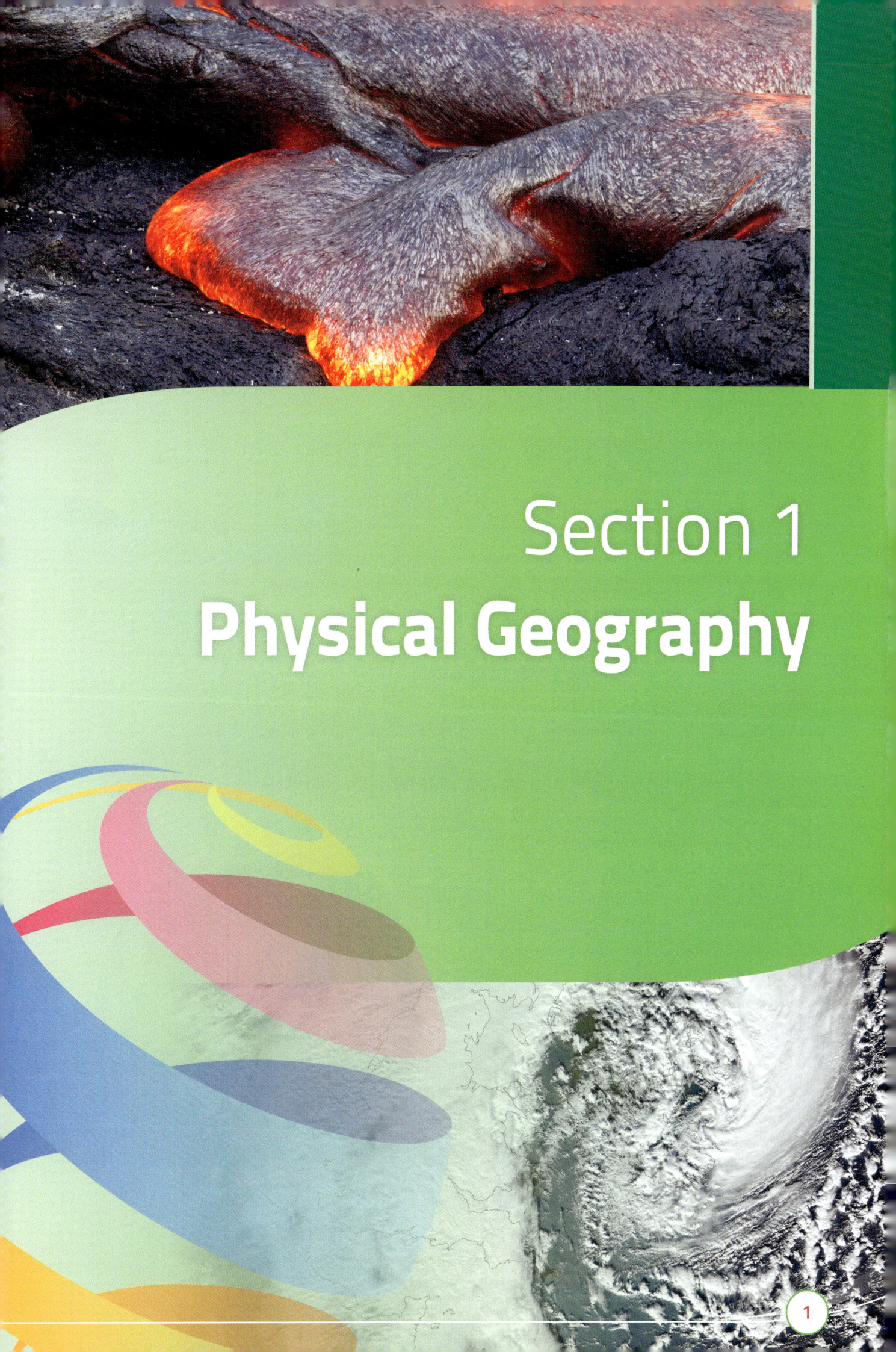

Chapter 1
Our Restless Earth

Learning outcomes

By the end of this chapter, you should be able to understand:

- The structure of the Earth
- That the Earth's crust is made up of a number of moving plates
- What happens at plate boundaries when these plates move (volcanoes, earthquakes, fold mountains)
- How people are affected by these events.

1.1 The structure of the Earth

KEYWORDS

- crust
- mantle
- core
- magma

The Earth is one of the eight planets of our solar system. It is the third planet from the sun.

The Earth was formed about **4.5 billion years** ago.

At first it was a giant, boiling sea of molten (melted) material. As it began to cool, the heavier material sank, while the lighter material floated to the surface. As a result, the Earth is made up of **three different layers**. These layers are:

- The **crust** – the layer that we live on
- The **mantle**
- The **core** (outer and inner).

The Earth is a sphere. It is shaped like a ball

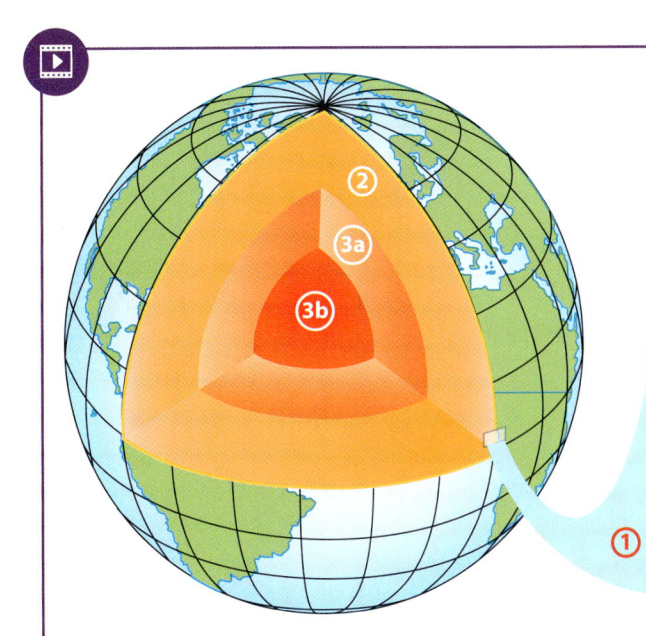

Chapter 1 · Our Restless Earth

1 The crust

The **crust** is the Earth's outer skin. It is made up of solid rock. It can be up to 60 km (kilometres) thick beneath the continents, but as thin as 10 km under the oceans.

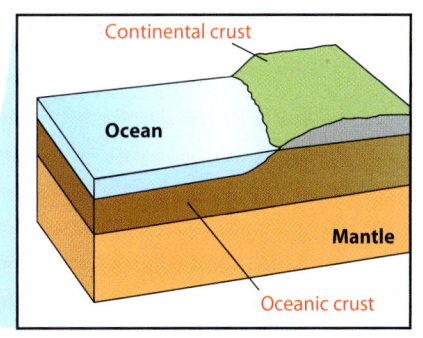

2 The mantle

Beneath the crust is a layer of hot, soft rock called the **mantle**. The temperature in the mantle is about 4,000°C. As a result, the rock is in a molten or semi-molten state and is called **magma**. The crust floats on top of the magma.

3 The core

The **core** is at the centre of the Earth. It is made of nickel and iron. At over 5,000°C, it is the hottest layer of the Earth. The outer core (3a) is molten, while the inner core (3b) is under so much pressure that it is solid.

Figure 1.1 The structure of the Earth

Questions

1. With the aid of a labelled diagram, show and name the **four** layers of the Earth.
2. (a) Name the **two** types of crust.
   (b) Describe **one** way in which they are different.
3. What is molten magma?

Definition

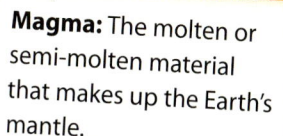

Magma: The molten or semi-molten material that makes up the Earth's mantle.

Activity

How can the layers of a peach be compared to those of the Earth? **Discuss** in class.

1.2 Plate tectonics

KEYWORDS

- plates
- plate tectonics
- convection currents
- transform boundary
- destructive boundary
- constructive boundary
- continental drift
- Pangaea

The crust of the Earth is broken up into different sections, called **plates**. There are seven large plates and several smaller ones.

The plates float on the semi-molten magma of the mantle. They fit together like a jigsaw and meet at **plate boundaries**. These plates are constantly moving.

The theory that attempts to explain the movements of the plates and the features that result is called **plate tectonics**. The plates are known as **tectonic plates**.

3

Section 1 · Physical Geography

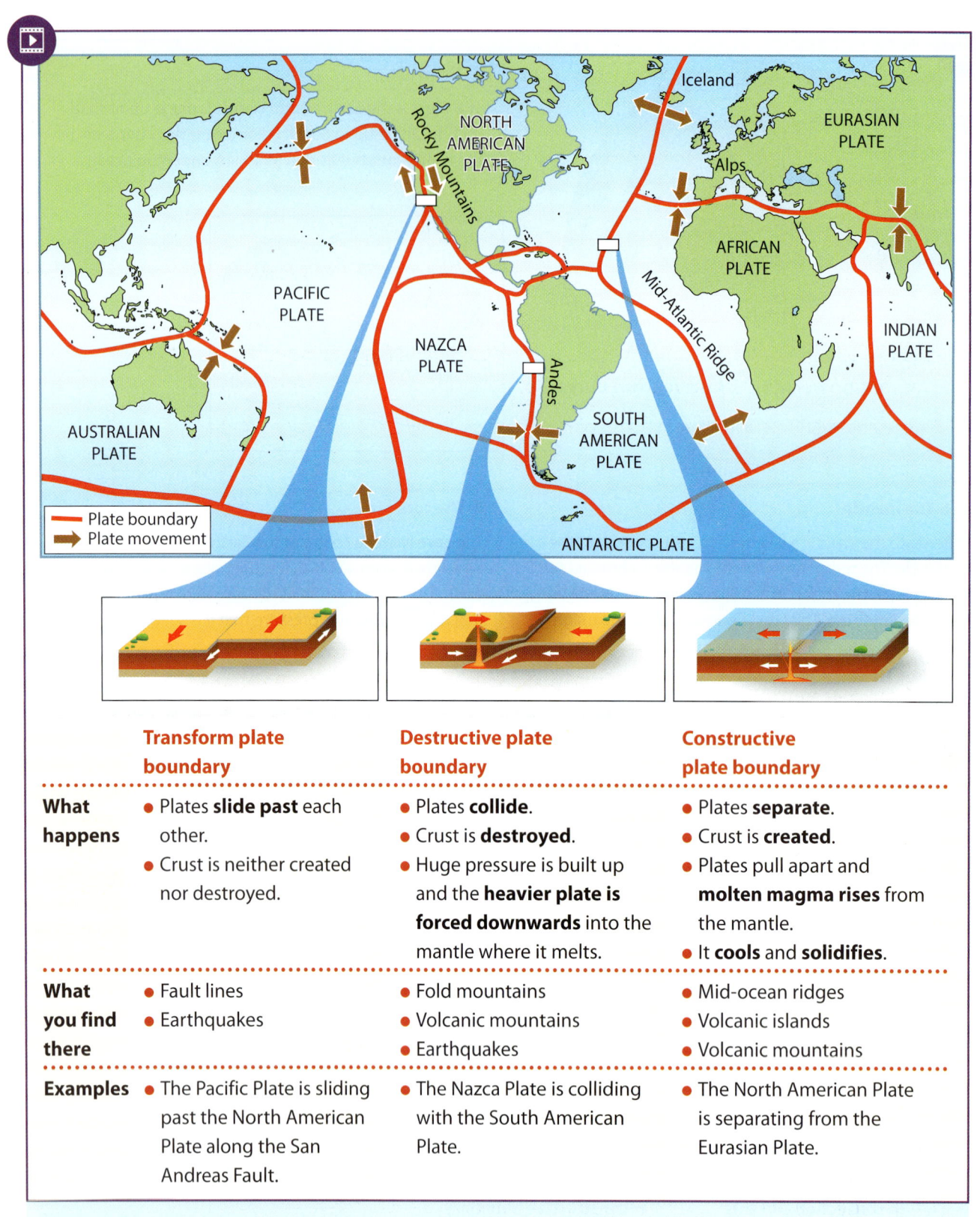

	Transform plate boundary	Destructive plate boundary	Constructive plate boundary
What happens	• Plates **slide past** each other. • Crust is neither created nor destroyed.	• Plates **collide**. • Crust is **destroyed**. • Huge pressure is built up and the **heavier plate is forced downwards** into the mantle where it melts.	• Plates **separate**. • Crust is **created**. • Plates pull apart and **molten magma rises** from the mantle. • It **cools** and **solidifies**.
What you find there	• Fault lines • Earthquakes	• Fold mountains • Volcanic mountains • Earthquakes	• Mid-ocean ridges • Volcanic islands • Volcanic mountains
Examples	• The Pacific Plate is sliding past the North American Plate along the San Andreas Fault.	• The Nazca Plate is colliding with the South American Plate.	• The North American Plate is separating from the Eurasian Plate.

Figure 1.2 The major plates of the Earth's crust and the three types of plate boundary

Activity

Examine Figure 1.2 and:

1 Suggest one reason why Ireland is unlikely to be a location for volcanoes and large earthquakes.

2 Name the plates on which Ireland, the USA and South Africa lie.

Geo fact

North America and Europe are drifting further apart at a rate of about 2 cm per year.

What happens at plate boundaries?

For most of the time, the plates are locked together and can't move. When they do move, an enormous amount of energy is let loose. As a result, a lot of activity takes place at plate boundaries. This includes:

- Mountain-building activity
- Volcanic activity
- Earthquake activity.

Link
You will deal with these topics in sections 1.3 to 1.5.

Why do plates move?

The plates float on the semi-molten magma in the mantle. The magma moves with a circular motion because of **convection currents**.

These convection currents cause the plates to move in different directions and at different speeds.

How do convection currents work?

- The very hot **core heats the magma** in the mantle.
- The magma nearest the core gets hotter first. It **expands**, gets **lighter** and **rises** towards the top of the mantle.
- As it rises it **cools**, because it is moving away from the heat source. It becomes **semi-molten**.

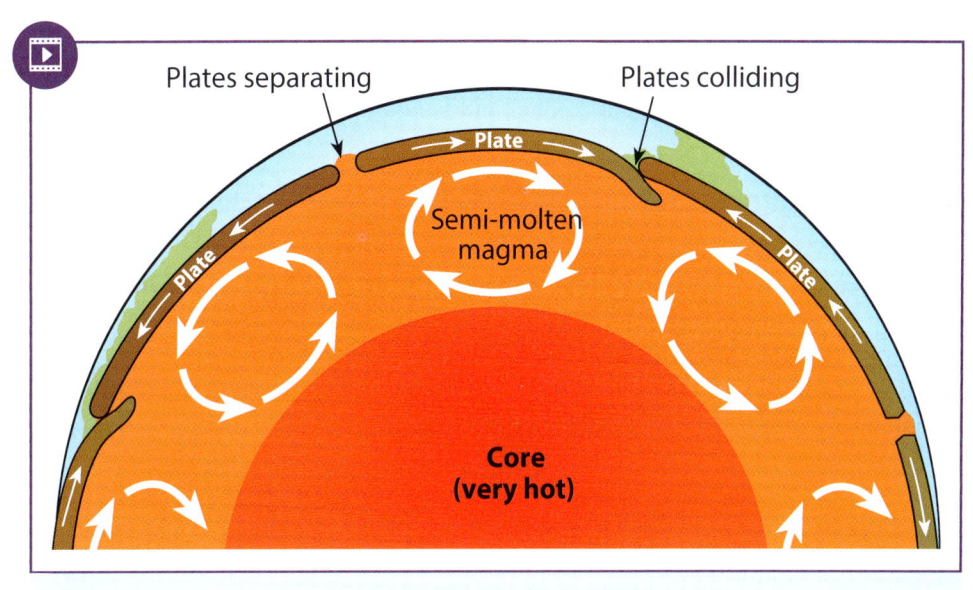

Figure 1.3 Convection currents in the mantle cause the plates of the crust to move

- The magma rises to the top of the mantle and **moves left or right** as it hits the bottom of the crust.
- The **friction** between the crust and the moving magma drags the plates with it.
- As the magma continues to **cool** it becomes more solid and **heavier**. It begins to **sink** back towards the core.
- When it reaches the core it **reheats** and the cycle starts all over again.

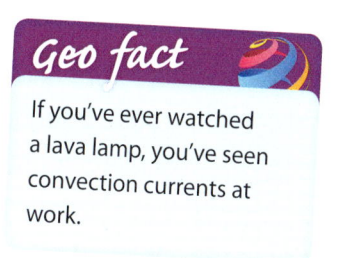

Geo fact
If you've ever watched a lava lamp, you've seen convection currents at work.

5

Section 1 · Physical Geography

Continental drift

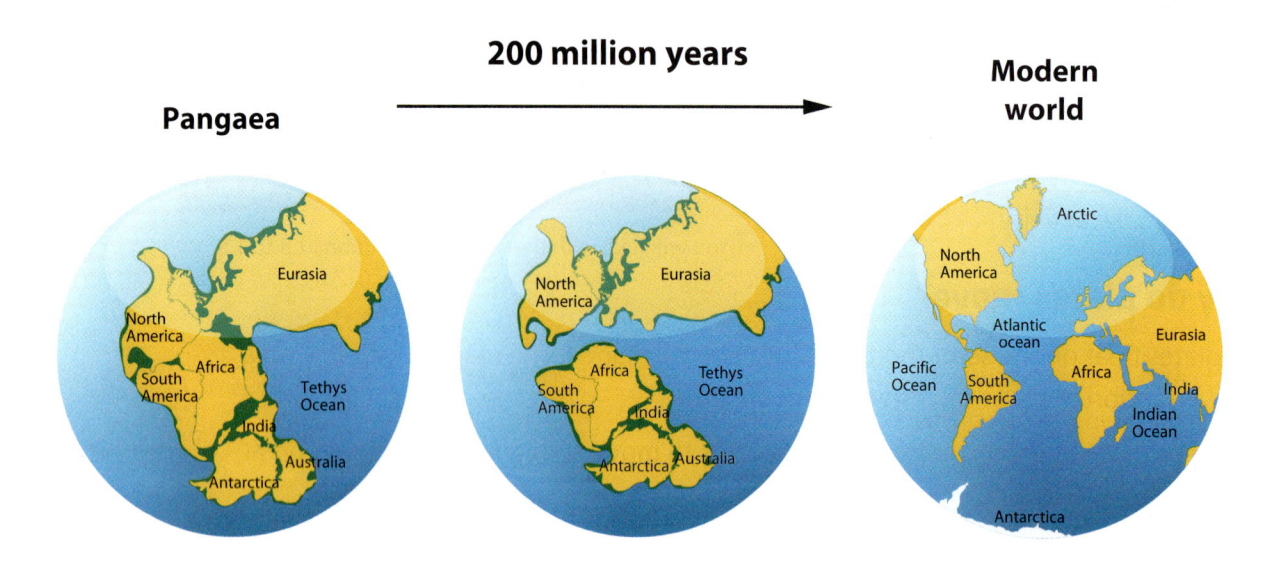

Figure 1.4 The continents as they might have looked about 200 million years ago, before continental drift (left); during the early stages of continental drift (centre); and a present-day map of the continents (right)

The Earth's **continents are passengers on the plates** that float beneath them. As the plates move, they carry the continents with them. This movement is very slow and it has taken millions of years for the continents to reach where they are today.

The continents began as one large landmass, called **Pangaea**. It gradually began to break up. The individual sections started to drift apart, carried along on the moving plates. This process is known as **continental drift**.

Continental drift continues today. For example, Europe is slowly moving away from North America, while India continues to push northwards into Asia.

> **Activity**
>
> **Examine** Figures 1.2 and 1.4. With the aid of an atlas, **identify** the Mediterranean Sea.
>
> What, in your opinion, will happen to the Mediterranean Sea over the next 50 million years?

Questions

1. Examine Figure 1.2 on page 4.
   (a) On which tectonic plate does Ireland lie?
   (b) Name **two** plates that are in collision.
   (c) Name **two** plates that are pulling apart.

2. With the aid of a labelled diagram, explain how the plates move.

3. List an activity that might take place at each of the following:
   (a) A destructive plate boundary
   (b) A constructive plate boundary
   (c) A transform plate boundary.

4. Briefly describe what happens during continental drift.

Chapter 1 · Our Restless Earth

1.3 Fold mountains

KEYWORDS

- fold mountains
- anticline
- syncline
- Alpine folding
- Armorican folding

Fold mountains are found along destructive plate boundaries.

When two plates move towards each other and collide, the pressure forces the rocks to buckle and crumple upwards into a series of folds. This happens in the same way as a tablecloth wrinkles as it is pushed across a table.

The upfolds are called **anticlines** while the downfolds are called **synclines**.

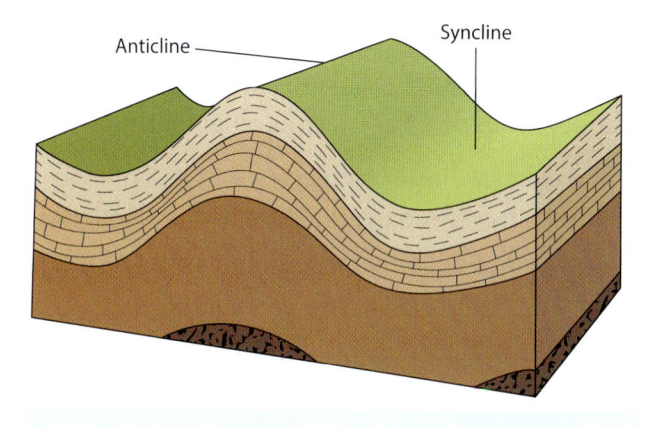

Figure 1.5 Fold mountains

Definition ✓

Fold mountains: Mountains formed when rocks buckled and folded as two plates collided.

How the Andes mountains were formed

- The heavier **Nazca Plate** and the lighter **South American Plate** collide.
- The Nazca Plate is **pushed down** into the mantle.
- The rocks that lie on the plates are compressed and **forced upwards**.
- The layers of rock buckle and crack into a series of **upfolds and downfolds**.

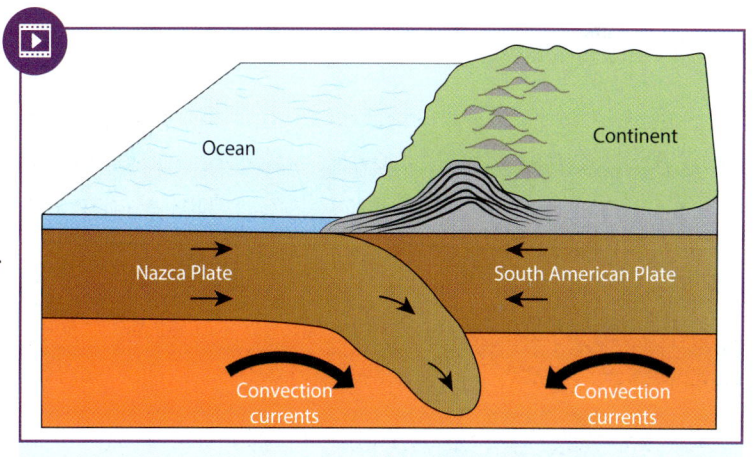

Figure 1.6 The Andes were formed when two plates collided

Activity

Fossils of sea creatures have been found thousands of metres up in the Andes. **Discuss** how this might have happened.

Definition ✓

A **fault** is a crack or fracture in the crust where the rocks on either side have moved past each other.

Folding has buckled the rocks to form anticlines and synclines. Note the **faults** that run up through the photograph

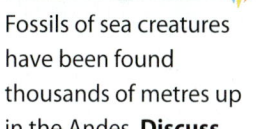

7

Section 1 · Physical Geography

Periods of folding

Alpine folding happened only about 30 to 35 million years ago. The mountains that were formed include:

- The Andes in South America
- The Rockies in America
- The Himalayas in Asia.

These mountains are very high and steep, as they have not yet been worn down as much as older fold mountains.

Armorican folding took place about 250 million years ago when the Eurasian and African plates collided. While these mountains were once as high as the Alps, they have been severely worn down over the years.

Most of **Ireland's fold mountains** were formed during this period. They include:

- MacGillycuddy's Reeks
- The Galtees
- The Comeraghs
- The Knockmealdowns.

The young folds of the Alps are still very high

The Galtees have been worn down by weathering and erosion over millions of years

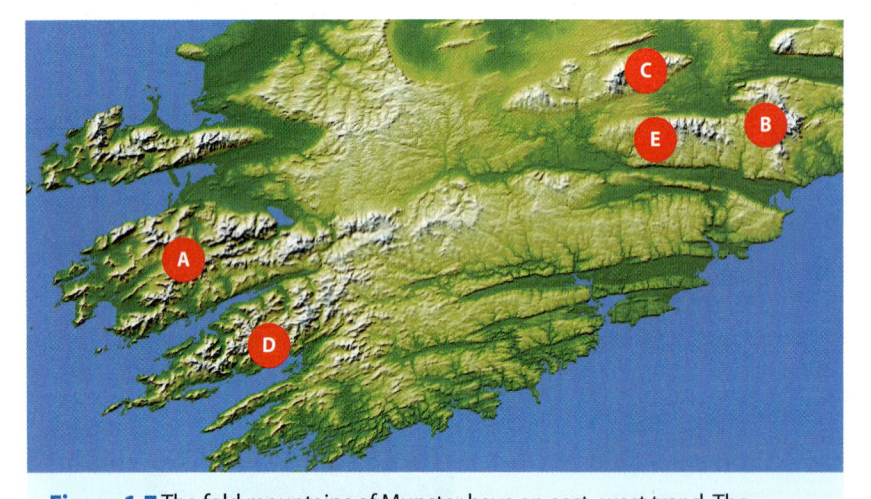

Figure 1.7 The fold mountains of Munster have an east–west trend. The pressure that folded them came from the African Plate as it pushed northwards

Activity

With the aid of an atlas, **identify** the mountain ranges:

A: Ma.........................
B: Co.........................
C: Ga.........................
D: Ca.........................
E: Kn.........................

Questions

1. Draw a simple, labelled sketch of a fold mountain. On it show and name: (i) an anticline, (ii) a syncline and (iii) a fold.

2. Examine the photograph at the bottom of page 7. What evidence does it show that folding has taken place?

3. (a) In what period of folding were the mountains of Munster formed?
   (b) Name the **two** plates that collided to form these mountains.
   (c) Name **three** fold mountain ranges found in Munster.

Chapter 1 · Our Restless Earth

1.4 Volcanic activity

KEYWORDS

- mid-ocean ridge
- geothermal energy
- volcanic cone
- Pacific Ring of Fire
- eruption
- vent
- pipe
- crater
- lava
- lava flow
- mudflow

Most volcanic activity takes place along the margins or boundaries of plates. Volcanic activity can result in:

- Mid-ocean ridges and islands
- Volcanic cones.

Mid-ocean ridge

A mid-ocean ridge is an **underwater mountain range**. It is formed where two plates separate.

As the plates move apart, molten magma rises from the mantle and fills the gap between the plates. When the magma meets the cold sea water, it cools and becomes solid to form a new ocean floor. As the eruptions of magma continue in an endless cycle, the ocean floor is built up to form a long ridge of mountains.

The **Mid-Atlantic Ridge** runs north to south for the full 16,000 km length of the Atlantic Ocean. It is so high in places that it is exposed above sea level. One such place is **Iceland**.

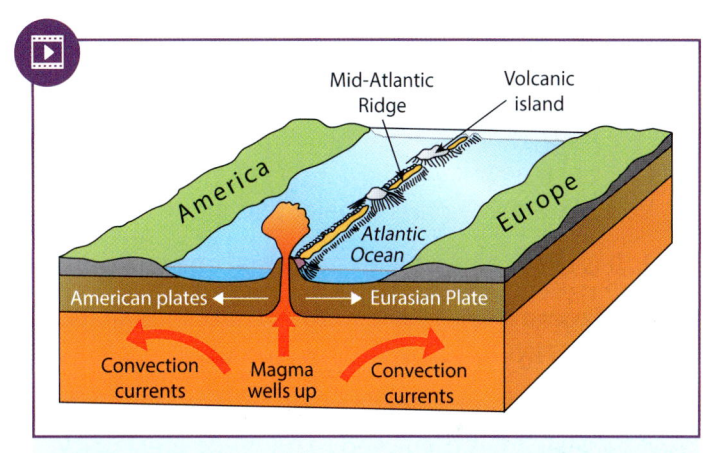

Figure 1.8 The Mid-Atlantic Ridge runs north–south on the floor of the Atlantic Ocean. It breaks the surface in places to form islands such as Iceland

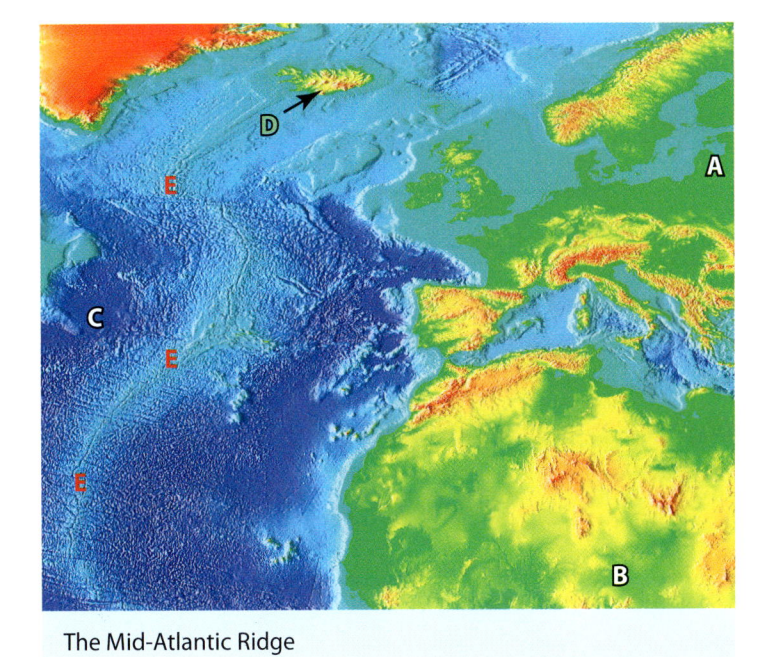

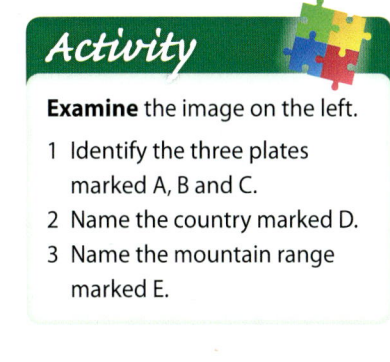

The Mid-Atlantic Ridge

Activity

Examine the image on the left.

1. Identify the three plates marked A, B and C.
2. Name the country marked D.
3. Name the mountain range marked E.

Section 1 · Physical Geography

Case study

Iceland: a volcanic island

Iceland is one of the few places where the Mid-Atlantic Ridge is exposed above the ocean. It is only about 20 million years old, making it the youngest country on Earth.

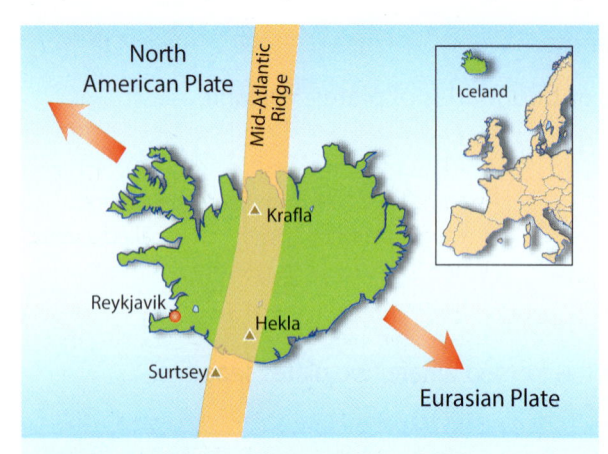

Figure 1.9 Iceland is a volcanic island where the Mid-Atlantic Ridge rises above the surface of the ocean

Fissure (crack) running through Iceland where the North American and Eurasian plates are pulling apart

Volcanic activity plays a major part in the economy of Iceland:

1 It is used to provide **geothermal energy**.

- **Magma** comes close to the surface and heats underground water to temperatures over 400°C.
- When the water reaches the surface, it turns to **steam**.
- The steam is then used to generate **electricity**.

Definition

Geothermal energy: Hot water or steam from deep beneath the Earth's surface is converted into electricity.

Geothermal energy provides up to 20 per cent of Iceland's electricity needs. It is used to:

- Heat homes and offices
- **Heat greenhouses**, enabling farmers to grow flowers and vegetables all year round
- Provide power for factories
- Help keep the pavements free of ice in winter.

2 It is an attraction for **tourism**.

- Tourists come to see Iceland's **volcanic landscape**.
- Tours by helicopter and coach are organised to visit active volcanoes.
- Some of the underground water comes to the surface as **hot springs** and **geysers** (fountains of hot water and steam).
- These are said to have healing powers due to the minerals in the water.
- Many tourists visit spas such as the **Blue Lagoon**.

Chapter 1 · Our Restless Earth

Volcanic mountains

Volcanic mountains are formed when molten magma emerges or **erupts** through a hole in the crust called a **vent**. They are generally found where plates are pulled apart or are in collision. Because the magma is under great pressure in the mantle, many eruptions are violent.

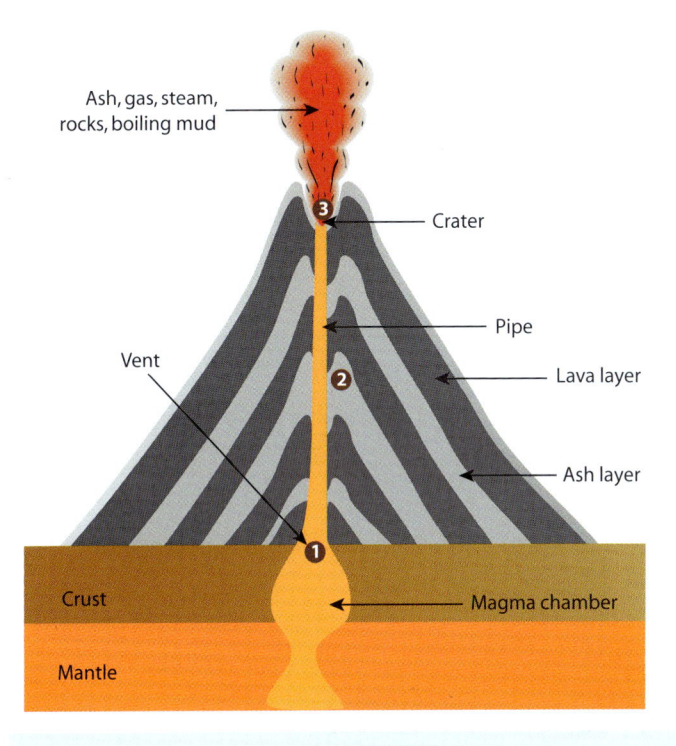

Geo fact

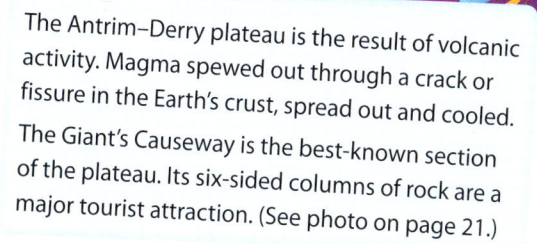

The Antrim–Derry plateau is the result of volcanic activity. Magma spewed out through a crack or fissure in the Earth's crust, spread out and cooled. The Giant's Causeway is the best-known section of the plateau. Its six-sided columns of rock are a major tourist attraction. (See photo on page 21.)

1 Magma finds its way towards the surface through an opening in the crust called a **vent**. When the magma reaches the surface, it is known as **lava**. Layers of lava build up around the vent, where it cools and hardens.

2 As the cone-shaped mountain builds up, the lava continues to make its way upwards through a **pipe**. Sometimes layers of **ash** also help to build the cone.

3 The lava continues to spill out of the volcano through an opening called a **crater**. Other materials, such as mud, gas, steam, rocks and boiling mud, can escape during an eruption.

Figure 1.10 The formation of a cone-shaped volcanic mountain

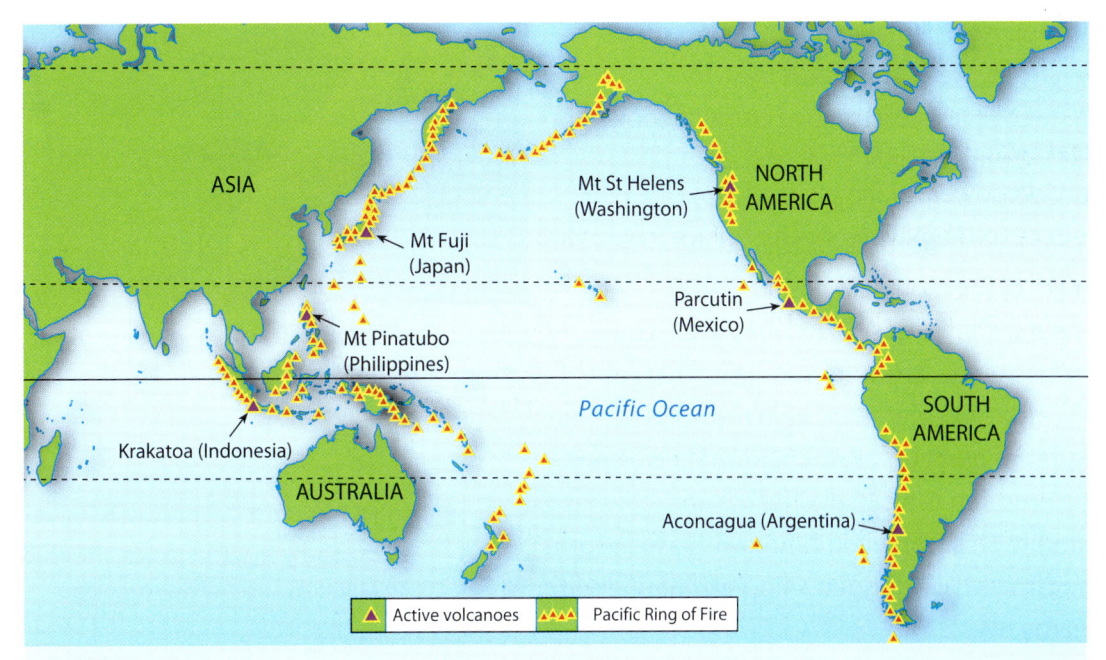

Figure 1.11 More than half of the world's active volcanoes are found along the **Pacific Ring of Fire**. This is a zone that encircles the Pacific Ocean, where many of Earth's plates are in collision

11

Section 1 · Physical Geography

Life cycle of a volcano

Volcanoes do not erupt forever. Some stopped erupting a long time ago. Volcanoes can be classed as:

- **Active**: The volcano is still erupting at regular intervals, e.g. Mount Etna, Mount Vesuvius and Mount St Helens.
- **Dormant**: The volcano has been quiet for hundreds of years but may erupt again. Mount St Helens had not erupted for over 120 years when it became active again in 1980.
- **Extinct**: The volcano has not erupted in recorded times (thousands of years). Slemish Mountain in Co. Antrim is an extinct volcano.

Geo fact
Stromboli, off Italy's Mediterranean coast, is a volcano that erupts so frequently that sailors have named it the Lighthouse of the Mediterranean.

Case study

Mount St Helens

Mount St Helens is a mountain peak in the Rocky Mountains, in the USA. It was formed by a series of volcanic eruptions over thousands of years. By 1980, it had been **dormant** for so long that people living in the region thought it would never erupt again.

- A series of earthquakes early in 1980 indicated that the mountain was beginning to rumble again. Soon **steam** and small **lava flows** began to appear from the crater. One side of the mountain began to bulge as **pressure** built up. It swelled outwards by over 100 metres before a massive eruption took place. Clouds of steam, gas and ash escaped in a huge volcanic explosion. The force of the eruption reduced the height of the mountain by 400 metres. A **new crater**, almost 3 km wide, was created.
- **Forests were stripped** from hills. Trees of two metres in diameter were mown down like blades of grass up to 25 km from the volcano.
- The eruption **melted glacial ice** and snow at the summit. This water combined with ash to form **mudflows** that clogged shipping channels in nearby rivers.
- The force of the blast and **poisonous gas** killed 57 people. Some were geologists, but the majority were so-called 'disaster tourists'.
- Almost **7,000 large animals** were **killed** in the blast.

A snow-capped Mount St Helens before the eruption. Note that it is surrounded by forest

Mount St Helens shortly after the eruption. Note the absence of forest, and the scars left by the mudflows

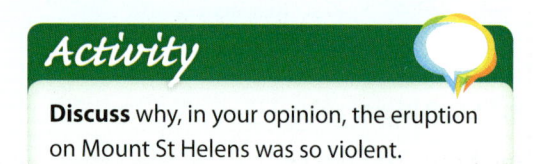

Activity
Discuss why, in your opinion, the eruption on Mount St Helens was so violent.

Questions

1. Describe, with the aid of a diagram, how a mid-ocean ridge is formed.
2. Describe how a volcanic mountain (cone) is formed.
3. Write a newspaper article (about 200 words) describing the Mount St Helens eruption.
4. Describe **two** positive effects (results) and **two** negative effects of volcanic activity.

1.5 Earthquakes

KEYWORDS
- plate boundary
- fault line
- focus
- tremors
- epicentre
- aftershocks
- seismometer
- Richter scale
- tsunami

An **earthquake** is a sudden movement or trembling of the Earth's crust. This movement takes the form of a series of shocks or **tremors**.

Earthquakes occur at **plate boundaries**, where plates collide or slide past one another. Pressure builds up until one of the plates slips. This eases the pressure and a huge amount of **energy is suddenly released**. The earthquake has occurred.

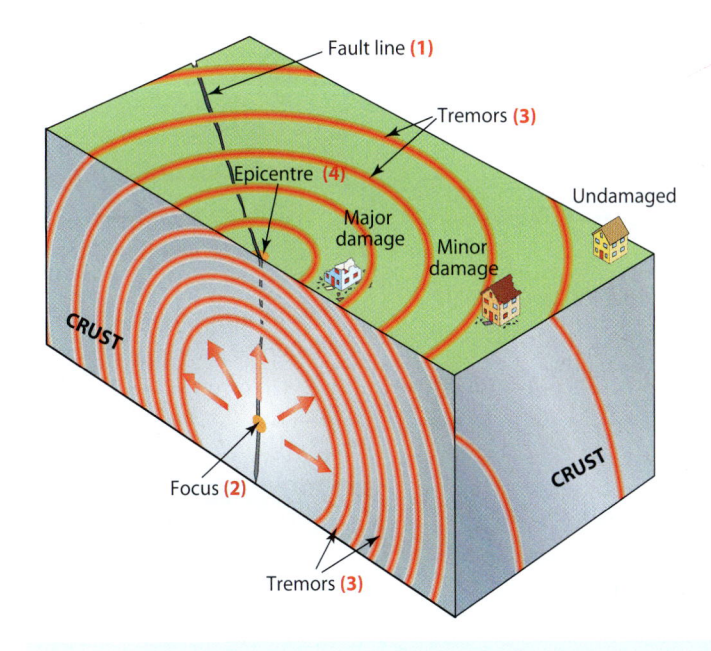

1. Plates suddenly move along the **fault line**.
2. The **focus** is the point deep underground where the earthquake occurs.
3. Shock waves or **tremors** begin to spread out from the focus, causing the Earth's surface to shake (or *quake*) for a period. Most tremors last from a few seconds up to a minute.
4. The tremors are usually strongest at the **epicentre**, the area on the surface directly above the focus.

Figure 1.12 The pattern of an earthquake

Aftershocks

Earthquakes rarely last for longer than one minute. Smaller tremors, called **aftershocks**, may occur in the hours or days after an earthquake. They often cause more damage than the original earthquake because buildings and structures have been weakened by the first tremors.

Activity

Discuss why aftershocks are as dangerous as the original tremors.

Section 1 · Physical Geography

Case study

Nepal earthquake (2015)

A very strong earthquake hit Nepal in April 2015. The epicentre was high in the Himalaya Mountains. The effects of the earthquake were felt up to 1,000 km away in China and India.

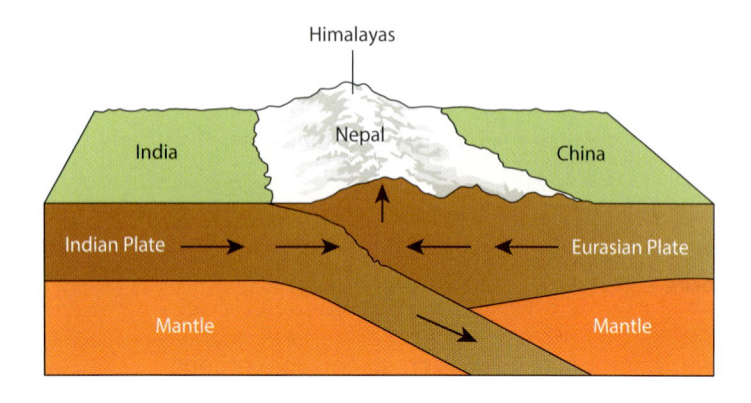

Nepal lies on the edge of the boundary between the **Indian Plate** and the **Eurasian Plate**. The Indian Plate is moving northwards at a speed of about 4 cm per year. This collision caused the solid rock on the surface of both plates to buckle and eventually built up to form the **Himalayas**.

As the plates continue to move, immense **pressure and stresses** build up in the rocks.

Figure 1.13 Earthquake in Nepal

The earthquake

The main earthquake registered **7.9 on the Richter scale** (see page 15) and lasted for less than a minute. More than a hundred **aftershocks**, some measuring as big as 6.7, were felt in the days following the initial earthquake.

The physical impact

- An area of the Earth's crust, about 120 km long, was moved forward by about two metres.
- Hundreds of **landslides** occurred, some of them large enough to be visible from space. Villages and roads were buried.
- **Avalanches** and ice falls occurred in many of the climbing regions.

Geo fact
Satellite measurements indicate that Mount Everest is now 3 cm smaller than it used to be before the earthquake.

The human impact of the earthquake

The greatest impact of the earthquake was felt in **poor, crowded urban areas**. These had lots of older and cheaply made buildings.

- More than 8,000 people are known to have died.
- More than 20,000 people were injured.
- Nearly three million people were made homeless.

Activity
Why is an earthquake in a developing country likely to cause more damage than one in a developed country? **Discuss** in pairs or groups.

The economic impact of the earthquake

- The **cost of rebuilding** after the earthquake could be more than €8 billion. This cost is shocking when the country's GNP is less than €20 billion.
- The **damage to cultural sites** and the deaths of climbers will harm the tourism industry. Tourism is crucial to the Nepalese economy, employing more than a million people.

Link
For more on **GNP** see Chapter 15, page 406.

Measuring earthquakes

Tremors from an earthquake can be detected and measured by a **seismometer** or **seismograph**. A pen on the tip of the seismometer records the tremors on a rotating drum.

The **Richter scale** is used to describe the strength or force of an earthquake. Each increase of one unit on the scale means that the strength of the earthquake is ten times more powerful.

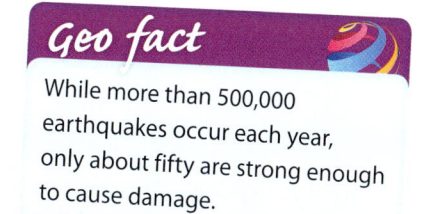

Geo fact
While more than 500,000 earthquakes occur each year, only about fifty are strong enough to cause damage.

Activity
If earthquake A measures 8 on the Richter Scale and earthquake B measures 6 on the Richter Scale, **calculate** how many times stronger earthquake A is.

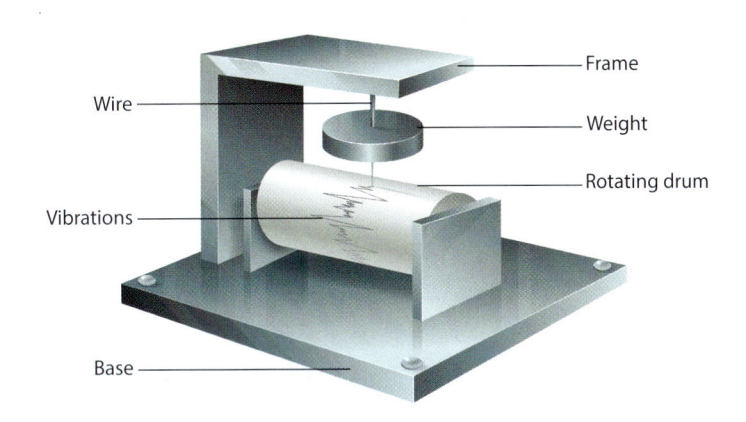

1. The base and frame of the **seismograph** vibrate during the earthquake.
2. The weight does not move because it is hanging freely from a thin wire.
3. A pen attached to the weight records the **tremors** (vibrations) on a rotating drum.

Figure 1.14 A seismograph

Predicting and preparing for earthquakes

Predicting earthquakes is not easy or accurate. However, there are still some ways of checking the chances of an earthquake:

- **Laser beams** can be used to detect **plate movement**.
- A **seismometer** can be used to pick up advance **vibrations** in the Earth's crust.

Preparing for earthquakes is vital in many parts of the world. People living in earthquake zones can:

- Hold **earthquake drills**, practising what to do in the event of an earthquake
- Put together **emergency kits** and store them in their homes.

Earthquake-proof structures can be built:

- Heavy furniture is **bolted** to the wall.
- Foundations of buildings have rubber **shock absorbers**.
- Concrete buildings are **reinforced** with steel.

Section 1 · Physical Geography

Case study

Tsunami in Japan (2011)

The most powerful earthquake ever to hit Japan, measuring 9.0 on the Richter scale, had its epicentre under the Pacific Ocean, just 70 km off the coast. Here, the Pacific Plate pushes against and slides beneath the Eurasian Plate on which Japan sits.

For a long time the plates had been locked and stresses were building up. In March 2011 the tension became too great and the plates suddenly slipped past one another. The tremors lasted for about six minutes. The earthquake created a huge **tsunami**.

The maximum height of the tsunami out at sea was about 40 metres. By the time it hit the coastline of Japan, the tsunami was between 6 and 10 metres high. The highest tsunami defence wall was 5 metres! The waves travelled inland for up to 10 km.

Impact of the tsunami

- More than 18,000 people were killed or reported missing, and more than 500,000 people were evacuated from their homes.
- Nuclear plants were shut down across the country as a safety measure. However, the cooling system of one nuclear plant failed, leading to radiation leaks.
- Entire towns were wiped off the map. At least 200,000 homes were damaged or destroyed.
- Roads, bridges and railways were washed away. Power plants and factories were damaged.

> **Definition** ✓
>
> **Tsunami:** A series of powerful ocean waves that are caused when an earthquake occurs under the sea.

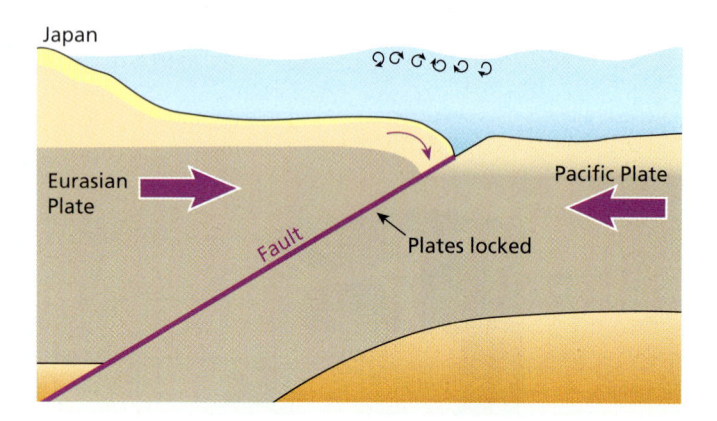

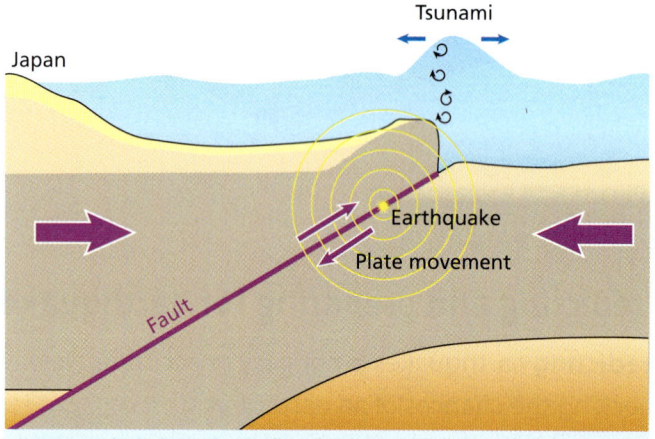

Figure 1.15 The earthquake occurred where the Eurasian Plate collided with the Pacific Plate. During the earthquake, the edge of the Eurasian Plate was pushed upwards by as much as 8 metres

Questions

1. Write **one** sentence to explain each of the following terms that are associated with earthquakes: (i) tremor, (ii) aftershock, (iii) focus, (iv) epicentre.
2. Describe how the strength of an earthquake is measured and recorded.
3. With the aid of a labelled diagram, explain how an earthquake can lead to a tsunami.

Chapter 1 · Our Restless Earth

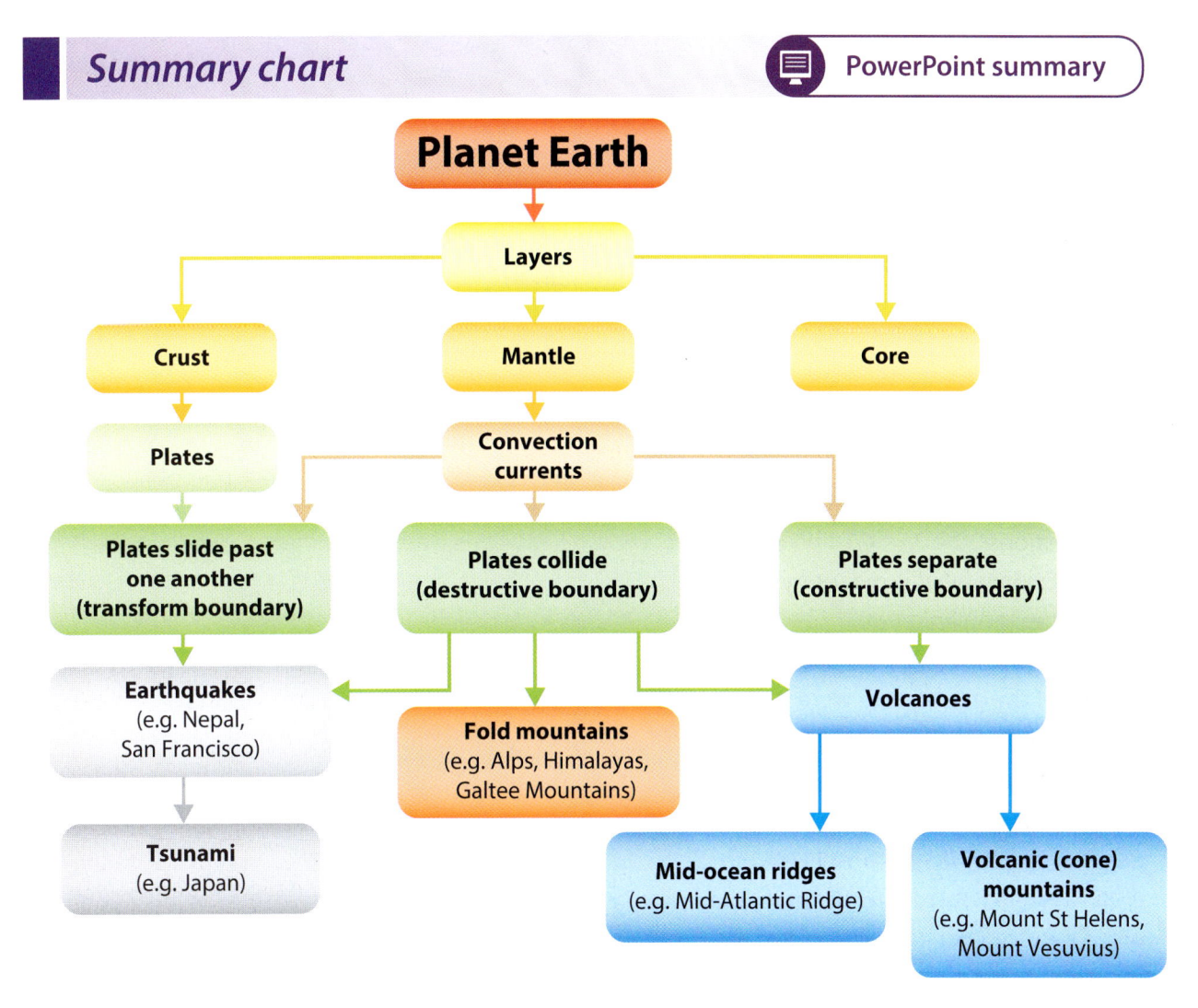

Summary chart

PowerPoint summary

Planet Earth → Layers
- Crust → Plates → Plates slide past one another (transform boundary) → Earthquakes (e.g. Nepal, San Francisco) → Tsunami (e.g. Japan)
- Mantle → Convection currents
  - Plates collide (destructive boundary) → Earthquakes / Fold mountains (e.g. Alps, Himalayas, Galtee Mountains) / Volcanoes
  - Plates separate (constructive boundary) → Volcanoes → Mid-ocean ridges (e.g. Mid-Atlantic Ridge) / Volcanic (cone) mountains (e.g. Mount St Helens, Mount Vesuvius)
- Core

Exam questions

1. (i) Name **one** feature formed where plates collide.
   (ii) Name **one** feature formed where plates separate.
   (iii) With the aid of a diagram, explain how **one** of the features named is formed.
   HL 2010

2. (i) With the aid of a diagram, explain how **fold mountains** are formed.
   (ii) Name **one** range of fold mountains in Ireland.
   HL 2007

3. (i) Examine the diagram (on the right) of a volcano and name each of the parts labelled **A, B, C** and **D**.
   (ii) Explain **one** positive impact and **one** negative impact of volcanoes.
   HL 2015

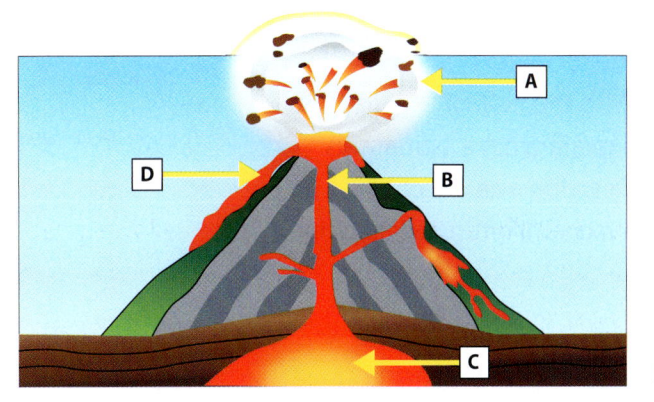

17

Section 1 · Physical Geography

Exam questions

4 (i) Name **one** example of a volcano.
(ii) With reference to the diagram on the right explain how volcanoes occur.

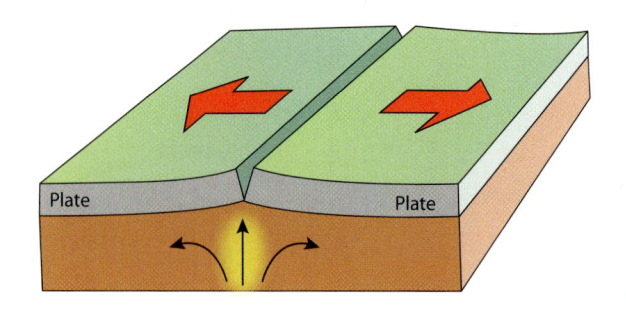

HL 2012

5 Examine the map (on the right) and answer each of the following questions.
(i) Explain what is meant by the term *epicentre*.
(ii) Explain why the effects of the earthquake were greater in Christchurch than in Wellington.
(iii) Describe **two** ways to reduce the impact of earthquakes.

HL 2015

6

Focus   Continental Drift   Richter Scale   Seismograph   Tsunami

(i) Explain any **two** of the terms listed in the box above.
(ii) Name **one** place in the world where earthquakes often happen.
(iii) Describe **two** effects of an earthquake on a large city.

OL 2014

7 On March 11, 2011, a tsunami struck the coast of Japan.
(i) Describe how an earthquake occurs, starting from the focus.
(ii) With the help of the diagram, explain what a 'tsunami' is.
(iii) Describe **one** effect of a tsunami hitting a large city.

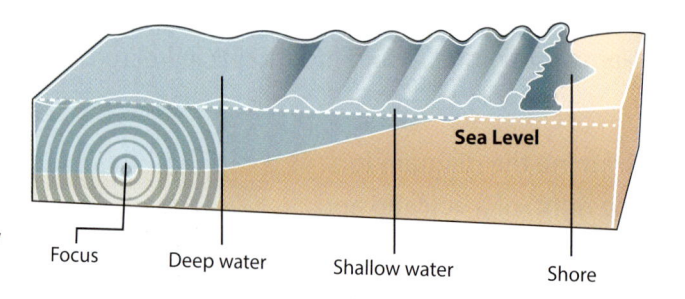

OL 2012

Chapter 2
Rocks

Learning outcomes

By the end of this chapter, you should be able to understand:

- That there are three groups of rocks, with several rock types in each group
- How the main types of rock are formed
- The location of these rocks in Ireland
- How we extract and use these rocks.

2.1 What is rock?

KEYWORDS

- minerals
- cemented
- sedimentary
- compressed
- igneous
- metamorphic

Rock is the hard material that forms the Earth's crust. All rocks:

- Are solid
- Occur naturally
- Are made up of one or more **minerals** that have been **compressed** and **cemented** together.

Rocks differ from each other in their:

- Mineral content
- Colour
- Hardness
- Texture (how they feel to the touch).

Rocks are made up of one or more minerals. Here you can see gold and quartz (bottom row, second from left) and copper (blue in bottom row, right)

Section 1 · Physical Geography

There are many different types of rock. However, they can be divided into **three groups**, according to **how they were formed**. These groups are:

- **Igneous** rocks
- **Sedimentary** rocks
- **Metamorphic** rocks.

There are many different rock types in each group.

Questions

1. (a) What is a rock?
   (b) What is rock made up of?
2. Name the **three** groups of rocks.
3. Why are rocks grouped in this way?

2.2 Igneous rocks

KEYWORDS

- granite
- basalt
- intrusive
- extrusive
- crystals

Igneous rocks are formed as a result of **volcanic activity**. Volcanic material cools down and solidifies, either within the crust or on the surface.

- **Intrusive** rocks are formed from material that cooled inside the crust.
- **Extrusive** rocks are formed from material that cooled on the surface.

Igneous rocks include **granite** and **basalt**.

Geo fact
The word igneous comes from the Latin word for fire.

Extrusive igneous rocks e.g. basalt

Intrusive igneous rocks e.g. granite

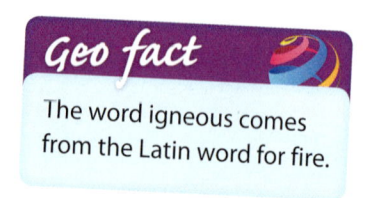

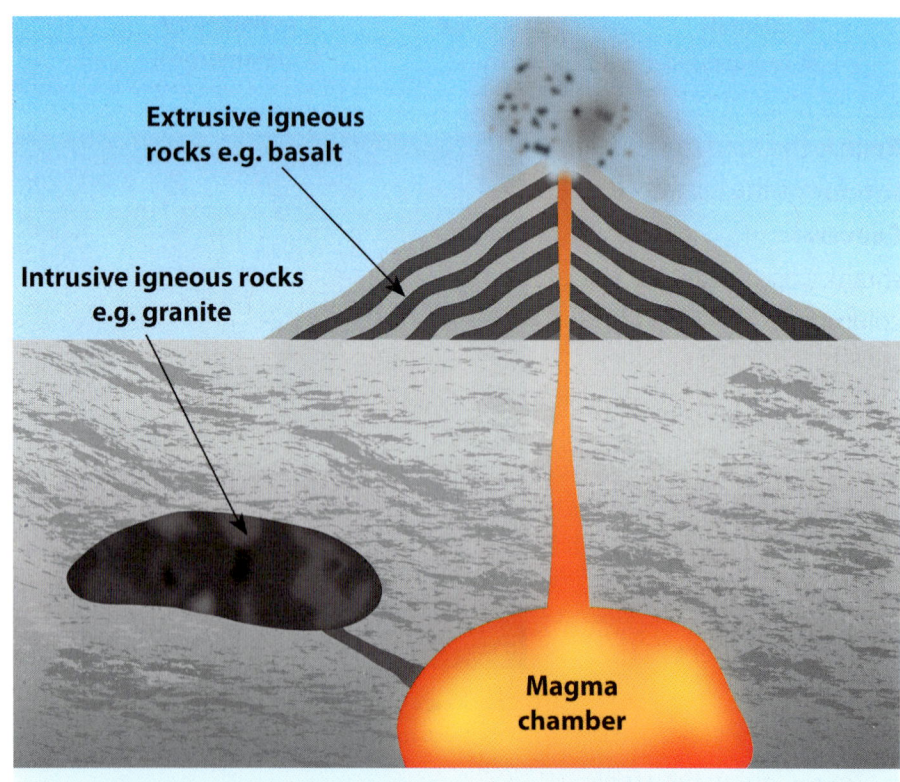

Magma chamber

Figure 2.1 Igneous rocks are formed from volcanic material

Granite

Granite is an **intrusive** rock. It formed when molten magma forced its way into the crust. It **cooled very slowly** over millions of years, allowing **large crystals** to form. These crystals include quartz. It eventually came to the surface when the overlying rocks were worn away.

Granite varies in colour from black or grey to pink. It is used in the building industry and for monuments. Granite is found in the Mourne and Wicklow Mountains.

Pink granite

Basalt

Basalt is an **extrusive** rock. It formed when lava spread out across the Earth's surface. The lava **cooled and solidified very quickly** because it was exposed to the air. As a result, basalt has **tiny crystals** that cannot be seen by the naked eye.

Basalt varies in colour from dark grey to black. It is found in the Antrim–Derry plateau. The most famous section of it is the **Giant's Causeway**. Here, as the lava cooled, it shrank and cracked to form six-sided columns.

There are about 40,000 hexagonal (six-sided) blocks of basalt in the Giant's Causeway

Questions

1. Explain the difference between molten magma and lava.
2. (a) Name **one** igneous rock.
   (b) With the aid of a diagram, explain how that rock was formed.
3. Briefly describe how the Giant's Causeway was formed.

Section 1 · Physical Geography

2.3 Sedimentary rocks

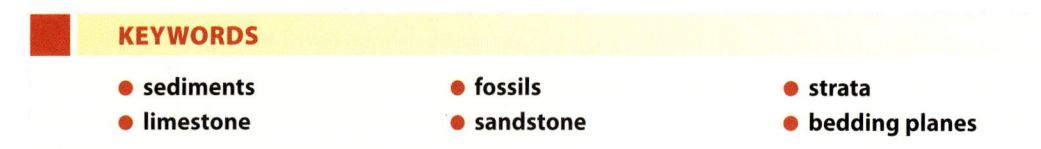

KEYWORDS

- sediments
- limestone
- fossils
- sandstone
- strata
- bedding planes

Sedimentary rocks are formed from the remains (**sediments**) of other rocks, plant life and animal life. These sediments are **deposited** on the beds of seas and lakes as well as on land. They are then **compressed** and **cemented** together.

Sedimentary rocks include **limestone**, **sandstone** and **coal**.

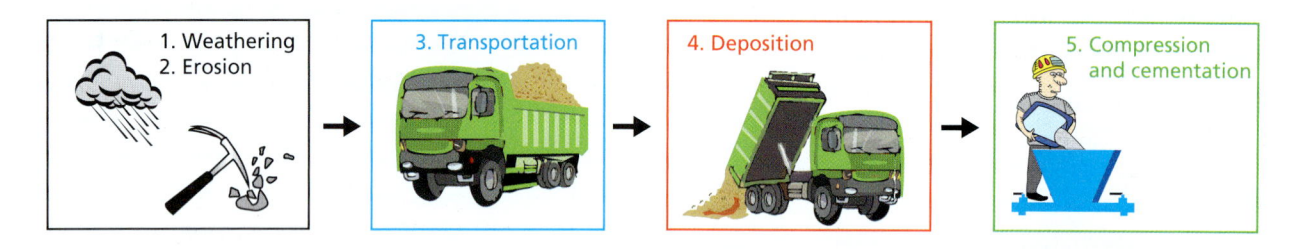

Figure 2.2 The making of sedimentary rocks

Limestone

Limestone formed on the beds of shallow, warm seas from the **skeletons of tiny sea creatures**, **fish** and **shells**. These piled up over millions of years. The particles were **compressed** and **cemented** together. The remains of some of the skeletons are preserved in the rock as **fossils**.

Limestone varies in colour from white to grey. It is **permeable** (allowing water to pass through it) and is laid down in layers, or **strata**.

Limestone is found in the Burren (Co. Clare) and under the soil and bogs that cover the Central Plain of Ireland. Limestone is used to make monuments and is the raw material for cement. Many public buildings are constructed of limestone.

Farmers use ground limestone to improve soil fertility.

Geo fact

Limestone is the most common rock in Ireland and is found in 31 of the 32 counties.

Limestone containing fossils

Sandstone

Sandstone formed when large amounts of sand were worn away from the surface of the Earth and transported by wind and rivers. The sand was then deposited on the beds of lakes and seas, as well as in deserts. The deposits built up and were **compressed** and **cemented** to form sandstone.

Sandstone varies in colour from **brown** to **red**. It is sometimes used as a building material. The mountains of Munster, including MacGillycuddy's Reeks, the Galtees and Comeraghs, are made of sandstone.

Sandstone is laid down in layers called **strata**. The divisions between the strata are called **bedding planes**

Questions

1. Explain the terms: (i) strata, (ii) fossils and (iii) permeable.
2. Describe how sandstone was formed.
3. Describe **two** uses to which limestone can be put.

Geo fact

Coal is a sedimentary rock that formed from decayed vegetation.

2.4 Metamorphic rocks

KEYWORDS
- heat
- pressure
- marble
- quartzite
- slate

Metamorphic rocks are formed when existing igneous or sedimentary rocks come into contact with great **heat** and **pressure**. They can change in both shape and form.

Metamorphic rocks include **marble**, **quartzite** and **slate**.

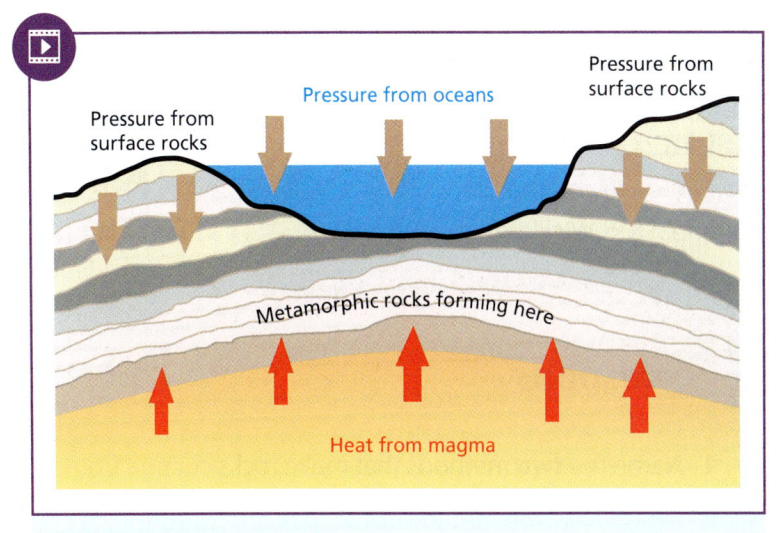

Figure 2.3 Metamorphic rocks are formed when existing rocks are changed by heat and pressure

Section 1 · Physical Geography

Marble

When molten magma forces its way into a body of limestone, it puts it under great heat and pressure. This changes the make-up of the limestone and it turns into **marble**.

Pure marble is white in colour, but, when other minerals are present, it can be red, green or black. Marble is a hard rock that also contains **crystals**.

Marble can be easily cut and polished. As a result, it is used for fireplaces, gravestones and ornaments. Marble is found in Rathlin Island (white), Connemara (green) and Cork (red).

Quarrying large slabs of marble at Carrara in Italy. The artist Michelangelo used Carrara marble

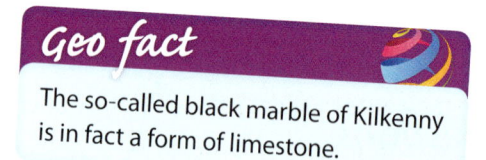

Geo fact
The so-called black marble of Kilkenny is in fact a form of limestone.

Quartzite

Quartzite was formed when sandstone came into contact with magma deep in the Earth's crust. This usually happened during periods of **folding**.

Quartzite consists mainly of grains of quartz that are packed tightly together. It varies in colour from grey to white.

It is an extremely hard rock so it remains as a cap on some of Ireland's mountains. These include Croagh Patrick (Co. Mayo), Errigal (Co. Donegal) and the Great Sugarloaf (Co. Wicklow).

Pilgrim path on the quartzite slope of Croagh Patrick

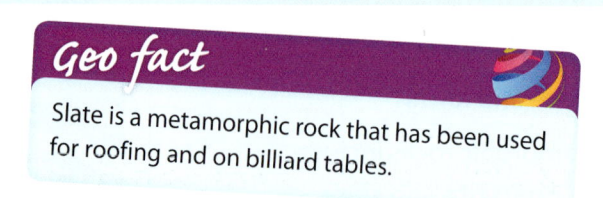

Geo fact
Slate is a metamorphic rock that has been used for roofing and on billiard tables.

Questions

1. Name the **two** methods that make rocks change from igneous or sedimentary to metamorphic.
2. Select any **one** metamorphic rock and describe its characteristics (what it looks like).
3. Select any **one** metamorphic rock and describe how it was formed.

2.5 Common rocks in Ireland

Figure 2.4 is a geological map. It shows where the most common rock types in Ireland can be found.

Questions

Examine Figure 2.4 and answer these questions:

1. (a) Name the most common rock type in Ireland.
   (b) Name **two** counties (or areas) where it is found.
2. (a) Name and locate your own county or area on the map.
   (b) Name the most common rock type found there.
3. Select **one** igneous, **one** sedimentary and **one** metamorphic rock type and name a location where each is found in Ireland.

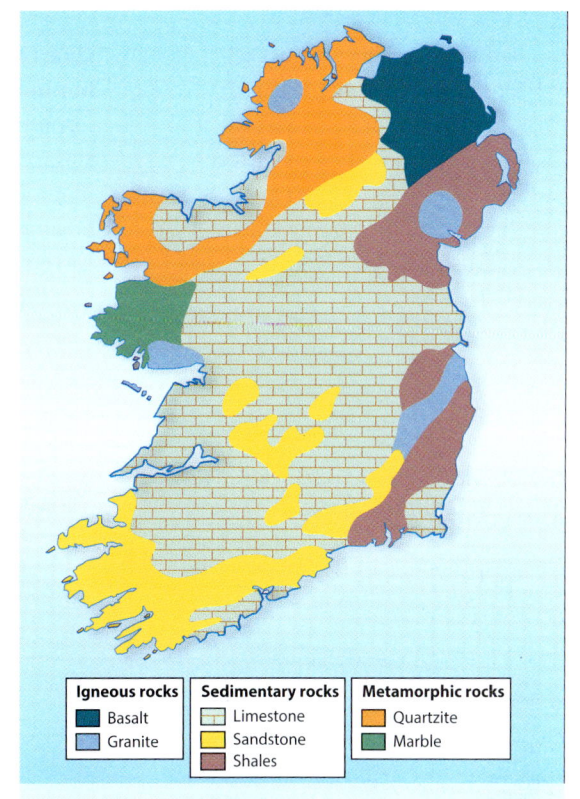

Figure 2.4 The locations of the most common rocks in Ireland

Igneous rocks	Sedimentary rocks	Metamorphic rocks
Basalt	Limestone	Quartzite
Granite	Sandstone	Marble
	Shales	

2.6 Resources from the Earth

KEYWORDS

- mining
- quarrying
- natural gas

Rocks provide us with a wide range of natural resources that can be extracted or mined.

The Earth's **natural resources** include:

- Metal ores: iron ore, copper, lead and zinc
- Precious metals and stones: gold, silver and diamonds
- Building materials: stone, sand and gravel
- Energy sources: uranium, oil, natural gas and coal.

The resources are recovered by **drilling**, **quarrying** and **mining**.

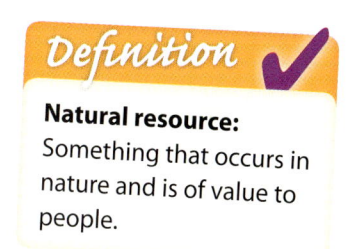

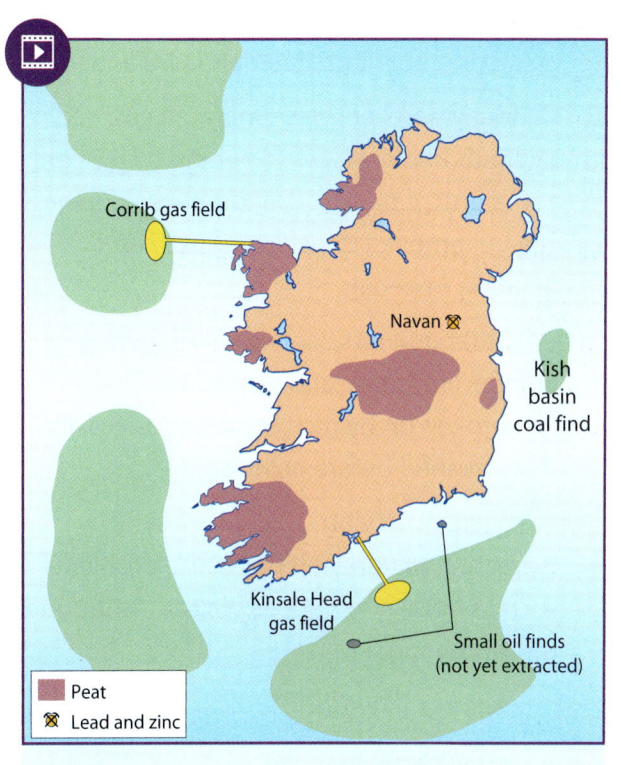

Definition ✓

Natural resource: Something that occurs in nature and is of value to people.

Figure 2.5 Some of Ireland's natural resources

25

Section 1 · Physical Geography

Drilling is used to extract **oil** or **gas** from an underground source. Most drilling takes place on land, but some takes place offshore. A pipeline on the seabed then brings the fuel ashore.

Quarrying and open-cast mining are used where the resource is on or close to the surface. These are a cheap method of mining but are not environmentally friendly. They can be noisy, give off dust and scar the landscape.

Shaft mining is used where the resource lies in seams deep beneath the surface. It is reached by constructing shafts down to the seams. Shaft mining is used to extract lead and zinc ores from the mines in Navan.

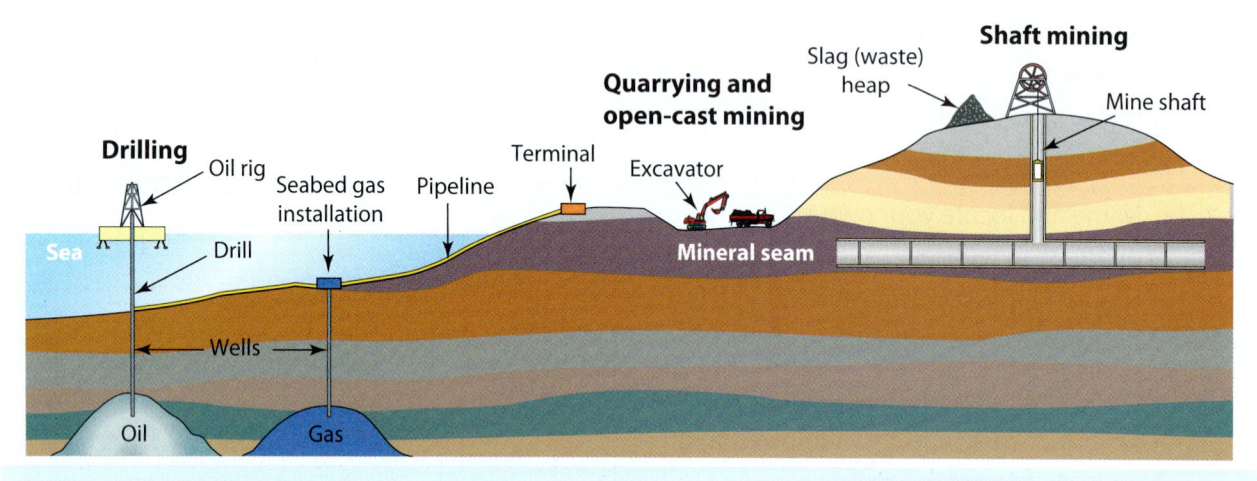

Figure 2.6 Extracting minerals by drilling, quarrying and mining

Case study

Quarrying

Quarrying is the most common way of extracting building materials in Ireland.

Many parts of the country are covered by sands and gravels left behind by glaciers at the end of the last Ice Age. These deposits can be removed directly and used as building materials.

Other quarries contain rocks such as granite, limestone and sandstone. This is first broken up by the use of explosives and then crushed before being sold.

While quarrying is a cheap way of extracting materials, it can cause problems such as noise and dust, as well as disfiguring the landscape.

Building materials are extracted by quarrying

Activity

Working in pairs, **outline arguments** (i) in favour of, and (ii) against, opening a quarry in your area.

Case study

Natural gas production in Ireland

Natural gas in Ireland in 2016

- Natural gas makes up about 25 per cent of total energy demand in Ireland.
- Until recently Ireland got most of its gas from the **North Sea** (Britain and Norway).
- Natural gas was first brought ashore from the **Kinsale Head** gas field in 1978, but that supply of gas is now almost completely used up.
- Natural gas is now in production at the **Corrib gas field** off the coast of Mayo.

History of the Corrib gas field

Natural gas was discovered about 80 km offshore and about 3 km beneath the seabed in 1998. Production of gas was due to start in 2005 but was delayed many times:

- By disputes over the route of the pipeline and the location of the processing terminal
- By concerns about health and safety on land
- By concerns about the environmental impact of the project.

This led to part of the route of the pipeline being changed and some of the pipeline being enclosed in a tunnel. Production finally began in late 2015.

The gas is processed at a newly built terminal at **Bellanaboy**.

Economic benefits

The discovery of natural gas off our coastline has major benefits for the Irish economy:

- It is expected that the Corrib field will provide up to 60 per cent of Ireland's annual gas demand.
- It will also provide a more secure gas supply.
- It will cut down on our imports of energy supplies.
- During the construction phase, between 700 and 1,400 people were employed on the project.
- About 150 full-time jobs have been created now that the terminal is in full production.

The Corrib gas terminal at Bellanaboy Bridge. Some of the onshore pipeline section runs in a tunnel under Sruwaddacon Bay (right background). Can you identify the route of the tunnel from the bay to the terminal?

Section 1 · Physical Geography

Questions

1. Name **three** natural resources that are extracted from the Earth.
2. Select any **one** of the natural resources named above and explain how it is extracted.
3. Describe **two** economic benefits of the resource that you selected.
4. Explain why some people might object to the extraction of that natural resource.

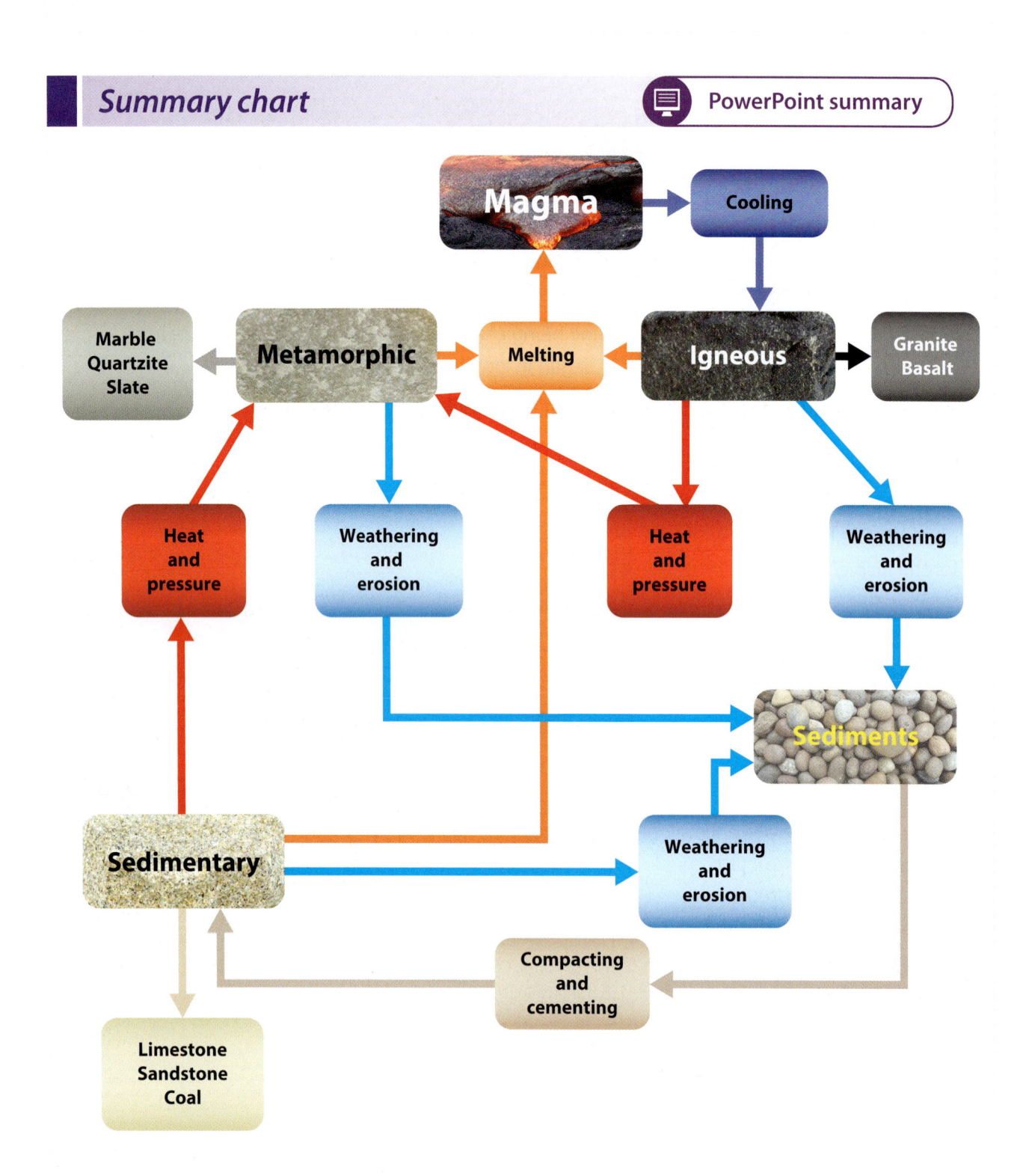

Summary chart

PowerPoint summary

Magma → Cooling

Metamorphic ← Melting ← Igneous → Granite, Basalt

Marble, Quartzite, Slate ← Metamorphic

Heat and pressure → Metamorphic

Weathering and erosion → Sediments

Heat and pressure → Metamorphic

Weathering and erosion → Sediments

Sedimentary → Weathering and erosion → Sediments

Compacting and cementing → Sedimentary

Limestone, Sandstone, Coal

28

Exam questions

1 (i) Name **one** rock and state **one** use of this rock.
   (ii) Explain how this rock was formed.
   (iii) Describe **one** advantage of quarrying.
   (iv) Describe **one** disadvantage of quarrying.

   OL 2015

2   A   B   C

   (i) State which of the images above **A**, **B** or **C** shows basalt rock.
   (ii) Name a location in Ireland where basalt is found.
   (iii) Describe and explain how basalt is formed.

   HL 2014

3 There are three major rock groups: **Igneous**, **Sedimentary** and **Metamorphic**.
   (i) Name **one** rock from each group.
   (ii) Choose any **one** rock that you have named and describe how it is formed.
   (iii) State **two** uses of this rock.

   OL 2013

4 (i) Name **one** area off the Irish coast where oil/natural gas has been found.
   (ii) Explain **one** positive effect and **one** negative effect of such a discovery for an area.
   (iii) State **one** reason why it is important to reduce the amount of fossil fuels being used.

   OL 2015

5 (i) Explain **two** advantages of oil and gas exploitation for the Irish economy.
   (ii) Describe **two** problems that may arise from oil and gas exploitation.

   HL 2014

6 Rocks are useful for economic activities.
   Name and explain **two** ways rocks may be used in economic activities.

   HL 2004

Chapter 3
Weathering and Mass Movement

Learning outcomes

By the end of this chapter, you should be able to understand:

- That the surface of the Earth is shaped by weathering, mass movement and erosion
- The difference between the processes of weathering and erosion
- How the various processes of weathering and mass movement operate
- That human activities can interfere with these processes.

3.1 Denudation: an introduction

KEYWORDS

- denudation
- weathering
- mass movement
- erosion

The process of breaking up and removing the rocks on the surface of the Earth is known as **denudation**. The three main processes of denudation are **weathering**, **mass movement** and **erosion**.

Denudation

Weathering

Weathering is the breakdown and decay of rocks that are exposed to the weather. There are two types of weathering:

- Mechanical weathering
- Chemical weathering.

Mass movement

Mass movement is the movement of loose material (**regolith**) down a slope under the influence of gravity. There are two types of mass movement:

- Slow (soil creep)
- Fast (landslide, bogburst, mudflow).

Erosion

Erosion is the wearing away of rocks and the removal of the materials that result. The main agents (causes) of erosion are:

- Moving water (rivers and sea)
- Moving ice (glaciers)
- Moving air (wind).

Questions

1. (a) What **three** processes make up denudation?
   (b) Explain the term weathering.
   (c) Explain the term erosion.
   (d) What is meant by mass movement?

2. (a) Name **two** types of weathering.
   (b) Name any **two** agents of erosion.
   (c) List **one** difference between weathering and erosion.

3.2 Mechanical weathering

KEYWORDS
- mechanical weathering
- freeze-thaw
- frost action
- scree

Mechanical weathering is the breaking down of rocks into smaller pieces. The pieces are not removed and remain in place. The most common type of mechanical weathering is **freeze-thaw**.

Freeze-thaw

Freeze-thaw is the break-up of rock by **frost action**. It occurs where:

- There is **precipitation** (rainfall) **and**
- The **temperature** rises above and falls below freezing point (0°C).

These conditions occur in Ireland during winter months, especially in upland areas. They also occur in snow-covered mountain ranges such as the Alps.

Geo fact

Trees can cause mechanical weathering. They may take root in cracks in rocks. As the roots grow, they wedge open the cracks. The rock can be split completely apart.

Activity

Why does freeze-thaw not occur when the temperature does not drop below freezing point (0°C)?

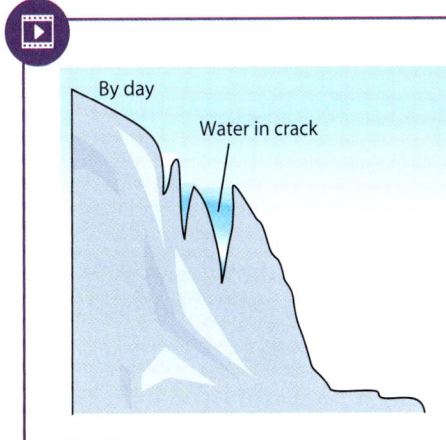

By day
During the day, water seeps into joints (cracks) in the rock.

By night
The temperature drops below freezing point (0°C). The water freezes and expands. This makes the crack bigger and puts strain on the rock.

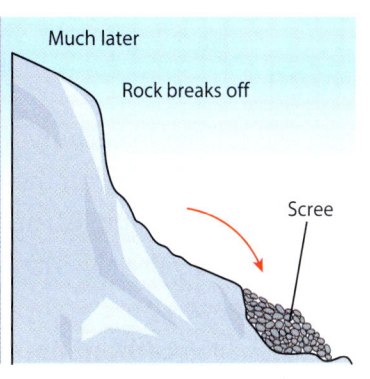

Over time
After repeated freezing and thawing, the rock splits. Sharp, jagged pieces break off. These pieces of rock are called **scree**. They roll down the mountainside and collect in piles at the bottom of the slope.

Figure 3.1 Freeze-thaw action

Section 1 · Physical Geography

> **Questions**
>
> 1. (a) Why does freeze-thaw nearly always take place in winter?
>   (b) Why is freeze-thaw most common in upland areas in Ireland?
>   (c) Why does freeze-thaw not occur in hot climate areas?
> 2. List the steps of freeze-thaw in order.
> 3. (a) Explain the term scree.
>   (b) Where would you most likely find a pile of scree?

Rock split by freeze-thaw action

3.3 Chemical weathering

KEYWORDS
- chemical weathering
- carbonation
- joint
- bedding plane
- karst
- Burren
- limestone pavement
- clint
- grike
- swallow hole
- cave
- stalactite
- stalagmite
- pillar

Chemical weathering occurs when rocks decay or are dissolved by chemicals. The most common type of chemical weathering is **carbonation**.

Carbonation

- When rain falls it takes in **carbon dioxide** as it passes through the air.
- The carbon dioxide mixes with the rainwater, turning it into a weak **carbonic acid**.
- Limestone contains **calcium carbonate**. The weak acid rain reacts with the calcium carbonate and slowly dissolves it.
- It then washes it away.
- This process is called **carbonation**.

The make-up of the limestone makes all this easier. It is **permeable**, so the rainwater can easily pass through it. It also has vertical cracks (called **joints**) and horizontal **bedding planes**, which make it easier for the water to pass through (see Figure 3.3, page 34).

Definition

Bedding plane: The line in rocks that separates two layers or strata.

Karst landscapes

The effects of carbonation are best seen in a **limestone landscape**, especially one where the soil cover has been removed and the rock is exposed to the weather. These areas are better known as **karst landscapes**, called after the limestone region of Slovenia. Ireland's best-known karst region is the Burren in Co. Clare.

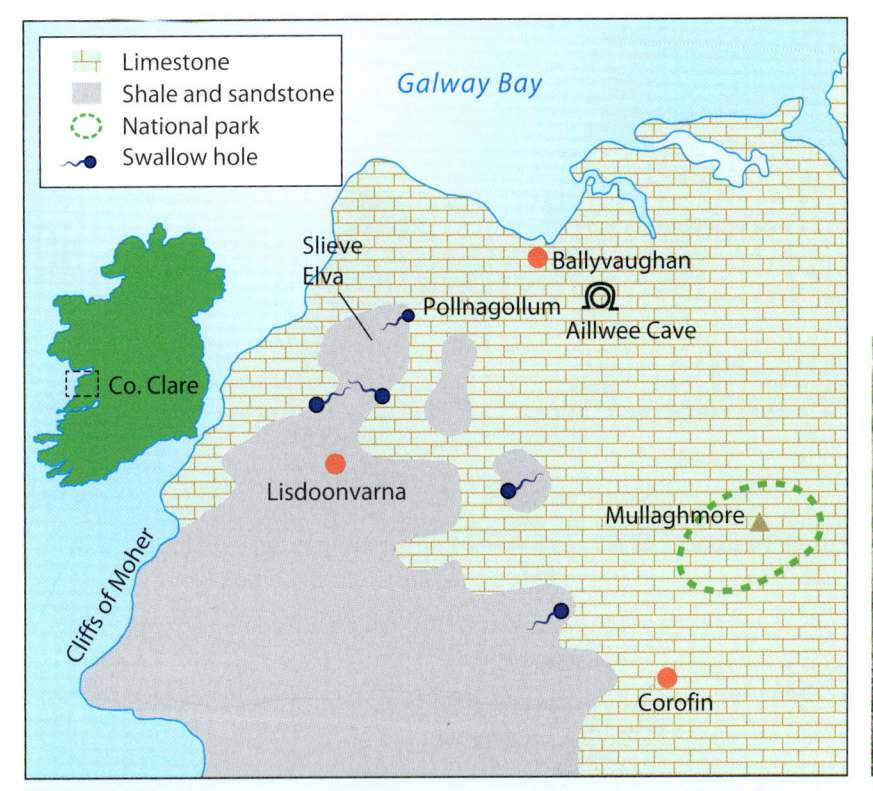

Figure 3.2 The Burren region of north Clare is a karst landscape of world importance

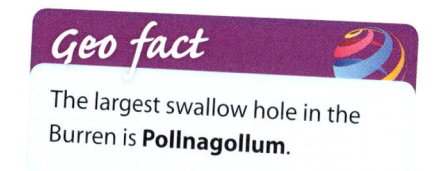

Limestone rocks showing strata (layers), bedding planes and joints (cracks)

Geo fact
The largest swallow hole in the Burren is **Pollnagollum**.

The Burren landscape

The Burren is a karst landscape of world importance. Its name comes from the Irish word for **rocky place**.

Most of the soil cover of the Burren was removed by erosion, leaving the limestone exposed. Weathering by **carbonation** has created a remarkable landscape, both on the surface and under the ground.

Clints and grikes on a limestone pavement in the Burren

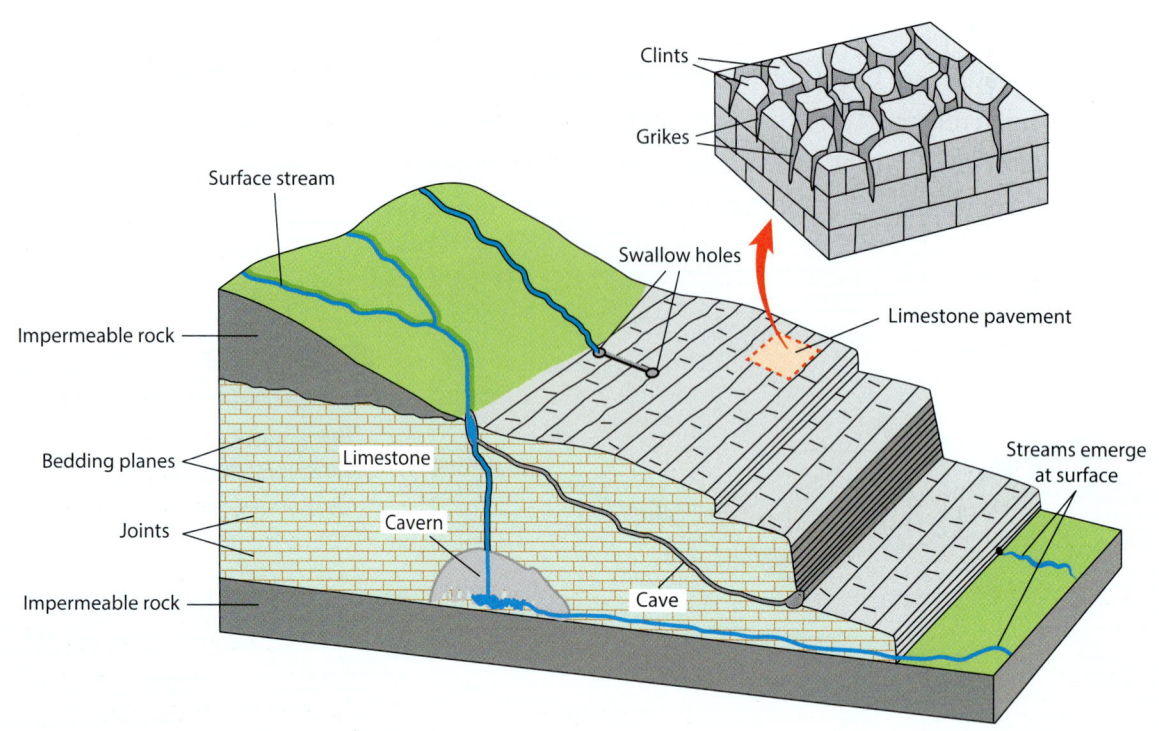

Section 1 · Physical Geography

Limestone pavement

The large area of exposed limestone is called a **limestone pavement**. It generally takes the form of almost flat terraces, but may also have steep cliff edges.

- As the rainfall seeps through the rock, it picks out the weakest points and weathers them by **carbonation**.
- The joints or cracks in the limestone are widened and deepened to form deep gashes called **grikes**.
- The blocks of limestone that remain are called **clints**.

Swallow hole

When a river flows onto a bare limestone surface, the water begins to dissolve the limestone by carbonation.

- The water widens the joints and bedding planes, opening them up.
- Soon the river disappears from the surface and begins to flow underground.
- The passage through which the river disappears is called a **swallow hole**.

Figure 3.3 The surface features of a karst region include a limestone pavement, clints, grikes and swallow holes

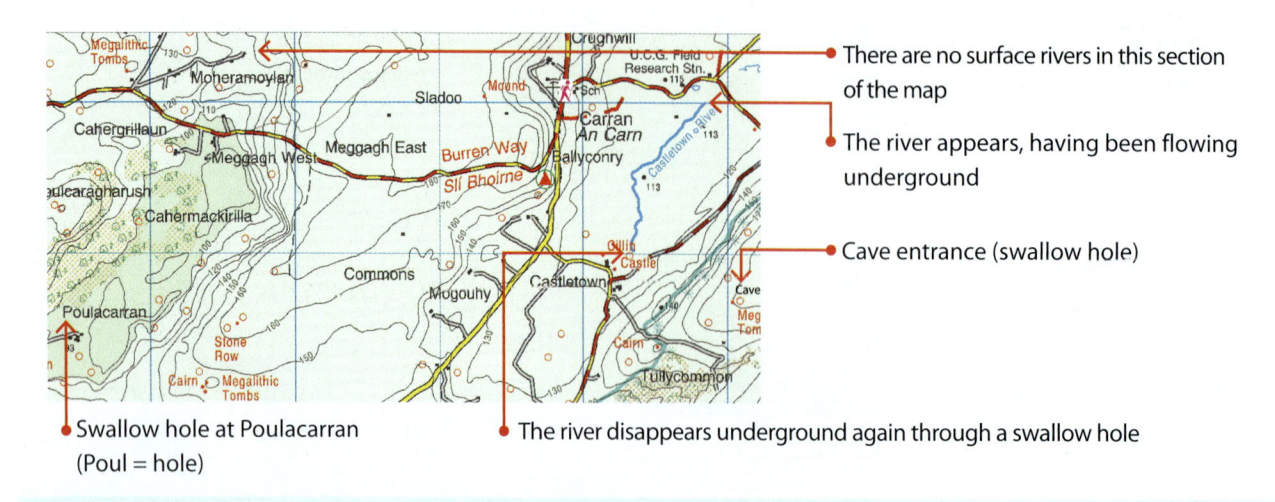

- There are no surface rivers in this section of the map
- The river appears, having been flowing underground
- Cave entrance (swallow hole)
- Swallow hole at Poulacarran (Poul = hole)
- The river disappears underground again through a swallow hole

Figure 3.4 Identifying surface features of a karst region on an Ordnance Survey map

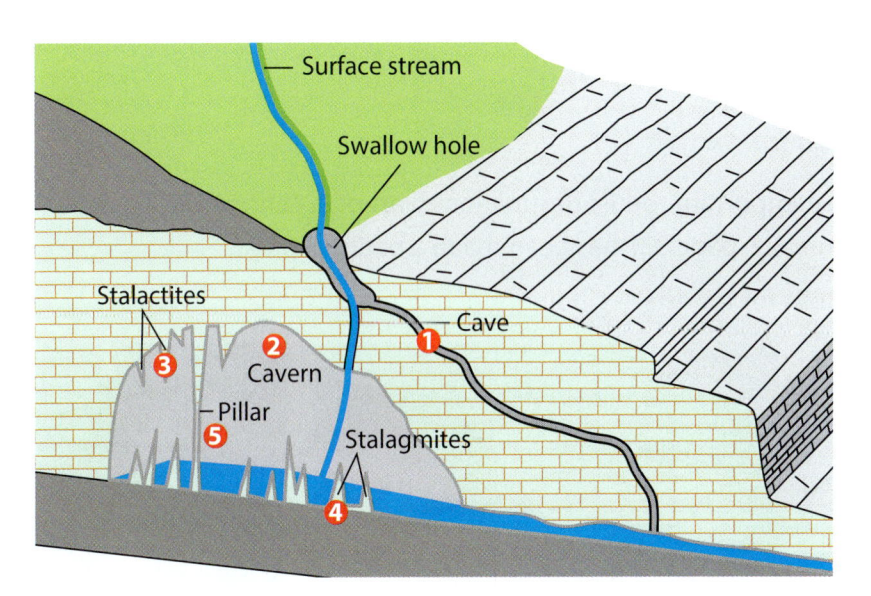

Chapter 3 · Weathering and Mass Movement

1. As the river flows underground, the carbonic acid in the water dissolves the limestone to cut out a long passage called a **cave**.

2. Sometimes the cave gets big enough to form a large chamber called a **cavern**.

3. When water containing dissolved limestone seeps through the limestone to the cave or cavern, some drops hang from the roof for a while.
   Some of the water evaporates, leaving behind tiny deposits of **calcite** (calcium carbonate) attached to the roof. These deposits build up slowly over thousands of years and hang from the roof in icicle-like shapes called **stalactites**.

4. When a drop of water falls to the floor of the cave, it also leaves behind a tiny amount of calcite. These deposits build up over time to form cone-shaped features called **stalagmites**.

5. As the stalactites and stalagmites continue to grow, they may join up to form **pillars.**

Figure 3.5 Underground features of a karst region include caves, caverns, stalactites, stalagmites and pillars

Underground features in a limestone cavern

Activity

Examine the photo on the left.
Identify the features labelled A, B and C.

Hint

Sta**c**tites: **c** for ceiling.
Stala**g**mites: **g** for ground.

Weathering in tropical regions

Chemical weathering also occurs in tropical regions such as the Amazon basin and the Congo basin.

It gives rise to a special kind of soil called **tropical red soil**.

Link

For more on **tropical red soil**, see Chapter 7, page 140.

Tropical red soils in Brazil. Note the dense forest growth. Note also how the river has washed away much of the soil

35

Section 1 · Physical Geography

Case study

The Burren National Park

The Burren is one of Ireland's most important tourist destinations. Part of it, centred on Mullaghmore mountain (see Figure 3.2, page 33), has been made a national park.

It has a wide range of attractions for tourists, including:

- **Landscape**: The Burren has a wide variety of scenery to attract tourists, cavers, walkers and rock climbers. These include the karst landscape, Aillwee Cave, the Cliffs of Moher and the Burren Way.
- **History**: The Burren has a wide variety of monuments and archaeological sites. They include high crosses, dolmens, ring forts and churches. They provide evidence that the Burren has had a long history of settlement.

Poulnabrone dolmen is one of the many historical monuments in the Burren

Flowers growing in a grike on the limestone pavement

The Burren is the only place in Ireland or Britain where the green moth is found

- **Flora**: The flora (plant life) of the Burren is remarkable because it has plants that are normally found in widely separate parts of Europe. Alpine, Mediterranean and native plants grow side by side. Orchids, ferns and avens are among the rare plants found there.
- **Fauna**: The fauna (wildlife) is also varied. It includes animals such as the pine marten and wild goat. Insects include many butterflies and the green moth, which is not found anywhere else in Ireland or in Britain.

Tourism in the Burren

The growth of tourism in the Burren must be carefully managed in the future. Tourism makes a valuable contribution to the local economy but tourist activity can also pose a threat to the fragile environment.

Benefits of increased tourism

- Increased tourism creates a rise in local employment, in both permanent and seasonal jobs.
- This, in turn, reduces out-migration.
- There are spin-off benefits for shops, coach owners, craftspeople and pubs.
- Both locals and visitors benefit from improved facilities, such as roads and leisure facilities.

Disadvantages of increased tourism

- Tourism increases the damage to flora, as people pick or trample on the rare flowers.
- The quiet, unspoilt nature of the Burren is changed by noise and air pollution.
- Road widening results in increased traffic, thus destroying the environment that attracted people in the first place.
- There is an increased risk of damage to ancient monuments.

Questions

1. (a) What is chemical weathering?
   (b) Explain the term carbonation.
   (c) Describe how carbonation occurs.

2. (a) What is a karst landscape?
   (b) Name Ireland's best-known karst landscape.
   (c) Name **one** surface landform and **one** underground landform found in the Burren.

3. With the aid of labelled diagrams, describe how each of the following were formed:
   (a) Clints and grikes
   (b) Stalactites and stalagmites.

4. The Burren region is a very important tourist region in Ireland.
   (a) Name **two** things that attract tourists to the Burren.
   (b) Explain **one** benefit of this tourism to the Burren area and the people living there.
   (c) Describe **one** problem that results from this tourism.

3.4 Mass movement

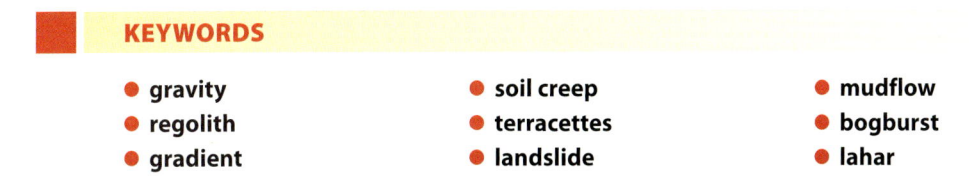

KEYWORDS

- gravity
- regolith
- gradient
- soil creep
- terracettes
- landslide
- mudflow
- bogburst
- lahar

Mass movement refers to the movement of any loose material downslope under the influence of **gravity**. This loose material includes loose rock produced by weathering, as well as soil and mud. It is known as **regolith**.

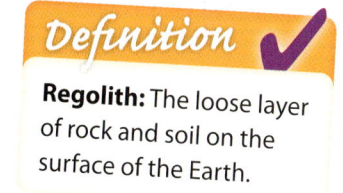

Definition
Regolith: The loose layer of rock and soil on the surface of the Earth.

Factors that influence mass movement

- **Gradient:** Gradient is a measure of the **steepness** of a slope. Mass movement is most likely when the gradient is steep. It is also **fastest**. On more gentle slopes, soil and rock will move very slowly.
- **Water:** After heavy rainfall, water makes the regolith **heavier** and also acts as a **lubricant**. This makes the material more likely to move downhill.
- **Vegetation:** The **roots** of trees and plants bind the soil together. This prevents or slows down mass movement.
- **Human activity:** People can cause mass movement by interfering with slopes. This may occur when the base of a slope is **undercut** during road building. The steeper slope means that material is more likely to collapse.

Section 1 · Physical Geography

Types of mass movement

Mass movements are grouped according to the **speed** at which they occur. They may be **fast or slow**. They may also be **wet or dry**.

Table 3.1

Speed	Moisture	Type of mass movement
Slow	Dry	Soil creep
Fast	Dry	Landslides
Fast	Wet	Mudflows

Soil creep

Soil creep is the slow movement of soil down a slope under the influence of gravity.

Creep is the **slowest** type of mass movement. The soil sometimes moves less than 1 cm per year. It is so slow that you can't see it happening. However, you can see its effects on the **landscape**:

- On grass-covered slopes, the soil piles up in a series of steps called **terracettes**.
- The lower parts of **tree trunks** are bent.
- **Fences and poles** lean downhill.
- **Walls** bulge and fall down.

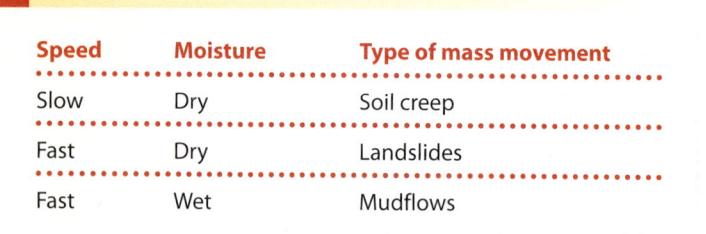

Activity

Examine Figure 3.6. Why, in your opinion, does soil creep occur slowly?

- Poles are tilted downslope.
- Tree trunks are bent.
- Fences are tilted and broken.
- Soil piles up in a series of steps called terracettes.
- Soil piles up behind walls, causing them to bulge and collapse.
- Soil creep is greatest at the surface.

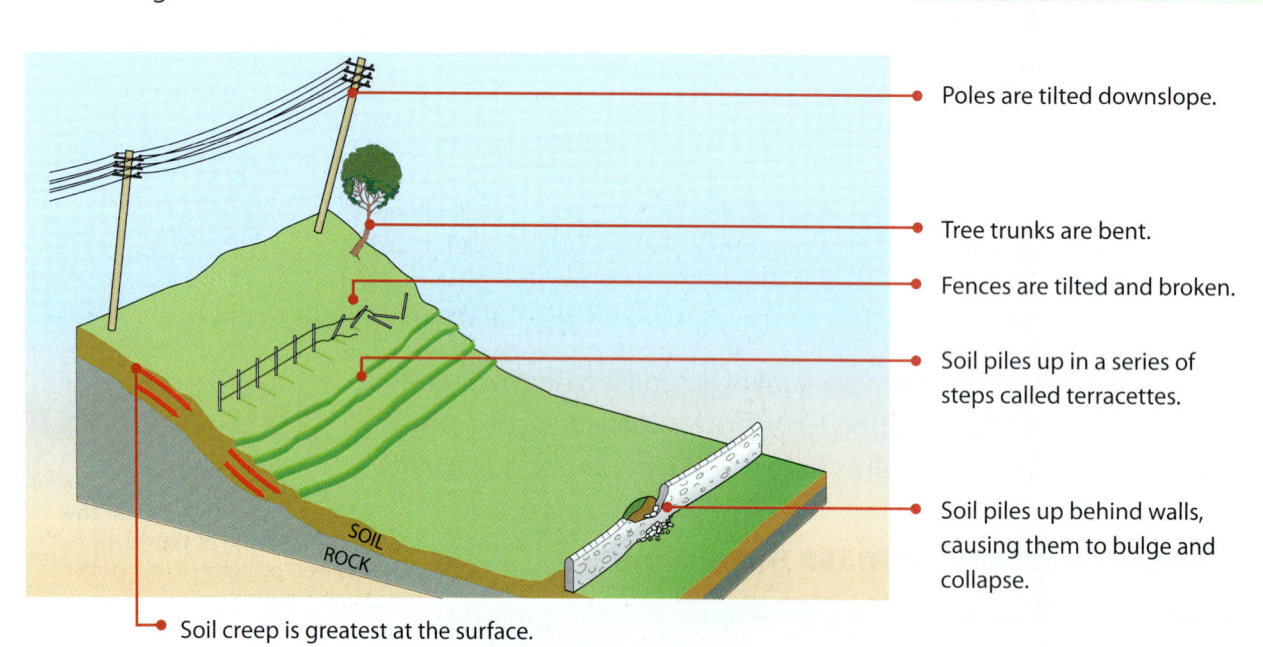

Figure 3.6 Some of the effects of soil creep on a slope

Landslides

A **landslide** takes place when large amounts of loose rocks and soil **suddenly** slide down a steep slope. They occur when slopes become unstable, and are most common in **upland** and **coastal** areas.

A landslide destroyed part of the town of Santa Tecla in El Salvador after the slope became unstable and failed

Most landslides occur when slopes are **undercut**, either by sea erosion or human activities such as quarrying and road building.

They also occur after heavy rainfall because the water loosens the hold that the regolith has on the rock beneath it.

Mudflows

Mudflows are flows of water that can contain rock, earth, silt, peat and other materials. They are the **fastest** forms of mass movement. The material can travel several kilometres from its starting point. The two main types of mudflow are:

- **Bogburst**
- **Lahar**.

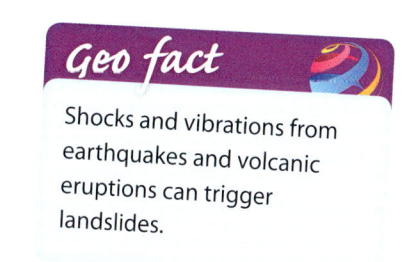

Geo fact
Shocks and vibrations from earthquakes and volcanic eruptions can trigger landslides.

Bogburst

A **bogburst** occurs in upland areas when **peat** (turf) becomes saturated with water **after heavy rainfall**. The peat loses its grip on the bedrock and begins to slide down the slope. The bogburst gains speed, forming a **slurry** that is strong enough to destroy everything in its path. Buildings and roads are damaged. Wildlife habitats are destroyed and rivers may be polluted.

Nature and human activity combined to contribute to a bogburst in the **Slieve Aughty Mountains** (Co. Galway) in 2003.

A construction company was engaged in preparing the ground for a large **wind farm**. It removed the coniferous trees on the site. In order to expose the bedrock, it also moved large areas of peat, and piled it into huge mounds.

A long spell of dry weather in summer was followed by heavy **downpours** in late autumn.

The peat became **saturated**, lost its grip on the bedrock and slid down the slope, following the course of a small stream. It caused a major fish kill, blocked roads and contaminated water supplies.

Lahar

A **lahar** is a type of mudflow that results after a **volcano** erupts in a **snow-capped mountain** region.

A sudden thaw of mountain snow due to a volcanic eruption can send a torrent of **mud, ash and hot water** down the slope of the volcano. As the water picks up more mud and rocks, it begins to look like a fast-flowing **river of concrete**.

Section 1 · Physical Geography

Case study

Lahar: the volcano of Nevado del Ruiz

The volcano of Nevado del Ruiz, a snow-capped mountain high in the **Andes**, erupted in 1985. The mountain was cloud-covered at the time, so the eruption went unnoticed.

- The volcano of Nevado del Ruiz erupted, throwing out huge amounts of ash and steam.
- The heat from the eruption melted the snow on the volcano.
- The meltwater rushed down the mountainside, picking up ash, soil and rocks on its way.
- Water + ash or soil = mudflow. The mud was up to 20 metres deep in places. It raced through the valley at speeds of up to 80 km per hour. Heavy rains also increased the size of the mudflow.
- The town of Armero was built on the plain at the foot of the mountain. It lay directly in the path of the mudflow, which struck just before midnight.

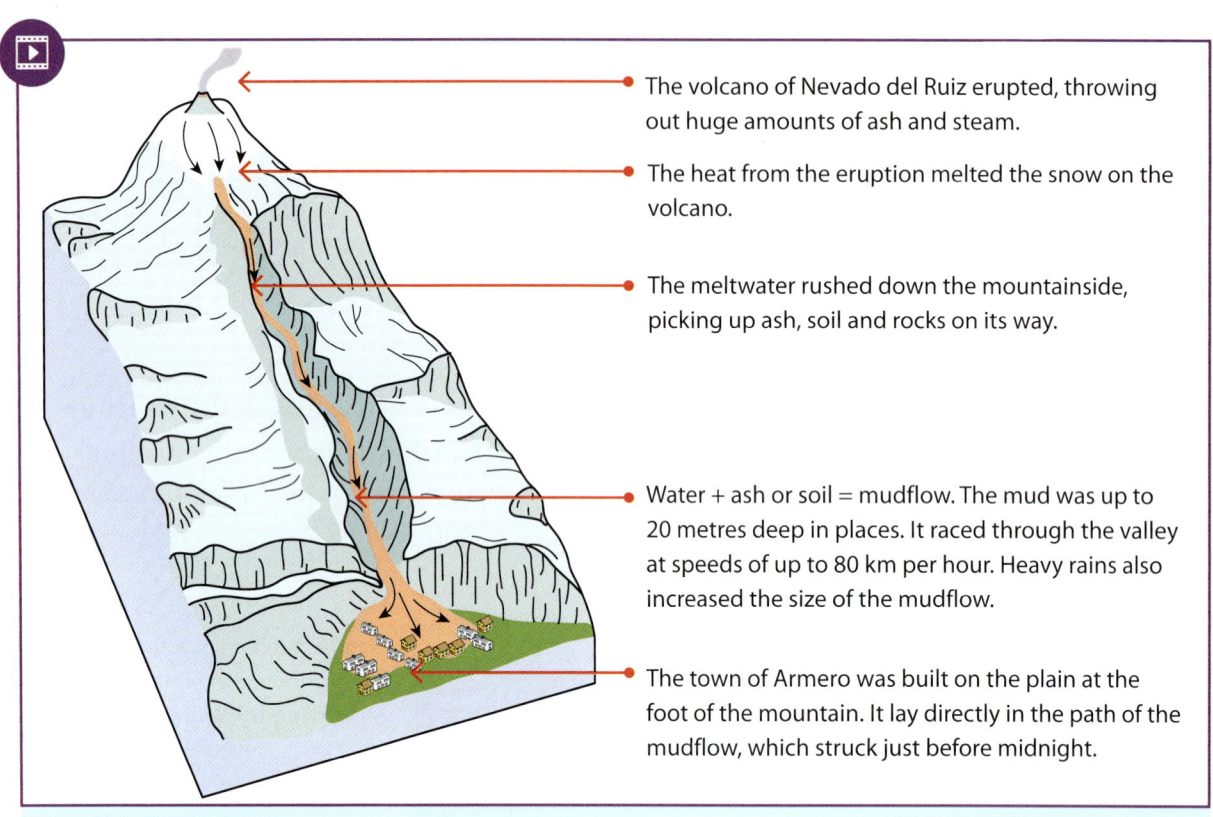

Figure 3.7 From eruption to lahar to destruction

Impact of the mudflow

It was the world's most deadly mudflow in the twentieth century. More than 21,000 people were killed. The death toll was so high because it occurred when people were asleep. More than 5,000 homes were destroyed and a further 6,000 people were made homeless. The cost of the disaster was $1 billion, about 20 per cent of Colombia's GNP.

The town of Armero in the foothills of the Andes after it was destroyed by a lahar

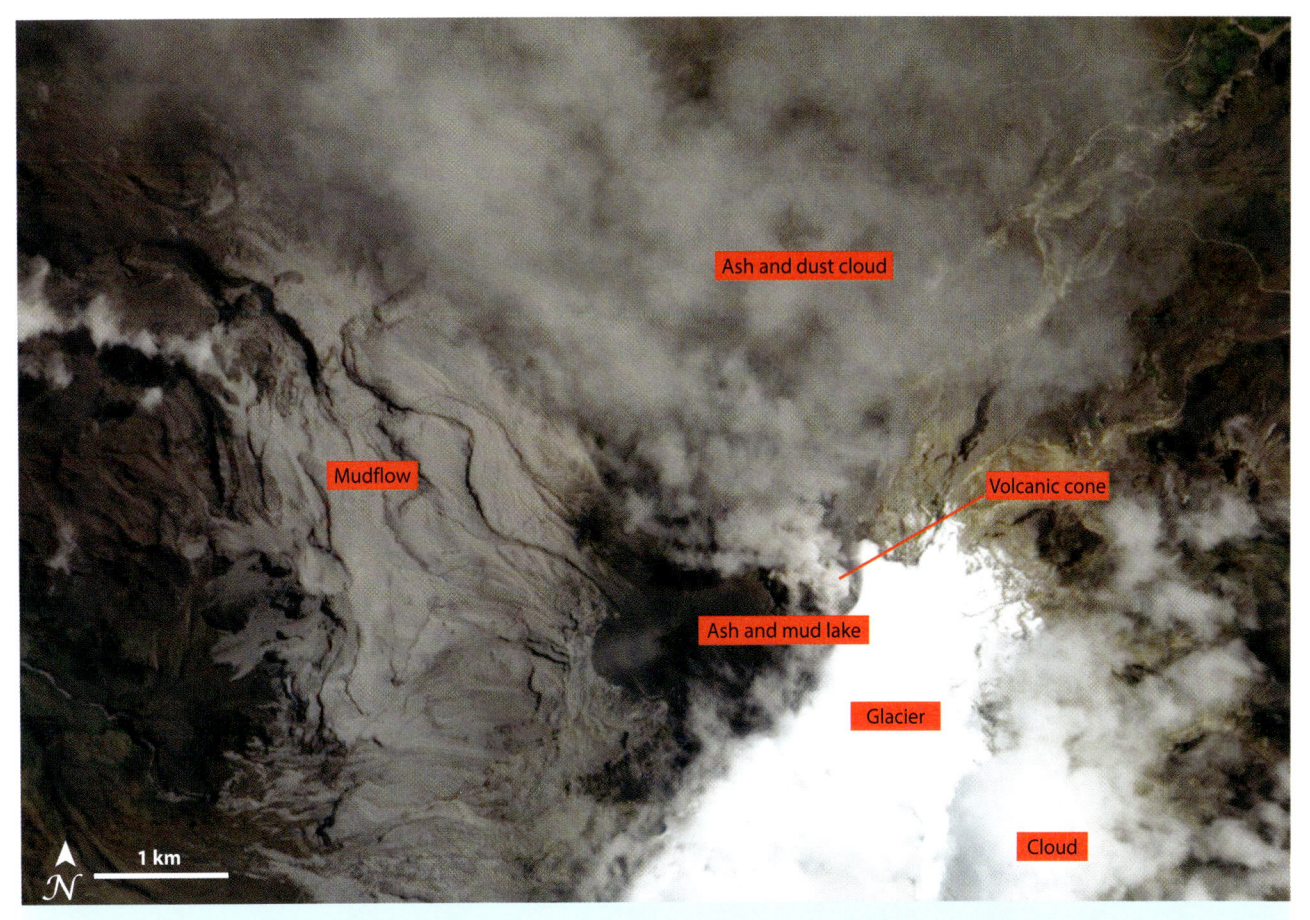

Nevado del Ruiz is still active, and erupted again in 2012. On this occasion, the mudflow was smaller and did not travel very far

Questions

1. (a) Explain the terms mass movement and regolith.
   (b) Name any **two** factors that contribute to mass movement.
   (c) How are the different types of mass movement grouped?

2. (a) What is soil creep?
   (b) Describe **three** ways in which soil creep affects the landscape.
   (c) List **two** differences between soil creep and a landslide.

3. (a) Why does water play such an important part in mudflows and bogbursts?
   (b) Describe how a bogburst might be caused.
   (c) Describe **two** impacts (effects) of a bogburst.

4. (a) What is a lahar?
   (b) Describe how a lahar might occur.
   (c) Why do lahars cause so much destruction?

Section 1 · Physical Geography

Summary chart

PowerPoint summary

Denudation

- **Weathering**
  - **Mechanical weathering**
    - Freeze-thaw
    - Scree slopes
  - **Chemical weathering**
    - Tropical red soils (Chapter 7)
    - Carbonation
      - **Surface landforms**
        - Limestone pavements
        - Clints & grikes
        - Swallow holes
      - **Underground landforms**
        - Caves & caverns
        - Stalactites
        - Stalagmites
        - Pillars
      - **The Burren & tourism**
        - Flora
        - Fauna
        - Landscape
        - History

- **Erosion (Rivers, Sea, Ice) (Chapter 4)**

- **Mass movement**
  - Influenced by:
    - Gradient
    - Water
    - Vegetation
    - Humans
  - **Slow**
    - Soil creep
      - Terracettes
      - Broken walls
      - Tilted poles
  - **Fast**
    - Landslides
    - Mudflows
    - Lahars
    - Bogbursts

42

Chapter 3 · Weathering and Mass Movement

Exam questions

1. With the aid of a labelled diagram(s), explain how frost action occurs.

    HL 2012

2. The diagram on the right shows a limestone landscape.
    (i) Name **one** example of a limestone landscape in Ireland.
    (ii) Name **one** *underground* feature found in a limestone area and explain how it was formed.
    (iii) Name **one** *surface* feature found in a limestone area and explain how it was formed.

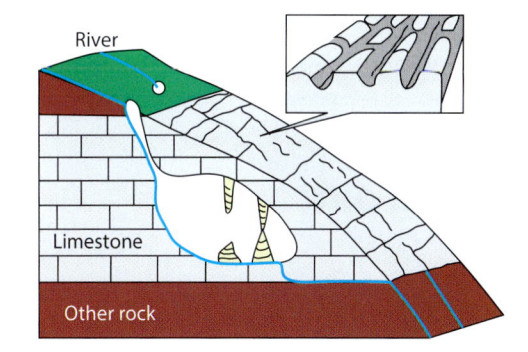

    OL 2014

3. Name the type of weathering most associated with the formation of the landscape shown (on the right) and explain this type of weathering.

    HL 2013

4. (i) Explain how precipitation and gradient influence mass movement.
    (ii) Name **one** type of slow mass movement and describe its effects.

    HL 2013

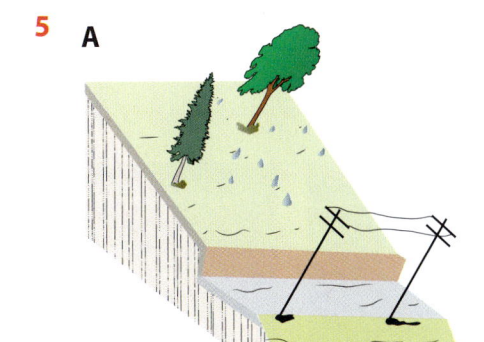

5. A   B

    Mass movement can be either slow or fast.
    (i) Name **each** type of mass movement shown in the pictures **A** and **B** above.
    (ii) Choose any **one** type of mass movement and explain how it happens.

    OL 2013

43

Chapter 4
Agents of Erosion

Learning outcomes

By the end of this chapter, you should be able to understand:

- That rivers, seas and ice shape the landscape
- That they do so by erosion, transportation and deposition
- How these processes operate
- That landforms (features) are formed as a result of these processes
- That human activities are influenced by these processes
- That human activities can interfere with these processes
- That these activities can have both positive and negative effects.

Introduction

The syllabus requires that you study the following topic:

Rivers (Sections 4.1–4.3)

The syllabus also requires that you study **one** of the following two sections:

The sea (Sections 4.4–4.6)

Glaciation (Sections 4.7–4.9)

Chapter 4 · Agents of Erosion

4.1 Rivers: shapers of our land

KEYWORDS

- drain
- landform
- channel
- bed
- bank
- youthful stage
- mature stage
- old stage
- erosion
- transportation
- deposition
- hydraulic action
- abrasion
- attrition
- load

Rivers **drain** rainwater from land and lakes and carry it to the sea. In doing so, they shape the landscape, creating **landforms** (or features) along the way.

Definitions

Rivers flow in **channels**. The bottom of the channel is called the **bed** and the sides of the channel are called the **banks**.

Figure 4.1 Common features of a river

Table 4.1 Features of a river

Feature	Definition
Source	The point where a river begins
Course	The route taken by a river as it flows into the sea
Tributary	A small river or stream that joins a larger one
Confluence	The place where two rivers meet
Mouth	The place where a river enters the sea
Estuary	The part of a river mouth that is tidal
Drainage basin	The area of land that is drained by a river and its tributaries
Watershed	The boundary between two drainage basins, often marked by hills or mountains

45

The three stages of a river

A river is often divided into three parts or **stages** as it flows from its source to its mouth. These are the **youthful** (or upper) stage, the **mature** (or middle) stage and the **old** (or lower) stage. Each stage has different features:

Table 4.2 The stages of a river

	Youthful stage	Mature stage	Old stage
The river	• is small • has a steep gradient	• is bigger • has a gentler gradient	• is much bigger • has an almost flat gradient
The valley has	• steep sides • a narrow floor	• gently sloping sides • a wider floor	• very gently sloping sides • a wide flat floor

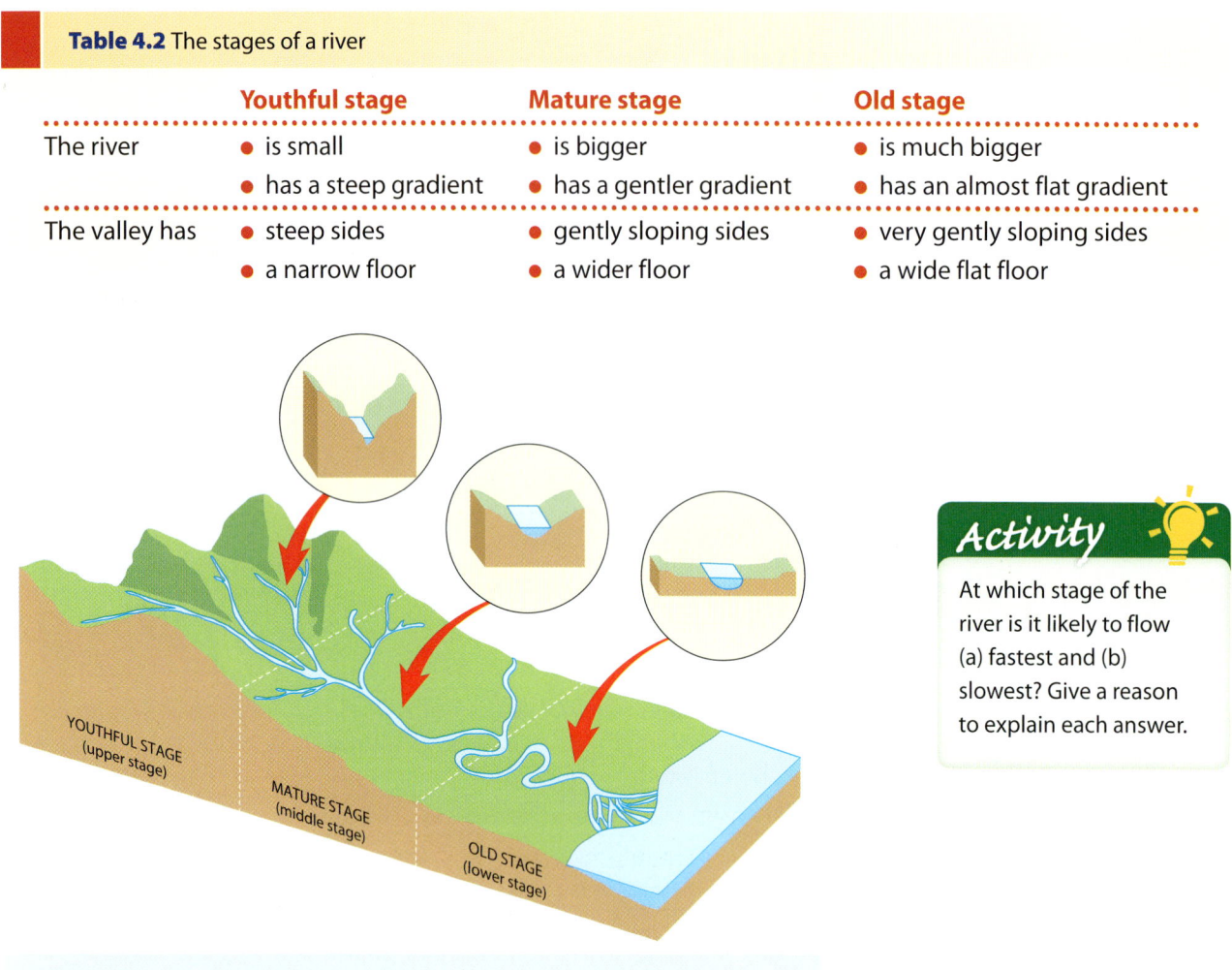

Figure 4.2 The gradient (slope) and shape of a river valley change along its course

Activity
At which stage of the river is it likely to flow (a) fastest and (b) slowest? Give a reason to explain each answer.

The work of rivers

As a river follows its course, it changes the landscape by the following processes:

- **Erosion** (wearing material away from the surface)
- **Transportation** (removing the material that it has eroded)
- **Deposition** (dropping the material it was transporting).

Erosion

The river **erodes** its bed and banks when:

- The force of the moving water breaks off material from the banks and bed of the river (**hydraulic action**).
- The material carried along by the river hits its banks and bed, wearing them away (**abrasion**).
- The material is worn down, smoothed and rounded as the stones bounce off each other (**attrition**).
- Acids in the water dissolve some rocks such as limestone (**solution**).

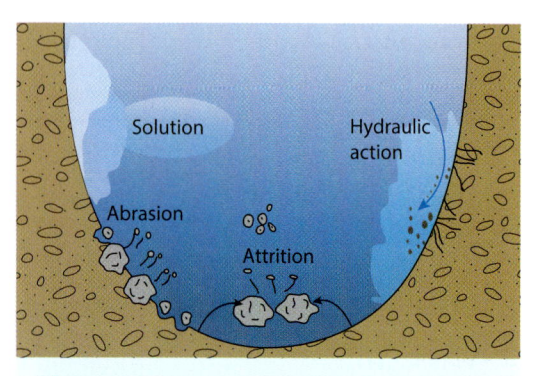

Figure 4.3 How a river erodes material in its banks and bed

Transportation

A river **transports** its **load** downstream in a number of ways:

- The largest load – boulders and rocks – is **rolled** along the bed of the river.
- The smaller particles – stones and pebbles – are **bounced** along the bed of the river.
- The lightest particles – silt and clay – are carried along, **suspended** in the water.
- Dissolved materials are carried in **solution**.

Deposition

The river drops or **deposits** its load when:

- It loses speed and has less energy
- Its volume decreases
- It enters a flat or gently sloping plain
- It flows into a lake or sea.

Definition
The material transported by a river is known as its **load**.

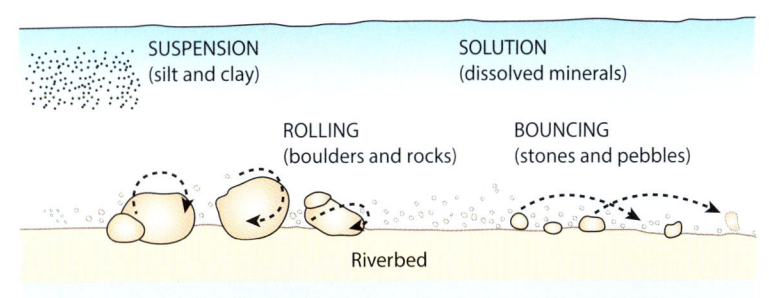

Figure 4.4 How a river transports its load of eroded material

Activity
At which stages of the river do (a) most erosion and (b) most deposition occur? Give a reason to explain each answer.

Questions

1. Rivers wear away the landscape by erosion.
   (a) Name **three** ways (processes) by which rivers erode the landscape.
   (b) Describe how any **two** of those processes erode the landscape

2. Rivers transport (or remove) the material that they have eroded.
   (a) Name **three** ways (processes) by which rivers transport this material.
   (b) Describe any **two** of those processes.

4.2 River landforms

KEYWORDS
- V-shaped valley
- interlocking spurs
- waterfall
- plunge pool
- gorge
- meander
- floodplain
- alluvium
- oxbow lake
- levee
- delta
- distributary

Landforms of a youthful river

The **youthful (or young) river** has a small volume of water and flows down a steep gradient. It may turn into a raging torrent after heavy rainfall. It uses most of its energy to **erode** the landscape. As a result, a number of features (or **landforms**) are created.

Section 1 · Physical Geography

V-shaped valley

A V-shaped valley has a **narrow floor** and **steep sides**.

- The river carries stones and rocks in its water.
- The force of the water and the grinding of rocks and stones cut down into the riverbed, and deepen it by **vertical erosion**.
- Meanwhile, **weathering** breaks up rock and soil on the valley sides. They eventually collapse and the material slides into the river.
- This gives the river valley its 'V' shape.
- The material is eventually worn down and transported by the river.

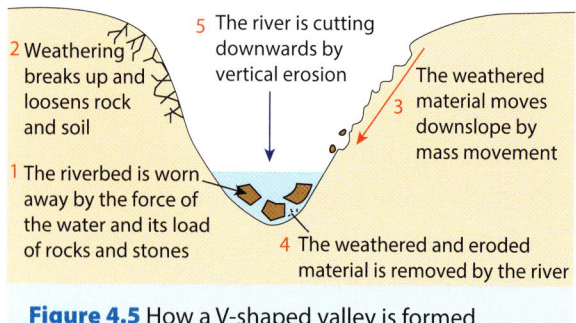

Examples are seen in the youthful stage of the rivers Moy, Lee, Liffey and Slaney.

Figure 4.5 How a V-shaped valley is formed

1 The riverbed is worn away by the force of the water and its load of rocks and stones
2 Weathering breaks up and loosens rock and soil
3 The weathered material moves downslope by mass movement
4 The weathered and eroded material is removed by the river
5 The river is cutting downwards by vertical erosion

Interlocking spurs

Interlocking spurs are a series of ridges that jut out from both sides of a young river valley and lock into one another like the teeth of a zip.

- When the river meets **hard or resistant rocks**, it is unable to erode through them.
- Instead, it **winds** and bends to avoid them.
- At the same time, the river continues to erode **downwards**.
- In this way, the river develops a **zigzag** course.

Examples are seen in the youthful stage of the rivers Moy, Lee, Liffey and Slaney.

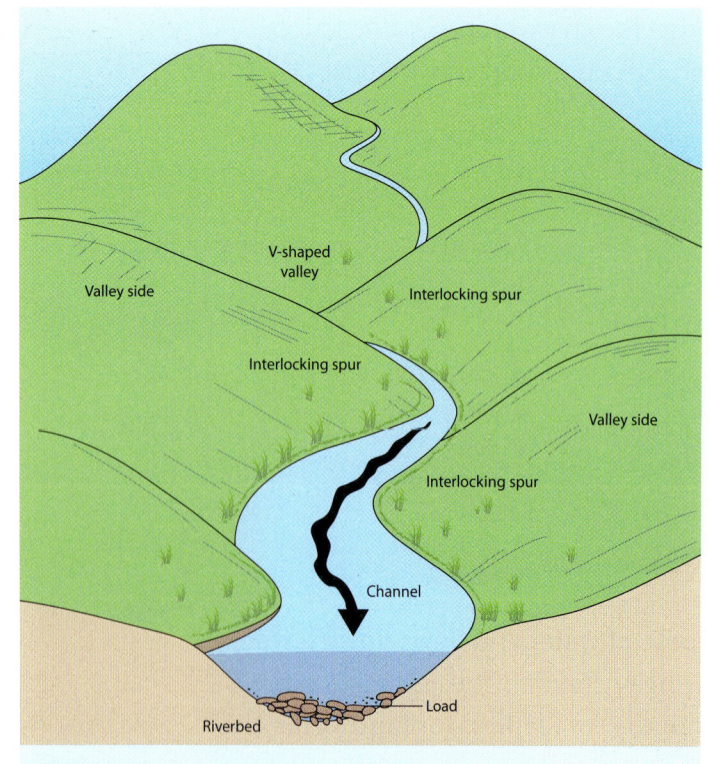

Figure 4.6 V-shaped valley with interlocking spurs

A V-shaped valley with interlocking spurs

Waterfall

A **waterfall** is a feature where the river flows or falls over a vertical slope.

- Waterfalls form when a layer of **hard** (or resistant) rock lies on top of a band of **softer** rock.
- Over thousands of years, the softer rock is eroded more quickly than the hard rock.
- Over time, the slope becomes steeper and a waterfall is formed.
- As the water drops over the waterfall, it carries its load with it. This helps the waterfall to erode a deep hole called a **plunge pool**.
- The falling water also cuts under the waterfall to form an **overhang** of hard rock. This eventually collapses.
- The process repeats itself and the waterfall **retreats upstream** to form a **gorge**.

Examples include Aasleagh Falls (Mayo), Torc Waterfall (Killarney) and Glencar Falls (Sligo).

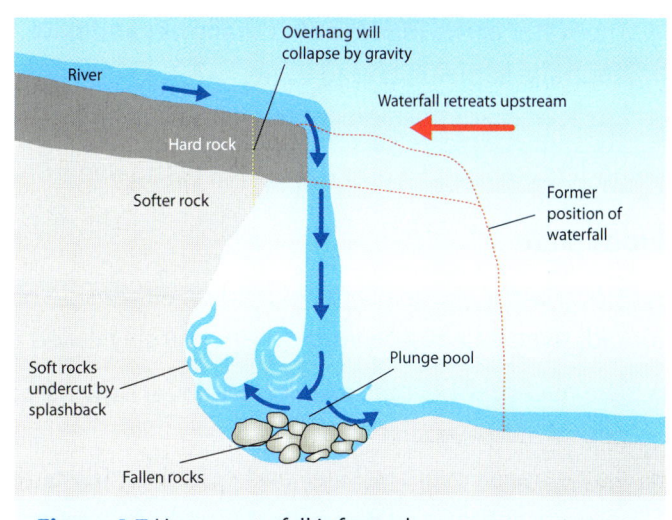

Figure 4.7 How a waterfall is formed

Geo fact
Niagara Falls is one of the world's most famous waterfalls. It is only about 50 metres high but is over 1 km wide. It retreats upstream by about 1 metre per year.

Landforms of a mature river

The **mature river** has a **greater volume** of water, now that many tributaries have joined it. It flows over a **gentler slope** (gradient) and has a **large load** of material to transport. As a result, it flows more **slowly** than in the youthful stage.

Wider valley

The sides of the mature valley are less steep. The valley floor is wider and is almost flat.

- At this stage, the river begins to swing from **side to side**, removing the interlocking spurs.
- As a result, the valley floor is widened by **lateral** (sideways) **erosion**.
- Weathering and mass movement continue, so the valley sides become **less steep**.

A wider valley may be seen in the mature stage of the rivers Nore, Boyne and Barrow.

Meanders

Meanders are curves or bends that develop along the mature (and old) course of a river. Meanders are formed by a combination of **erosion** and **deposition**.

- As the water flows around a slight bend, the water at the outer bank is deeper and flows more quickly. As a result, it has more power to **erode** the bank.

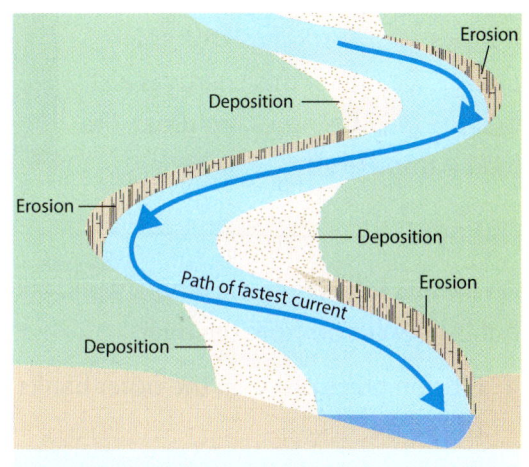

Waterfall and gorge at Niagara Falls

Figure 4.8 How meanders form

Section 1 · Physical Geography

- The water at the inner bank is shallower and flows more slowly. As a result, the river **deposits** some of its load there.
- Erosion and deposition continue and the **meander** becomes more prominent.

Meanders are found along the course of the rivers Shannon, Moy and Avoca.

Floodplain

A **floodplain** is the level area of land on either side of a mature (or old) river. It has a covering of very fine clay called **alluvium**.

- The river may become swollen and **overflow its banks** after a period of heavy rain.
- As it spreads over the level land on either side of the river, it quickly loses its energy and **deposits its load** of alluvium.
- Over many periods of flooding, a thick layer of alluvium builds up to form the **floodplain**.

Floodplains have developed along the rivers Shannon, Liffey, Boyne and Suir.

Definition
Alluvium: Material transported and deposited by a river when it floods.

Geo fact
Well-developed meanders and wide floodplains are also found in the old stage of a river.

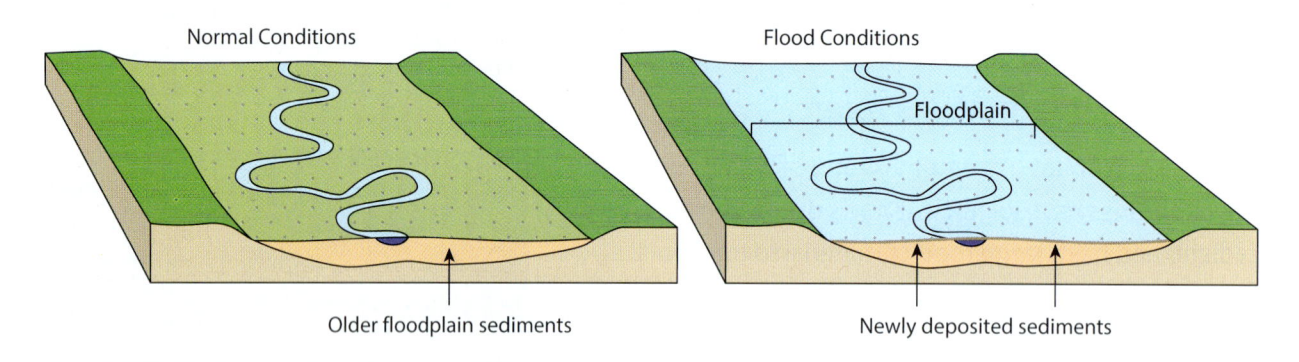

Figure 4.9 How a floodplain is formed

Landforms of an old river

The **old river** transports a **large load of alluvium** as it flows over land that is almost **level**. As a result, it **flows slowly** and has little spare energy. If some of this energy is lost or if the load becomes too great, the load is **deposited**.

Old river and its floodplain during a period of flooding

Oxbow lake

An **oxbow lake** is a horseshoe-shaped lake that was **once part of a river meander**, but is now cut off from the river.

- Erosion takes place on the outer banks of the river where **two meanders are close together**.
- Slowly the **neck** of land between two meanders gets narrower.
- During a flood, when the river has more energy, the neck of land is finally cut through.

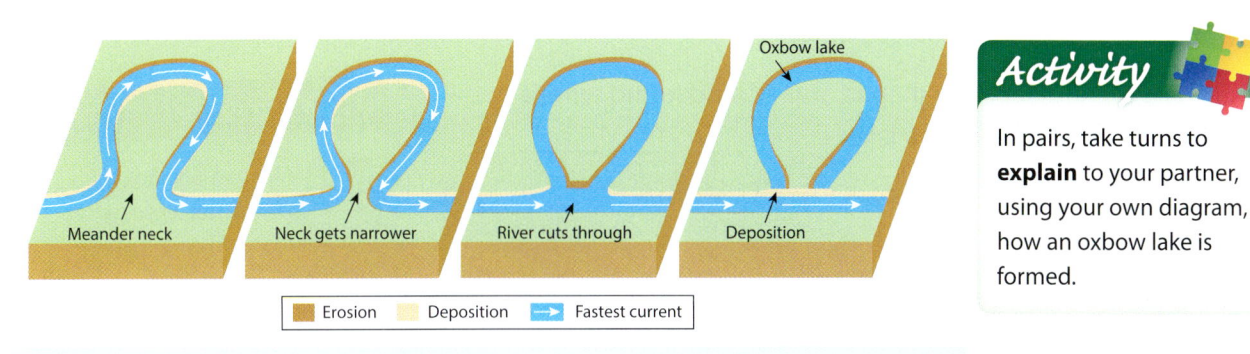

Figure 4.10 How an oxbow lake is formed

Activity

In pairs, take turns to **explain** to your partner, using your own diagram, how an oxbow lake is formed.

- When this happens, a new, straighter river channel is created. The meander is abandoned.
- The river has little energy at this stage and deposits some of its load of **alluvium**.
- Both ends of the meander are cut off from the river channel to form an **oxbow lake**.

Oxbow lakes can be seen at the old stage of the rivers Mississippi, Liffey and Moy.

Levees

Levees are raised banks of **alluvium** that are found along the banks of some rivers in their old stage.

- When a river **floods** and begins to spread out over the floodplain, it quickly loses its energy and begins to **deposit its load**.
- Most of the load, especially its **heavier particles**, is deposited **close to the banks** of the river. The lighter particles are carried further.
- After many periods of flooding, these deposits build up to form **levees**.

Levees are found along the old stage of the rivers Mississippi, Moy and Liffey.

Oxbow lakes already formed and also about to form on a tributary of the Mississippi

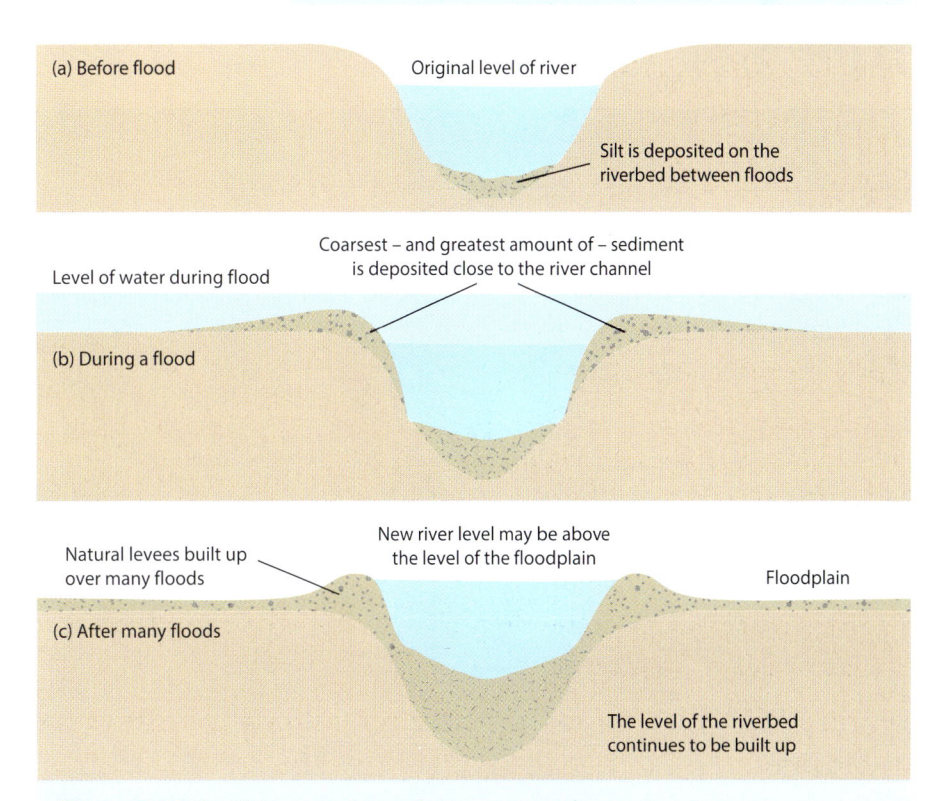

Figure 4.11 How levees are formed

Section 1 · Physical Geography

Delta

A **delta** is a triangular or fan-shaped area of land found **where a river flows into the sea** (or a lake).

- When a river flows into the sea, it loses its speed and **deposits its load**.
- If a river has a big load, the tides and currents may not be strong enough to carry it all out to sea.
- The mouth of the river becomes clogged and the river breaks up into smaller channels called **distributaries**.
- The deposits build up gradually and eventually rise above sea level to form a **delta**.

Deltas are found at the mouths of the rivers Nile, Po, Mississippi and Amazon.

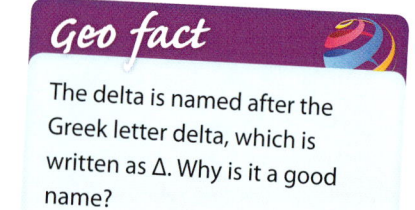

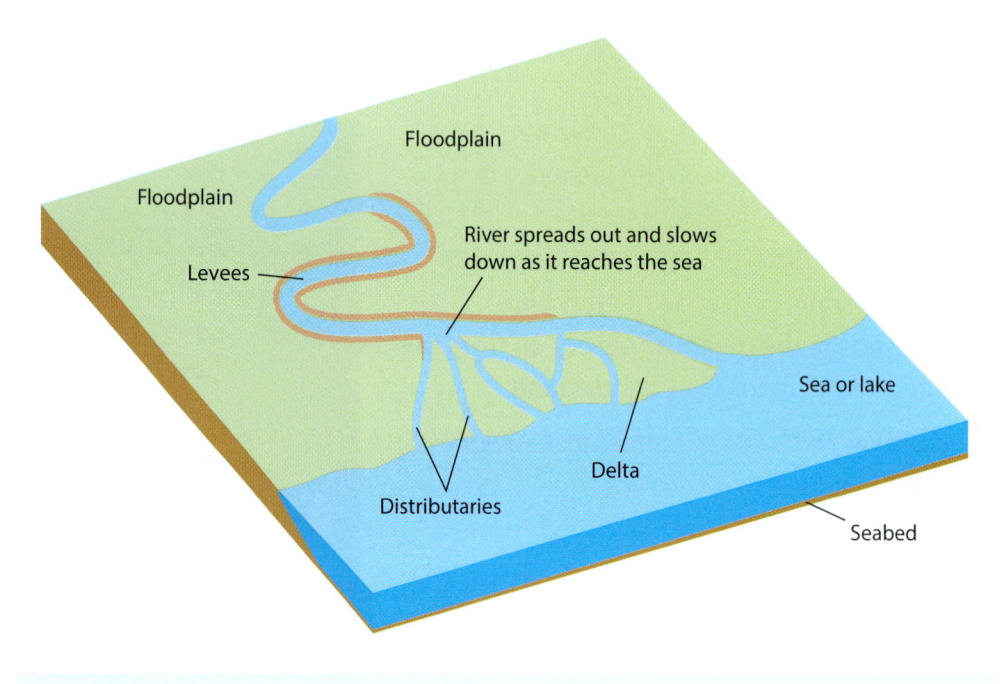

Geo fact
The delta is named after the Greek letter delta, which is written as Δ. Why is it a good name?

Figure 4.12 How a delta is formed

Delta forming at the mouth of a river

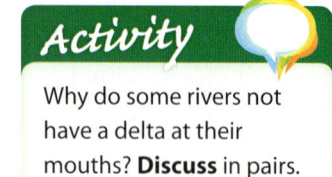

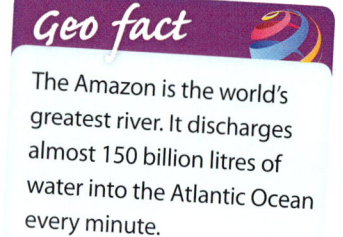

Activity
Why do some rivers not have a delta at their mouths? **Discuss** in pairs.

Geo fact
The Amazon is the world's greatest river. It discharges almost 150 billion litres of water into the Atlantic Ocean every minute.

Chapter 4 · Agents of Erosion

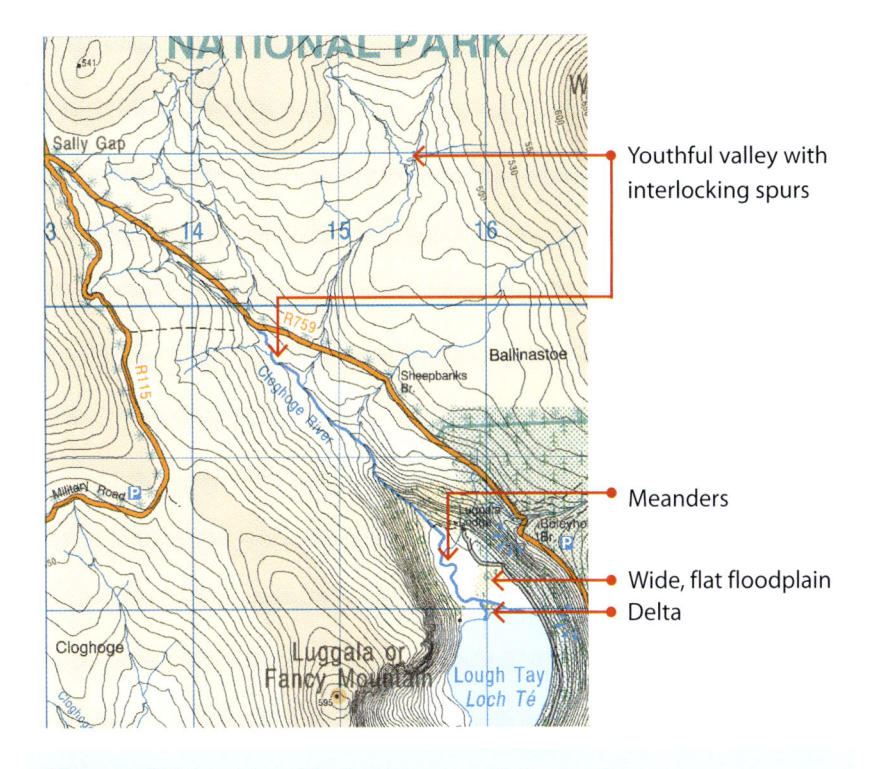

Figure 4.13 Identifying river features on an Ordnance Survey map

Labels on map:
- Youthful valley with interlocking spurs
- Meanders
- Wide, flat floodplain
- Delta

Activity

Examine Figure 4.13. Can you identify another example of one of the landforms labelled on the map?

Questions

1. (a) Name **one** landform of river erosion.
   (b) At what stage of the river is it found?
   (c) Name **one** example of that landform.
   (d) Draw a labelled diagram of that landform.
   (e) Explain how that landform was formed.

2. (a) Name **one** landform of river deposition.
   (b) At what stage of the river is it found?
   (c) Name **one** example of that landform.
   (d) Draw a labelled diagram of that landform.
   (e) Explain how that landform was formed.

4.3 Rivers and people

KEYWORDS

- dam
- flooding
- hydroelectric power (HEP)

People interact with the natural processes of rivers in a number of ways.
- Building dams and weirs
- Flooding: its impact and people's response to it.

Section 1 · Physical Geography

Case study

The River Shannon

The Shannon is the longest river in Ireland. For most of its course, the **River Shannon** has a very gentle gradient.

It also receives large amounts of water from tributaries such as the Inny, Suck and Brosna (see map on page 281). The Shannon and its tributaries drain an area of almost 16,000 km².

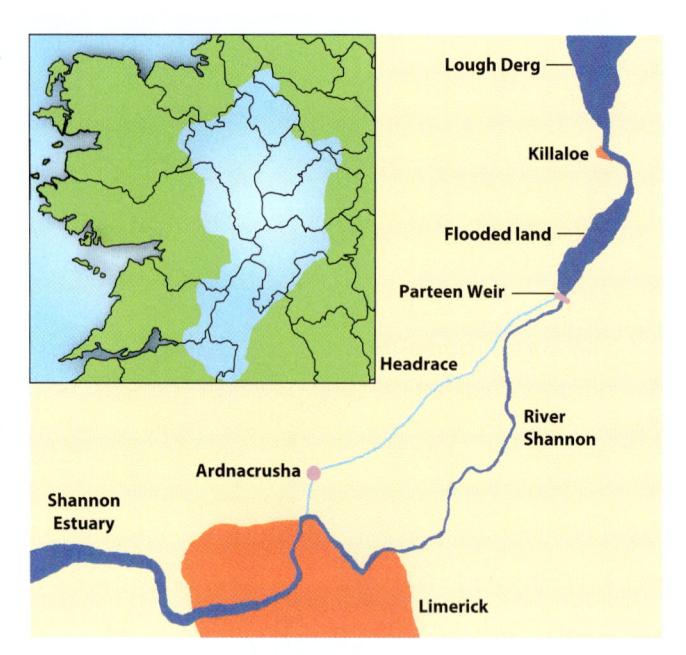

The Shannon hydroelectric scheme

The **Shannon Scheme** was a plan by the Irish government in the 1920s to provide a cheap, reliable and plentiful supply of electricity for the country.

The main parts are:

Parteen Weir

- The raising of the water levels created a large **reservoir** south of Killaloe.
- The weir diverts much of the flow of the River Shannon into a **headrace canal** leading to the power station at Ardnacrusha.

> **Definitions**
>
> **Dam:** A barrier built across a river to raise the level of the river on the upstream side.
> **Weir:** A low dam that serves the same purpose but also allows water to flow over its top.

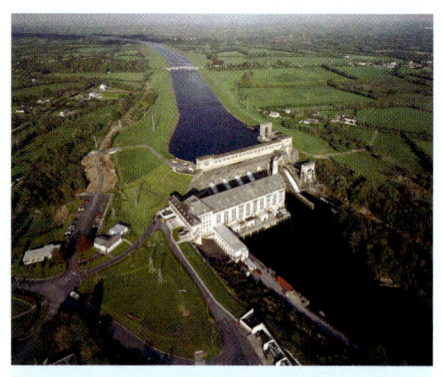

The power station at Ardnacrusha, with the headrace in the background

The headrace canal

- This is a canal, that brings water from the weir at Parteen to the dam at Ardnacrusha.

Ardnacrusha Dam

- This is where electricity is generated, using the water in the headrace canal.
- The water rapidly spins the **blades** in the turbines. These are connected to generators that make electricity as they spin.

Table 4.3 Benefits and disadvantages of the Shannon dam and weirs

Benefits	Disadvantages
• They enable the generation of **HEP**. This is a clean source of renewable energy.	• Thousands of hectares of **farmland** were lost when the artificial lake was created.
• They are used to **manage the risk of flooding** in the lower Shannon catchment area.	• Families had to evacuate their homes and be **relocated** elsewhere.
	• New roads and bridges had to be built, while others were buried beneath the water.

Case study

Flooding on the Shannon

Causes

The River Shannon is liable to serious flooding. Some flooding now occurs every winter and for some period every second summer on average. There are a number of reasons for this:

- The river has a very **gentle gradient** so water is slow to leave the channel.
- The river channel is both narrow and shallow in places. Silt from bogs has settled on the bed. Vegetation has blocked some of the lower channel.
- There are narrow **choke points** where water leaves the lakes on the Shannon.
- The huge **floodplains** are barely above normal water levels in places. During the building boom, construction took place on some of the floodplains.

The **worst flooding** ever experienced along the Shannon took place in December 2015 and early January 2016.

It followed very heavy rainfall that was three times the average for the period. The rainfall resulted from six back-to-back storms that began in November. The ground soon became saturated and most water flowed quickly from the land as run-off.

The effects

The floods affected both rural areas and urban areas that included Carrick-on-Shannon and Athlone. The main effects of the flooding were:

- Four hundred **homes** were abandoned after being flooded. Another 150 homes were marooned and cut off by floodwaters.
- **Shops** were flooded and stock destroyed.
- **Roads** were flooded, with many impassable for weeks.
- Large areas of floodplain were flooded. **Animals** had to be moved to higher ground. Stocks of winter feed were destroyed.

Flooding would have been more extensive but for the widespread use of **sandbags**. Nevertheless, the cost of repairing the damage caused by the floods was more than €100 million.

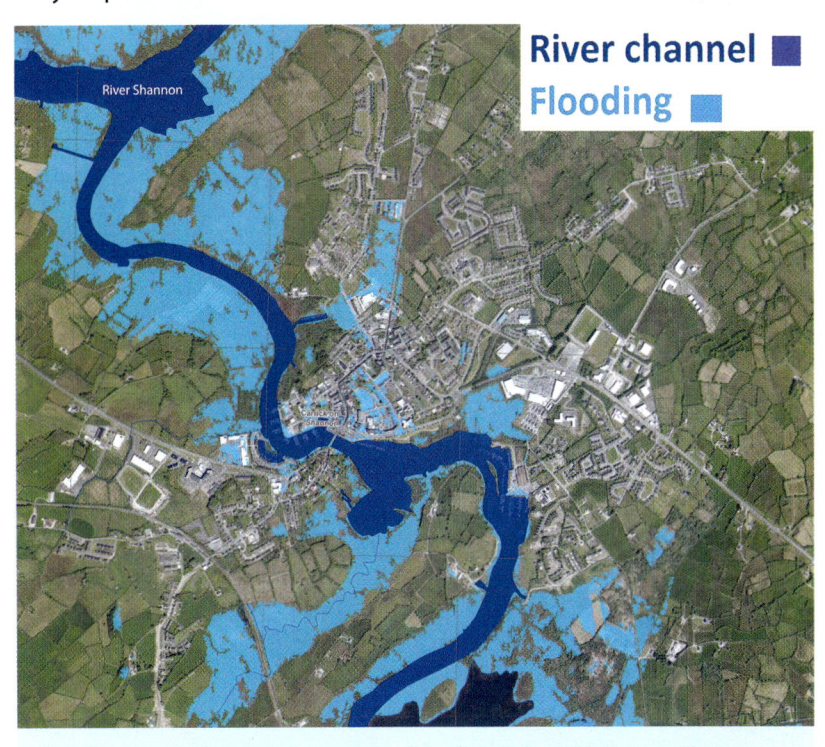

Satellite image showing the extent of the flooding at Carrick-on-Shannon

Section 1 · Physical Geography

Questions

1. Large rivers are used to generate hydroelectricity.
   (a) Describe what needs to be done to the river to enable this to happen.
   (b) Describe **one** positive effect of this.
   (c) Describe **one** negative effect of this.

2. (a) Describe **two** reasons why a river might burst its banks and flood.
   (b) Describe any **two** effects of that flooding on people and property.

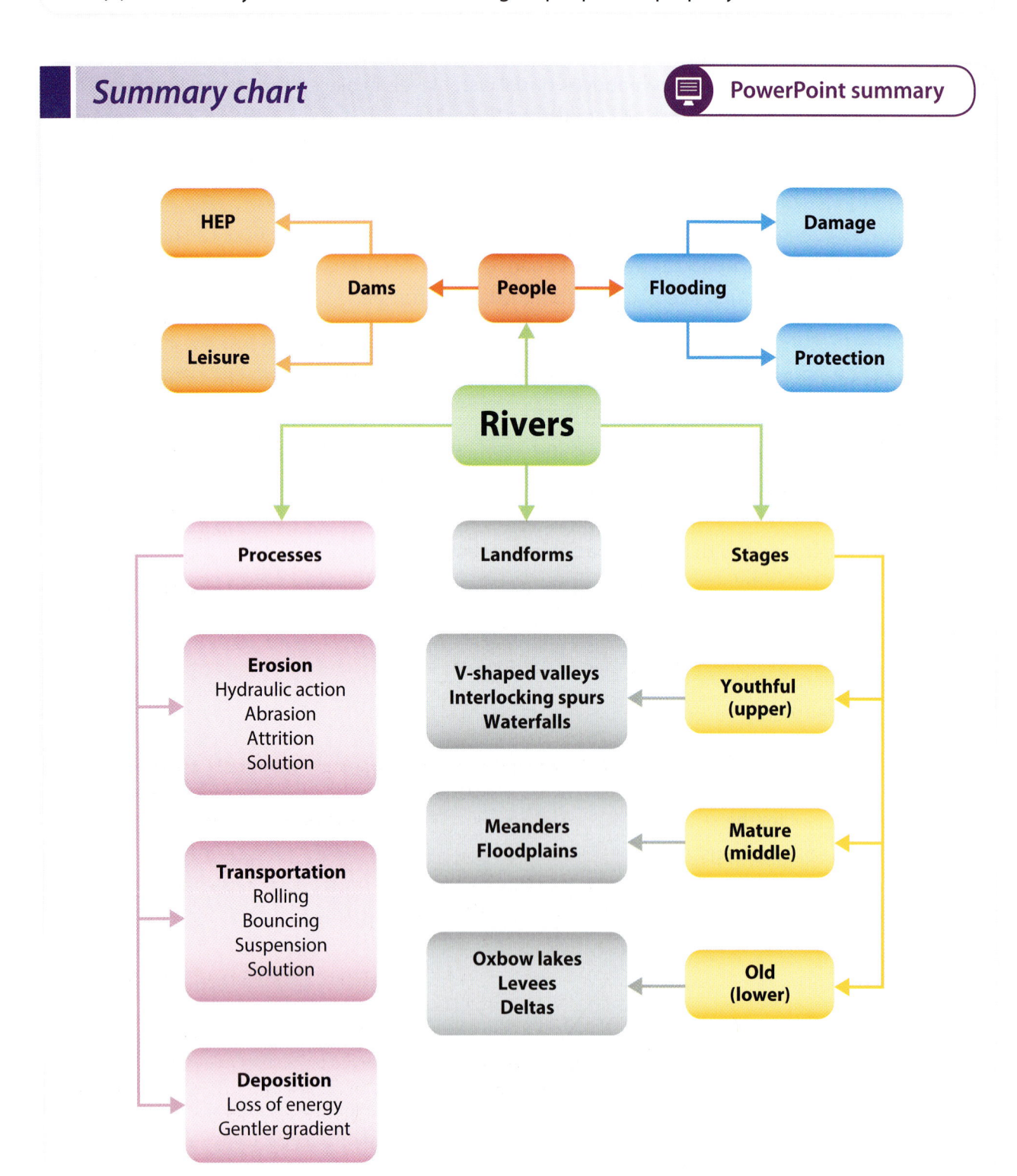

Summary chart

PowerPoint summary

Rivers

People → Dams → HEP / Leisure
People → Flooding → Damage / Protection

Processes
- Erosion: Hydraulic action, Abrasion, Attrition, Solution
- Transportation: Rolling, Bouncing, Suspension, Solution
- Deposition: Loss of energy, Gentler gradient

Landforms
- V-shaped valleys, Interlocking spurs, Waterfalls
- Meanders, Floodplains
- Oxbow lakes, Levees, Deltas

Stages
- Youthful (upper)
- Mature (middle)
- Old (lower)

4.4 Sea: the destroyer

KEYWORDS
- swash
- backwash
- destructive waves
- constructive waves
- hydraulic action
- compressed air
- bay
- headland
- sea cliff
- notch
- wave-cut platform
- sea cave
- sea arch
- sea stack
- blowhole

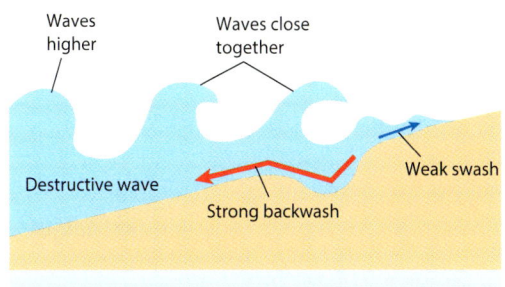

Figure 4.14a Destructive waves operate during stormy weather. They have a lot of energy and a strong backwash. As a result, these waves cause **erosion**

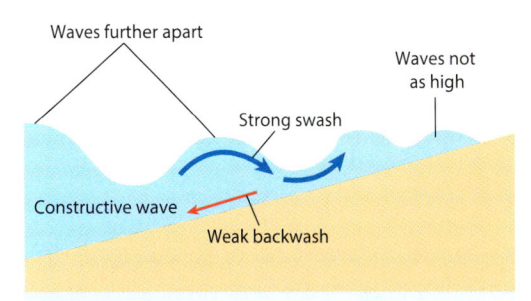

Figure 4.14b Constructive waves operate in calm weather. They have limited energy and most of it is used by the swash to transport and **deposit** material

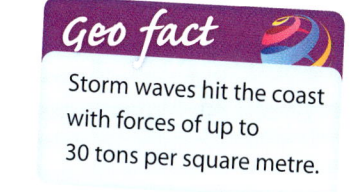

The coastline is constantly changing. This is due to the action of waves as they **erode**, **transport** and **deposit** material along the coastline.

Waves

When wind blows over the smooth surface of the sea, it causes ripples in the water and these grow into **waves**. The size of the wave increases with the **strength of wind** and the **length of sea** over which it passes.

When waves reach shallow water, they **break** or tumble onto the shore. The frothy water that rushes onto the shore is called the **swash**. The water that runs back out from the wave is called the **backwash**.

- A **destructive wave** is one where the backwash is stronger than the swash and material is **eroded**.
- A **constructive wave** is one where the swash is stronger than the backwash and material is **deposited**.

How waves erode

Waves **erode** by the following four methods (or **processes**).

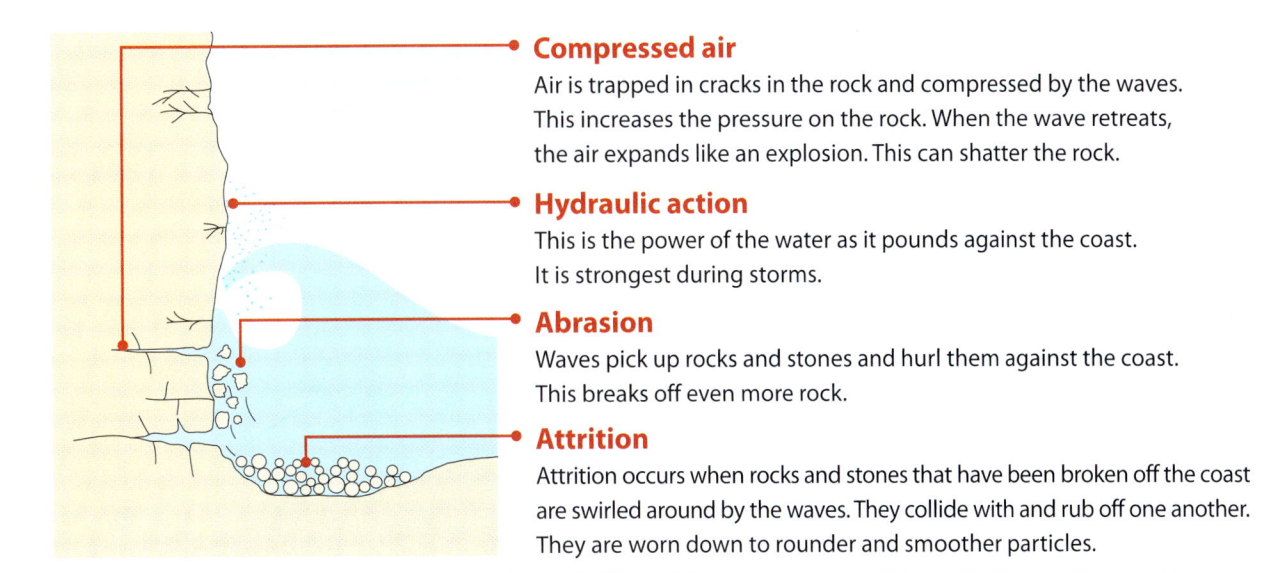

Geo fact
Storm waves hit the coast with forces of up to 30 tons per square metre.

Compressed air
Air is trapped in cracks in the rock and compressed by the waves. This increases the pressure on the rock. When the wave retreats, the air expands like an explosion. This can shatter the rock.

Hydraulic action
This is the power of the water as it pounds against the coast. It is strongest during storms.

Abrasion
Waves pick up rocks and stones and hurl them against the coast. This breaks off even more rock.

Attrition
Attrition occurs when rocks and stones that have been broken off the coast are swirled around by the waves. They collide with and rub off one another. They are worn down to rounder and smoother particles.

Figure 4.15 The ways in which waves erode the coastline

Section 1 · Physical Geography

Landforms of coastal erosion

A number of landforms are created as a result of coastal erosion.

Bays and headlands

A **bay** is a wide, curved opening into the coast.
A **headland** is a neck of high land that juts out into the sea.

Bays and headlands are formed where there are different bands of rock along the coast. If the rock is **soft**, such as shale, it is eroded very quickly and a **bay** is formed. If the rock is **hard**, such as sandstone, it is eroded much more slowly and stands out as a **headland**. If the headlands are big, they shelter the bay and a small **beach** may form in the bay.

Examples of bays include Dublin Bay and Galway Bay. Examples of headlands include Mizen Head and Malin Head.

Sea cliffs

A **sea cliff** is a vertical or steep slope on the coast.

Destructive waves attack the coast and cut into the rock, eroding a **notch**. They do this by the processes described on the previous page. When the notch becomes deeper, the overhanging rock above it will collapse under its own weight.

As the processes of **undercutting and collapse** continue, the cliff gradually retreats.

As the cliff retreats, a gently-sloping rock surface remains between the high-water mark and the low-water mark. This is called a **wave-cut platform**.

The best known cliffs in Ireland are the Cliffs of Moher in Co. Clare. The highest cliffs in the country are at Slieve League in Co. Donegal.

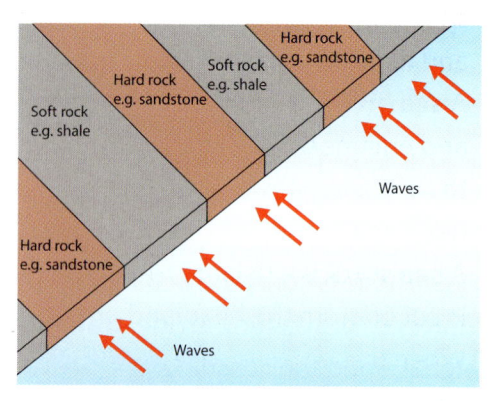

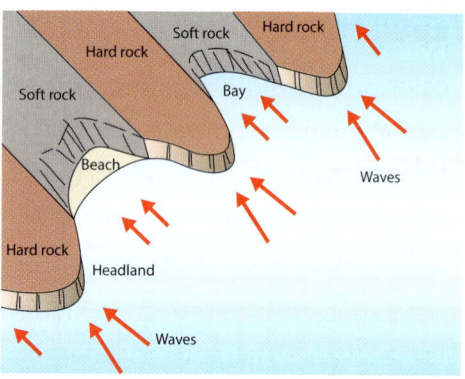

> **Geo fact**
> Headlands are also known as 'points', e.g. Rosses Point.

Figure 4.16 Headlands and bays are formed when soft rock is eroded more quickly than hard rock

> **Activity**
> What processes (methods) of erosion are active when bays and headlands are formed?

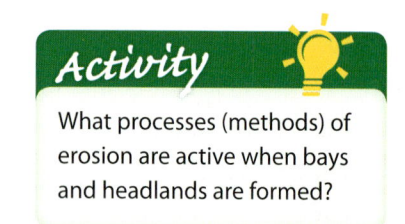

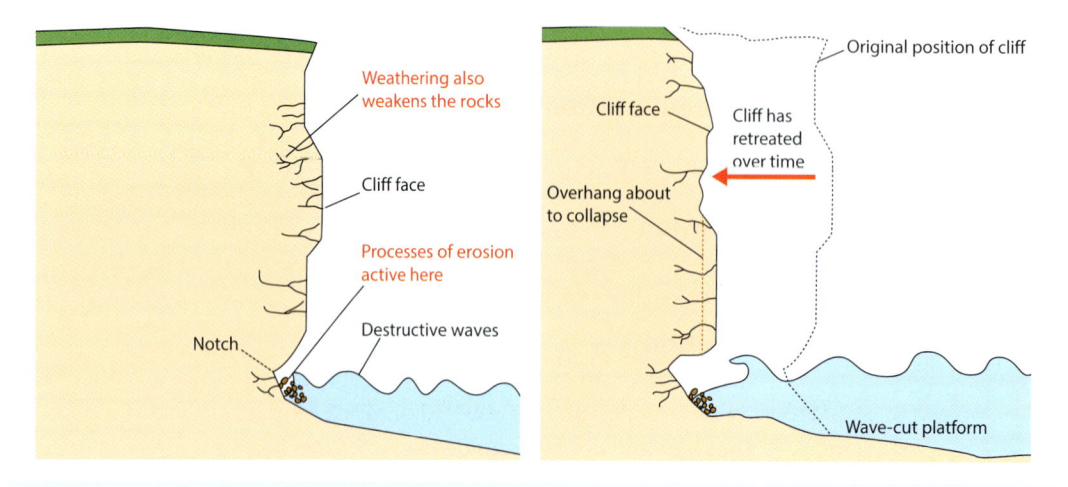

Figure 4.17 How a cliff and wave-cut platform are formed

58

Sea cave, sea arch, sea stack and blowhole

A number of landforms that are all linked together are found on a **cliff coastline**. They are **sea caves**, **sea arches**, **sea stacks** and **blowholes**.

- A **sea cave** is a tunnel or passage in the rock at the foot of a cliff. If the rock has a weak spot such as a crack (fault), the waves will attack it by hydraulic action, compressed air and abrasion. The crack gets larger and develops into a small cave.
- A **sea arch** is a passage that runs right through a headland. If the cave is deepened and enlarged by erosion, it may cut through to the other side of the headland to form a sea arch. A sea arch may also form if two caves on opposite sides of a headland meet.
- A **sea stack** is a pillar of rock that is cut off from the headland or cliff. When the waves erode the base of a sea arch, they widen it. Eventually the roof is unable to support itself and it collapses, leaving the former tip of the headland cut off as a sea stack. If the base of the sea stack is eroded, it will collapse to leave a **stump** of rock that is visible at low tide.

Sea caves, sea arches and sea stacks can all be seen close together at **Hook Head** in Co. Wexford and at the **Bridges of Ross** in Co. Clare.

A spout of water blowing through a blowhole

- A **blowhole** is a passage that links the roof of a cave with the surface of the cliff top.

Air is trapped and **compressed** in the cave by powerful storm waves. This builds up pressure and helps to loosen and shatter the rock at the back of the cave. The rock eventually **collapses**, forming a blowhole.

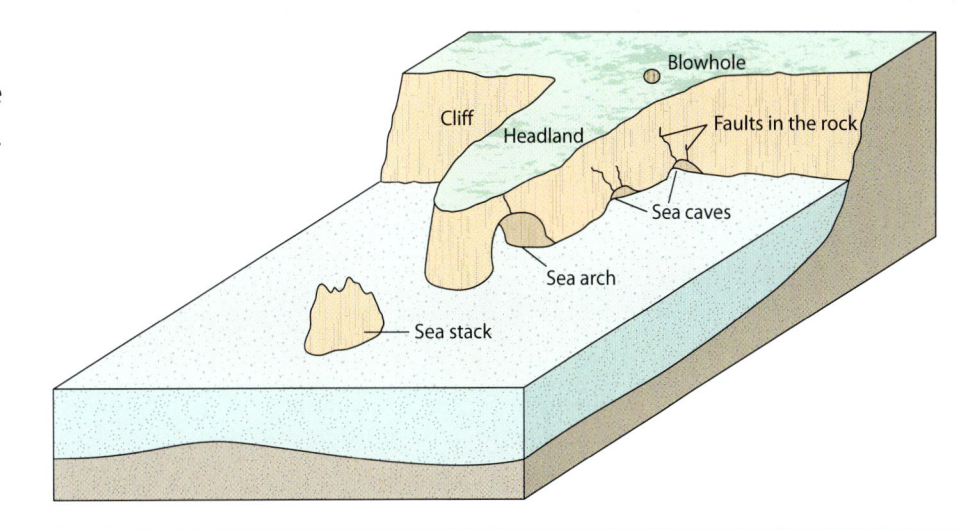

Figure 4.18 Features of erosion found on a cliff coastline

During stormy weather, sea spray may spurt out from the blowhole.

Some blowholes have very descriptive names such as 'The Two Pistols' and 'McSweeney's Gun' on the Co. Donegal coast.

Section 1 · Physical Geography

Features of coastal erosion

Activity

Examine the photograph on the left. Link each of the following landforms with one of the letters:
- Notch
- Sea cave
- Sea arch
- Stack
- Cliff.

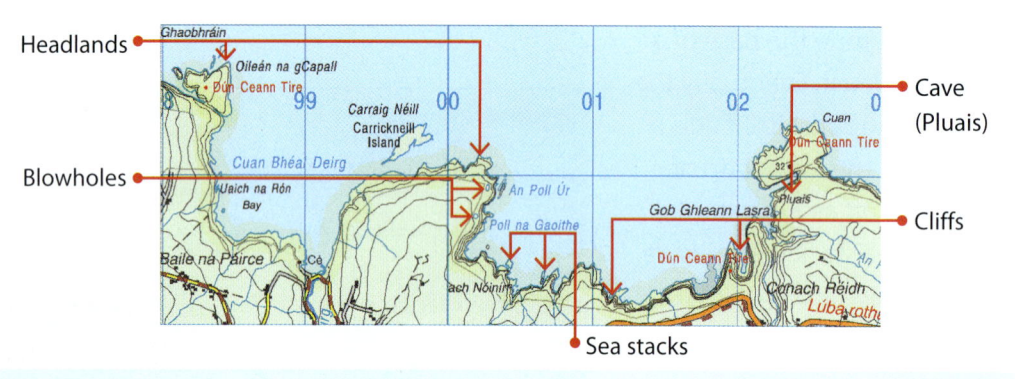

Figure 4.19 Landforms of coastal erosion on an Ordnance Survey map extract

Questions

1. Waves wear away the coastline by erosion.
   (a) Name **three** ways (processes) by which waves erode.
   (b) Describe how any **two** of those processes erode the coastline.

2. (a) Name **one** landform of coastal erosion.
   (b) Name **one** example of that landform.
   (c) Draw a labelled diagram of that landform.
   (d) Explain how that landform was formed.

4.5 Sea: the builder

KEYWORDS
- load
- longshore drift
- beach
- sand dunes
- sand spit
- lagoon
- tombolo

Transport by the sea

All the material that is transported by the waves is called the **load**. The load includes stones, pebbles, sand and silt.

The waves transport the load in two types of movement:

1. Up the shore by the **swash** and back down the shore by the **backwash** (see page 57).
2. Along the shore by **longshore drift**. This occurs when the waves approach the shore at an angle.

2 The **swash** from the breaking waves moves material up the shore and deposits some of it there. Because of the direction of the waves, the material is also moved along the shore.

3 The **backwash** brings some of the material straight out, following the slope of the beach.

4 These processes are repeated over time and the material is gradually moved along the shore in a **zigzag** fashion. This movement is known as **longshore drift**.

1 The waves approach the shore at an **angle**.

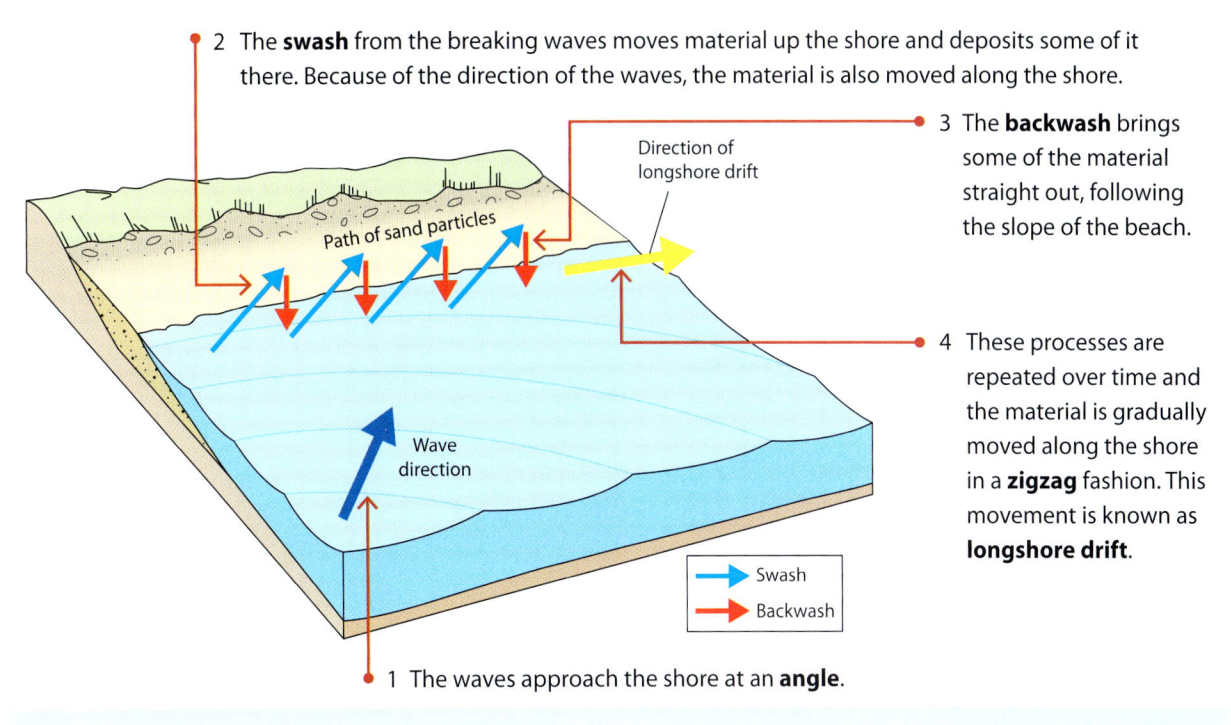

Figure 4.20 Waves move their load by swash, backwash and longshore drift

Landforms of coastal deposition

Waves **deposit** their load when they lose some of their **energy** and can no longer transport such a large load. This may occur in **sheltered areas** like bays or where the shore **slopes very gently** out to sea.

A number of landforms are created as a result of **coastal deposition**.

Activity

Examine Figure 4.20. Would longshore drift occur if the waves came straight in towards the shore? Explain your answer.

Beach

A **beach** is a build-up of sand and shingle (small pebbles) deposited by **constructive waves** between low and high tide levels.

- When waves break, the swash carries its load of both coarse and fine material up the shore and deposits it.
- The backwash is weaker and it drags some of the finer material back towards the sea.

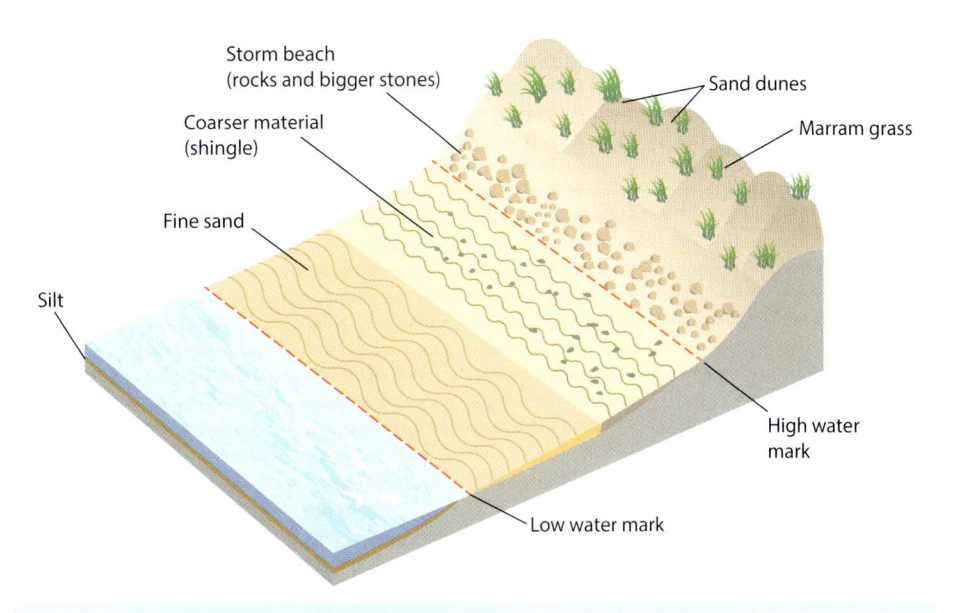

Figure 4.21 Features of coastal deposition

Section 1 · Physical Geography

- As a result, **finer** beach material is found **lower** down the beach, while **coarser** beach material is found at the **upper** beach.
- In stormy weather, the swash is strong enough to be able to hurl large stones and rocks up past the normal high tide level, where they remain to form a **storm beach**.

Sandy beaches and storm beaches can be seen at Greystones (Co. Wicklow), Keel (Achill Island) and Tramore (Co. Waterford).

Sand dunes

Sand dunes are hills of sand that pile up on the shore, just beyond the high tide level.

- When winds blow in from the sea, they **dry** the sand on the beach, making it lighter.
- It then blows the dry sand inland until it is **trapped** by a wall or vegetation.
- The sand then **piles up** to form low hills or dunes.

Marram grass is sometimes planted on the dunes. It has deep roots that help bind the sand particles together, preventing them from blowing further inland and covering farmland and buildings.

Sand dunes are found at Inch (Co. Kerry), Rosslare (Co. Wexford) and Tramore (Co. Waterford).

Sand dunes and a sandy beach in Co. Donegal

Activity

1 **Examine** the photograph above and identify three landforms of coastal deposition.
2 **Examine** the photograph below. What evidence is there to suggest that longshore drift is occurring?

Sand spit

A **sand spit** is a ridge of sand or shingle that is connected to the land at one end and extends across a bay.

- A spit begins where there is a **change in the direction** of a coastline.
- Longshore drift loses some of its energy and **deposits** material at a faster rate than it can be removed.
- These deposits gradually **build up** above the level of the water.
- As deposition continues, the spit **extends** further across the bay.

Sand spits stretch across the bays at Tramore (Co. Waterford), Inch (Co. Kerry) and Portmarnock (Dublin).

A sand spit growing across a bay

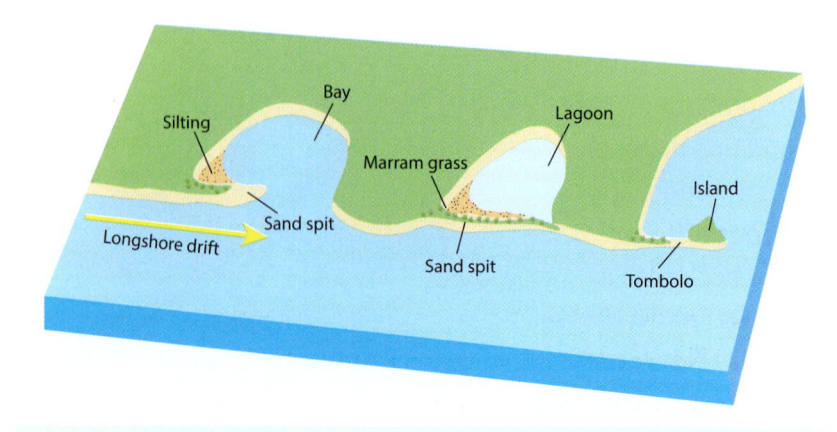

Figure 4.22 A sand spit grows across a bay. Its growth can also lead to the formation of a lagoon or a tombolo

Lagoon

A **lagoon** is an area of water that has been cut off from the sea by a bank of sand.

If a sand spit continues to grow, it eventually reaches the far side of the bay to form a **sand bar**. Some of the bay is now sealed off from the sea. A lake, called a **lagoon**, is formed. Over time the lagoon begins to fill with silt and mud from rivers that may flow into it.

Lagoons have formed at Our Lady's Island (Co. Wexford) and Lough Gill (Co. Kerry).

Tombolo

A **tombolo** is a ridge of sand or shingle that leads from the mainland to a nearby island.

A tombolo is formed when a **sand spit** grows **outwards** from the mainland. Material is moved by **longshore drift** and is deposited in the sheltered waters between the mainland and the island.

Howth (Co. Dublin) was once an island but it was then connected to the mainland by a tombolo. The suburb of Sutton is built on the tombolo.

A tombolo linking an island to the mainland

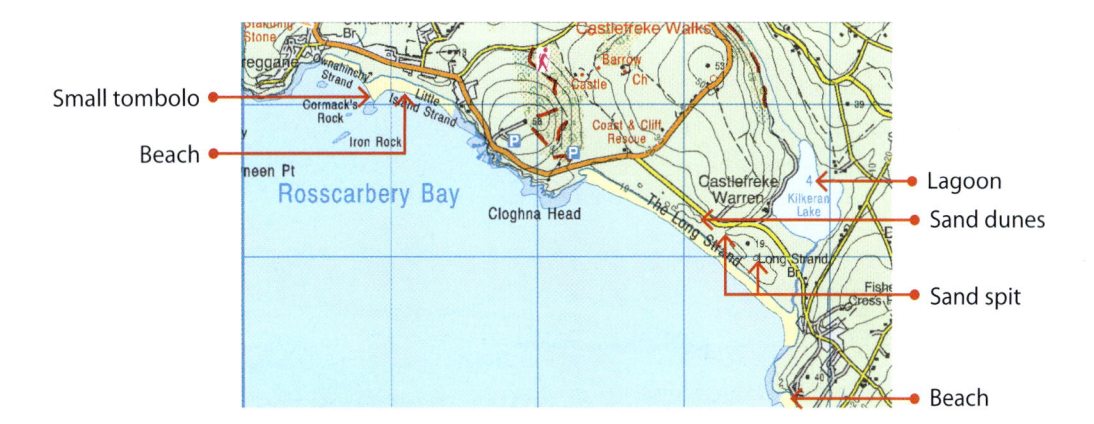

Figure 4.23 Landforms of coastal deposition in Rosscarbery Bay, Co. Cork

Questions

1. (a) Name the process by which waves move material up and down the shore.
   (b) Name and describe the process by which waves move material along the shore.

2. (a) Name **one** landform of coastal deposition.
   (b) Name **one** example of that landform.
   (c) Draw a labelled diagram of that landform.
   (d) Explain how that landform was formed.

Section 1 · Physical Geography

4.6 People and the sea

KEYWORDS

- sea wall
- rock armour
- groyne
- gabion

The sea plays an important role in a range of human activities. In turn, people interfere with the natural processes of the sea. In both situations, there are positive and negative effects.

The sea and economic activity

Table 4.4 How people use the sea

Activity	Positive effect	Negative effect
Recreation and leisure	• The sea and beaches allow for a wide range of activities that include sailing, fishing and sunbathing. • Businesses in resort towns benefit when tourists come to stay.	• Tourism can result in litter and pollution. • The sewage systems of some tourist resorts are unable to cope with the increase in summer population. • Tourists can damage sand dunes while walking on them.
Transport	• Bulky goods, including oil, ores and containers, can be transported quite cheaply over long distances. • Ferries transport people, cars and trucks.	• Oil spillages, both from pipelines and tankers, can cause pollution. This can damage the coastal environment. • Spillages also lead to the destruction of fish and other sea creatures.
Food supply	• The sea is an important source of food, both from fish caught in the wild and fish reared on fish farms. • Employment is provided in the fishing and processing sectors.	• Overfishing, especially by super-trawlers, can lead to the depletion of fish stocks. • The cages of fish farms can be an eyesore when located in scenic areas.

Coastal protection

Sea walls

Concrete **sea walls** are built to **protect coastal towns** from attack by the sea. They have a **curved top** to deflect the waves back out to sea. However, the sea may also destroy these walls, especially during severe storms. Sea walls have been built at Bray, Tramore and Galway.

Sea wall, rock armour and groynes on the English coast

Rock armour

Large boulders (or **rock armour**) are placed at the base of **soft cliffs** or in front of **sand dunes**. They help to prevent erosion because the power of the waves is reduced as they hit the boulders. Rock armour has been used to protect the coastline at Tramore and Youghal.

Groynes

Groynes are low walls, often made of wood, that are built at right angles to the coast. They **reduce longshore drift** by trapping sand. The sand accumulates and builds up the level of the beach. Groynes have been constructed at Youghal and Rosslare.

Gabions

Gabions are **wire cages** that are filled with small stones placed along beaches or sand dunes. They break the power of the waves and help to slow down the rate of erosion. Gabions protect sections of beach at Rosslare, Tramore and Lahinch.

Case study

Rosslare

Rosslare has two distinct settlements that lie just 8 km apart.

- **Rosslare Strand** has been a major holiday resort for nearly a century. It is situated along 8 km of safe, sandy beaches with Blue Flag status. The area enjoys the most hours of sunshine in Ireland and has a wide range of attractions for tourists.
- **Rosslare Harbour** is the site of Rosslare-Europort, a major ferry terminal. It has roll-on roll-off (RORO) passenger and freight services to Britain and France.

While both settlements make use of the sea and the coast, each has different needs. Sometimes, there is a conflict of interest in these needs.

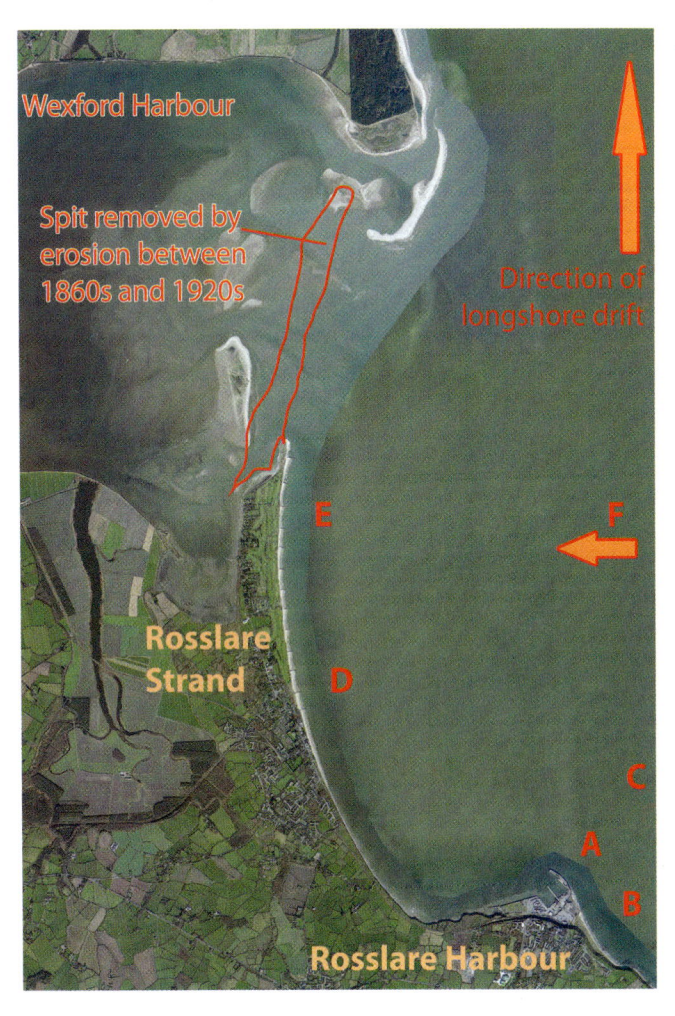

Geo fact
Nearly 3.5 km of the northern section of the Rosslare sand spit have been lost to coastal erosion.

A A **sea wall** was built at Rosslare Harbour, jutting out into the bay. It was built to provide shelter for the ferry terminal and to prevent silting in the harbour. Over the years it has been extended and new piles built.

B Some sand was trapped and a new beach began to develop ahead of the sea wall.

C The wall deflected longshore drift away from the coast. Most of the sand was deposited offshore in very deep water.

D The supply of sand to Rosslare Strand, to the north, was interrupted. Erosion of the beaches and sand dunes resulted. Parts of the golf course were flooded and some of the course was washed away.

E Expensive measures were taken to prevent further erosion. These included the use of groynes (wooden and stone), rock armour and gabions.

F Beach nourishment was also undertaken. Sand was dredged from the seabed about 6 km offshore and placed on the beach to build it up.

Aerial photograph of Rosslare

Section 1 · Physical Geography

Questions

1. (a) Describe **two** ways in which coastal areas are of benefit to people.
   (b) Describe **two** ways in which people can have a negative impact on a coastal area.
2. (a) Name an area of the Irish coastline that is at risk from coastal erosion.
   (b) Describe **two** methods by which people attempt to prevent or reduce the effects of coastal erosion.

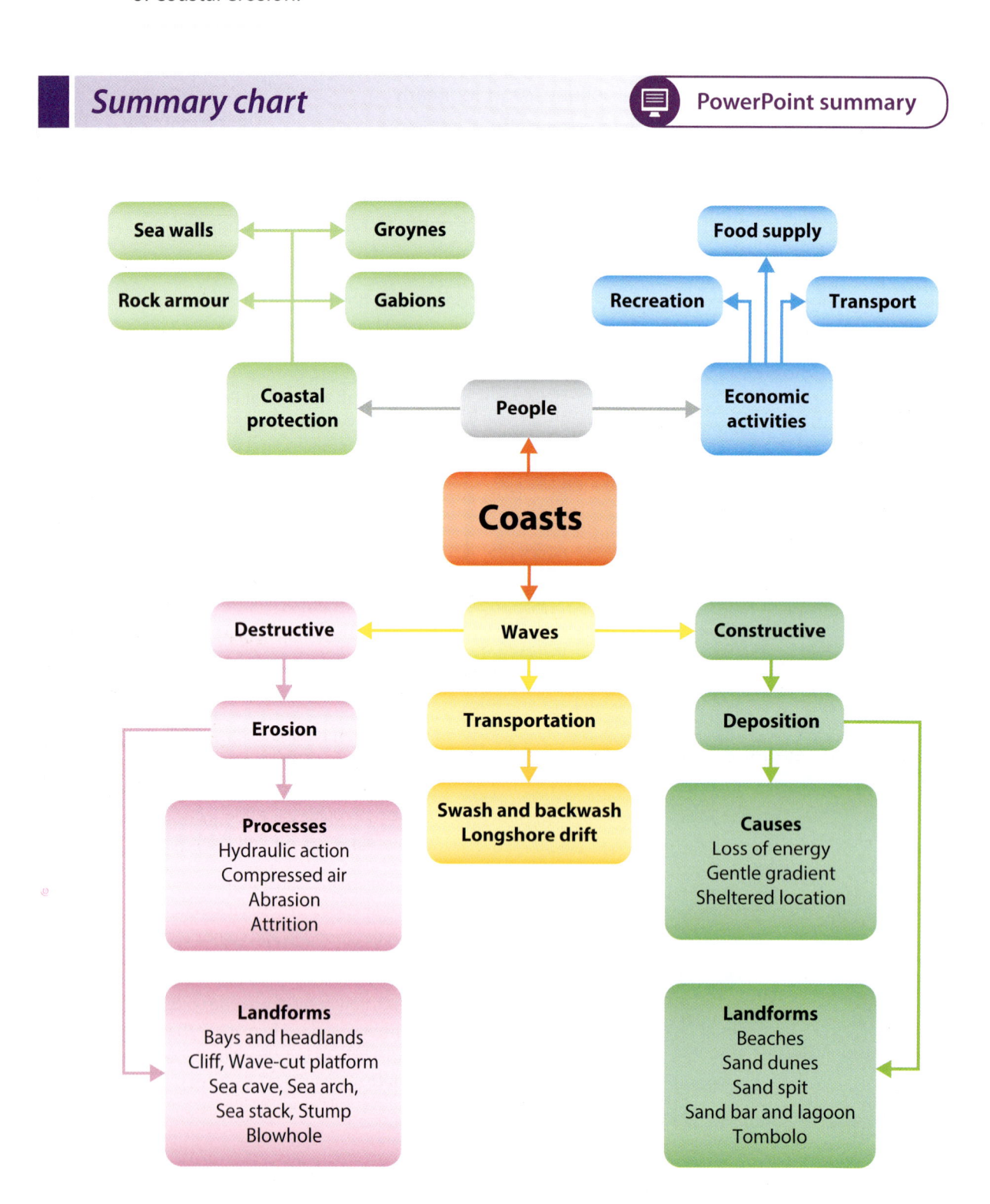

Summary chart — PowerPoint summary

Coasts

People:
- Coastal protection: Sea walls, Groynes, Rock armour, Gabions
- Economic activities: Food supply, Recreation, Transport

Waves:
- **Destructive** → Erosion
  - Processes: Hydraulic action, Compressed air, Abrasion, Attrition
  - Landforms: Bays and headlands, Cliff, Wave-cut platform, Sea cave, Sea arch, Sea stack, Stump, Blowhole
- **Transportation**: Swash and backwash, Longshore drift
- **Constructive** → Deposition
  - Causes: Loss of energy, Gentle gradient, Sheltered location
  - Landforms: Beaches, Sand dunes, Sand spit, Sand bar and lagoon, Tombolo

4.7 Glaciation: the work of erosion

> **KEYWORDS**
> - glaciation
> - glacier
> - ice sheet
> - Ice Age
> - plucking
> - abrasion
> - striae
> - cirque
> - tarn
> - arête
> - pyramidal peak
> - U-shaped valley
> - ribbon lake
> - paternoster lakes
> - hanging valley
> - fiord

About two million years ago, the climate of many countries became much colder. There was only one season – winter – and all precipitation took the form of **snow**.

- Snow began to collect on colder **upland** areas.
- As more snow fell, the weight of the upper layers compressed the bottom layers into **ice**.
- Great rivers of ice, called **glaciers**, moved down from the uplands under the influence of gravity.
- While some glaciers melted, others joined together to cover lowland areas with **ice sheets**.
- Another **Ice Age** had begun.

During the Ice Age, up to **one third** of the Earth's surface was covered with ice. Today, Greenland and Antarctica are still covered with ice sheets. Glaciers can be found in the higher parts of mountain ranges such as the Alps and Himalayas.

Ireland was covered by ice sheets on at least two occasions. The ice was up to 1,000 metres thick in places. The last of this ice melted just 10,000 years ago.

The results of **glaciation** are widespread over the Irish landscape.

> **Definition** ✓
> **Ice Age:** A period when large parts of several continents were covered by ice sheets.

> **Geo fact**
> The ice sheets of the Arctic and Antarctic are now under threat from climate change.

The Franz Josef glacier in New Zealand. Note the stream of meltwater flowing away from its snout (front)

How glaciers erode

As ice moves, it erodes the landscape by the processes of **plucking** and **abrasion**.

Plucking

As the ice moves, there is **friction** between it and the rock beneath it. This causes some of the ice to **melt**, and the water seeps into cracks in the rock. This meltwater then freezes again and sticks to the glacier. As the glacier moves forward, it pulls or **plucks** chunks of rock away with it.

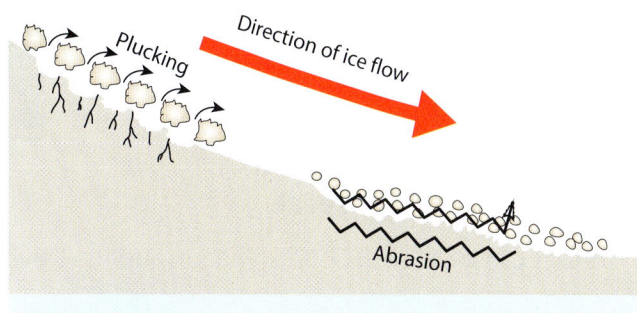

Figure 4.24 Glaciers erode by the processes of plucking and abrasion

67

Section 1 · Physical Geography

Abrasion

As the ice carries the plucked rocks away, they **scrape** or **scratch** the rock surface over which the glacier passes. This sandpaper effect wears down the rock. The scratches are called **striae.** They show us the direction in which the ice moved.

Landforms of glacial erosion

Most landforms of erosion are found in upland areas.

Cirques

A **cirque** (also called coom) is a large hollow that is found high up in a mountain. It has three steep sides and may contain a lake. It was the **birthplace of a glacier**.

A cirque is formed when snow collects in mountain hollows and is compressed to form ice. The ice **plucks** rocks from the sides of the hollow, causing the walls to become steep. These rocks are then used as a tool to deepen the hollow by **abrasion**. The ice builds up until it overflows the hollow and begins to flow downhill under its own weight. When the ice finally melts, a lake, called a **tarn**, is trapped in the cirque.

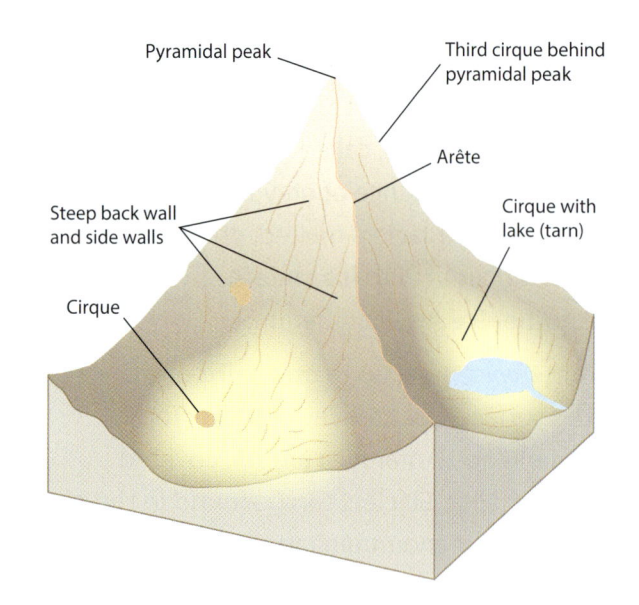

Coomshingaun, in the Comeragh Mountains, is the largest cirque in either Ireland or Britain. Other cirques include the Devil's Punchbowl near Killarney and Lough Nahanagan in Co. Wicklow.

Scratches (or **striae**) on the rock surface following abrasion by a glacier

Figure 4.25 Cirques, arêtes, tarn and pyramidal peak

Arête

An **arête** is a narrow, **steep-sided ridge**.

When two cirques develop side-by-side or back-to-back, the ground between them is gradually eroded backwards until just a narrow ridge, called an **arête**, remains.

When three or more cirques form around a mountain, only a steep-sided peak, with several arêtes, remains as a result of erosion. This is called a **pyramidal peak**.

Arêtes can be seen at Coomshingaun and the Devil's Punchbowl. The upper slopes of Carrauntoohill form a pyramidal peak.

A mountain landscape that is being shaped by glaciation

Activity

Link each of the following with a letter in the picture: **arête, cirque, glacier, pyramidal peak**.

U-shaped valley

A glaciated or **U-shaped** valley has a wide, flat floor and steep sides.

When the glacier moves out of a cirque, it takes the easiest route down the mountainside. This is usually through a former river (V-shaped) valley. The glacier uses its load to reshape the river valley by **plucking** and **abrasion**.

The glacier widens, deepens and straightens the V-shaped valley, changing it to a U-shaped valley. In doing this, it cuts the heads off the interlocking spurs, leaving them as **truncated spurs**.

Glendalough (Co. Wicklow), Doo Lough Valley (Co. Mayo) and the Black Valley (Co. Kerry) are amongst the best examples of **glaciated valleys** in Ireland.

Ribbon lake

A **ribbon lake** is a long, narrow lake that occupies the floor of a glaciated valley. If a river links a number of them, they are called **paternoster** (or rosary bead) **lakes**.

They are formed when a glacier scoops out hollows in the valley floor. This happens where the rock on the valley floor is softer and the glacier is able to pluck and remove large amounts of rock. When the glacier melts, the hollows fill with water to form lakes.

Ribbon lakes occupy the floors of glaciated valleys at the Gap of Dunloe and Black Valley (Co. Kerry).

Activity

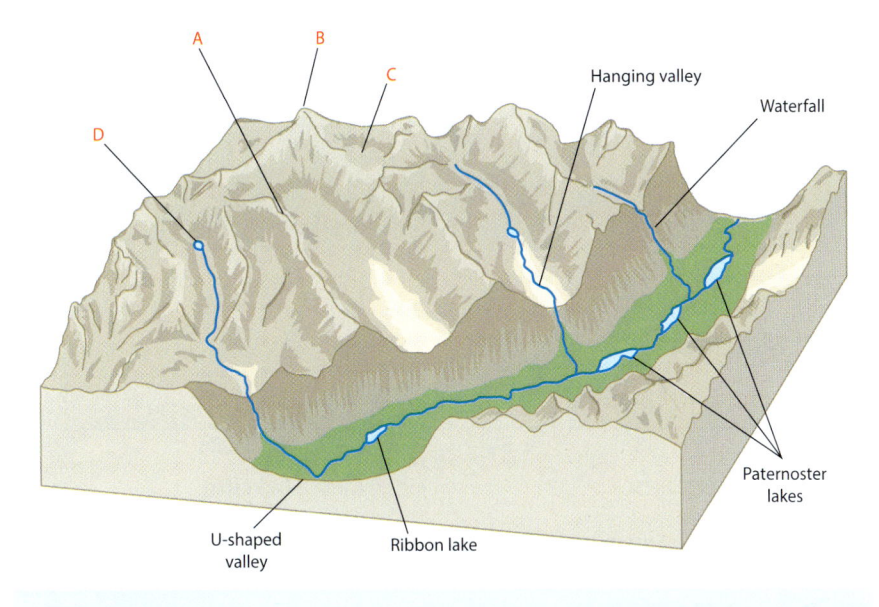

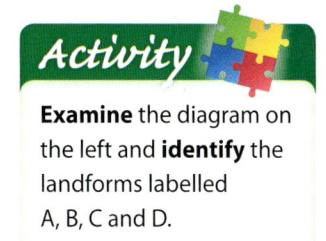

Examine the diagram on the left and **identify** the landforms labelled A, B, C and D.

Figure 4.26 Landforms associated with a glaciated (U-shaped) valley

Hanging valley

A **hanging valley** is a small tributary valley that hangs above the main glaciated valley.

This valley was occupied by a small glacier that was unable to erode as deeply as the main glacier did. When the ice melted, the floor of the tributary valley was left high above the floor of the main valley. If a stream leaves the hanging valley, it drops into the main valley as a **waterfall**.

The Polanass Waterfall in Glendalough is located where a hanging valley meets the main valley.

Section 1 · Physical Geography

Fiords

Fiords are long, narrow inlets that are very deep and have steep sides.

Fiords were once glaciated valleys that ended as the glacier reached the coast. When the Ice Age ended, the glaciers melted. This caused sea levels to rise, **drowning glaciated valleys** near the coast.

Killary Harbour (Co. Mayo) is the best example of a fiord in Ireland.

A fiord is a drowned glaciated valley

Activity

Examine the photo above.

In which direction did the glacier travel: foreground towards background or background towards foreground?

Explain your choice.

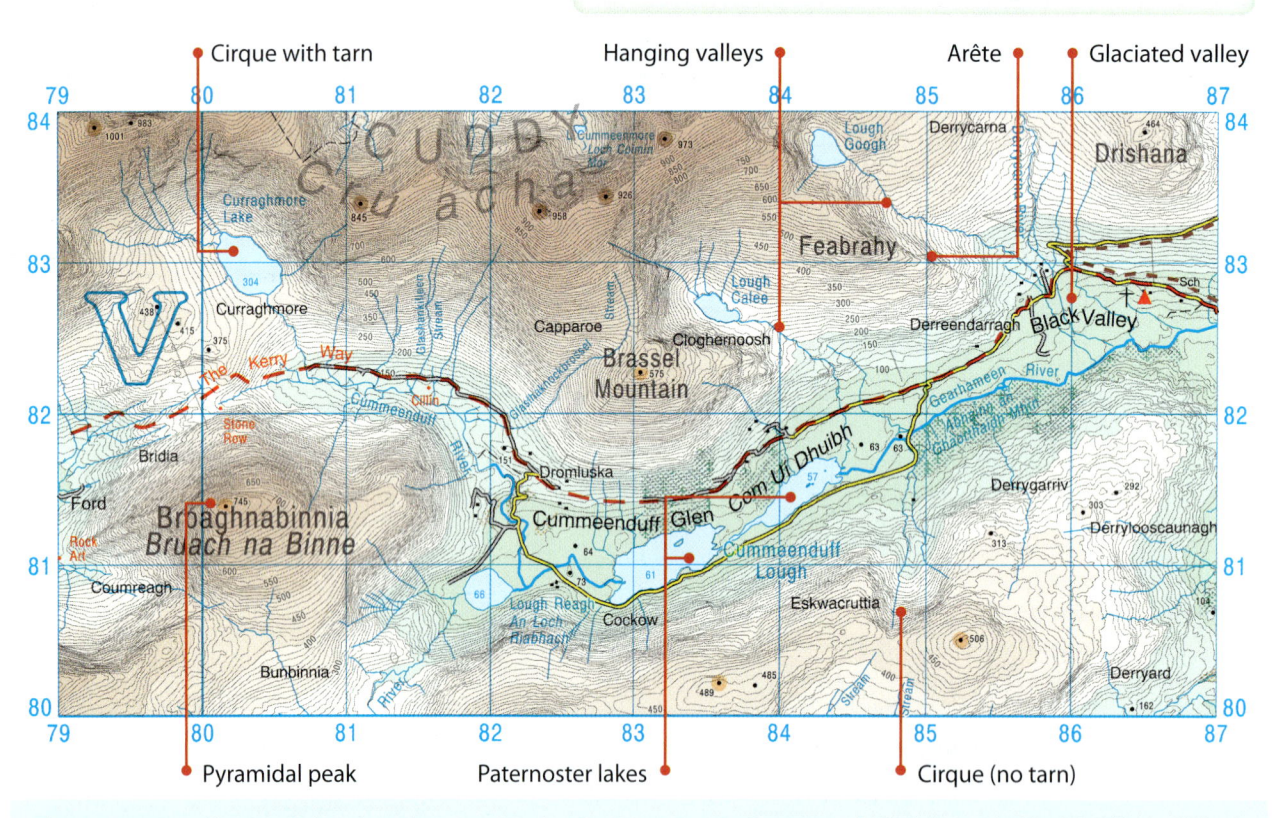

Figure 4.27 Landforms of glacial erosion on an Ordnance Survey map. Cummeenduff Glen is a U-shaped valley

Questions

1. Explain the following terms: (i) Ice Age, (ii) ice sheet, (iii) glacier.

2. Ice wears away the landscape by erosion.
   (a) Name the **two** ways (processes) by which ice erodes.
   (b) Describe how **each** of these processes erodes the landscape.

3. (a) Name **one** landform of glacial erosion.
   (b) Name **one** example of that landform.
   (c) Draw a labelled diagram of that landform.
   (d) Explain how that landform was formed.

4.8 Glaciation: the work of deposition

KEYWORDS
- moraine
- boulder clay
- drumlin
- erratic
- esker
- outwash plain

How glaciers transport their load

Glaciers are able to carry large amounts of eroded material. The term **moraine** describes the load of loose rock that is transported and later deposited by the glacier.

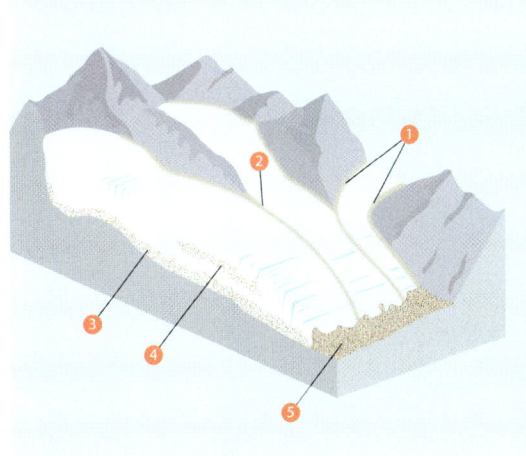

1. **Lateral moraines** are carried along the side of the glacier.
2. **Medial moraines** are formed when two lateral moraines join together.
3. **Ground moraines** are carried along beneath the glacier.
4. Some material is **carried inside** the glacier.
5. Some material is **pushed ahead** of the glacier.

Figure 4.28 How glaciers transport their load

Lateral and medial moraines on a glacier

Landforms of glacial deposition

Landforms of glacial deposition are usually found in **lowland areas**. Here the temperature is warmer and the ice begins to melt. It is unable to transport its load so it begins to **deposit** it.

Erratics

Erratics are **large boulders** that are deposited by ice in an area where the rock type is different. As a result, they look a little out of place in the landscape.

Erratics can tell us **how far** the ice travelled and the **direction** from which it came. Erratics made of Connemara marble have been found perched on limestone in the Burren.

Boulder clay plains

Boulder clay plains are lowland areas that have been covered by a layer of **boulder clay**. This is a mixture of boulders, stones and clay.

As the ice sheet melts, it loses some of its energy and begins to deposit its load on the lowland areas over which it passes.

All the **fertile farming areas** of Ireland, including the Golden Vale, have a covering of boulder clay.

Granite erratics deposited on a limestone surface

The Golden Vale is one of Ireland's main farming regions

Drumlins

Drumlins are oval-shaped hills that are made of **boulder clay**.

Drumlins are formed when the ice deposits some of its load of boulder clay. As the remaining ice moves over the boulder clay, it **smooths** and **shapes** it, forming small hills called drumlins. As a result, one end of a drumlin is steep, while the other end has a gentle slope. Drumlins occur in groups, forming what is called a **'basket-of-eggs' landscape**.

The largest drumlin region in Ireland stretches from Clew Bay (Co. Mayo) through to Strangford Lough (Co. Down).

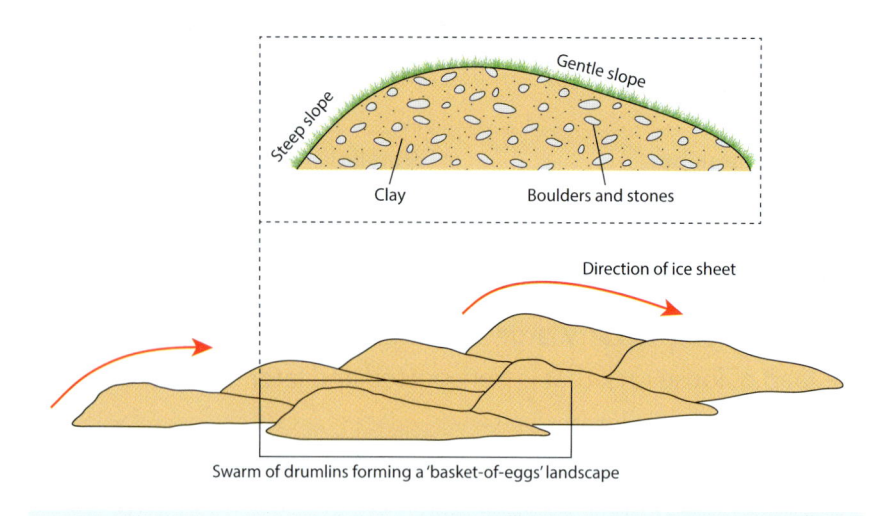

Figure 4.29 Drumlins are oval-shaped hills made of boulder clay

Some drumlins, such as those at Clew Bay, have been **drowned** after the sea level rose and flooded the land between them

Moraines

Moraine is the name given to the load of rock, stones and clay that was transported and later deposited on a valley floor by a glacier.

When the glacier begins to melt, it deposits its load. There are four main types of moraine, named according to where they were deposited by the melting glacier:

- **Lateral moraines** are found along the sides of the valley.
- A **medial moraine** is found along the middle of the valley.
- A **ground moraine** covers the floor of the valley.
- A **terminal moraine** marks the furthest point to which the glacier advanced.

Moraines are found in most glaciated valleys, including Glendalough (Co. Wicklow).

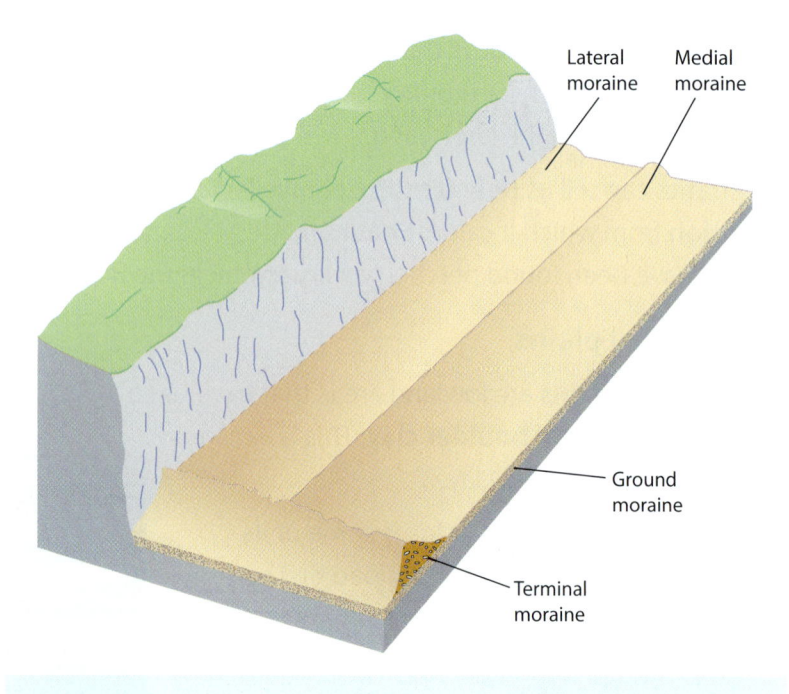

Figure 4.30 Moraines are named according to where they are deposited

Landforms of meltwater deposition

Temperatures began to rise towards the end of the Ice Age and glaciers began to melt. Vast quantities of **meltwater** flowed away from them. This carried away the smaller particles (sand and gravel) and spread them over the landscape to form **eskers** and **outwash plains**.

Eskers

Eskers are long, narrow ridges made of **sand and gravel**.

When the ice began to melt, huge streams of **meltwater** flowed through **tunnels beneath the ice**, transporting sand and gravel. Some of this material was deposited on the beds of the meltwater streams if the load got too great. As the water escaped from the tunnels, it lost more of its energy and deposited the remainder of its load. The deposited material built up to form **ridges** called eskers.

The Esker Riada runs through the bogs of the Midlands, where it provides a dry foundation for the Dublin–Galway road.

Cross-section of an esker showing layers of sand and gravel

Outwash plains

An **outwash plain** is a low, flat area made of sand and gravel deposits, which is found in front of a terminal moraine.

When the ice sheet began to melt, huge quantities of meltwater flowed away from its front. The meltwater carried large amounts of **sand and gravel** with it. As the meltwater spread out, it lost most of its energy. It then deposited the heavier material first, followed by the lighter material.

The Curragh of Kildare is an outwash plain.

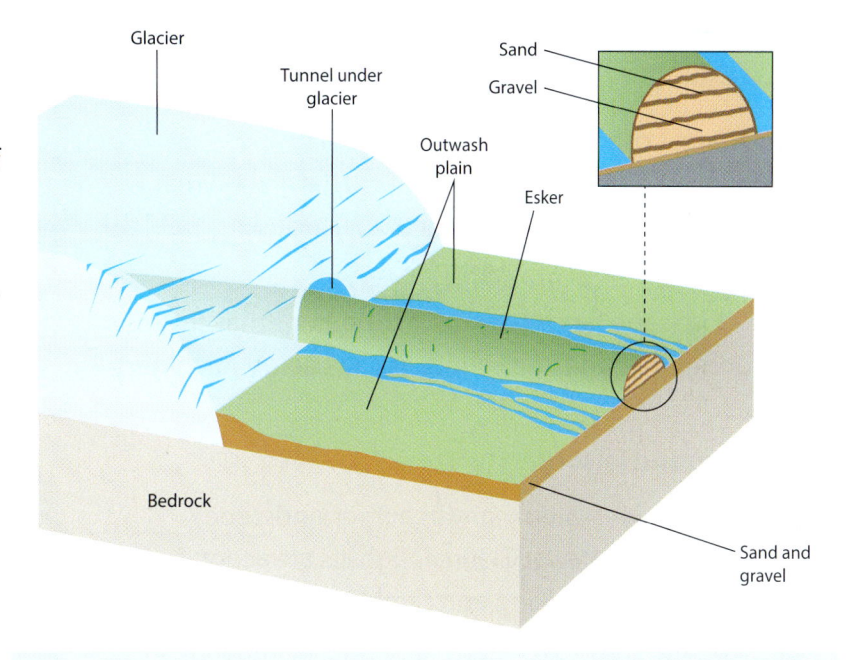

Figure 4.31 Eskers and outwash plains are formed from sand and gravel deposited by meltwater from glaciers

Questions

1. Glaciers transport (or remove) the material that they have eroded.
   (a) What term describes this load of material?
   (b) Describe any **two** ways by which a glacier transports its load.

2. (a) Name **one** landform of glacial deposition.
   (b) Name **one** example of that landform.
   (c) Draw a labelled diagram of that landform.
   (d) Explain how that landform was formed.

3. (a) Name **one** landform of meltwater deposition.
   (b) Name **one** example of that landform.
   (c) Draw a labelled diagram of that landform.
   (d) Explain how that landform was formed.

Section 1 · Physical Geography

4.9 Glaciation and people

The effects of glaciation have had a huge influence on human activity. These influences have had both positive and negative effects.

Co. Wicklow is one region of Ireland that has been influenced by glaciation.

Case study

Wicklow: the effects of glaciation

The positive effects of glaciation

Hydroelectricity

Lough Nahanagan is a **tarn** (cirque lake) whose waters are used as part of the ESB's pumped storage scheme at Turlough Hill.

A man-made reservoir was built at the top of the hill. Water is released from this reservoir and flows through four turbines buried in the mountain, generating electricity.

Agriculture

Large areas of south Co. Wicklow have a thick covering of boulder clay. This makes a fertile soil that is suitable for many types of agriculture, including arable and dairy farming.

The landscape has a very gentle gradient that makes for good drainage. It also makes the use of machinery easier.

Tourism and leisure

Glaciation has created many beautiful landscapes, including the valley of Glendalough. Its attractions include two lakes, hiking and climbing.

It is also the site of an ancient monastic settlement, attracted there by the remote and peaceful setting.

Water supply

Large glacial lakes provide water supply for urban areas. These lakes can also be used for leisure purposes, including boating and fishing.

The Blessington Lakes provide much of the water supply for Dublin.

Sand and gravel

Eskers and lake beds that are now exposed are valuable sources of sand and gravel for the building industry.

Case study

The negative effects of glaciation

Poor agriculture

Upland areas that were affected by glaciation are not good for many types of agriculture. Ice removed much of the soil cover from the landscape. Many of these areas now have a covering of blanket bog, while some areas are also badly drained.

The result is that many of these upland areas are suitable only for sheep farming and forestry.

Flooding

The impact of glaciation on the landscape of Wicklow may not yet be over.

One of the impacts of **climate change** is that ice sheets and glaciers are melting at an increasing rate. This will lead to a global rise in sea levels.

Low-lying coastal areas, such as those near Wicklow Town, are at risk of being flooded.

Questions

1. Describe **two** ways in which glaciated landscapes are of benefit to people.
2. Describe **two** ways in which glaciated landscapes can have a negative impact on people.

Section 1 · Physical Geography

Summary chart

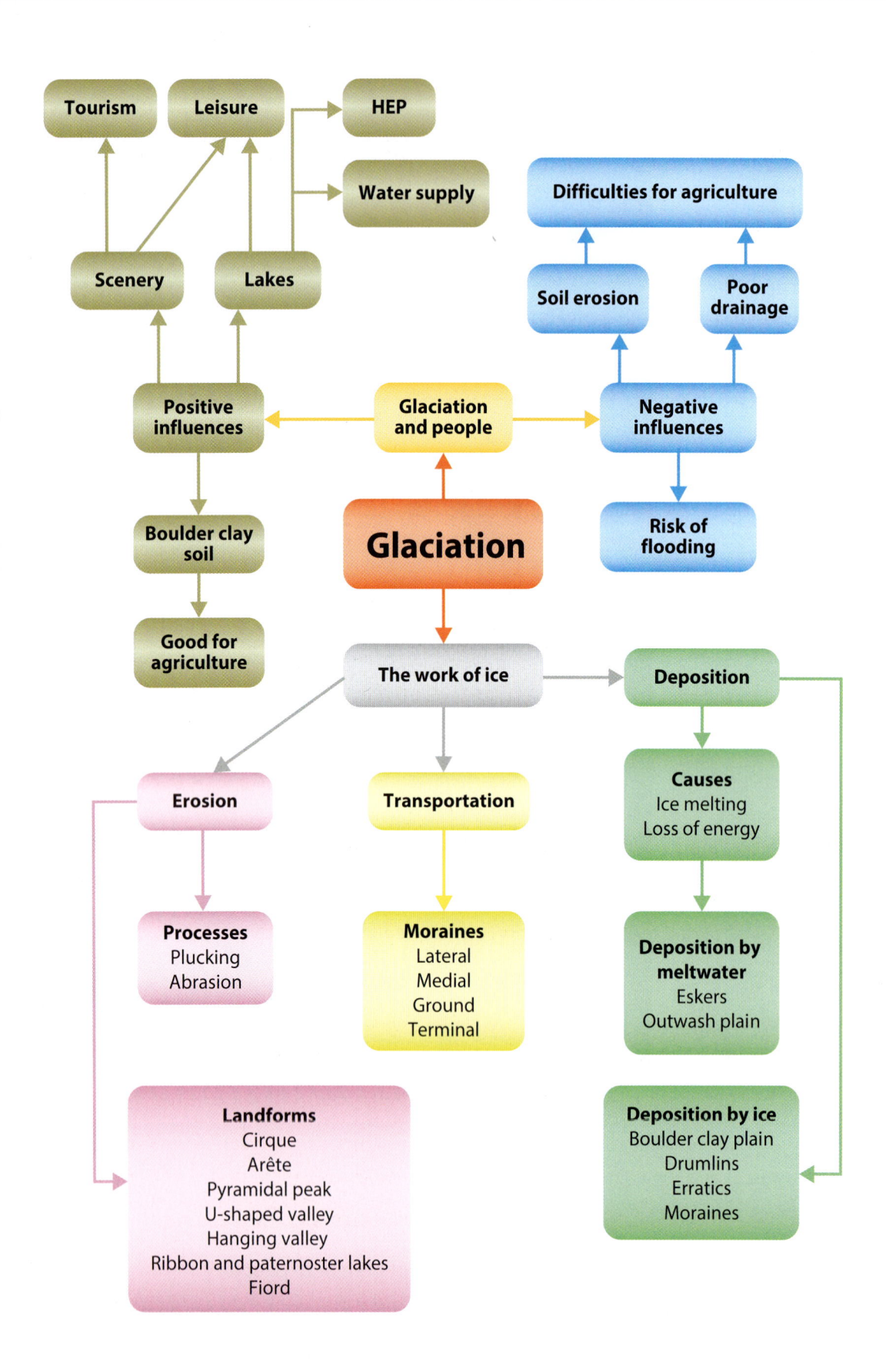

PowerPoint summary

Glaciation

Glaciation and people

Positive influences
- Tourism
- Leisure
- HEP
- Water supply
- Scenery
- Lakes
- Boulder clay soil
- Good for agriculture

Negative influences
- Difficulties for agriculture
- Soil erosion
- Poor drainage
- Risk of flooding

The work of ice

Erosion

Processes
- Plucking
- Abrasion

Landforms
- Cirque
- Arête
- Pyramidal peak
- U-shaped valley
- Hanging valley
- Ribbon and paternoster lakes
- Fiord

Transportation

Moraines
- Lateral
- Medial
- Ground
- Terminal

Deposition

Causes
- Ice melting
- Loss of energy

Deposition by meltwater
- Eskers
- Outwash plain

Deposition by ice
- Boulder clay plain
- Drumlins
- Erratics
- Moraines

Exam questions

1. Name **one** feature formed by **river erosion** and explain, with the aid of a labelled diagram, how it was formed.

   HL 2012

2. Name **one** feature formed by **river deposition** and explain, with the aid of a labelled diagram, how it was formed.

   HL 2013

3. (i) Describe **one** advantage of rivers for people.
   (ii) Describe **one** disadvantage of rivers for people.

   OL 2015

4. Examine the photograph of a hydroelectric power station with its dam and lake.
   (i) Describe **one** advantage of dam building.
   (ii) Describe **one** disadvantage of dam building.

   OL 2010

5. (i) Name and briefly explain **one** way that people use rivers.
   (ii) Name and briefly explain **one** way that people pollute rivers.

   HL 2007

6. Name **one** feature formed by coastal erosion and explain, with the aid of a labelled diagram, how it was formed.

   HL 2014

7. (i) Name one feature formed by coastal deposition **or** glacial deposition.
   (ii) Explain, with the aid of a diagram(s), how this feature was formed.

   OL 2015

8. (i) Name and briefly explain **one** way that people use coastal areas.
   (ii) Name and briefly explain **one** way that people pollute coastal areas.

   HL 2008

9. (i) Name and briefly explain **one** way that people benefit from the results of glaciation.
   (ii) Name and briefly explain **one** disadvantage of the results of glaciation.

   HL 2008

Chapter 5
The Restless Atmosphere

Learning outcomes

By the end of this chapter, you should be able to understand:

- That the Earth is surrounded by a mixture of gases that make up the atmosphere
- That the Earth is heated unequally and how this leads to the global wind pattern and ocean currents
- How air masses influence the weather
- That precipitation occurs as part of the water cycle
- The elements of weather and how they are measured
- The greenhouse effect
- Global warming and how we humans contribute to climate change.

5.1 The atmosphere

KEYWORDS

- atmosphere
- troposphere
- weather
- ozone layer

A blanket of air, which we call the **atmosphere**, surrounds planet Earth. The atmosphere is made up of various gases, including nitrogen and oxygen.

Why the atmosphere is important

Without the atmosphere, there would be no life on Earth.

- The atmosphere provides us with the air we breathe.
- It absorbs heat from the sun by day.
- It retains heat at night.
- It protects us from harmful rays from the sun.

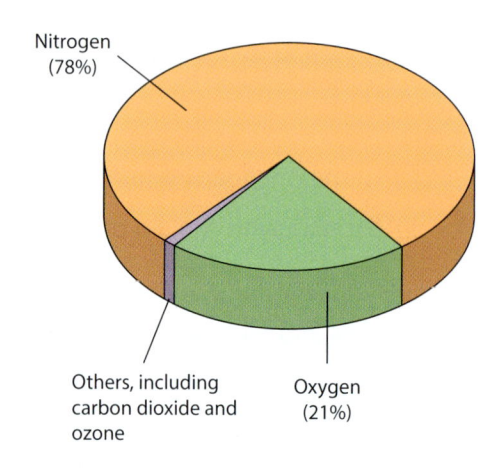

Figure 5.1 The main gases of the atmosphere

Nitrogen (78%)
Oxygen (21%)
Others, including carbon dioxide and ozone

78

Troposphere

The lowest layer of the atmosphere is called the **troposphere**. It is about 12 km thick. Over 75 per cent of the Earth's gases are found in the troposphere. Almost all the **water vapour** and **clouds** are found here. As a result, the troposphere is the layer of the atmosphere in which **weather** forms.

> **Definition** ✓
> The **ozone layer** is part of the atmosphere. It absorbs the sun's harmful ultraviolet (UV) rays, and prevents most of them from reaching the ground.

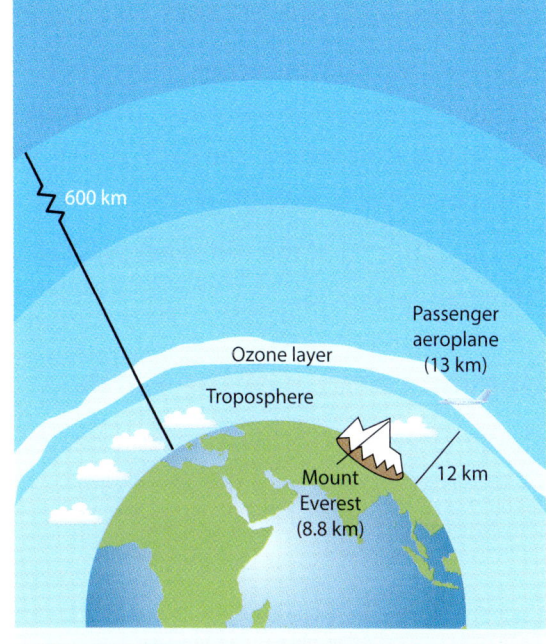

Figure 5.2 The layers of the Earth's atmosphere

Questions

1. (a) What is the atmosphere?
   (b) Name the **two** main gases of the atmosphere.
   (c) Name the lowest layer of the atmosphere.

2. Describe **two** reasons why the atmosphere is important to life on Earth.

5.2 The heat machine

KEYWORDS
- solar energy
- latitude
- seasons
- greenhouse effect
- axis

The **sun** is a huge mass of burning gases that give off **solar energy**. This energy provides **heat** and **light** to the atmosphere and to the Earth's surface. It also influences our climate and weather.

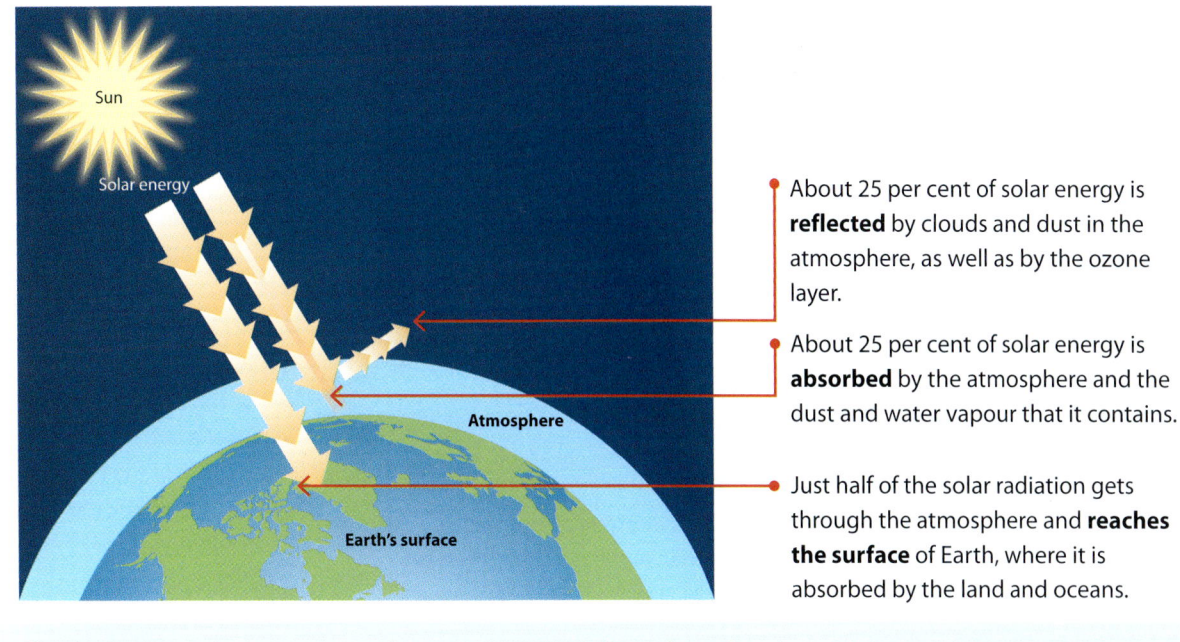

> **Geo fact**
> Snow-covered areas and ice caps reflect much of the solar energy that reaches them.

- About 25 per cent of solar energy is **reflected** by clouds and dust in the atmosphere, as well as by the ozone layer.
- About 25 per cent of solar energy is **absorbed** by the atmosphere and the dust and water vapour that it contains.
- Just half of the solar radiation gets through the atmosphere and **reaches the surface** of Earth, where it is absorbed by the land and oceans.

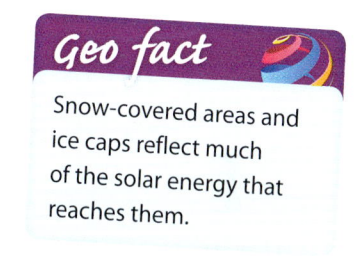

Figure 5.3 How solar energy heats the atmosphere and the surface of Earth

Section 1 · Physical Geography

The greenhouse effect

We have seen how the **gases** of the atmosphere absorb solar energy. Some of these gases act like a blanket. They **trap** and **retain heat**. By keeping this heat in the atmosphere, the Earth is warmer than it would otherwise be. This is essential to support life.

This trapping of the sun's energy is called the **greenhouse effect**. It is a natural process.

> **Link**
> For more on **the greenhouse effect** see Section 5.8 on page 104.

Uneven heating of the Earth

The surface of the Earth is unevenly heated by the incoming solar energy. The amount received at any place on the Earth's surface depends on the **latitude** of that place and the angle of the sun's rays.

Latitude and heat

Places that are near to the **equator** (low latitudes) are much warmer than places that are near to the **poles** (high latitudes). This is due to:

- The angle of the sun in the sky
- The curve of the Earth's surface
- The layer of atmosphere that surrounds the Earth.

> **Definition**
> **Latitude:** The distance north or south of the equator of a place on the Earth's surface. It is measured as an angle, in degrees.

> **Activity**
> Use your atlas to **find** the latitudes between which Ireland lies.

Diagram labels: North Pole; Sun's rays are parallel; Equator; Rays are direct (vertical); Small area; Large area; Rays are oblique (at an angle); South Pole

- Ireland's position is in the mid-latitudes. As a result, it has a moderate average temperature, one that is neither very hot nor very cold.
- At or near the equator, the sun is at a high angle in the sky. It shines straight downwards so its rays have less ground to cover. As a result, the ground warms up rapidly and becomes very hot.
- Near the poles, the sun is at a lower angle in the sky. Its rays have to spread their heat over a large area due to the curve of the Earth's surface. As a result, these places get much less heat than the equator.

The sun's rays pass through a greater depth of atmosphere near the poles, so they lose more heat than at the equator.

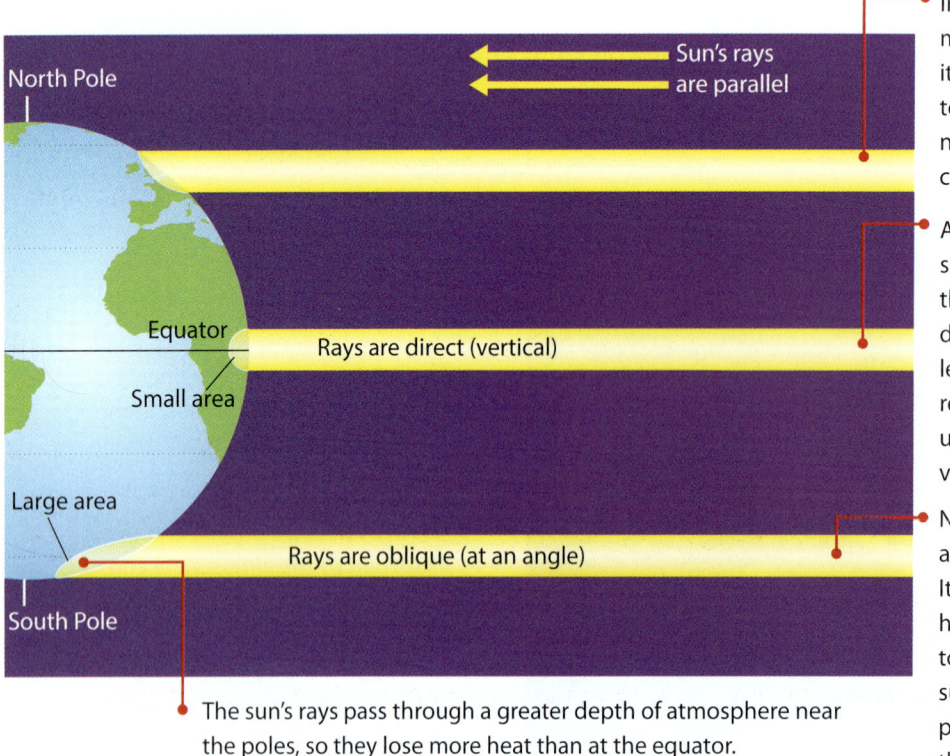

Figure 5.4 The link between latitude and the uneven heating of the Earth's surface

Seasons and the sun

The Earth **orbits** (moves round) the sun once every 365¼ days. This is what determines the length of a year. During this orbit, different parts of the Earth are **tilted** towards the sun at different times of the year. These parts receive more direct sunlight than those that are tilted away from the sun.

Geo fact
Earth spins on its **axis** once every 24 hours, giving us day and night (light and dark).

Definition
The **axis** of the Earth is an imaginary line linking the North Pole and South Pole.

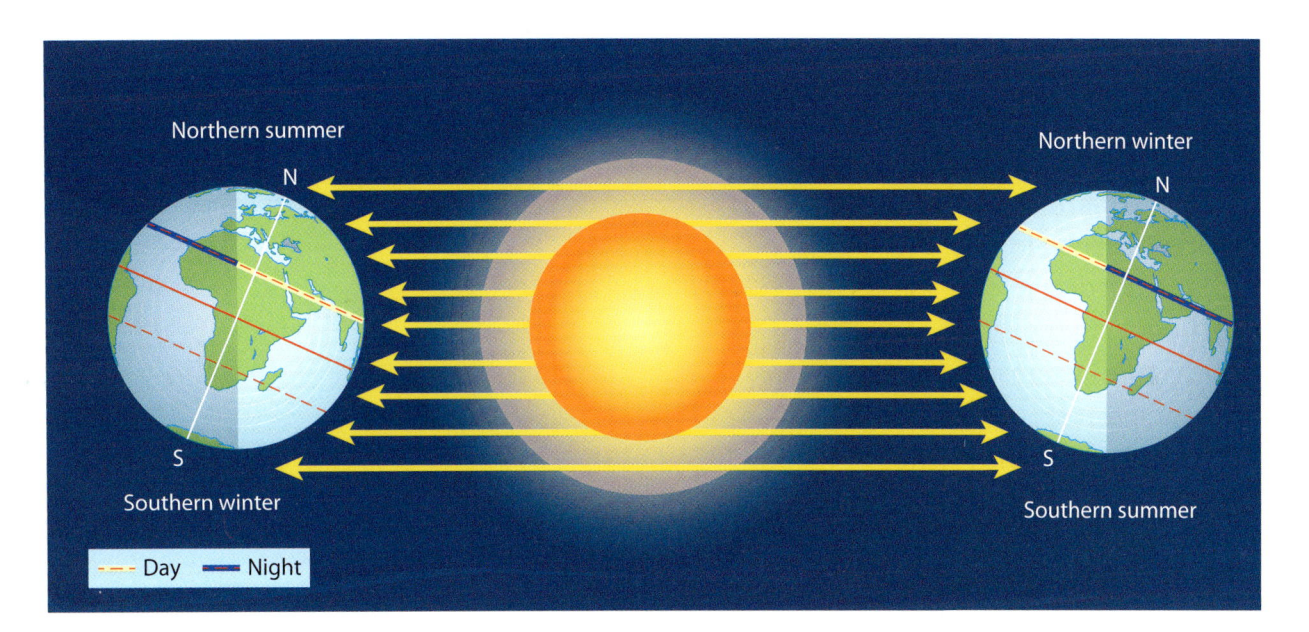

Summer in the northern hemisphere
- The northern hemisphere is tilted towards the sun.
- Days are long, while nights are short.
- It receives much more solar energy, so its weather is warmer.

Winter in the northern hemisphere
- The northern hemisphere is tilted away from the sun.
- Days are short, while nights are long.
- It receives much less solar energy, so its weather is colder.

Figure 5.5 Why summers are warmer than winters

Questions

1. (a) What is solar energy?
   (b) Describe how the sun heats the atmosphere.

2. (a) List **two** factors that cause heat to be unevenly distributed over the Earth?
   (b) Explain why places near the equator receive more solar energy than places close to the poles.
   (c) Describe **three** differences between summer and winter in the northern hemisphere.

Section 1 · Physical Geography

5.3 Wind: the atmosphere on the move

KEYWORDS

- wind
- atmospheric pressure
- low pressure
- high pressure
- prevailing wind
- wind pattern
- wind belt
- Coriolis effect
- the doldrums
- trade winds
- westerlies
- polar winds

The atmosphere is not a calm place. Its lower layer is always in motion. This moving air is called **wind**. The faster the air moves, the more wind there is. And, as the winds move around the globe, they **transfer heat**.

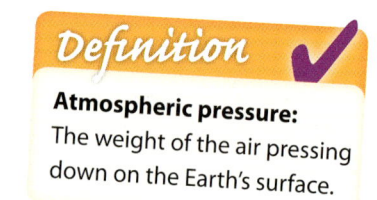

Definition

Atmospheric pressure: The weight of the air pressing down on the Earth's surface.

How winds form

Winds form because the sun heats different parts of the Earth unequally. Places closer to the equator get much more heat than places near the poles (see Figure 5.4, page 80).

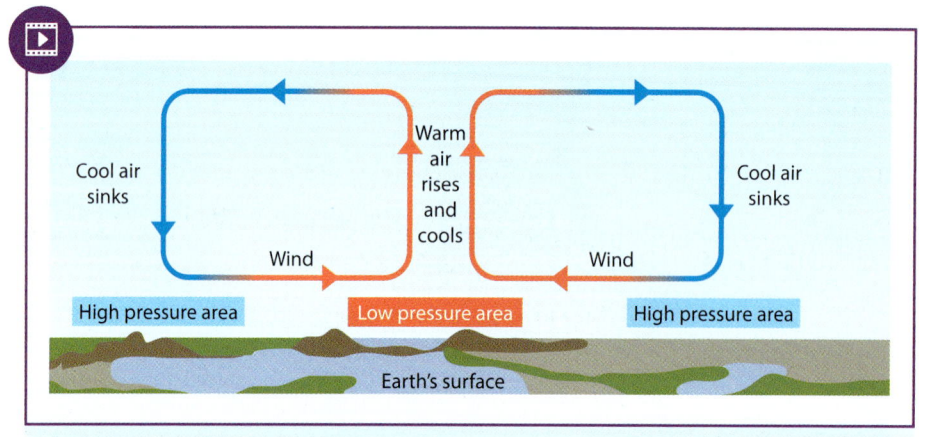

- When air is **heated**, it expands and becomes **lighter**. It rises and creates an area of **low atmospheric pressure** (LP).

Figure 5.6 Warm air rises to create a low pressure area. Cold air from a high pressure area moves in to take its place. This is wind

- When air is **cooled**, it becomes **heavier** and descends. It presses down on the Earth's surface and creates an area of **high atmospheric pressure** (HP).
- Air moves **from high** pressure areas **to low** pressure areas. This is **wind**.

When air is heated, it rises

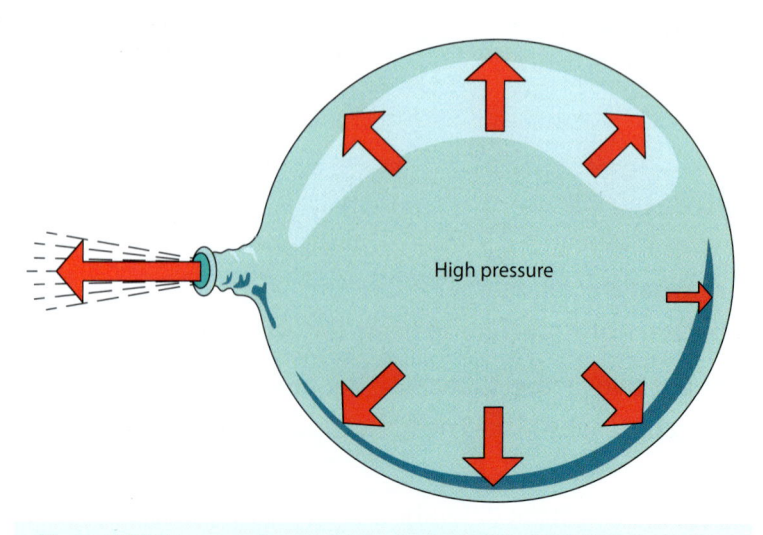

Figure 5.7 Air moves from a high pressure area to a low pressure area

82

Some facts about winds

- Winds are named after the direction **from which they blow**.
- The wind that is most frequent in an area is called the **prevailing wind**.
- Winds that blow from the equator towards the poles are **warm winds**.
- Winds that blow from the poles towards the equator are **cold winds**.

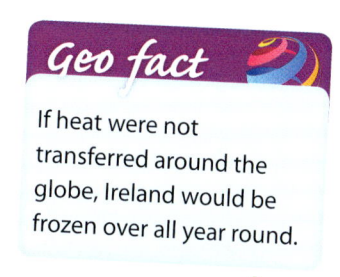

Geo fact
If heat were not transferred around the globe, Ireland would be frozen over all year round.

Activity
What is the direction of the prevailing wind at:
- Dublin Airport?
- Malin Head?
- Shannon Airport?
- Rosslare?

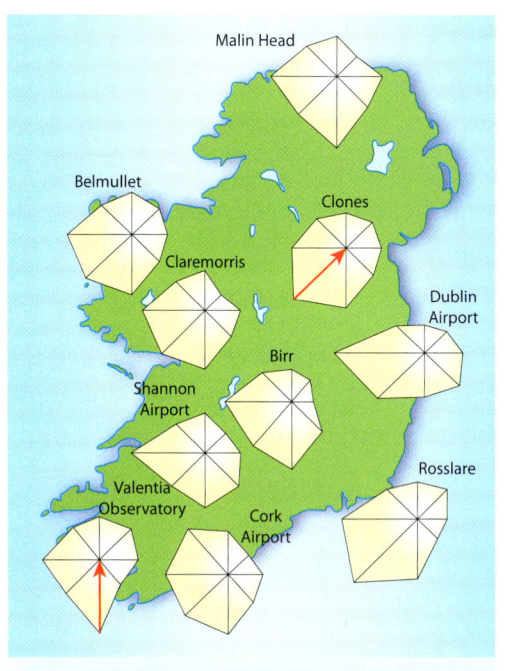

Figure 5.8 The prevailing wind direction at Valentia Observatory is **southerly**. The prevailing wind direction at Clones is **south-westerly**

Global wind patterns

Winds blow from high pressure areas to low pressure areas (see Figure 5.6, page 82). These differences in pressure result in the development of a global **wind pattern**.

The winds in the northern and southern hemispheres are divided into three **wind belts**. We will now examine how the wind belts of the northern hemisphere develop.

1. Near the equator, the air is heated and **rises**. As it does so, it creates a belt of **low pressure** (LP).
2. The warm air begins to move in a **polar direction**. As it does so, it begins to **cool**.
3. The air is now cooler and heavier. It begins to **sink**, producing an area of **high pressure** (HP) at about **30° N**.
4. The **cool air** then **blows** along the surface of Earth, away from the area of high pressure, to replace the rising air at the equator.
   The **first wind belt** has now developed.
5. At the North Pole, cold polar air sinks to form an area of **high pressure**.
6. The cold air moves away from the pole (as **wind**) and begins to heat up.
7. By latitude **60° N** the air is warmer, so it rises to create an area of **low pressure**.
8. The warm air begins to move back towards the North Pole. A **second wind belt** has now developed.
9. A **third wind belt** develops between the high pressure (HP) belt at latitude 30° N and the low pressure (LP) belt at latitude 60° N.
10. A similar pattern develops in the southern hemisphere.

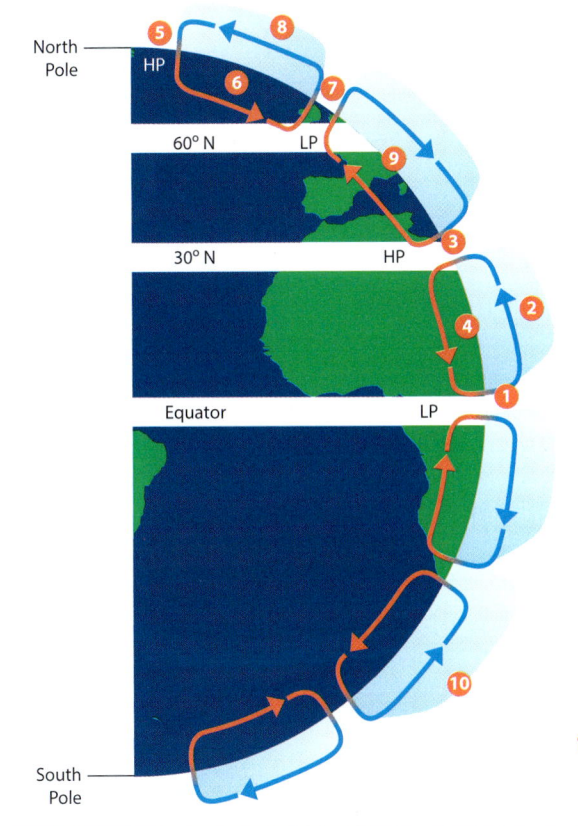

Figure 5.9 How global wind patterns develop

83

Section 1 · Physical Geography

Coriolis effect

The differences in pressure tend to push winds in **straight paths**. If the Earth did not spin on its axis, all the winds would blow straight from the north or straight from the south.

In fact, the Earth spins on its axis (**rotates**) from west to east. This changes the direction of the winds, making them follow **slanted paths** across the Earth.

- Winds are **deflected to the right** in the **northern** hemisphere.
- Winds are **deflected to the left** in the **southern** hemisphere.

This is called the **Coriolis effect**.

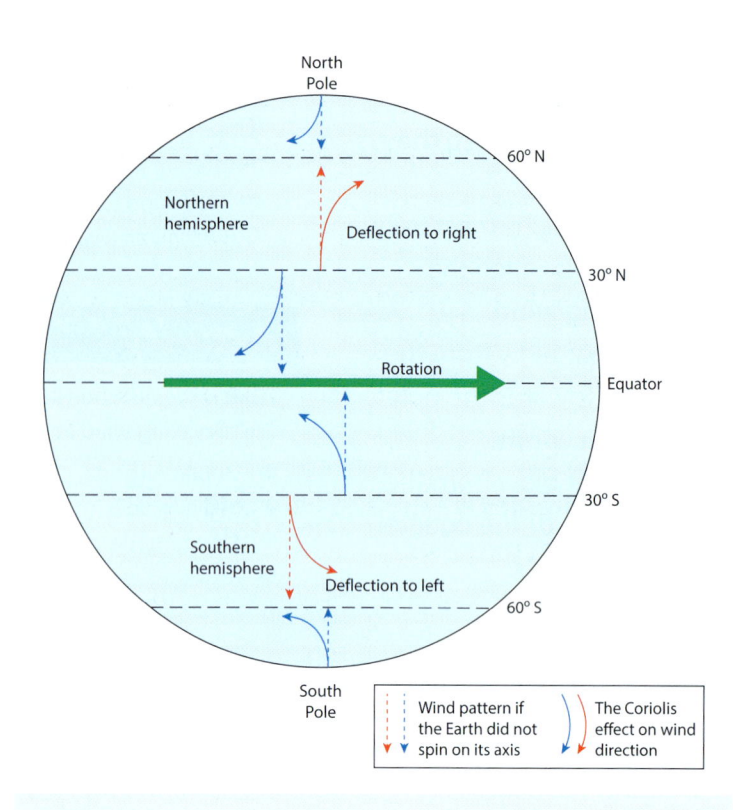

Figure 5.10 The Coriolis effect on the wind system

Global winds

A combination of unequal heating of the atmosphere and the Coriolis effect gives us the global patterns that we have today.

Trade winds

The **trade winds** are movements of air **towards the equator**, from the north-east in the northern hemisphere and from the south-east in the southern hemisphere.

The winds do not move directly north or south because they are deflected by the Coriolis effect. As a result they blow towards the west. That means that they are **easterlies**.

These were the **sailor's favourite winds**, since the weather was warm, and the winds usually blew steadily.

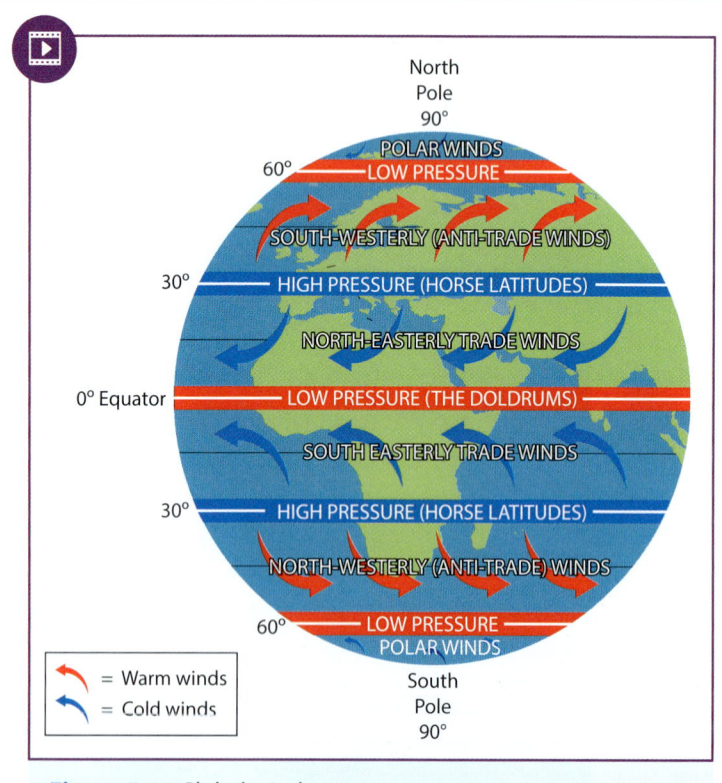

Figure 5.11 Global wind patterns

Activities

1. Which wind belt affects Ireland most frequently?
2. What is the direction of these winds?
3. Are they warm or cold winds?

Definition

The doldrums: An area close to the equator that has very **calm weather**. Winds are very light or have died out entirely. This is because the air is heated and rises straight up rather than blowing along the surface.

The westerlies

The **westerlies** are movements of air from about latitude 30° towards latitude 60°.

- In the **northern hemisphere** they are deflected by the Coriolis effect to blow from the **south-west**.
- In the **southern hemisphere** they blow from the **north-west**.

It is because of the direction from which they originate that they are called **westerlies**.

The south-westerlies are the **prevailing winds** in Ireland. It is these winds that are responsible for most of the weather conditions across the country.

The polar easterlies

The **polar easterlies** are **dry** and **very cold** winds that blow outwards from the high pressure areas at the poles.

Since the winds originate in the east, they are known as **easterlies**.

Questions

1. (a) What is wind?
   (b) How are winds named?
   (c) What is atmospheric pressure?
   (d) How do winds form?
2. (a) Why do winds blow from high pressure areas to low pressure areas?
   (b) What is the Coriolis effect?
   (c) What are the doldrums?
3. Describe, with the aid of a labelled diagram, how any **one** of the global wind belts developed.

5.4 Ocean currents

KEYWORDS

- ocean current
- warm current
- cold current
- Gulf Stream
- North Atlantic Drift
- Canaries Current
- Labrador Current

The water of the ocean surface moves in regular patterns called surface **ocean currents**. These currents are like giant rivers that flow slowly through the oceans.

The movement of ocean currents results from:

- Unequal heating of the oceans
- The prevailing winds
- The rotation of the Earth.

Unequal heating of the oceans

Solar heating causes the ocean water to heat and expand. Near the equator the water is about 8 cm higher than in middle latitudes. This causes a very slight slope and water wants to flow down the slope. By the time it reaches the poles, it is cold and heavy so it sinks.

Section 1 · Physical Geography

The prevailing winds

As the winds blow over the surface of the oceans, there is **friction** between the water and the wind. This causes some of the water to be dragged along, roughly following the global wind pattern. For example, the south-westerly winds help to drag the **North Atlantic Drift** towards Ireland.

The rotation of the Earth

As the Earth rotates on its axis from west to east, it causes the currents of the northern hemisphere to move to the right. As a result, a **clockwise pattern** has developed in the currents of the North Atlantic.

Effects of ocean currents

The most important effect of ocean currents is their impact on **climate**. They transfer heat around the globe.

Currents that flow from the equator towards higher latitudes bring warm water and are called **warm currents**. Currents that flow from the direction of the poles bring cold water and are called **cold currents**.

Case study

Currents of the North Atlantic

There are five major systems of rotating ocean currents around the world. The currents of the North Atlantic make up one of these systems. The currents of the North Atlantic system include the Gulf Stream, North Atlantic Drift, Labrador Current and Canaries Current.

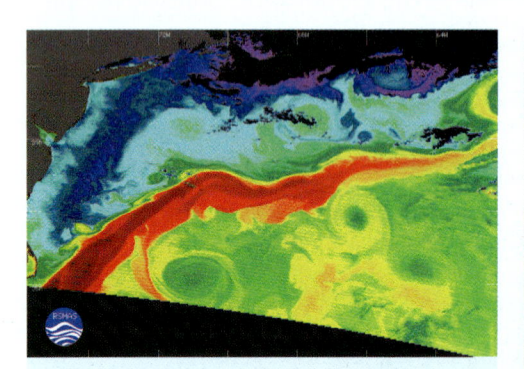

An infra-red satellite image showing the Gulf Stream and and North Atlantic Drift (red). The Greenland and Labrador currents are seen in blue

Ship among icebergs and floating ice

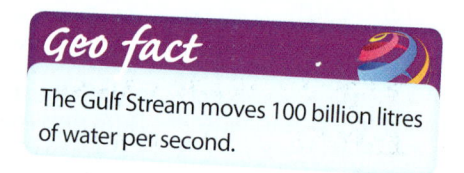

Geo fact
The Gulf Stream moves 100 billion litres of water per second.

Chapter 5 · The Restless Atmosphere

Case study

- The **Labrador Current** is a **cold current** that flows **south** from the Arctic Ocean. It passes the coasts of Greenland, Canada and the north-east USA.

  It lowers the temperature of the oceans and, as a result, many ports in Canada and the USA are frozen over for several months of the year.

  It also brings icebergs into the shipping lanes of the Atlantic. As it mingles with the Gulf Stream, it produces coastal fog.

- The **Gulf Stream** is a **warm current** that begins in the Gulf of Mexico and flows in a **north-easterly** direction towards the North Atlantic Ocean. Here it splits in two to form the North Atlantic Drift and the Canaries Current.

- The **North Atlantic Drift** is a continuation of the Gulf Stream. It flows in a north-easterly direction past the coast of Western Europe.

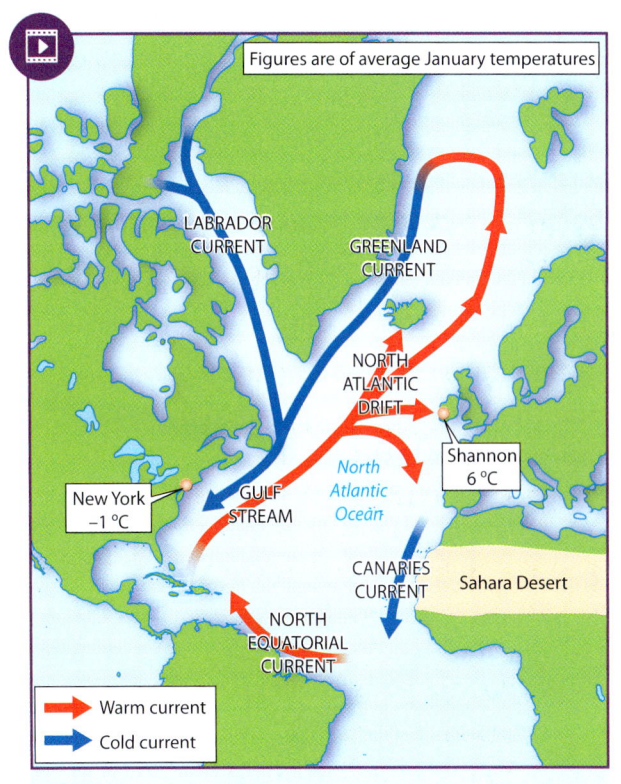

Figure 5.12 Currents of the North Atlantic

The North Atlantic Drift raises the temperature of the waters off the coasts of Ireland, Scotland and Norway by about 8°C. This keeps them ice-free all year round.

The warm waters also transfer some heat to the air. The prevailing south-westerly winds that blow over Ireland are much warmer than they would otherwise be. This warm air can hold more moisture, thus bringing us more rainfall.

- The **Canaries Current** is a cold current that flows in a **southerly** direction off the coast of West Africa.

  When winds blow over this cold current, they lose their moisture. As a result, they bring very little rainfall to the Sahara, thus adding to the desert conditions.

Activity

Even though it is closer to the equator, New York has colder winters than Shannon. Give two reasons why this is so.

Questions

1. Explain what causes ocean currents to flow. In your answer, refer to:
   - Unequal heating of the oceans
   - Prevailing winds.
2. (a) Name **two** currents found in the North Atlantic.
   (b) Name the current that flows off the west coast of Ireland.
   (c) Explain **two** ways that this current influences the climate of Ireland.

Section 1 · Physical Geography

5.5 Air masses and weather systems

KEYWORDS

- weather
- front
- warm front
- isobar
- cold sector
- air mass
- cold front
- depression
- warm sector
- anticyclone

Air masses are large bodies of air that have similar temperature, pressure and moisture throughout. They can be thousands of kilometres across.

Air masses move around and **influence the weather** that a country experiences.

- **Maritime** air masses tend to bring rain.
- **Continental** air masses tend to be dry.
- **Polar** and **Arctic** air masses are cold.
- **Tropical** air masses are warm.

Definition
Weather: The word used to describe the state of the atmosphere at any particular time and place.

Arctic Maritime air mass
Polar Maritime air mass
Polar Continental air mass
Tropical Maritime air mass
Tropical Continental air mass

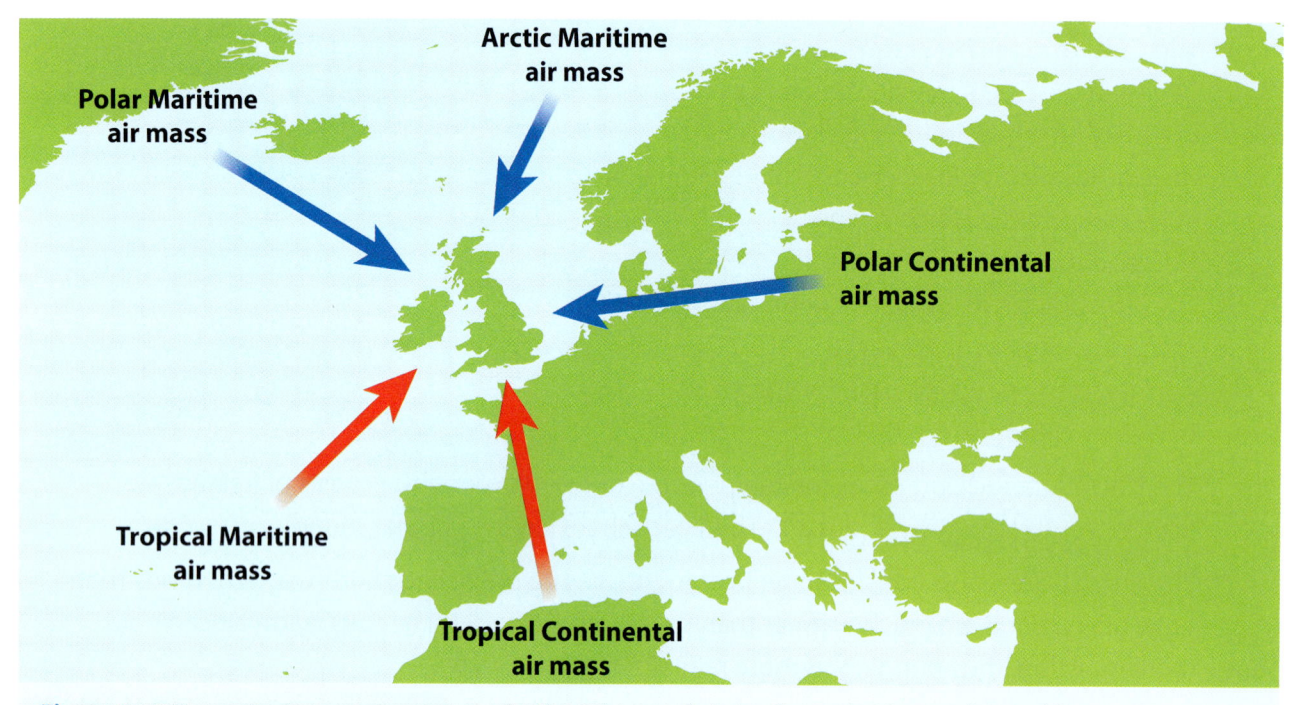

Figure 5.13 Five main air masses meet around Ireland. As a result, Ireland's weather is very changeable

Table 5.1 Air masses and weather

Air mass	From	Winter conditions	Summer conditions
Arctic Maritime	Arctic region	Very cold with snow	Cold showers (rare)
Polar Maritime	Greenland & Arctic	Cold and wet	Cool and wet
Polar Continental	Central Europe	Cold and dry	Hot and dry
Tropical Continental	North Africa	Mild and dry	Hot and dry
Tropical Maritime	Atlantic	Mild and wet	Warm and rainy

88

Fronts

When two air masses meet, they do not mix very well because of the differences between them. The boundary area between two air masses is called a **front**. Fronts can be **cold** or **warm**.

Cold front

- A **cold front** occurs when a cold air mass pushes in and replaces a warm air mass. The warm air mass is lighter so it is forced to rise rapidly into the atmosphere.
- As the **warm air rises**, it cools and condensation takes place. Masses of cloud develop. **Heavy rain** falls along the front.

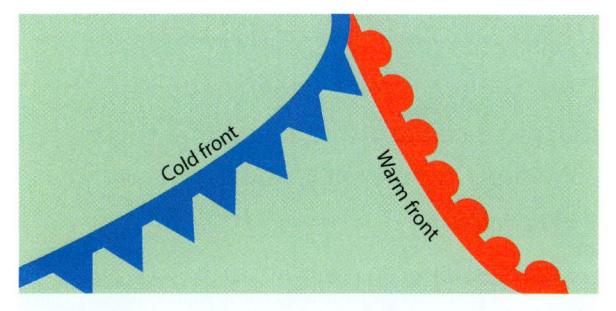

Figure 5.14 Cold and warm fronts on a weather map

Showing fronts on a weather map

- A cold front is shown on a weather map by a solid blue line with triangular teeth.
- A warm front is shown on weather maps by a solid red line with semicircles.

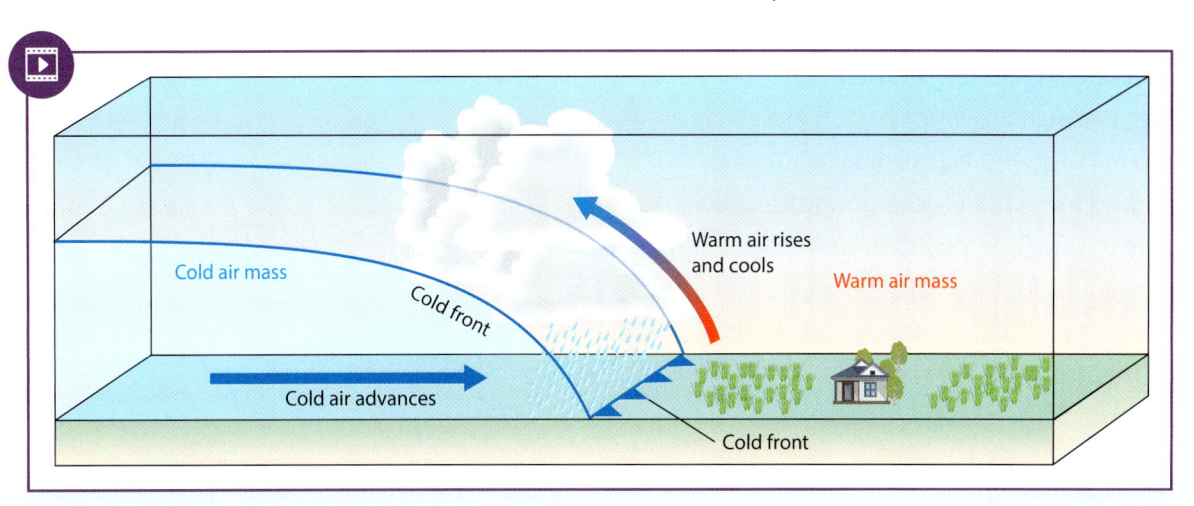

Figure 5.15 The formation of a cold front

Warm front

- A **warm front** occurs when a warm air mass approaches a cold air mass. The warm air is lighter so it rises up over the cold air.
- As the warm air rises, it cools and condenses to form dark, rain-bearing clouds. **Periods of rain** soon follow.

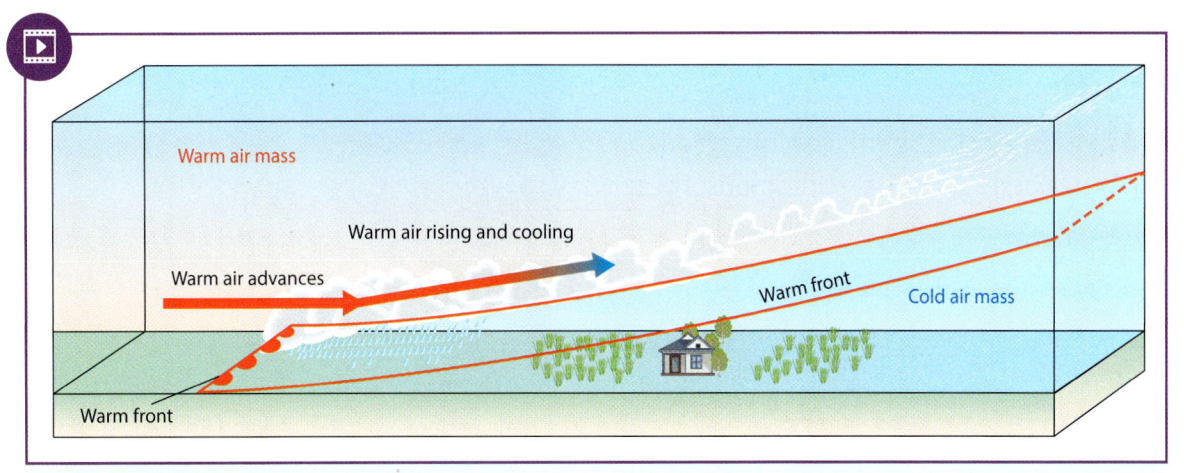

Figure 5.16 The formation of a warm front

Section 1 · Physical Geography

Depressions (low pressure)

Depressions are areas of **low pressure** that produce **unsettled** conditions. These conditions include rainy, cloudy and windy weather.

Depressions can measure up to 2,000 km across and tend to have an oval shape. Pressure is lowest in the centre. The depressions that affect Ireland develop in the mid-Atlantic and move eastwards.

- Depressions develop when a warm tropical air mass meets a cold polar air mass, creating **warm and cold fronts**.
- At the **cold front**, the cold air mass moves faster and is heavier than the warm air. It cuts in beneath it, thus forcing the warm air upwards.
- At the **warm front**, the warm air is being pushed forward. As it is lighter than the cold air ahead of it, it is forced upwards.
- The depression is formed where these two fronts meet. Here the warm air is rising upwards and out of the cold air's way. This creates an area of **low pressure**.

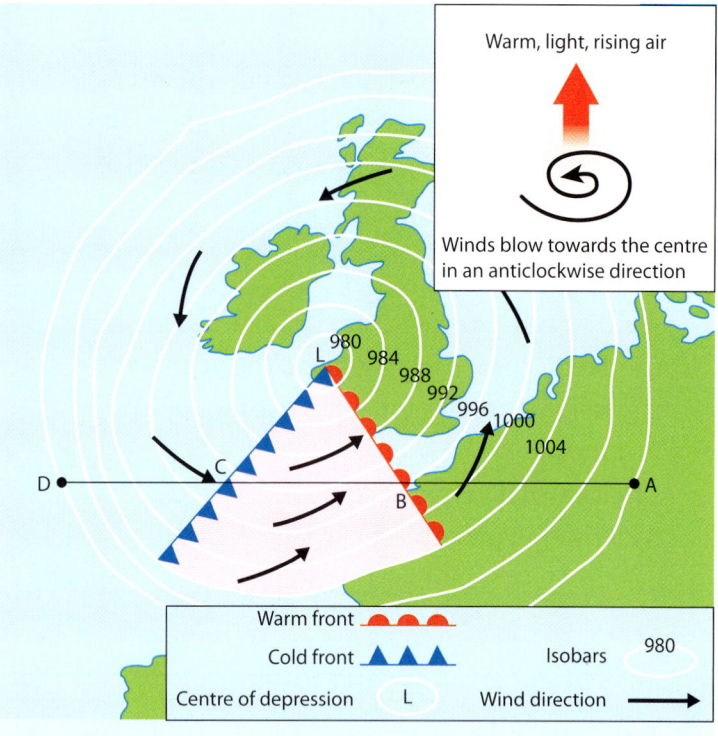

Figure 5.17 Weather map showing a depression

Activity

Examine Figure 5.17.
1. What is the atmospheric pressure at L?
2. What is the atmospheric pressure at D?

Definition ✓

Isobars: Lines drawn on a weather map connecting places of equal atmospheric pressure, measured in **millibars**.

Geo fact

When isobars on a weather chart are close together, it will be a windy day.

Weather in a depression

We have seen that depressions bring very unsettled weather, with wet, cloudy and windy conditions. These conditions change quite rapidly as the depression passes.

A major depression over Ireland. This was Storm Darwin as it hit the country in February 2014

90

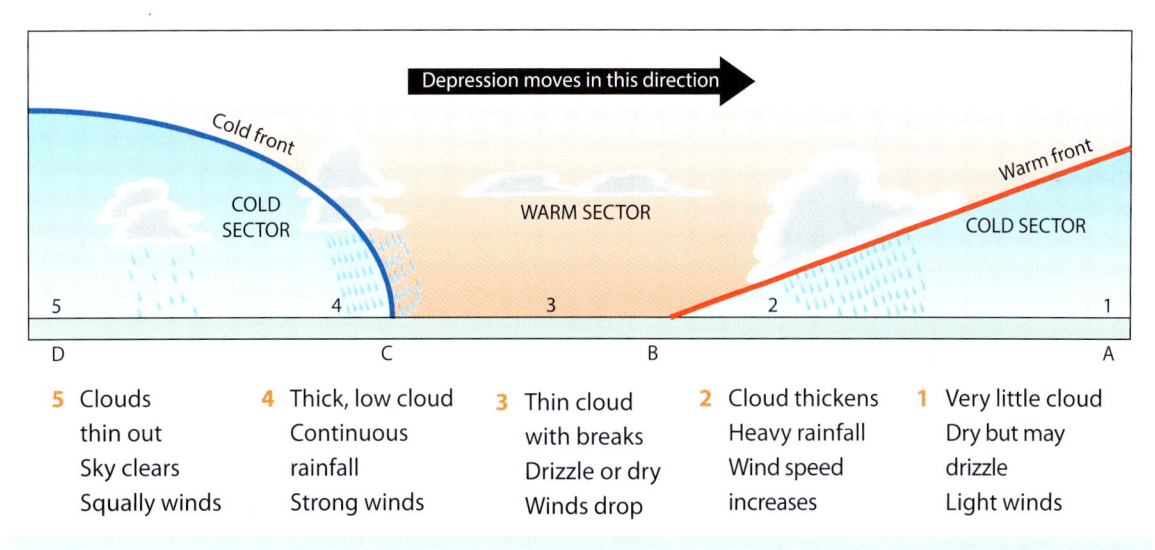

5 Clouds thin out / Sky clears / Squally winds	**4** Thick, low cloud / Continuous rainfall / Strong winds	**3** Thin cloud with breaks / Drizzle or dry / Winds drop	**2** Cloud thickens / Heavy rainfall / Wind speed increases	**1** Very little cloud / Dry but may drizzle / Light winds

Figure 5.18 Profile across a depression (between A and D in Figure 5.17), showing the general weather conditions that occur. Please read both diagrams **from right to left** (i.e. from A to D and from 1 to 5)

Anticyclones (high pressure)

An anticyclone is an air mass with **high pressure** at the centre. It is also known as a **high**. Since an anticyclone consists of a single air mass, there are no fronts.

In the centre, the air is descending slowly on to the Earth's surface, where it is compressed to form an area of high pressure.

Anticyclones appear on weather charts as a series of closed, widely spaced isobars of 1000 millibars and above. The isobar at the centre of the anticyclone is the area of highest pressure.

Weather in an anticyclone

Anticyclones are usually slow-moving features. As a result, they bring **settled weather** for days, sometimes even weeks.

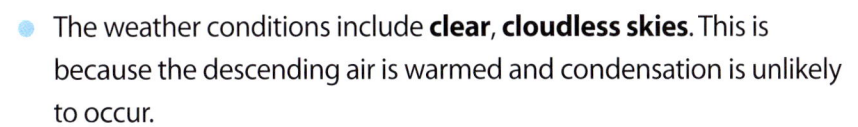

- The weather conditions include **clear**, **cloudless skies**. This is because the descending air is warmed and condensation is unlikely to occur.
- Winds, if any, are very light and blow in a **clockwise** direction in the northern hemisphere.
- In **summer**, the clear skies bring **hot, sunny weather**.
- In **winter**, the clear skies bring low temperatures. The lack of cloud cover means that nights are **cold** and **frosty**.

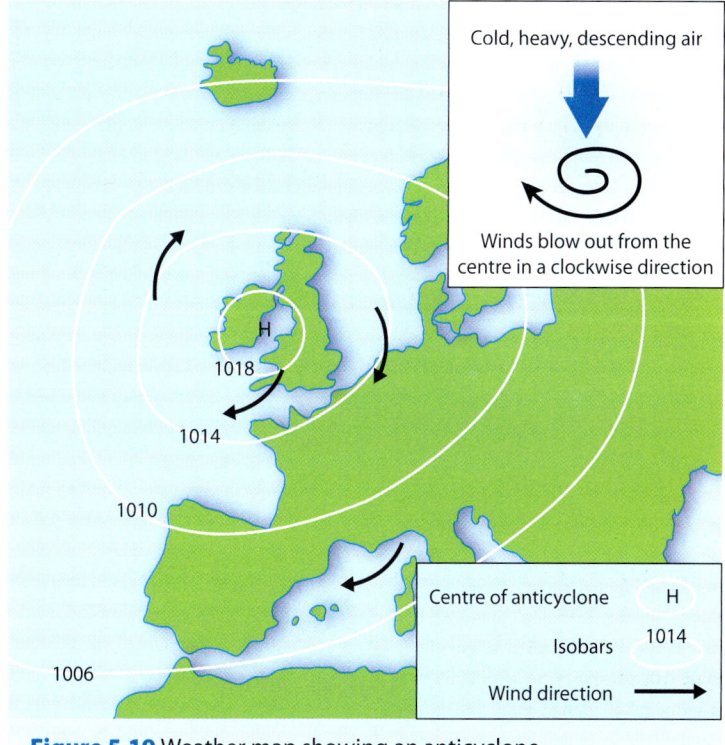

Figure 5.19 Weather map showing an anticyclone

Activities

Examine Figure 5.19.
1. What is the atmospheric pressure along the west coast of Ireland?
2. Is the pressure at H likely to be 1016 or 1020? Explain why.

Section 1 · Physical Geography

Clear skies over Ireland as an anticyclone (area of high pressure) is centred on the country

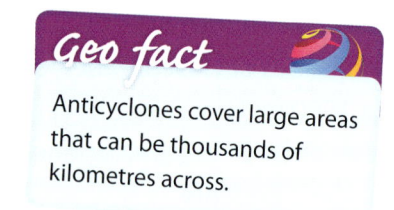

Geo fact

Anticyclones cover large areas that can be thousands of kilometres across.

Questions

1. (a) What is an air mass?
   (b) Name **two** air masses that affect Ireland.
   (c) Briefly describe the weather associated with each of them.

2. (a) What is a weather front?
   (b) With the aid of a labelled diagram, describe how a warm front or a cold front develops.

3. (a) Draw a diagram of a depression. On it show and label the warm front, the cold front, the centre of the depression (L) and the direction of the winds.
   (b) Describe the weather that is associated with a depression.

4. (a) What is an anticyclone?
   (b) Describe the weather conditions associated with an anticyclone.

5.6 Water in the atmosphere

KEYWORDS

- water cycle
- evaporation
- condensation
- precipitation
- clouds
- cirrus
- cumulus
- stratus
- relief rainfall
- rain shadow
- cyclonic rainfall
- convectional rainfall

Water is a renewable **natural resource**, vital for the survival of life on the planet. Less than 3 per cent of the Earth's water is fresh water; the remainder is salt water.

The water cycle

The **water cycle** is the Earth's way of recycling water. It describes the journey water takes as it constantly passes between the atmosphere, the oceans and the land.

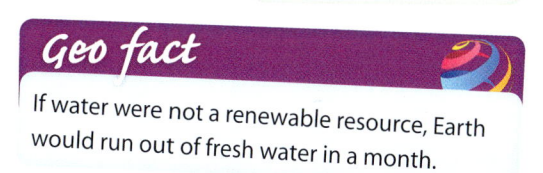

Activity

Why, do you think, is this group of processes called a cycle?

Geo fact

If water were not a renewable resource, Earth would run out of fresh water in a month.

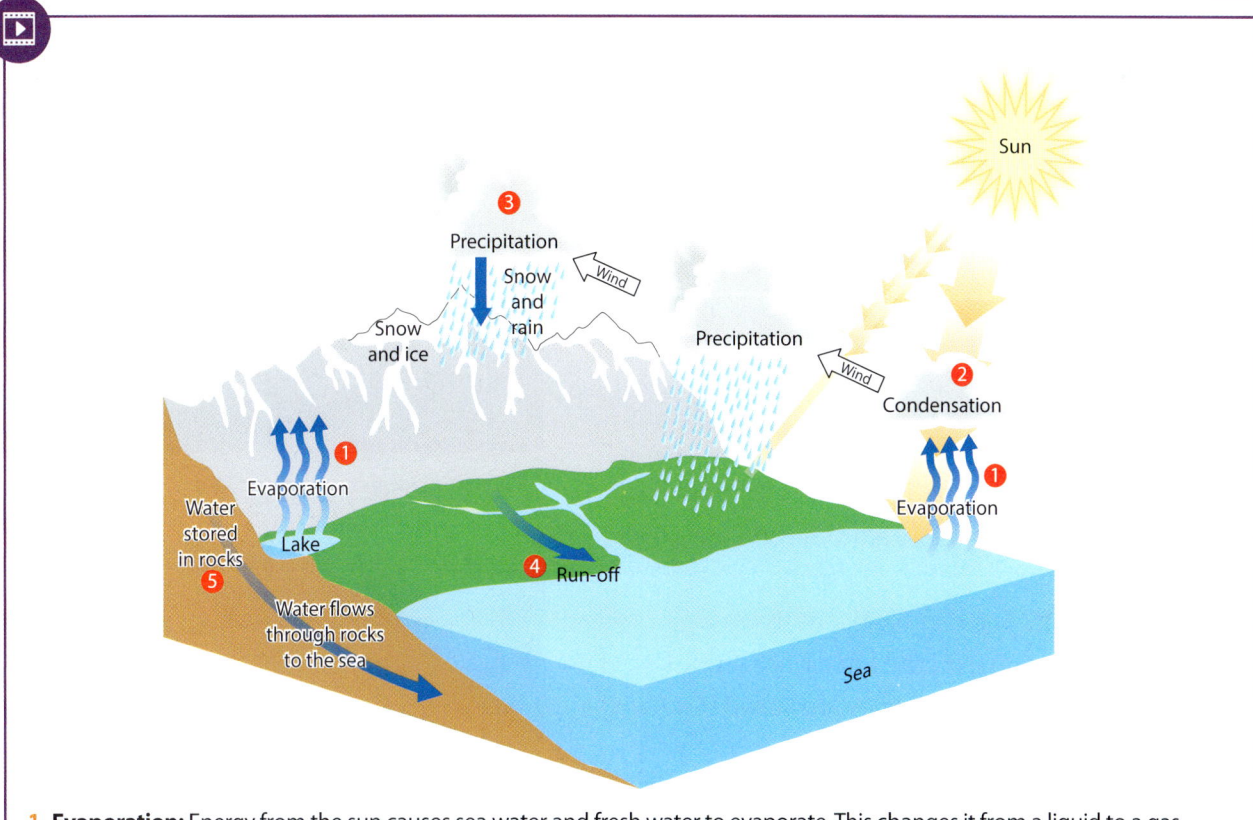

1. **Evaporation:** Energy from the sun causes sea water and fresh water to evaporate. This changes it from a liquid to a gas (water vapour) in the atmosphere.
2. **Condensation:** The water vapour is so light that it rises into the atmosphere. As it rises, it cools and **condenses** into tiny water droplets to form **clouds**.
3. **Precipitation:** The droplets join up and become heavier. Eventually the water falls and returns to Earth (**precipitates**) in the form of rain, snow, sleet or hail.
4. **Run-off:** Some precipitation evaporates immediately. More of it soaks into the ground. The rest of the water finds its way back to the sea by rivers and streams. This is known as surface **run-off**.
5. **Underground water:** The bulk of the water soaks into the ground, where it is held in the soil or in pores (tiny holes) in the rocks. From there it can return to the sea or people can drill wells for a water supply.

Figure 5.20 The water cycle

Section 1 · Physical Geography

Clouds

The atmosphere contains moisture in the form of **water vapour**. When the water vapour condenses, it forms tiny water droplets or ice crystals. These are so small and light that they can float in the air. When billions of them come together they become a visible **cloud**.

Clouds are grouped according to their **shape** and the **height** at which they occur. The darker the colour of the cloud, the more likely it is that precipitation is about to occur. There are three main types of cloud:

- Cirrus
- Cumulus
- Stratus.

Cirrus

The word **cirrus** comes from the Latin word for curl.

- Cirrus clouds are wispy like a lock of hair.
- They occur at high altitude.
- They are made of ice crystals.
- They are associated with good weather.

Cumulus

The word **cumulus** comes from the Latin word for heap.

- Cumulus clouds are fluffy or woolly in appearance.
- They occur at medium altitude.
- They are also known as fine weather clouds.
- They can bring rain if they darken in colour.

Stratus

The word **stratus** comes from the Latin word for layer.

- Stratus clouds occur at low altitude, and are grey in colour.
- They form layers and can block out the sky.
- They bring continual drizzle and light rain.
- If they reach ground level, they are called fog.

Precipitation

When cloud particles become too heavy to remain suspended in the air, they fall to Earth as **precipitation**. Precipitation occurs in a variety of forms: rain, hail, sleet or snow.

Rainfall is by far the most common form of precipitation. There are three types of rainfall:

- Relief rainfall
- Cyclonic (frontal) rainfall
- Convectional rainfall.

Cirrus clouds along the Connemara coast

Cumulus clouds over north Clare

Stratus clouds over the Giant's Causeway

Relief rainfall

Relief rainfall occurs when an air mass is forced to rise over a **mountain range**.

- Warm, **moist air** blows in from over the sea.
- If it meets a coastal **mountain range**, it is forced to rise.
- This causes the air to **cool** and **condensation** occurs.
- Clouds form and eventually **rain falls** on the **windward** side of the mountain.
- The air that descends on the sheltered (**leeward**) side of the mountain has very little moisture left. Condensation ceases and a **rain shadow** is created.

Ireland receives relief rainfall throughout the year; most of it falls in the mountainous areas of the west coast.

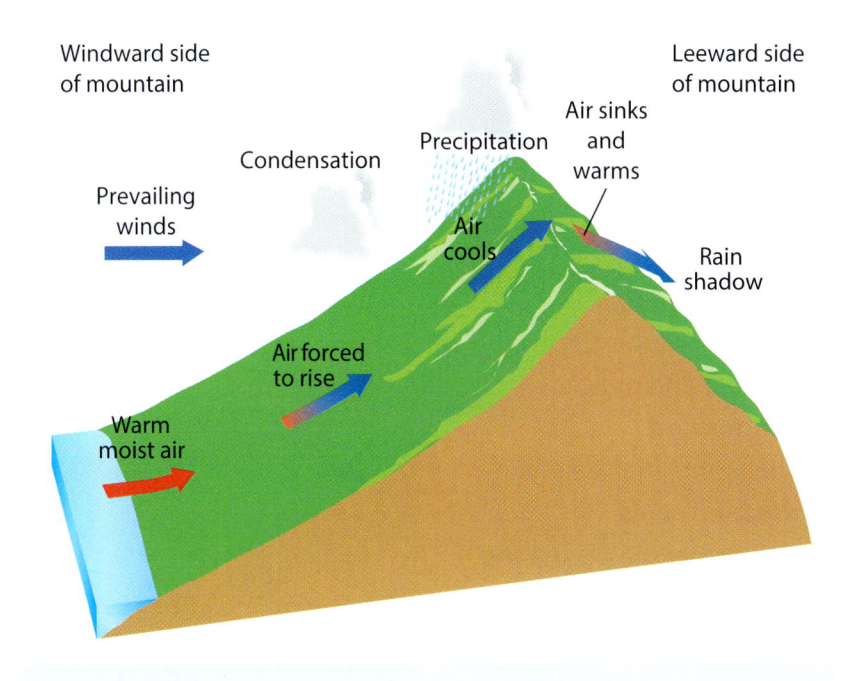

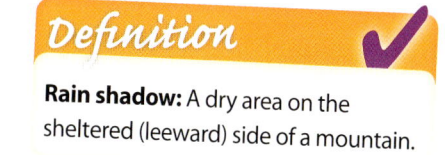

Figure 5.21 Relief rainfall

Definition ✓

Rain shadow: A dry area on the sheltered (leeward) side of a mountain.

Cyclonic (frontal) rainfall

Cyclonic (frontal) rainfall occurs when an **air mass is forced to rise** at a front.

- Cold, polar air and warm, moist tropical air masses meet at a **front**.
- The light, warm air mass rides up over the cold, heavy air mass.
- This causes the warm air to **cool** and **condensation** occurs.
- Clouds form and eventually **rain falls**.
- Rain is light at first, but eventually becomes heavier.

Fronts develop over the Atlantic and, when they move in, they bring changeable weather to Ireland. Rainfall is most frequent during winter.

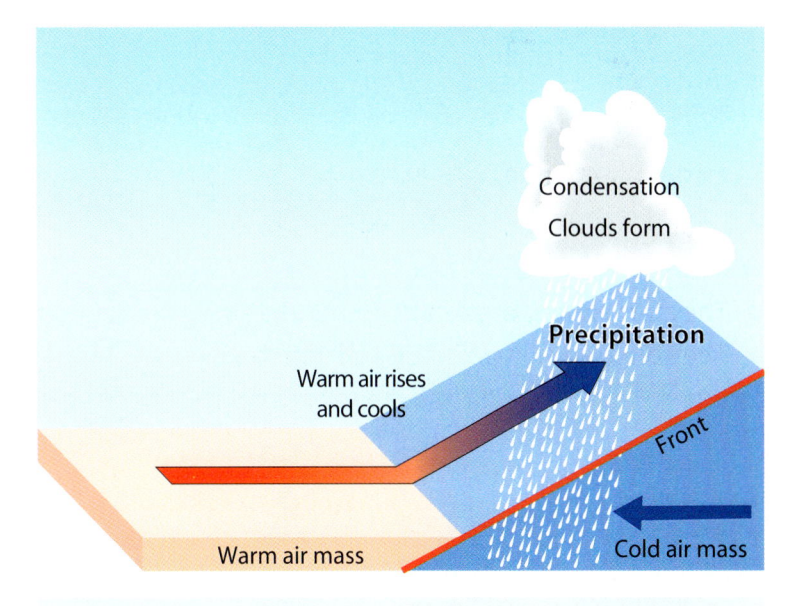

Figure 5.22 Cyclonic (frontal) rainfall

Geo fact

The west of Ireland receives over 2,000 mm of rainfall annually, while parts of the east and Midlands receive as little as 800 mm.

Section 1 · Physical Geography

Convectional rainfall

Convectional rain occurs when the surface layer of the atmosphere is heated, causing moisture-laden air to rise.

- The Earth's surface is heated by **solar energy**.
- The land warms the air above it and moisture is **evaporated**.
- This warm, moist air then rises and **cools**.
- **Condensation** occurs and clouds form.
- Heavy **showers** follow. They are sometimes accompanied by thunder.

Convectional rainfall occurs each afternoon in equatorial regions. It also occurs in Ireland, but only in summer during hot and sunny days.

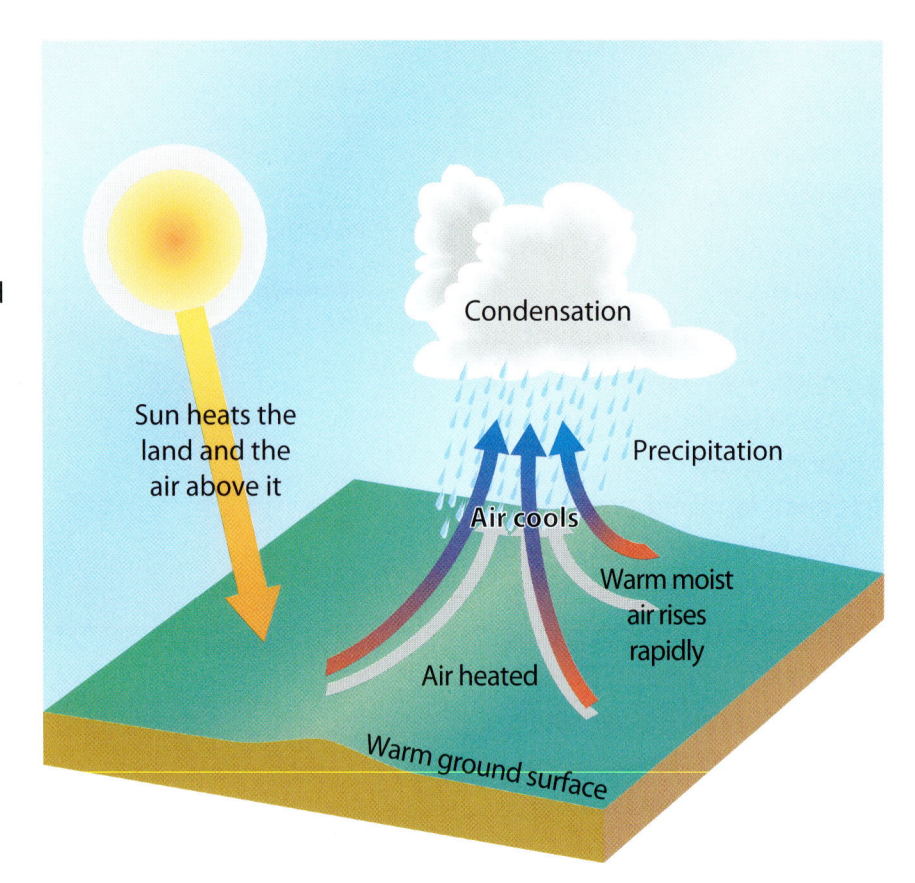

Figure 5.23 Convectional rainfall

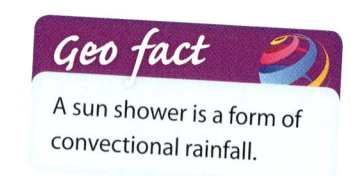

Geo fact
A sun shower is a form of convectional rainfall.

Questions

1. Explain each of the following terms:
   - Evaporation
   - Condensation
   - Precipitation.

2. Describe, with the aid of a simple labelled diagram, how the water cycle works.

3. (a) Name **three** types of cloud.
   (b) Select **one** cloud type and briefly describe it.

4. (a) Why does precipitation occur?
   (b) Name **three** types of precipitation.
   (c) What is the most common type of precipitation?

5. Select any **one** type of rainfall and, with the aid of a labelled diagram, explain how it occurs.

Chapter 5 · The Restless Atmosphere

5.7 Weather

KEYWORDS
- weather
- meteorology
- synoptic chart
- weather station
- Stevenson screen
- temperature
- atmospheric pressure
- relative humidity
- wind speed/direction
- precipitation
- sunshine

Weather is the word used to describe the state of the atmosphere at any particular time and place. Weather conditions can change every day and can vary over short distances.

Elements of weather

The study of weather is called **meteorology**. It involves measuring the elements of weather at least once a day. These include:

- Temperature
- Atmospheric pressure
- Relative humidity
- Wind speed and direction
- Precipitation
- Sunshine.

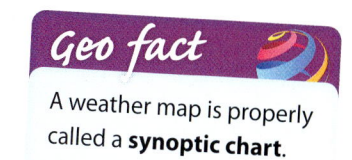

Geo fact
A weather map is properly called a **synoptic chart**.

Weather forecasts

A weather forecast predicts what the weather will be for a particular place.
Meteorologists prepare weather forecasts. They study information that is collected from a number of sources. These sources include weather stations, satellites, radar stations, gas rigs and shipping.

Ground
Weather stations
Radar stations

Air
Weather satellites
Weather balloons

Sea
Weather buoys
Shipping

The information is transmitted to **Met Éireann** headquarters

Information on the elements of weather is collected from many sources

Meteorologists analyse the information and prepare the weather forecast

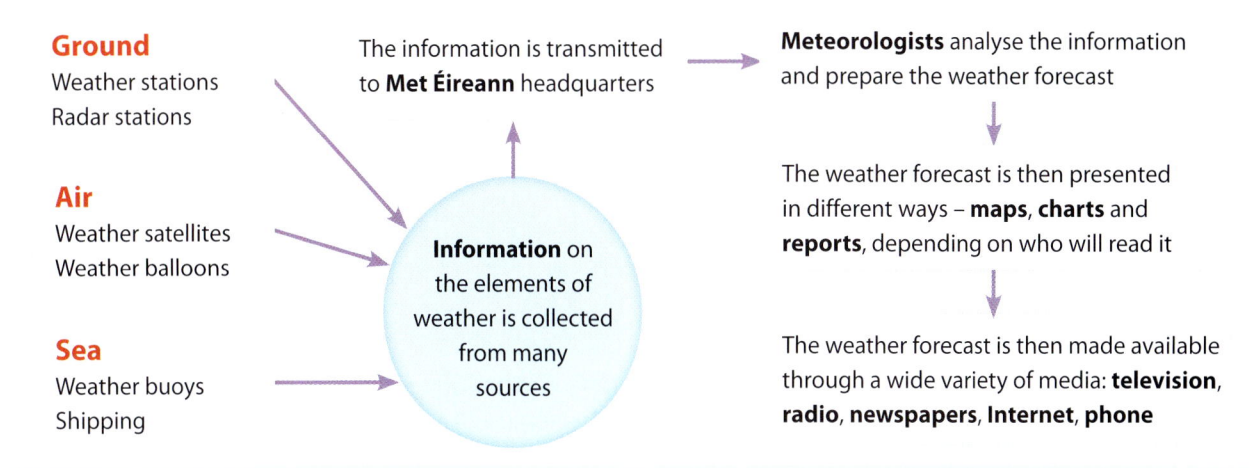

The weather forecast is then presented in different ways – **maps**, **charts** and **reports**, depending on who will read it

The weather forecast is then made available through a wide variety of media: **television**, **radio**, **newspapers**, **Internet**, **phone**

Figure 5.24 Preparing a weather forecast

The importance of weather forecasts

We are all interested in the weather forecast for our local area. The upcoming weather will influence what we wear and the activities that we undertake. It may even affect our mood.

Some occupations require very accurate weather forecasts, e.g. farming, fishing, tourism, air traffic and sport.

Activity
Explain why these people would need an accurate weather forecast: farmer, fisherman, airline pilot and tourist.

Section 1 · Physical Geography

The weather station

A **weather station** is a place where information about the elements of weather is gathered and recorded using many different instruments. **Met Éireann** currently gathers data from 25 land-based weather stations.

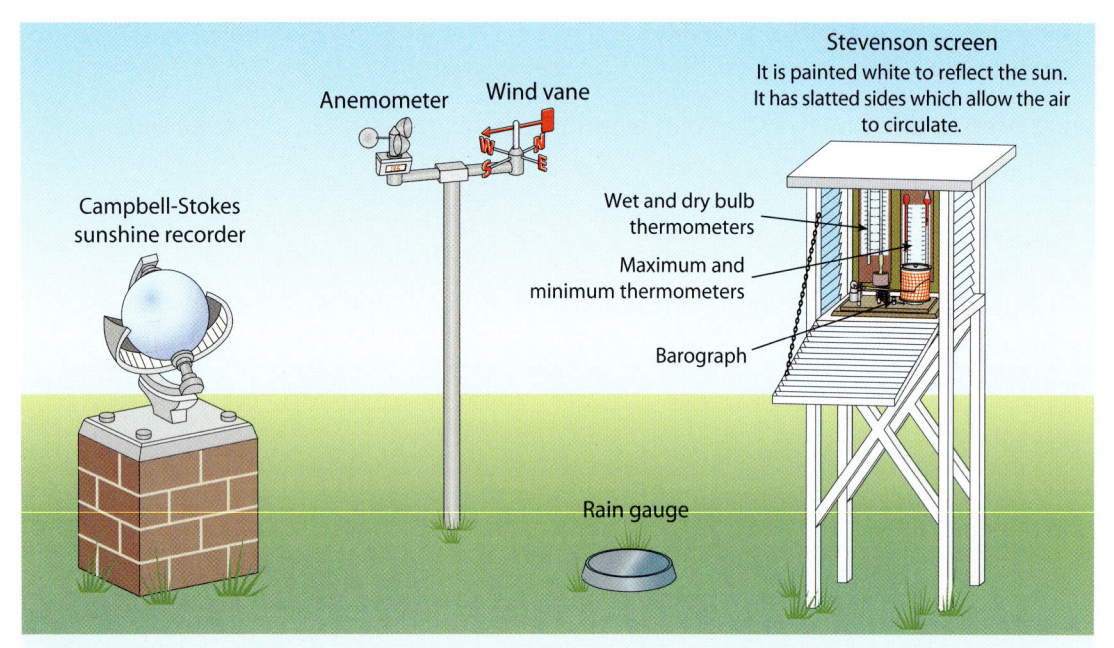

Figure 5.25 The weather instruments found in a typical land-based weather station. The Stevenson screen does not measure any element of weather. It is a home for some instruments

Measuring weather

We will now examine how each element of weather is measured. In doing this, we will look at the following:

- The **element** that is being measured
- The **instrument** used to measure it
- The **unit** of measurement
- **How it is shown** on a weather (synoptic) chart.

Measuring temperature

Temperature is the degree of hotness or coldness of the atmosphere.

- Temperature is measured with a **thermometer**.
- The unit of measurement of temperature is **degrees Celsius/Centigrade** (°C).
- **Isotherms** are lines on a weather chart that join places of equal temperature.

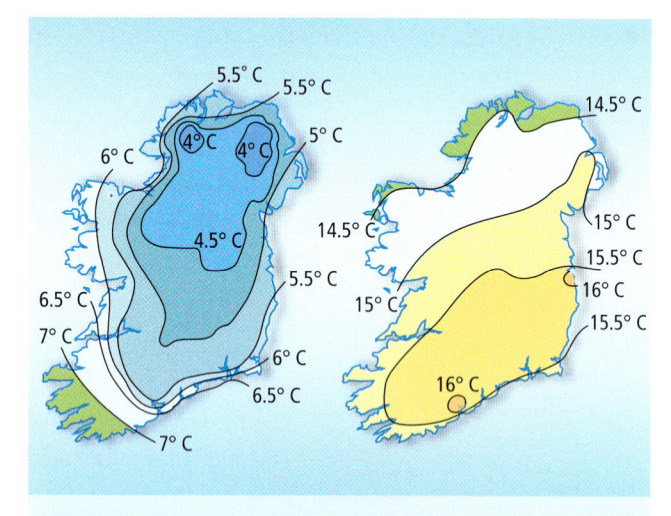

Figure 5.26 Isotherms showing average air temperatures for Ireland in January (left) and in July (right)

Activity

Examine Figure 5.26.

1. What province has the highest temperatures in January?
2. What is the difference between the maximum and minimum temperatures in July?

98

Chapter 5 · The Restless Atmosphere

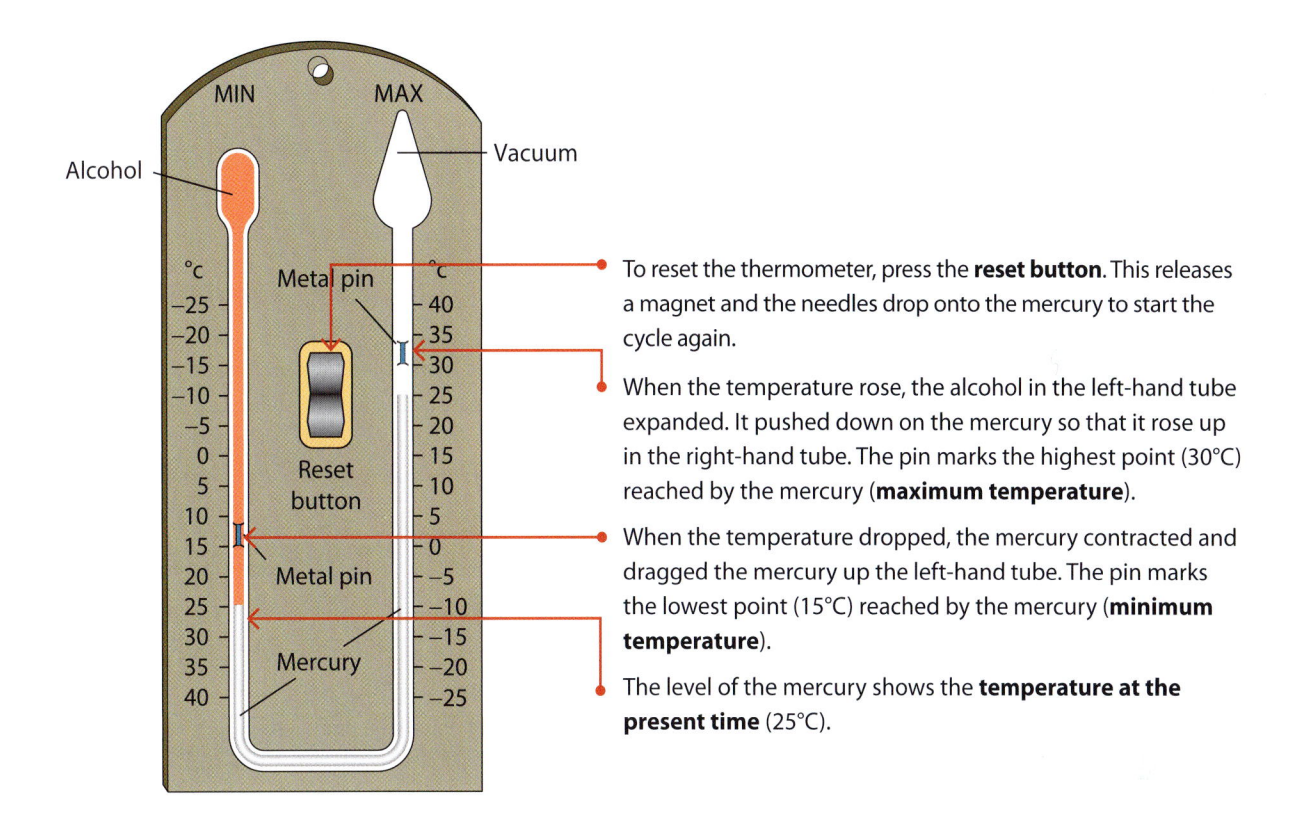

To reset the thermometer, press the **reset button**. This releases a magnet and the needles drop onto the mercury to start the cycle again.

When the temperature rose, the alcohol in the left-hand tube expanded. It pushed down on the mercury so that it rose up in the right-hand tube. The pin marks the highest point (30°C) reached by the mercury (**maximum temperature**).

When the temperature dropped, the mercury contracted and dragged the mercury up the left-hand tube. The pin marks the lowest point (15°C) reached by the mercury (**minimum temperature**).

The level of the mercury shows the **temperature at the present time** (25°C).

Figure 5.27 Maximum-minimum thermometer

Calculating mean (or average) annual temperature and temperature range

Table 5.2 Temperature table

Months	Jan	Feb	Mar	Apr	May	Jun	Jul	Aug	Sep	Oct	Nov	Dec
Mean monthly temperature (°C)	10	13	16	18	20	23	25	27	22	16	14	12

Table 5.3 Calculations

Mean temperature = $\frac{\text{Sum of monthly temperatures}}{\text{Divided by 12}} = \frac{216}{12} = 18°C$

Temperature range = Maximum temperature − minimum temperature = 27°C − 10°C = 17°C

Activities

1. Calculate the mean monthly temperature and the temperature range for:
   (a) The first three months of the year
   (b) The last four months of the year.
2. In the example on the right, why is the temperature range 18°C rather than 14°C?

Example

Maximum temperature = 16°C
Minimum temperature = −2°C
Temperature range = 18°C

Section 1 · Physical Geography

Measuring atmospheric pressure

Atmospheric pressure is the **weight of the atmosphere** as it presses down on the Earth.

- Atmospheric pressure is measured with a **barometer**. A **barograph** is a barometer that is connected to a chart to record the atmospheric pressure.
- The unit of measurement of atmospheric pressure is **millibars** (mb) or **hectopascals**.
- **Isobars** are lines on a weather map that join places of equal atmospheric pressure.

- The corrugated drum is flexible. When the pressure of the air increases, the drum is pushed down slightly. When the pressure of the air decreases, the drum rises slightly.
- The movement of the drum is transferred to a pointer by a series of levers.
- A drum slowly rotates, with a page of graph paper attached.
- The end of the pointer has an inked nib that records the pressure on the graph paper.

Atmospheric pressure is measured and recorded on a barograph

Weather (synoptic) charts

These charts provide information on **elements of weather** that include air pressure, rainfall, sunshine, wind (see Figure 5.8, page 83) and temperature (see Figure 5.26, page 98). The information is shown using symbols.

The most common type of weather chart is the one that shows **atmospheric pressure** (see Figure 5.28).

These charts show the atmospheric pressure pattern using **isobars** (lines of equal pressure) and indicate areas of high pressure (H) and low pressure (L), along with the associated **fronts** (see Figure 5.14, page 89).

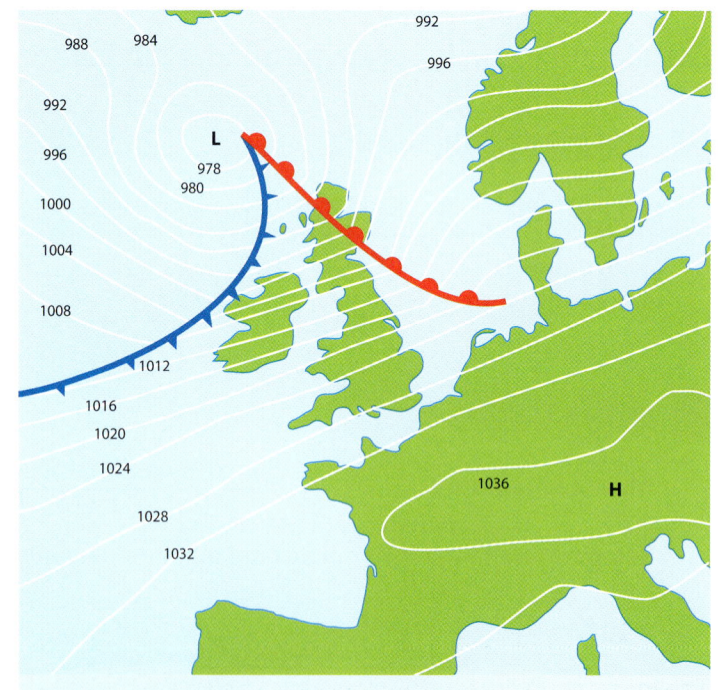

Figure 5.28 Weather map showing atmospheric pressure in the Atlantic and Western Europe

Activities

Examine Figure 5.28.
1 Which letter, L or H, represents a low pressure centre?
2 Which area, L or H, has very little wind?
3 Describe briefly the weather conditions that are approaching the west coast of Ireland.
   Hint: refer to Figure 5.18, page 91.

Chapter 5 · The Restless Atmosphere

Measuring relative humidity

Relative humidity refers to the amount of water vapour in the air compared to the amount it would contain if it were **saturated**.

- Relative humidity is measured with a **hygrometer**. The most common type of hygrometer uses **wet and dry bulb thermometers**.
- The measurement is expressed as a **percentage**.
- If the air has all the moisture that it can hold at a given temperature, the relative humidity is 100 per cent. If it has half the moisture that it can hold, the relative humidity is 50 per cent.
- The difference in temperature between the dry bulb and the wet bulb is used to calculate the relative humidity of the air using a special table.
- When both temperatures are the same, the air has the maximum amount of moisture that it can hold. As the difference between the two temperatures increases, relative humidity decreases and the air is drier.

Definition

Saturated: Full of water; saturated air holds the maximum amount of water vapour possible.

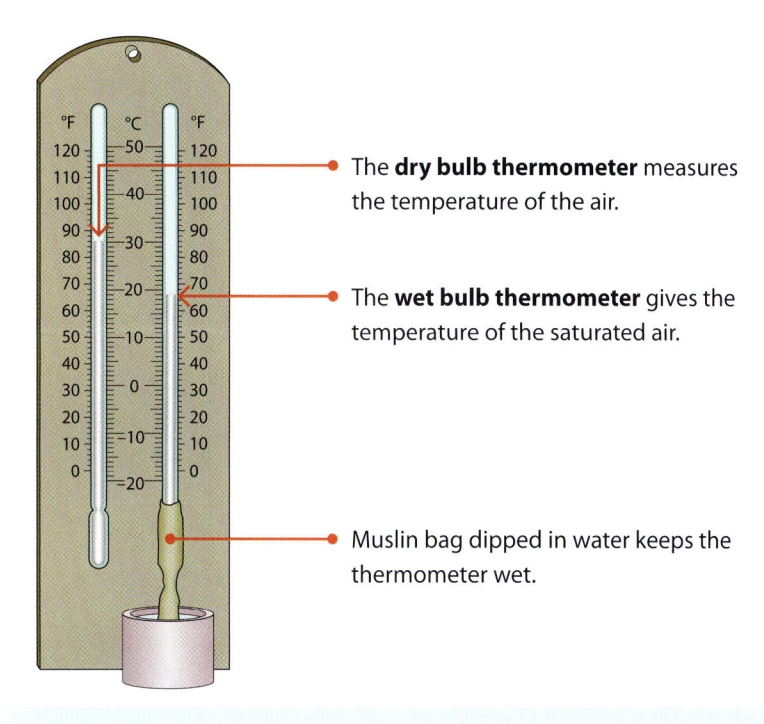

- The **dry bulb thermometer** measures the temperature of the air.
- The **wet bulb thermometer** gives the temperature of the saturated air.
- Muslin bag dipped in water keeps the thermometer wet.

Figure 5.29 Wet and dry bulb thermometers are used to measure relative humidity

Measuring wind speed and direction

The lower layer of the atmosphere is always in motion. This moving air is called **wind**.

- The **speed** of the wind is measured with an **anemometer**.
- The unit of measurement is either miles or **kilometres per hour** (kph).
- The **direction** of the wind is indicated by a **wind vane**.
- Wind direction is described by the direction **from** which the wind is blowing.

Section 1 · Physical Geography

The **Beaufort scale** was devised to estimate wind speed by describing its effects on the landscape. The scale ranges from 0 (calm conditions where smoke rises vertically) to 12 (hurricanes with widespread damage).

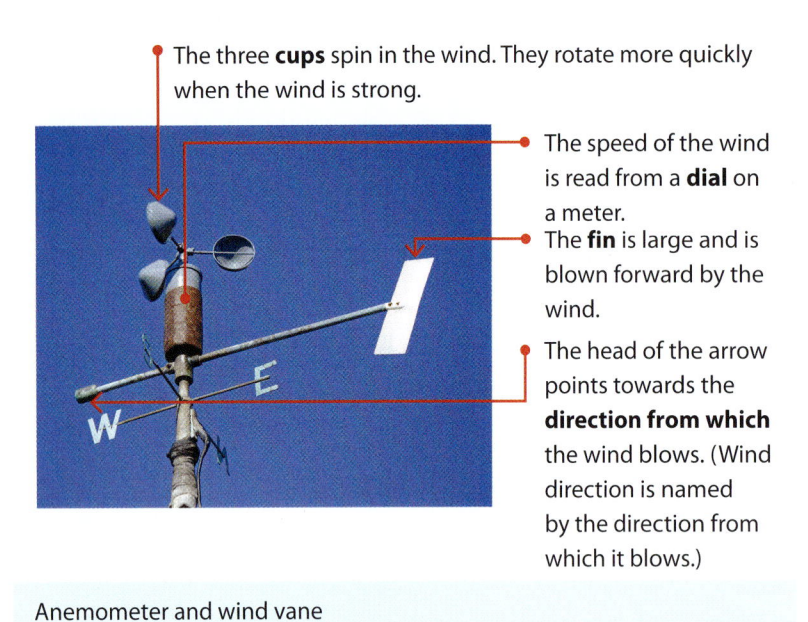

> **Geo fact**
> The **Beaufort scale** was named after the Irishman who devised it.

- The three **cups** spin in the wind. They rotate more quickly when the wind is strong.
- The speed of the wind is read from a **dial** on a meter.
- The **fin** is large and is blown forward by the wind.
- The head of the arrow points towards the **direction from which** the wind blows. (Wind direction is named by the direction from which it blows.)

Anemometer and wind vane

Measuring precipitation

Moisture that results from the condensation of water vapour in the atmosphere returns to Earth as **precipitation**. It occurs in a variety of forms, including rain, hail, sleet and snow.

- Precipitation is measured with a **rain gauge**.
- The unit of measurement is **millimetres** (mm).
- **Isohyets** are lines on a weather chart that join places of equal precipitation.

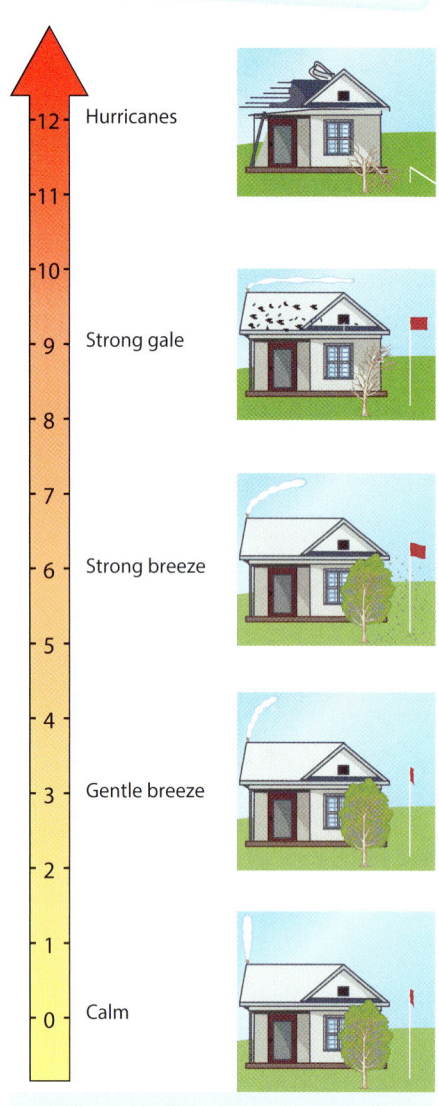

Beaufort scale:
- 12 Hurricanes
- 11
- 10
- 9 Strong gale
- 8
- 7
- 6 Strong breeze
- 5
- 4
- 3 Gentle breeze
- 2
- 1
- 0 Calm

Figure 5.30 The Beaufort scale

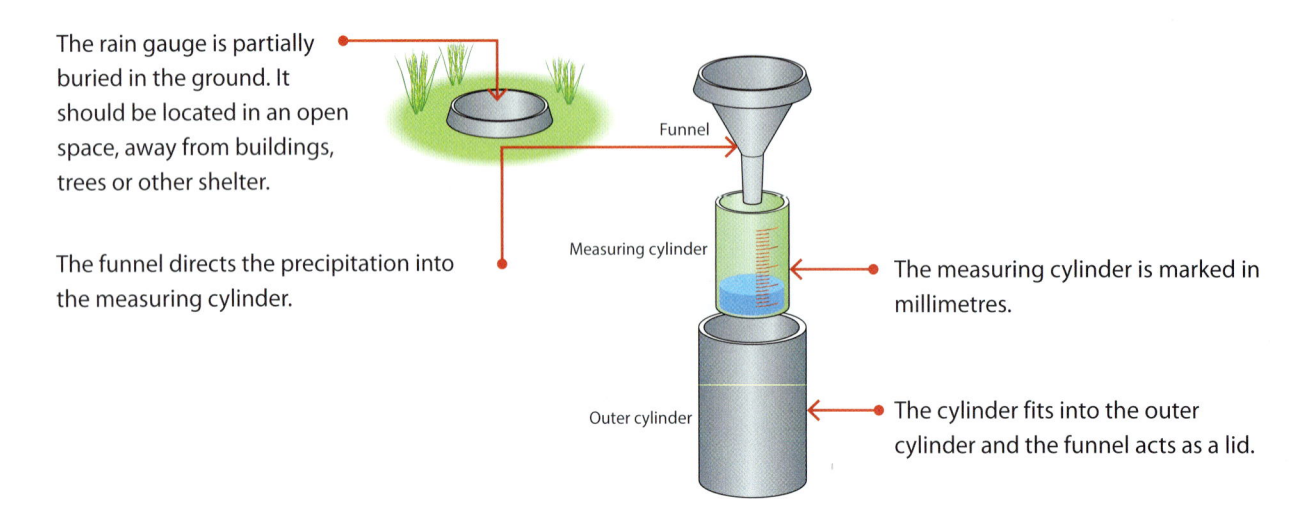

- The rain gauge is partially buried in the ground. It should be located in an open space, away from buildings, trees or other shelter.
- The funnel directs the precipitation into the measuring cylinder.
- Funnel
- Measuring cylinder
- The measuring cylinder is marked in millimetres.
- Outer cylinder
- The cylinder fits into the outer cylinder and the funnel acts as a lid.

Figure 5.31 A rain gauge

Chapter 5 · The Restless Atmosphere

Measuring sunshine

- Sunshine is measured with a **Campbell-Stokes sunshine recorder**.
- The unit of measurement is **hours per day**.
- **Isohels** are lines on a weather chart that join places of equal sunshine.

Activity
Examine Figure 5.32. For how many hours did the sun shine on the strip of paper?

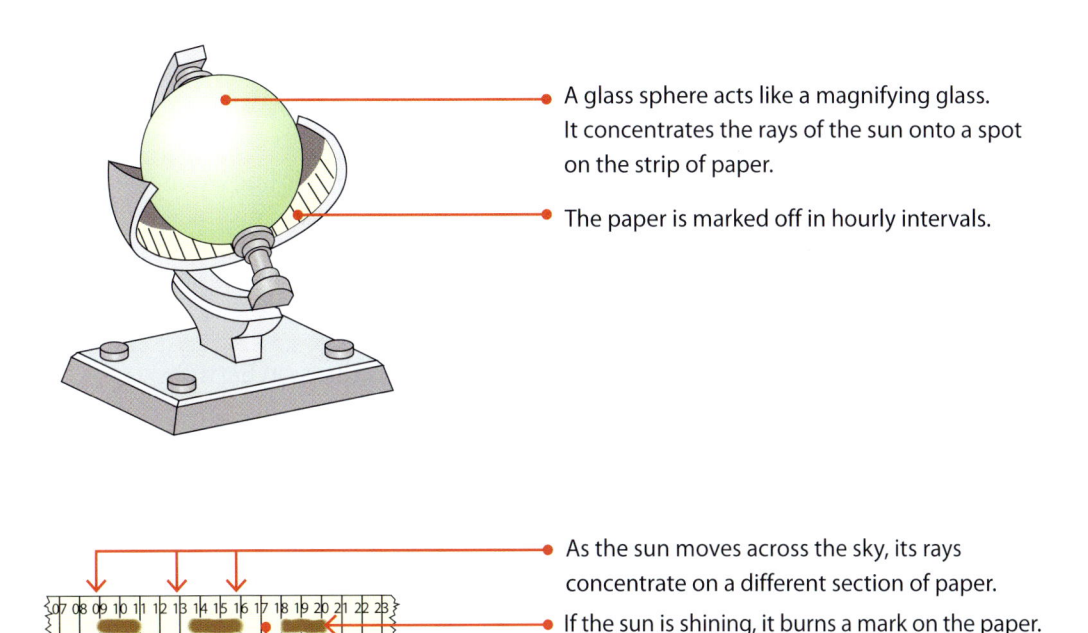

- A glass sphere acts like a magnifying glass. It concentrates the rays of the sun onto a spot on the strip of paper.
- The paper is marked off in hourly intervals.
- As the sun moves across the sky, its rays concentrate on a different section of paper.
- If the sun is shining, it burns a mark on the paper.
- If the sun does not shine, the paper is unmarked.

Figure 5.32 Campbell-Stokes sunshine recorder

Questions

1. (a) What is meant by the term 'weather'?
   (b) What is a weather forecast?
   (c) Briefly describe how a weather forecast is prepared.
   (d) Select any occupation and explain why an accurate weather forecast is important for it.

2. (a) Name any **three** weather instruments and state which element of weather each is used to measure.
   (b) What is a Stevenson screen?

3. Select the weather element of your choice and:
   (a) Name the unit of measurement in which that element is measured.
   (b) Name the weather instrument that is used to measure it.
   (c) With the aid of a labelled diagram, explain how that instrument works.

Section 1 · Physical Geography

5.8 The greenhouse effect and global warming

KEYWORDS

- natural greenhouse effect
- greenhouse gases
- carbon dioxide
- methane
- nitrous oxide
- global warming
- fossil fuels
- CFCs
- climate change

The Earth is heated by solar energy. The atmosphere, the land and the oceans absorb this energy.

Some of the energy is lost back into space, but the **gases** of the atmosphere **trap** much of it. The gases act like the glass on a greenhouse, letting heat in but preventing most of it from getting out. This is nature's way of keeping the Earth warm. It is known as the **natural greenhouse effect**.

Carbon dioxide, methane and nitrous oxide are the most effective gases at trapping heat. As a result, they are known as the **greenhouse gases**.

The greenhouse effect is important because, without it, the temperatures on Earth would be more than 30°C colder than they are today and the Earth would not be warm enough to support life.

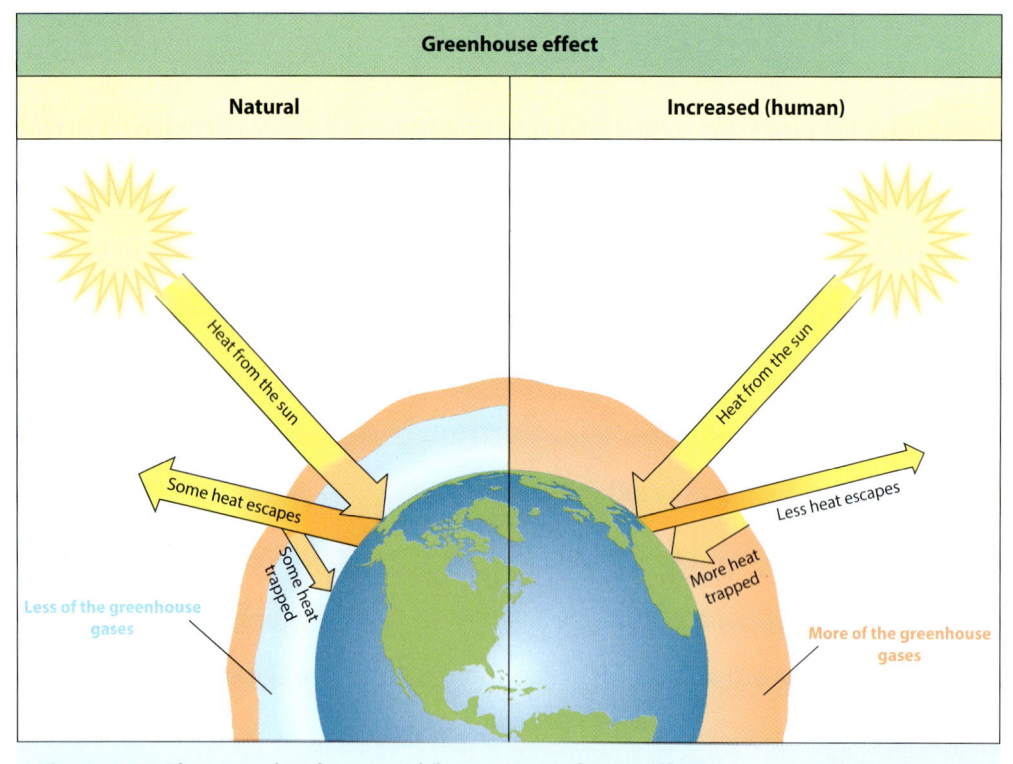

Figure 5.33 The natural and increased (human) greenhouse effect

Global warming

Over the years there was a balance between the incoming energy and the outgoing energy. As a result, the Earth's temperatures remained more or less constant.

The Earth is now warmer than it has been for thousands of years. Scientists believe that global temperatures will continue to rise. The heating up of planet Earth is called **global warming**.

Geo fact

2015 was the Earth's hottest year on record.

Evidence for global warming

Scientists are agreed that there is good evidence for global warming. These are some of the facts they take into account:

- 15 of the 16 warmest years globally have occurred since 2000.
- The area of Greenland's ice sheets that melt each summer has increased by 30 per cent.
- Droughts have become more common in Africa.

Causes of global warming

Global warming is thought to be due to an **increased greenhouse effect**. The volume of greenhouse gases in the atmosphere has increased enormously in recent years. They trap more heat and so the world's temperatures are gradually increasing.

Most of the increase in greenhouse gases is as a direct result of **human activity**.

Carbon dioxide

- **Carbon dioxide** is the most common of the greenhouse gases.
- The main source of carbon dioxide is the burning of **fossil fuels** such as coal, oil and natural gas. These fuels are used in transport, generating electricity, industry and homes.
- **Deforestation**, especially in tropical rainforests, also contributes to the increase in carbon dioxide in the atmosphere.

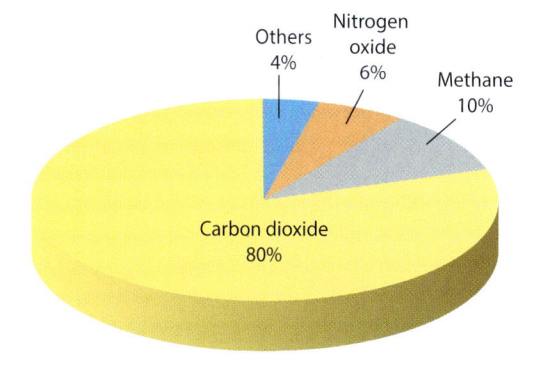

Figure 5.34 The main greenhouse gases

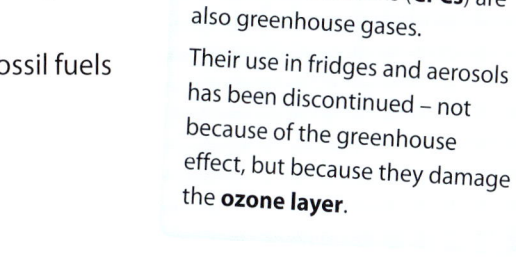

Methane

- **Methane** is a very powerful greenhouse gas, one unit of which can trap 30 times as much heat as a unit of carbon dioxide.
- **Agriculture**, mainly through cattle farming and rice growing, is the main cause of the increase in methane gas.
- Methane is also produced by the extraction and use of fossil fuels and the decay of organic waste in **landfill sites**.

Nitrous oxide

- **Nitrous oxide** is even more potent than methane.
- Its sources include agriculture (especially the use of nitrogen **fertilisers**) and industry (production of **nylon**).

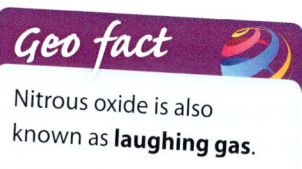

Geo fact

Chlorofluorocarbons (**CFCs**) are also greenhouse gases.

Their use in fridges and aerosols has been discontinued – not because of the greenhouse effect, but because they damage the **ozone layer**.

Geo fact

Nitrous oxide is also known as **laughing gas**.

Section 1 · Physical Geography

Effects of global warming

We have already listed some evidence showing that global warming is taking place. This increase in world temperatures will also have other effects. The two main ones are:

1. A **rise in sea levels:** As global temperatures increase, the ice caps and sea ice will melt. The temperatures of the oceans will rise, causing their waters to expand. As a result, sea levels are rising.

2. **Climate change:** Apart from global warming, other aspects of climate are changing also. These include changes in **wind and precipitation patterns**.
   - Tropical storms and **hurricanes** will become more frequent and stronger.
   - Rainfall patterns will change, with some areas getting wetter and other areas suffering increased **drought**.

Global warming will also affect Ireland

- On average, **sea levels** will rise by about 3.5 cm per decade around Ireland (A).
- **Storm activity** will become more severe and frequent, with extreme wave heights (B).
- Low-lying coastal areas and some river floodplains will be open to more **flooding** ( ).
- Increased levels of **erosion** will affect soft coastline areas ( ).
- Drier summers may lead to **drought and water shortages** in the east of the country (C).
- **Heavier winter rainfall** will affect the coastal areas of the west and north (D).
- **Agriculture**, especially arable and pastoral farming, will have to adapt to the new climatic conditions as crops will begin to replace grass (E).

North Atlantic Drift

Increased rainfall, added to snow and ice melt, would send more fresh water into the North Atlantic. This would change the character of the ocean and cause the **North Atlantic Drift** to begin to **slow down** gradually. Temperatures around Ireland would drop by at least 5°C. At its best, this would balance the effect of global warming. At its worst, it would bring the region close to Ice Age conditions.

Figure 5.35 Some of the likely effects of global warming on Ireland

Solutions to global warming

The Paris climate conference, held in December 2015, resulted in the first ever global agreement in the fight against global warming. The main aim of the agreement is to ensure that average global temperatures increase by not more than 2°C above pre-industrial levels. The agreement also requires that, by 2050, man-made emissions should be reduced to levels that can be absorbed by our forests and oceans.

There are many ways in which the impact of global warming can be reduced:

- **Clean energy:** Reduce dependence on fossil fuels. Use cleaner and renewable energy sources such as solar, wind, wave and hydro power.
- **Reduce deforestation:** This should be accompanied by reforestation (replanting trees), especially in tropical regions.
- **Reduce, reuse and recycle:** This reduces the need for goods, as well as the energy and resources used in their manufacture.
- **Use energy-efficient appliances:** These include lights, fridges and heaters.

Geo fact
Between them, China and the USA are responsible for more than 40 per cent of global emissions of carbon dioxide into the atmosphere.

Activity
Find out what is meant by your 'carbon footprint'.

Geo fact
In 2015, global temperatures reached 1°C above pre-industrial levels for the first time.

Questions

1. Explain each of the following terms:
   - Greenhouse effect
   - Global warming
   - Ozone layer.

2. (a) Name the **three** main greenhouse gases.
   (b) Why is the greenhouse effect important to life on Earth?

3. Explain **three** human activities that have contributed to global warming.

4. Describe any **two** impacts of global warming.

5. Describe **two** ways by which global warming could be reduced.

Section 1 · Physical Geography

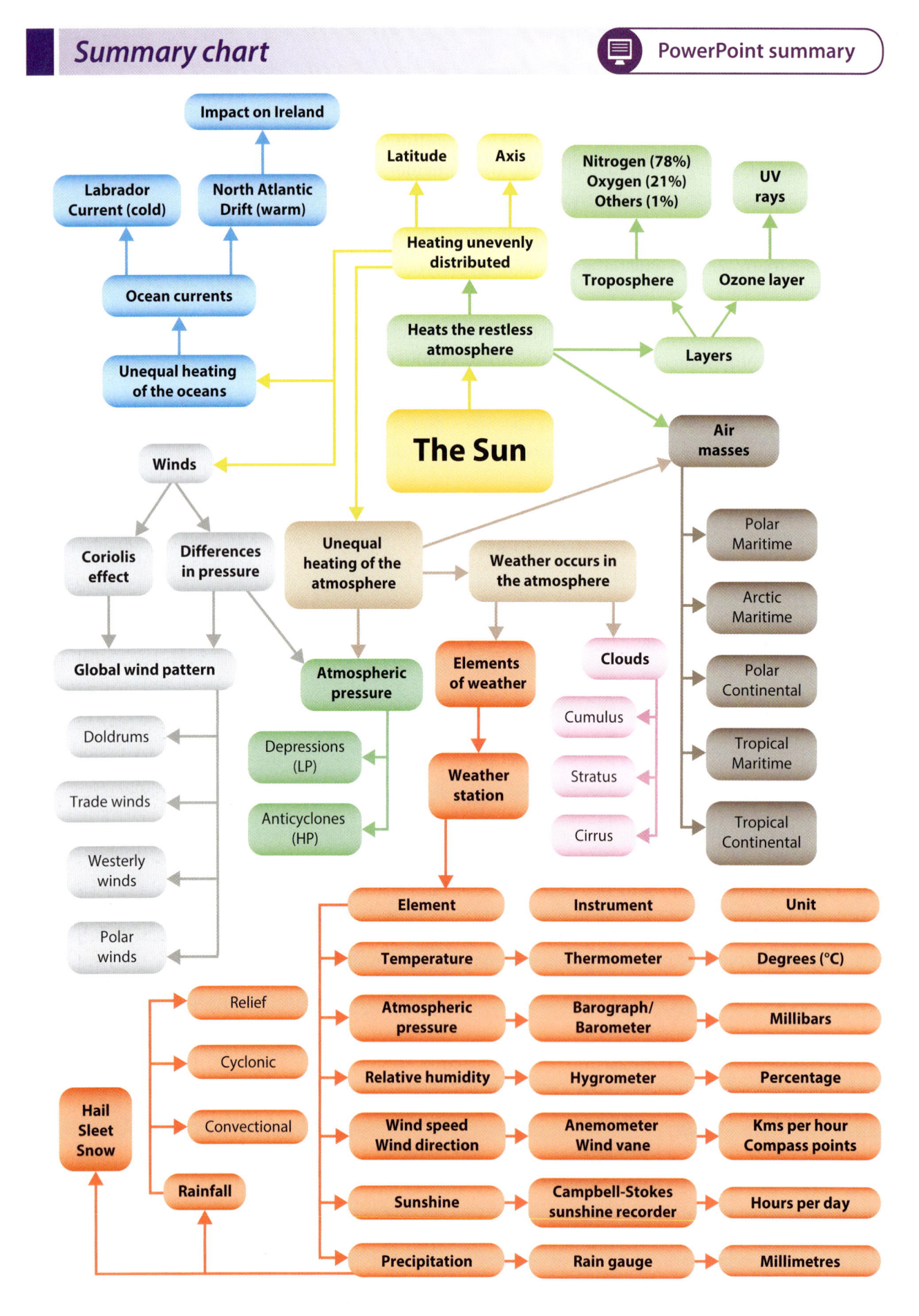

Summary chart

PowerPoint summary

The Sun

- Impact on Ireland
- Labrador Current (cold) → Ocean currents
- North Atlantic Drift (warm) → Ocean currents
- Ocean currents ← Unequal heating of the oceans
- Latitude, Axis → Heating unevenly distributed
- Heats the restless atmosphere
- Nitrogen (78%), Oxygen (21%), Others (1%) → Troposphere
- UV rays → Ozone layer
- Troposphere, Ozone layer → Layers

Winds
- Coriolis effect
- Differences in pressure
- Global wind pattern
  - Doldrums
  - Trade winds
  - Westerly winds
  - Polar winds

Unequal heating of the atmosphere → Atmospheric pressure
- Depressions (LP)
- Anticyclones (HP)

Weather occurs in the atmosphere
- Elements of weather → Weather station
- Clouds
  - Cumulus
  - Stratus
  - Cirrus

Air masses
- Polar Maritime
- Arctic Maritime
- Polar Continental
- Tropical Maritime
- Tropical Continental

Element	Instrument	Unit
Temperature	Thermometer	Degrees (°C)
Atmospheric pressure	Barograph/Barometer	Millibars
Relative humidity	Hygrometer	Percentage
Wind speed / Wind direction	Anemometer / Wind vane	Kms per hour / Compass points
Sunshine	Campbell-Stokes sunshine recorder	Hours per day
Precipitation	Rain gauge	Millimetres

Rainfall
- Relief
- Cyclonic
- Convectional

Hail / Sleet / Snow

108

Chapter 5 · The Restless Atmosphere

Exam questions

1. Study the diagram, which shows how the sun heats the Earth. The line **X** shows the Equator.

   Explain why the temperature at **A** is lower than the temperature at **B**.

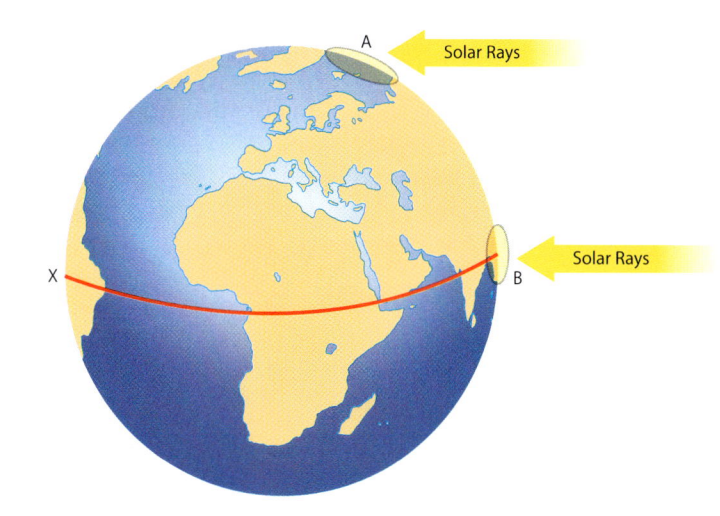

   OL 2015

2. Explain why places near the Equator are **hotter** than places near the Poles.

   (If it helps, you can draw a diagram as part of your answer.)

   OL 2009

3. (i) What name is given to the numbered lines shown on the map?
   (ii) What name is given to the feature labelled **A** on the map?
   (iii) What name is given to the feature labelled **B** on the map?
   (iv) What is the atmospheric pressure at **C** on the map?
   (v) Describe the weather conditions that you would expect to find at **D** on the map?

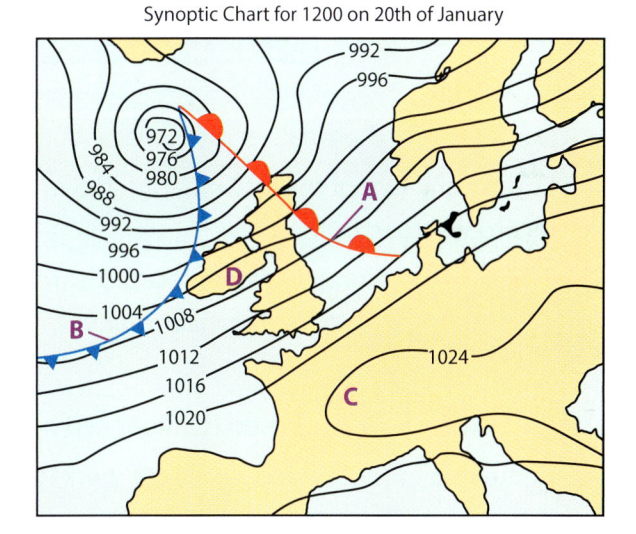

   HL 2008

4. (i) Explain the water cycle with reference to each of the stages labelled **A**, **B**, **C** and **D** in the diagram on the right.
   (ii) Name **two** cloud types.

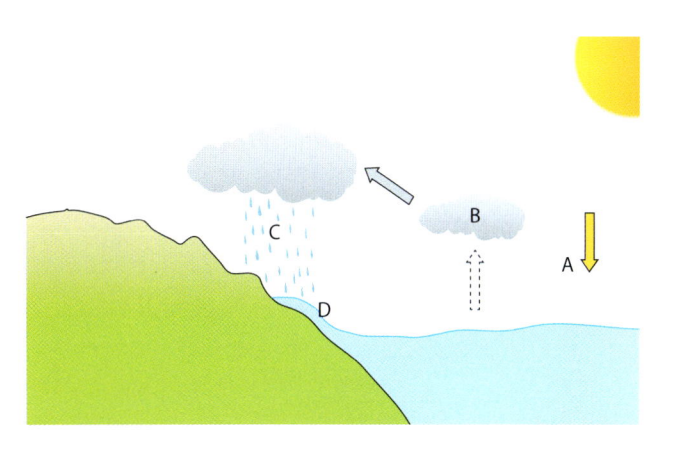

   HL 2013

109

Section 1 · Physical Geography

Exam questions

5 (i) Name the type of rainfall shown in the diagram.

(ii) Describe how this type of rainfall occurs.

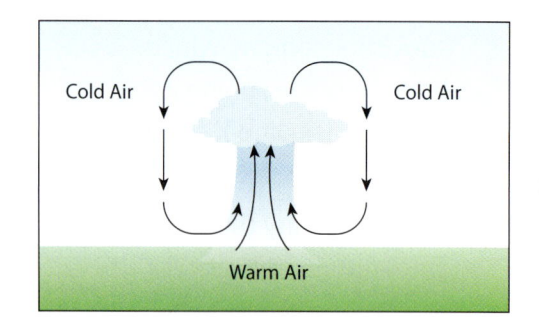

HL 2012

6 Describe and explain, with the aid of a labelled diagram, how relief rainfall occurs.

HL 2015

7

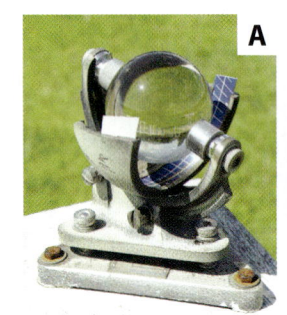

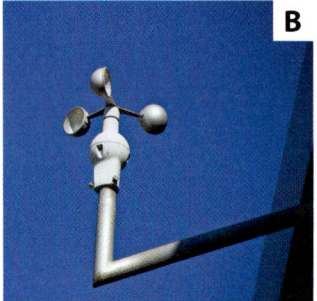

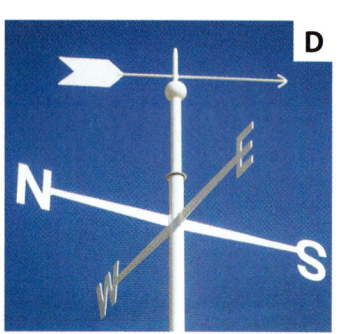

(i) Name each of the weather instruments **A**, **B**, **C** and **D** shown above.

(ii) Choose any **two** of the instruments shown above **and** describe how they are used to record weather.

(iii) Explain why accurate weather forecasts are important for any **two** of the following: *Fishermen, Farmers, Tourists, Airline pilots.*

HL 2014 / OL 2014

8 The work that many people do is influenced by weather.

(i) Name **two** groups of people whose work is influenced by the weather.

(ii) For **each** group, explain how the weather influences them.

OL 2010

9 (i) Name **two** major gases found in the atmosphere.

(ii) Explain, with the aid of a diagram, how the greenhouse effect occurs.

(iii) Name **two** ways in which the greenhouse effect can be reduced.

HL 2011

Chapter 6
Climates and Natural Regions

Learning outcomes

By the end of this chapter, you should be able to understand:

- The different factors that influence climate
- That natural regions have unique characteristics
- That there are three climate zones: hot, temperate and cold
- That human activities are influenced by climate.

6.1 Introducing climate

KEYWORDS

- climate
- latitude
- temperate
- continental
- local climate
- aspect
- altitude

Climate is the average condition of the weather over a long period of time – usually 35 years – across a large area of the world's surface.

Factors that influence world climates

There are several different climates across the world, each with its own characteristics of **temperature** and **precipitation**. The way that different climates develop is influenced by the following factors:

- Latitude
- Distance from the sea
- Prevailing winds and air masses.

111

Section 1 · Physical Geography

Latitude

The **latitude** of a place is its **distance north or south of the equator**. Latitude is measured in **degrees**.

- Areas near the equator receive more sunlight than anywhere else on Earth. The sun is high in the sky and its rays are concentrated on a smaller area of the Earth's surface, giving greater heat.
- Away from the equator, the sun's rays are more slanted. Its heat is spread over a wider area, so it is cooler.

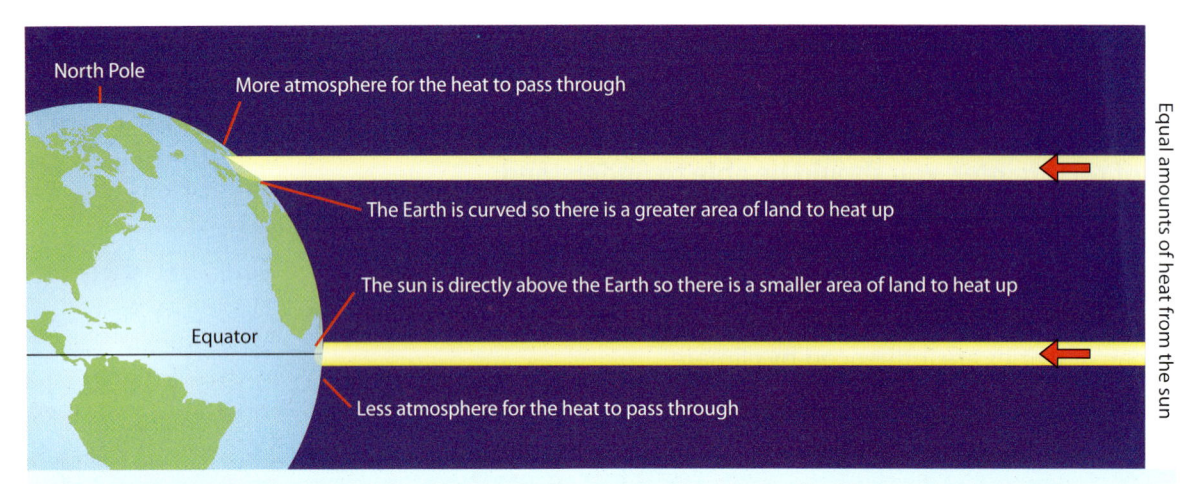

North Pole — More atmosphere for the heat to pass through

The Earth is curved so there is a greater area of land to heat up

The sun is directly above the Earth so there is a smaller area of land to heat up

Equator — Less atmosphere for the heat to pass through

Equal amounts of heat from the sun

Figure 6.1 How latitude influences temperature

Distance from the sea

The sea takes longer to warm than land does during summer. It also takes much longer to cool during winter.

- As a result, **coastal areas** have **cooler summers** and **milder winters** than inland areas. This means that coastal areas also have a **smaller temperature range** than inland areas. This type of climate is described as **temperate**.
- Areas that are **further inland** have **hotter summers** and **colder winters** than coastal areas. This means that they have a **larger temperature range** than coastal areas. This type of climate is described as **continental**.

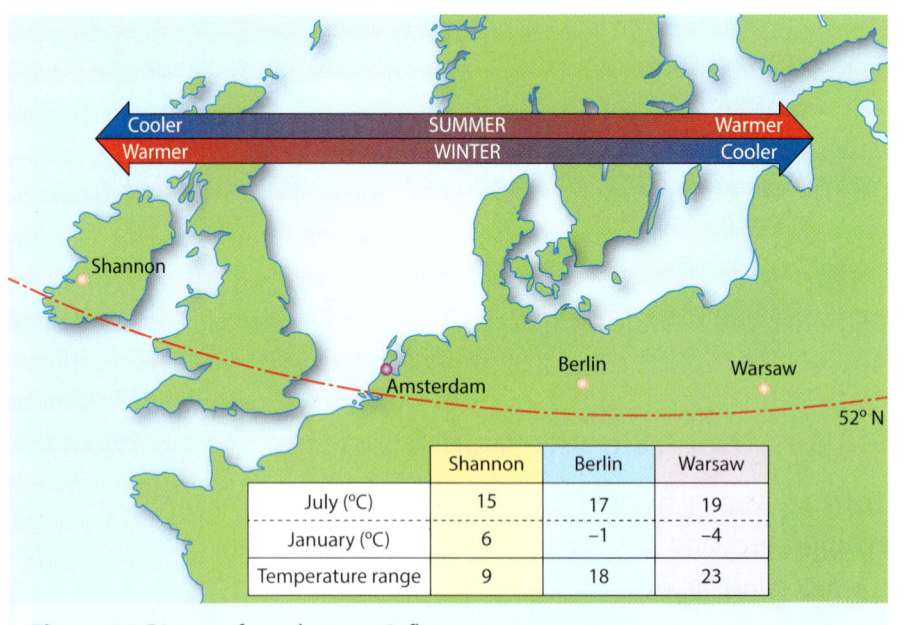

Cooler SUMMER Warmer
Warmer WINTER Cooler

	Shannon	Berlin	Warsaw
July (°C)	15	17	19
January (°C)	6	−1	−4
Temperature range	9	18	23

Figure 6.2 Distance from the coast influences temperature

Activity

Examine Figure 6.2.

1. What is the annual temperature range at:
   (a) Shannon?
   (b) Berlin?
2. Is winter in Amsterdam warmer or cooler than in Shannon? Give a reason for your answer.

Prevailing winds and air masses

Winds influence the temperature and precipitation that an area receives. This influence depends on two factors:

- The **direction from which the winds blow**
- Whether they pass over **land or sea**.

Northerly winds
- Northerly winds are cold because they come from cold, high latitudes.
- While they are normally dry, they may bring snow in winter.

South-westerly winds
- South-westerly winds are cool in summer because the sea takes longer to heat than the land.
- They are mild in winter because the sea cools more slowly than the land.
- They are rain-bearing because they absorb moisture as they pass over the ocean.

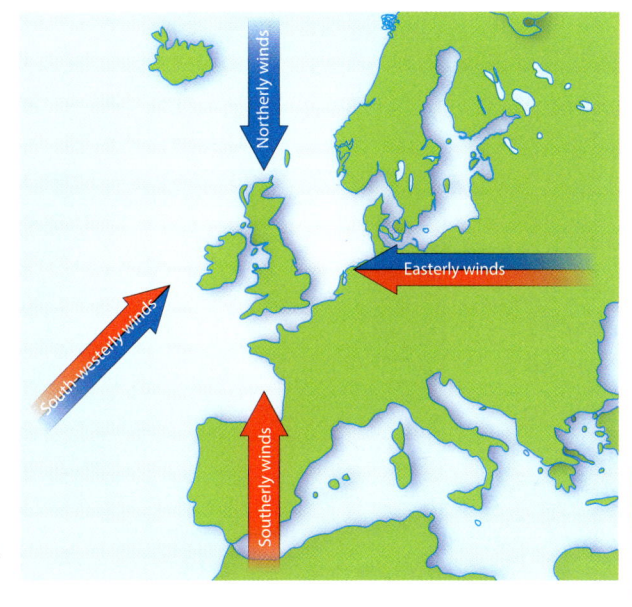

Southerly winds
- Southerly winds are warm because they come from the lower latitudes.
- They may bring some rainfall because they cool as they move towards the higher latitudes.

Easterly winds
- Easterly winds are warm in summer because the land has absorbed heat quickly.
- They are cold in winter because the land loses heat quickly.
- They are usually dry because they absorb little moisture as they pass over the land.

Activity

Examine Figure 6.3. In pairs, decide which of these winds is likely to be (a) coldest and (b) warmest.

Give one reason for each answer.

Figure 6.3 How different winds affect Ireland's climate

Factors that influence local climates

Sometimes a small area can experience a climate that is different from that of the whole region. This is known as a **local climate**. Local climates are influenced by:

- Aspect
- Altitude.

Aspect

Aspect refers to the **direction a slope faces** in relation to the sun's rays. In the **northern hemisphere:**

- **South-facing slopes are warmer** because the sun's rays strike the ground at a more direct angle. These slopes are also influenced by **warm, southerly winds**.
- **North-facing slopes are colder** because they do not get the direct rays of the sun and may be in the shade. These slopes may also be in the path of **cold, northerly winds**.

Section 1 · Physical Geography

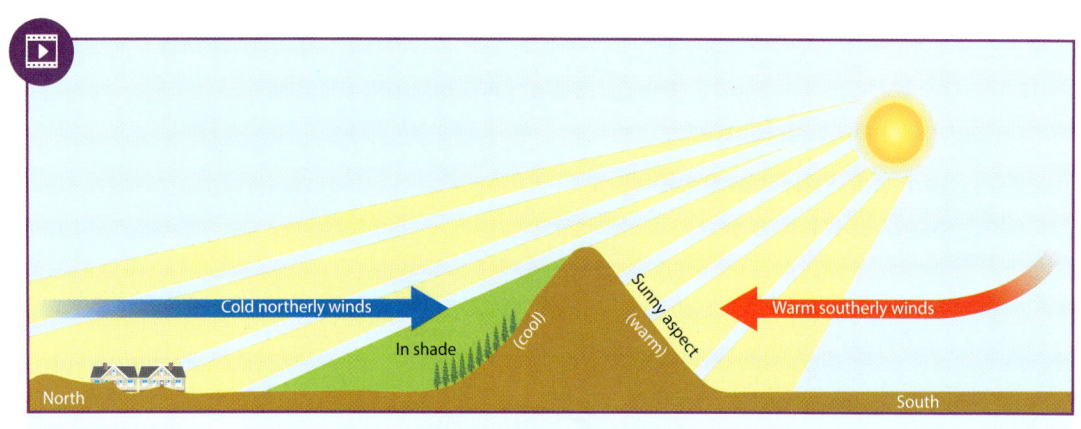

Figure 6.4 How aspect can affect a local climate

Altitude

Altitude refers to **height above sea level**. The higher the place is above sea level the colder it is. This is because, as altitude increases, air becomes thinner and is less able to absorb and hold heat. Temperatures drop by about 1°C for every 100-metre increase in altitude.

Upland areas:

- Are **more exposed to wind** than sheltered lowland areas, which reduces temperatures even further
- Receive **more precipitation** because, as the air is cooled, it can hold less water vapour.

Even though it lies close to the equator, the summit of Mount Kilimanjaro is snow-capped. It is the tallest freestanding mountain in the world and rises 4,700 m above the surrounding plains

Activity

Calculate the difference in temperature between the summit of Mount Kilimanjaro and the surrounding plain.

What is the temperature at sea level?

Questions

1. (a) What is climate?
   (b) Explain the difference between a world climate and a local climate.
2. (a) List **three** factors that influence world climates.
   (b) Explain how each of them affects climate.
3. Explain any **two** ways in which winds influence Ireland's climate.
4. (a) List the **two** factors that influence local climates.
   (b) Explain how each of them affects local climate.

Chapter 6 · Climates and Natural Regions

6.2 Natural regions and world climates

KEYWORDS

- natural region
- natural vegetation
- hot climates
- temperate climates
- cold climates

A **natural region** is a region of the world that has its own unique characteristics that make it different from other regions. These characteristics include:

- Climate
- Natural vegetation
- Wildlife
- Human activities.

Climate is the most important of these characteristics. The climate of a region influences what vegetation grows there, what animals inhabit it and the activities of the people who live there.

Definition

Natural vegetation: The cover of plants and trees that grow in an area before it is changed by human activity.

World climates

The Earth can be divided into different climatic zones. Each of these has its own **temperature** and **rainfall pattern**.
There are three broad climate zones:

- Hot climates
- Temperate climates
- Cold climates.

Geo fact

Most of the world's people inhabit regions with a temperate climate because they are the most comfortable regions to live in.

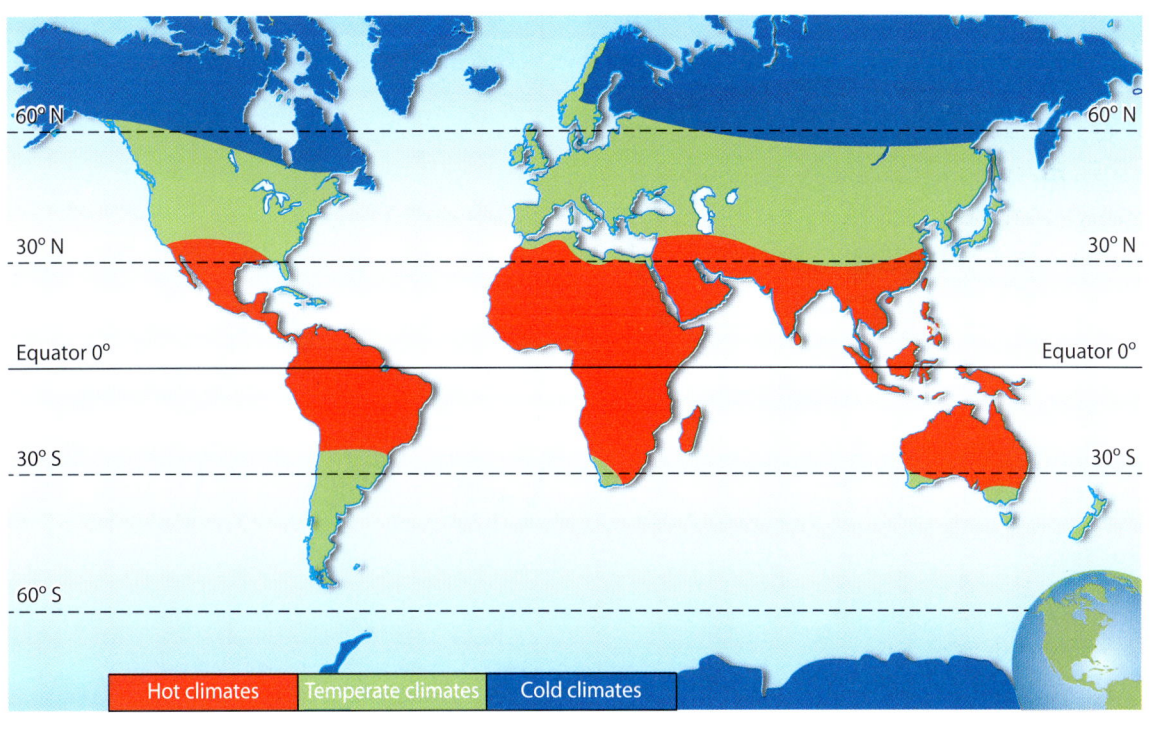

Hot climates are found close to the equator. They include:
- Equatorial climate
- Hot desert climate
- Savanna climate.

Temperate climates are found in the mid-latitudes. They include:
- Cool temperate oceanic climate
- Warm temperate oceanic climate (also called Mediterranean climate).

Cold climates are found close to the poles. They include:
- Tundra climate
- Boreal climate.

Figure 6.5 There are three broad climate zones: hot, temperate and cold

115

Section 1 · Physical Geography

> **Questions**
>
> **1** (a) What is a natural region?
> (b) List **four** characteristics of a natural region.
>
> **2** (a) Name the **three** broad climate zones.
> (b) With the aid of an atlas, identify the climate zone in which the following countries are located: Ireland, Brazil, Canada, Spain, Iceland, Sudan.

6.3 Hot climates of the world

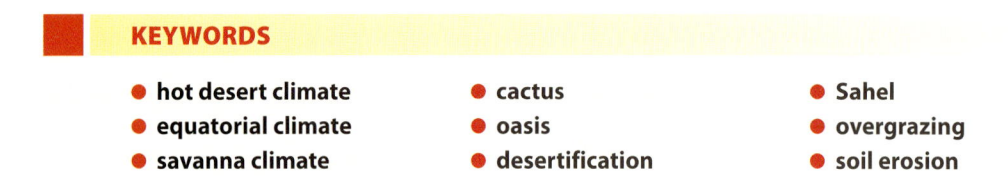

KEYWORDS

- hot desert climate
- equatorial climate
- savanna climate
- cactus
- oasis
- desertification
- Sahel
- overgrazing
- soil erosion

Most hot climates are found between latitudes 30° N and 30° S. They include **hot desert** climate, **equatorial** climate and **savanna** climate.

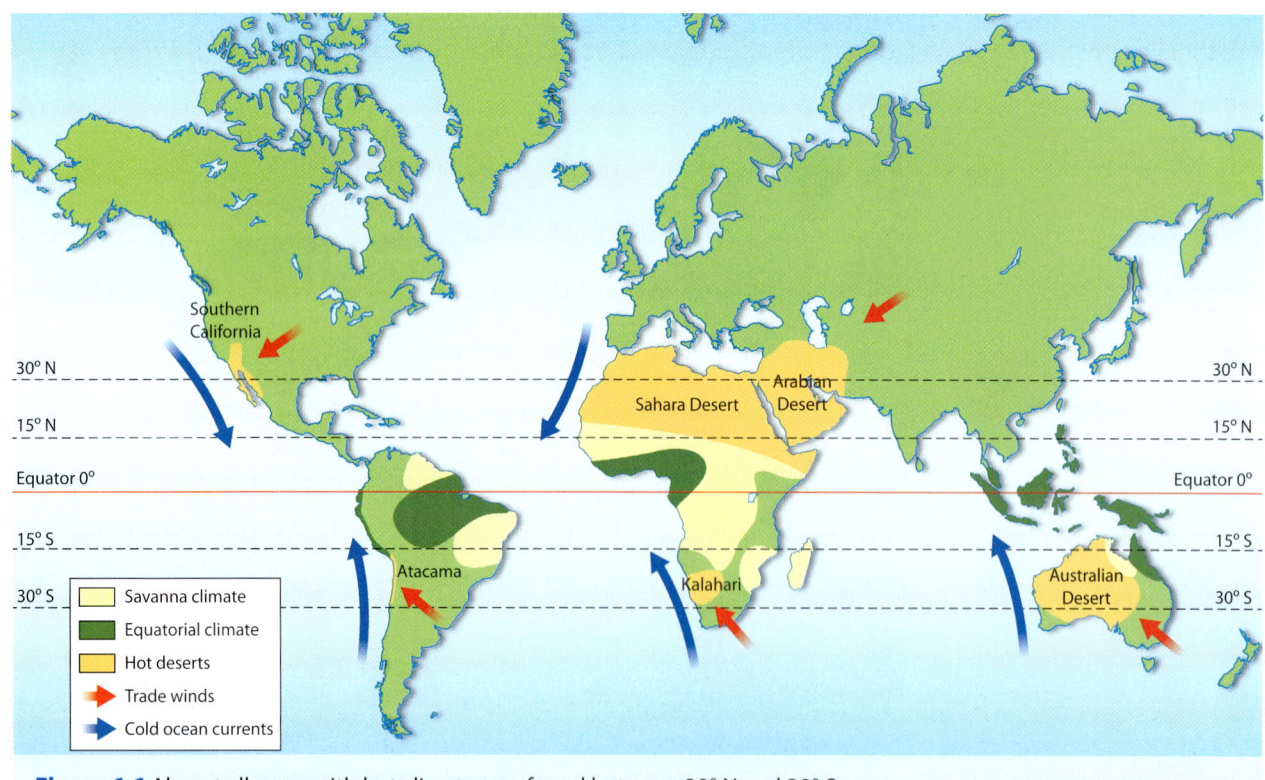

Figure 6.6 Almost all areas with hot climates are found between 30° N and 30° S

Chapter 6 · Climates and Natural Regions

Table 6.1 Characteristics of equatorial and savanna climates

	Equatorial climate	**Savanna climate**
Temperature	• Hot all year round (averaging 27°C) • One-season climate	• Hot all year round (averaging around 30°C) • Two-season climate
Rainfall	• Rainfall every afternoon • Annual total: over 2,000 mm • High level of humidity	• Annual total: over 800 mm • Summers wet (monsoon rains) • Winters dry
Natural vegetation	• Rain forest (jungle) • Hardwoods (mahogany, teak, cherry)	• Scattered trees • Grassland (green and brown, depending on the season)
Wildlife	• Exotic birds (parrots etc.) • Snakes, monkeys, butterflies	• Herds of cattle • Lions, cheetahs, giraffes

Focus on hot desert climate

Location

The **hot deserts** of the world are found **between 15° and 30° north and south** of the equator and lie along the **western sides of the land masses**.

Geo fact

One in every four ingredients in our medicines comes from rainforest plants.

Table 6.2 Characteristics of a hot desert climate

Temperature	
Daytime temperatures are high, varying between 30°C and 50°C.	• Hot deserts are located in the tropics, where the sun is always high in the sky. • Cloudless skies allow for long hours of sunshine.
Night-time temperatures are as low as 5°C.	• The absence of cloud cover and vegetation means that there is a rapid loss of heat at night. • Night is said to be the 'winter of the desert'.
There is a large daily temperature range.	
Rainfall	
Rainfall is rare. The annual total can be less than 100 mm. There are long periods of drought, broken by sudden downpours.	• The hot deserts are in the path of the trade winds. These blow overland towards the equator. Thus, they become warmer and hold their moisture. As a result, they are dry winds. • Some deserts are in the path of winds that blow over cold currents. As they do so, they are cooled and lose their moisture over the ocean.

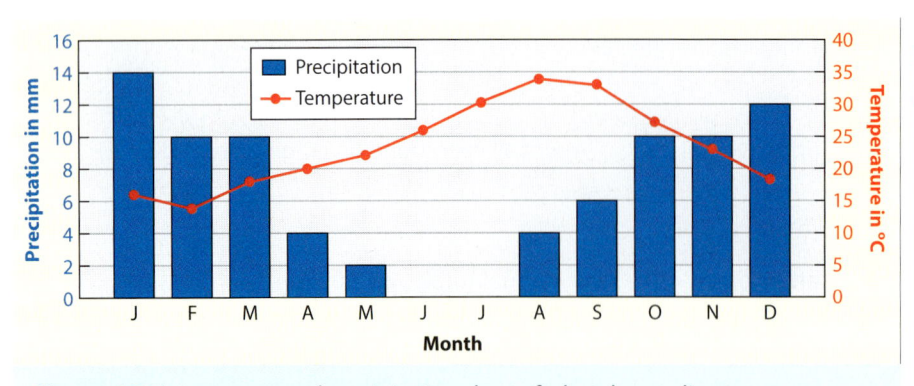

Section 1 · Physical Geography

Figure 6.7 Temperature and precipitation chart of a hot desert climate

Activity

Examine Figure 6.7 and answer the following questions.
1. Which is the wettest month?
2. How many months are without rainfall?
3. Which is the hottest month?
4. What is the highest temperature reached?

Vegetation in hot deserts

There is very little vegetation (**flora**) in deserts due to the shortage of moisture. Plants are almost all ground-hugging shrubs and short woody trees. The plants are able to survive because they have adapted to desert conditions.

- Some plants, such as the cactus, have a **thick waxy skin** and **needles**. These reduce the loss of moisture and protect against animals.
- Some plants, such as the date palm, have **taproots** that grow deep into the ground to find moisture.
- Other plants, such as the Joshua tree, have **juicy flesh** that stores water.

Different types of cactus, with a date palm tree in the background

Animals in hot deserts

Animals (**fauna**) that live in deserts have adapted to the harsh climatic conditions of intense heat and lack of water.

- Animals like the desert fox stay in cool **underground burrows** by day and come out in the cool of the night.
- Animals have changed their body form. The jack-rabbit and desert fox have **long ears** that help them **lose body heat**.
- Rattlesnakes get moisture from the small creatures that they eat.

Definition

Oasis: A fertile area in a desert where water is found close to the surface.

The desert fox stays underground by day and has developed large ears

- Camels store fat in their humps for times when water and food are scarce.
- They have long eyelashes and nostrils that open and close, giving protection in sandstorms.
- They have wide hooves that enable them to walk on dry sand.
- They have thick lips, enabling them to eat prickly plants.

Camel caravan at an **oasis** in the Sahara

Desertification

Desertification means **turning land into desert**. It occurs when desert conditions spread into areas that were once fertile.

The areas most affected by desertification are those at the **edge of existing deserts**. This is especially true in the case of the **Sahel**, a region at the southern edge of the Sahara Desert.

Activity

With the aid of your atlas, **identify** the countries marked A to E that make up part of the Sahel.

Causes of desertification

Desertification is caused by a combination of **climate change** and **human factors**. This has affected many groups of people, including the **Tuareg** who live in a number of countries in the Sahel region.

Figure 6.8 The Sahel lies to the south of the Sahara Desert

Climate change

The climate of the Sahel has changed over the last 30 years.

- Rainfall in the region is unreliable. Rains may come late or not come at all.
- **Higher temperatures**, as a result of global warming, lead to increased evaporation and less condensation.
- As a result, several **droughts** have occurred.
- Rivers and water holes have dried up.

Human factors

The countries of the Sahel have a high birth rate, leading to **rapid population growth** and an **increased demand for food**.

In the Sahel region, animal ownership was seen as a sign of wealth. Large herds of poor quality cattle and goats destroyed the vegetation by overgrazing

- People keep large herds of cattle and goats, leading to **overgrazing** of the land.
- Farmers change their way of farming. They change from grazing to growing food crops. Without fertilisers, the soil soon loses its **nutrients** and the crops fail.
- Trees and shrubs are cut down for cooking and heating. As a result, **soil erosion** is speeded up.

Section 1 · Physical Geography

Results of desertification

Desertification has had very serious results for the people of the Sahel.

- Vast areas of land are now unable to support agriculture.
- Towns and villages have been swallowed up by the advancing sands.
- Hundreds of thousands of people have died as a result of **famine**.
- Millions of people have been forced to migrate in search of food or aid. Many of these people still live in **refugee camps**.
- Many people have moved into urban areas, leading to the **growth of slums**.
- Millions of animals have died.

Solutions to desertification

Most solutions to desertification are carried out at local level rather than in the region as a whole. These include:

- Slowing down soil erosion by planting trees and building walls as **shelter belts**.
- Binding the soil particles by **planting grasses** that are resistant to drought.
- Digging **deeper wells** to find water for irrigation.
- Introducing **new breeds of animals** to produce more milk, but with smaller herds.
- **Growing crops** as well as keeping animals. Animal manure is used to fertilise the soil.

Land has been abandoned as the desert sands have advanced

Locals build stone walls to slow down soil erosion by winds. Note the shallow trench that has been dug both to trap rainfall and to prevent the loose soil from being washed away

Questions

1. (a) Describe the general location of hot deserts (refer to latitudes).
   (b) Name **two** hot deserts.
   (c) Explain the climate conditions found in hot deserts. Refer to:
      - Daytime temperature
      - Night-time temperatures
      - Precipitation.

2. (a) Name **one** desert animal and **one** desert plant.
   (b) Describe **two** ways in which each of them has adapted to desert conditions.

3. (a) What is desertification?
   (b) Name **one** region that is affected by desertification.
   (c) Describe any **two** causes of desertification in that region.

6.4 Temperate climates of the world

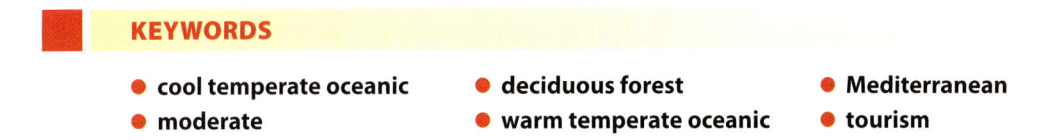

> **KEYWORDS**
> - cool temperate oceanic
> - moderate
> - deciduous forest
> - warm temperate oceanic
> - Mediterranean
> - tourism

Most temperate climates are found in the **mid-latitudes**. They include the warm temperate oceanic climate and the cool temperate oceanic climate.

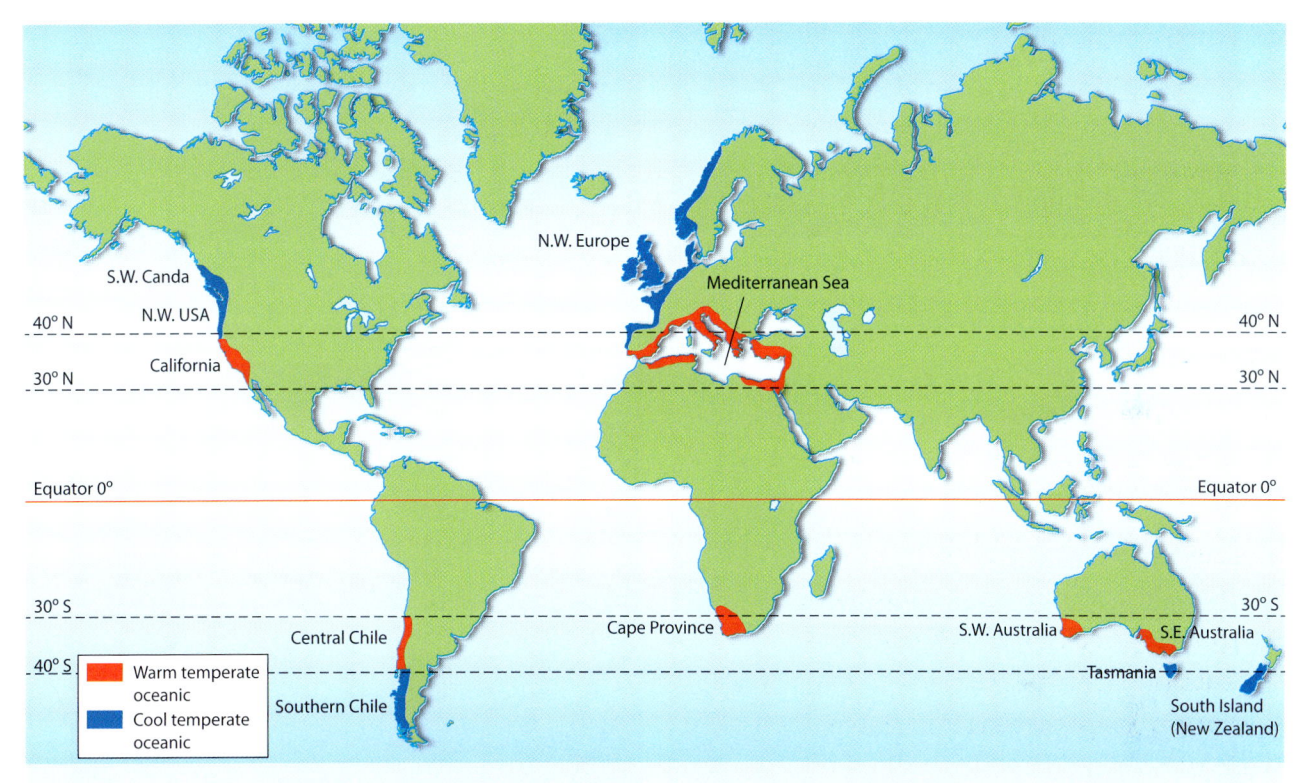

Figure 6.9 Regions with temperate climates. **Ireland** has a cool temperate oceanic climate

Table 6.3 Characteristics of a cool temperate oceanic climate

Temperature	• Summers are warm, with temperatures averaging 15°C to 17°C. • Winters are mild, with temperatures averaging 4°C to 6°C. • Annual temperature range is about 11°C. • Overall it is a moderate climate, neither too hot nor too cold.
Rainfall	• Rain falls throughout the year, but there is a winter maximum. • Annual total varies between 800 mm and 2,000 mm, reducing from west to east. • The weather conditions are cloudy and changeable.
Natural vegetation	• Deciduous forest is the main form of natural vegetation. • Tree species include oak, ash, elm and willow. • Most of it has been removed for farming, transport and settlement.

Section 1 · Physical Geography

Case study

Ireland and its cool temperate oceanic climate

Winters in Ireland are mild. Rainfall has a winter maximum and is highest in upland areas

Summers in Ireland are warm. The sunniest part of the country is the south-east. Some rain also falls

Ireland's natural vegetation is deciduous forest. Species include oak, ash and elm

Ireland's native wildlife includes the hare, red squirrel and red deer, seen here in Killarney National Park

Most of the natural vegetation has been removed to make way for agriculture and settlement

All of these factors have enabled settlements to develop in Ireland over a long period of time

Chapter 6 · Climates and Natural Regions

Focus on warm temperate oceanic climate

Regions that have a **warm temperate oceanic climate** are found along the **western edges** of the continents and lie **between 30° and 40°** north and south of the equator.

The warm temperate oceanic climate is also known as the **Mediterranean climate** because the area surrounding the Mediterranean Sea is the largest region that experiences this climate.

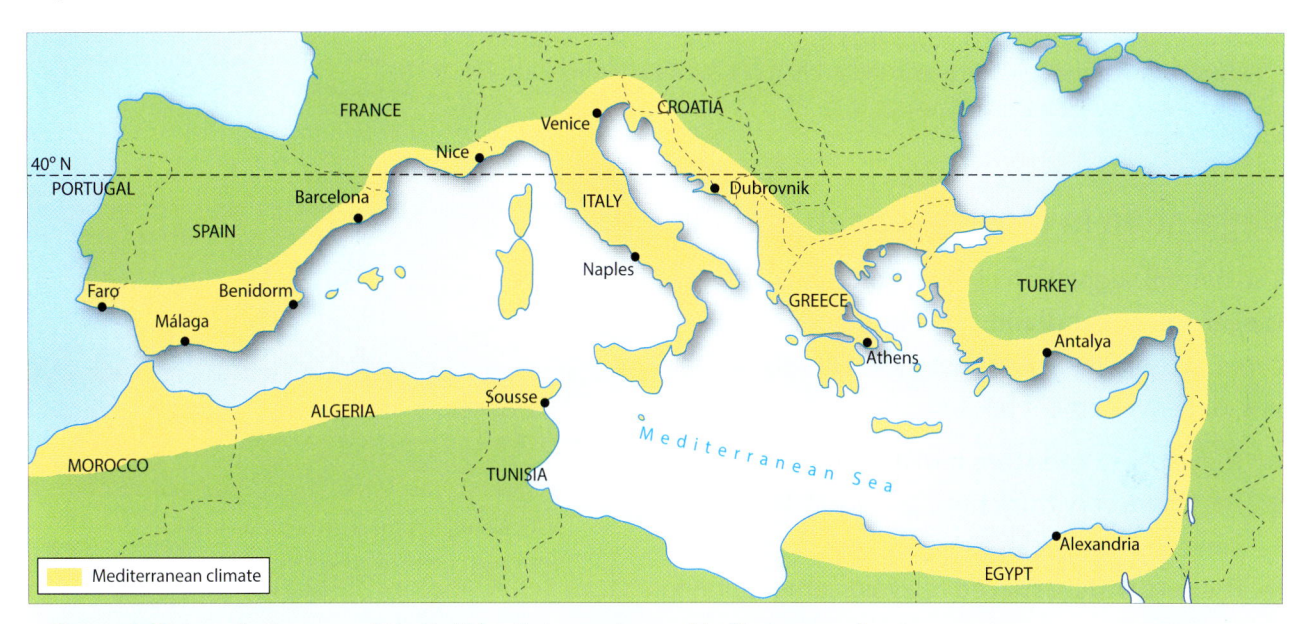

Figure 6.10 Areas in Europe and North Africa that experience a Mediterranean climate

Table 6.4 Characteristics of a warm temperate oceanic climate

Summer Summers are hot with temperatures averaging 30°C.	• These regions are reasonably close to the equator and the sun is still high in the sky, especially in summer. • Cloudless skies allow for long hours of sunshine.
Summers are generally dry, with some drought.	• High-pressure belts dominate these regions. • They are under the influence of the trade winds that blow over dry land masses.
Winter Winters are mild, with temperatures averaging between 10°C and 15°C.	• The sun is still high enough in the sky to give warm conditions. • The prevailing wind in winter is the south-westerly. As it blows from lower latitudes, it is a warm wind.
Winters are moist, with rainfall between 400 mm and 700 mm.	• The prevailing winds blow in over the Atlantic Ocean, bringing moist air. • Depressions form over the Mediterranean Sea. • Rain falls in heavy showers.

Section 1 · Physical Geography

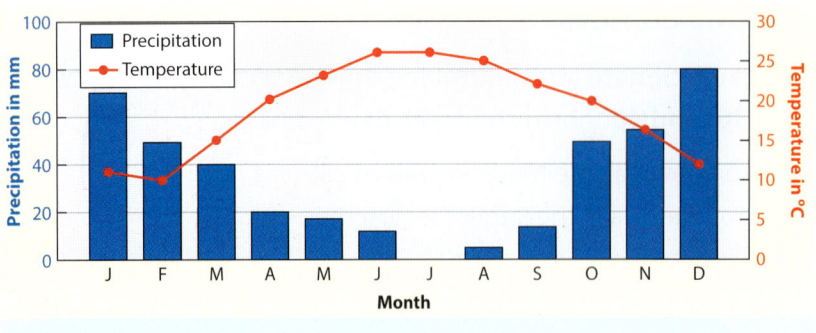

Figure 6.11 Temperature and precipitation chart of a Mediterranean (warm temperate oceanic) climate

Activity

Examine Figure 6.11.

1. What is the highest temperature?
2. What is the lowest temperature?
3. What is the temperature range?
4. In how many months does precipitation exceed 50 mm?
5. Which month experiences total drought?

Vegetation in Mediterranean regions

The natural vegetation of the Mediterranean region is **evergreen woodland**. Trees include the cork oak, cypress, cedar and olive. These are adapted to their hot, dry environment because:

- They absorb and **store moisture** during winter.
- They have very **thick bark** and **waxy leaves** to prevent moisture loss.
- They are **widely spaced** to avoid competition for moisture.

Native Mediterranean vegetation includes evergreen trees, heathers and herbs

As the woods were cleared, a new type of natural vegetation took over. It consisted of low-lying **heathers** and **herbs**. These include thyme, lavender and rosemary.

The changing Mediterranean landscape

Human activity has changed the Mediterranean landscape over thousands of years and most of the woodland has been cleared for **agriculture**.

- **Sheep and goats** are the animals most commonly reared.
- **Overgrazing** has damaged the scant vegetation and the soil has been exposed to erosion by sudden downpours of rain.
- Fruit and vegetable farming takes place throughout the year. **Irrigation schemes** have been introduced to overcome the problems of summer drought.
- The main crops grown are **citrus fruits** (oranges, lemons and grapefruit), **tomatoes** and **vines**.
- Other crops that are produced include **wheat**, **maize** and **sunflowers**.

Growing vegetables with the aid of irrigation in southern Spain

Chapter 6 · Climates and Natural Regions

Tourism in the Mediterranean

The hot, dry, sunny weather of the Mediterranean climate is very attractive to holidaymakers. As a result, **tourism** is the most important industry in many coastal areas, including the Costa del Sol, the Riviera and Majorca. While it has brought wealth and jobs to these regions, it has also led to worries because of pollution, water shortages and badly planned developments.

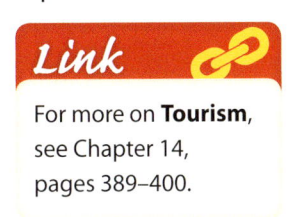

Link
For more on **Tourism**, see Chapter 14, pages 389–400.

Geo fact
Spain attracted almost 65 million tourists in 2015. The majority came from Britain, France and Germany.

Hotels and apartments fronting the beach in Benidorm, a resort on Spain's Mediterranean coast

Questions

1. Briefly describe the differences between cool temperate oceanic climates and warm temperate oceanic climates. In your answer, refer to:
   - Temperature
   - Rainfall
   - Natural vegetation.

2. (a) Give another name for warm temperate oceanic climates.
   (b) Name **two** regions that experience this climate.
   (c) In your copybook, copy and complete these sentences relating to warm temperate oceanic climates:
   Summers are warm because . . .
   Summers are dry because . . .
   Winters are mild because . . .
   Winters are moist because . . .

3. (a) Describe the natural vegetation of a region that has a warm temperate oceanic climate.
   (b) Explain **two** ways in which human activity has changed the rural landscape.
   (c) Describe **two** aspects of Mediterranean climate that are attractive to tourists.

Section 1 · Physical Geography

6.5 Cold climates of the world

KEYWORDS

• tundra   • boreal   • taiga   • permafrost   • hibernation

Activity
The word tundra means 'without trees'. Why don't trees grow there?

The cold climates of the world are found mainly in the northern hemisphere because, apart from Antarctica, there is no matching land mass in the southern hemisphere.

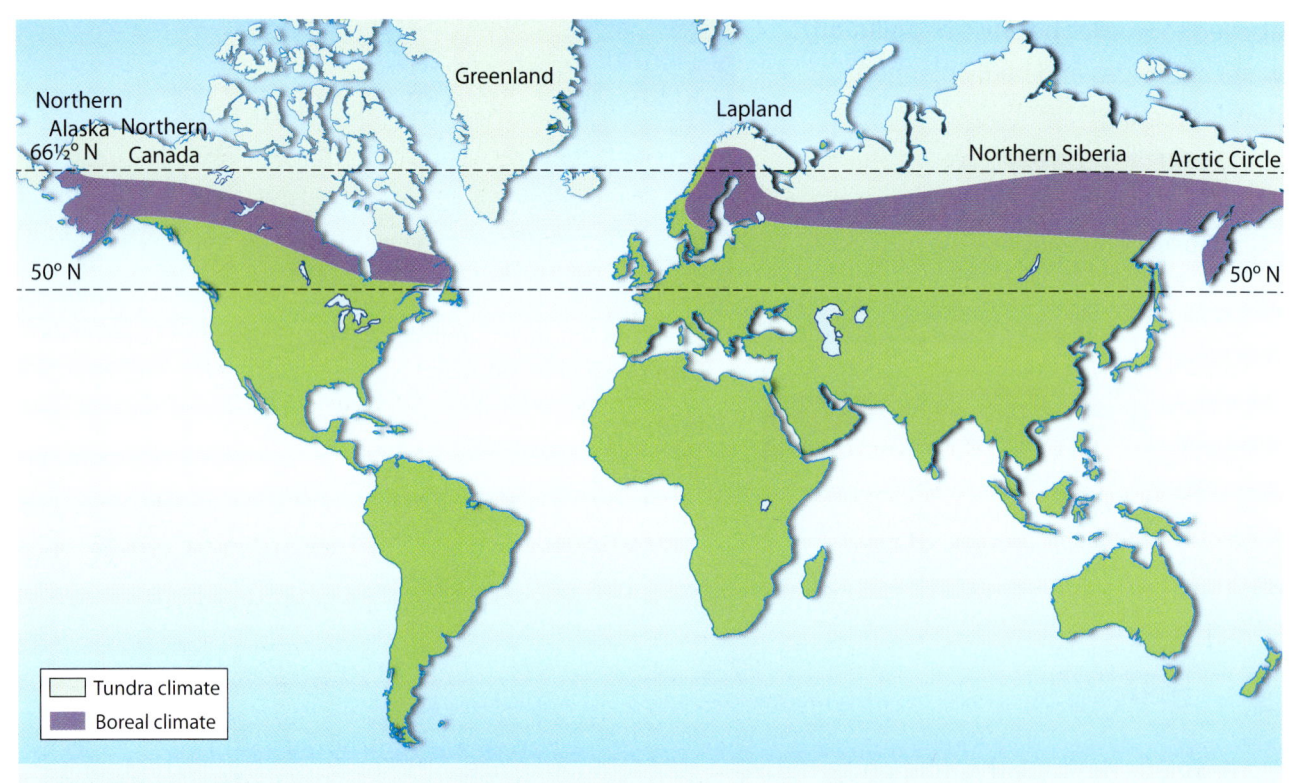

Figure 6.12 Cold climates are found in the high latitudes of the Eurasian and American land masses

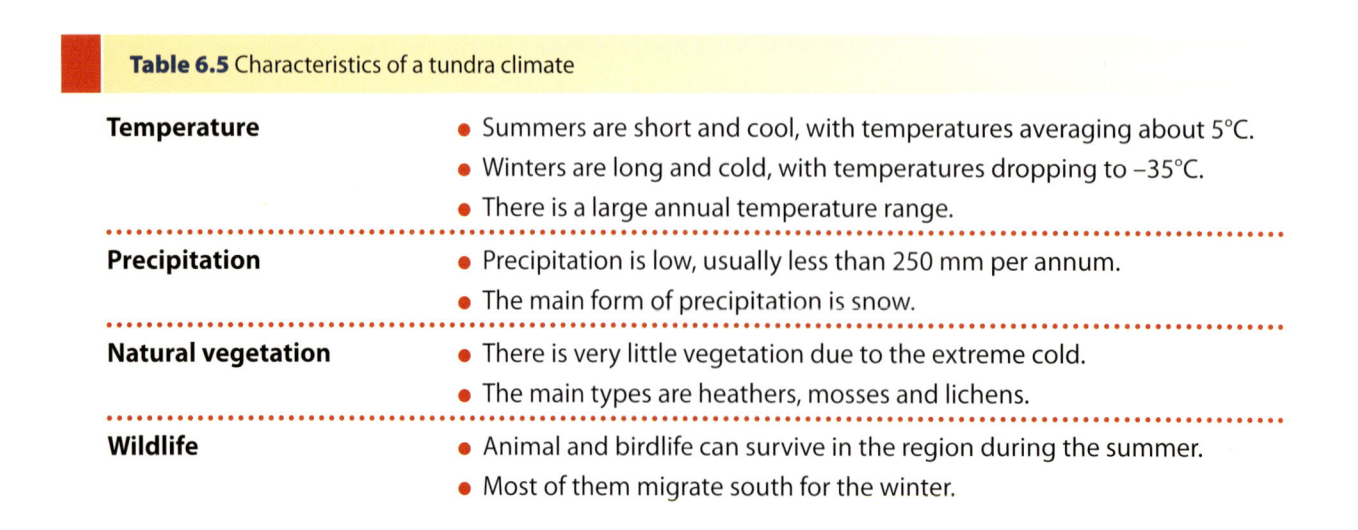

Table 6.5 Characteristics of a tundra climate

Temperature	• Summers are short and cool, with temperatures averaging about 5°C. • Winters are long and cold, with temperatures dropping to −35°C. • There is a large annual temperature range.
Precipitation	• Precipitation is low, usually less than 250 mm per annum. • The main form of precipitation is snow.
Natural vegetation	• There is very little vegetation due to the extreme cold. • The main types are heathers, mosses and lichens.
Wildlife	• Animal and birdlife can survive in the region during the summer. • Most of them migrate south for the winter.

Chapter 6 · Climates and Natural Regions

Focus on boreal climate

Location

The word **boreal** means 'northern'. Boreal climate is found in a high latitude belt that runs across America and Eurasia between 55° N and the Arctic Circle.

Table 6.6 Characteristics of a boreal climate

Temperature

Summers are short and have long hours of daylight. Coastal areas are cool (about 10°C). Inland areas are warmer (about 15°C).
- The northern hemisphere is tilted towards the sun.
- The long hours of sunshine allow the land to gradually absorb some of the heat.

Winters are cold and have long hours of darkness. Temperatures can reach as low as −25°C.
- The northern hemisphere is tilted away from the sun.
- The sun is low in the sky, so its rays have to cover a large area of ground, giving little heat.

Precipitation

Precipitation is generally less than 400 mm per annum. It is mainly in the form of snow. Maximum precipitation occurs in summer.
- Polar winds are too cold to hold much moisture.
- Many boreal regions are very far from the sea, so the winds that blow over them are dry.

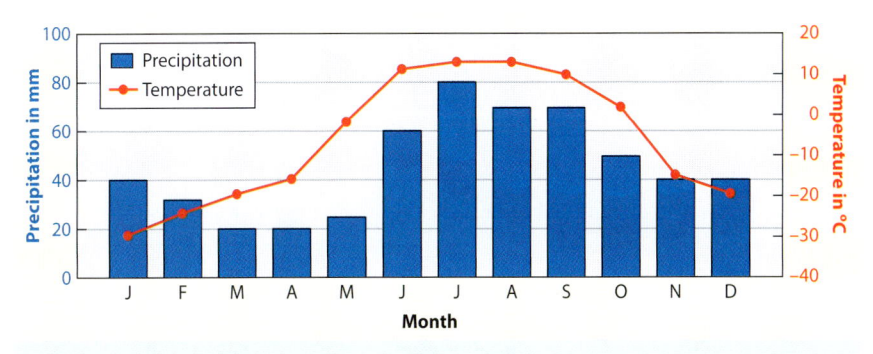

Figure 6.13 Temperature and precipitation in the boreal climate

Activities

Examine Figure 6.13.

1. Which month has:
   (a) The highest temperature?
   (b) The lowest temperature?
2. **Calculate:**
   (a) Annual temperature range.
   (b) Total precipitation for January to April inclusive.

Vegetation in a boreal climate

The natural vegetation of the boreal climate is an evergreen forest called **taiga**. Some trees in the taiga are **coniferous**.

Since the climate is too harsh for agriculture, the forests have survived largely intact. The taiga accounts for over **20 per cent of the world's forested area**.

Definition

Coniferous: Trees that bear cones.

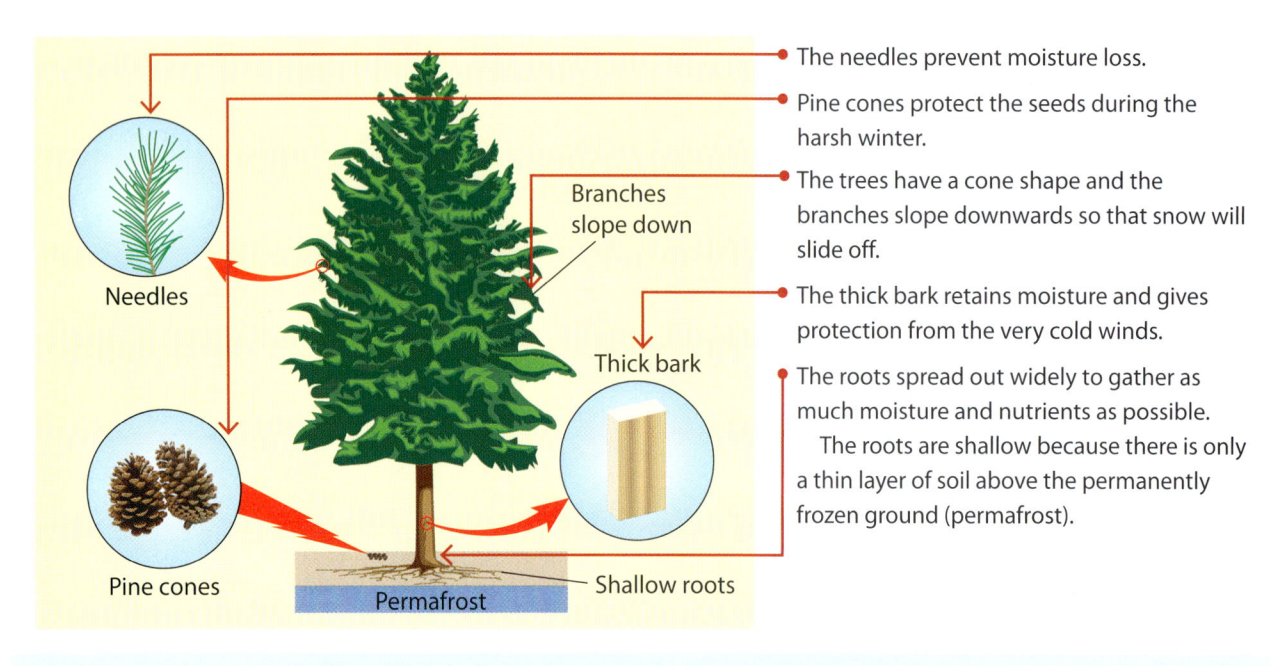

Section 1 · Physical Geography

- The needles prevent moisture loss.
- Pine cones protect the seeds during the harsh winter.
- The trees have a cone shape and the branches slope downwards so that snow will slide off.
- The thick bark retains moisture and gives protection from the very cold winds.
- The roots spread out widely to gather as much moisture and nutrients as possible.
  The roots are shallow because there is only a thin layer of soil above the permanently frozen ground (permafrost).

(Labels on diagram: Needles, Pine cones, Branches slope down, Thick bark, Shallow roots, Permafrost)

Figure 6.14 The trees of the taiga have adapted to harsh winters in a number of ways

Wildlife in the boreal

The taiga is home to a rich variety of wildlife, including the mink, bear, wolf and eagle. They have adapted to their environment in a number of ways:

- Some animals, such as the grizzly bear, avoid the stresses of winter by spending the cold season in **hibernation**.
- Fur acts as an **insulating layer**, keeping an animal's body warm in winter and cool in summer.
- Some animals have **wide hooves** that act as snowshoes.
- Birds **migrate** to the south during winter.

Activity

Examine the photograph on the right. Explain how the trees of the taiga have adapted to the severe climate.

Winter in the boreal forest

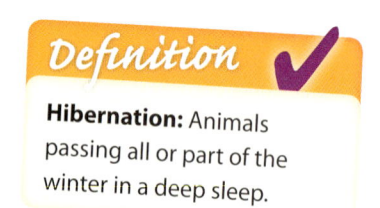

Definition

Hibernation: Animals passing all or part of the winter in a deep sleep.

Arctic foxes change the colour of their fur with the seasons. In summer they are brown but in winter they change to white to blend in with the snow

128

People in the boreal

Very few people live in the boreal forest because of the harsh climate. Miners, foresters and small groups of native peoples populate this remote landscape.

For many years most of the boreal forest was untouched by human interference. Today, the boreal forests of Russia and Canada are at risk from **logging companies**, many of which clear the forests of all trees. The wood is in huge demand for paper and chipboard. The forest areas are also at risk of **environmental damage** from mining and oil exploration.

The **Sami** are Europe's last tribe. More than 50,000 of them live in Lapland. They have a long tradition of herding reindeer which is why they used to be **nomadic**, often travelling long distances. However, with the invention of the snowmobile, the Sami are now able to cover long distances in a shorter time. As a result, most families have now settled in towns

Geo facts
Only the Sami can legally own reindeer in Finland.
None of the reindeer in Finland are actually wild.

Activity
Lapland is spread over parts of several countries. Can you **identify** three of them? Use an atlas.

Definition
Nomadic: Moving in large groups from place to place in search of grazing for their animals.

Questions

1. Explain each of the following characteristics of a boreal climate:
   - Winters are very cold.
   - There are long hours of darkness in winter.
   - Precipitation occurs mainly in the form of snow.

2. (a) What is the taiga?
   (b) Describe the vegetation of the taiga.
   (c) Explain **two** ways in which the vegetation of the taiga has adapted to its environment.

3. (a) Describe any **two** ways in which wildlife has adapted to the climate conditions of the taiga.
   (b) Briefly describe the lifestyle of a people who live in the taiga.

Section 1 · Physical Geography

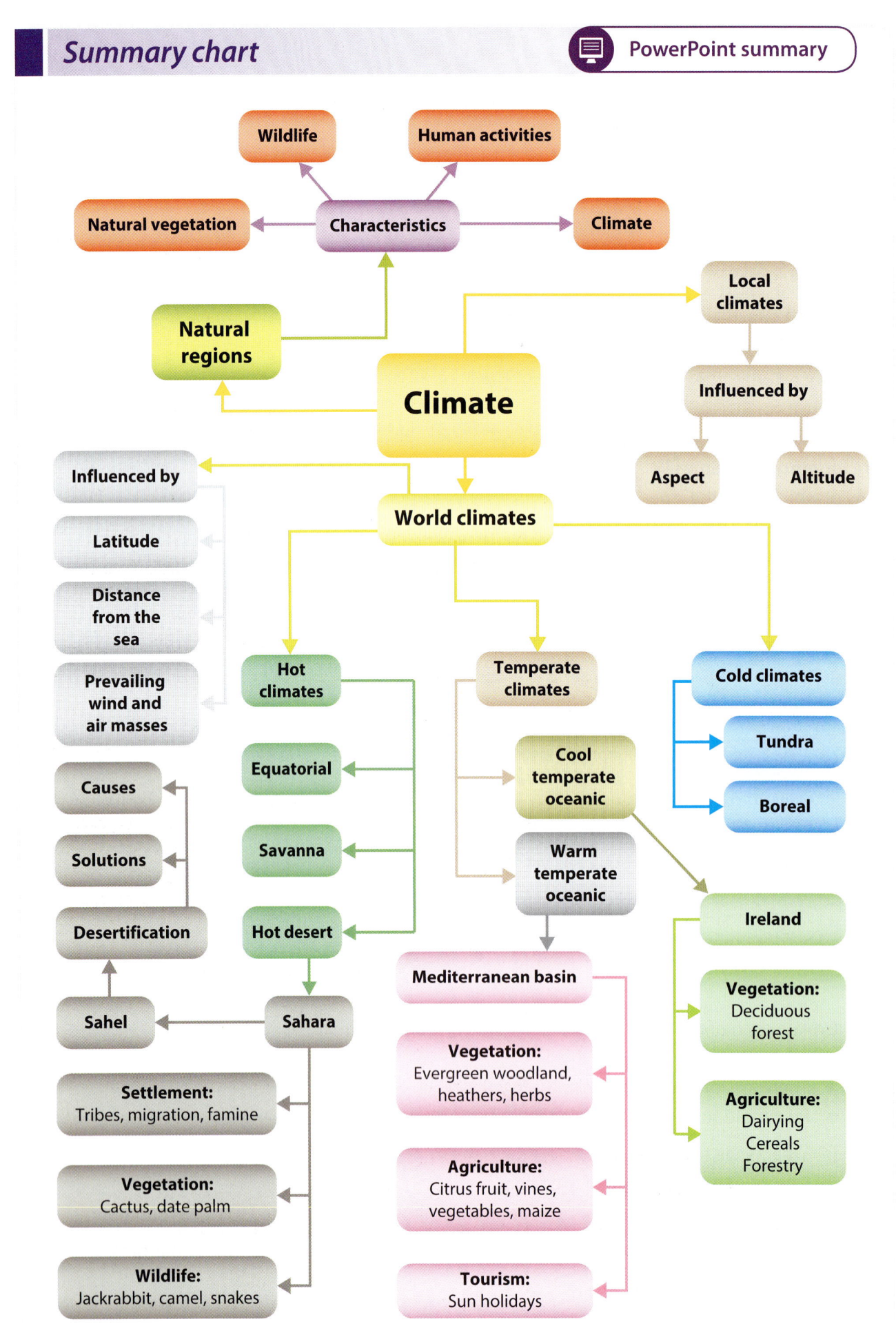

Summary chart

PowerPoint summary

- **Climate**
  - Characteristics
    - Wildlife
    - Human activities
    - Natural vegetation
    - Climate
  - Natural regions
  - Local climates
    - Influenced by
      - Aspect
      - Altitude
  - World climates
    - Influenced by
      - Latitude
      - Distance from the sea
      - Prevailing wind and air masses
    - Hot climates
      - Equatorial
      - Savanna
      - Hot desert → Sahara
        - Sahel → Desertification
          - Causes
          - Solutions
        - Settlement: Tribes, migration, famine
        - Vegetation: Cactus, date palm
        - Wildlife: Jackrabbit, camel, snakes
    - Temperate climates
      - Cool temperate oceanic
      - Warm temperate oceanic → Mediterranean basin
        - Vegetation: Evergreen woodland, heathers, herbs
        - Agriculture: Citrus fruit, vines, vegetables, maize
        - Tourism: Sun holidays
    - Cold climates
      - Tundra
      - Boreal
    - Ireland
      - Vegetation: Deciduous forest
      - Agriculture: Dairying, Cereals, Forestry

130

Chapter 6 · Climates and Natural Regions

Exam questions

1. Explain how any **three** of the following factors influence climate:
   - Latitude
   - Altitude
   - Prevailing winds
   - Relief
   - Distance from seas and oceans.

   HL 2013

2. The diagram shows a mountainous area in Europe.

   Explain **two** reasons why you would expect the place labelled **X** on the diagram to be colder than the place labelled **Y**.

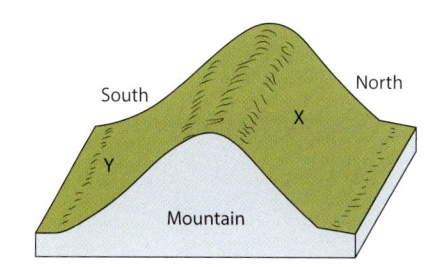

   HL 2008

3. (i) Name **one** hot climate, **one** temperate climate and **one** cold climate.

   (ii) Select **one** climate and describe it in detail, referring to temperatures and precipitation.

   HL 2010

4. Name **one** type of climate that you have studied (e.g. Hot desert, Mediterranean).

   (i) Describe briefly the climate and the vegetation found there.

   (ii) Describe **one** way in which the climate affects people living there.

   OL 2008

5. The photographs above show vegetation in three different hot climate areas.

   (i) Name **one** hot climate that you have studied and describe this hot climate.

   (ii) Describe the vegetation resulting from this hot climate.

   (iii) Name **one** way in which this climate affects people.

   OL 2013

6. (i) Name **one cold** climate that you have studied.

   (ii) Explain the temperature **and** precipitation characteristics of this **cold** climate.

   (iii) Describe **one** way that natural vegetation has adapted to this **cold** climate.

   HL 2014

Exam questions

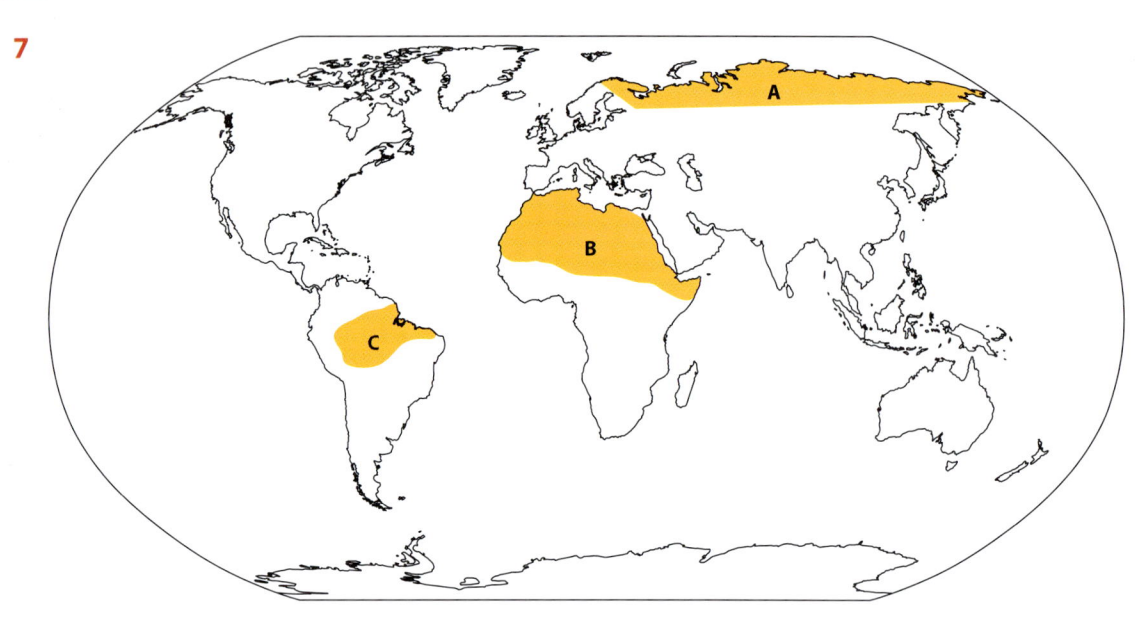

7

Examine the map above which shows the location of three of the world's climatic regions.

(i) Name the type of climate at each of the locations **A**, **B** and **C**.

(ii) Explain the characteristics of any **one** climate type that you have studied.

HL 2012

8 (i) Name an area that experiences severe drought **and** explain why drought occurs in this area.

(ii) Describe and explain the impacts of drought on human activity in this area.

HL 2014

9 Explain how climate has hindered (slowed down) the development of **one** named **developing country**.

HL 2008

Chapter 7
Soils

Learning outcomes

By the end of this chapter, you should be able to understand:

- What soil is and what it is made of
- How soils are formed
- Soil profiles and leaching
- The characteristics of Ireland's main soil types
- How soil and vegetation influence each other.

7.1 What is soil?

KEYWORDS

- mineral matter
- living organisms
- humus
- parent material
- soil profile
- soil horizon
- bedrock
- plant litter
- topsoil
- subsoil
- soil texture
- leaching
- impermeable
- hardpan

Soil is the thin layer of loose material on the Earth's surface. It is one of the world's most important **natural resources**. Plants obtain their minerals from the soil, so without soil there would be no food for animals or people.

Soil has five main ingredients, both living and non-living:

- Mineral matter
- Air
- Water
- Living organisms
- Humus.

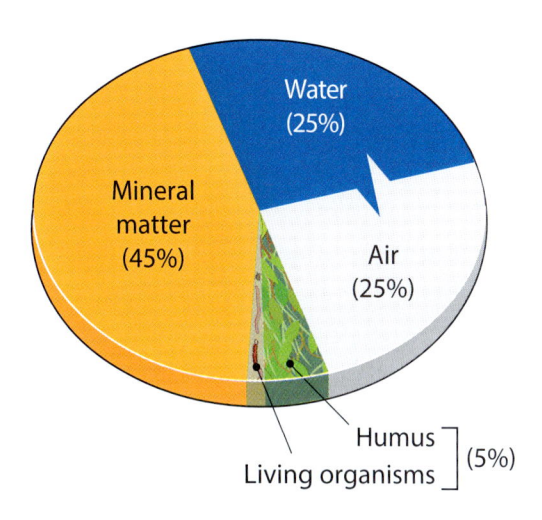

Figure 7.1 The amount of water and air in soil varies, depending on the weather and how well the soil can hold water

- Water (25%)
- Mineral matter (45%)
- Air (25%)
- Humus, Living organisms (5%)

133

Section 1 · Physical Geography

Mineral matter

Mineral matter is the **biggest ingredient** in soil. It is made up of **rock particles** that have been broken down by weathering and erosion. It includes stones, sand, silt and clay.

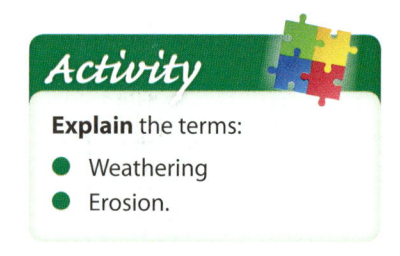

> **Activity**
> **Explain** the terms:
> - Weathering
> - Erosion.

Air

Air fills the spaces (or **pores**) between the mineral particles in the soil. Air contains **oxygen** and **nitrogen**. These are vital for the growth of plants. Air also allows living organisms to survive in the soil.

Water

Water helps to bind the soil particles together. Water is important for plant growth because it contains **dissolved minerals**. Plants absorb these minerals through their roots.

Living organisms

Soil is home to creatures such as earthworms, woodlice and slugs. It is also home to millions of tiny creatures, too small to be seen by the naked eye, called **micro-organisms**. They include bacteria and fungi.

> **Geo fact**
> There are more micro-organisms in one handful of soil than there are people on Earth.

When **worms** burrow through the soil, they mix it and also make it easier for water and air to pass through. Micro-organisms help to break down dead plants into humus.

Humus

Organic matter is composed of the remains of dead creatures and plants. It is broken down and mixed into the soil by the living organisms.

As the organic matter begins to decay, it turns into a dark brown or black substance called **humus**. Humus provides **nutrients** that make the soil fertile. It also helps to bind the soil particles together.

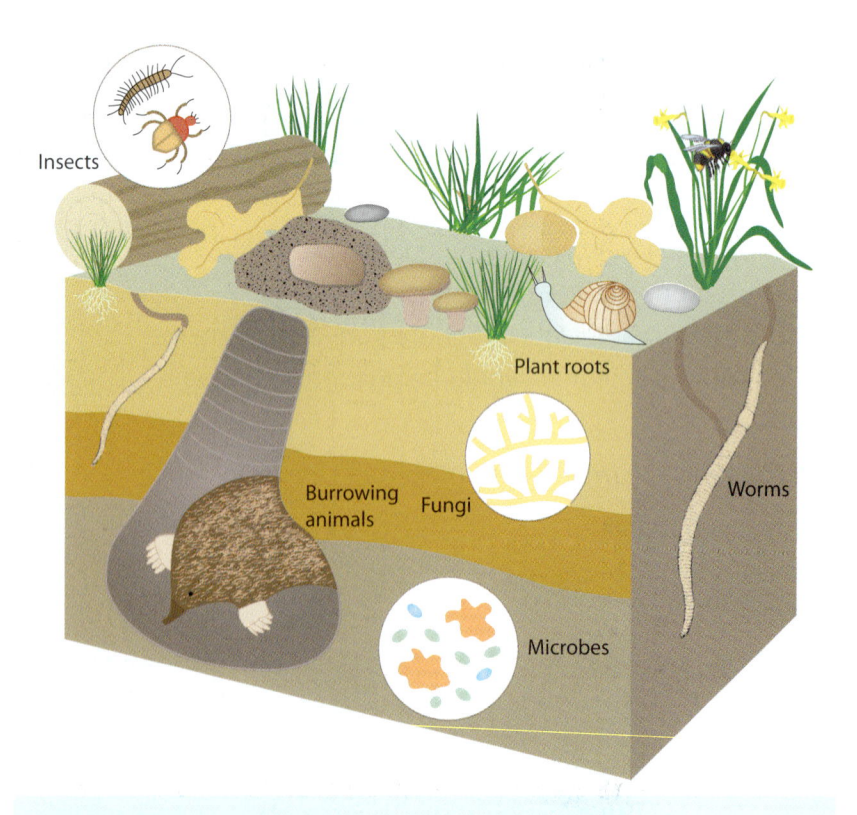

Figure 7.2 Living organisms help to make soil more fertile

How are soils formed?

A number of factors work together over a period of time to form soil. They are:

- Climate
- Parent material
- Vegetation
- Living organisms
- Landscape
- Time.

Climate

Temperature and rainfall influence the rate at which the parent rock is broken down by weathering. Hot climates experience **chemical weathering**, while cold climates experience **freeze-thaw**.

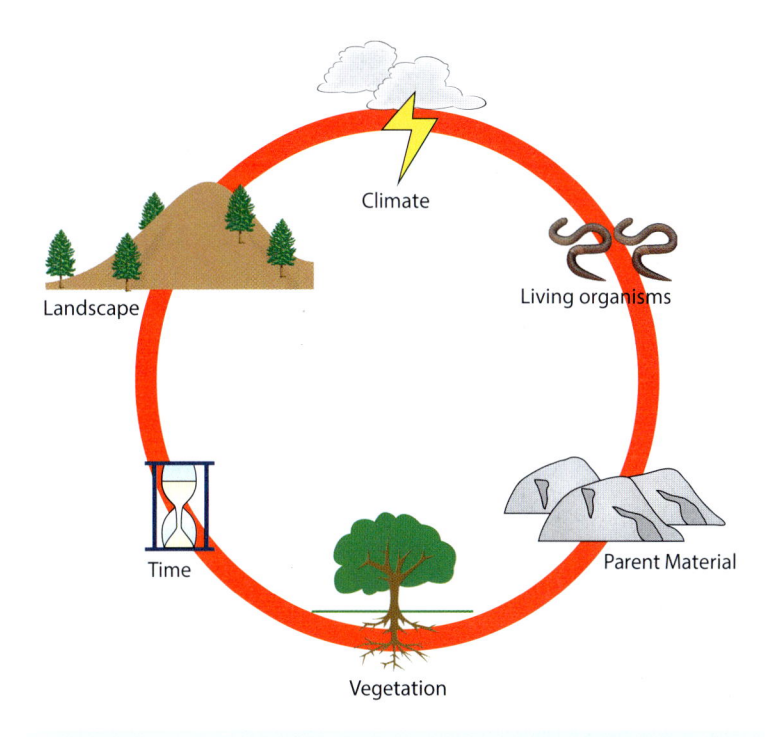

Figure 7.3 The factors that influence how soil is formed

Parent material

The **type of rock** in an area also affects soil formation. For example, granite is slow to break down by weathering, while sandstone breaks down easily and forms soil quickly.

Soils that develop from limestone are more fertile than those that develop from granite or sandstone.

Vegetation

When vegetation dies, it is broken down and decays to add **humus** and **nutrients** to the soil. Deciduous vegetation provides more leaf fall than coniferous vegetation.

Living organisms

Micro-organisms such as **bacteria and fungi** help to break down the dead plant and animal life in the soil, turning it into humus.

As animals such as **earthworms** dig through the soil, they break it up and mix it, allowing more water and air to enter the soil. When these creatures die, their remains add nutrients to the soil.

Landscape

Upland areas are cold and wet, so soils are often waterlogged. There is little plant and animal life, so there is less humus.

Lowland soils are generally deeper and well drained. They have more humus as there is plentiful plant and animal life.

Time

Time is one of the most important factors in soil formation. The longer a rock is exposed to the forces of **weathering**, the more it is broken down. It may take up to 400 years for 1 cm of soil to form.

Geo fact

People can also influence the make-up of soil. They can make it more fertile by drainage, adding fertiliser, ploughing and irrigation. They can make it less fertile by overusing it or by removing vegetation.

135

Section 1 · Physical Geography

Soil profiles

If you dig down into the ground as far as the **bedrock**, you will find a number of different layers. Each layer is called a **horizon**. They can be seen along road cuttings and other areas where the soil is exposed.

Apart from the surface layer of **plant litter**, there are usually three horizons in a soil profile. They differ from one another in colour, content and texture.

Definition

Bedrock: The hard layer of rock that lies beneath looser rocks and soil.

Plant litter: Dead plant material, such as leaves and twigs, that has fallen to the ground.

Geo fact

Soil texture refers to the feel of a soil: the size and type of particles that make it up.

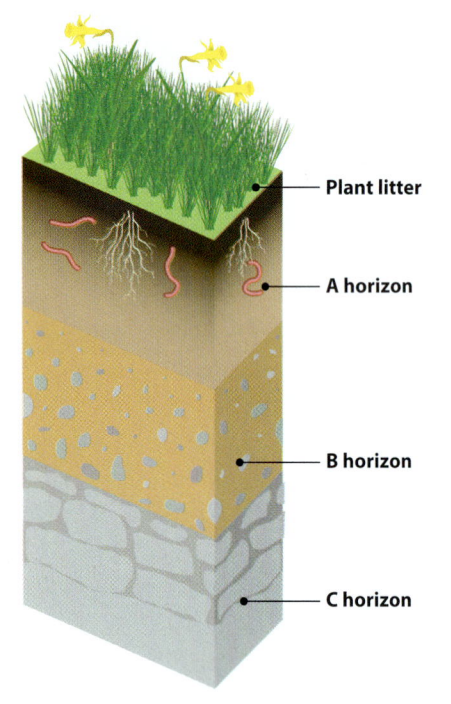

A horizon
The upper layer of soil is called the **topsoil**. It is usually darker than lower layers as it has a high humus content. It is **loose and crumbly**. Most of the organisms live in this layer. It is generally the most **fertile** layer of soil.

B horizon
Found beneath the A horizon, this is called the **subsoil**. It is usually lighter in colour because it has less humus. It has more **stones** than the A horizon because it is closer to the parent material and is protected from weathering.

C horizon
This consists of the **parent rock** of the soil. The upper section may be broken down into rock particles, but the lower section consists of solid **bedrock**.

Figure 7.4 A typical soil profile. Compare with the photograph below

Activity

Examine the picture on the right.
1 Name the horizons that you can identify.
2 Describe the plant litter.

Leaching

In wet climates, such as in Ireland, water soaks down through the soil. As it does so, it washes minerals, humus and nutrients down into the B horizon. This process is known as **leaching**.

Leaching can cause the A horizon to lose its fertility because it washes the nutrients down beyond the reach of plant roots. This leaves the soil without the minerals that may be essential for plant growth.

A soil profile

Hardpan

If leaching is very severe, minerals such as clay and iron oxide (rust) build up at the bottom of the A horizon. They cement together to form a crust called **hardpan**. Since hardpan is **impermeable**, it causes the soil above it to become **waterlogged**.

Definition

Impermeable: Rocks that do not let water soak through them are called impermeable.

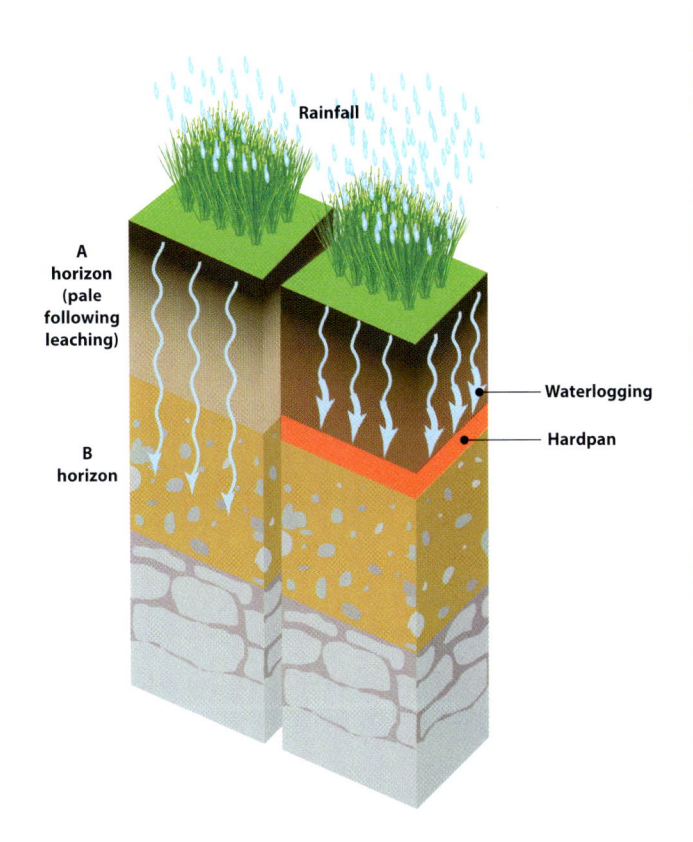

Figure 7.5 Leaching (left) and hardpan (right)

The upper layer consists of a dark humus layer with plant roots and a greyish layer below. All the nutrients have been leached from this layer

Questions

1. (a) What is soil?
   (b) List the **five** ingredients of soil.
   (c) The volumes of which **two** ingredients vary according to the weather?

2. Draw a labelled diagram of a typical soil profile.

3. Explain each of the following terms:
   - Micro-organisms
   - Plant litter
   - Humus.

4. Describe how any **two** of the following affect the fertility of a soil:
   (a) humus, (b) micro-organisms, (c) air and water.

5. Explain any **two** effects of leaching and hardpan on soils.

137

Section 1 · Physical Geography

7.2 Soils of Ireland

KEYWORDS

● brown earth soils   ● podzol soils   ● peaty soils   ● gley soils

There are four main soil types in Ireland:

- Brown earth soils
- Peaty soils
- Podzol soils
- Gley soils.

Students are required to study **two** Irish soils.

Brown earth soils

- Brown earth soils developed on the **boulder clays** deposited after the last Ice Age. These areas were formerly covered by **deciduous forest**.
- There was a plentiful supply of plant litter available. This decayed rapidly to form **humus**, giving the soil its dark brown colour.
- Rainfall is limited so there is **very little leaching** of minerals.
- Brown earth soils are well drained and **fertile**. They are suited to a wide range of farming types, including arable and pastoral farming.
- Brown earth soils are the most common soil in Ireland and are found in the **drier lowlands** of the south, Midlands and east.

Activity

With the aid of your atlas, **identify**:

1. Two counties with brown earth soils.
2. Two counties with podzol soils.

Activity

Why, do you think, are peaty soils found along the western part of the country?

Hint: Examine a physical map of Ireland.

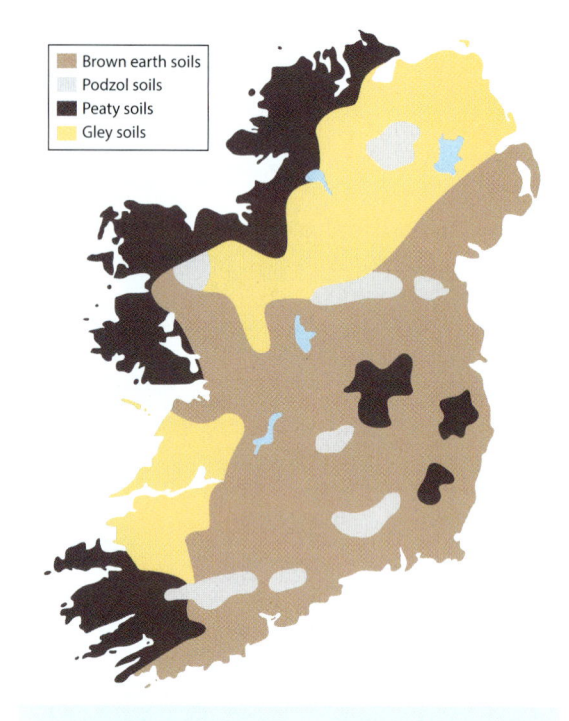

Figure 7.6 This map shows the general locations of the main soil types in Ireland

Deciduous trees
Thick layer of plant litter
A horizon is rich in humus
A horizon blends into the **B horizon** due to worm action
Bedrock in the **C horizon**

Brown earth soil covers much of the Irish landscape. It is a fertile soil that is suited to both arable and pastoral farming

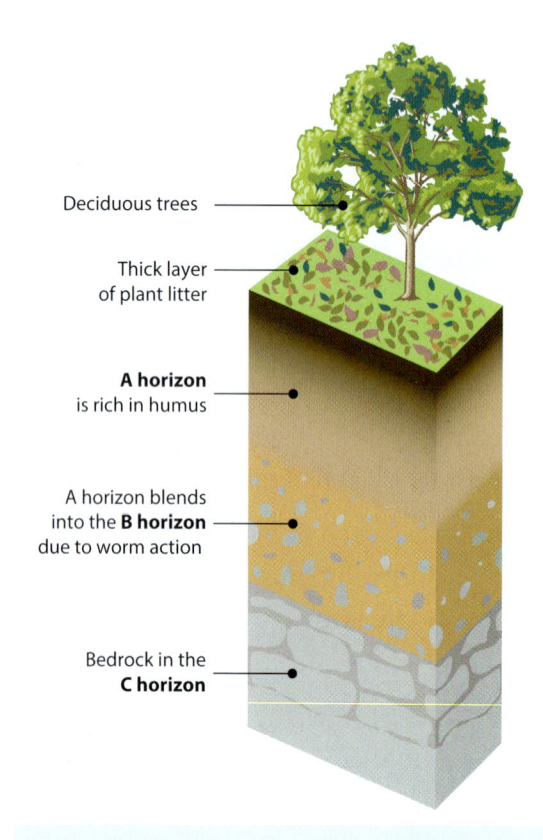

Figure 7.7 A soil profile of brown earth soil

138

Chapter 7 · Soils

Podzol soils

- Podzol soils developed in cold and wet areas that were covered by **coniferous forest**.
- The forest provided only limited amounts of plant litter in the form of pine leaves. The plant litter decayed very slowly in the colder temperatures, to form only **small amounts of humus**. The cold also limits earthworm activity.
- The heavier rainfall causes **leaching** and hardpan may develop. This gives the A horizon a greyish colour.
- Podzol soils are **relatively infertile** and are also slightly acidic.
- They are found in the damp, **poorly-drained upland areas** of Cork, Galway and Tipperary.

Figure 7.8 A soil profile of podzol soil

The plant litter on the floor of a coniferous forest consists mainly of needles. This leads to limited amounts of humus in podzol soils

Geo fact
Peat (or turf) consists of partially decayed organic matter and is used as fuel and garden compost.

Other soils in Ireland

Gley soils (above) develop in areas where the bedrock or the clay above it is impermeable. As a result, the rain is unable to drain away. These soils become waterlogged and are suitable only for pastoral farming

Peaty soils are dark in colour. They are full of organic matter that has not broken down. They develop in cold, upland areas that have very high rainfall. They retain the water and are easily waterlogged

Questions

1. Examine Figure 7.6 on page 138 and, with the aid of an atlas, answer the following questions:
   (a) Which is the most common soil type in Ireland?
   (b) What is the main soil type in your county?
   (c) Name **one** soil type common in lowland areas.

2. Name **one** Irish soil type that you have studied.
   (a) Describe **three** characteristics (features) of this soil.
   (b) Draw a labelled soil profile of this soil.

Section 1 · Physical Geography

7.3 A world soil: tropical red soil

KEYWORDS
- tropical red soil
- chemical weathering
- iron oxide
- deforestation
- latosol

This section is for **Higher Level** students only.

Tropical red soils are found in areas that have a tropical or equatorial climate. Their formation is influenced mainly by the **hot, wet** climatic conditions. As a result, **chemical weathering** is very active. This causes the rock to decompose very rapidly, forming soil that is several metres deep.

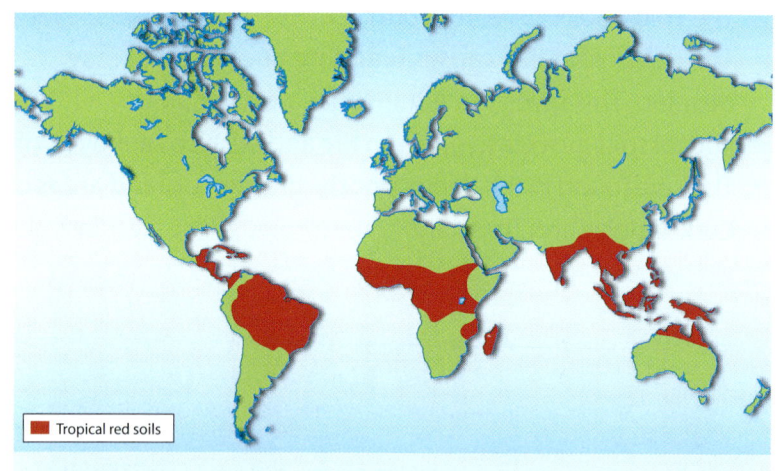

- There is continuous leaf fall in the forest throughout the year, giving a **thick layer of plant litter**. This is rapidly broken down, partly by organisms in the soil.
- The acids from the decaying humus speed up the **weathering** of the bedrock.
- Weathering breaks down the iron in the soil into **iron oxide** (rust), giving the soil its **reddish colour**.
- The soil is **heavily leached** due to very heavy rainfall.

Figure 7.9 Tropical red soils are found in regions that are close to the equator

Geo fact
The soils of the humid tropical and equatorial zones are called **latosols**.

Deforestation

Tropical soils are very fertile. However, when the forests are cut down, the soil loses the source of its humus. It is leached by the heavy rainfall and soon loses its fertility. Without its cover of vegetation, the soil is unprotected. It is quickly eroded by surface water.

Definition
Deforestation: The large-scale cutting down of trees, transforming a forest into cleared land.

Tropical red soil (**latosol**) exposed beneath a tropical forest in India. Here the soil is being mined. It will be mixed with water and baked under the sun to make building bricks.

Activity
Examine the picture on the left. Apart from its colour, what evidence suggests that this is a tropical red soil?

Questions

1. (a) Name **two** regions where tropical red soils are found.
   (b) Why do tropical red soils have a reddish colour?
2. (a) Describe how tropical red soils are formed.
   (b) Why is the climate so important in the formation of tropical red soils?
3. Describe how tropical red soils lose their fertility so quickly.

7.4 Natural vegetation and soil

Soil conditions can influence vegetation and vegetation, in turn, can influence soil conditions.

Table 7.1 How soil influences vegetation

Drainage	**Sandy** soils are free-draining and can support a wide range of vegetation.
	Clay soils become waterlogged and support a limited range of vegetation.
Nutrients	**Fertile** soils contain a wide range of nutrients, including nitrogen and calcium, and can support a wide range of vegetation.
	Infertile soils can support only a limited range of vegetation.
Depth	**Deep** soils support vegetation with long roots such as deciduous forests.
	Shallow soils are limited in the vegetation that they can support (e.g. conifers).

Table 7.2 How vegetation influences soil

Plant litter	**Deciduous** trees provide lots of plant litter to form humus and brown earth soils.
	Coniferous trees provide little plant litter, leading to the formation of podzols.
Soil erosion	**Roots** bind soil particles together, thus slowing down or preventing soil erosion.
	When **vegetation cover** is lost, the soil is liable to be eroded by surface water.
Leaching	**Vegetation** can absorb surface water, thus reducing the amount of leaching.
	Without vegetation, the water moves downward in the soil, leaching nutrients.

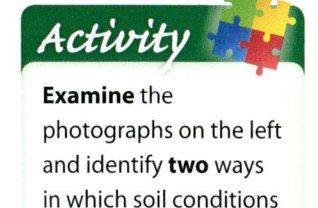

Activity

Examine the photographs on the left and identify **two** ways in which soil conditions and vegetation have influenced one another.

Section 1 · Physical Geography

Questions

1. Describe **two** ways in which soils influence vegetation.
2. Describe **two** ways in which vegetation influences soil.

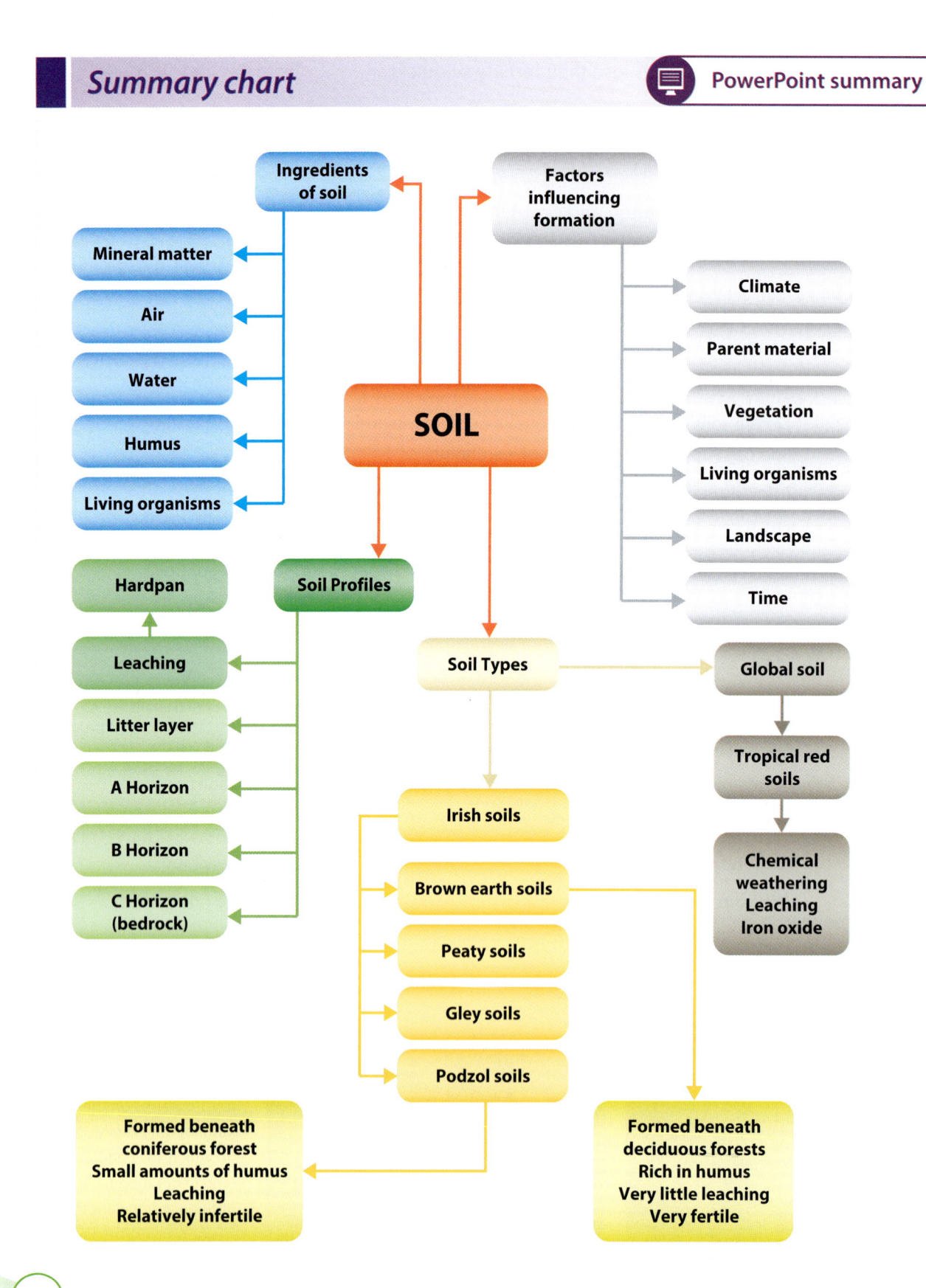

Summary chart

PowerPoint summary

SOIL

Ingredients of soil:
- Mineral matter
- Air
- Water
- Humus
- Living organisms

Factors influencing formation:
- Climate
- Parent material
- Vegetation
- Living organisms
- Landscape
- Time

Soil Profiles:
- Hardpan
- Leaching
- Litter layer
- A Horizon
- B Horizon
- C Horizon (bedrock)

Soil Types:
- Irish soils
  - Brown earth soils
  - Peaty soils
  - Gley soils
  - Podzol soils
- Global soil
  - Tropical red soils
    - Chemical weathering
    - Leaching
    - Iron oxide

Podzol soils: Formed beneath coniferous forest. Small amounts of humus. Leaching. Relatively infertile.

Brown earth soils: Formed beneath deciduous forests. Rich in humus. Very little leaching. Very fertile.

142

Chapter 7 · Soils

Exam questions

1. Look carefully at this diagram showing the main ingredients of soil.
   (i) What percentage of soil is made up of mineral particles?
   (ii) Describe the importance of any **three** of the following in the composition of soil:
   - Mineral particles
   - Air
   - Water
   - Plant remains.

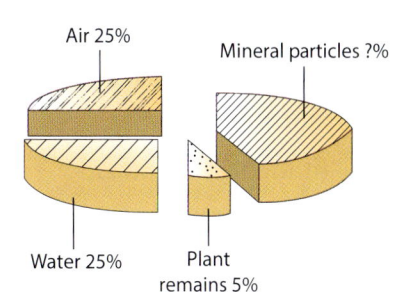

   OL 2007

2. (i) Explain the role in soil formation of any **two** of the following factors:
   - Climate
   - Vegetation
   - Parent rock
   - Micro-organisms.

   (ii) Describe **one** way that soil is important to people.

   HL 2015

3. (i) Describe and explain the formation of the soil profile shown (on the right).
   (ii) Name **two** soil types commonly found in Ireland.

   HL 2013

4. (i) Examine the diagram of a soil profile. Name the layers labelled **X**, **Y** and **Z**.
   (ii) Describe the composition of any **one** soil you have studied.

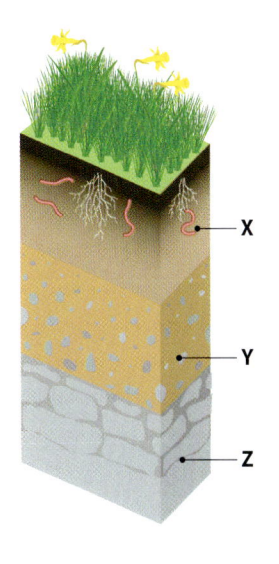

   HL 2011

143

Section 1 · Physical Geography

Exam questions

5 Examine the map, which shows some of Ireland's principal soil types.

(i) Identify the most common soil type in the south-east of Ireland.

(ii) Choose **two** Irish soil types and describe any **three** differences between them.

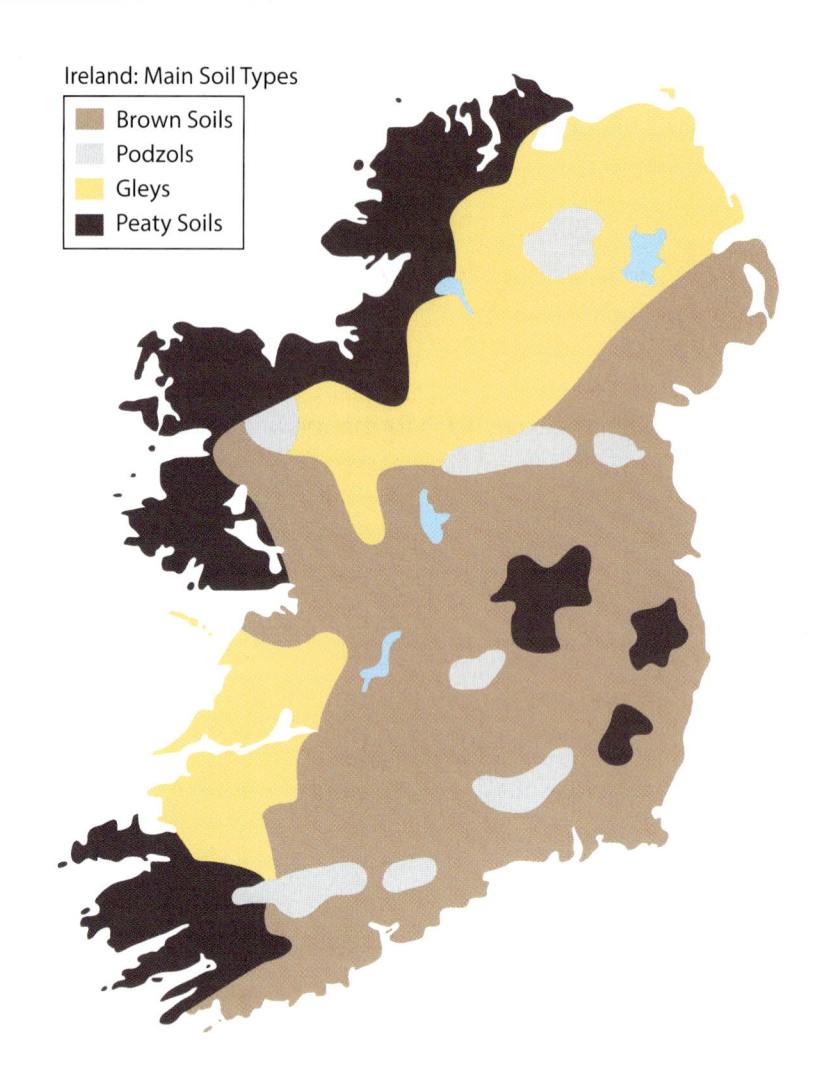

Ireland: Main Soil Types
- Brown Soils
- Podzols
- Gleys
- Peaty Soils

HL 2007

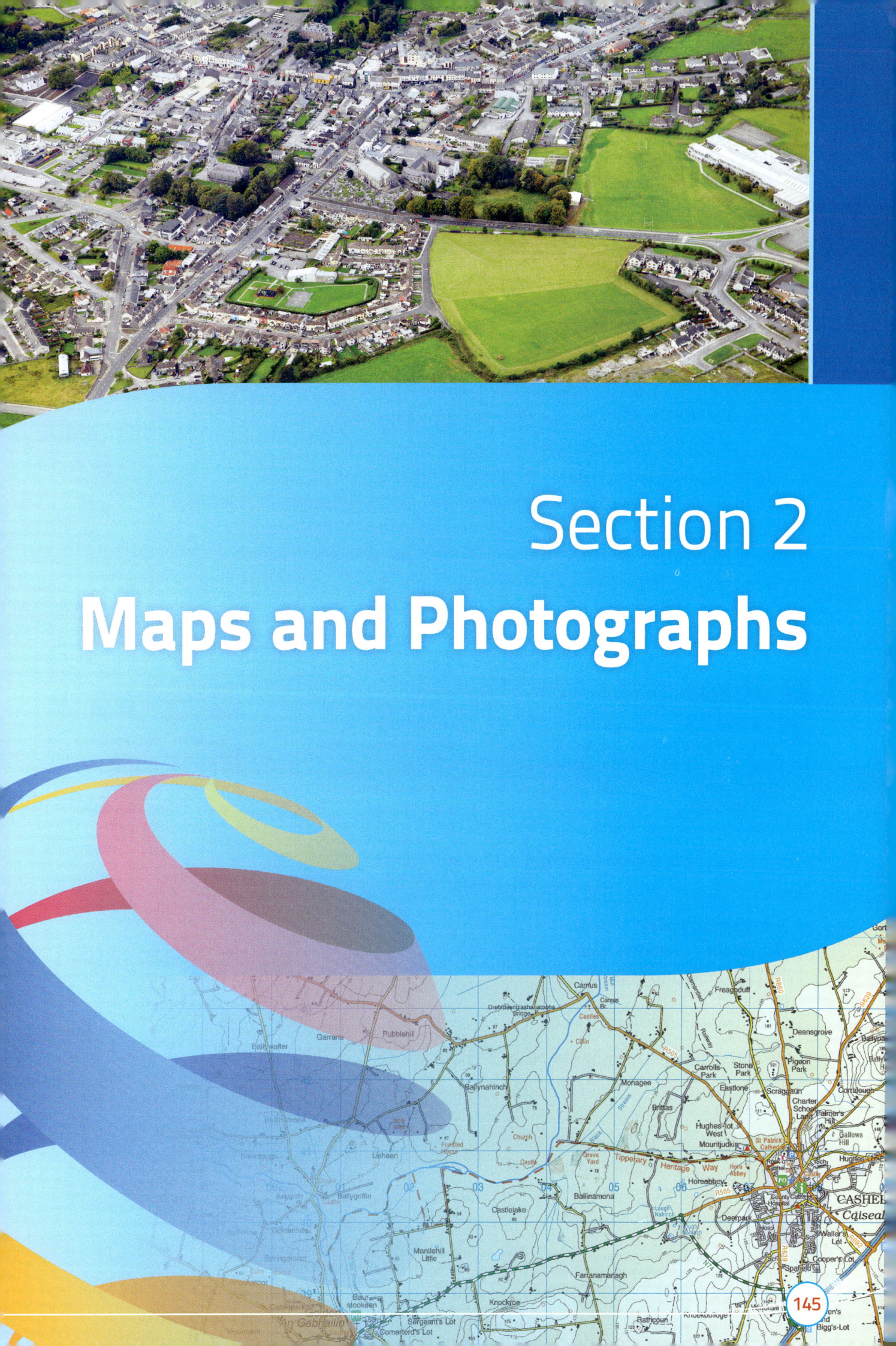

Section 2
Maps and Photographs

Chapter 8
Maps and Photographs

Learning outcomes

By the end of this chapter, you should be able to understand:

- How symbols and colour are used to present information on OS maps
- How to accurately locate features on OS maps and aerial photographs
- How to use the skills of measurement and drawing on OS maps and aerial photographs
- How to interpret the physical landscape in OS maps and aerial photographs
- How to interpret the human landscape in OS maps and aerial photographs.

8.1 Ordnance Survey maps

KEYWORDS

- map
- Ordnance Survey
- scale
- legend
- distance
- area
- National Grid
- grid reference
- compass point
- contours
- spot height
- triangulation pillar
- gradient
- cross-section
- sketch map

Activity

Examine the maps in Figures 8.1 and 8.2.

Can you identify one purpose for which each map could be used?

A **map** is a drawing or plan of part or all of the Earth's surface.

Maps:

- Are drawn to **scale**
- Use **colours**, **symbols** and **labels** to represent features found on the landscape.

Scale

Scale is the ratio or relationship between a distance on the map and the corresponding distance on the ground.

Maps are drawn to different scales, depending on the amount of information that is required and the area of ground that the map must cover.

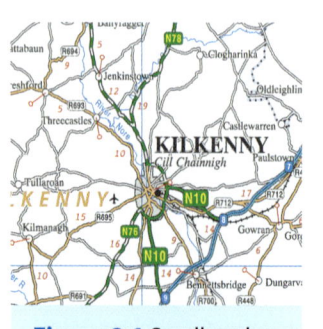

Figure 8.1 Small-scale maps show a large area but have little detail. This map, centred on Kilkenny, is drawn to a scale of 1:400,000

Figure 8.2 Large-scale maps show a smaller area but have great detail. This map, showing the centre of Kilkenny, is drawn to a scale of 1:7,000

146

Chapter 8 · Maps and Photographs

Discovery Series of maps

The Ordnance Survey of Ireland (OSI) publishes a series of maps, called the **Discovery Series**. These maps are drawn at a scale of **1:50,000**. This means that each centimetre on the map represents 50,000 centimetres (or 500 metres) on the ground.

Figure 8.3 The Discovery Series of maps are designed for tourists and leisure activities. They are drawn to a **scale of 1:50,000**. This map shows the centre of Kilkenny

Scale on a map

Scale on a map may be shown in three ways:

1. Representative fraction (RF)
2. Linear scale
3. Statement of scale.

1 Representative fraction (RF)
The scale is written as a ratio. In this case, the scale is 1:50,000.

2 Linear scale
The scale is shown along a ruled line that is divided into kilometres and miles. One section of the linear scale divides miles and kilometres into tenths.

SCALE 1:50 000   SCÁLA 1:50 000

2 ceintiméadar sa chiliméadar (taobh chearnóg eangaí) 2 centimetres to 1 Kilometre (grid square side)

3 Statement of scale
The map gives a written description of the scale. In this case, 2 centimetres on the map represent 1 kilometre on the ground.

Figure 8.4 The three methods of showing scale on the Discovery Series maps all say the same thing, but in different ways

OS map legend

Ordnance Survey maps use **symbols** to show information on a map. All the symbols used can be found in the map **legend**.

The symbols are used to represent both natural features (such as beaches, mountains and rivers) and man-made features (such as roads, buildings and airports). The symbols vary from map to map, depending on the scale.

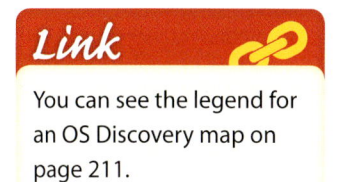

Link
You can see the legend for an OS Discovery map on page 211.

Section 2 · Maps and Photographs

Measuring distance

Scale is the same for all parts of a map. This is important because it enables us to measure distances on the map.

Straight-line distance

Straight-line distance is the shortest distance between any two points. It is often called 'as the crow flies'.

To measure a straight-line distance between two points on a map:

1 Place a strip of paper on the map so that its edge passes through the two points.
2 Mark the edge of the paper where it touches the two points on the map.
3 Place the paper against the linear scale on the map and read the distance in kilometres (km).

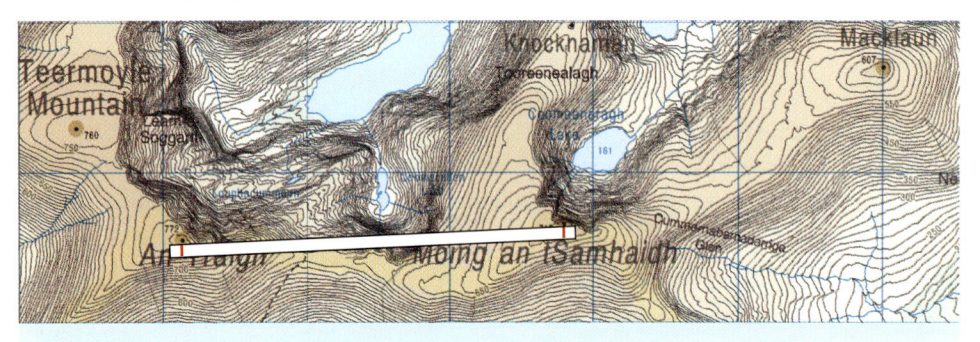

Figure 8.5a Measuring straight-line distance (as the crow flies) on a map. Measure the distance between the summits of An Traigh and Moing an tSamhaidh, Co. Kerry

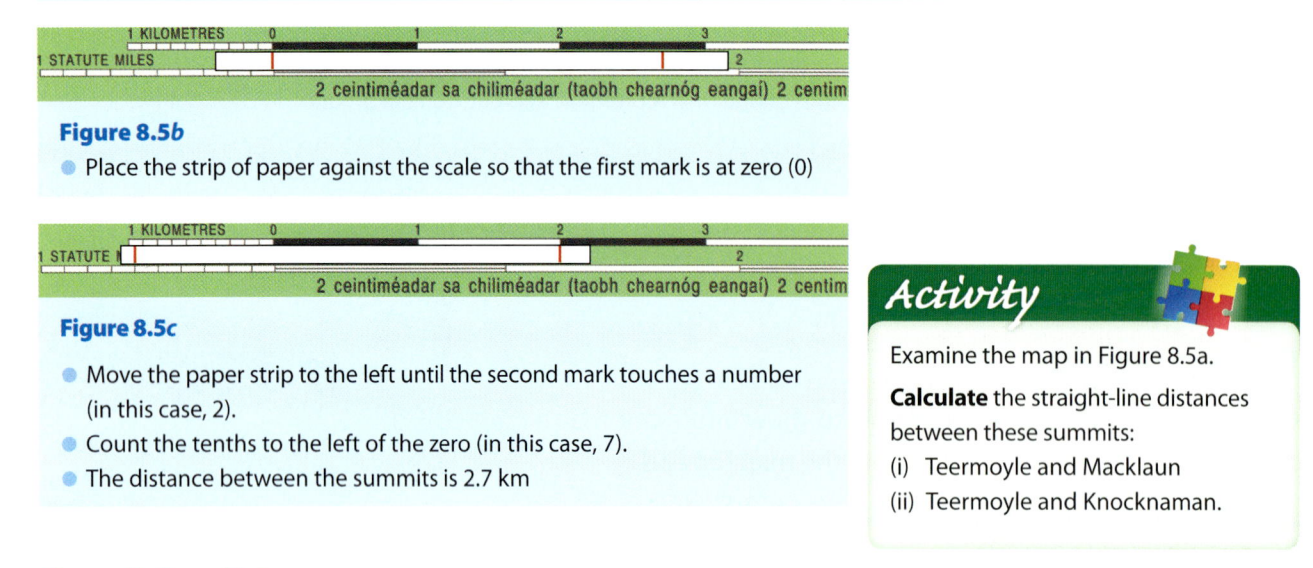

Figure 8.5b
- Place the strip of paper against the scale so that the first mark is at zero (0)

Figure 8.5c
- Move the paper strip to the left until the second mark touches a number (in this case, 2).
- Count the tenths to the left of the zero (in this case, 7).
- The distance between the summits is 2.7 km

Activity

Examine the map in Figure 8.5a.
Calculate the straight-line distances between these summits:
(i) Teermoyle and Macklaun
(ii) Teermoyle and Knocknaman.

Curved-line distance

Curved-line distance is used to measure a distance along any line that is not straight, e.g. roads, railways and rivers.

Chapter 8 · Maps and Photographs

To measure a curved-line distance between two points on a map:

1 Place the edge of your paper strip at the start point and put a pencil mark on both the map and the paper (A).

2 Hold the edge of the paper along the line until you reach the first bend or turn. Put a pencil mark on both map and paper (B).

3 Keep the marks at (B) in line with one another. Move the paper strip so that it is in line with the next section of the line. Put a pencil mark on both map and paper (C).

4 Repeat this process until you have measured the required distance.

5 Place the paper strip on the linear scale and read the distance in kilometres.

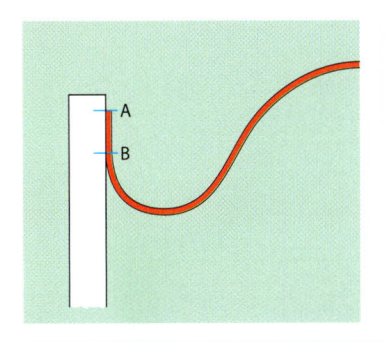

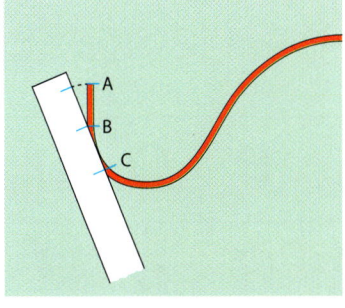

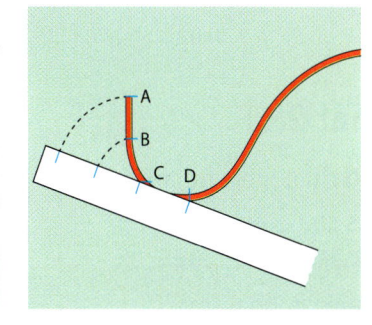

Figure 8.6 Measuring a curved-line distance on a map

Calculating area

Two types of area can be measured on an OS map:

- A regular-shaped area such as the actual map extract
- An irregular-shaped area such as an island, lake or mountain.

Geo fact
The side of each square on an OS map has a length of 1 kilometre.
Each square on an OS map has an area of 1 square kilometre (km^2).

To calculate the area of a map extract

1 Count the number of squares along the base of the map.

2 Count the number of squares along the vertical side of the map.

3 Multiply the two totals. This gives you the area of the map extract in square kilometres (km^2).

Example

Calculate the area of the map extract shown in Figure 8.7.

Number of grid squares along base of map = 5

Number of grid squares up the side of the map = 5

Total number of squares = 5 × 5 = 25

Area of map extract = 25 km^2

Figure 8.7 Measuring area

149

Section 2 · Maps and Photographs

To calculate the area of an irregular shape

1. Count all the complete squares.
2. Count each square where the shape covers half or more of its area. Ignore those squares where the shape takes up less than half its area.
3. Add the totals from steps 1 and 2 to find the total area in square kilometres (km^2).

Example

Calculate the area of the island in the map extract shown in Figure 8.7.

Number of complete squares = 5

Number of areas that take up half or more of a square = 4

Area of island = 5 + 4 = 9 km^2

Activity

Calculate the sea area in the map extract shown in Figure 8.7.

The National Grid

The **National Grid** covers Ireland and some of its sea areas. It consists of twenty-five squares called **sub-zones**, each named by a letter of the alphabet. Each sub-zone is 100 km by 100 km.

Finding location with grid references

The sides of each sub-zone are divided into 100 equal parts by a series of lines. These lines are called **co-ordinates** and are numbered from 00 to 99.

We use these co-ordinates together with the sub-zone letter to find a location on a map. This location is called a **grid reference**.

Grid references are made up of three parts (call them **LEN**).

- **L** refers to the sub-zone **Letter**.
- **E** refers to the **Easting**. This is the vertical line. Its value is read from left to right (going east) along either the base or top of the map.
- **N** refers to the **Northing**. It is the horizontal line. Its value is read from bottom to top (going north) along the sides of the map.

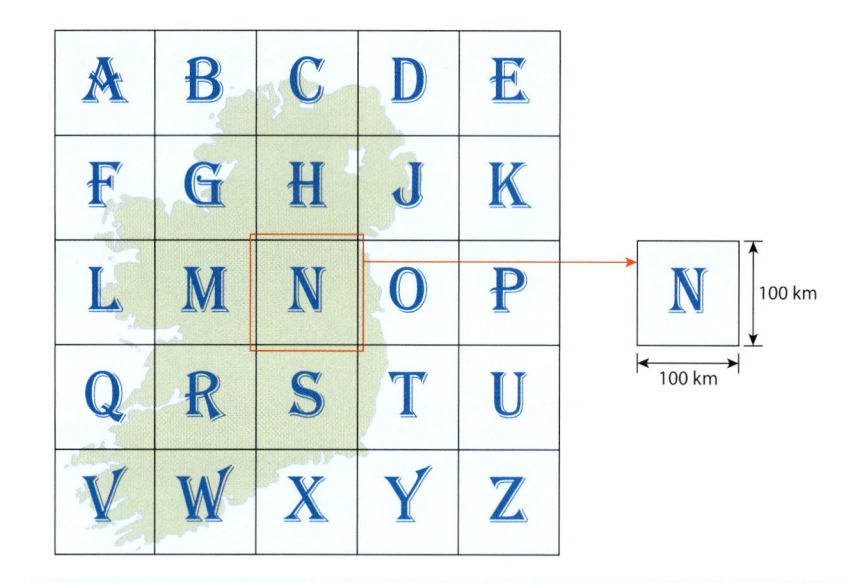

Figure 8.8 The National Grid

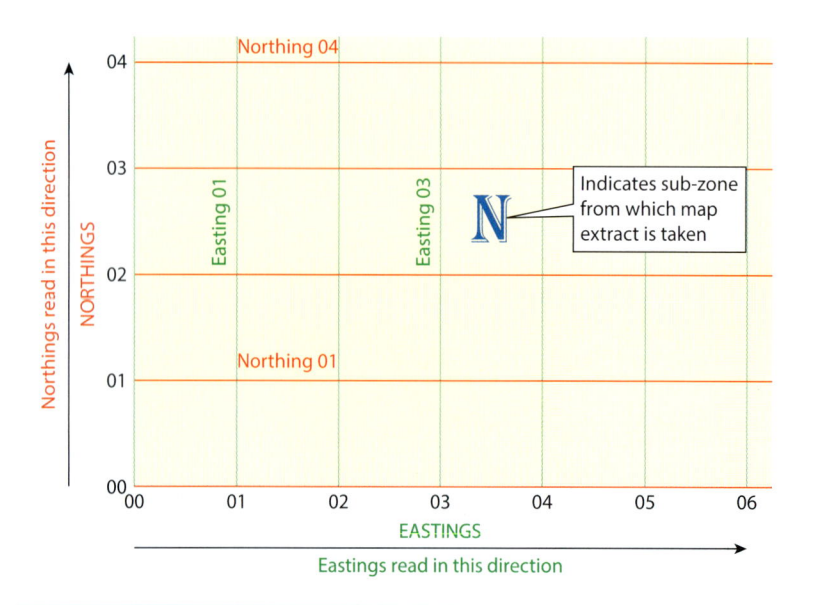

Figure 8.9 A grid reference consists of a sub-zone letter, an easting and a northing (LEN)

Chapter 8 · Maps and Photographs

Four-figure grid references

A **four-figure grid reference** will give you the location of any single **square** on the map. The easting and the northing each have two digits.

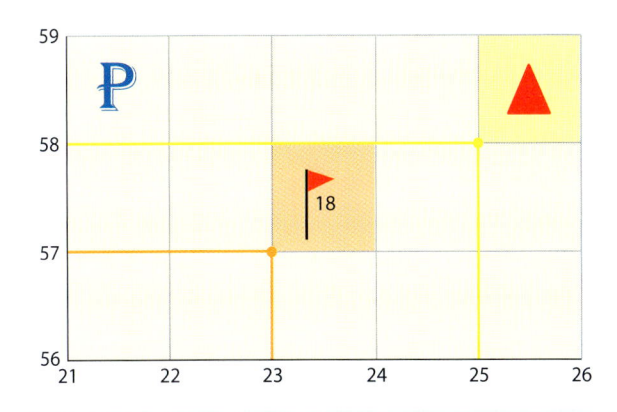

Figure 8.10 Four-figure grid references

Golf Course
Sub-zone:	P
Easting:	23
Northing:	57
Grid reference:	P 23 57

Hostel
Sub-zone:	P
Easting:	25
Northing:	58
Grid reference:	P 25 58

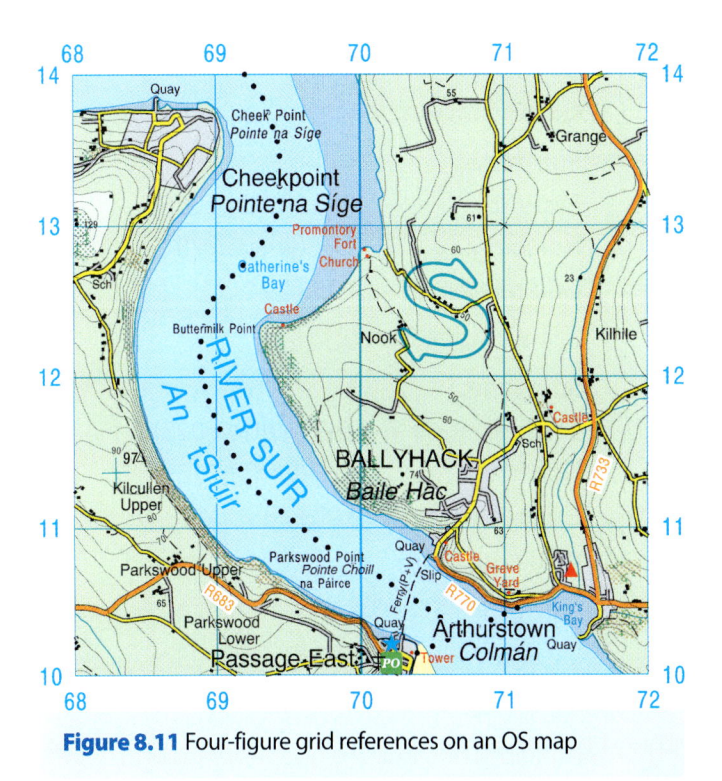

The following are examples of four-figure grid references from Figure 8.11.

Ballyhack
Sub-zone:	S
Easting:	70
Northing:	11
Grid reference:	S 70 11

Cheekpoint
Sub-zone:	S
Easting:	68
Northing:	13
Grid reference:	S 68 13

Figure 8.11 Four-figure grid references on an OS map

Activity

Examine Figure 8.11. Give a four-figure grid reference for:
- Passage East
- Arthurstown
- Buttermilk Point
- Promontory Fort.

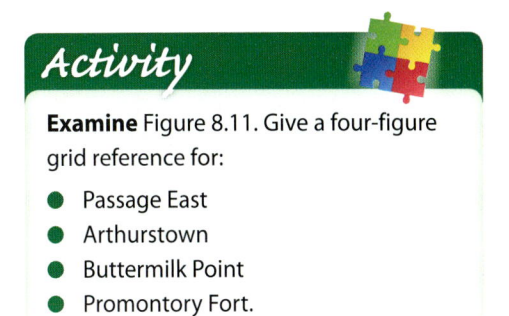

Hint

In a four-figure grid reference, the easting and northing cross at the bottom left corner of the square

151

Section 2 · Maps and Photographs

Six-figure grid references

A **six-figure grid reference** gives a more exact location than a four-figure grid reference. It refers to a definite point within a grid **square**.

Imagine that each side of the grid square is divided into ten equal parts, as in decimal measurement. This will then give a third digit for both the easting and the northing (see Figure 8.12).

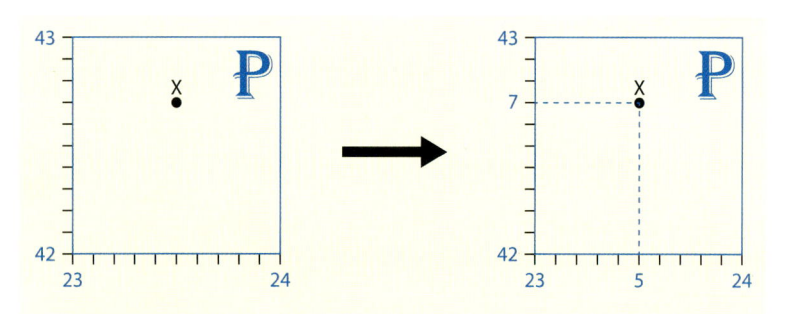

The sub-zone letter is **P**
The easting is **23.5**
The northing is **42.7**
Ignore the decimal point when writing the grid reference.
The six-figure grid reference for **X** is **P 235 427**.

Figure 8.12 Getting a six-figure grid reference

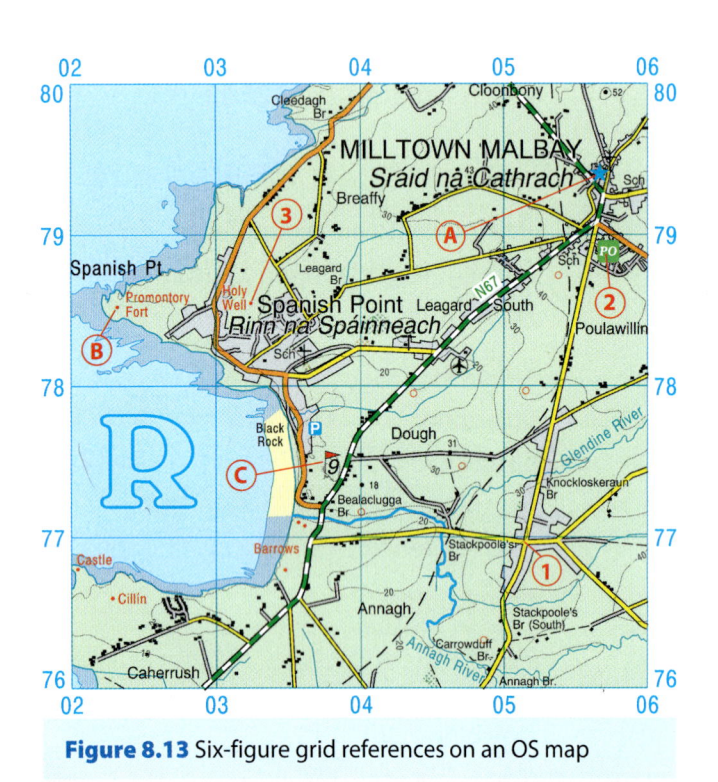

Figure 8.13 Six-figure grid references on an OS map

The following are examples of six-figure grid references from Figure 8.13.

Garda Station (A)

Sub-zone:	R
Easting:	05.6 (written 056)
Northing:	79.4 (written 794)
Grid reference:	R 056 794

Promontory Fort (B)

Sub-zone:	R
Easting:	02.3 (written 023)
Northing:	78.5 (written 785)
Grid reference:	R 023 785

Golf course (C)

Sub-zone:	R
Easting:	03.7 (written 037)
Northing:	77.5 (written 775)
Grid reference:	R 037 775

Activity

Examine Figure 8.13.

1 Give a six-figure grid reference for:
   - Crossroads (1)
   - Post office (2)
   - Holy Well (3).

2 Identify the feature at each of these six-figure grid references:
   - R 036 777
   - R 023 766
   - R 040 772

152

Chapter 8 · Maps and Photographs

Directions

Directions on a map are described by using **compass points**. The four main points of the compass – **north**, **east**, **south** and **west** – are called the **cardinal points**.

If the spaces between the cardinal points are divided, four more compass points are created. These are NE, SE, SW and NW.

A further division creates eight more minor compass points.

Activity

1. What do the letters NE, SE, SW and NW stand for?
2. What direction lies between:
   - E and NE?
   - SW and W?
   - N and NE?

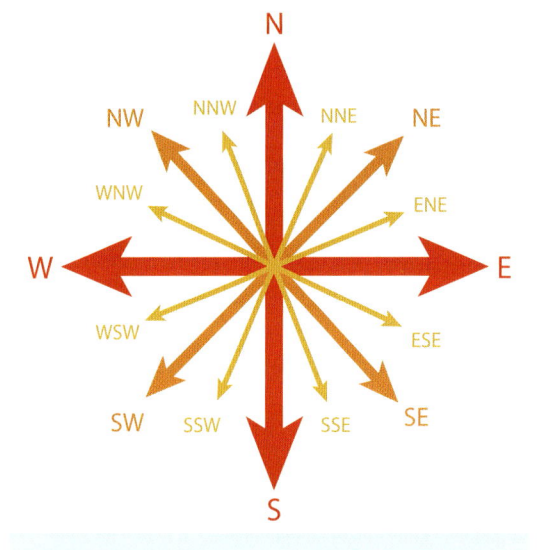

Figure 8.14 Points of the compass shown on a compass rose

The following are examples of directions from Figure 8.15.

- **A:** Rabbit Island lies to the **east** of the quay.
- **B:** The camping site lies to the **north** of Cribby Island.
- **C:** The R362 runs in a **north-easterly** direction.
- **D:** Rabbit Island lies to the **north-west** of the castle.

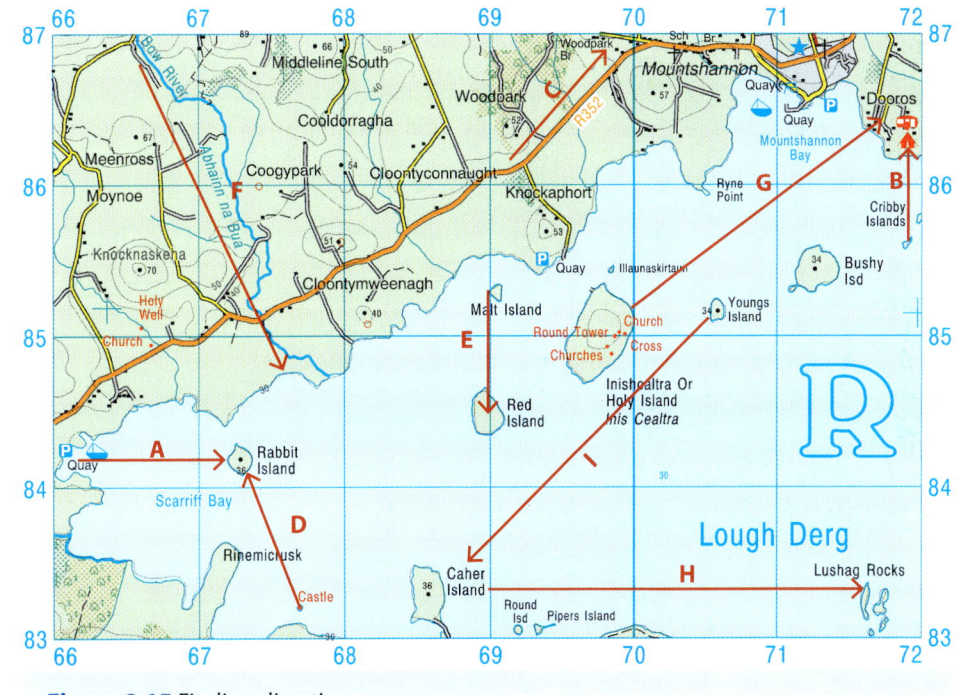

Figure 8.15 Finding direction on a map

Activity

Examine Figure 8.15 and fill in the blanks.

- **E:** Red Island lies to the _____ of Malt Island.
- **F:** Abhainn na Bua flows in a _____ direction.
- **G:** The caravan park lies to the _____ of Holy Island.
- **H:** Lushag Rocks lie to the _____ of Caher Island.
- **I:** Caher Island lies to the _____ of Youngs Island.

153

Section 2 · Maps and Photographs

Height

Height (or altitude) on an Ordnance Survey map is shown in **metres above sea level**.

Height is shown on a map in four ways:

1 Colour
2 Contours
3 Spot heights
4 Triangulation pillars.

Triangulation pillar on the summit of Nephin Mountain, Co. Mayo

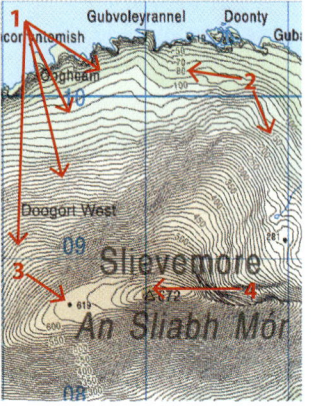

1 **Colour coding** gives a general picture of height. Different shades of green are used to show lowland areas under 200 metres in height. Cream indicates land between 200 and 300 metres. Next come various shades of brown, with the shade becoming darker as height increases.

2 **Contours** are **lines** on a map that join places of equal height. They are usually drawn at intervals of 10 metres. The height is written next to some of the contours.

3 **Spot heights** give the exact height of a point. They are shown on a map by a small **black dot** with the height of the ground at that point written next to it.

4 **Triangulation pillars** can be found at the top of a hill or mountain. They are shown on a map by a **black triangle** with the exact height of the ground at that point written next to them.

Figure 8.16 Showing height on an OS map

Slope

Slope is also called **gradient**. Changes in slope are identified by the spacing of the contours.

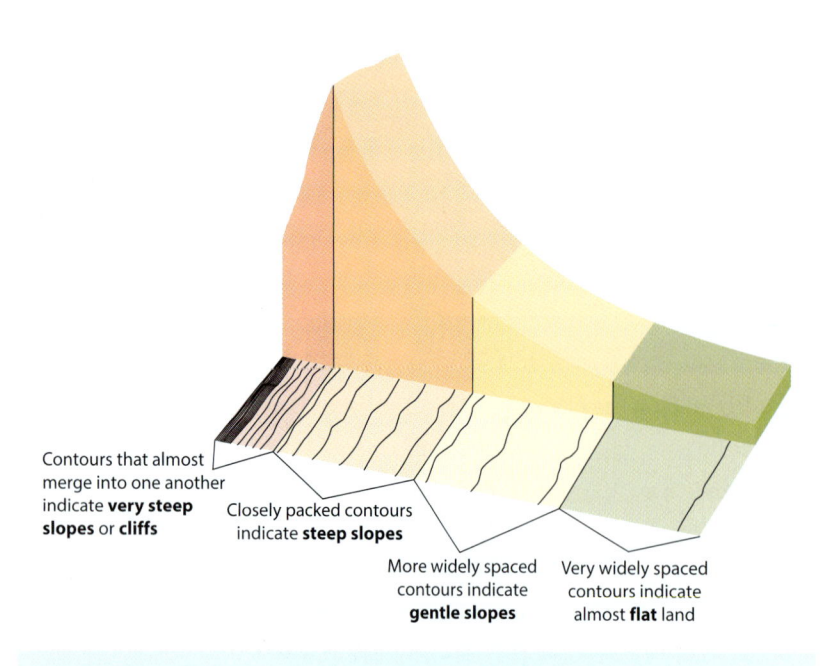

Contours that almost merge into one another indicate **very steep slopes** or **cliffs**
Closely packed contours indicate **steep slopes**
More widely spaced contours indicate **gentle slopes**
Very widely spaced contours indicate almost **flat** land

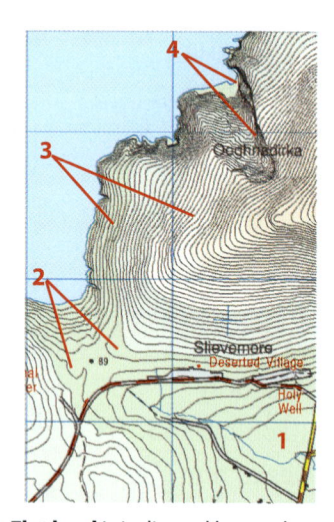

1 **Flat land** is indicated by an absence of contours.

2 **Gentle slopes** are indicated by contours that are widely spaced.

3 **Steep slopes** are indicated by contours that are closely packed together.

4 **Cliffs** are indicated by contours that are 'on top of one another'.

Figure 8.17 The spacing of contours gives an indication of how steep or gentle a slope is

Figure 8.18 Different slopes on an OS map

Types of slope

There are three types of slope. They can be identified by the pattern of the contours.

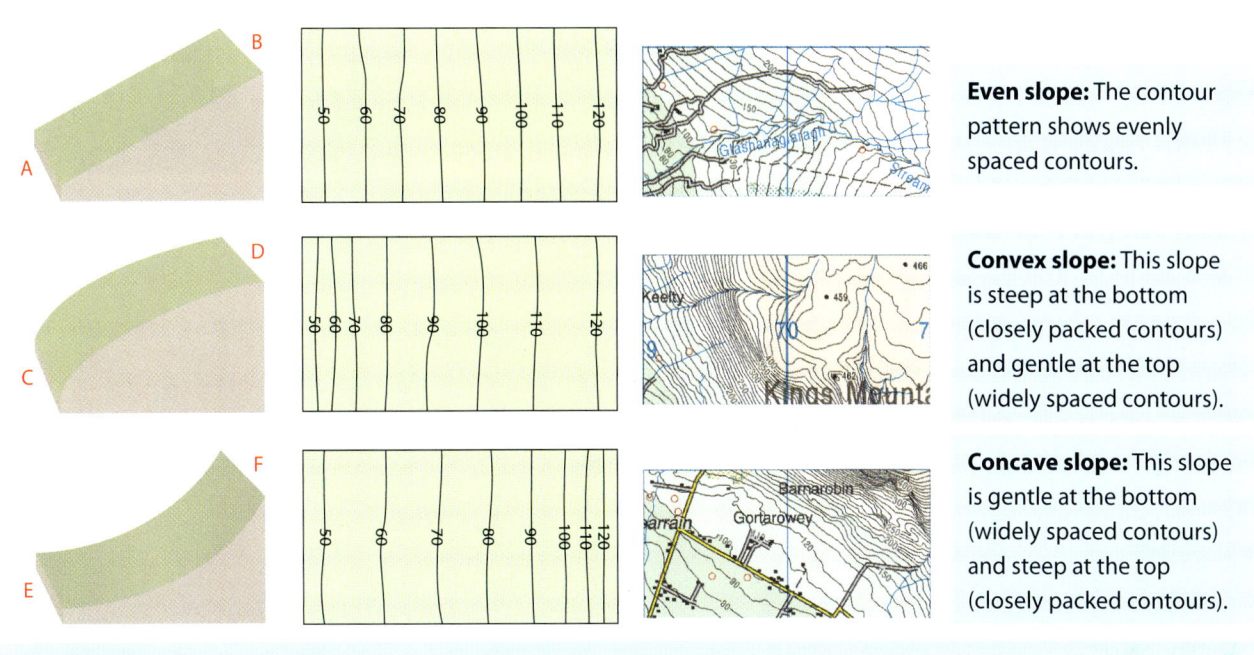

Even slope: The contour pattern shows evenly spaced contours.

Convex slope: This slope is steep at the bottom (closely packed contours) and gentle at the top (widely spaced contours).

Concave slope: This slope is gentle at the bottom (widely spaced contours) and steep at the top (closely packed contours).

Figure 8.19 We can identify the type of slope from the contour pattern

Calculating gradient

We can give a more accurate description of the slope by expressing it as a ratio. It is calculated as follows:

$$\frac{\text{The difference in height between any two points}}{\text{The distance between the points}}$$

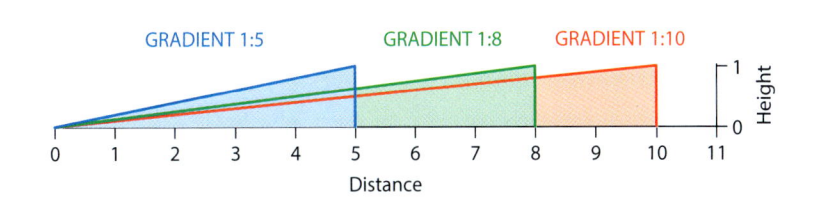

Figure 8.20 A gradient of 1:8 (1 in 8) means that the slope rises (or falls) by 1 unit for every 8 units travelled along the ground

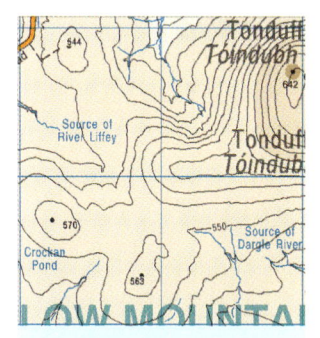

Figure 8.21 Calculating gradient

Example

Look at Figure 8.21. Calculate the average gradient between .642 and .563.

$$\frac{\text{Difference in height}}{\text{Distance between points}} = \frac{642 - 563 \text{ m}}{1.8 \text{ km}} = \frac{79 \text{ m}}{1,800 \text{ m}} = \frac{1}{22.8}$$

This can be written as 1 : 22.8 (there is a gradient of 1 in 22.8).

Activity

Calculate the average gradient between:
(a) .642 and .570
(b) .544 and .563.

Section 2 · Maps and Photographs

Cross-sections

A cross-section shows a section of landscape that is viewed from the side as if it was cut through with a knife. It gives us a very good idea of the general shape, height and slope of that section of landscape.

Cross-sections are usually drawn on **graph paper** from a line that links two points on a map.

Figure 8.22 A cross-section of a city skyline

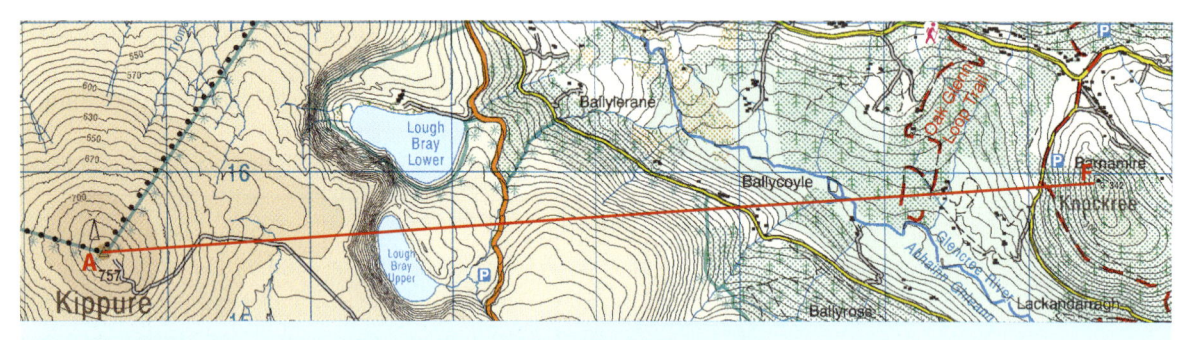

Figure 8.23 The cross-section below is drawn along the line from A to B

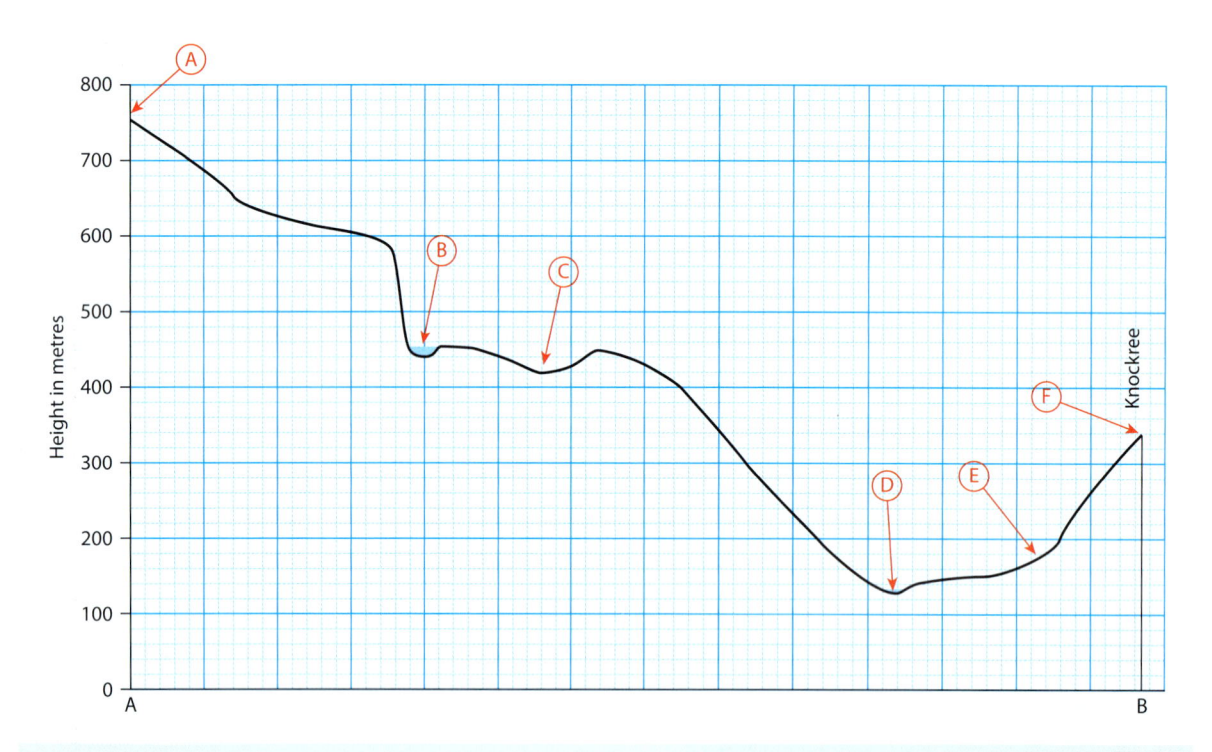

Figure 8.24 A cross-section drawn from A to F on the map extract above (Figure 8.23)

Activity

Examine the map **and** the cross-section above.
- Name the mountain peak at A.
- Name the lake at B.
- Name the road at C.
- Name the river at D.
- Name the type of vegetation at E.
- What is the height of the hilltop at F?

Drawing a sketch map

To draw an Ordnance Survey map extract follow these steps:

1 Always use **pencils**.
2 Draw a frame that is the **same shape** as the map extract. It may be smaller than the map extract.
3 Give the sketch a **title** and indicate **north** with a direction arrow.
4 Draw the **coastline** (if there is one on the map extract). Insert the features that you were asked for. Do not insert any extra features.
5 **Identify** each feature by name or by a legend or key.

Hint

In order to help you to position the features correctly, draw the sketch map on **graph paper**. Each square on the graph paper will correspond to a square on the map

Example

Draw a sketch map of the Millstreet area showing the following features:

- A river
- A named road
- The built-up area of Millstreet
- An area of land above 200 metres in height
- The railway
- An antiquity
- A tourist attraction.

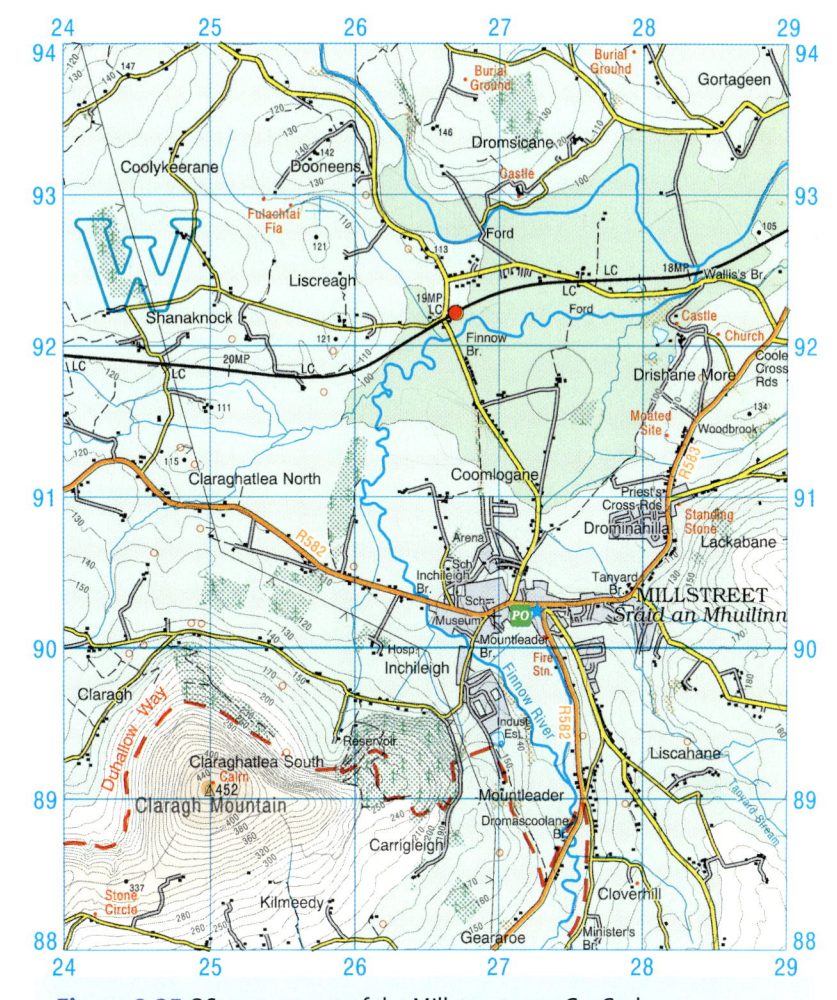

Figure 8.25 OS map extract of the Millstreet area, Co. Cork

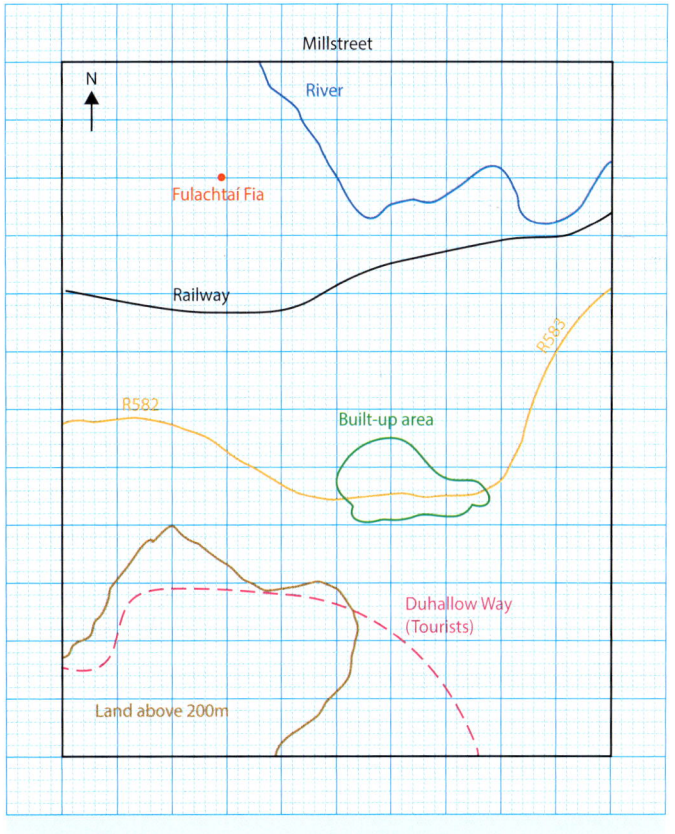

Figure 8.26 A sketch map of the Millstreet area

157

Section 2 · Maps and Photographs

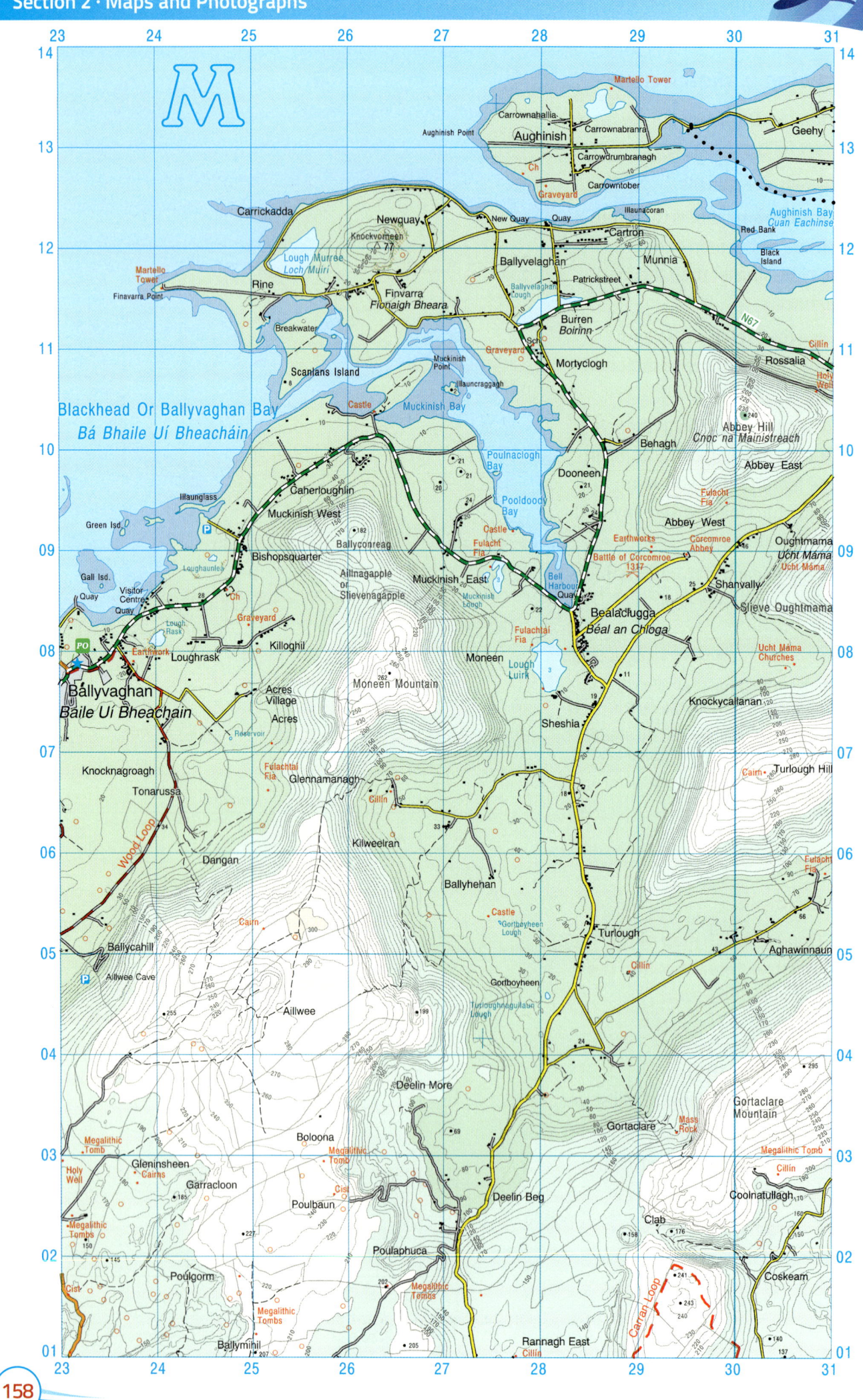

Chapter 8 · Maps and Photographs

Questions

1. Calculate the following distances:
   (a) The straight-line distance between the tops of Abbey Hill and Turlough Hill.
   (b) The straight-line distance between the post office at Ballyvaughan and the quay at Bealaclugga.
   (c) The distance along the N67 between the post office at Ballyvaughan and the quay at Bealaclugga.

2. Calculate the area of each of the following:
   (a) The full map extract
   (b) The area of sea shown on the map extract
   (c) The area of land on the map – using the information from (a) and (b) above.

3. Identify **one** feature at each of the following four-figure grid references:
   (a) M 30 06
   (b) M 29 03
   (c) M 24 11
   (d) M 26 01
   (e) M 23 04
   (f) M 28 13.

4. Give a four-figure grid reference for each of the following:
   (a) The quay at Bealaclugga
   (b) The summit of Abbey Hill
   (c) The car park at Aillwee Cave
   (d) Ballyvaughan
   (e) Green Island
   (f) Lough Luirk.

5. Identify the feature at each of the following six-figure grid references:
   (a) M 244 093
   (b) M 248 071
   (c) M 235 086
   (d) M 287 136
   (e) M 280 111
   (f) M 280 080.

6. Give a six-figure grid reference for each of the following:
   (a) The quay at Bealaclugga
   (b) The summit of Abbey Hill
   (c) The car park at Aillwee Cave
   (d) The cairn on the summit of Turlough Hill
   (e) A holy well
   (f) A castle along the coast.

7. (a) List **three** ways in which height is shown on this map extract.
   (b) What is the height of the highest contour shown on the map extract?

Opposite: **Figure 8.27** Ballyvaughan (also spelled Ballyvaghan) OS map extract, Co. Clare

Section 2 · Maps and Photographs

Chapter 8 · Maps and Photographs

Questions

1. True or false?
   (a) Freagh Hill lies to the north on the map.
   (b) An area of woodland is shown in the south-west of the map extract.
   (c) Brandon Hill lies to the south-east on the map.
   (d) The Leinster Way runs to the south of Mount Brandon.

2. Identify each of the following directions (all locations are hilltops, shown in brown):
   (a) Freagh Hill lies to the _____ of Coppanagh Hill.
   (b) Coppanagh Hill lies to the _____ of Brandon Hill.
   (c) Brandon lies to the _____ of Mount Alto.
   (d) Mount Alto lies to the _____ of Brandon Hill.
   (e) Brandon Hill lies to the _____ of Croghan.
   (f) Croghan lies to the _____ of Bishop's Hill.

3. (a) List **four** ways in which height is shown on this map extract.
   (b) What is the name and height of the highest point on the map?
   (c) Two hilltops have a height of 365 metres. Name them.
   (d) List **two** ways in which height is shown at each of these locations:
      (i) S 651 434
      (ii) S 621 345.

4. Select the correct answers from the brackets:
   (a) The higher slopes of Mount Brandon are (gentle / steep).
   (b) The slope in grid square S 63 45 is (gentler / steeper) than that in G 64 45.
   (c) The grid square with the gentlest slope in the map extract is (S 63 39 / S 63 45).
   (d) The slope in S 65 37 is (even / convex / concave).
   (e) The slope in S 64 42 is (even / convex / concave).
   (f) The slope in S 68 39 is (even / convex / concave).

5. Draw a sketch map of the area shown on the OS map. On it show and name:
   (a) The River Nore
   (b) The R703
   (c) The summit of Brandon
   (d) An area of land above 300 metres in height
   (e) The built-up area of Inistioge
   (f) A riverside parking area
   (g) A castle
   (h) An area of woodland.

Opposite: **Figure 8.28** Inistioge OS map extract, Co. Kilkenny

Section 2 · Maps and Photographs

8.2 Reading the physical landscape

KEYWORDS

- relief
- landform
- plateau
- gap
- ridge
- drainage
- river
- well drained
- marsh

By understanding colour, contours and gradient on OS maps, it is possible to identify different features of the physical landscape. These relate to **relief** and **drainage**.

Relief

Relief refers to the **shape of the physical landscape**. It includes references to:

- Height and slope (see page 154)
- Landforms or shapes in the landscape.

If you refer back to these maps, you will find that we have already identified some landforms on OS maps:

- Map showing fluvial (river) landforms (see page 53).
- Maps showing coastal landforms (see pages 60 and 63).
- Map showing glacial landforms (see page 70).

We can also identify a number of other relief features on an OS map.

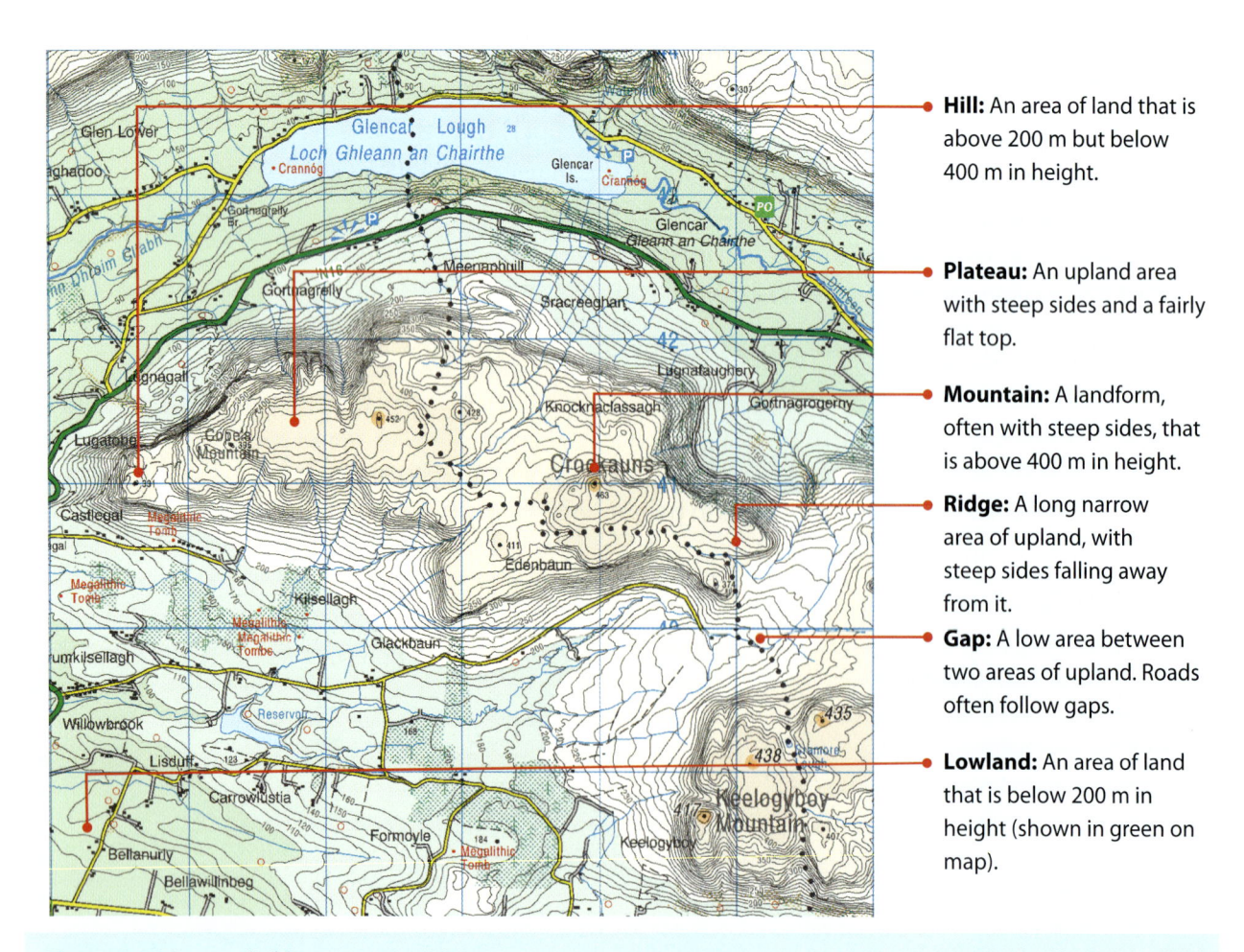

Hill: An area of land that is above 200 m but below 400 m in height.

Plateau: An upland area with steep sides and a fairly flat top.

Mountain: A landform, often with steep sides, that is above 400 m in height.

Ridge: A long narrow area of upland, with steep sides falling away from it.

Gap: A low area between two areas of upland. Roads often follow gaps.

Lowland: An area of land that is below 200 m in height (shown in green on map).

Figure 8.29 Some relief features on an OS map

Drainage

Drainage refers to the ways that water flows in the landscape. It includes **rivers**, **lakes** and **marshy areas**.

We can identify areas that are well drained or badly drained by the characteristics labelled in Figure 8.31 and Figure 8.32.

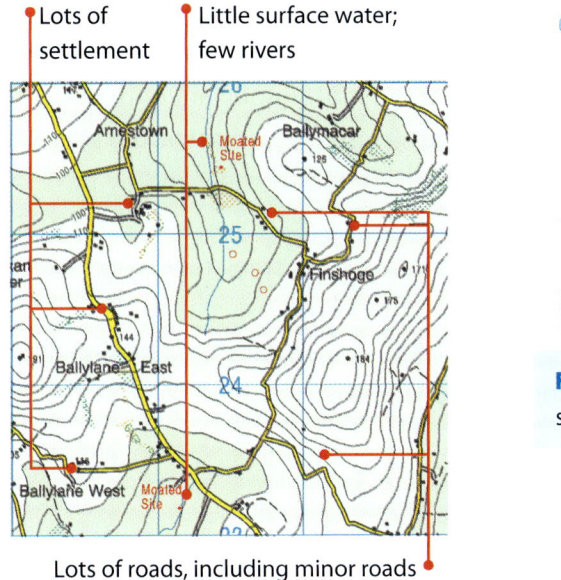

- Lots of settlement
- Little surface water; few rivers
- Lots of roads, including minor roads

Figure 8.30 Water symbols on an OS map

- Loch / Lake
- Canáil, canáil (thirim) / Canal, Canal (dry)
- Abhainn nó sruthán / River or Stream
- Líne bharr láin / High Water Mark
- Líne lag trá / Low Water Mark (shingle, mud sand or loose rock)

Figure 8.31 Evidence of a well-drained landscape

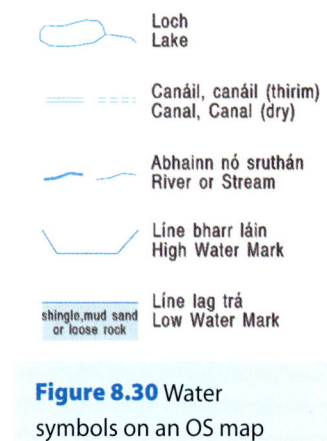

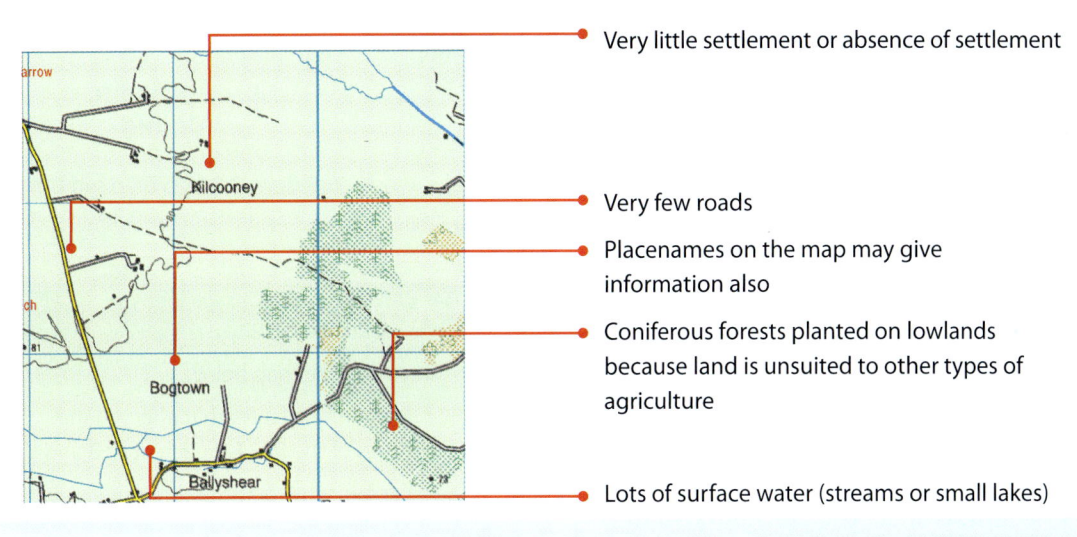

- Very little settlement or absence of settlement
- Very few roads
- Placenames on the map may give information also
- Coniferous forests planted on lowlands because land is unsuited to other types of agriculture
- Lots of surface water (streams or small lakes)

Figure 8.32 Evidence of a badly drained landscape

8.3 Reading the human landscape

KEYWORDS

- transport
- bridging point
- settlement
- ancient settlement
- rural settlement
- patterns of settlement
- nucleated settlement
- linear settlement
- dispersed settlement
- urban settlement
- urban functions
- land use

The **human landscape** refers to the changes that humans have made to the natural landscape. In particular it refers to:

- Transport
- Settlement
- Urban functions
- Land use.

163

Section 2 • Maps and Photographs

Transport

Transport on an OS map refers to **roads**, **railways**, **canals**, **ferries** and **airports**. The road network is by far the most important of these.

- **Motorways and national routes (primary and secondary)** link cities and large towns. The motorways are relatively new and by-pass towns rather than pass through them.
- **Regional roads and third-class roads** link small towns and villages as well as connecting them to the national routes.
- **Third-class roads and other roads** serve rural areas and link them to the more important routes listed above.

Influences on road network

1 **Few roads are built in upland areas.**
   - Very few people live in these areas so there is no need for roads.
   - The steep gradients make road building both difficult and expensive.
2 **Most roads are built in low-lying areas.**
   - Roads are built to serve people and most people live in low-lying areas.
   - The gentler gradients make road building easier.
   - Roads are often built to follow the contours at the foot of a hill, giving them a level course.
3 **Roads cut through mountains at their lowest point.**
   - Roads take the easiest and lowest route through mountains. This is along a valley floor or through a **gap**, again following the contours where possible.
4 **Roads are influenced by rivers.**
   - When roads follow a river valley, they are built at the **edge of the floodplain**, well back from the river, where possible. This is to avoid the risk of flooding.
   - Bridges are built where there is a need for a road to cross a river. These locations are called **bridging points**.

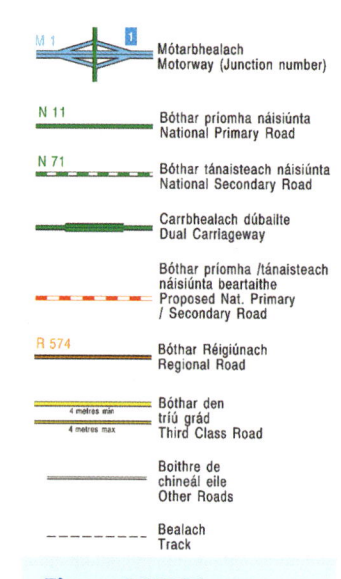

Figure 8.33 OS map symbols for the different classes of road

Figure 8.34 OS map symbols for airport and airfield

Activity

Examine the map below.
1 Explain one factor that affected the route of the R584 at each of **A**, **B** and **C**.
2 Explain why roads have not been built at **D** and **E**.

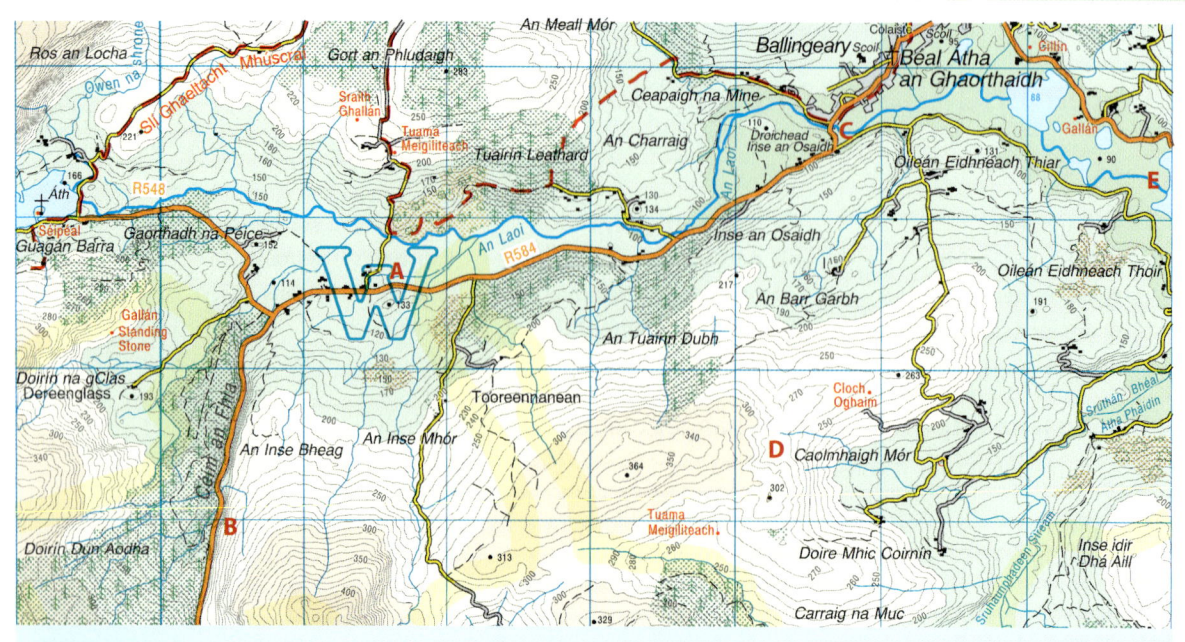

Figure 8.35 Road system in and around Ballingeary, Co. Cork

164

Settlement

A **settlement** is a place where people live. It can vary in size from a single house to a large city. The study of settlement can be divided into three sections:

- Ancient settlement
- Rural settlement
- Urban settlement.

Ancient settlement

Ancient settlements are places that are no longer occupied. They include historical sites and antiquities. Most are **shown** and **named in red** on Ordnance Survey maps. Others are identified by a **symbol**, also in red.

Examples of ancient settlement are shown in the table below.

Séadchomhartha
Ainmnithe
Named Antiquities

Clós, m.sh. Ráth nó Lios
Enclosure, e.g. Ringfort

Láthair Chatha (le dáta)
Battlefield (with date)

Figure 8.36 Symbols for antiquities on OS maps

Table 8.1 Ancient settlements, listed by period of history and function

Period	Function	Examples
Pre-Christian	Defence	Fort, Dún, Rath, Lios, Crannóg, Enclosures (O)
	Burial places	Standing stone (gallaun), Ogham stone, Megalithic tomb, Cairn, Dolmen, Barrow, Mound
	Domestic	Fulacht fia, Midden
	Worship	Bullaun stone, Standing stone (gallaun), Stone circle, Stone row
Christian	Defence	Round tower
	Religion	Holy well, Cill, Church, Abbey, Monastery
	Burial	High cross, Cross base, Graveyard
Norman and Plantation	Defence	Castle, Town wall, Motte, Moat(ed site)
	Religion	Friary, Monastery, Mass rock
	Residential	House, Demesne, Placenames ending in –*town*

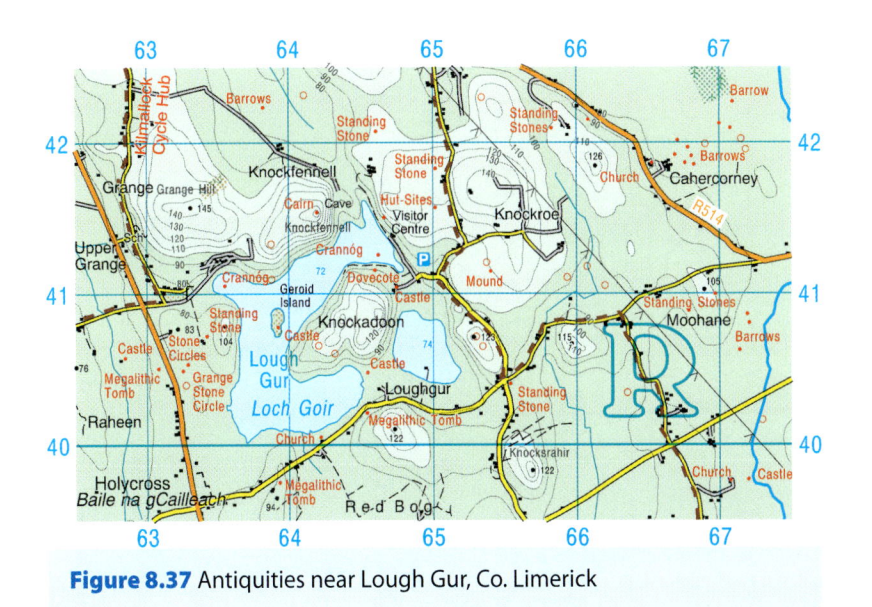

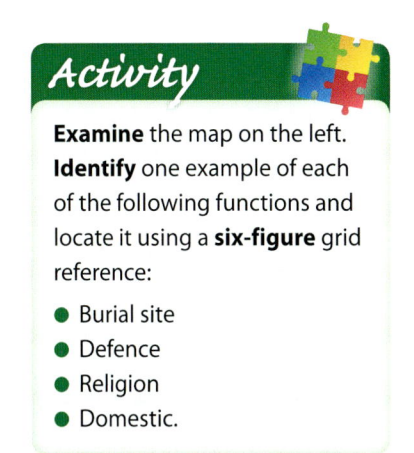

Figure 8.37 Antiquities near Lough Gur, Co. Limerick

Activity

Examine the map on the left. **Identify** one example of each of the following functions and locate it using a **six-figure** grid reference:

- Burial site
- Defence
- Religion
- Domestic.

Section 2 · Maps and Photographs

Rural settlement

The **location** and **density** of rural settlement is influenced by a number of factors. When people first decided where to settle, they were attracted by some **physical factors** and put off by others.

Altitude

Most people live on land that is **below 200 metres** in Ireland (green on an OS map). Above 200 metres, the weather can be too cold, too wet and too windy to attract settlement. Soils in upland areas tend to be thin and infertile, making them difficult for agriculture.

Slope

People are attracted to **flat or gently sloping land**. The soil is usually very **fertile**, making it attractive for agriculture. It is also easier to build houses and roads. Steep slopes have poor soil and are difficult to build on and use machinery on.

Shelter

Settlement tends to develop in areas that are **sheltered** from the worst effects of winds. These locations include **valley floors** and the foot (bottom) of a hill or mountain. Settlement along the coast tends to be located near **harbours**.

Drainage

People prefer to settle in areas that are well drained. Poorly drained land is likely to flood or be marshy and, as a result, may not be suitable for agriculture.

Aspect

The direction in which a settlement faces is called its **aspect**. South-facing slopes attract settlement because they get more sunshine and are warmer than north-facing slopes (see Figure 6.4, page 114).

> **Definition**
>
> **Population density** on an OS map refers to the number of houses (shown by black squares) per km^2.

Clonmacnoise is an ancient monastic site in Co. Offaly that was founded almost 1,500 years ago

> **Activity**
>
> **Examine** the photograph above. List three pieces of evidence that indicate that Clonmacnoise is an ancient religious settlement.

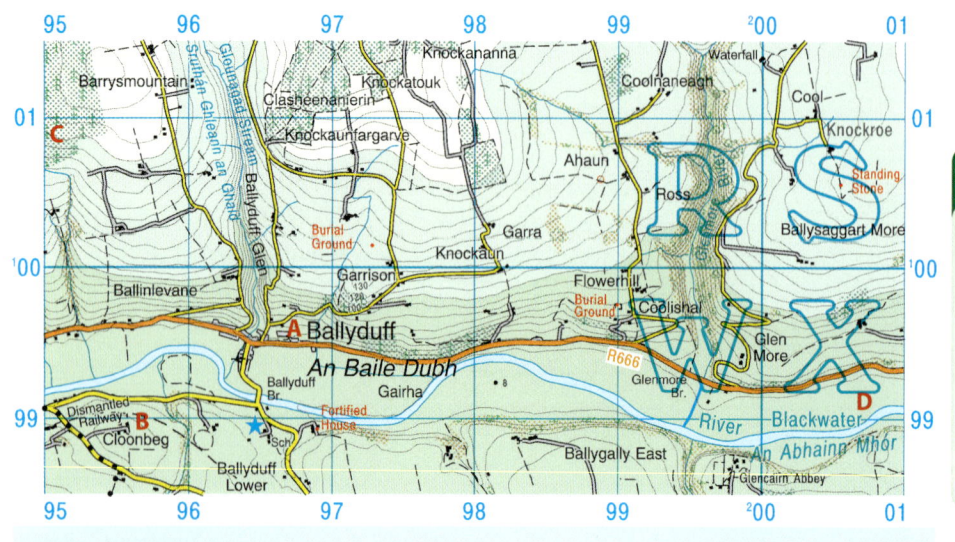

Figure 8.38 Influences on rural settlement

> **Activity**
>
> **Examine** Figure 8.38.
>
> 1. What factors have attracted settlement to A and B?
> 2. Explain why there is an absence of settlement at C and D.

Patterns of rural settlement

There are three patterns of rural settlement:

- Nucleated settlement
- Linear settlement
- Dispersed settlement.

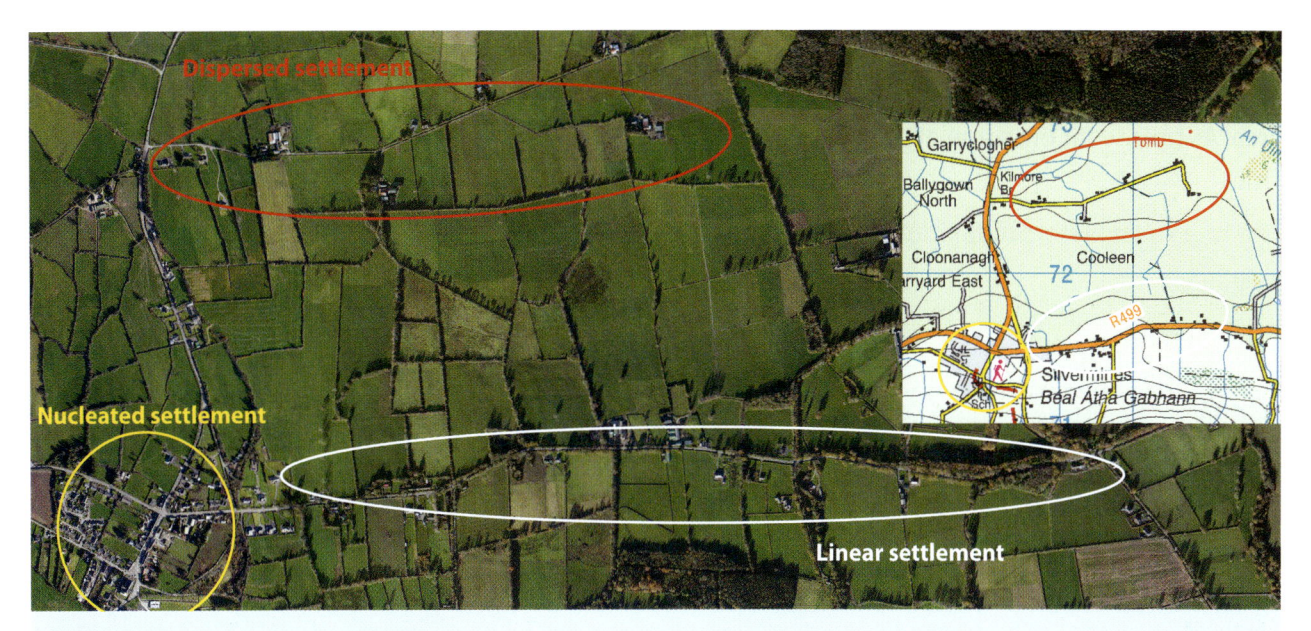

Figure 8.39 Rural settlement patterns

Nucleated settlement

In nucleated settlements houses are **clustered** together in groups. This generally happens at a small village or at a point where roads meet.

Linear settlement

Linear settlement can also be called **ribboned** settlement. Houses are built **in a line** along a road. This pattern is usually found along a coastline, at the foot of a mountain or at the edge of a village or town.

Dispersed settlement

In dispersed settlement **individual houses** are scattered around the countryside in a random pattern. Many are **farmhouses**, each on their own farm and with their own outbuildings. Others are **one-off houses**.

Section 2 · Maps and Photographs

Urban settlement

Urban settlement refers to **cities**, **towns** and **large villages**. These are built-up areas where the buildings are grouped closely together. Built-up areas are identified on an OS map by the grey-coloured symbol in Figure 8.40.

Figure 8.40 Symbol for a built-up area on an OS map

Location and development of urban settlements

Location refers to the place where an urban settlement is built, as well as its surrounding area. As time went on, some of these settlements grew or **developed** into large towns and cities.

The four main factors that influence the development of urban settlements are:

- Relief
- Drainage
- Transport
- Coast.

Urban settlement is influenced by relief

Most towns developed on flat or gently sloping lowland areas.

- The **construction** of roads and buildings was easier and cheaper.
- The surrounding area was more likely to have fertile agricultural land to supply food, and enable the town to become a **market centre**.

Urban settlement is influenced by rivers

Most towns developed near rivers.

- In times past, rivers were used for water supply and **transport**.
- Rivers provided **defence** from attack.
- Towns developed at places where bridges could be built (**bridging points**).

Good transport links allow trade to develop

Towns developed where:

- A number of roads met (**route focus**)
- The town was on a **rail** route (with a railway station)
- The town had a **canal** link (look for locks).

Definition ✓
Route focus: Where several roads meet, e.g. at a bridging point.

A coastal location attracts water-based activities

Towns developed on the coast because:

- Sheltered harbours enabled them to develop as **ports** (trade and fishing)
- They were able to provide **tourist attractions** such as beaches and scenery.

Chapter 8 · Maps and Photographs

Case study

Location of Ballina

Why did the town of Ballina develop at that location?

Relief and drainage

- Ballina is built on **very gently sloping land** between the 20 metre contour and sea level. This made the construction of roads and buildings easier.
- Ballina is surrounded by land that is gently-sloping and low-lying (below 50 metre contour). The town may have served as a **market centre** for agricultural produce.

Transport

- Ballina is built at a **bridging point** on the River Moy. The river becomes too wide to cross below the two bridges.
- Ballina is a **route focus**. It developed at the meeting point of several roads, including the N26, N59, R314 and R294. This enabled trade to develop.
- A **railway line** runs to Ballina, with the railway station at G 241 183. This enabled the town to continue to grow.

> **Hint**
>
> When explaining something on an OS map, always use some evidence (names, grid reference, etc.) taken directly from the map.

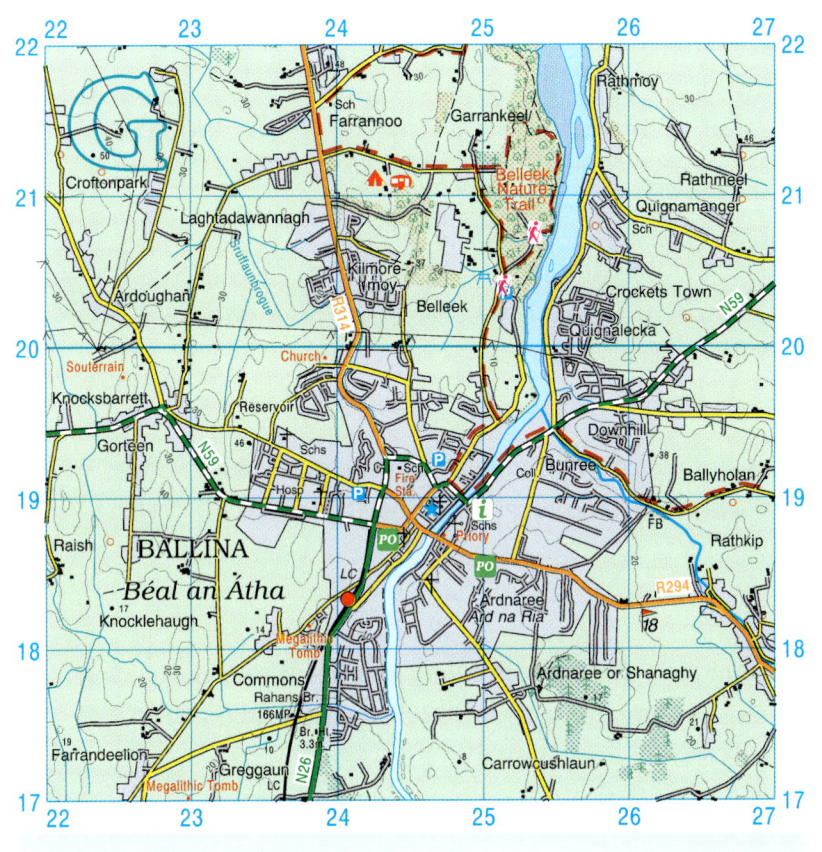

Figure 8.41 Location of Ballina, Co. Mayo

169

Section 2 · Maps and Photographs

Urban functions on OS maps

The term **function** refers to the **services and activities** that the town provides for the people who live or work there or in the surrounding area.

Most Irish towns have several functions. Many can be identified by the symbols on the OS map. A wide range of functions attracts people and helps the town to develop.

Table 8.2 Present-day functions of urban areas

Function	Map evidence
Industrial	• Is there an industrial estate in or near the town? • Are any raw materials available locally?
Transport	• What roads meet in the town? • Is there a railway and railway station? • Are there car parks in the town?
Port	• Is the harbour deep and sheltered? • Are there piers, quays or lighthouses?
Tourist	• What attractions in or around the town would encourage people to visit and stay? • For more details, see **Tourism and leisure**, pages 173 and 174.
Educational	• Is there a range of schools and colleges? • Is there a university?
Religious	• Is there a cathedral, as well as a number of churches?
Medical	• Is there a hospital in or near the town?
Residential	• Are there residential suburbs on the outskirts of the town?
Recreational	• Is there a golf course, stadium or park?

Some functions are not shown on a map but we can assume that they are present in most towns. They include **retail** (shops), **commercial** (offices) and **financial** (banks).

Functions change over time

Functions may change over time, and a function that was once very important may no longer be relevant. These former functions include **defence** and **ecclesiastical**. In many cases, evidence for these former functions is shown on OS maps.

Table 8.3 Former functions of urban areas

Function	Map evidence
Defence	• Is there a castle, tower, town wall or town gate?
Ecclesiastical	• Is there an abbey, round tower, priory, monastery or friary?

Chapter 8 · Maps and Photographs

Case study

Urban functions of Drogheda

Figure 8.42 Urban functions of Drogheda, Co. Louth

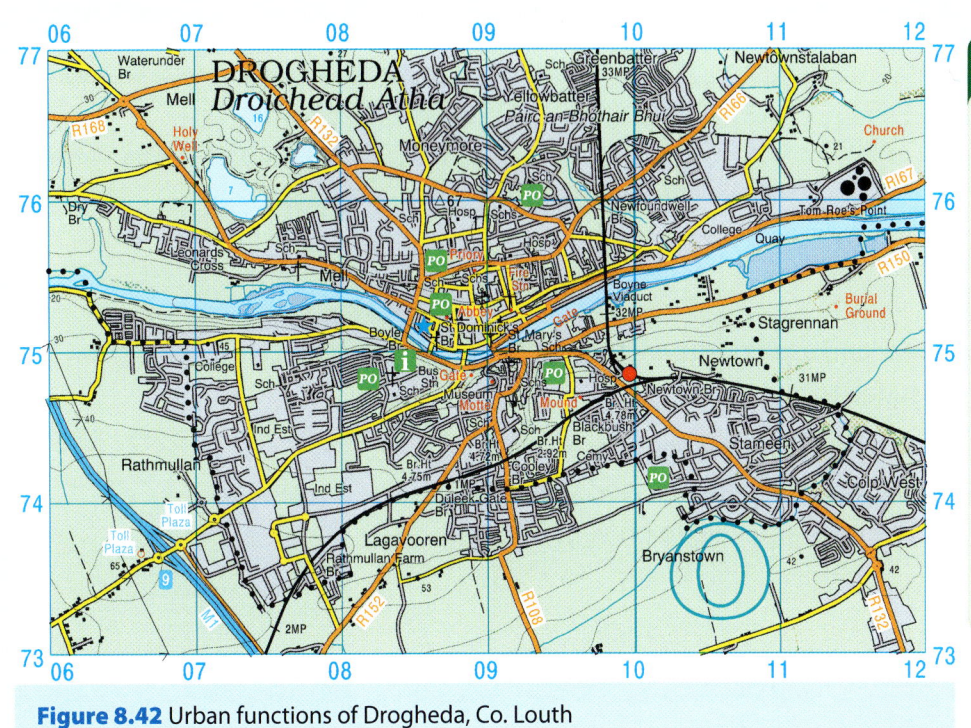

Activity

Examine the OS map on the left. **Identify** and **locate** by grid reference:

(a) Two functions of Drogheda that have not been listed in the case study.

(b) Any four pieces of map evidence that show that Drogheda has a tourist function.

Table 8.4 Some present-day functions of Drogheda

Function	Map evidence
Industrial	• Two industrial estates
Transport	• Motorway (M1), national roads (N51), regional roads (R152, R166) • Railway junction and station • Bus station
Tourist	• Tourist information office • Wide range of antiquities (motte, gate, etc.) • Youth hostel • Museum
Educational	• Several schools and colleges
Residential	• Residential estates (Newtown, Yellowbatter, etc.)

Table 8.5 Some past functions of Drogheda

Function	Map evidence
Defence	• Motte, gates, mound
Ecclesiastical	• Priory, abbey

171

Section 2 · Maps and Photographs

Land use

Land use refers to **the way in which people use land**. We have already studied two land uses: settlement and communications. We can identify or interpret a number of other land uses, including:

- Forestry
- Agriculture
- Bogs
- Industry
- Tourism and leisure.

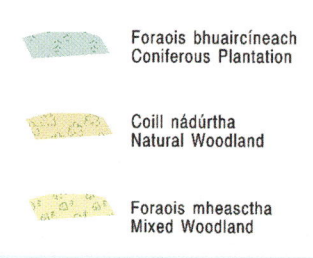

Figure 8.43 Forestry symbols on an OS map

- Foraois bhuaircíneach Coniferous Plantation
- Coill nádúrtha Natural Woodland
- Foraois mheasctha Mixed Woodland

Forestry

Forestry is rarely the preferred land use. Forests are usually planted on land that is not suited to agriculture.

Coniferous forests are planted on upland slopes. These areas are unsuited to agriculture because the gradient is too steep and the soil quality is poor. The trees also help to prevent soil erosion.

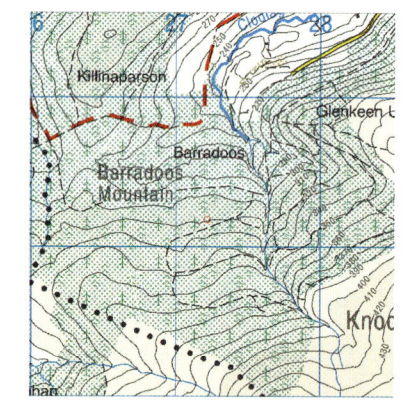

Coniferous forests are also planted on lowland areas where the land is poorly drained. The marshy land is likely to flood and is unsuited to agriculture. The trees also absorb much of the excess moisture.

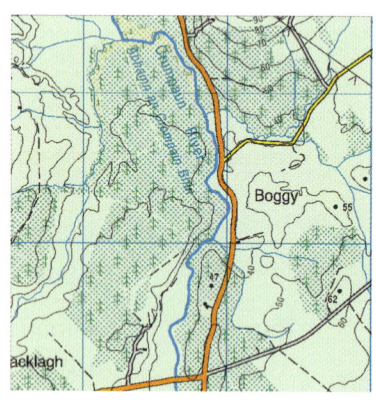

Natural woodland (deciduous trees) and **mixed woodland** are mainly associated with country estates and demesnes. They were often planted for privacy and to enhance the scenery. Many date back to the time of the **plantations**.

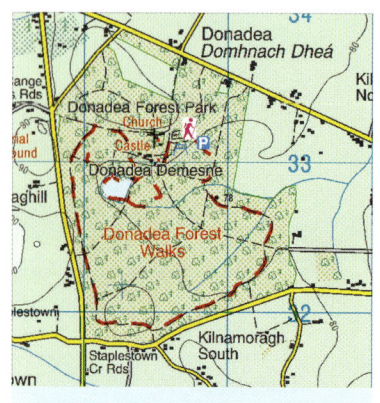

Figure 8.44 Forested areas as shown on OS maps

Agriculture

Agriculture is the main land use in Ireland. It is not shown on OS maps, but we can deduce its presence.

Most agriculture takes place in **lowland** areas that are **well drained**. Dispersed rural settlements, especially when the houses are set back from main roads, are usually **farmhouses** with their outbuildings. See Figure 8.39 on page 167.

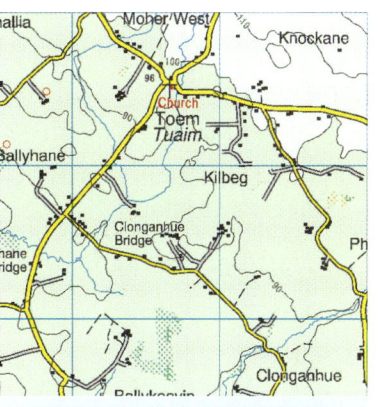

Figure 8.45 Agricultural land as implied on OS maps

Bogs

Raised bogs are deep, level bogs that are found in the Midlands of Ireland. They contain peat up to a depth of about seven metres.

The area is very **flat** (absence of contours). Much of the area does not have any settlement. Part of the area may be planted with **coniferous forests**. Some **names** may also give information.

In Figure 8.46, note also the railway that is used to transport milled peat.

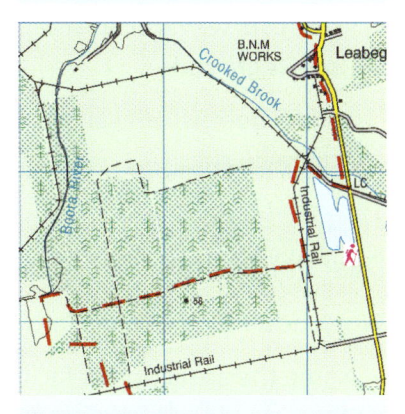

Figure 8.46 Bogland as shown on OS maps

Industry

Many towns have **industrial estates**. These are usually located at the edge of the town. They are nearly always located next to **good transport links**.

Tourism and leisure

A wide range of tourist attractions and leisure facilities can be seen on Ordnance Survey maps. Many of them are identified on the legend by **symbols**.

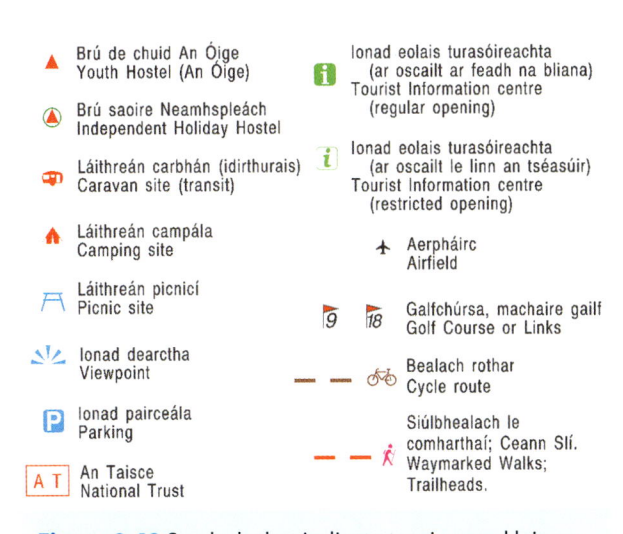

- ▲ Brú de chuid An Óige Youth Hostel (An Óige)
- Brú saoire Neamhspleách Independent Holiday Hostel
- Láithreán carbhán (idirthurais) Caravan site (transit)
- Láithreán campála Camping site
- Láithreán picnici Picnic site
- Ionad dearctha Viewpoint
- P Ionad pairceála Parking
- AT An Taisce National Trust
- Ionad eolais turasóireachta (ar oscailt ar feadh na bliana) Tourist Information centre (regular opening)
- Ionad eolais turasóireachta (ar oscailt le linn an tséasúir) Tourist Information centre (restricted opening)
- Aerpháirc Airfield
- Galfchúrsa, machaire gailf Golf Course or Links
- Bealach rothar Cycle route
- Siúlbhealach le comharthaí; Ceann Slí. Waymarked Walks; Trailheads.

Figure 8.48 Symbols that indicate tourism and leisure facilities on OS maps

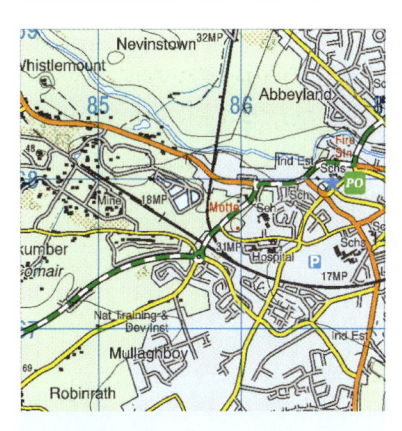

Figure 8.47 Industry on an OS map

Link
See also **Factory location** on page 362.

Activity

Examine Figure 8.47. Apart from the industrial estates, can you find any other evidence that suggests that the town has an industrial function?

Section 2 · Maps and Photographs

Table 8.6 Tourism and leisure on OS maps

Feature	Activities/Attraction
Mountains	Scenery, hill walking, rock climbing
Rivers and lakes	Sailing, canoeing, fishing, scenery
Coast/beaches/harbours	Boating, swimming, fishing, windsurfing, sunbathing, playing on beach
Forests	Forest parks, nature trails, picnic sites, walking
Nature reserves	Wildlife, plants, scenery, bird-watching
Antiquities/demesnes	Visiting historic attractions, interest in history
Golf courses/racecourses/sports grounds	Playing sports, watching sports
Youth hostels/caravan parks/camping sites	Accommodation while visiting

Describing tourist attractions

When describing a tourist attraction or leisure facility:

1 Name the attraction or facility.
2 Locate it using a grid reference.
3 Explain why it is attractive to tourists and what activities it could be used for.

Figure 8.49 Tourist attractions in and around Rosses Point, Co. Sligo

Activity

Can you **name** and **locate**, using six-figure grid references, any five tourist attractions in the Rosses Point area?

Placenames

Placenames on an OS map can give information about the physical or the human landscape.

While most placenames were originally Gaelic, some have English, Norman or Viking origins. When we know the meaning of the original root word, we can understand the origin of many placenames.

Table 8.7 Placenames with Gaelic root words

Root word	Meaning	Examples
Áth	Crossing point of a river	Athlone, Athy, Baile Átha Cliath
Cnoc	Hill	Knock, Knockree
Carraig	Rock	Carrick-on-Suir, Carrigaline
Drum/Drom	Hill	Drumcliffe, Drumcondra
Gleann	Glen/valley	Glendalough, Glenmore, Glencar
Loch	Lake	Loughrea, Lochbeg
Port	Harbour/landing place	Portmarnock, Portlaw, Portumna
Trá	Beach	Tramore, Tralee
Baile	Small town/townland	Ballybunion, Ballyshannon
Cill	Church	Kilkenny, Killarney
Dún	Fort	Dunmore, Dungarvan
Lios	Fort	Lismore, Liscannor
Rath	Fort	Rathgar, Rathmore

Table 8.8 Some placenames with non-Gaelic root words

Root word	Meaning	Examples
Castle–	Defensive site	Castlebar, Castlecomer
–town	Plantation town/estate	Rochestown, Grantstown
–land	Land given during plantations	Archersland, Butlersland
–ford	Inlet	Waterford, Wexford

Section 2 · Maps and Photographs

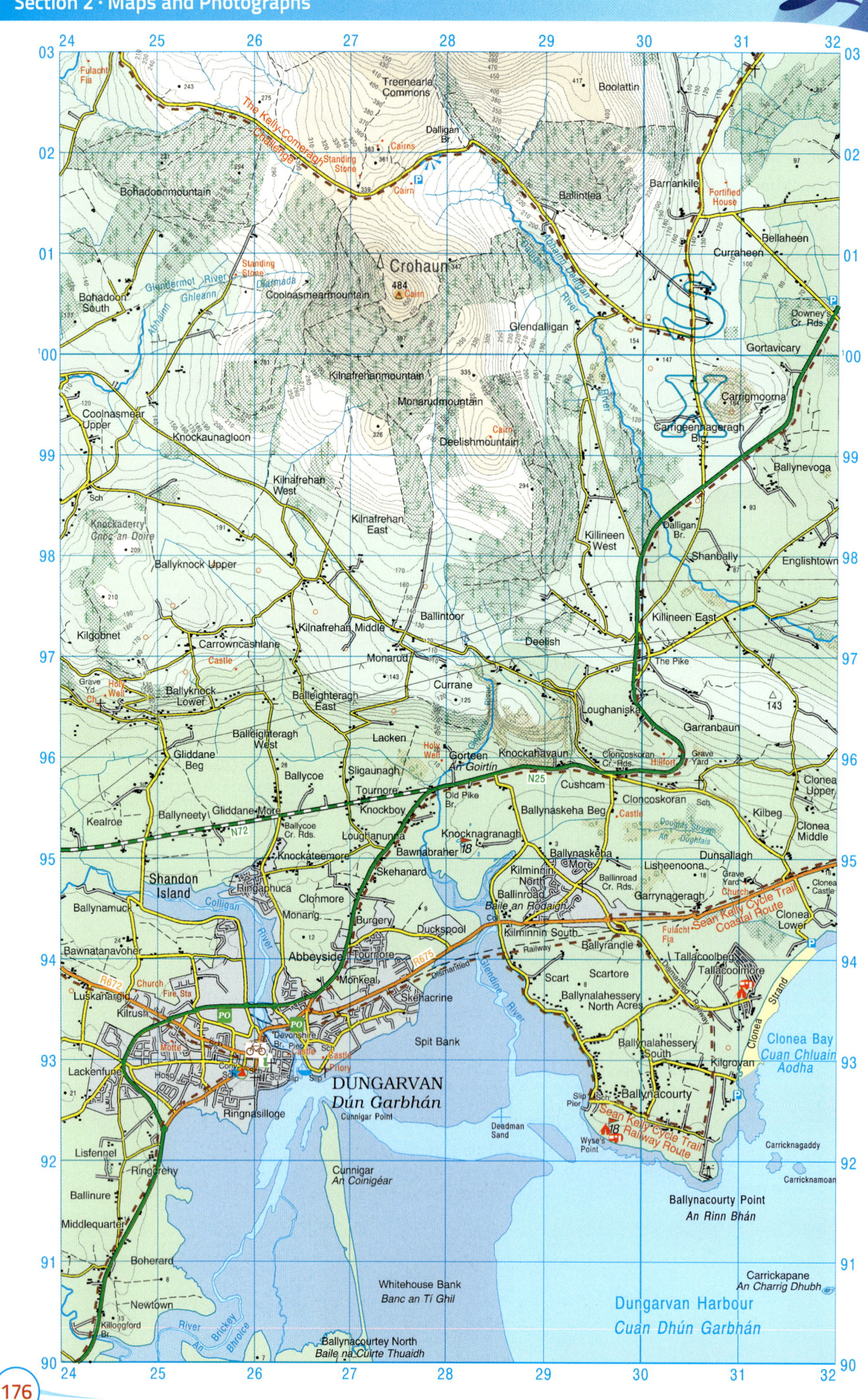

Chapter 8 · Maps and Photographs

Questions

Examine the OS map extract on the left and answer the questions that follow.

Section 8.2

1. Identify the coastal features at the following grid references:
   (a) X 31 93
   (b) X 26 91

2. Give a four-figure grid reference for each of the following river features: young (V-shaped valley), meander, flood plain.

3. Link each of the following to one of the four-figure grid references that follow: mountain, hill, gap, lowland.
   (a) X 28 99
   (b) S 27 01
   (c) X 30 96
   (d) S 27 00

4. What map evidence suggests that the land at X 28 97 is badly drained?

Section 8.3

1. What is the main form of transport in the area shown on the map?
   Name **three** different examples of this type of transport.

2. Why is there an absence of transport at grid references S 26 00 and S 27 00?

3. Name and locate by a six-figure grid reference **one** example of each of the following types of ancient settlement: (a) burial, (b) defence, (c) religion/worship, and (d) domestic.

4. Identify and describe the pattern of rural settlement at each of the following locations:
   (a) X 30 92
   (b) X 31 93
   (c) X 31 99

5. Suggest **two** reasons why there is an absence of settlement at S 26 00.

6. Describe **three** reasons why Dungarvan developed at this location.

7. Identify and describe any **two** former functions of Dungarvan. Use map evidence to support your answer.

8. Identify and describe any **two** current functions of Dungarvan. Use map evidence to support your answer.

9. Dungarvan and the area that surrounds it have a wide range of tourist and leisure facilities. Identify and describe any **two** of them. Use map evidence to support your answer.

Opposite: **Figure 8.50** Dungarvan OS map extract, Co. Waterford

Section 2 · Maps and Photographs

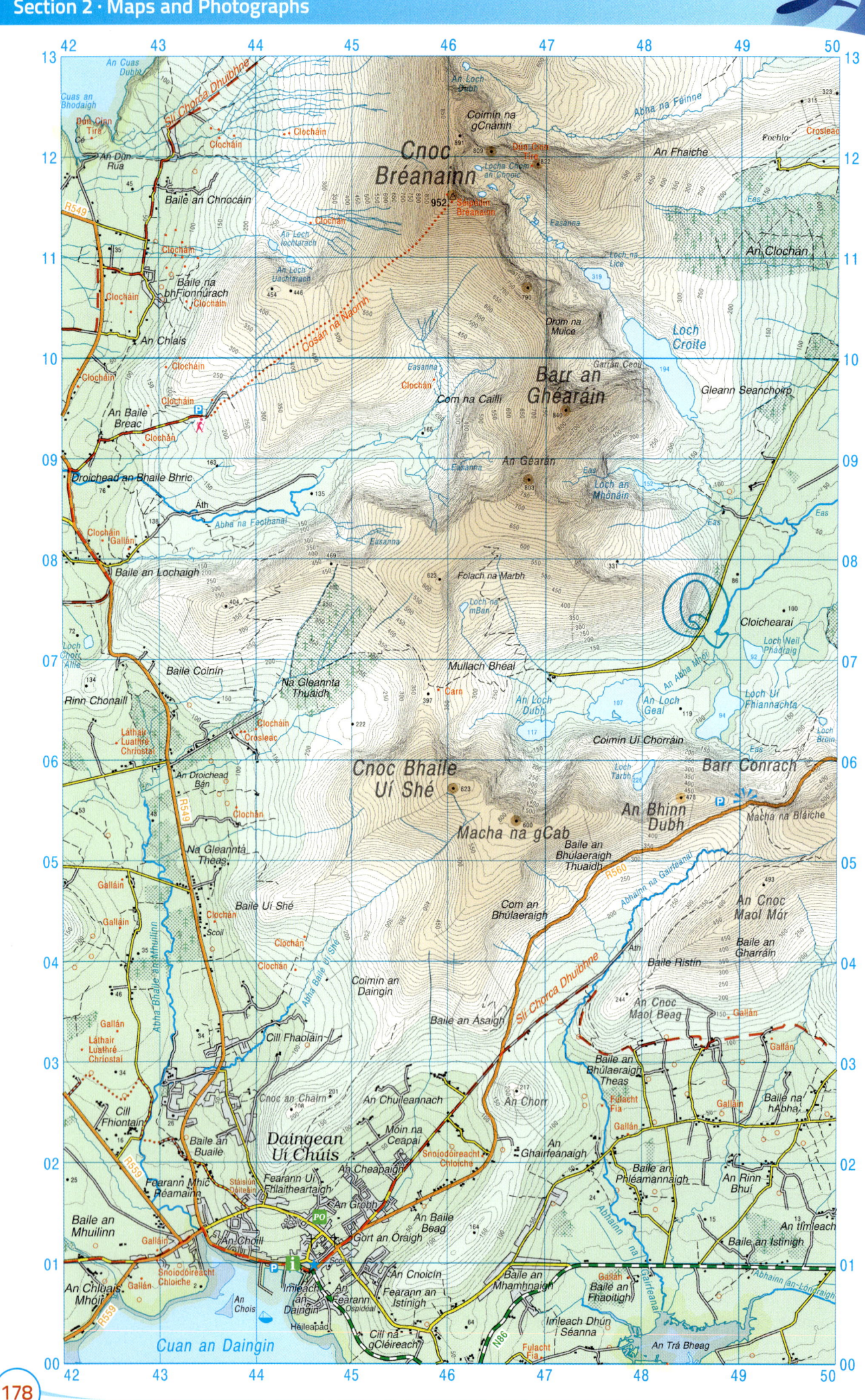

Chapter 8 · Maps and Photographs

Questions

Examine the OS map extract on the left and answer the questions that follow.

Section 8.2

1. Identify **two** landforms of coastal erosion at Q 42 12.
2. Give a four-figure reference for each of the following glacial features:
   (a) Cirque with a lake
   (b) Arête
   (c) Paternoster lakes
   (d) U-shaped valley.
3. Identify and describe any **two** features along the course of the Garfinny River.
4. What map evidence suggests that the land at Q 49 07 is badly drained?

Section 8.3

1. It is clear that settlement has existed in this area for a long time. With reference to the OS map, identify **two** pieces of evidence to support this statement.
2. What is the main form of transport in the area shown on the map?
   Name **two** different examples of this type of transport.
3. Why is there an absence of transport at Cnoc Bhaile Uí Shé and Macha na gCab (Q 45 05 and Q 46 05)?
4. Identify and locate by a six-figure grid reference any **two** patterns of rural settlement in the map extract. Briefly describe each pattern.
5. Suggest **two** reasons why there is an absence of settlement at Q 48 11.
6. Describe **three** reasons why Dingle (Daingean Uí Chúis) developed at this location.
7. Identify and describe any **two** current functions of Dingle (Daingean Uí Chúis). Use map evidence to support your answer.
8. Dingle (Daingean Uí Chúis) and the area that surrounds it have a wide range of tourist and leisure facilities. Identify and describe any **two** of them. Use map evidence to support your answer.

This is an OS map extract of a Gaeltacht region. Many of the names are shown in Irish only, for example:

- Staisiún dóiteáin (fire station)
- Scoil (school)
- Ospidéal (hospital)
- Gallán (standing stone)
- Crosleac (stone cross)
- Snoíodóireacht chloiche (stone carving).

Opposite: **Figure 8.51** OS map of the Dingle and Brandon district, Co. Kerry

Section 2 · Maps and Photographs

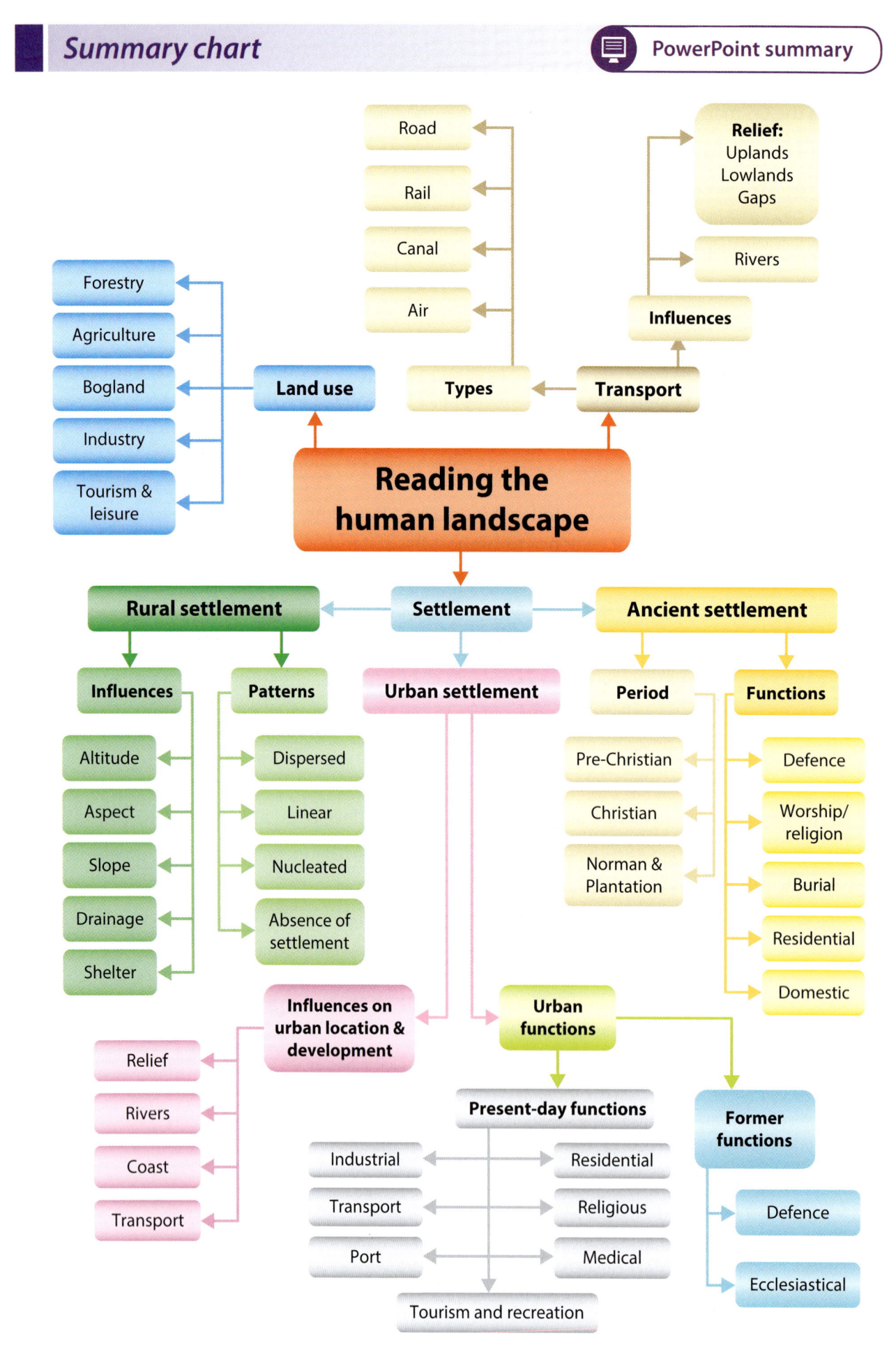

Summary chart

PowerPoint summary

Reading the human landscape

- **Land use**
  - Forestry
  - Agriculture
  - Bogland
  - Industry
  - Tourism & leisure

- **Transport**
  - Types
    - Road
    - Rail
    - Canal
    - Air
  - Influences
    - Relief: Uplands, Lowlands, Gaps
    - Rivers

- **Settlement**
  - **Rural settlement**
    - Influences
      - Altitude
      - Aspect
      - Slope
      - Drainage
      - Shelter
    - Patterns
      - Dispersed
      - Linear
      - Nucleated
      - Absence of settlement
  - **Urban settlement**
    - Influences on urban location & development
      - Relief
      - Rivers
      - Coast
      - Transport
    - Urban functions
      - Present-day functions
        - Industrial
        - Transport
        - Port
        - Residential
        - Religious
        - Medical
        - Tourism and recreation
      - Former functions
        - Defence
        - Ecclesiastical
  - **Ancient settlement**
    - Period
      - Pre-Christian
      - Christian
      - Norman & Plantation
    - Functions
      - Defence
      - Worship/religion
      - Burial
      - Residential
      - Domestic

180

8.4 Aerial photographs

> **KEYWORDS**
>
> - aerial photograph
> - vertical photograph
> - oblique photograph
> - foreground
> - middle ground
> - background

An **aerial photograph** is a view of the land surface taken from the air.

Aerial photographs provide a great deal of information about the landscape, especially when they are used alongside Ordnance Survey maps.

There are two types of aerial photograph:
- Vertical aerial photograph
- Oblique aerial photograph.

Vertical aerial photograph

A vertical aerial photograph is taken with the camera pointing **directly downwards** at the ground.

- It shows a view taken from directly above the landscape.
- The dominant feature is the **roofline of buildings**.
- It does not show the horizon.
- The scale on a vertical aerial photograph is true throughout the whole photograph.

Oblique aerial photograph

An oblique aerial photograph is taken with the camera pointing **downwards at an angle**.

- It gives a view that is similar to viewing the landscape from the top of a high hill or a very tall building.
- It shows both the **roofline** and the **sides** of buildings.
- It may also show the horizon.
- Features at the bottom (foreground) of the photograph appear much larger than those at the top (background) of the photograph.

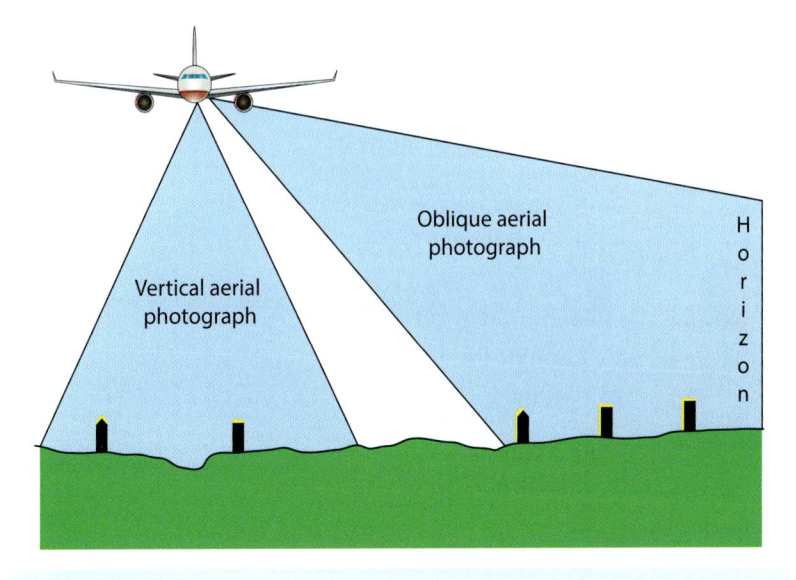

Figure 8.52 Taking vertical and oblique aerial photographs

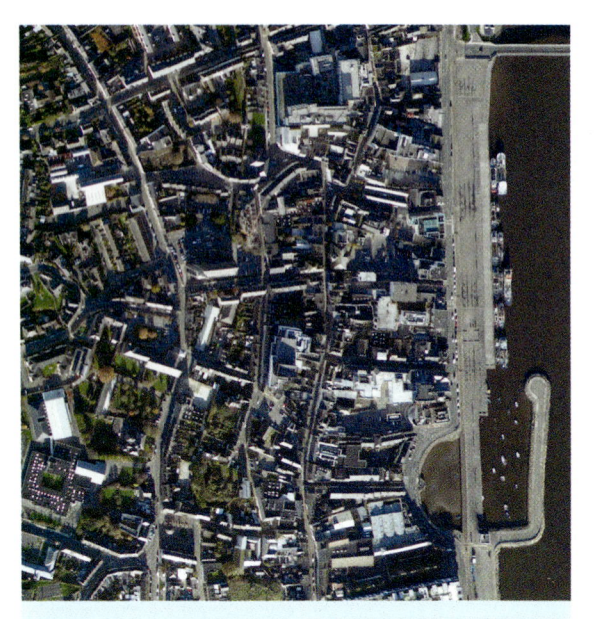

Section 2 · Maps and Photographs

Vertical aerial photograph of Wexford

Oblique aerial photograph of Wexford

Locating features on photographs

Divide the photograph into nine equal sections. The names given to these sections depends on the type of photograph.

The vertical aerial photograph will have an arrow that points to the north. Use compass directions (see page 153) to describe the location of features

To describe location on an oblique aerial photograph, use the names of the nine sections as shown in the picture

Activity

Examine the vertical aerial photo above.

Give the location of the following:

A Factory

B Open fields

C School

D Church.

Activity

Examine the oblique aerial photo above.

Give the location of the following:

A Factory

B Open fields

C School

D Church.

Identifying the season

It is possible to identify the season when an aerial photograph was taken by using the following pointers.

Summer
- Deciduous trees have full foliage.
- High summer sun casts short shadows.
- Cattle are seen grazing in the fields.
- Ripening crops are identified by bright colours.
- Bales of hay or silage may be seen in the fields.

Winter
- Deciduous trees have lost their foliage.
- Low winter sun casts long shadows.
- Cattle have been moved indoors.
- Fields have been freshly ploughed.
- Chimney smoke from houses indicates cold weather.

The Irish countryside in the summer

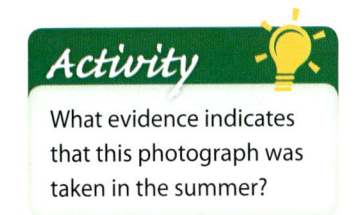

Activity
What evidence indicates that this photograph was taken in the summer?

Drawing a sketch map

To draw a sketch map of an aerial photograph, follow these steps:
1. Always use a pencil (or coloured pencils).
2. Draw a frame that is the same shape as the photograph. It may be smaller than the photograph.
3. Give the sketch map a title.
4. Divide the photo and sketch map frame into nine sections (using a light pencil).
5. Draw the coastline (if there is one on the map).
6. Draw the outline of the required features in a shape similar to the original.
7. Identify each feature either by name or by using a labelled key.

Remember: Do not trace the photograph. Do not include features that you were not asked for.

Section 2 · Maps and Photographs

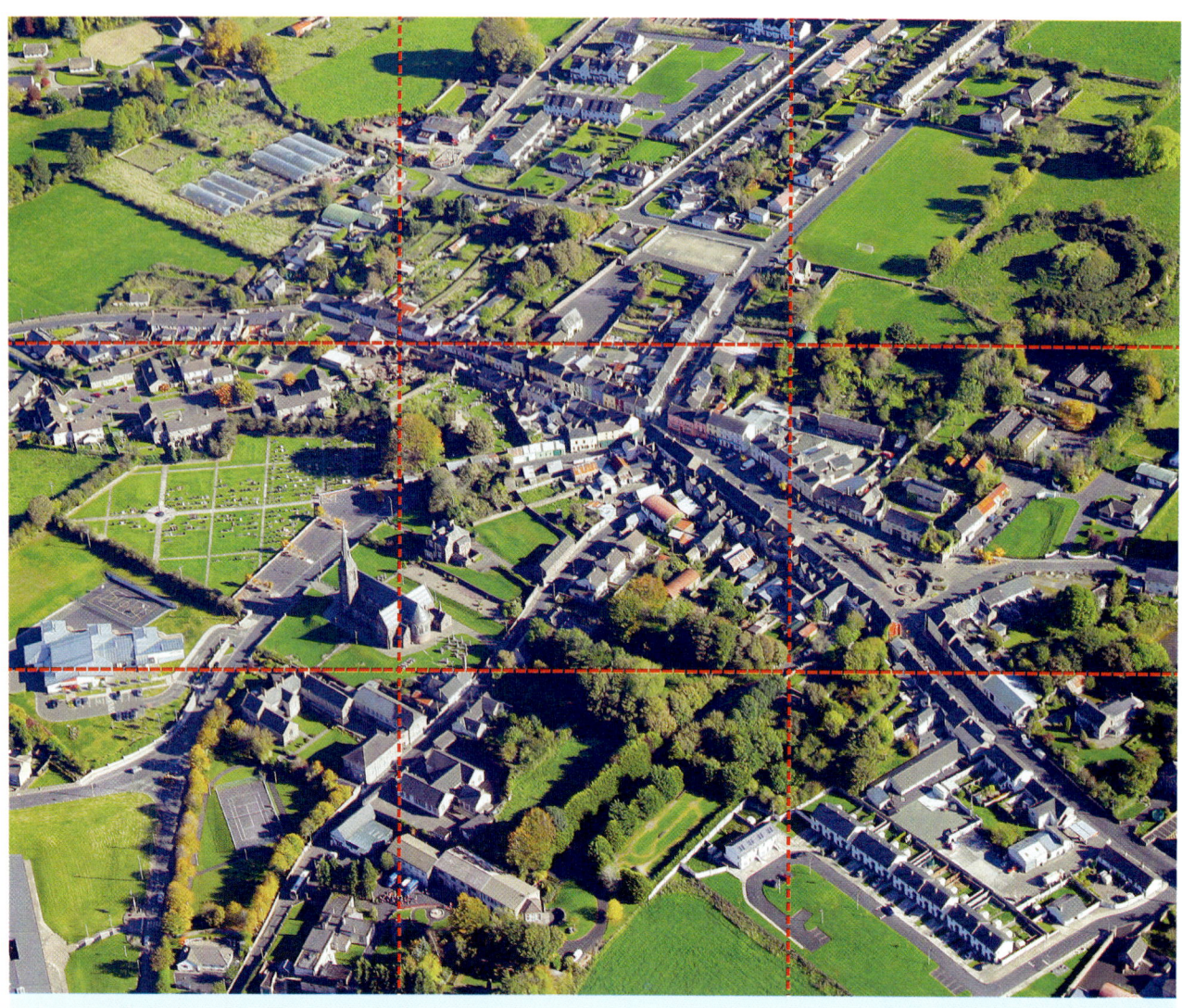

Aerial photograph of Kilfinane, Co. Limerick

Example
Draw a sketch map of the area shown on the photograph. On it show and name the following:

- The town square
- A church
- A clump of trees
- A cemetery
- Polytunnels
- A terrace of houses
- An antiquity.

Hint
Remember to draw light lines to divide the photograph frame into nine sections. This makes it easier to locate features on the sketch.

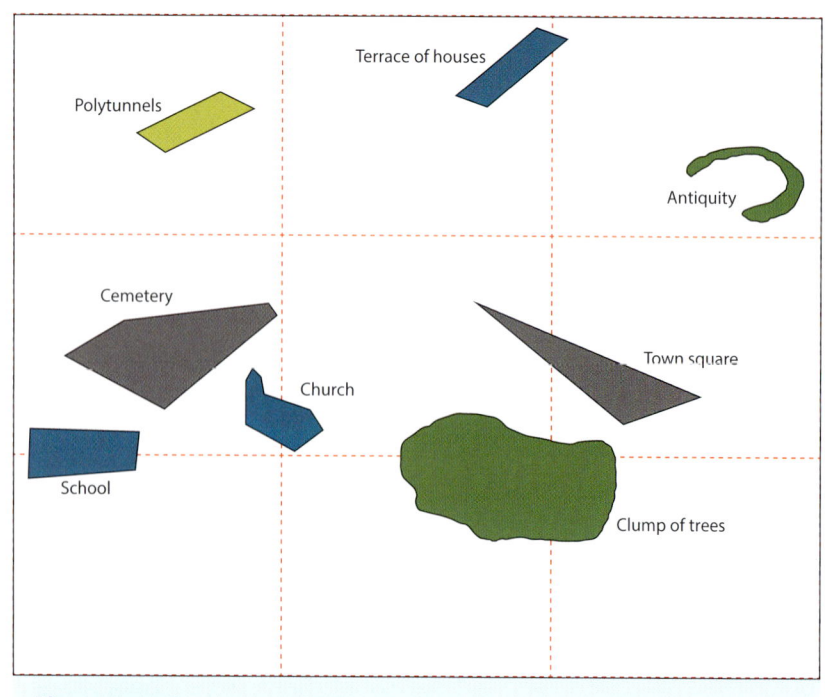

Figure 8.53 Sketch map of Kilfinane, drawn from the aerial photograph above

184

Chapter 8 · Maps and Photographs

Questions

Blarney, Co. Cork

1. What type of photograph is this: vertical or oblique? Explain your answer.

2. Give a location for each of the following:
   (a) The car park at A
   (b) The church at B
   (c) Pasture at C
   (d) The houses at D
   (e) The school at E
   (f) The shops at F.

3. (a) At what time of the year was the photograph taken?
   (b) Give **two** pieces of evidence to support your answer.

4. Draw a sketch map of the area shown in the photograph. On it show and name the following features:
   (a) Two connecting streets
   (b) An old factory building
   (c) A church
   (d) A car park
   (e) A line of shops
   (f) A clump of trees
   (g) A housing estate.

Section 2 · Maps and Photographs

8.5 Rural settlement and land use

> **KEYWORDS**
> - defensive settlement
> - historic settlement
> - land use

It is possible to identify evidence of **rural settlement** (historic and present-day) as well as **land use** on aerial photographs.

Historic settlement

Historic rural settlement includes the following defensive, burial and religious features.

Table 8.9 Historic rural settlements

Defensive settlements	Burial sites	Religious settlements
• Castles	• Graveyards	• Monasteries/abbeys
• Stone forts	• Standing stones	• Church ruins
• Round towers	• Dolmens	• Crosses

Present-day settlement

Most present-day settlement in rural areas consists of individual houses. Some are farmhouses. They can be identified by their farm buildings and the farmland that surrounds them. They form a **dispersed** settlement pattern.

Some houses are built along the sides of rural roads, where they form a **linear** pattern.

Where houses are grouped together at a village or crossroads, they form a **nucleated** (or clustered) pattern.

> **Link**
> For more on **Patterns of rural settlement**, see page 167.

Land use

Some rural land uses can also be identified in aerial photographs.

- **Pastoral farming:** identified by green fields in which grass is growing and animals are grazing.
- **Arable farming:** identified by ploughed fields or by fields where crops are ripening or have been harvested.
- **Woodland:** identified by areas of coniferous or deciduous trees.
- **Market gardening:** identified by areas of polytunnels or glasshouses.
- **Mining or quarrying:** identified where large areas have been excavated.

> **Activity**
> **Examine** the photograph below.
> (a) Identify two different examples of historic rural settlement.
> (b) Identify two rural land uses.

Historic rural settlement at Ardmore, Co. Waterford

Chapter 8 · Maps and Photographs

Questions

Present-day rural settlement and land use near Ballyduff, Co. Waterford and the River Blackwater

1. (a) Identify **two** patterns of rural settlement in the photograph.
   (b) Select **one** of these patterns and explain how it developed.
2. (a) Identify **two** land uses in the photograph.
   (b) Describe any **one** of them.
3. Draw a sketch map of the area shown on the photograph. On it show and name the following:
   (a) The river
   (b) Two roads
   (c) A bridge
   (d) Linear settlement
   (e) An area of pastureland
   (f) An area of woodland
   (g) Farmhouse and buildings.

8.6 Urban settlement and land use

KEYWORDS
- urban settlement
- location
- urban function
- traffic management
- urban planning

Many of the aspects discussed here are similar to those that apply to Ordnance Survey maps (see pages 168–71).

Location of urban settlement

The location and growth of urban settlement is influenced by a combination of the following factors: relief, transport, rivers, coast and defence.

Section 2 · Maps and Photographs

Relief

- The construction of roads and buildings is easier on **flat or gently sloping lowlands**.
- The surrounding area is likely to have **fertile agricultural land** to supply food.

Transport

- A number of roads may meet there (**route focus**).
- A **railway** may pass through the town.
- The town may be built next to a **canal**.

Rivers

- In times past, rivers were used for **water supply**.
- Towns developed at points where the river could be crossed (**bridging point**).
- Large rivers were used for **trade** and transport.
- Rivers are important for **tourism** and leisure.

Coast

- The town may have developed as a **fishing port**.
- The town may have developed as a **tourist resort**.
- The town may have developed as a **commercial port**.

Defence

- The town may have developed near a **castle** as it provided defence in times past.

> **Activity**
>
> **Examine** the photograph below. Describe three reasons why the town of Trim developed at this location.

Aerial photograph of Trim, Co. Meath

Urban functions

The term **function** refers to the services and activities that a town provides for people who work or live in the town or surrounding areas. (See also **Urban functions on OS maps**, page 170).

Some urban functions that can be identified on aerial photographs include:

- **Residential** (houses, apartments)
- **Transport** (roads, rail, car parks, port, canal)
- **Retail** (shops, shopping centres)
- **Commercial** (office blocks)
- **Religious** (churches, abbeys, convents)
- **Port** (docks, cranes, containers, ships)
- **Industrial** (factories, industrial estates)
- **Educational** (schools, colleges and universities)
- **Recreational** (playing fields, tennis courts, golf courses)
- **Tourist** (marinas, beaches, golf courses, historic buildings)
- **Medical** (hospitals).

It is also possible to identify **past functions** of a town. These include:

- **Defensive** (town walls, castles, towers, mottes)
- **Industrial** (mill-races or wheels, weirs, old mill buildings)
- **Market** (market squares, market houses, warehouses near a river or canal).

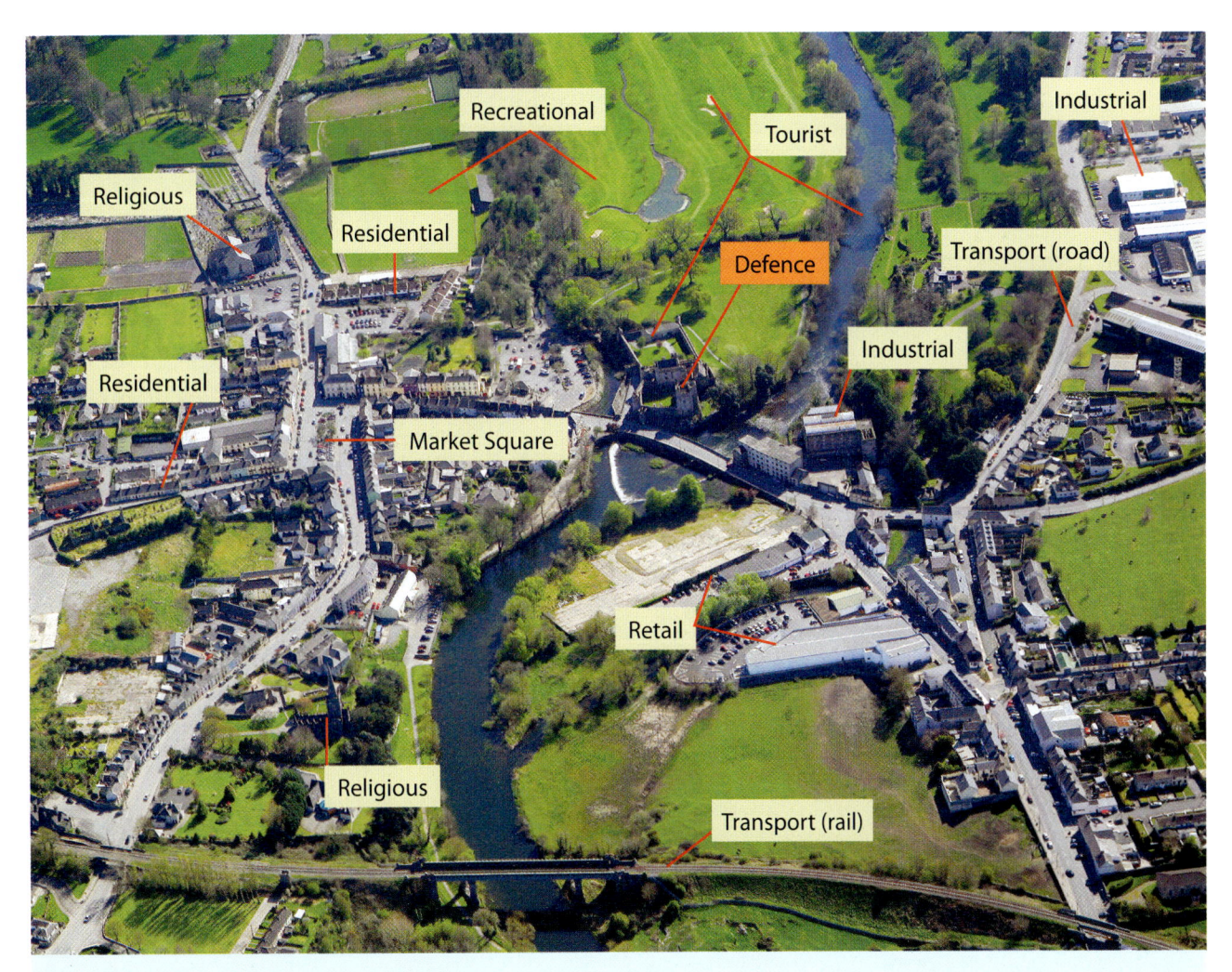

Some of the functions of Cahir, Co. Tipperary

Section 2 · Maps and Photographs

Identifying tourism and recreational attractions

Photographs also provide details of some of the tourist and leisure attractions that may be available in the town and surrounding area.

Table 8.10 Tourism and leisure on an aerial photograph

Feature	Activities/Attraction
Golf courses/racecourses/sports grounds/tennis courts	Playing and watching sports
Rivers and lakes	Cruising, canoeing, fishing, scenery
Coast/beaches/harbours	Boating, swimming, fishing, windsurfing, sunbathing, playing on beach
Forests	Nature trails, picnic sites, walking
Antiquities/demesnes/architecture	Visiting historic attractions
Caravan parks/camping sites/holiday homes	Accommodation while visiting
Shopping centres/shops	Shopping

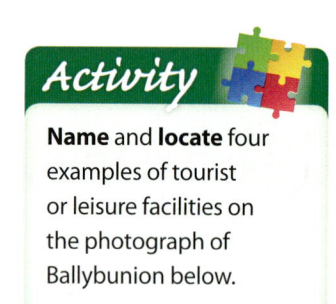

Activity

Name and **locate** four examples of tourist or leisure facilities on the photograph of Ballybunion below.

Ballybunion, Co. Kerry

Managing traffic

The increase in the number of cars on Irish roads has led to an increase in **traffic congestion** in urban areas. It is possible to pinpoint places where this congestion is likely to occur. These include:

- The main shopping streets
- Places where several streets meet
- Points where streets become narrow
- Points close to schools and shopping centres.

Measures that have been taken to reduce traffic congestion include the following:

- Controlling traffic flow with **traffic lights**
- **Yellow boxes** to ease congestion where roads intersect
- **Double yellow lines** to prevent on-street parking
- **One-way streets** to regulate the flow of traffic
- **Pedestrianisation** of some streets
- **Roundabouts** to reduce delays at intersections
- **Bypasses** and **ring roads** to reduce the amount of traffic passing through a town
- Off-street car parking and multi-storey **car parks**
- **Bus lanes** for buses and taxis during busy periods of the day
- **Filter lanes** reserved for vehicles making a turn at the next junction
- **Cycle lanes** to allow a space on the road that is reserved for cyclists.

Activity

Examine the photograph below. Identify four ways by which the local authority has attempted to manage traffic flow in this part of Dublin.

Managing traffic on the quays in Dublin

Section 2 · Maps and Photographs

Identifying house types

A number of different housing types can be identified on aerial photographs, including:

- Terraced houses
- Semi-detached houses
- Detached houses
- Apartment blocks.

We can give more information on the houses by referring to some of the following points.

Table 8.11 Identifying house types

Factors	What to look for
Gardens	Front garden, back garden, no garden
Location	In the town centre, on an outlying street, in the suburbs
Density	High density (apartments and terraces), low density (detached and semi-detached houses)
Pattern	In a set or planned pattern (suburban estates), one-off housing
Open space	Green or open space (suburban estates), fronting directly on to streets (terraces)

Activity

1. **Identify** one example of each of the housing types listed above in the photograph of Kilkenny.
2. Select any two housing types and **give a brief description** of each.

Different housing types in Kilkenny

Urban planning

Urban areas are rapidly expanding. Most of this is accounted for by the growth in residential areas and industrial estates. Other facilities, including shopping centres and schools, are also part of urban growth.

This expansion needs to be properly planned and controlled.

Table 8.12 Planning considerations

You are locating a	Site	Transport	Environment
Factory	A large greenfield site for factory buildings, storage space, parking and future expansion.	Access to major roads, a railway or a port is required for transporting raw materials and finished products, as well as ease of access for workers.	The location should be at a reasonable distance from residential areas, schools and hospitals because of noise and traffic considerations.
Residential area	Level sites are preferred for ease of construction. Space for the provision of recreational facilities is required.	Access to main roads for car owners and the availability of public transport are essential.	The location should be at a reasonable distance from industrial areas because of noise and traffic considerations.
School	A large site is required for school buildings, sports facilities and parking.	Schools should be (a) away from main routeways because of traffic danger, noise and air pollution and (b) close to residential areas to reduce the need for transport.	The location should be at a reasonable distance from industrial areas because of noise, air pollution and traffic considerations.
Shopping centre	A large site is required for the shopping centre, customer car park and delivery trucks.	Access to major roads for delivery trucks as well as customers' cars is essential.	Many shopping centres are built close to residential areas, reducing the need for transport.

A shopping centre at Blackpool in Cork

Activity

Explain two reasons why a shopping centre was built at this location.

Section 2 · Maps and Photographs

Questions

Aerial photograph of Drogheda, Co. Louth

1. Give a location for each of the following features: the railway station, the railway bridge, a mound and tower, a church, a rooftop car park.

2. Draw a sketch map of the area shown on the photograph. On it show and name: the river, the railway, a church, a tower, a warehouse, oil tanks, an area of farmland.

3. (a) Identify and locate any **four** functions of Drogheda.
   (b) Describe any **two** of them.

4. The functions of Drogheda have changed over time. Discuss this statement, referring to **one** past function and **one** present function.

Chapter 8 · Maps and Photographs

Questions

Aerial photograph of Nenagh, Co. Tipperary

1. Draw a sketch map of the area shown on the photograph. On it show and name: the main street, a church, a school, a shopping centre, an area of terraced housing, a factory.

2. Describe and explain **three** of the main services available in the town of Nenagh.

3. Explain **two** reasons why the shopping centre in the foreground was built in that location.

4. (a) Name and locate using the correct terms (right background, etc.) an example of each of the following economic activities: (i) primary; (ii) secondary; (iii) tertiary.

   (b) Choose **one** of the examples of the economic activities named above and explain **two** reasons why it is at its present location.

Section 2 · Maps and Photographs

8.7 Comparing maps and photographs

Ordnance Survey maps and aerial photographs provide a large amount of information for the user. The type of information and the way it is used vary between maps and photographs.

Table 8.13 Getting information from maps and photographs

Ordnance Survey map	Factor	Aerial photograph
• Shown exactly by grid reference	**Location**	• General location can be described
• National and regional roads and some services are named	**Names**	• Features are not named
• Map is true to scale at all times	**Scale**	• Vertical photographs are true to scale • Scale varies in oblique photographs from foreground to background
• Easy to calculate accurately	**Distance**	• Can only be estimated
• Map shows a larger area of land	**Area**	• Photograph shows a smaller area of land. • Important buildings are named
• Individual buildings in built-up areas are not shown	**Buildings**	• Shape and size of individual buildings are shown. • Height in storeys can be seen
• Some shown, but only by symbol	**Land use**	• Clearly shown or can be guessed
• Altitude is clearly shown • Gradient can be calculated accurately	**Altitude and gradient**	• Altitude is not shown • Gradient is not clear, especially in vertical aerial photographs

Questions

1. (a) Identify and locate an area of woodland on the aerial photograph of Kilmallock.
   (b) Identify the location of that woodland on the OS map by a six-figure grid reference.

2. (a) Identify and locate an antiquity on the aerial photograph.
   (b) Name and locate that antiquity on the OS map by a six-figure grid reference.

3. Describe **three** differences in the way that information about Kilmallock is shown on the OS map and on the aerial photograph.

4. Refer to the OS map and the aerial photograph. Describe and explain **three** of the main services available in Kilmallock.

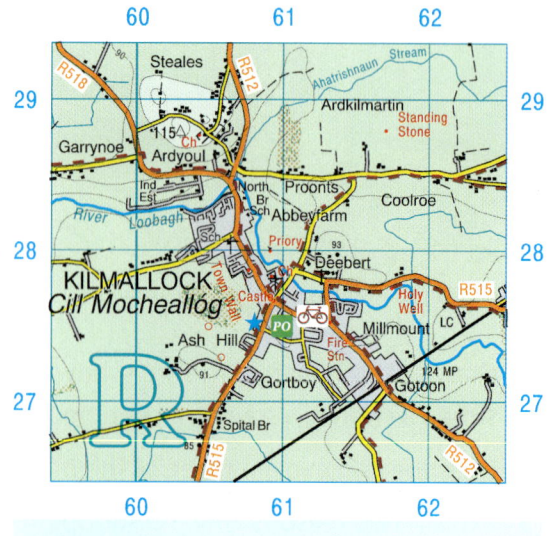

Figure 8.54 Kilmallock, Co. Limerick

Chapter 8 · Maps and Photographs

Questions

Aerial photograph of Kilmallock, Co. Limerick

5 Refer to the OS map and the aerial photograph.
Explain **three** reasons why Kilmallock (and the surrounding area) is a **tourist** destination.

6 Describe **two** differences in the way that roads are shown on the OS map and on the photograph.

7 Refer to the OS map and the aerial photograph.
Explain **three** reasons why Kilmallock developed at this location.

Section 2 · Maps and Photographs

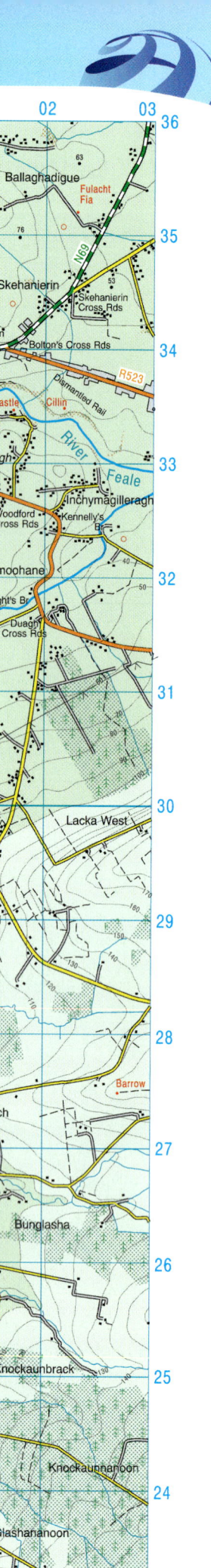

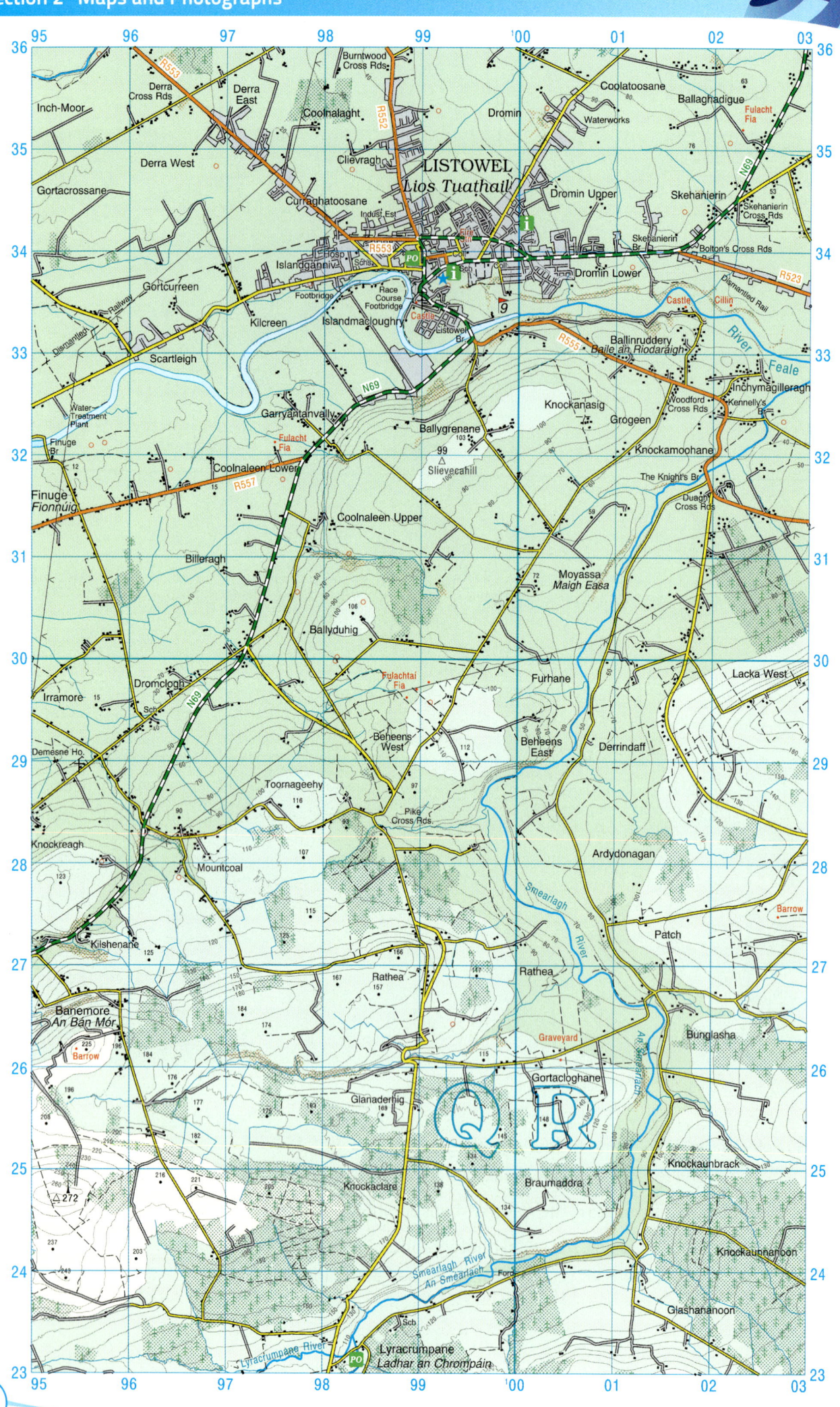

Chapter 8 · Maps and Photographs

Aerial photograph of Listowel, Co. Kerry (Opposite: Listowel OS map extract, Co. Kerry)

Section 2 · Maps and Photographs

Questions

OS map of Listowel

1. Draw a **sketch map** of the area shown on the Ordnance Survey map. On your sketch map show and label each of the following:

   - N69
   - A named river
   - Built-up area of Listowel
   - An area of forest
   - A named antiquity
   - A golf course.

2. (a) What is the general **direction** from the town of Listowel towards Lyracrumpane (Q 98 23)?
   (b) What is the **height** in metres of the highest point shown on the map?
   (c) Measure the **distance** in kilometres along the N69 from the point where it enters the map at Q 950 271 to its junction with the R555.

3. Explain two reasons why there is very little **settlement** in the south-western section of the map (between eastings 950-980 and northings 230-250).

4. Explain three reasons for the location of the **industrial estate** at Q 985 344.

5. (a) Name and locate, using six-figure grid references, two rural **settlement patterns** evident on the Ordnance Survey map.
   (b) Explain why one of the settlement patterns has developed at that location.

6. Explain three reasons why the town of Listowel **developed** at this location, using evidence from the map to support each reason.

7. Name and explain two possible ways in which the River Feale might have influenced the **development** of Listowel.

OS map and photograph of Listowel

Refer to the OS map **and** the aerial photograph in each answer.

1. Describe and explain three of the main **services** available in Listowel.
2. Explain three reasons why Listowel (and the surrounding area) is an important **tourist** destination.

Aerial photograph of Listowel

1. Draw a **sketch map** of the area shown on the aerial photograph.
   On your sketch map show and label each of the following:

   - Two connecting streets
   - The river
   - A bridge
   - A racecourse
   - An off-street car park
   - A church
   - A large office block
   - A castle.

2. (a) At what **time of year** was this photograph taken?
   (b) Explain one reason for your answer.

3. (a) Name and locate two **tourist attractions** shown on the aerial photograph.
   (b) Explain why each of the attractions you have named in (a) is attractive to tourists.

4. Identify two ways that Listowel uses **traffic management** to reduce traffic problems. Use evidence from the photograph to support your answer.

5. It is proposed to build a **factory** in the field on the extreme left background.
   (a) Explain one argument in support of this site.
   (b) Explain one objection that might be raised against building the factory at this site.

6. Describe and explain three of the main **services** available in this part of the town.

Chapter 8 · Maps and Photographs

Questions

OS map of Wexford

1. Draw a **sketch map** of the area shown on the Ordnance Survey map. On your sketch map show and label each of the following:
   - The coastline
   - The River Slaney
   - Built-up area of Castlebridge
   - N25
   - A golf course
   - A sandy beach.

2. (a) Name the transport feature located at **grid reference** T 047 224.
   (b) What is the general **direction** of Wexford Town from Murrintown (T 005 160)?
   (c) Measure the **distance** in kilometres of the stretch of the N25 shown on the map.

3. Explain three reasons why the town of Wexford **developed** at this location, using evidence from the OS map to support each reason.

4. (a) Name and locate, using six-figure grid references, two rural **settlement patterns** evident on the Ordnance Survey map.
   (b) Explain why one of the settlement patterns has developed at that location.

5. A business park has been **developed** at T 052 184.
   (a) Explain two advantages of this location.
   (b) Explain one disadvantage of the location.

6. The town of Wexford provides a variety of **services**.
   (a) Name and locate, using grid references, three of these services.
   (b) State how each of these services can be used by the local people.

OS map and photograph of Wexford

Refer to the OS map **and** the aerial photograph in each answer.

1. Describe and explain three of the main **services** available in Wexford.
2. Explain three reasons why Wexford (and the surrounding area) is an important **tourist** destination.

Aerial photograph of Wexford

1. Draw a **sketch map** of the aerial photograph. On your sketch map show and label each of the following:
   - The coastline
   - A pier
   - A church
   - A recreational area
   - An off-street car park
   - A residential area
   - A school
   - An area of waste ground.

2. (a) Identify and locate three types of **urban land use** to be seen in the photograph.
   (b) Give two reasons why one of the land uses you named above might benefit local people or tourists.

3. Name and locate two different **rural land-uses** shown on the aerial photograph.

4. It is proposed to build a **school** in the field on the centre background.
   (a) Give two arguments in support of this site.
   (b) State one disadvantage of the site.

5. Explain two reasons why Wexford **developed** at this location, making reference to the aerial photograph for each reason.

6. (a) Explain two reasons why **traffic congestion** happens so often in Irish towns and cities.
   (b) Imagine you are in charge of traffic for Wexford. Describe one method you might use to ease traffic congestion.

201

Section 2 · Maps and Photographs

Chapter 8 · Maps and Photographs

Aerial photograph of Wexford (Opposite: Wexford OS map extract)

203

Section 2 · Maps and Photographs

Cashel OS map extract, Co. Tipperary

Chapter 8 · Maps and Photographs

Aerial photograph of Cashel, Co. Tipperary

Section 2 · Maps and Photographs

Questions

OS map of Cashel

1. Draw a **sketch map** of the area shown on the Ordnance Survey map. On your sketch map show and label each of the following:
   - N69
   - A named river
   - Built-up area of Listowel
   - An area of forest
   - A named antiquity
   - A golf course.

2. (a) What is the **area** in square kilometres of the map extract?
   (b) What is the **distance** in kilometres measured in a straight line (as the crow flies) between the post offices in Golden and Cashel?
   (c) Measure the **distance** in kilometres along the N74 from the Garda Station in Golden to Junction 9 on the M8.

3. The area shown on the Ordnance Survey map has a long history of settlement. Name, locate and explain, using six-figure grid references, any two examples of **historic settlement** on the map.

4. Explain three reasons why the town of Cashel **developed** at this location, using evidence from the map to support each reason.

5. (a) Name and locate, using six-figure grid references, two rural **settlement patterns** evident on the Ordnance Survey map.
   (b) Explain why one of the settlement patterns has developed at that location.

6. The town of Cashel provides a variety of **services**.
   (a) Name and locate, using grid references, three of these services.
   (b) State how each of these services can be used by the local people.

Aerial photograph of Cashel

1. Draw a **sketch map** of the aerial photograph. On your sketch map show and label each of the following:
   - Two connecting streets
   - A church
   - An antiquity
   - A recreational area
   - An off-street car park
   - A residential area
   - A clump of trees
   - An area of shops.

2. (a) Identify and locate three types of urban **land use** to be seen in the photograph.
   (b) Give two reasons why one of the land uses you named above might benefit local people or tourists.

3. (a) Name and locate two **tourist attractions** shown on the aerial photograph.
   (b) Explain why each of the attractions you have named in (a) is attractive to tourists.

4. It is proposed to build a **factory** in the field on the extreme right background.
   (a) Give two arguments in support of this site.
   (b) State two objections that might be raised against building the factory at this site.

5. Explain two reasons why Cashel **developed** at this location, making reference to the aerial photograph for each reason.

OS map and photograph of Cashel

Refer to the OS map **and** the aerial photograph in each answer.

1. Outline three reasons for the **development** of Cashel.
2. Explain three reasons why Cashel (and the surrounding area) is an important **tourist** destination.

Questions

OS map of Galway

1. Draw a **sketch map** of the area shown on the Ordnance Survey map. On your sketch map show and label each of the following:
   - The coastline
   - The River Corrib
   - N18
   - A railway
   - A named island
   - A golf course.

2. (a) What is the general **direction** from Galway Airport (M 374 284) to the road roundabout at M 352 258?
   (b) What is the **area** of Galway Bay that is shown on the map?
   (c) Measure the **distance** in kilometres of the N18 shown on the map.

3. (a) Name and describe the type of **settlement pattern** found at M 36 26.
   (b) Explain one reason why there is an absence of settlement in the area around M 340 260.

4. Explain three reasons why the city of Galway **developed** at this location, using evidence from the map to support each reason.

5. Galway and the area that surround it provide a variety of **attractions** for tourists.
   (a) Name and locate, using grid references, three of these attractions.
   (b) State how each of these services can be used by the local people.

Aerial photograph of Galway

1. Draw a **sketch map** of the aerial photograph. On your sketch map show and label each of the following:
   - A river
   - A bridge
   - A railway station
   - A marina
   - A car park
   - A church
   - An industrial zone.

2. (a) Identify and locate three types of urban **land use** to be seen in the photograph.
   (b) Give two reasons why one of the land uses you named above might benefit local people or tourists.

3. (a) Name and locate two **tourist attractions** shown on the aerial photograph.
   (b) Explain why each of the attractions you have named in (a) is attractive to tourists.

4. Explain two reasons why Galway **developed** at this location, making reference to the aerial photograph for each reason.

5. (a) Name and locate using the correct terms (right background, etc.) an example of each of the following **economic activities:**
   - Primary
   - Secondary
   - Tertiary.

   (b) Choose one of the examples of the economic activities named above and explain two reasons why it is at its present location.

OS map and photograph of Galway

Refer to the OS map **and** the aerial photograph in each answer.

1. Outline three reasons for the **development** of the city of Galway.

2. Describe and explain three of the main **services** available in this part of Galway City.

Section 2 · Maps and Photographs

Galway OS map extract

Chapter 8 · Maps and Photographs

Aerial photograph of Galway

Section 2 · Maps and Photographs

Summary chart

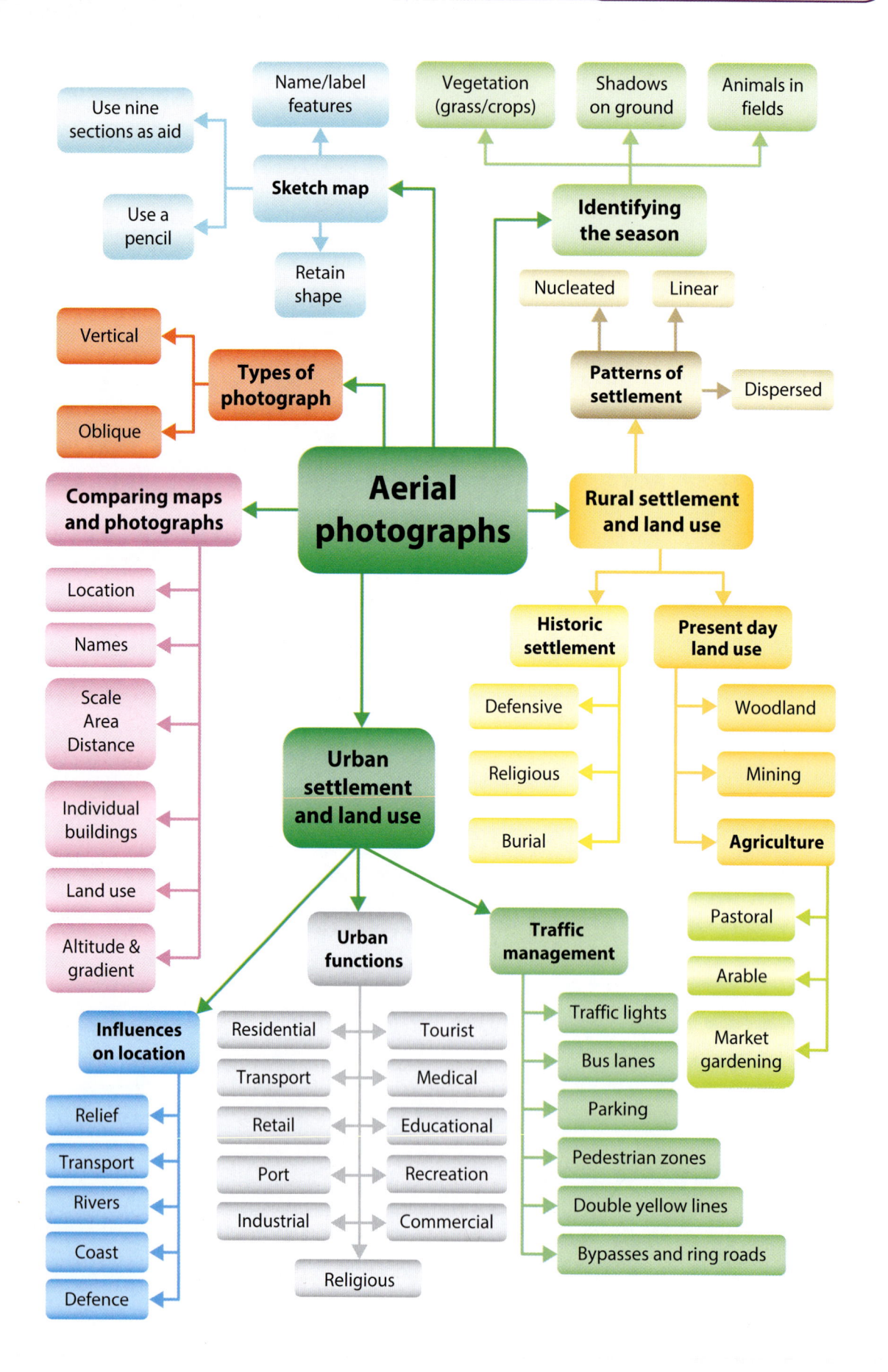

PowerPoint summary

Aerial photographs

- Sketch map
  - Use nine sections as aid
  - Use a pencil
  - Name/label features
  - Retain shape

- Identifying the season
  - Vegetation (grass/crops)
  - Shadows on ground
  - Animals in fields

- Types of photograph
  - Vertical
  - Oblique

- Rural settlement and land use
  - Patterns of settlement
    - Nucleated
    - Linear
    - Dispersed
  - Historic settlement
    - Defensive
    - Religious
    - Burial
  - Present day land use
    - Woodland
    - Mining
    - Agriculture
      - Pastoral
      - Arable
      - Market gardening

- Comparing maps and photographs
  - Location
  - Names
  - Scale / Area / Distance
  - Individual buildings
  - Land use
  - Altitude & gradient

- Urban settlement and land use
  - Urban functions
    - Residential ↔ Tourist
    - Transport ↔ Medical
    - Retail ↔ Educational
    - Port ↔ Recreation
    - Industrial ↔ Commercial
    - Religious
  - Traffic management
    - Traffic lights
    - Bus lanes
    - Parking
    - Pedestrian zones
    - Double yellow lines
    - Bypasses and ring roads
  - Influences on location
    - Relief
    - Transport
    - Rivers
    - Coast
    - Defence

210

Chapter 8 · Maps and Photographs

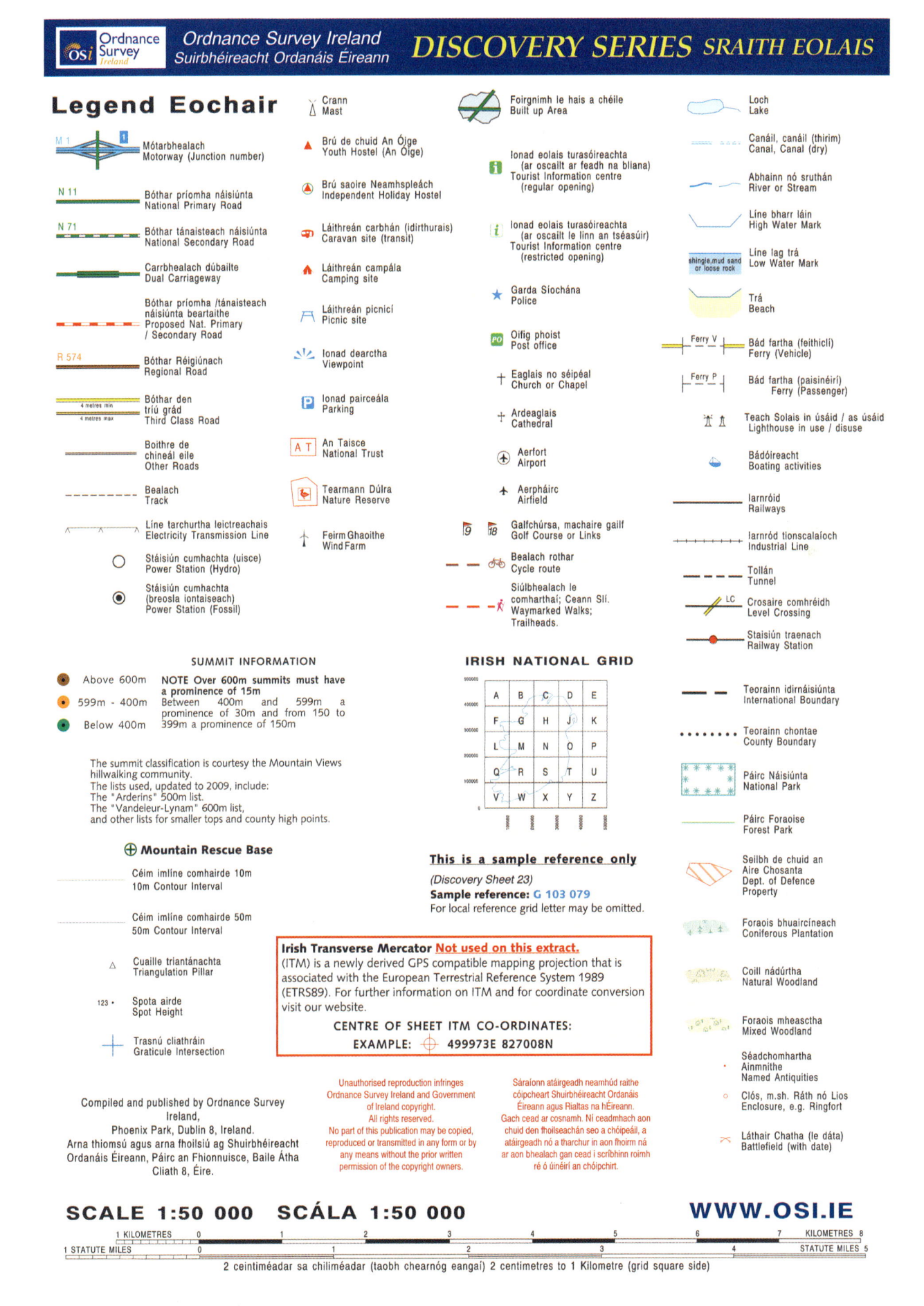

Ordnance Survey Ireland
Suirbhéireacht Ordanáis Éireann

DISCOVERY SERIES SRAITH EOLAIS

Legend Eochair

Roads and Routes
- M 1 — Mótarbhealach / Motorway (Junction number)
- N 11 — Bóthar príomha náisiúnta / National Primary Road
- N 71 — Bóthar tánaisteach náisiúnta / National Secondary Road
- Carrbhealach dúbailte / Dual Carriageway
- Bóthar príomha / tánaisteach náisiúnta beartaithe / Proposed Nat. Primary / Secondary Road
- R 574 — Bóthar Réigiúnach / Regional Road
- Bóthar den tríú grád (4 metres min / 4 metres max) / Third Class Road
- Bóithre de chineál eile / Other Roads
- Bealach / Track
- Líne tarchurtha leictreachais / Electricity Transmission Line
- Stáisiún cumhachta (uisce) / Power Station (Hydro)
- Stáisiún cumhachta (breosla iontaiseach) / Power Station (Fossil)

Tourism and Services
- Crann / Mast
- Brú de chuid An Óige / Youth Hostel (An Óige)
- Brú saoire Neamhspleách / Independent Holiday Hostel
- Láithreán carbhán (idirthurais) / Caravan site (transit)
- Láithreán campála / Camping site
- Láithreán picnicí / Picnic site
- Ionad dearctha / Viewpoint
- Ionad páirceála / Parking
- An Taisce / National Trust
- Tearmann Dúlra / Nature Reserve
- Feirm Ghaoithe / Wind Farm

Buildings and Features
- Foirgnimh le hais a chéile / Built up Area
- Ionad eolais turasóireachta (ar oscailt ar feadh na bliana) / Tourist Information centre (regular opening)
- Ionad eolais turasóireachta (ar oscailt le linn an tséasúir) / Tourist Information centre (restricted opening)
- Garda Síochána / Police
- Oifig phoist / Post office
- Eaglais nó séipéal / Church or Chapel
- Ardeaglais / Cathedral
- Aerfort / Airport
- Aerpháirc / Airfield
- Galfchúrsa, machaire gailf / Golf Course or Links
- Bealach rothar / Cycle route
- Siúlbhealach le comharthaí; Ceann Slí / Waymarked Walks; Trailheads

Water and Coast
- Loch / Lake
- Canáil, canáil (thirim) / Canal, Canal (dry)
- Abhainn nó sruthán / River or Stream
- Líne bharr láin / High Water Mark
- Líne lag trá (shingle, mud sand or loose rock) / Low Water Mark
- Trá / Beach
- Ferry V — Bád fartha (feithiclí) / Ferry (Vehicle)
- Ferry P — Bád fartha (paisinéirí) / Ferry (Passenger)
- Teach Solais in úsáid / as úsáid / Lighthouse in use / disuse
- Bádóireacht / Boating activities

Railway and Boundaries
- Iarnród / Railways
- Iarnród tionscalaíoch / Industrial Line
- Tollán / Tunnel
- LC — Crosaire comhréidh / Level Crossing
- Stáisiún traenach / Railway Station
- Teorainn idirnáisiúnta / International Boundary
- Teorainn chontae / County Boundary
- Páirc Náisiúnta / National Park
- Páirc Foraoise / Forest Park
- Seilbh de chuid an Aire Chosanta / Dept. of Defence Property
- Foraois bhuaircíneach / Coniferous Plantation
- Coill nádúrtha / Natural Woodland
- Foraois mheasctha / Mixed Woodland
- Séadchomhartha Ainmnithe / Named Antiquities
- Clós, m.sh. Ráth nó Lios / Enclosure, e.g. Ringfort
- Láthair Chatha (le dáta) / Battlefield (with date)

SUMMIT INFORMATION
- Above 600m
- 599m – 400m
- Below 400m

NOTE: Over 600m summits must have a prominence of 15m. Between 400m and 599m a prominence of 30m and from 150 to 399m a prominence of 150m.

The summit classification is courtesy the Mountain Views hillwalking community.
The lists used, updated to 2009, include:
The "Arderins" 500m list.
The "Vandeleur-Lynam" 600m list,
and other lists for smaller tops and county high points.

- Mountain Rescue Base
- Céim imlíne comhairde 10m / 10m Contour Interval
- Céim imlíne comhairde 50m / 50m Contour Interval
- Cuaille triantánachta / Triangulation Pillar
- 123 • Spota airde / Spot Height
- Trasnú cliathráin / Graticule Intersection

IRISH NATIONAL GRID

A	B	C	D	E
F	G	H	I	J
L	M	N	O	P
Q	R	S	T	U
V	W	X	Y	Z

This is a sample reference only
(Discovery Sheet 23)
Sample reference: **G 103 079**
For local reference grid letter may be omitted.

Irish Transverse Mercator Not used on this extract.
(ITM) is a newly derived GPS compatible mapping projection that is associated with the European Terrestrial Reference System 1989 (ETRS89). For further information on ITM and for coordinate conversion visit our website.

CENTRE OF SHEET ITM CO-ORDINATES:
EXAMPLE: 499973E 827008N

Compiled and published by Ordnance Survey Ireland, Phoenix Park, Dublin 8, Ireland.
Arna thiomsú agus arna fhoilsiú ag Shuirbhéireacht Ordanáis Éireann, Páirc an Fhionnuisce, Baile Átha Cliath 8, Éire.

Unauthorised reproduction infringes Ordnance Survey Ireland and Government of Ireland copyright. All rights reserved. No part of this publication may be copied, reproduced or transmitted in any form or by any means without the prior written permission of the copyright owners.

Sáraíonn atáirgeadh neamhúd raithe cóipcheart Shuirbhéireacht Ordanáis Éireann agus Rialtas na hÉireann. Gach cead ar cosnamh. Ní ceadmhach aon chuid den fhoilseachán seo a chóipeáil, a atáirgeadh nó a tharchur in aon fhoirm ná ar aon bhealach gan cead i scríbhinn roimh ré ó úinéirí an chóipchirt.

SCALE 1:50 000 — SCÁLA 1:50 000

WWW.OSI.IE

2 ceintiméadar sa chiliméadar (taobh chearnóg eangaí) 2 centimetres to 1 Kilometre (grid square side)

Figure 8.55 Map legend for the 1:50,000 series of OS maps

Section 2 · Maps and Photographs

Ireland Relief

© Collins Bartholomew 2016

Ireland Political

Section 2 · Maps and Photographs

Europe Relief

Cross-section

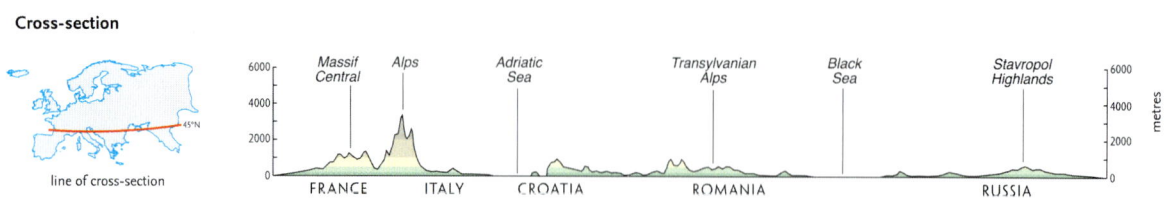

line of cross-section

Massif Central — Alps — Adriatic Sea — Transylvanian Alps — Black Sea — Stavropol Highlands

FRANCE — ITALY — CROATIA — ROMANIA — RUSSIA

Scale 1 : 25 000 000
Conic Equidistant projection

© Collins Bartholomew 2016

Chapter 8 · Maps and Photographs

Europe Political

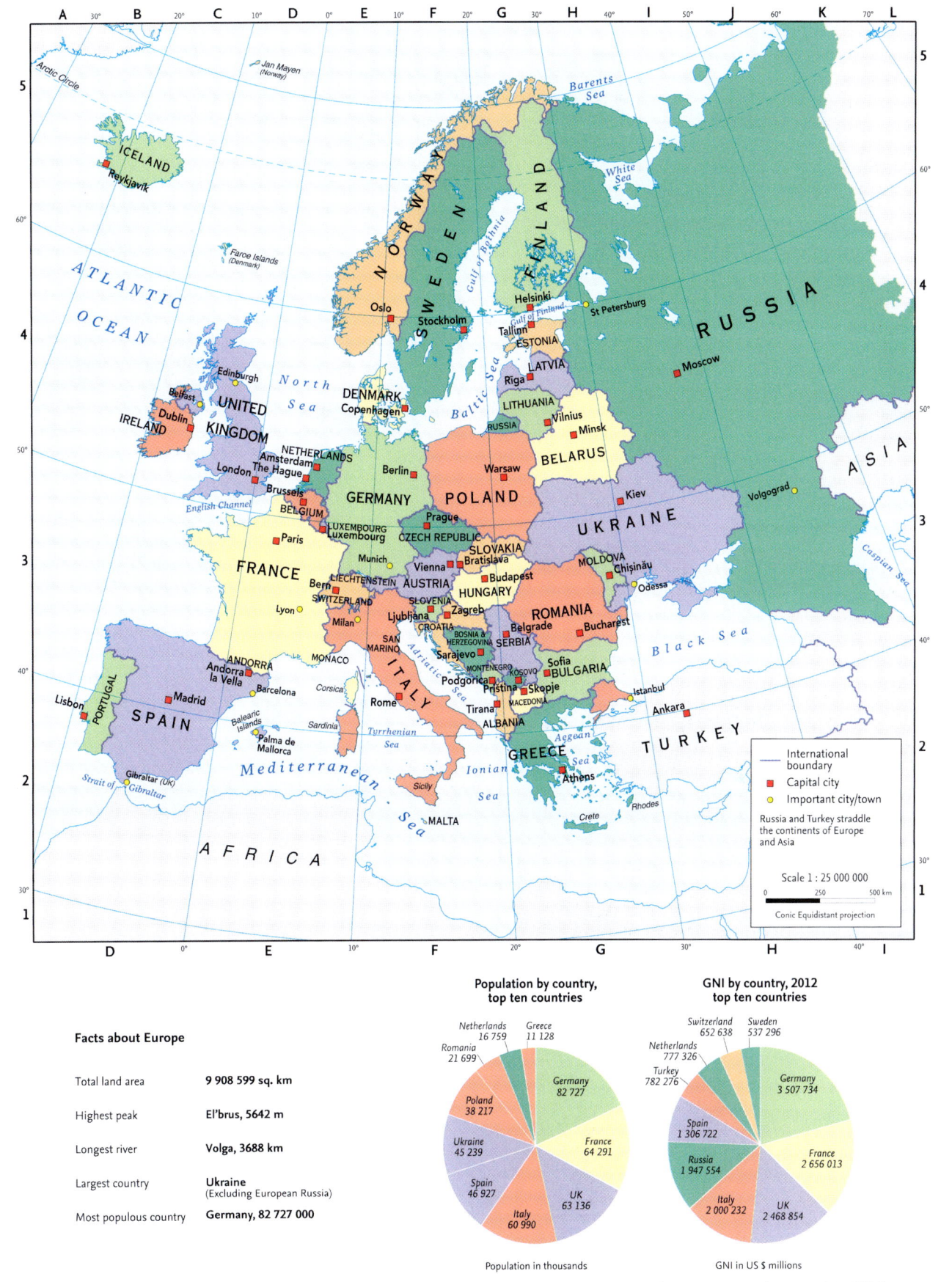

Facts about Europe

Total land area	9 908 599 sq. km
Highest peak	El'brus, 5642 m
Longest river	Volga, 3688 km
Largest country	Ukraine (Excluding European Russia)
Most populous country	Germany, 82 727 000

Population by country, top ten countries (Population in thousands)
- Netherlands 16 759
- Greece 11 128
- Romania 21 699
- Germany 82 727
- Poland 38 217
- France 64 291
- Ukraine 45 239
- UK 63 136
- Spain 46 927
- Italy 60 990

GNI by country, 2012, top ten countries (GNI in US $ millions)
- Switzerland 652 638
- Sweden 537 296
- Netherlands 777 326
- Turkey 782 276
- Germany 3 507 734
- Spain 1 306 722
- France 2 656 013
- Russia 1 947 554
- UK 2 468 854
- Italy 2 000 232

GNI (Gross national income) in US $

Scale 1 : 25 000 000
Conic Equidistant projection

Russia and Turkey straddle the continents of Europe and Asia

© Collins Bartholomew 2016

Section 2 · Maps and Photographs

Mountain heights

	metres
Mt Everest (Nepal/China)	8848
K2 (China/Pakistan)	8611
Kangchenjunga (Nepal/India)	8586
Dhaulagiri (Nepal)	8167
Annapurna (Nepal)	8091
Cerro Aconcagua (Argentina)	6959
Nevado Ojos del Salado (Arg./Chile)	6908
Chimborazo (Ecuador)	6310
Denali (USA)	6190
Mt Logan (Canada)	5959

Island areas

	sq. km
Greenland	2 175 600
New Guinea	808 510
Borneo	745 561
Madagascar	587 040
Baffin Island	507 451
Sumatra	473 606
Honshū	227 414
Great Britain	218 476
Victoria Island	217 291
Ellesmere Island	196 236

Continents

	sq. km
Asia	45 036 492
Africa	30 343 578
North America	24 680 331
South America	17 815 420
Antarctica	12 093 000
Europe	9 908 599
Oceania	8 923 000

World Relief

216

Chapter 8 · Maps and Photographs

Oceans	sq. km
Pacific Ocean	166 241 000
Atlantic Ocean	86 557 000
Indian Ocean	73 427 000
Arctic Ocean	9 485 000

Lake areas	sq. km
Caspian Sea	371 000
Lake Superior	82 100
Lake Victoria	68 800
Lake Huron	59 600
Lake Michigan	57 800
Lake Tanganyika	32 900
Great Bear Lake	31 328
Lake Baikal	30 500
Lake Nyasa	30 044

River lengths	km
Nile (Africa)	6695
Amazon (S. America)	6516
Chang Jiang (Asia)	6380
Mississippi-Missouri (N. America)	5969
Ob'-Irtysh (Asia)	5568
Yenisey-Angara-Selenga (Asia)	5500
Huang He (Asia)	5464
Congo (Africa)	4667
Río de la Plata-Paraná (S. America)	4500
Mekong (Asia)	4425

© Collins Bartholomew 2016

Section 2 · Maps and Photographs

World Political

Chapter 8 · Maps and Photographs

The Continents

© Collins Bartholomew 2016

Section 2 · Maps and Photographs

Satellite image of planet Earth. This image is made up of 10,000 individual satellite scenes collected over 100 days

Section 3
Social Geography

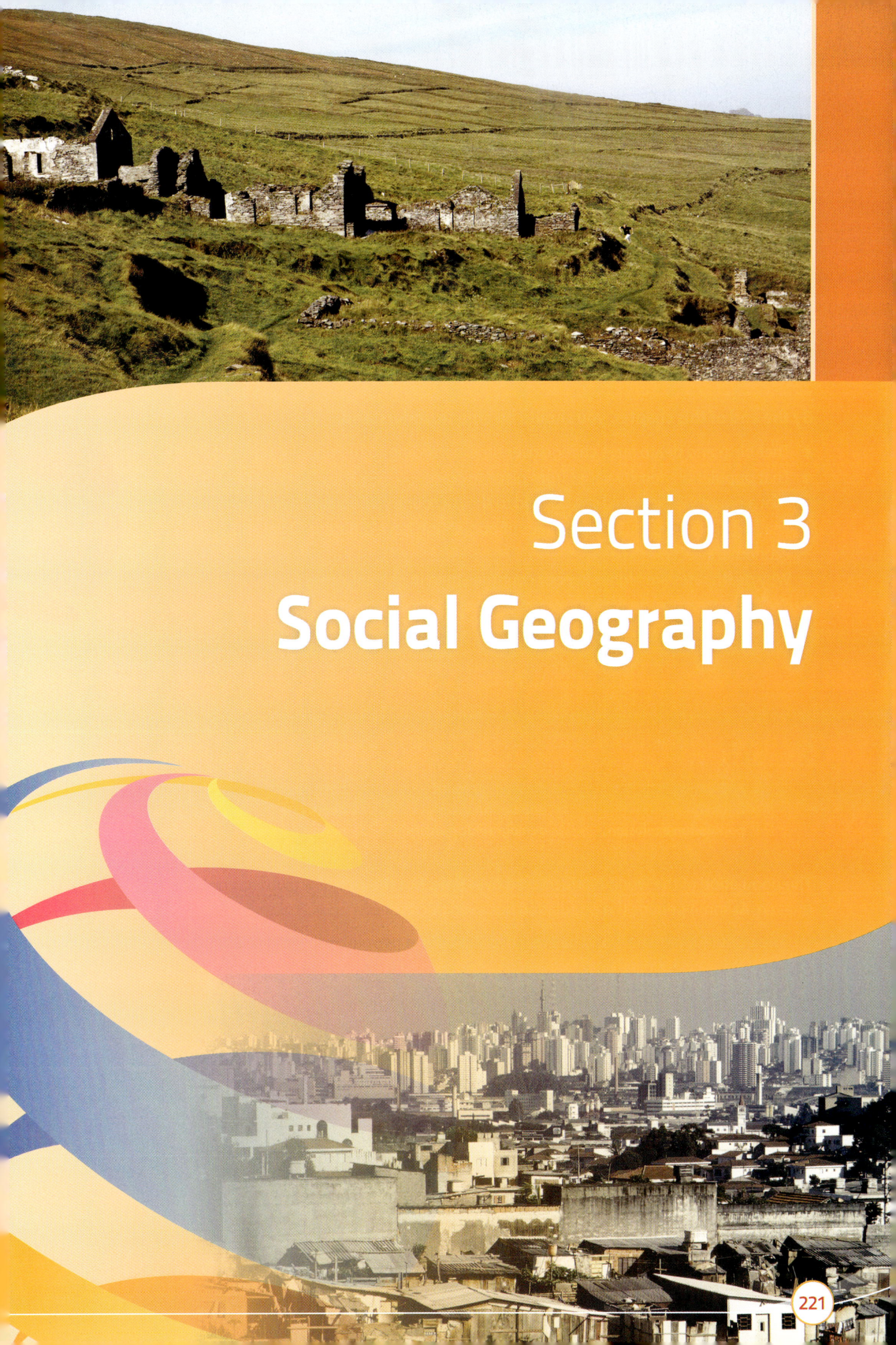

Chapter 9
Population: Distribution, Diversity and Change

Learning outcomes

By the end of this chapter, you should be able to understand:

- That birth and death rates change over time, according to the population cycle
- That population density varies from place to place
- That a population pyramid can be used to show a country's population structure
- That high densities and low densities of population have different social and economic effects
- Why death rates are higher in poor countries than in rich countries
- That migration can be individual or organised.

9.1 Population growth

KEYWORDS

- population
- fluctuate
- population explosion
- developing world
- population cycle
- demographic transition
- birth rate
- death rate
- natural increase

The population of the world has increased over time, but the rate of growth has been uneven. At some periods the population has even decreased.

The population of the world had reached **7.3 billion** people by the end of 2015. At present, the population is **increasing** by about 76 million every year or about **1.5 million people every week**.

The population has not always increased so quickly. In the past people died at almost the same rate as others were born. Population growth was **slow and uneven** because famine, wars and plagues killed many people. The population **fluctuated**.

Definition ✓

Fluctuate: To rise and to fall in an uneven way.

Geo fact

The **Black Death** in the fourteenth century was so severe that it may have **halved** the population of Europe.

Chapter 9 · Population: Distribution, Diversity and Change

Since about 1900, however, the world's population has **increased dramatically**. This is because most babies who are born survive to become adults and to have children of their own. This population growth is called the **population explosion**.

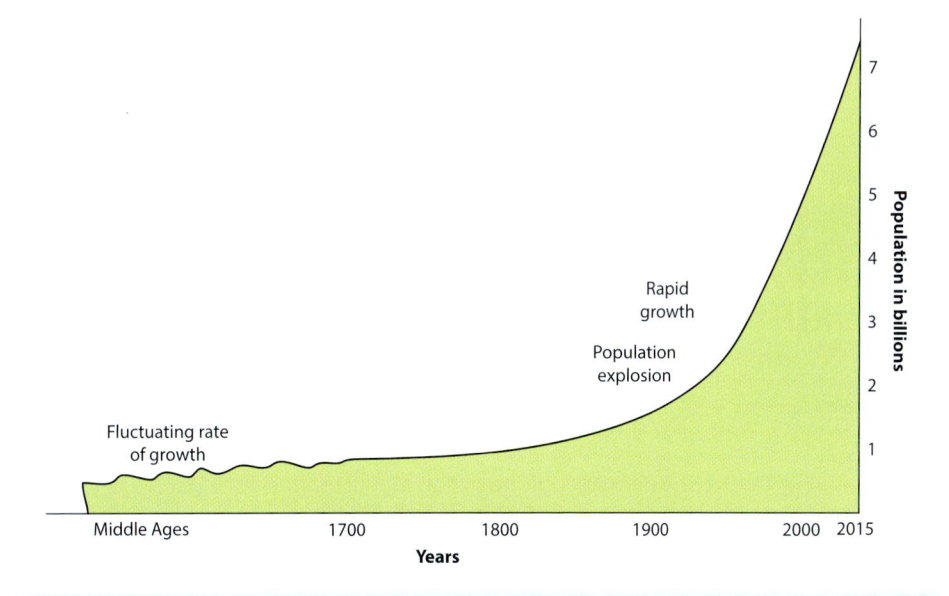

Figure 9.1 Population increase from the Middle Ages to the present

Where is population growth greatest today?

- Today, almost all population growth is in poorer countries, also known as the **developing world**. The populations of many countries in south and south-west Asia and in Africa are growing rapidly.
- On the other hand, the populations of **wealthier countries**, such as those in Europe and North America, are **growing very slowly**, because parents are having very few children.
- In some countries, such as **Japan**, the population is **falling**.

A crowded beach scene on China's east coast

The population cycle

The study of population is called **demography**. People who study population have drawn up a diagram or '**model**' to help us to understand how a population increases over time. This is called the **demographic transition model** or **population cycle**.

The demographic transition model shows the **changes in the birth rates, death rates and total population** of a country over time.

What is the message here?

> **Definitions** ✓
>
> **Birth rate:** The number of births per 1,000 people in one year.
>
> **Death rate:** The number of deaths per 1,000 people in one year.

223

Section 3 · Social Geography

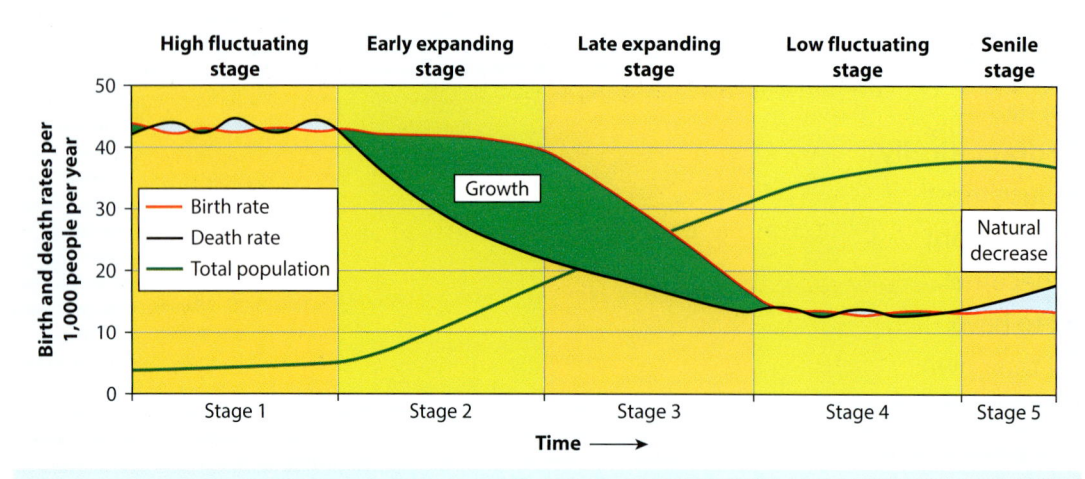

Figure 9.2 The demographic transition model (population cycle)

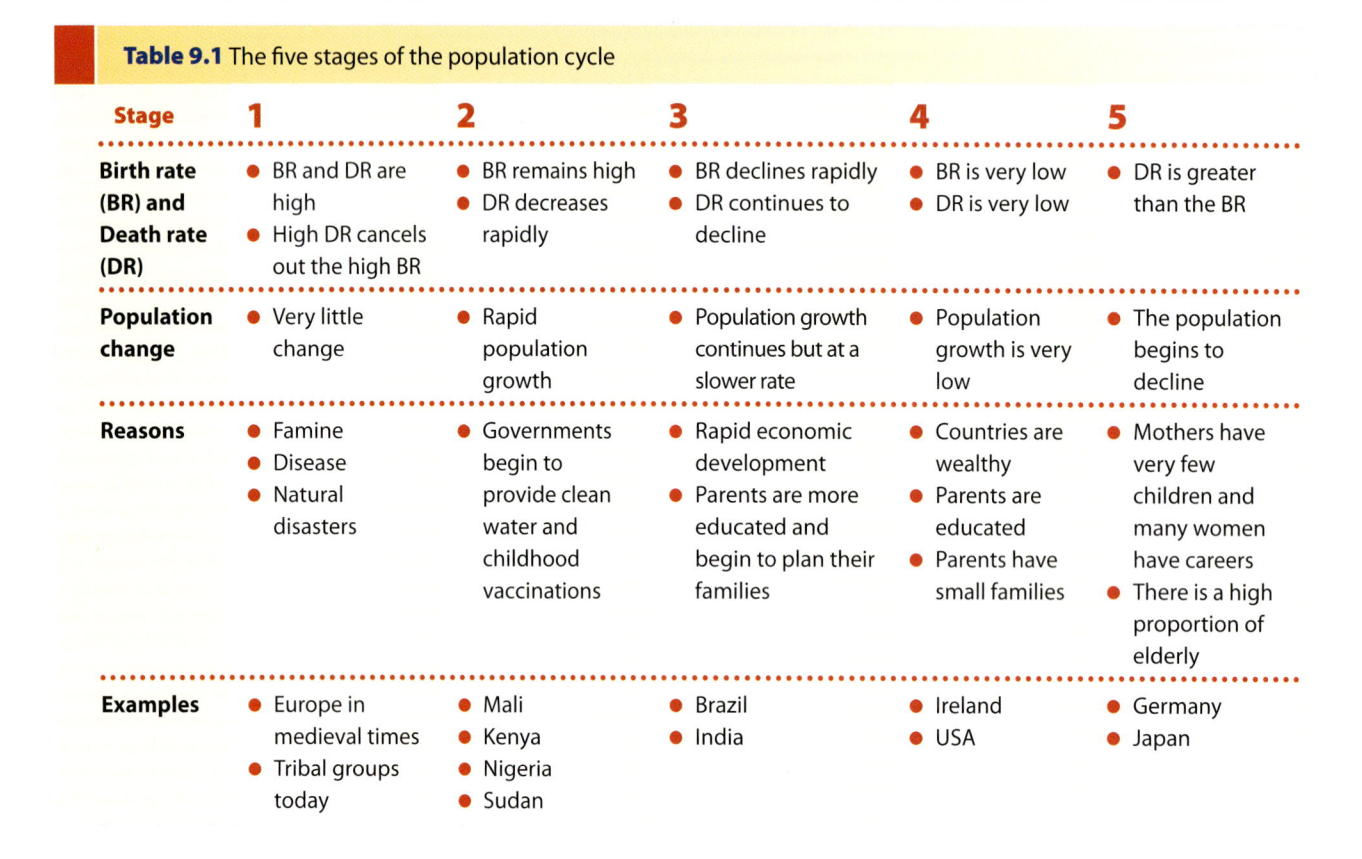

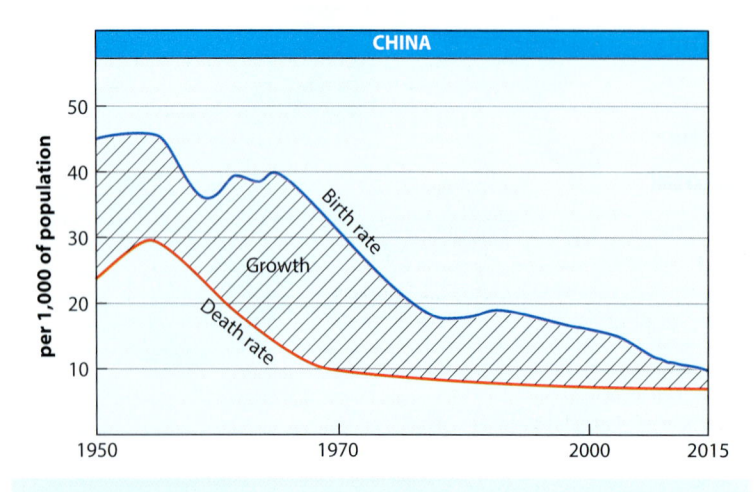

Table 9.1 The five stages of the population cycle

Stage	1	2	3	4	5
Birth rate (BR) and Death rate (DR)	• BR and DR are high • High DR cancels out the high BR	• BR remains high • DR decreases rapidly	• BR declines rapidly • DR continues to decline	• BR is very low • DR is very low	• DR is greater than the BR
Population change	• Very little change	• Rapid population growth	• Population growth continues but at a slower rate	• Population growth is very low	• The population begins to decline
Reasons	• Famine • Disease • Natural disasters	• Governments begin to provide clean water and childhood vaccinations	• Rapid economic development • Parents are more educated and begin to plan their families	• Countries are wealthy • Parents are educated • Parents have small families	• Mothers have very few children and many women have careers • There is a high proportion of elderly
Examples	• Europe in medieval times • Tribal groups today	• Mali • Kenya • Nigeria • Sudan	• Brazil • India	• Ireland • USA	• Germany • Japan

Figure 9.3 Population cycle of China over time

Activity

Examine Figure 9.3. At what stage was China in the population cycle in 2015?

Chapter 9 · Population: Distribution, Diversity and Change

Natural increase

Natural increase occurs when the **birth rate is higher than the death rate**.

Natural increase is given as a **percentage**, and can be calculated by subtracting the death rate from the birth rate.

When the death rate is higher than the birth rate, there is a **natural decrease** in population.

A family in France, a developed country

Example

In a country at stage 2, the birth rate may be 40 per 1,000 and the death rate may be 15 per 1,000.

Growth = 40 − 15 = 25 per 1,000

Convert to percentage:

$$\frac{25}{1,000} \times \frac{100}{1} = 2.5\%$$

The natural increase is **2.5% per year**.

Activity

What is the percentage increase in a country with the following rates?

- Birth rate per 1,000 = 30
- Death rate per 1,000 = 20

Questions

1. Explain **one** reason why population growth was low during the Middle Ages.
2. Name **one** region in the world where population growth is still very high.
3. Look at the demographic transition model in Figure 9.2 and Table 9.1, page 224, and answer these questions:
    (a) At what stage is Brazil in the model?
    (b) At what stage is Ireland in the model?
    (c) Why is stage 1 called the high fluctuating stage?
    (d) What happens at the low fluctuating stage?
    (e) Explain one reason for the decline in birth rates in stage 3.
    (f) Why does a natural decrease take place in stage 5?
    (g) Name a country that is now at stage 5.

9.2 Factors that affect the rate of population change

KEYWORDS

- crop rotation
- colonisation
- food supply
- irrigation
- sanitation
- vaccination
- shanty town
- feminist movement
- replacement level
- family planning
- female literacy

A number of factors influence the rate of population change:

1. Food supply
2. Improved technology
3. Health
4. War
5. The place of women in society
6. Education

Section 3 · Social Geography

1 Food supply

Extra food helps a population to grow.

- Modern farmers use better **seeds** than before.
- They use **crop rotation** to stop the soil from losing minerals.
- **Fertilisers** greatly increase food output per **hectare**.
- Farmers have learned to store grain in **silos** so that it is not spoiled by rain or eaten by pests.

With additional food supplies, the population of Europe and North America increased rapidly in the nineteenth and early twentieth centuries. **Colonisation** by Europeans brought modern agricultural advances to Africa, South America and Asia.

The potato in nineteenth-century Ireland

The population of Ireland grew from 4.5 million in 1800 to more than 8 million in 1845. This was because a hectare of land could produce enough **potatoes** and vegetables to support a family.

However, when the potato crop failed during the **Great Famine** of 1845–48, **food supply declined**. As a result, almost a million people died.

Increased food supply in Brazil

The population of Brazil grew from 17 million in 1900 to 203 million in 2015. This was due to **high inward migration** from Europe and because of a **high birth rate**.

Brazilian farmers cleared land for agriculture. This meant that they could increase supplies of rice, maize, vegetables and fruit to feed the rapidly growing population.

Geo fact

One hectare = 10,000 square metres, or half the size of Croke Park stadium.

Definitions

Crop rotation: Growing a different crop in the same field each year in order to reduce the risk of pests and to prevent all the nutrients in the soil being used up.

Silo: A tall tower in a farm that is used to store grain.

Colonisation: When one country takes control of another country and its people go there to live and govern.

2 Improved technology

Better technology can boost population growth.

- Tractors, better ploughs, combine harvesters and other equipment have made **farming** more efficient. This increases the **food supply**.
- In **Germany** and other advanced countries, cereals such as wheat are grown using modern technology and **chemical fertilisers**. Output of wheat per hectare is very high.
- **Irrigation** has meant that vast areas of dry land can now be farmed.
- **Drones** are now used by farmers to check crops and equipment on large farms.
- New technology has also produced **medical equipment and medicines** that save lives and decrease the death rate.

Definition

Irrigation: Supplying dry land with water through canals or piping, so that crops can grow.

A modern irrigation system in Tunisia, North Africa

Workers use modern technology to plant lettuces in a field

Chapter 9 · Population: Distribution, Diversity and Change

3 Health

The health of a population affects death rates. People's health can be improved in several ways, including:

- Clean **drinking water**
- Proper **sanitation**
- Childhood **vaccinations**
- A good **health service**.

> **Definition**
>
> **Sanitation:** The treatment and disposal of sewage to protect people's health.

Rich countries

In wealthy countries, **safe drinking water** has been available since the end of the nineteenth century.

In Ireland, Germany and other developed countries, treated domestic water supplies and **modern sanitation** are available to almost all of the population.

Tuberculosis (TB) caused the deaths of more than 3,000 adults in Ireland every year until the middle of the twentieth century. However, after 1948 it was stamped out in a major campaign using **new drugs**.

Poor countries

In Brazil, clean water is widely available in cities, but not in many **rural areas**. People who live in the countryside depend on a well. This water may be unsafe if it is contaminated by animals.

Millions of Brazilians also live in **shanty towns** outside the large cities. In shanty towns, safe drinking water is often unavailable. This can lead to outbreaks of diseases such as **cholera**.

> **Definition**
>
> **Shanty town:** A poor area at the edge of a city where people live in houses made of old timber, plastic and recycled materials.

A baby being weighed in a rural clinic in Brazil

A girl drinking filtered water in rural Brazil. Filtered water helps people to stay healthy

227

Section 3 · Social Geography

4 War

War has a major impact on people's lives.

- It disrupts farming, health services, water supplies and sanitation systems.
- People's **health** is therefore affected.
- The **food supply** is also reduced.
- Modern **weapons** and **bombing** campaigns can also lead to death on a terrible scale for soldiers and civilians alike.

War is a common occurrence in the **developing world** today, especially in Africa. More than five million people died as a result of the civil war in the Democratic Republic of the Congo (1998–2003). By September 2015, after four years of war in Syria, at least 210,000 people had been killed.

Germany took part in two world wars in the twentieth century. More than five million Germans died during the Second World War. These included soldiers at the front and civilians who died from the Allied bombing of German cities. These deaths reduced the German population during the 1940s.

5 The place of women in society

Women in **developed countries** today have a far higher status (position) in society than their grandmothers had. This change was brought about by:

- The **feminist movement** that began in the 1960s
- Higher levels of female **education**.

Two generations ago in Ireland and Germany, most women were confined to the roles of mothers and full-time homemakers. However, today many mothers pursue a career. They also **plan their families**.

- In 1970, Irish mothers had an average of four children each.
- In 2015, Irish mothers had an average of two children each, the highest in the EU.
- In Germany, the average number of children per mother is 1.4. This figure is well below the **replacement level** of 2.1 children per mother.

In **developing countries**, mothers have much more traditional roles. Women in many of these countries have **low status**. Many women do not have access to **family planning**.

- In many African countries mothers have more than five children each.

> **Definition**
>
> **Feminist movement:** A social and political campaign started by women to achieve equality with men.

> **Definitions**
>
> **Replacement level:** The average number of children that mothers must have so that a population does not decline in the next generation.
>
> **Family planning:** When couples use contraception to plan the number of children they will have and when they will have them.

6 Education

In general, the **more educated** the population, the **smaller the family** and the **lower the population growth**. When parents, especially women, are educated, they are more likely to be aware of family planning and to raise healthy children. In addition, educated women are more likely to pursue a career outside the home. It is easier to do that with a small family.

- In **Ireland and Germany**, everyone goes to school and most complete second-level education. Many women combine careers with raising a family. Parents also tend to have fewer children because raising children is expensive.
- In **Brazil**, great strides have been made in girls' education in recent decades. At this time, 98 per cent of girls aged 15–24 are literate, while 47 per cent of girls complete secondary school. This helps to explain why the number of children per mother in Brazil today has fallen from **5 children in 1970 to 1.8 today**.

Geo fact
The German population would decline without **inward migration**. There were 8.2 million non-nationals living in Germany at the end of 2015.

Girls on their way to school in rural Brazil. Education helps them to make choices in their lives

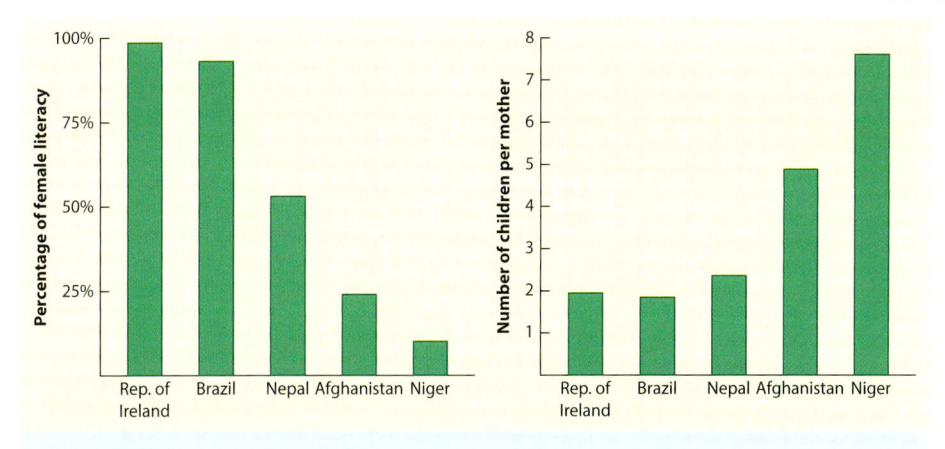

Figure 9.4 Female literacy and the number of children per mother in selected countries

Activity
Study the bar charts in Figure 9.4. **Explain** the connection between female literacy and the number of children per mother.

Figure 9.5 Annual rates of population growth today in selected countries

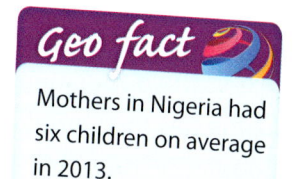

- Poland −0.1%
- Russia −0.5%
- USA 0.7%
- China 0.5%
- India 1.2%
- Sudan 2.2%
- South Sudan 4.1%
- Nigeria 2.8%
- Uganda 3.3%
- Brazil 0.9%

Geo fact
Mothers in Nigeria had six children on average in 2013.

229

Section 3 · Social Geography

> **Questions**
>
> 1 Explain how fertilisers help to increase food supply.
>
> 2 Explain how the following factors have reduced infant deaths in poor countries in recent decades:
>   - Vaccinations
>   - Clean water.
>
> 3 Give **two** reasons why educated women are more likely to plan their families.

9.3 Future rates of population increase

> **KEYWORDS**
>
> - Sub-Saharan Africa
> - fertility rate

People who study populations have different views about population growth in the future.

The population of the world has grown from **1.6 billion in 1900 to 7.3 billion in 2015**. Will that rate of increase continue into the future? If it does, the population will reach 10 billion by the middle of the twenty-first century. There are **pessimistic** and **optimistic** views about this.

The optimistic view

The more hopeful (optimistic) view is that the present growth rate in the world's population will continue to slow down and that the population will reach a steady level within a few decades. Optimists make the following points:

- The population in several **developed countries**, such as Japan and Russia, is decreasing as the population ages. Many more wealthy countries, especially in Europe, will show the same trend over the next decade.
- Many **developing countries**, such as Brazil, have seen dramatic declines in births per mother in only a few decades. This will happen in many other countries as they move across the population cycle.
- **China** has the world's largest population – almost 1.4 billion. However, Chinese population growth has slowed and the population is likely to begin to fall after 2030.
- As **Sub-Saharan Africa** develops and mothers become literate, this region will also see a decline in births per mother. It is already happening in South Africa, where female literacy is 94 per cent among young women.

Table 9.2 Population increase per annum

Year	Additional population
1990	87 million
2002	79 million
2015	76 million

The global rate of increase is slowing down

> **Definition**
>
> **Sub-Saharan Africa:** Africa south of the Sahara desert.

Chapter 9 · Population: Distribution, Diversity and Change

The pessimistic view

The less hopeful (pessimistic) view is that the population of the world will continue to expand quickly. Pessimists make the following points:

- The population of the world is still **growing at more than 1 per cent** a year.
- **India** will add more than 300 million to its present population by 2050 and surpass China's population.
- The population of **Africa** is likely to increase by 900 million by 2050 because the birth rate is still high. Mothers in most countries in Sub-Saharan Africa have an average of five children each. These children will grow up to have children of their own.

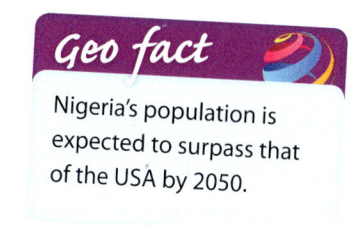

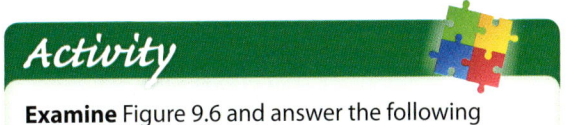

Geo fact

Nigeria's population is expected to surpass that of the USA by 2050.

Activity

Examine Figure 9.6 and answer the following questions:

1. What was the population in 1980?
2. What was the increase in the population between 1980 and 2016?
3. According to the optimistic view of the world's projected population, what figure will the population of the world reach by 2050?

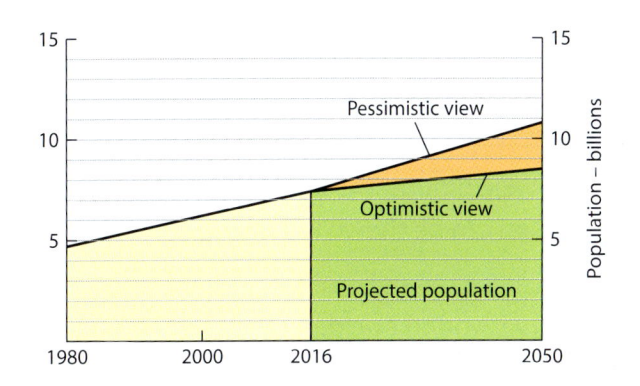

Figure 9.6 Forecasts for future population growth

What happens to the number of humans will depend on how fast **fertility rates** fall.

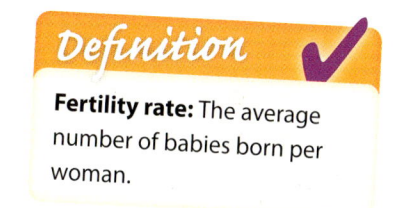

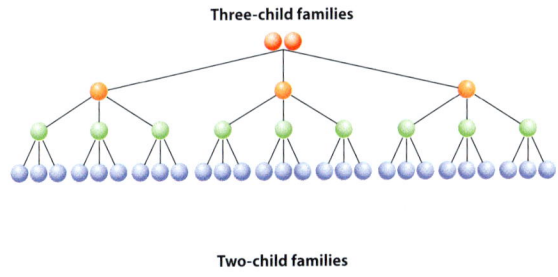

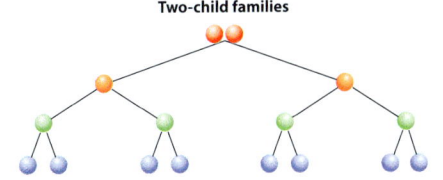

Definition

Fertility rate: The average number of babies born per woman.

Figure 9.7 In three generations, three-child families produce more than three times the number of people that two-child families produce

The world may reach the limit of the population it can hold during this century

231

Section 3 · Social Geography

> **Questions**
>
> 1 Give **two** reasons why optimists believe that the global population will stabilise (level off) within a few decades.
> 2 Give **one** reason why pessimists believe that global population will continue to grow rapidly.

9.4 Population pyramids

KEYWORDS
- population structure
- population pyramid
- life expectancy
- dependent population
- ageing population

How to read a population pyramid
- Age groups are arranged in bars for each age group.
- The length of each bar shows the numbers of people in each age group.
- Children's age groups are at the bottom of the pyramid. The oldest age groups are at the top.
- The male population is on the left and the female population is on the right.

Population structure means the make-up of a population. The population is divided up to show males and females of different age groups. The **age and sex structures** of a country's population can be shown with a **population pyramid**.

We can see at a glance whether the population of a country is young or elderly. We can also work out the percentage of people aged over 65 and the percentage of children of 14 and younger in a country. These groups are called the **dependent population**.

We will look at the population pyramid for three countries at different stages of the population cycle: Brazil, Ireland and Germany.

Table 9.3

	Fertility rate	Life expectancy
Brazil:	1.8	73.6 years
Ireland:	2.0	80.9 years
Germany:	1.4	80.9 years

The population pyramid of Brazil

- The pyramid of Brazil has a **fairly broad base** and a **young age structure**. This is because, until recent years, Brazil had a high birth rate.
- The pyramid gets **narrower at the base**. This is because mothers in Brazil have had fewer babies in recent years as parents plan their families. This shows that the birth rate is falling.
- The bars of **young adult** age groups are wide. This is good for the **economy** of the country because Brazil has a large, young and energetic labour force.
- The pyramid of Brazil is very **narrow at the top**. This is because Brazil has a **low life expectancy**, so the percentage of Brazilians aged over 65 is low.

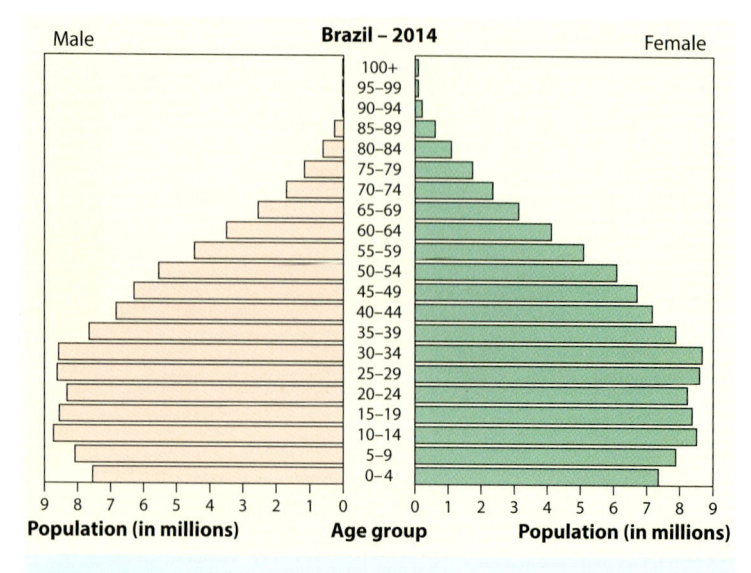

Figure 9.8 Population pyramid of Brazil

232

The population pyramid of Ireland

- The pyramid is narrow in the age groups from 15 to 29. One reason is because the **fertility rate was in decline** when those age groups were born.
- However, the **birth rate has increased** in recent years. We see this because the bars for the three youngest age groups have widened. One reason is that thousands of young adults migrated into Ireland during the **Celtic Tiger years** and became parents.
- The bars showing the 30–44 age groups are wide. This is because birth rates were higher when those people were born. **Inward migration** of East European adults also helps to explain the high numbers in those age groups.
- **Life expectancy is high** in Ireland. At the top of the pyramid, we can see that great numbers of people live into their eighties in Ireland. However, **women live longer than men**, as the top of the pyramid shows.

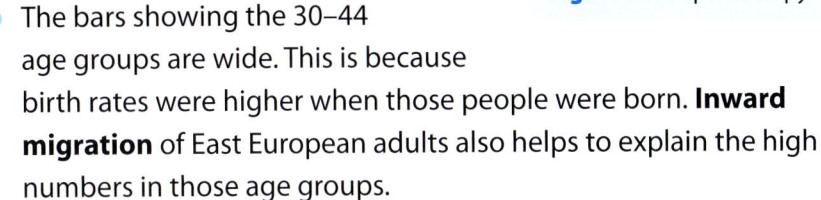

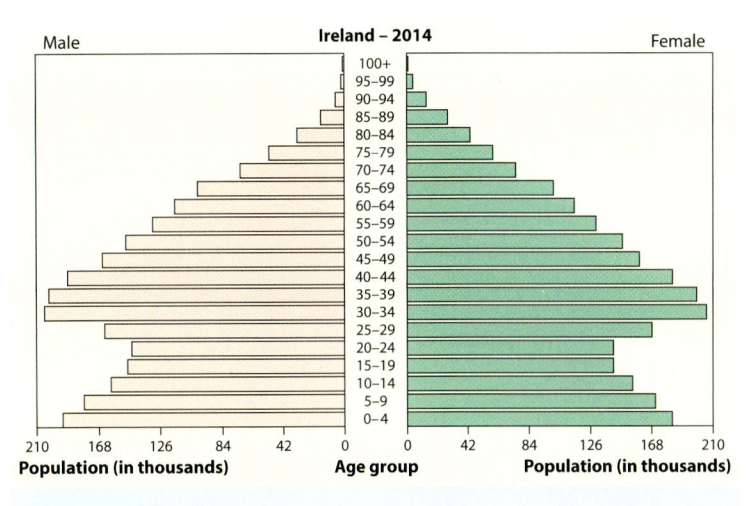

Figure 9.9 Population pyramid of Ireland

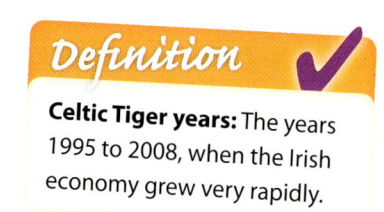

> **Definition** ✓
>
> **Celtic Tiger years:** The years 1995 to 2008, when the Irish economy grew very rapidly.

The population pyramid of Germany

- Germany's population pyramid has a **narrow base**. This shows that Germany has a **low birth rate**.
- The base of the pyramid is also **getting narrower**. This shows that the birth rate is continuing to decrease. Because of **family planning**, mothers had very few children during recent decades.
- The percentage of older people is high. This is because of **high life expectancy**. Germany has an **ageing population**.
- Women live longer than men in Germany. This is shown by the **wider top bars on the top right-hand side**.

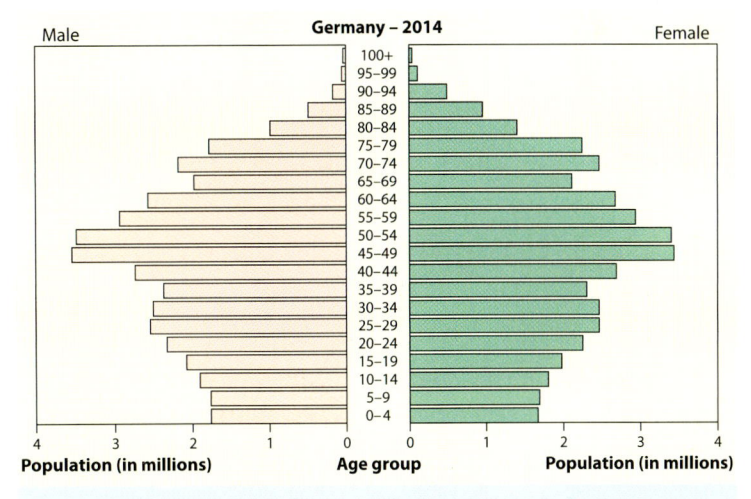

Figure 9.10 Population pyramid of Germany

Section 3 · Social Geography

Who uses population pyramids?

Population pyramids are used by people who **plan for the future needs of a population**.

- Brazil has a high percentage of young people. Government planners can see that schools have to be built for them and teachers trained to teach Brazil's young people.
- In Germany, many people are elderly. The government has to plan for their health and transport needs. Caring for the elderly will also be a challenge for health services.
- If a country has a low birth rate, this can mean that there may not be enough workers in the future. Governments may need to make plans to attract workers from other countries.

Elderly people practising tai chi in Berlin. Germany has an ageing population

Geo fact
Because of its ageing population, Singapore is offering financial benefits to couples who have a third child.

Questions

1. Look at the three population pyramids of Brazil, Ireland and Germany, pages 232–33, and answer the following questions:
   (a) How many women in Brazil are aged 30–34?
   (b) How many Irish children, including boys and girls, are in the 0–4 age group?
   - About 200,000
   - About 400,000
   - About 350,000

   (c) Which age group in Ireland had more people than any other age group?
   (d) Roughly how many women in Germany are aged 90–94?
   (e) Which country has the youngest population structure? Explain your answer.
   (f) Which country has the oldest population structure? Explain your answer.

2. Explain **one** reason for the increase in the population of children in Ireland.

3. Explain **one** effect of an ageing population in a country such as Germany.

9.5 Variations in population distribution and density

KEYWORDS
- population distribution
- population density
- resources
- terrain
- the Great Famine
- rural depopulation
- settler
- migration
- biofuel

The population of the world is unevenly **distributed**. In other words, the **density** of population is not the same everywhere. Even in the same area, population density can vary over time.

Some of the factors that cause this variation are:
- **Social and historical**
- To do with **resources and terrain**.

Definitions ✓
Population distribution: How people are spread over a region.

Population density: The average number of people living in a square kilometre.

Resources and terrain

People avoid regions that are very high, very wet and humid or very dry. For example, Greenland has very few people because most of it is covered by an ice cap. The Sahara and other deserts are too dry for farming.

On the other hand, there is high population density in many of the great **floodplains** of the world. These include the Ganges basin in India and the Nile valley in Egypt.

Western Europe has a high population density. This is due to its moderate climate, many excellent soils and large industrial cities.

Definitions

Resources: Any material or product that people find useful.

Terrain: The physical features of an area of land.

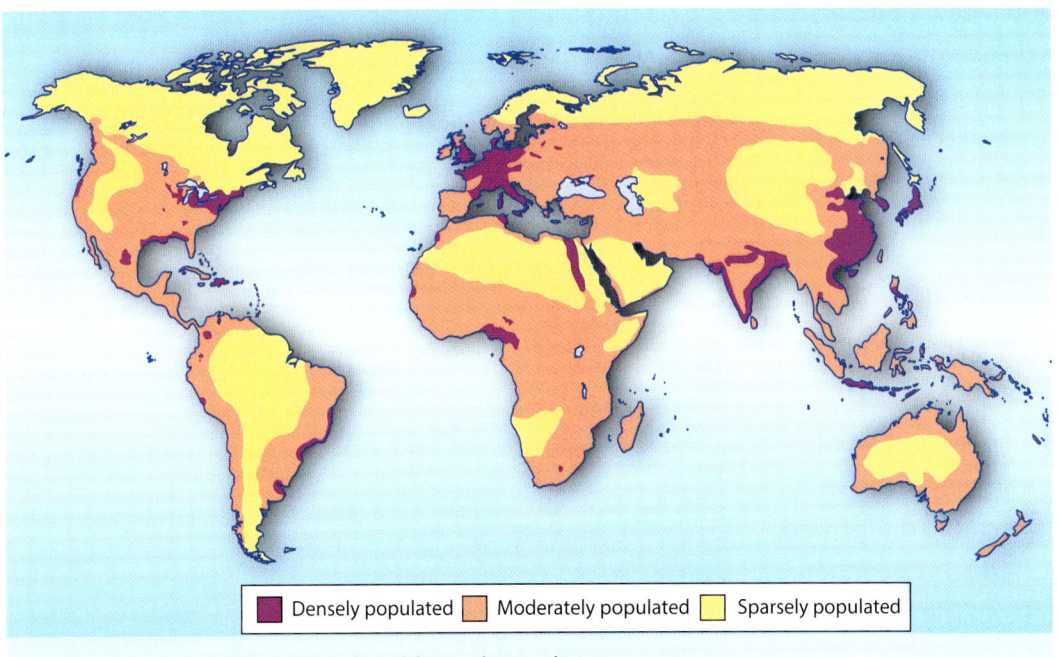

Figure 9.11 A simplified map of world population density

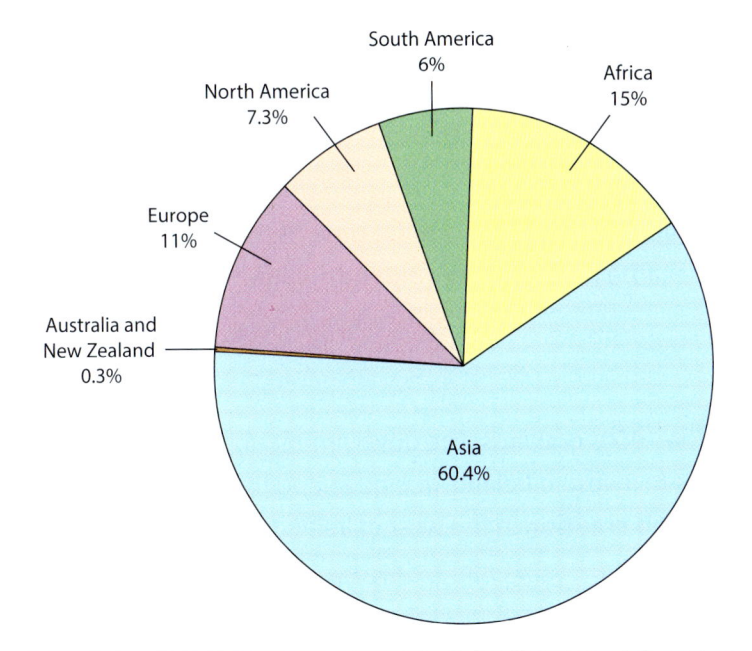

Figure 9.12 Percentage share of the world's population by continent

- North America 7.3%
- South America 6%
- Africa 15%
- Europe 11%
- Australia and New Zealand 0.3%
- Asia 60.4%

Geo fact

India and China have 37% of the world's population between them.

Activities

Examine Figure 9.12. What percentage of the world's population is found in North and South America combined?

Section 3 · Social Geography

Social and historical factors 1: west of Ireland

The population density of the west of Ireland has changed dramatically over the last two centuries.

Population growth before the Famine

After 1800, the population of the west of Ireland **grew very rapidly**. This was because:

- People married early and had **large families**.
- The **subdivision** of farms into **small plots of land** meant that every son got land and nobody had to emigrate to get a job.
- The small plots of land could grow enough **potatoes** to feed the large families.

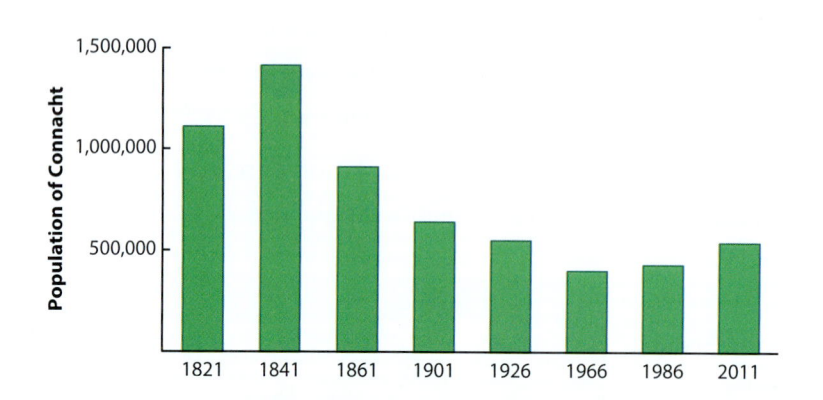

Figure 9.13 The population change of Connacht over time. People emigrated in the past because of the lack of resources

The impact of the Famine

The **Great Famine** of the 1840s halted population growth.

- Many thousands of people **died of hunger** and famine fever in the west of Ireland and many more **emigrated**.
- After the Famine, farmers no longer subdivided their land. The **eldest son** inherited the family farm.
- People **married later**. The eldest son married only after the younger family members had left. Therefore, **families got smaller**.
- People continued to **emigrate** for the next hundred years, and others left the rural areas to live in **towns and cities**.

Abandoned houses in Great Blasket Island off the coast of Kerry. The last remaining inhabitants left the island in 1953

As a result, the population of the west of Ireland declined steadily from the time of the Famine until the 1960s. Population distribution became more uneven, and population density decreased.

Population growth in recent decades

Population decline was halted and reversed from the 1960s onwards. The government under **Seán Lemass** encouraged multinational companies to invest in Ireland. Ireland joined the **EEC** (later the EU) in 1973. These two factors helped **job creation** in the west of Ireland.

The **Celtic Tiger** years that began in 1995 also helped to create jobs in the West. Irish and international companies invested in the West, particularly in Galway City. The population of **urban centres** such as Letterkenny, Sligo, Galway and Ennis grew very rapidly.

However, some rural areas in the west of Ireland continued to lose people to nearby towns and to the Dublin region, where many jobs were available. When rural areas lose people to towns and cities, **rural depopulation** takes place.

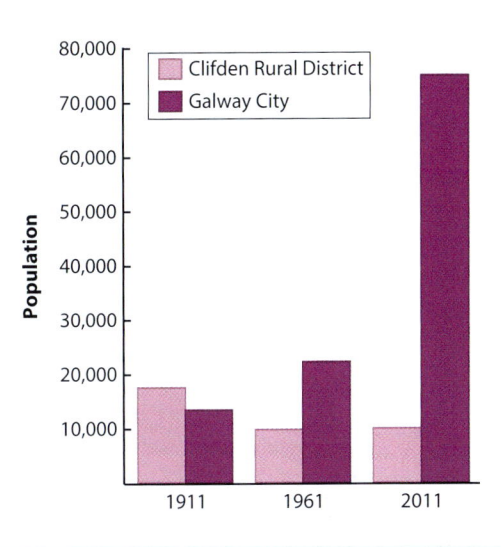

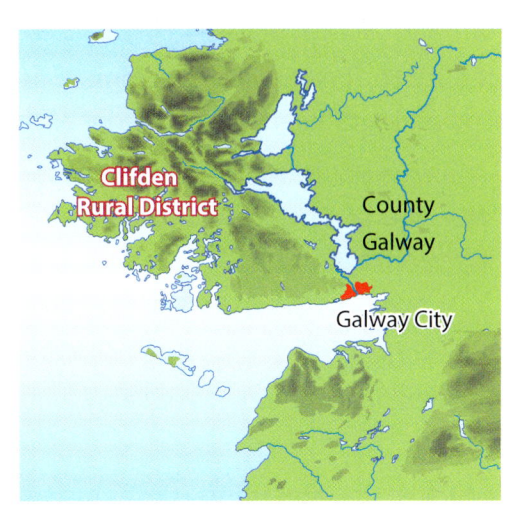

Figure 9.14 Population change in Clifden Rural District and Galway City

Social and historical factors 2: Brazil

Population density varies across Brazil and has also varied over time.

Table 9.4 Brazil's population in figures

Population 2015	203 million
Population density	24 per km² (Rep. of Ireland: 67)

Original inhabitants

The first people to live in Brazil crossed the Bering Strait from Asia and spread down through the American continent. It is estimated that **five million** inhabitants lived in Brazil before the European discovery of the Americas. They were mainly **hunter-gatherers**. Brazil had a very low population density, spread throughout the country.

Geo fact

Brazil covers almost half of South America.

European settlers

After the European discovery of the Americas, waves of **Portuguese** colonists arrived and settled along the **east coast of Brazil**.

- The **coastal climate** was suitable for growing coffee, cotton and sugar cane.
- Ports such as **Rio de Janeiro** were built so that sugar, coffee and other produce could be exported to Europe.
- **Population density rose sharply** on the east coast because of the **high birth rate** and also because people continued to **migrate** from Europe into the twentieth century. Many migrants from Germany, Italy and Switzerland settled on the cooler coast of southern Brazil.

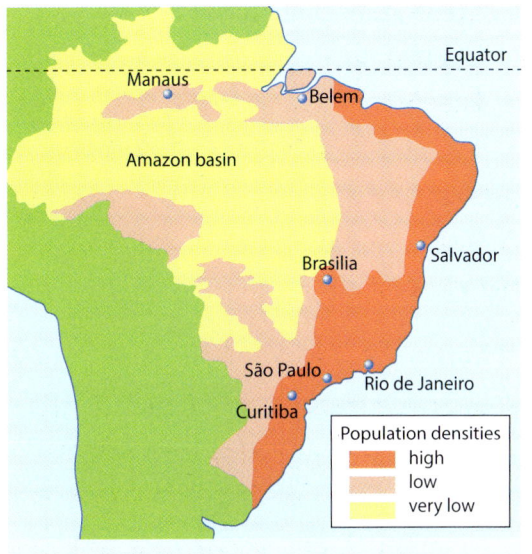

Figure 9.15 Population density in Brazil; 84 per cent of the population live in urban centres

237

Section 3 · Social Geography

Migration into the interior

In the 1960s, the Brazilian government began to encourage settlement in the interior of the country.

- A new capital, **Brasilia**, was built 1,000 km inland.
- New **roads** were opened up and settlers were offered **free land**.
- Vast **mineral resources**, such as iron ore and precious metals, were also discovered.

Settlement in the interior is not easy for the following reasons:

- Much of the **land is infertile** as heavy rains leach away the minerals from the soil.
- The natural vegetation of the Amazon basin is dense **tropical rainforest**.
- The **climate is extreme**, with high temperatures and humidity.

For those reasons, the Amazon basin has been called a **green hell**. The result is that many new settlers have sold their farms in the interior to large companies and ranchers. Vast estates now raise cattle or grow **soya beans** and **crops for biofuels**. A small number of workers use machines to work these estates.

Therefore, fifty years after the modern attempt to settle the interior began, **population density in the interior remains low**. East coast cities continue to expand.

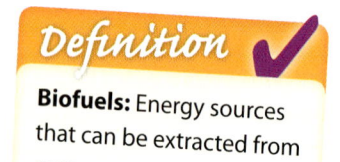

A road cuts through a recently deforested area. Roads have been built through the Amazon rainforest to encourage migration into the interior

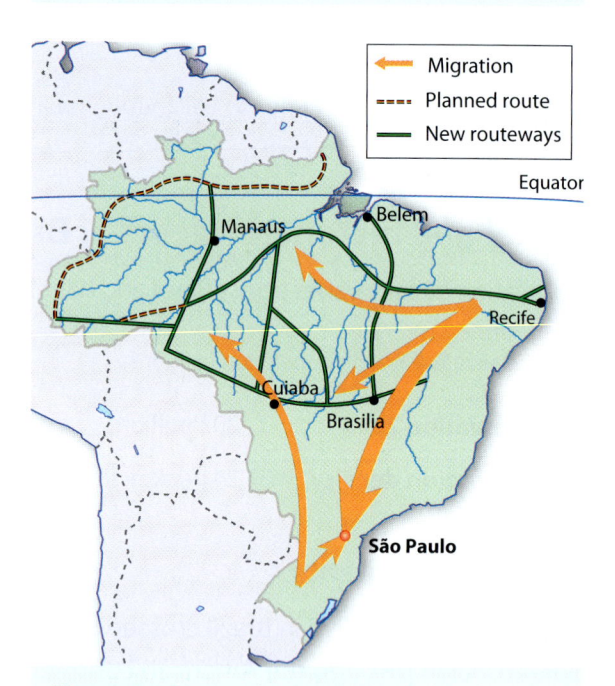

Figure 9.16 Internal migration in Brazil

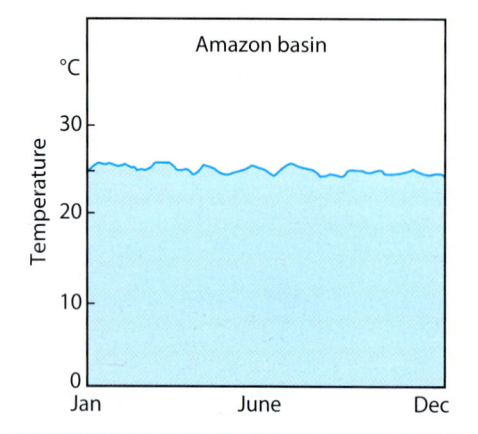

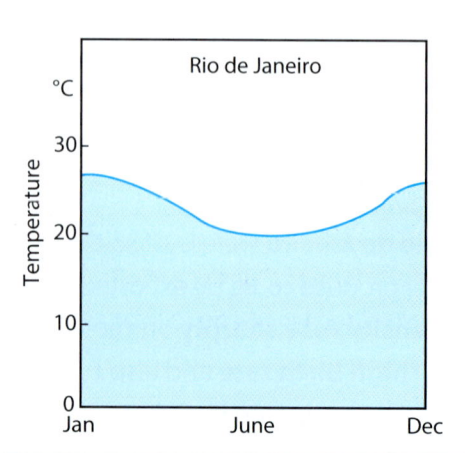

Definition

Biofuels: Energy sources that can be extracted from corn, sugar cane, grasses and organic waste.

Figure 9.17 Temperatures in the Amazon basin are hot all year round. Temperatures along the coast of Brazil vary, e.g. in Rio de Janeiro

Chapter 9 · Population: Distribution, Diversity and Change

The fate of native tribes

Native tribes of the interior have fared very badly. Over the centuries their population has fallen to 200,000 – a fraction of what it was 500 years ago.

Native people have low resistance to European diseases such as measles, which has resulted in many thousands dying.

Members of a Brazilian tribe in a reserve in Brazil

Resources and terrain 1: Dublin region

Dublin City and County contained more than 1.2 million people in 2011. This is more than twice the population of Connacht. In the Dublin region, population density is just over 1,000 people per km².

Scenes such as this are found in north Co. Dublin market gardens

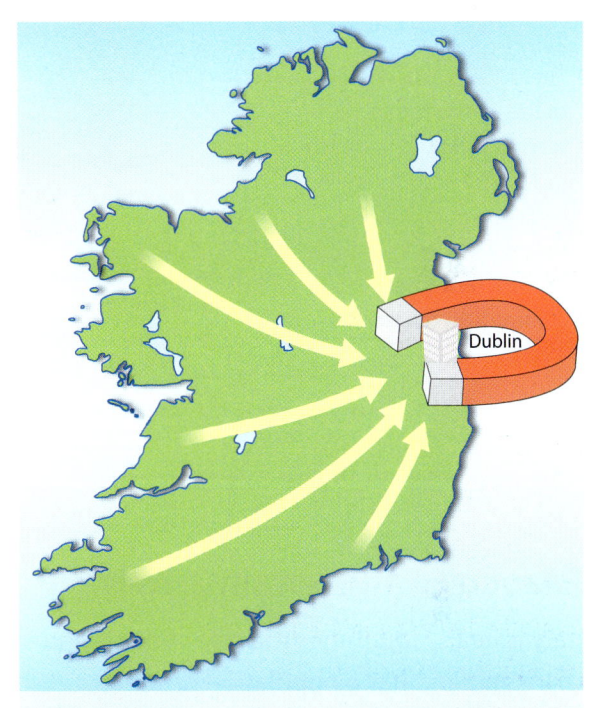

Figure 9.18 The magnetic pull of Dublin is due to the many jobs in the region

However, population density in the Dublin region varies from place to place and has changed over time. The population of the city has **grown dramatically since 1960** as the economy of the country has grown.

Coastal towns, such as Malahide, are expanding as the population of the region grows.

The Dublin region has many **resources**. It is Ireland's largest port. The city provides thousands of jobs in the civil service, media, shops and in transport.

The expanding city of Dublin showing low-rise suburbs; new towns have grown around Dublin in recent decades

239

Section 3 · Social Geography

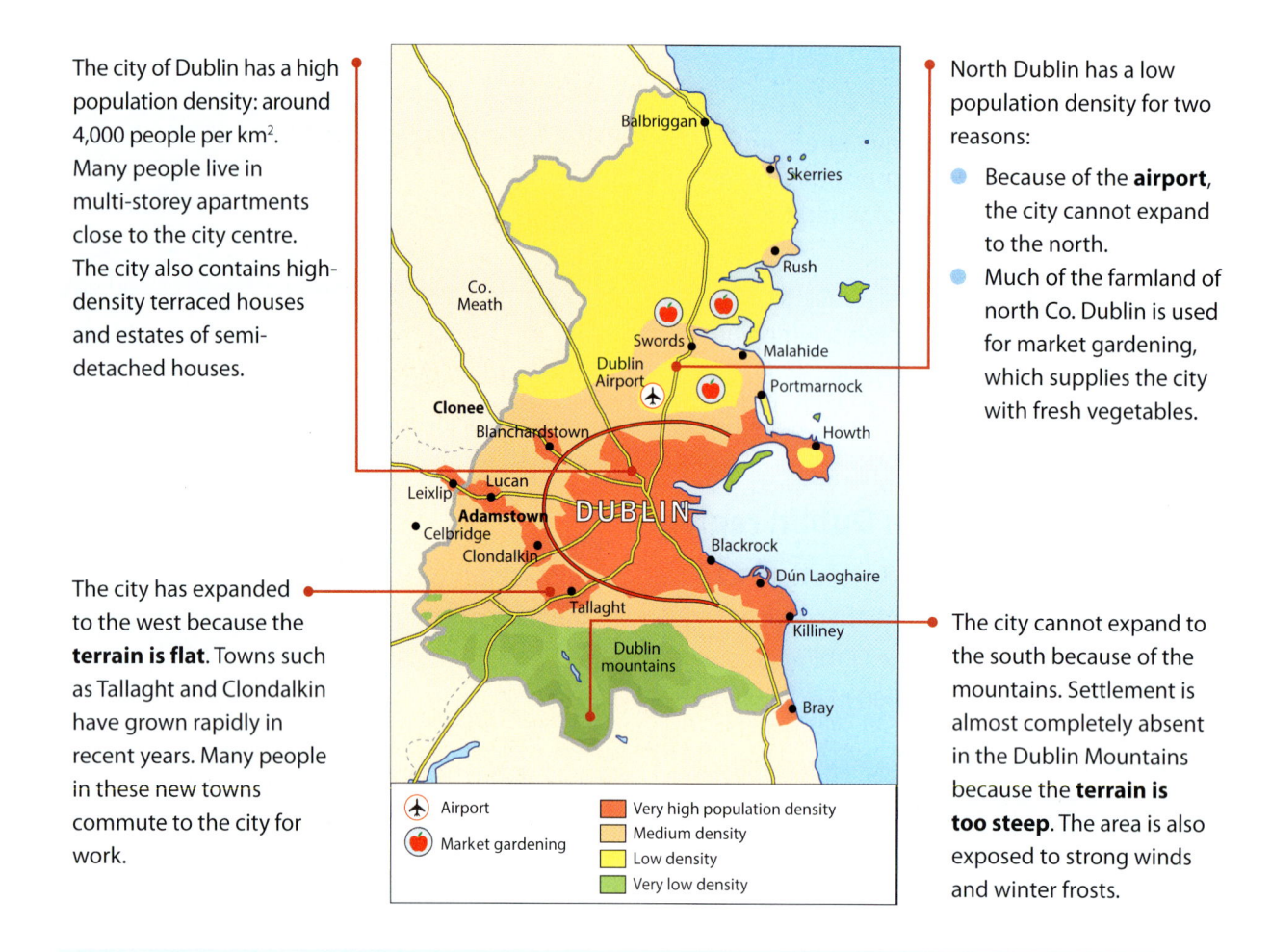

The city of Dublin has a high population density: around 4,000 people per km². Many people live in multi-storey apartments close to the city centre. The city also contains high-density terraced houses and estates of semi-detached houses.

The city has expanded to the west because the **terrain is flat**. Towns such as Tallaght and Clondalkin have grown rapidly in recent years. Many people in these new towns commute to the city for work.

North Dublin has a low population density for two reasons:
- Because of the **airport**, the city cannot expand to the north.
- Much of the farmland of north Co. Dublin is used for market gardening, which supplies the city with fresh vegetables.

The city cannot expand to the south because of the mountains. Settlement is almost completely absent in the Dublin Mountains because the **terrain is too steep**. The area is also exposed to strong winds and winter frosts.

Figure 9.19 Dublin City and County: varying population densities

Resources and terrain 2: Italy

Italy is nearly four times the size of the island of Ireland and has a population of some 61 million (2015). However, the population is **not evenly distributed**. The population from Rome to the Alps is 40 million people while the peninsula south of Rome and the islands of Sardinia and Sicily have a combined population of 21 million.

Natural conditions such as **climate**, **resources and terrain** help to explain why population distribution and density is uneven in Italy.

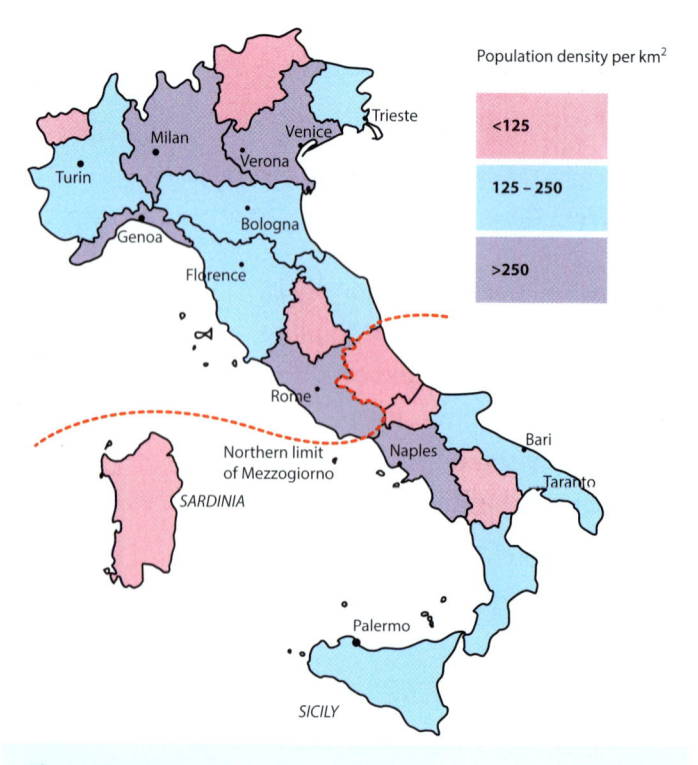

Figure 9.20 Population density in Italy

240

Northern and central Italy

Large areas of northern and central Italy have **high population density**.

The **Po valley** in the north is one of the most fertile and productive agricultural regions in the world for the following reasons.

- **Climate:** The **growing season** is about 270 days in length. Average summer **temperatures** of 22°C are ideal for crops such as wheat, corn and sunflowers. **Rainfall** is well distributed throughout the growing season.
- **Resources:** It has excellent **alluvial soils** – a great natural resource.
- **Terrain:** The **landscape** of the Po valley is flat or rolling – ideal for large machinery such as combine harvesters.
- **Location:** Farmers have a very large **market** in northern Italy and produce vast quantities of cereals, dairy products, vegetables and wines.

Intensive agriculture in the Po delta in northern Italy. Much of the land is under plastic to protect crops and help them grow

For all these reasons, the Po valley can support a large population.

In addition, the Alps produce **hydroelectricity**, another very important **natural resource**, which is used in the industries of the great cities of the north. These cities include Milan, Turin, Genoa and Bologna.

Manufacturing companies in these cities include Fiat, Olivetti, Lamborghini, Ferrari, Gucci and Benetton. These companies **employ a large number** of people. Their products are sold all over the world. For generations, migrants have fled the poverty of the south and have settled in northern Italy, where they have found work.

The Alps have wonderful scenery and winter snows, which support the **tourist industry**. These, in addition to the beaches of the Adriatic, are also **natural resources**.

The artistic and cultural treasures of Venice, Milan, Florence and Rome are not natural resources but they support more than one million workers.

Section 3 · Social Geography

Southern Italy, Sardinia and Sicily

These areas are together known as the **Mezzogiorno**. The Mezzogiorno is the poorest region in Italy.

- **Climate:** The climate is very extreme. Summer **drought** reduces crop yields as fields become parched and grass dries up. Only goats and a few sheep survive in the hills. Many farms have an output per hectare that is only **one fifth** that of the north of Italy. Irrigation helps, but this is confined to small areas.
- **Resources:** The south has **few natural resources**. Only the area around Naples supports a population density of more than 250 per km². This is because of the area's **rich volcanic soils**. Naples also has a good natural harbour.
- **Terrain:** Unlike the north, 85 per cent of the Mezzogiorno terrain is either **hilly or mountainous**. The Apennine Mountains extend southwards along the Italian peninsula. The **soil** in much of the south is thin and stony. Farms are small with low yields of wheat, olives and grapes. Slopes are steep with much **soil erosion** due to deforestation.
- **Location:** The Mezzogiorno has many beaches, historic ruins and volcanic mountains, but only 13 per cent of visitors to Italy go south of Rome.

In general, **manufacturing** in the south is small-scale and manufacturing industries are much less efficient than those in the north. Very few foreign firms locate in the south. For that reason, the south remains poorer and less populated than the north. The young continue to **migrate** to the north of Italy and to other EU countries.

The landscape of southern Italy. The land is hilly, with small farms and fields

Geo fact
'Mezzogiorno' is the Italian for 'midday'. It is a name given to the south of Italy because the sun shines from the south at midday.

Questions

1. Study Figure 9.12 on page 235 and answer the following questions:
   (a) Name the continent with the largest population.
   (b) What percentage of the world's population is in Africa and South America combined?

2. Look at Figure 9.13 on page 236 showing population change in Connacht over time.
   (a) Why did the population decline during the years 1861 to 1966?
   (b) Explain **one** reason for the gradual increase in the population of Connacht from 1966 to the present time.

3. Name **one** area of Brazil where population density is low.

4. Look at Figure 9.19, the population density map of Co. Dublin on page 240.
   (a) Explain **two** reasons for the lower population density in north Co. Dublin.
   (b) Explain **one** reason for the expansion of the urban area into west Dublin.

5. (a) What effect do the Alps and the Apennine Mountains have on population density in Italy?
   (b) Give **two** reasons why the Po valley supports high population densities.
   (c) Explain **one** reason for the outward migration of young people from the south of Italy.

9.6 Low population densities

KEYWORDS
- marriage rate
- political isolation
- economic isolation
- export crop
- nomadic herder
- desertification

Very low populations densities can lead to:
- Low marriage rates
- Abandonment of agricultural land
- Political and economic isolation.

1 The west of Ireland

As we have seen, the population density of the west of Ireland is very low in comparison with that of the east coast counties. This has had important consequences for the west of Ireland.

Low marriage rates in rural areas

Before the 1930s, a **matchmaker** arranged some marriages in rural areas. A marriage guaranteed a wife for the eldest son on the farm, but matchmaking had little to do with romance. Marriages were business deals.

- A young farmer finished his education at age 13 and stayed at home. He eventually **inherited the family farm**. However, with the decline in matchmaking, it was up to a young farmer to seek a wife.
- Many young people left the west of Ireland because there were so few **job opportunities** there.
- Females with secondary education moved to the cities to find jobs in the **civil service, teaching or nursing**.
- A poorly educated farmer was very unlikely to persuade a young female teacher, civil servant or nurse back from Dublin to live in a small house on a poor, remote farm.
- As a result, large numbers of **bachelor farmers** in the West lived lonely lives with their ageing parents.
- Because of low marriage rates, **birth rates fell** and the **population decreased**.

The introduction of mass secondary education in the late 1960s meant that young men were better educated and gained confidence. As a result, the number of bachelors fell significantly. In recent decades, young people have become more mobile, because many of them own cars. This has made it easier to find a partner in the West.

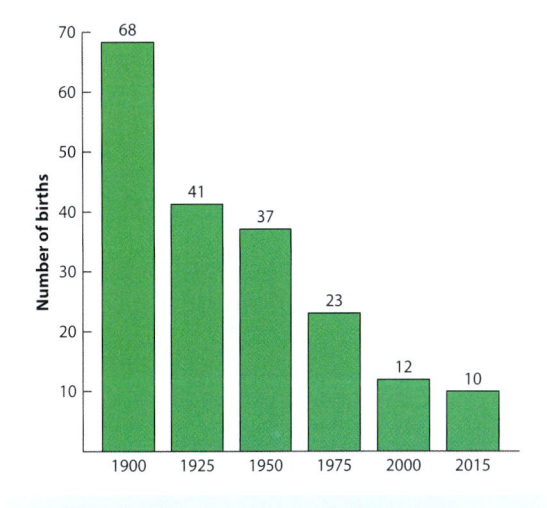

Figure 9.21 The number of babies born in a rural parish in the west of Ireland in selected years

The landscape in Connemara is beautiful but the population density there is very low. Can you explain why?

'A match was made when a farm needed a woman.'

Traditional saying

Section 3 · Social Geography

Abandonment of agricultural land

A lot of agricultural land in the west of Ireland is no longer being farmed.

- Many farms in the West are **too small** to make a living out of them.
- Many farmers' children now go on to **third-level education**.
- The economic opportunities in **manufacturing and services** in **urban centres**, such as Letterkenny, Sligo and Ennis, allow many young people the opportunity to work in jobs other than agriculture.
- The result is that many small farms in the West are now being used for **forestry**.
- Near the western seaboard, some land is being turned over to **tourism**, e.g. caravan parks and golf courses.

Political and economic isolation

The west of Ireland is distant from Dublin – the economic centre of the state. Because of its low population, the West has only a small number of TDs and Senators in the Dáil. Therefore, the West **lacks** the **political influence** of the Dublin region.

Communications in the West are not as modern as those in the east of Ireland:

- In 2016, only two of the western seaboard counties, Galway and Clare, had **motorways**.
- Many rural areas in the West still did not have **broadband** in 2016, which is vital to business today.

The West's position on the edge of Ireland and Europe means that companies are less likely to locate there, because of the distance from markets at home and abroad.

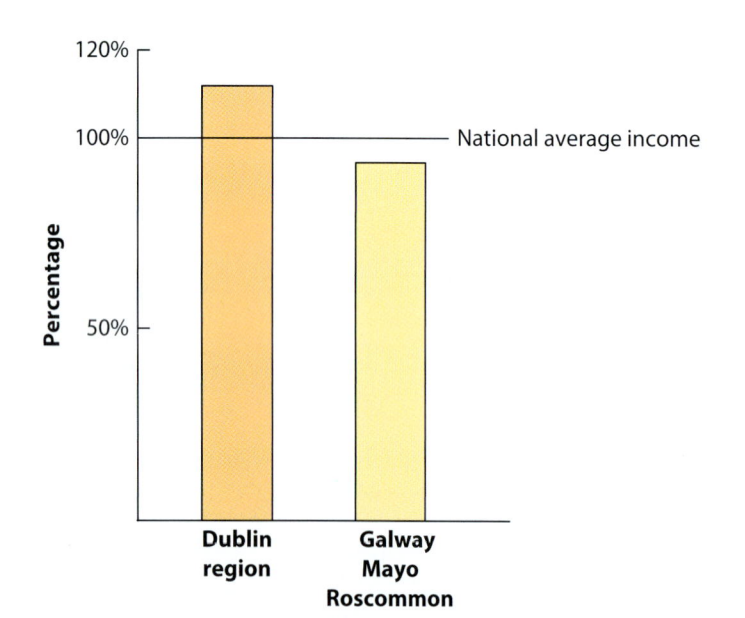

Figure 9.22 The disposable income of people in western counties was much less than that of people in Dublin in 2011

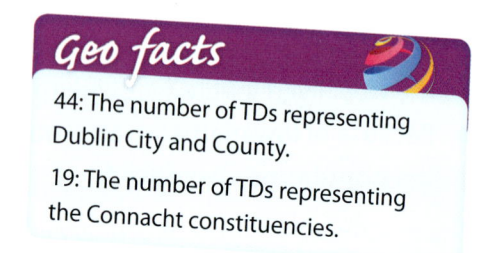

Geo facts

44: The number of TDs representing Dublin City and County.

19: The number of TDs representing the Connacht constituencies.

Chapter 9 · Population: Distribution, Diversity and Change

2 Mali: a country with low population density

Mali in West Africa is a **landlocked** state. Northern Mali forms part of the Sahara desert, while central Mali is part of the Sahel (see page 119). It is one of the world's poorest countries. Mali is more than twelve times the size of the island of Ireland, but it has a **very low population density**.

Mali's population is composed of many cultural groups.

- Most people live in the **south** because of the **higher rainfall**.
- In the south, farmers live along the **River Niger**, where they grow food with the help of irrigation canals. They also raise cattle. **Cotton** is grown as an **export crop**.
- **Nomadic herders** live in the desert and semi-desert regions of the **north**. Their animals include camels, donkeys, sheep and goats.

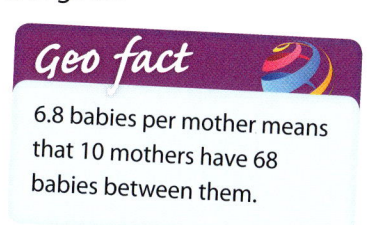

Definitions

Export crop: A crop such as cotton or cocoa that is grown for export.

Nomadic herders: People who move from place to place with their animals in search of grass.

Geo fact
6.8 babies per mother means that 10 mothers have 68 babies between them.

Table 9.5 Mali in figures

Area	1,240,100 km^2
Estimated population 2015	16.2 million
Population density	12.6 per km^2
Urban population	36%
Annual population growth	2.6%
Babies per mother (average)	6.8

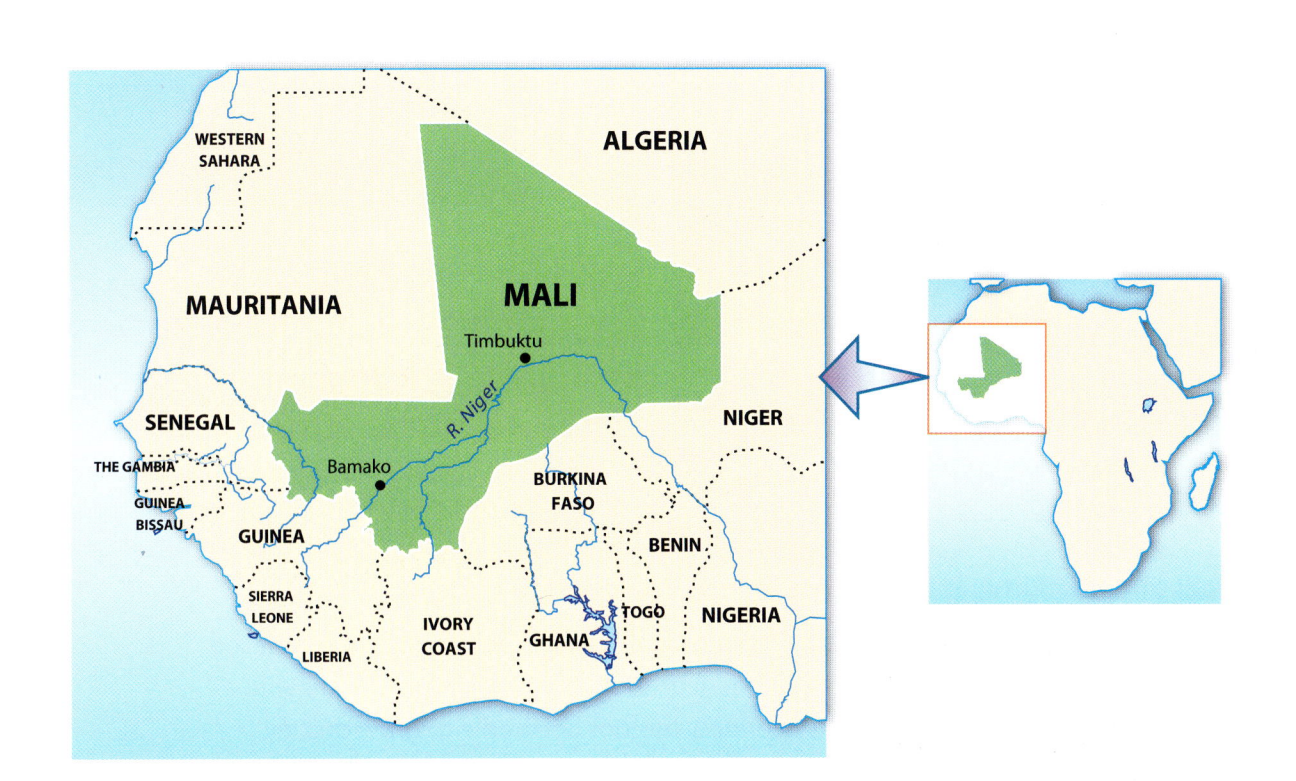

Figure 9.23 Mali and surrounding countries

245

Section 3 · Social Geography

Low marriage rates in rural areas

Life in remote, semi-desert areas of Mali is very difficult. Remote areas in northern Mali are losing young people, **especially young men**, to the cities, where they go in search of work. The **drift to the cities** by young men leads to a mismatch: too many men in the cities and too many women in the countryside. This makes it more difficult for some young people to find spouses.

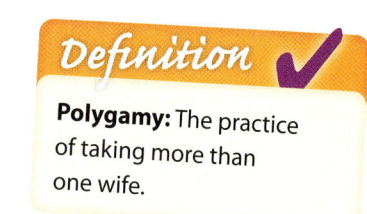

Polygamy, allowed in some societies, is still a frequent occurrence in Malian society. Polygamy has a long tradition in Mali and neighbouring countries. It gives women the opportunity to marry in areas where there is a shortage of men.

> **Definition**
> **Polygamy:** The practice of taking more than one wife.

Abandonment of agricultural land

Mali suffers from frequent **droughts**.

- When drought occurs, the already sparse scrub is quickly stripped bare by **grazing animals**.
- People cut the already scarce **timber** for firewood.
- Long periods of drought, overgrazing and cutting of firewood lead to **desertification** in the Sahel.
- When animals die in times of drought, herders are forced to **abandon agricultural land** and head for the towns and cities in the south to find work. This leads to **low population density** in rural areas.

> **Link**
> For more on **Desertification,** see Chapter 6, pages 119–20.

Desert scene in Mali where population densities are very low

A village in south-eastern Mali where the Dogon tribe live. The climate is not as arid here as in the north

Political and economic isolation

For most of the twentieth century Mali was a **colony** of France. It was **politically isolated** and **underdeveloped**. Mali became independent in 1960, but it is a poor country with a widely spread population. As a result, its economy has not been able to grow quickly.

- Mali's **transport system** is not well developed. It has very **poor road and rail links** with its neighbours. Therefore, foreign trade is very low.
- It has **no known reserves of oil or gas**, and therefore is of little interest to the outside world. However, **gold mines in the south** of the country have created employment and led to an increase in exports.

The government of Mali has attempted to reduce its political and economic isolation in recent years with the following steps:

- Mali is now a member of the **African Union**, an organisation of states. This has helped to reduce its isolation from its neighbours.
- Mali joined the **World Trade Organization** (WTO) to help it to increase foreign trade.
- The Malian government has established **good relations with the USA**.

Questions

1 Give **one** reason why some men found it difficult to find a partner in the west of Ireland after the tradition of matchmaking ended.

2 Can you explain **one** reason why income in the west of Ireland is lower than it is in the Dublin region?

3 Draw a map of West Africa. Mark in and name:
- Mali
- The River Niger
- The city of Bamako
- Three countries that share a border with Mali.

9.7 High population densities

KEYWORDS
- pavement dweller
- water supply
- dysentery
- bustee
- apartment block
- air pollution
- red tide

The density of population in an area has significant effects on the social and economic geography of that area.

Very high densities can lead to:

- Overcrowding
- Shortage of clean water
- Pollution
- Lack of open space.

We will examine high population densities in **Kolkata** and **Hong Kong**.

Higher Level students must study Kolkata **and** Hong Kong. **Ordinary Level** students study Kolkata **or** Hong Kong.

Geo fact
Calcutta was renamed **Kolkata** in 2001.

Section 3 · Social Geography

1 Kolkata (Calcutta)

Kolkata is one of the largest cities in India, a **developing country**. It is a great manufacturing city and a major port. It has a famous university and modern hospitals. However, it is **very densely populated**, and wealth and poverty exist side by side in the city. Kolkata has many problems.

Overcrowding

- Many areas of the city have a density of more than 24,000 people per km^2.
- A large number of people from the countryside have **migrated** to Kolkata because of evictions, famine, floods, violence and poverty.
- **Three generations** of one family often live in a very small home. When weather permits, many people sleep on the street or on the roof.
- Newly arrived, poor **migrants** to the city live in makeshift dwellings made of plastic and waste timber in the **shanty towns**. These are found near railway stations and in open ground at the edge of the city.
- Some even sleep under bridges or live on pavements. They are known as **pavement dwellers**.
- Kolkata's **high birth rate** has also contributed to the rapid growth of the population.

Figure 9.24 Kolkata stretches for 64 km along the River Hooghly

Table 9.6 Population growth in the Kolkata urban area

Year	1820	1931	1961	2015
	250,000	1.2 m	4.4 m	14.5 m

The smells from refuse heaps, smoke from the cooking stalls that line many streets, and monsoon rains that flood the streets, are some of the challenges that people in the city face.

Shortage of clean water

- Providing a **clean water supply** for a rapidly growing population has been a major challenge for the city.
- Middle-class homes and hotels have **water on tap**. However, most people who can afford it use an electrically powered **water filter** as well.
- Poor districts do not have water piped to homes. Instead, shared water pipes on the pavement provide drinking water.
- If this water becomes polluted it can lead to outbreaks of diseases such as **dysentery**.
- People in poor districts wash clothes and take showers in washing areas located on pavements, using water that has been pumped from the polluted **River Hooghly**.
- Shanty town residents have to travel to nearby streets for drinking water.

Men using a tap on the pavement in Kolkata to wash with

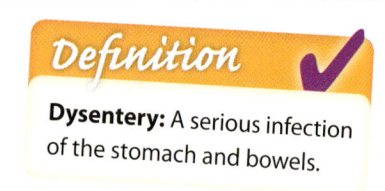

Definition

Dysentery: A serious infection of the stomach and bowels.

248

Chapter 9 · Population: Distribution, Diversity and Change

Lack of open space

The centre of Kolkata has a large park, most of which is open to the public. It is located on the banks of the River Hooghly and also contains a racetrack and sports grounds.

However, open space is in short supply in Kolkata because of population pressure:

- In most areas front and back gardens are non-existent. Children play on the side streets beside their homes.
- Much of city life is lived on the **pavements**. Thousands of people sleep on them; craftspeople conduct their business on them. Many people cook and sell food on the pavements.
- The shanty towns, known as **bustees**, have occupied any spare space at the edges of the city.

Kolkata people are very proud of their city and of its tolerance for different cultures. They do not welcome the image of poverty that Kolkata has in many countries and think that it is undeserved.

The city has an excellent and cheap **underground railway** line. The **Internet** is widely available.

Newcomers to the city live anywhere they can find space, in this case beside a railway track

Kolkata people are friendly, cheerful and extremely hard working. Most people make great sacrifices to send their children to school, which they see as an escape route from poverty.

2 Hong Kong

Hong Kong had a population of about **7.28 million** people in 2015 in an area not much bigger than Co. Dublin. It has very high population density because most of its population is crowded into two districts, **Kowloon** and **Victoria**. These two districts make up a mere 10 per cent of the land area of Hong Kong. Therefore, **overcrowding** in those areas is severe.

However, Hong Kong is a **wealthy city** in comparison with Kolkata. The figures below indicate that the standard of living in Hong Kong is quite high. Irish people, used to low-rise dwellings, would consider Hong Kong to be extremely crowded.

Table 9.7 Hong Kong in figures

Life expectancy in years	84
Number of children per mother	1.1
Child mortality rate per thousand live births	2.3
Income per head in US$	40,320
Percentage of Internet users	74%
Population density	6,897 per km^2

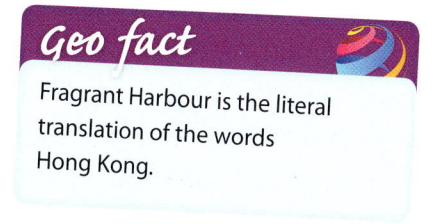

Geo fact
Fragrant Harbour is the literal translation of the words Hong Kong.

Geo fact
54 million tourists visited Hong Kong in 2013, most of them from mainland China.

Section 3 · Social Geography

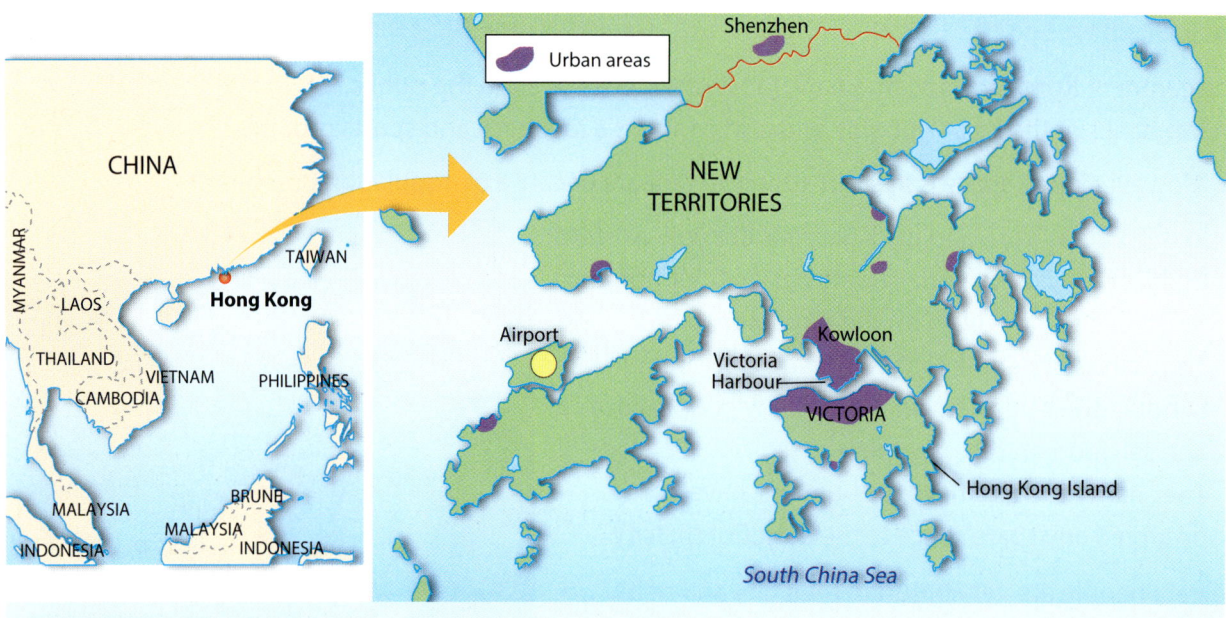

Figure 9.25 China and Hong Kong

High-rise apartment living

Hong Kong grew rapidly in the **twentieth century**, from 500,000 people in 1920 to 7.28 million in 2015. For much of the twentieth century, the city had a **high birth rate**. The population also grew because of a large influx of **migrant workers** from mainland China.

- Most of the population live in **high-rise apartment blocks**. Each apartment block houses hundreds of families. With births averaging one child per mother, most apartments have just two small bedrooms.
- In the city centre, thousands of old people without a family sleep in **overcrowded dormitories** in bunks that may be three tiers high.
- Others live in tiny caged spaces big enough for a single bunk. These are known as **bedspace apartments** or **cage homes**.

Water supply

Providing more than 7 million people with enough safe water has been achieved in the following ways:

- A bay on the coast known as Plover Cove was dammed to store fresh water from streams and became a huge **reservoir** of fresh water.
- China agreed to provide water from a nearby river. Modern **filter systems** make the water supply safe.
- **Seawater** is used for flushing toilets using separate mains and piping. This accounts for 15 per cent of water use.

A Hong Kong street with multi-storey apartment buildings

Pollution

Hong Kong is a hive of economic activity. The city is teeming with factories and workshops.

- **Air pollution** is a major problem. At street level, traffic emissions can be very difficult for residents.
- Many beaches and bays around Hong Kong are heavily polluted from **industrial waste and sewage**.
- Several beaches sometimes have algae known as a **red tide**. These algae continue to be a health hazard for bathers.

Lack of open space

- Buildings in Hong Kong are often so high that they **block the sunlight** at street level.
- **Land has been reclaimed** from the sea to create space for new industrial zones. The only place to locate the new international airport was an **artificial island** in the bay.
- However, on Hong Kong island the hills outside the city are too steep for buildings and are covered in trees. These areas have forest tracks, which provide a **peaceful area** for people to escape the bustle of the city.

A red tide in the seawater in Hong Kong. This type of algae kills farmed fish and closes beaches to bathers

Questions

1. Explain **two** reasons for the overcrowding in Kolkata.
2. Write down **one** reason why people in some parts of Kolkata are short of clean water.
3. Explain **one** reason why many people live in high-rise apartments in Hong Kong.
4. Describe **two** examples of pollution that people in Hong Kong have to face in their daily lives.

9.8 Global patterns: the North/South divide

KEYWORDS
- the North
- the South
- child mortality
- life expectancy
- balanced diet
- malnutrition
- HIV/AIDS

In the world as a whole, there are sharp social inequalities among regions, related in part to population characteristics.

An unequal world

There are two major economic regions in the world: the developed world (**the North**) and the developing world (**the South**).

In the **developed world**, almost all **babies survive infancy** and most people have long lives. People have clean water, plenty of food and a good quality of life.

Definition

The North: The developed world/the First World.

The South: The developing world/the Third World.

Section 3 · Social Geography

In the **developing world**, most **children are born to poor parents**. Many babies die in infancy and many children, especially girls, do not attend school.

Therefore, it is an unequal world. We will examine how unequal it is in relation to:

- Child mortality
- Life expectancy.

Child mortality in the developed world

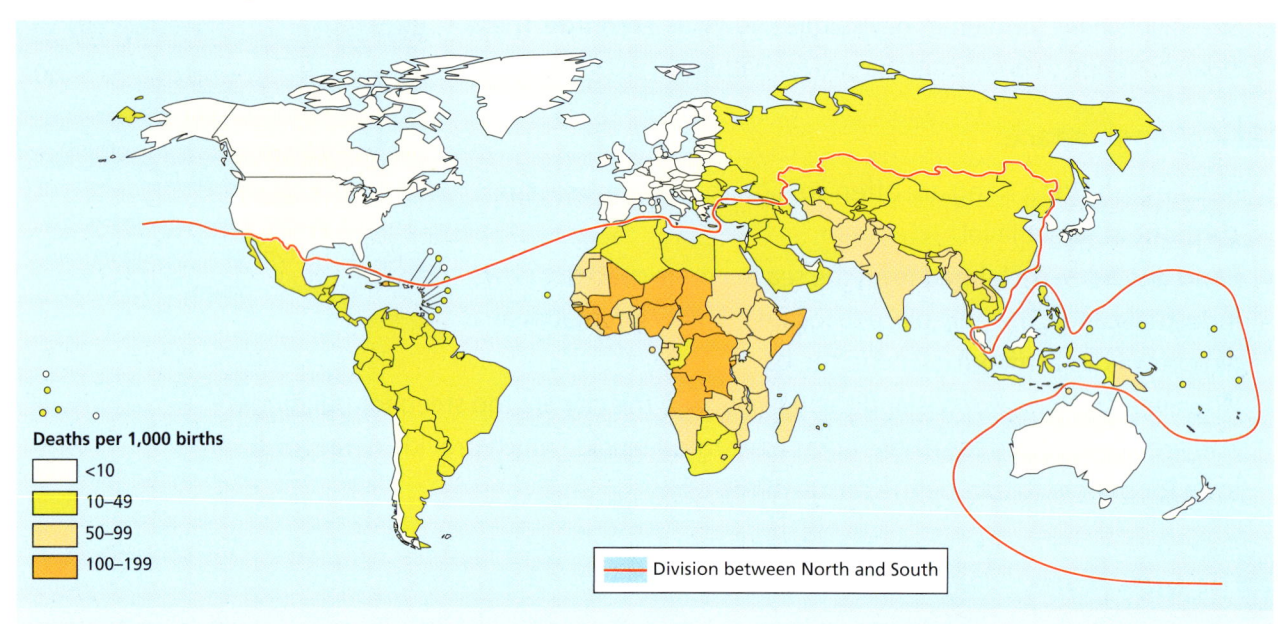

Deaths per 1,000 births
- <10
- 10–49
- 50–99
- 100–199

Division between North and South

Figure 9.26 World map of child mortality (deaths of children under the age of five) © WHO

The child mortality rate is the average number of children who die under the age of five for every 1,000 born per year. This rate is **very low in the developed world** (the North) because children's health is a priority. There are several reasons for low child mortality:

- **Healthy mothers** have healthy babies.
- Mothers receive **excellent care** during pregnancy.
- Most women have their babies in **maternity hospitals** where the health of mothers and babies can be monitored around the clock.
- Young children receive many **vaccinations** to protect them against diseases that used to kill. These include the **6 in 1** and **MMR** vaccines.
- **Safe water** – free of harmful bacteria – is available on tap.
- **Sanitation systems** keep cities free of health hazards.
- Parents are well educated and know the importance of providing a **balanced diet** for their infants.
- There is good access to a **wide range of foods** to make sure that children have a healthy diet.

Newborn babies in Germany

Activity

Find out:
- What vaccinations are given in the 6 in 1.
- What the letters MMR stand for.

Activity

What are the most important features of a balanced diet? **Discuss** this in class.

Child mortality in the developing world

Why do so many babies and children die in the developing world (the South)? There are several reasons for this, many of them related to **poverty**:

- Many **mothers give birth at home** in villages where medical care is unavailable. Therefore, many babies die if there is a birth complication.
- The poorer the family, the more likely it is that a mother's health is poor. **Unhealthy mothers** are more likely to have babies who are underweight. These babies are at risk from measles, whooping cough and other infections.
- There may not be access to a wide range of foods, so children **may not have a balanced diet**.
- There is often **little access to clean water**.
- In many countries, **mothers are uneducated**. They may be unaware of the importance of hygiene. Therefore, they often use **unboiled water** to feed babies and young children. This can cause stomach infections, which can lead to diarrhoea, dehydration and the death of a young child in a short time.
- **Poor sanitation** systems can also lead to outbreaks of disease.
- Major efforts are being made to vaccinate babies and young children against killer infections, even in the poorest countries. However, **malaria** and **measles** still cause many young children to die in the developing world, especially in Africa.
- The best way to prevent malaria is to sleep under a treated **mosquito net**. However, in Sub-Saharan Africa, most children do not have mosquito nets. This leads to many deaths.

A very poor part of Nairobi, Kenya.

Activity
Look at the photo above. Can you think of one reason why illness is common here?

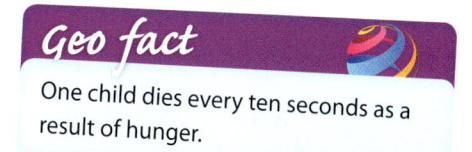

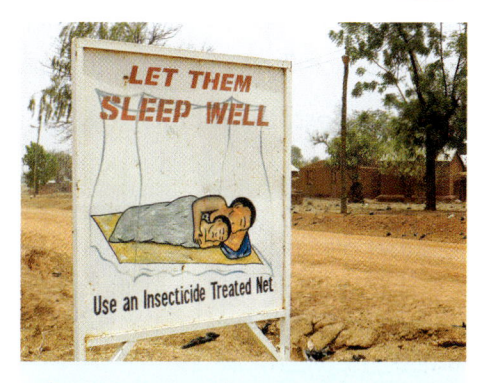

Geo fact
One child dies every ten seconds as a result of hunger.

A poster encouraging parents to use mosquito nets to protect themselves and their children from malaria

Life expectancy in the developed world

The age at which people die depends on where in the world they live. People live much longer in rich countries than in poor countries.
Life expectancy in developed countries (the North) is high for many reasons:

- **Child mortality is very low** because of vaccinations against childhood infections.
- People have a **balanced diet** that helps to keep them healthy.
- **Safe water** supplies and **sanitation** systems are available to all.
- Excellent **medical services** help people to live longer.
- **Smoking bans** in workplaces are reducing the health risks that are linked to smoking in many countries.

Smoking kills. Smoke-free zones are becoming more widespread for that reason

253

Section 3 · Social Geography

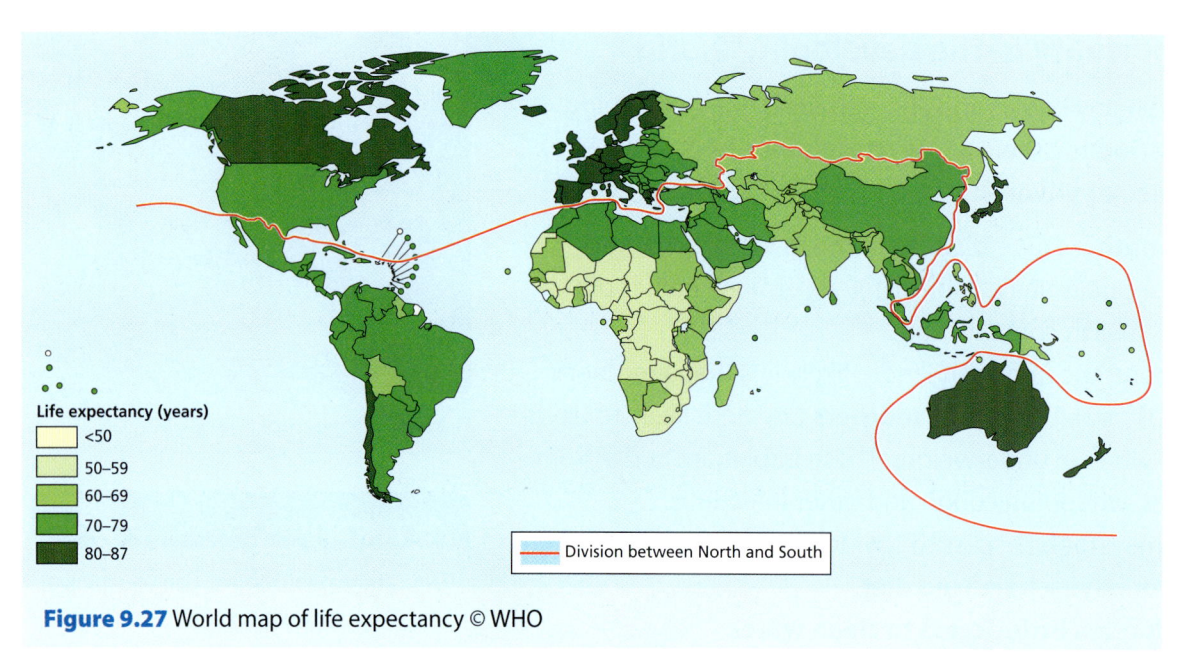

Figure 9.27 World map of life expectancy © WHO

Life expectancy in the developing world

Life expectancy **varies greatly** between countries in the developing world (the South). This is because countries in the developing world are at different stages of development. However, countries where life expectancy is low have some common characteristics:

- **Child mortality is high**.
- **Malnutrition** affects the poor in developing countries. Malnourished people are more likely to die of malaria, TB and other diseases.
- Tens of millions of people drink **water that is unsafe** and contains bacteria. This leads to continuous infections that can shorten people's lives.
- Over 500,000 **women die in childbirth** each year, most of them in poor countries.
- In 2014, 35 million people suffered from **HIV/AIDS**. The majority are in Sub-Saharan Africa, the world's poorest region. This condition has reduced life expectancy in several countries. This is because there are poor health services and most victims cannot afford **expensive drug treatments**.

Many countries in the developing world experience terrible **wars**. The civil war in the Democratic Republic of Congo between 1998 and 2003 caused the deaths of about five million people. Many other countries, including Sudan, South Sudan, Liberia, Iraq and Syria, have experienced conflicts in recent years.

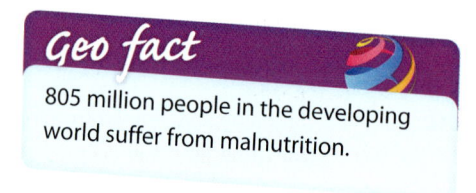

Geo fact
In Ireland in 2015, life expectancy was 78.7 years for men, 83.2 years for women.

A grandmother in Tanzania caring for the two children of her deceased daughter

Geo fact
805 million people in the developing world suffer from malnutrition.

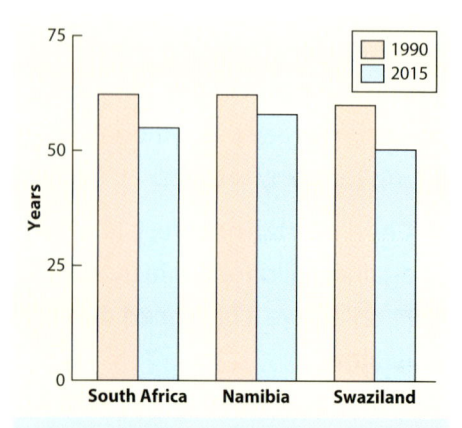

Figure 9.28 The reduced life expectancy 1990–2015 for three countries due to deaths caused by HIV/AIDS

Improvements in life expectancy

Almost all developing countries outside Sub-Saharan Africa have seen increased life expectancy in recent decades. This is because of the efforts made by governments, the World Health Organization, and other organisations to improve life expectancy. China and India are examples of countries that have longer life expectancy today.

Table 9.8 Life expectancy

Country	1990	2015
China	68	75
India	59	66

Questions

1. Explain **two** reasons for low child mortality in the developed world.
2. Explain **two** reasons why babies and young children face great health challenges in the South.
3. Can you suggest **two** reasons why life expectancy is increasing in countries such as China?

9.9 People on the move

KEYWORDS
- migration
- push and pull factors
- individual migration
- migrant
- emigrant
- immigrant
- organised migration
- plantation
- colonisation
- forced migration

Migration is the **movement of people from one place to another**.

- They may move from one country to another (**international migration**), or within a country (**internal migration**).
- They may leave the city for the suburbs or they may move from rural areas to towns because of economic opportunities.
- Movement of people has occurred throughout history and continues today.

Migration may be **individual** or **organised**.

Individual migration

People migrate from one place to another because some things about where they live are **repellent** to them. Repellent reasons **push** them away. These are called **push factors**. They may include:

- Overcrowding
- Unemployment
- Poverty
- Hunger
- Drought
- War
- A dull social scene.

Definition ✓

Individual migration: When people either as **individuals or families** decide to move.

People also migrate because the places to which they move are **attractive** in some way. Attractive reasons **pull** migrants to a particular place or region. These are called **pull factors**. They may include:

- Better job opportunities
- A better climate
- Fertile land
- A peaceful society
- A lively social scene
- The presence of friends and family members who have already migrated to that place.

> **Definitions** ✓
>
> **Migrant:** A person who moves from one country or place to another.
>
> **Emigrant:** An outward migrant who leaves his or her own country and travels to another.
>
> **Immigrant:** An inward migrant who enters a country from another country.

There are often **barriers to migration** which may stop or slow down people who want to move.

- **Poverty:** travel costs can be high.
- **Family:** there may be somebody at home who needs looking after.
- **Visas:** many countries require a foreigner to have a visa in order to enter the country.

Many Irish people have **emigrated** to Britain and the USA, especially since the Famine. At the present time, many **immigrants** from Eastern Europe now live in Ireland.

Migration from the west to the east of Ireland

People have migrated from the west to the east of Ireland for generations. This was because of the poor job prospects in the west and the better job prospects that existed in the east, especially in Dublin.

From the 1940s to the 1960s, few people sat the Leaving Certificate and career choices were limited. Jobs that were available included:

- Civil service jobs in Dublin
- Teaching
- Nursing
- Life as a priest, nun or missionary.

Ireland was a poor country for most of the twentieth century. Many parents from the west of Ireland encouraged their children to take up secure public sector jobs. **Primary teaching** was an example.

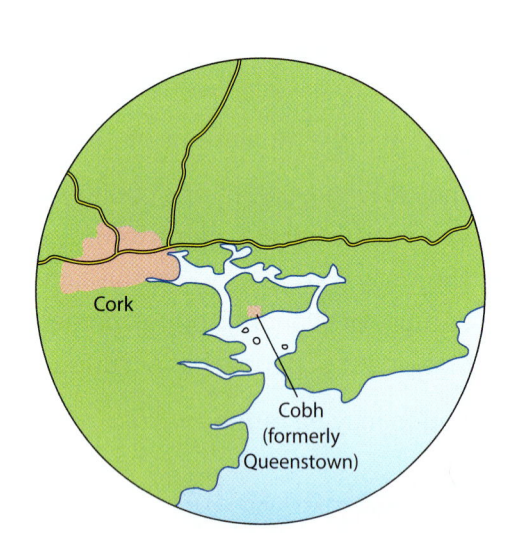

Figure 9.29 From 1848 to 1950 over 6 million adults and children emigrated from Ireland. Of these, 2.5 million left from Cobh in Cork Harbour

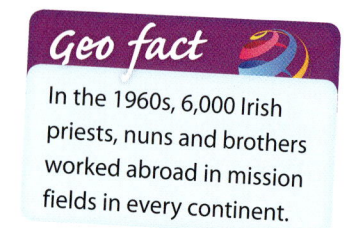

> **Geo fact**
>
> In the 1960s, 6,000 Irish priests, nuns and brothers worked abroad in mission fields in every continent.

Primary teaching

Primary teaching was a career that **led to migration** from the west to the east of Ireland. This was because:

- There were two **teacher-training colleges** in Dublin.
- There were relatively **few teaching posts in the West** because the population was falling rapidly due to outward migration.
- On the other hand, **Dublin's population was growing** and schools were expanding.

Therefore, young teachers from the West began their teaching careers in Dublin and many remained there all their lives. With the rapid increase in the population of Dublin City and County since the 1960s, this trend has continued to the present time.

Emigration from Ireland to the UK and the USA

Ireland – the push factors
- Hunger
- Poverty

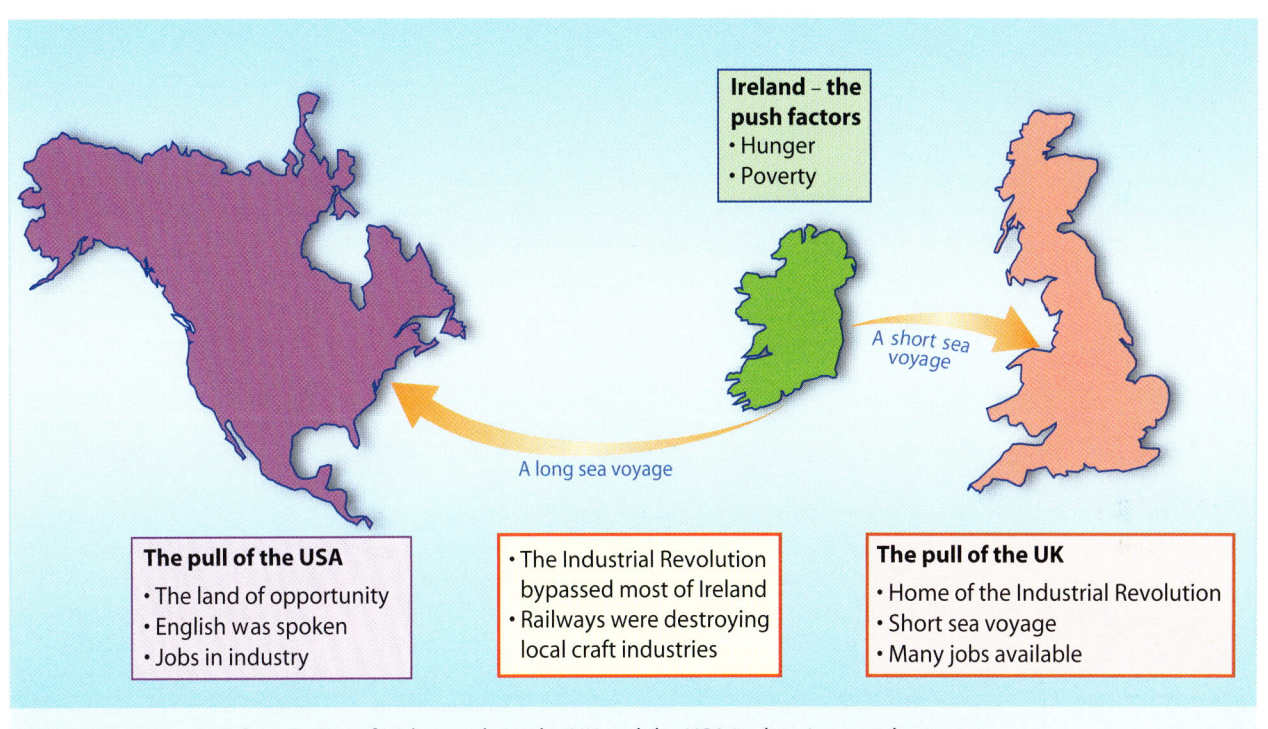

A short sea voyage

A long sea voyage

The pull of the USA
- The land of opportunity
- English was spoken
- Jobs in industry

- The Industrial Revolution bypassed most of Ireland
- Railways were destroying local craft industries

The pull of the UK
- Home of the Industrial Revolution
- Short sea voyage
- Many jobs available

Figure 9.30 Outward migration of Irish people to the UK and the USA in the nineteenth century

People with Irish blood are found in many countries abroad, from Britain to the USA, Canada and Australia. This is because many Irish people have **emigrated**, especially since the Famine of the 1840s. The push of **poverty** and **overcrowding** at home, and the pull of **economic opportunities** abroad, were the reasons for this **mass outward migration**.

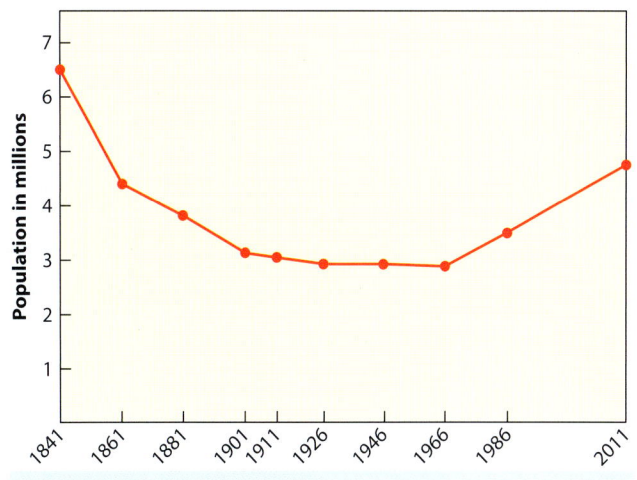

Figure 9.31 The population of the 26 counties that became the Republic of Ireland. After the Famine, emigration caused the population to decline

Section 3 · Social Geography

Irish emigrants are **economic migrants**.
- Recession at home leads to **outward migration**.
- An economic boom at home leads to **inward migration**.

Activity

Look up Ellis Island on the Internet and find out where exactly it is.

Migrants from Europe waiting to be processed at Ellis Island in New York Harbour in 1907. Thousands of Irish people sat on the same chairs

Table 9.9 Ireland: Migration from 1950s onwards

1950s	1960s	1970s	1980s	1990s	2000–2008	2008–2015
Loss of population	Population began to grow for the first time since the Great Famine	Population continued to grow	Outward migration began again	Population began to grow again	Population growth continued with inward migration	Outward migration began again
• Migrants left by boat for the UK and USA. • A disastrous decade for Ireland's people. • 411,000 emigrated because of the lack of jobs. • Governments failed to provide jobs.	• During the Lemass era (1958–66), a golden age dawned. • Programmes for economic expansion led to jobs at home. • Emigration was greatly reduced.	• Inward migration exceeded outward migration by 104,000. • Ireland joined the EEC. • EEC funds helped the economy to grow. • This was a decade of optimism.	• A recession at home, with job numbers down to 1.1 million, led to outward migration of more than 200,000. • Emigrants were now well-educated and moved into well-paid jobs abroad.	• The Celtic Tiger provided at least 50,000 new jobs every year. • Migrants returned. • People from the EU and other countries also came to work in Ireland. • The economy grew to more than 2 million workers.	• By 2008, people from many nations, such as Poland, were living and working in Ireland. • The population was at its highest figure since 1871.	• The banking crisis led to an economic recession. • Tens of thousands of young people left the country. • From 2014, the economy began to recover and jobs were created.

Dublin Airport, familiar to many young people who left Ireland during the economic problems that occurred after 2008

Migration studies

Here are some real-life experiences of young people who **emigrated** out of or **immigrated** into Ireland in recent years. These are people speaking in 2015.

Case studies

1 Nicola

I am an Irish doctor and I am 30 years old. I did medicine in UCD. I worked in hospitals in Dublin for five years after becoming a doctor. Some of my doctor friends had already gone to Australia to work in hospitals and for further training. I took the plunge at the end of 2013 and I am working in Melbourne in a large hospital. The work is challenging. However, I am well paid and the outdoor lifestyle suits me. I have many friends, both Irish and Australian. I applied for residency in Australia at the end of 2014.

I keep in touch with my family using Skype and with my friends on Facebook and Twitter. For that reason, I am not really lonely, even though Australia is very far away. I returned to Ireland to spend Christmas with my family in December 2014. In five years I will be a medical consultant and I hope to return to Ireland then to continue my career.

When Nicola comes home to work, how will her experience in Australia help in her work?

2 Stanislaw

My name is Stanislaw. I am Polish and am in my late thirties. I came to Ireland in 2004 when Poland joined the EU. Why Ireland? Ireland in 2004 was booming and was known as the Celtic Tiger. In addition, I had free movement throughout the EU.

I am a mechanic and had many years' experience when I came to Ireland. I had no trouble getting a job in a large town in the Midwest region of Ireland. I have worked in the same garage since I came to Ireland. The pay is fine – a lot better than in Poland – but the cost of living is high here as well. I do a little overtime when I need extra cash.

I returned to Poland to marry my girlfriend, Zofia, in 2006. She then came to Ireland with me. Learning English is a major challenge for me. I was never very good at languages in school. Zofia, who is much better at English, is helping me to write this.

We have two children; both are Irish citizens and their English is excellent. Zofia works part time in a crèche.

Ireland has been good to us and we have many Polish friends and some Irish friends here. A Polish priest is attached to this parish. He says Mass in Polish every Sunday and we meet the Polish community at Mass.

We now have enough money to return to Poland to buy a house. Both our parents are getting on in years and they miss us and their grandchildren. Ireland has been good to us and when eventually we leave, we will be sorry to go.

How has Stanislaw contributed to the Irish economy?

Section 3 · Social Geography

Organised migration

In the past, migration was frequently **organised by governments** in order to **colonise** distant lands. By doing this, a government could extend its territory and its power.

Two such organised migrations were:

1 The Plantation of Ulster
2 The Spanish colonisation of part of South America.

> **Definition** ✓
>
> **Organised migration:** When a government undertakes the settlement or colonisation of territory abroad, e.g. the Plantations by English and Scottish settlers in Ireland.

Case study

1 The plantation of Ulster

In order to **extend their rule over Ireland**, English monarchs took over parts of Ireland that had belonged to rebellious Irish chiefs. They gave this land to **English and Scottish settlers** who were loyal to the Crown. This transfer of land was known as a **plantation**.

Many plantations took place in the sixteenth and seventeenth centuries. One of the best organised was the **Ulster Plantation**.

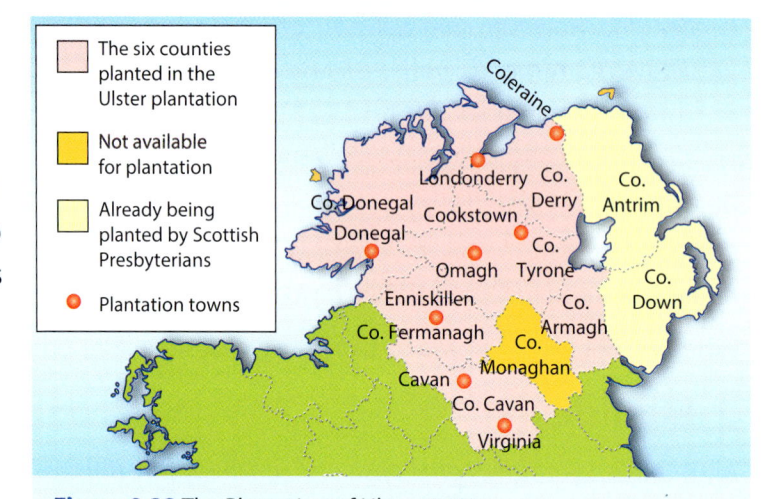

Figure 9.32 The Plantation of Ulster, 1609

Background to the Ulster Plantation

After an unsuccessful rebellion, Gaelic chieftains from Ulster left Ireland for Rome in 1607. This event is known as the **Flight of the Earls**. The counties of Donegal, Derry, Tyrone, Fermanagh, Armagh and Cavan were now available for plantation.

How did the plantation work?

- Mapmakers appointed by the Crown **surveyed** the land.
- Estates were given to English and Scottish settlers known as **undertakers** and **servitors**.
- The **first planters arrived in 1609** with tools, seeds and animals to settle on the land.
- They had to build **fortified dwellings** with roofs of slate to protect themselves against attacks from the native Irish.
- They brought with them their own **language**, **religion** and **farming methods**.

Why did the settlers come to Ulster?
They wanted a **better life** than they could have at home. They were given **fertile land** at **low rents**.

Chapter 9 · Population: Distribution, Diversity and Change

Case study

Results of the plantation

- **Fortified and planned towns** such as Londonderry, Donegal town, Belfast and Enniskillen were built.
- Despite attacks from the native Irish, the planters prospered and **the Crown tightened its grip on Ulster**.
- The ownership of much of the land of Ulster was transferred to English and Scottish settlers. The **native Irish became tenants** on land they had previously regarded as their own.
- Planters brought the **English language** and **Protestant religion** to Ulster.
- The **Irish language**, together with **Gaelic laws** and customs, **declined**.
- The relationship between the two cultures remained very hostile. This **hostility** led to much **conflict and bloodshed**, which has continued up until recent times.

The Peace Line wall separating the nationalist and unionist communities in west Belfast

Case study

2 European colonisation of South America

The New World, already settled by native Americans, was 'discovered' by Christopher Columbus in 1492. In the years that followed, the Spanish and Portuguese set their sights on creating **new empires in the New World**. At this time, the Incas had a vast empire in Peru. The Spanish conquistador **Francisco Pizarro** destroyed the Inca Empire and claimed its territory for Spain. The Portuguese colonised Brazil.

Activity

How did it come about that Portugal seized Brazil and that Spain conquered the rest of South America?

Link

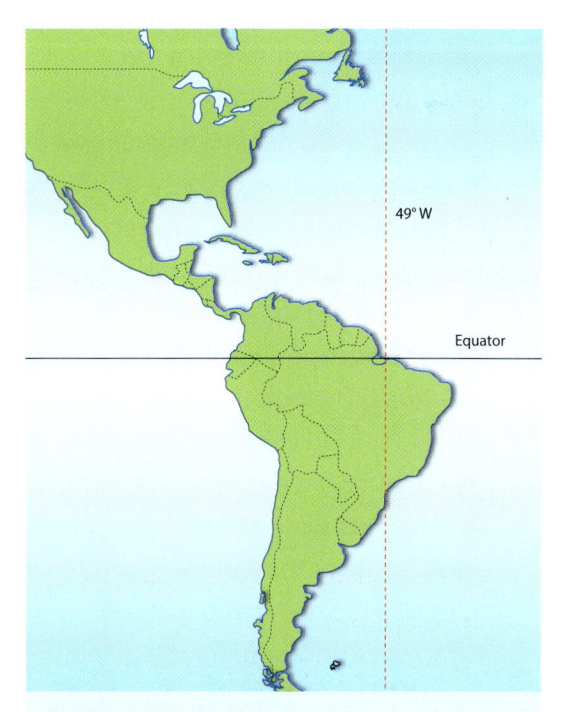

See also the section on **Brazil**, pages 237–39.

Figure 9.33 In 1494, Spain and Portugal divided the New World between them. All lands east of the line shown were to be Portuguese while lands west of the line were to belong to Spain

continued on next page

Section 3 · Social Geography

Case study

Many of the colonists were **adventurers**, known as **conquistadors**. They came to South America to get rich.

- They took **gold and silver** from the native powers.
- They set up huge **plantations** to grow coffee, cotton, sugar cane and bananas for export back to Europe.

The results of colonisation

- Native empires were no match for the superior weapons and cavalry of the invaders. The native people of the Andes were conquered by the Spaniards and become little better than slaves.
- Great numbers of native people died from **European diseases**, such as measles, brought by the conquerors.
- Spain and Portugal ruled separate portions of South America for 300 years. **Spanish and Portuguese** became the **languages of rule** of the South American continent.
- The **cross followed the sword**. Spanish and Portuguese missionaries followed the soldiers, bringing the **Catholic religion**, which is still powerful in South America today.
- **European architecture** was used in the building of cathedrals and other buildings all over South America.
- The Spanish and Portuguese brought European animals such as **horses and cattle** to South America for the first time.
- Ships returning to Europe carried **new foods to Europe** such as **potatoes and tomatoes**. The potato became a very important food in Europe, especially in Ireland during the nineteenth century.
- **Settlements** were established **along the coast**. Some of these have become major cities, like Rio de Janeiro in Brazil.
- To provide the labour for the plantations, many **African slaves** were forcibly brought from West Africa to Brazil and the Caribbean. This was **involuntary** or **forced migration**. The descendants of those slaves live in Brazil and in other regions today.
- The mixture of native people, Africans and Europeans has created a **multiracial society** in South America.

Figure 9.34 The racial composition of South America today

Map legend:
- People of European blood
- Mixed European and native people
- Native Andean peoples
- Native Amazon tribes
- High proportion of African Americans

A group of people doing exercises in multiracial São Paulo

262

Chapter 9 · Population: Distribution, Diversity and Change

Questions

1. Suggest **one** push factor and **one** pull factor that caused many young people to migrate from the west of Ireland to Dublin over many decades.
2. Explain **two** results of the Ulster Plantation.
3. Name **one** country that was colonised by the Portuguese in South America.
4. Give **two** effects of colonisation on the native peoples of South America.

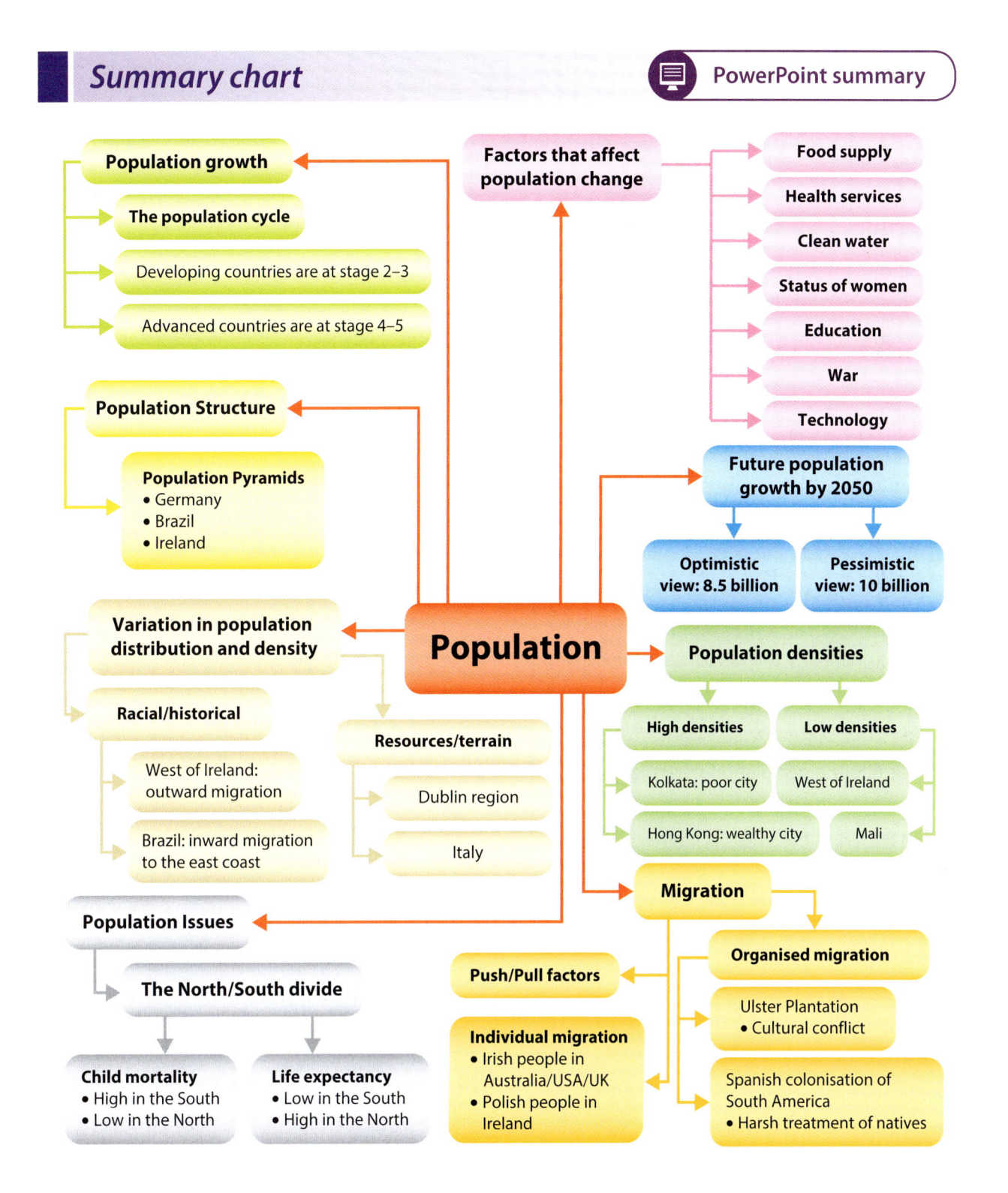

Summary chart

PowerPoint summary

Population growth
- The population cycle
- Developing countries are at stage 2–3
- Advanced countries are at stage 4–5

Population Structure
- Population Pyramids
  - Germany
  - Brazil
  - Ireland

Variation in population distribution and density
- Racial/historical
  - West of Ireland: outward migration
  - Brazil: inward migration to the east coast
- Resources/terrain
  - Dublin region
  - Italy

Population Issues
- The North/South divide
  - Child mortality
    - High in the South
    - Low in the North
  - Life expectancy
    - Low in the South
    - High in the North

Population

Factors that affect population change
- Food supply
- Health services
- Clean water
- Status of women
- Education
- War
- Technology

Future population growth by 2050
- Optimistic view: 8.5 billion
- Pessimistic view: 10 billion

Population densities
- High densities
  - Kolkata: poor city
  - Hong Kong: wealthy city
- Low densities
  - West of Ireland
  - Mali

Migration
- Push/Pull factors
- Individual migration
  - Irish people in Australia/USA/UK
  - Polish people in Ireland
- Organised migration
  - Ulster Plantation
    - Cultural conflict
  - Spanish colonisation of South America
    - Harsh treatment of natives

263

Section 3 · Social Geography

Exam questions

1 The diagram (on the right) shows population change over time.

(i) What name is given to this diagram that shows population change?

(ii) Explain each of the following:

(a) Why the death rate fluctuates (goes up and down) in Stage 1.

(b) Why the death rate declines rapidly in Stage 2.

(c) Why there is a natural decrease in population in Stage 5.

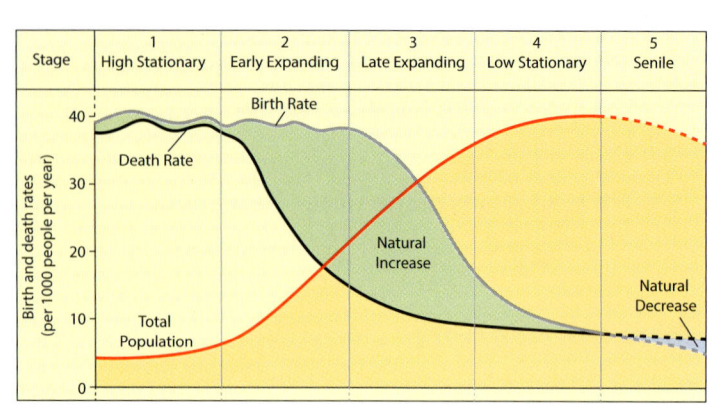

HL 2014

2 % of Population by Age Group in Germany and Brazil in 2013

Age Group	0–14 years (%)	15–64 years (%)	65+ years (%)
Germany	13.1	66.1	X
Brazil	24.2	68.5	7.3

US Census Bureau

Examine the table above and answer each of the following questions.

(i) Calculate **X**, the percentage of the population in Germany aged 65 and over.

(ii) Describe **two** challenges facing Germany in the future, given the percentage of its population aged 65 years and over.

(iii) Explain why the percentage of the population in the 0–14 year age group in Brazil is significantly higher than that in Germany.

HL 2015

3 Examine the population pyramids (on the right).

(i) Describe the impact of birth rates **and** death rates on the structure of each of the **Pyramids A** and **B**.

(ii) Explain **two** reasons why life expectancy is higher in some countries.

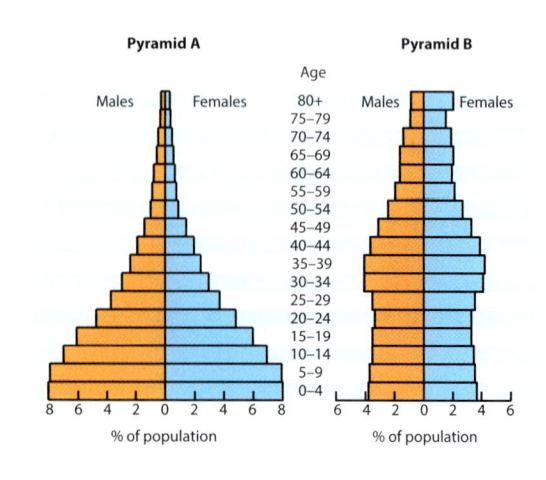

HL 2014

Chapter 9 · Population: Distribution, Diversity and Change

Exam questions

4. Study the pyramid (on the right) showing the age and sex structure of the population in Ethiopia.

    (i) What percentage of males are in the 40–44 year age group?

    (ii) Explain why there is a high percentage of Ethiopia's population in the younger age groups.

    (iii) Explain why there is a very low percentage of Ethiopia's population aged 65 years and over.

    (iv) State **one** way in which information from the Census of Population can be used.

    OL 2015

5. Describe **two** effects of very low population density in a region that you have studied.

    HL 2014

6. (i) Name **one** city with a high population density, that you have studied.

    (ii) Describe and explain **two** problems experienced as a result of the high population density, in the city named in part (i) above.

    HL 2012

7. Examine the map (on the right) which shows world life expectancy.

    (i) What is the life expectancy for **each** of the following countries?
    - Ireland
    - Mali

    (ii) Explain the term 'life expectancy'.

    (iii) Explain **two** reasons why life expectancy is longer in Ireland than in countries such as Mali.

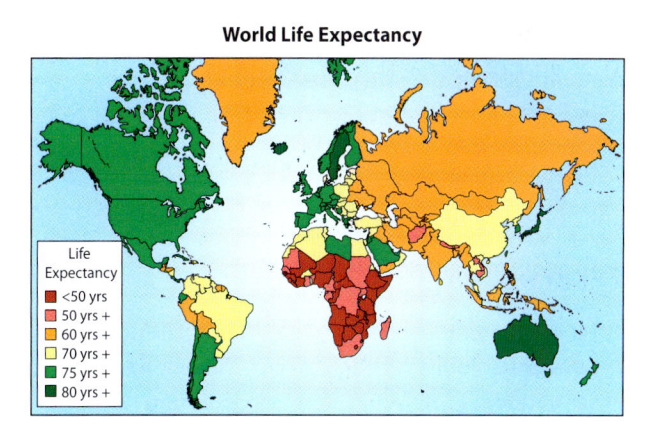

    HL 2011

8. (i) Name **one** example of organised migration that you have studied.

    (ii) Describe **two** effects of this organised migration on the area to which people migrated.

    (iii) Explain **one** barrier to migration in the present day.

    HL 2013

Chapter 10
Settlement

Learning outcomes

By the end of this chapter, you should be able to understand:

- The reasons why early settlers chose settlement sites
- The historical or physical reasons for the distribution of nucleated settlements in Ireland
- That nucleated settlements have distinct functions
- That the functions of settlements may change over time
- That settlements are linked to each other by transport routes.

Students must study an example of settlement from one of the following eras:
- Pre-Christian
- Viking
- Norman
- Plantation.

We will study pre-Christian settlement.

10.1 Early settlers in Ireland

KEYWORDS

- settlement
- archaeologist
- midden
- megalithic tomb
- fulacht fia
- crannóg
- communications
- togher
- esker

The landscape today shows evidence of human settlement, past and present. The location of initial settlement in an area is related to:

- Where people were coming from
- Their need for water, food, defence and communication.

Pre-Christian settlement

Where did early settlers come from?

Archaeologists think that the first settlers started coming to Ireland about 9,000 years ago. They may have come on foot via land bridges that connected Ireland with Britain after the Ice Age. The sea level was much lower at that time.

We know that many very early settlers remained near the north-east coast because of excavations at **Mount Sandel** on the River Bann in Co. Derry.

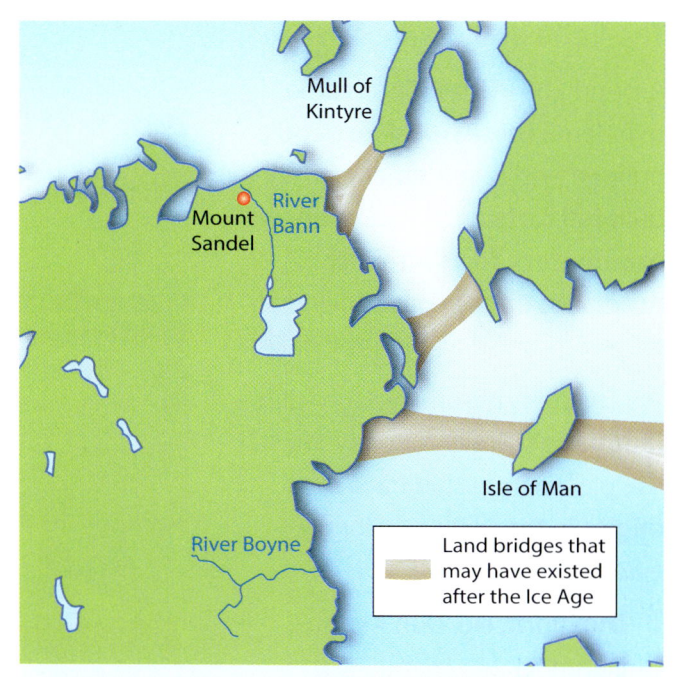

Figure 10.1 Land bridges probably connected Ireland to Britain after the Ice Age

Where did early settlers live?

Archaeologists have uncovered many sites of early settlements. Many of them are found along river valleys and lakes where water was available, e.g. Mount Sandel; Lough Gur in Co. Limerick.

What did early settlers eat?

Early settlers were hunters and food-gatherers. They gathered food from the seashore. They hunted wild pigs, caught salmon and collected hazelnuts. They used simple stone weapons to kill and skin animals.

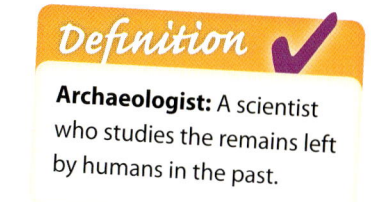

Archaeologists have also found bones of small birds, hares and deer at early sites. Early people threw the discarded bones of animals into rubbish heaps that are called **middens**.

> **Definition**
>
> **Archaeologist:** A scientist who studies the remains left by humans in the past.

Early farmers

New Stone Age farmers came to Ireland around 4000 BC. These farmers brought seed and domesticated (tame) animals with them. They cooked meat in **fulachtaí fia**. They built large stone graves known as **megalithic tombs** that still exist. These are older than the pyramids of Egypt.

Many of these tombs are found in the Burren, Co. Clare and along the River Boyne. The valley of the Boyne had soil that was excellent for growing crops.

Fulacht fia

Fulacht fia means 'the cooking pit of the deer'.

- People dug a hole in the ground and filled it with water.
- They lined the hole with flat stones.
- A fire heated large stones nearby.
- These very hot stones were thrown into the fire and caused the water to boil.
- They then cooked meat in the boiling water.

Section 3 · Social Geography

The Celts and defence

Around 500 BC, the **Celts** came to Ireland. These **Iron Age** people built defensive settlements. They built **hill forts** on high ground and **promontory forts** on small headlands on the coast. They built **crannógs** on small islands in lakes.

The Celts introduced the **Irish language** to Ireland. Today, we still use placenames that have their origins in the Celtic era, for example:

- **Dún** (fort), e.g. Dún Aengus, Dunmore
- **Inis** (island), e.g. Inishmore, Inishfree.

A crannóg in Knockalough Lake, Kilmihil, Co. Clare

Definition

Crannóg: A man-made island in a lake on which people built houses, kept animals, and lived in safety from hostile clans.

Communications

The greater part of pre-Christian Ireland was **covered in forests**. Therefore, settlers lived on the coast and along river valleys. They used flimsy boats to travel from place to place. Vast areas remained completely untouched. However, over time, some forests were cut down and tracks became established.

The Celts used oak timbers to make **paths** through short sections of bogland in the Midlands. These were known as **toghers**.

Dún Aengus, an ancient Celtic fort, sits high on the cliffs of Inishmore, Aran Islands. Coastal erosion caused the cliffs to retreat

People travelled along **eskers** in the centre of Ireland. These were ridges left by meltwater from glaciers (see page 73) that enabled people to cross the boglands of the Midlands and the floodplain of the Shannon. **Esker Riada** was the name given by the Celts to describe an ancient east–west route through the Midlands. In Christian times, this route became An Slí Mór (the Great Highway).

Chapter 10 · Settlement

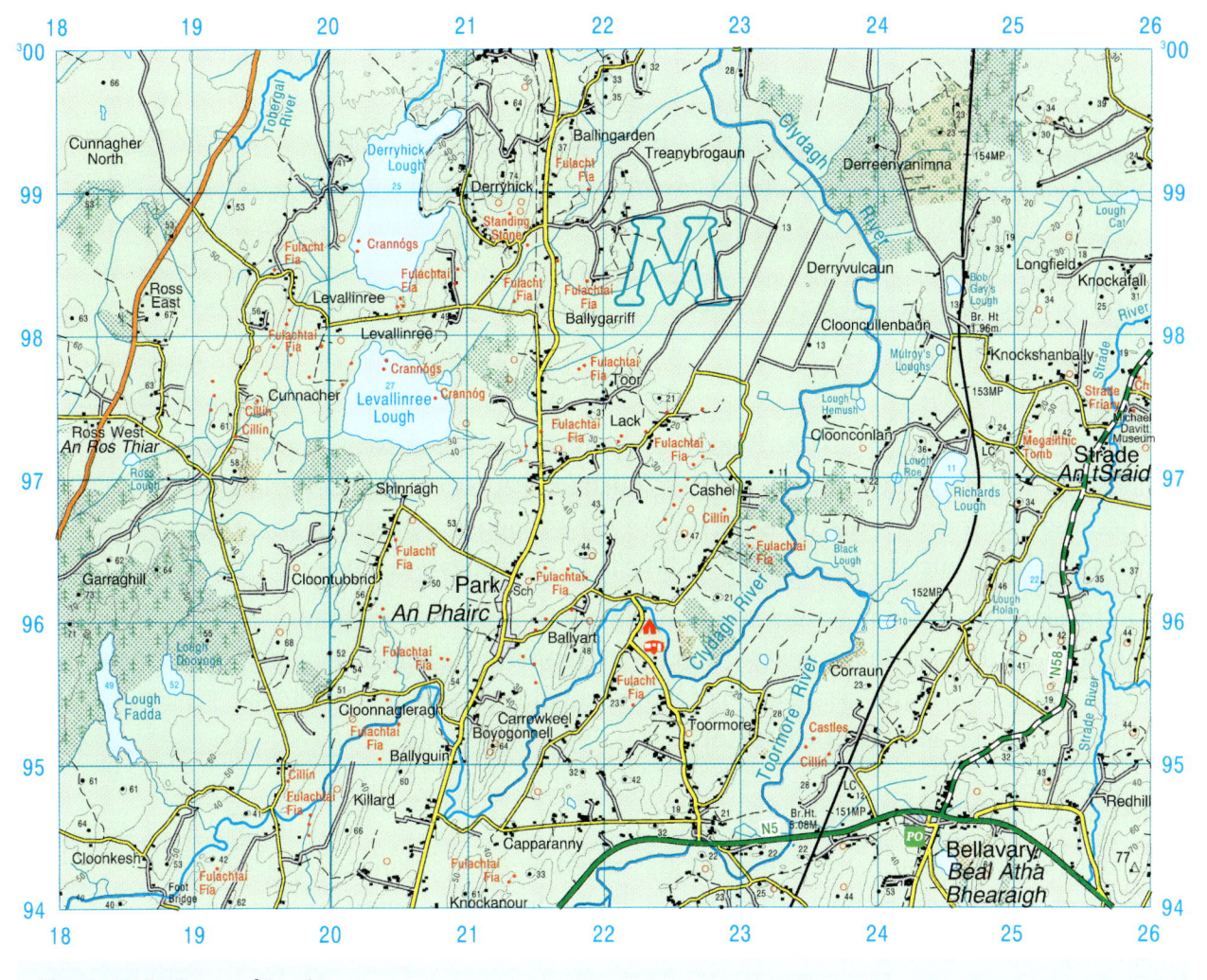

Figure 10.2 OS map of East Mayo

Questions

Study the ancient pre-Christian sites marked in red on the OS map above and answer the following questions:

1 Give a six-figure grid reference for each of the following pre-Christian features found in the OS map:
   - A crannóg
   - A fulacht fia
   - A megalithic tomb.

2 Using evidence from the OS map, explain why water was readily available for early settlers.

3 Can you explain why fulachtaí fia were close to lakes and streams?

4 Look at the ring fort at Boyogonnell, M 212 952.
   (a) At what altitude in metres is the ring fort located?
   (b) Can you suggest **one** reason why it was built at that location?
   (c) Give a grid reference for another ring fort built on a similar site.

Section 3 · Social Geography

10.2 Nucleated settlements

KEYWORDS

- nucleated settlement
- Viking
- monastic settlement
- Norman
- plantation settlement
- landlord town
- primate city
- decentralisation

Where people settled in Ireland depended on:

- Social and historical factors
- Resources and terrain.

As we saw in Chapter 8 (page 167), **nucleated** or **clustered settlements** are houses and buildings that are grouped together in a cluster (**nucleus**). People chose to settle in a place because it possessed a vital or useful feature, e.g. a spring, a dry point or an easily defended site. These nuclei (plural) grew over time to form villages and towns.

In this chapter we will look at **nucleated settlements** and the reasons they developed where they did. In the next section we will examine the influence of **resources and terrain** on the distribution of settlements. In this section we will concentrate on **social and historical factors**.

Social and historic influences

Over a long period of time, many different groups of settlers came to Ireland from abroad. Most of these groups built settlements that grew into towns over a long period. Each wave of settlers chose particular locations in which they established settlements.

Viking settlements

The **Vikings** arrived in Ireland at the end of the eighth century. They were a Scandinavian **sea-faring people** with settlements in Britain, the Faroe Islands and Iceland. They were plunderers of monasteries at first. Later, they established settlements **along the coast** in bays, and in harbours at the **mouths of rivers**. This meant that they could maintain contact with Vikings in other areas.

The placenames of many coastal towns today indicate their Viking origin. Many of their settlement names ended with the Norwegian word **fjord**, meaning an inlet. This later became **ford**, e.g. Carlingford, Wexford and Waterford.

The **low** used at the end of Wicklow and Arklow was the Viking word for low-lying land.

Dublin was also a Viking settlement, chosen because of its good harbour at the mouth of the River Liffey.

Figure 10.3 Settlements of Viking origin are located along the coast and on estuaries

Monastic settlements

The ruins of early monasteries are found all over Ireland. Many of these monasteries were established by Irish monks in **remote areas**, e.g. Scattery Island, Glendalough and Skellig Michael.

Some monasteries became **centres of trade and learning**, as well as religion. The monastery at **Clonmacnoise** in Co. Offaly was an important cultural centre between the eight and twelfth centuries, and was visited by scholars from all over Europe.

The ruins of the monastery at Clonmacnoise

Activity
Look up Skellig Michael on the Internet and see how the monks lived in beehive cells on the island long ago.

Norman settlements

The Normans invaded Ireland in the twelfth century. Unlike the Vikings, they were interested in fertile land.

They brought with them a tradition of **castle-building**. They built many castles with a **keep** and **bailey**. A town developed around the castle. The Normans also developed towns that the Vikings had established, e.g. Dublin.

Towns that were founded or developed by the Normans include Trim, Carrickfergus, Kilkenny and Athenry.

Roscommon Castle, a Norman castle that dates from the thirteenth century

Figure 10.4 Some of the towns that were developed by the Normans

Plantation settlement

Plantations by English settlers took place in the sixteenth and seventeenth centuries. Examples include the plantations of Laois-Offaly, Munster and Ulster (see page 260).

Where plantations occurred, towns were built to provide protection for settlers. These settlements have grown into modern towns.

Table 10.1 Some plantation towns

Plantation	Town
Laois-Offaly	Portarlington, Daingean
Munster	Youghal, Mallow
Ulster	(London)Derry, Strabane, Virginia, Co. Cavan

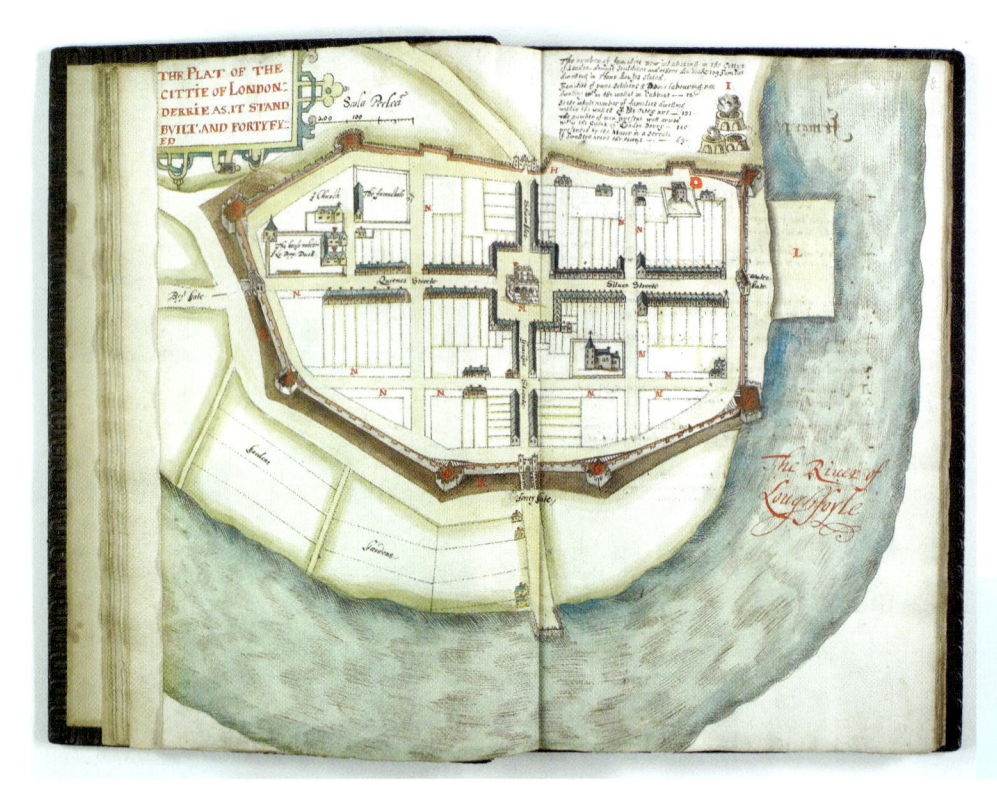

Section 3 · Social Geography

A plan of Londonderry. The city was built after the Ulster Plantation of 1609

Landlords' towns

After the Cromwellian Plantation of the seventeenth century, **landlords** became the most important people in Irish society. Several landlords built towns on their estates. These **towns were planned**, with straight streets, town squares and English architecture, e.g. Abbeyleix, Birr, Kilrush and Strokestown.

The importance of Dublin

Dublin is a **primate city**. A primate city is at least twice as big as the next city in the same state. Paris and Copenhagen are other examples of primate cities in Europe.

John's Mall, Birr, Co. Offaly, shows evidence of a planned town

As we have seen, Dublin began as a Viking settlement. It grew during Norman times, and became the **colonial capital** of British rule in Ireland for hundreds of years.

Dublin is the **economic heart** of the state. It is a capital with many functions:

- It is the **seat of government**. The Dáil, Seanad and most of the civil service are in Dublin.
- Dublin is Ireland's **chief port**. It also has the **largest airport** in the state, with thousands of employees.
- Dublin is at the centre of Ireland's road and rail network. The **transport system** radiates outward to the provinces from Dublin.
- Dublin is Ireland's most important **financial centre**. Large banks and insurance companies have their headquarters there.
- Dublin is the most important centre for **shopping**, **tourism**, **education** and **health** in the state.

Leinster House, Dublin, is the seat of government in the Republic of Ireland

Therefore, Dublin is **multi-functional**. It is growing very rapidly. From 1981 to 2011, the population of Dublin City and County grew by a quarter of a million people. During the Celtic Tiger years that began in 1995, many major companies from abroad chose Dublin as the location of their European headquarters. More than 27 per cent of the population of the Republic now live in Dublin City and County.

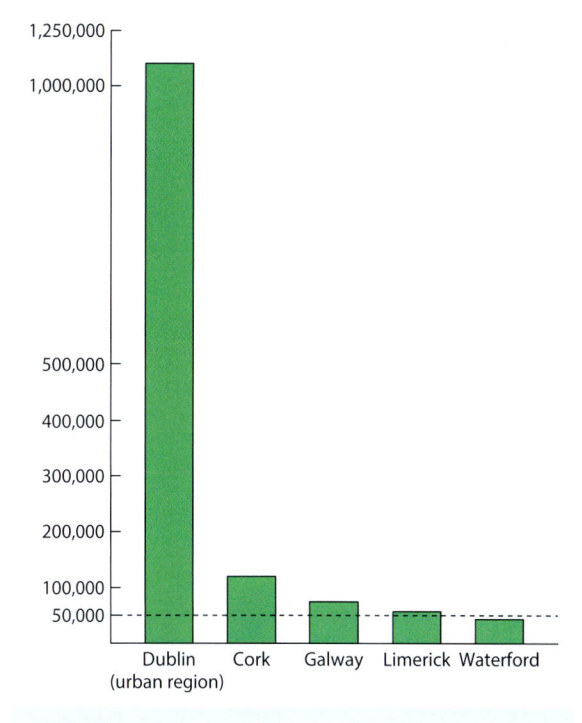

Figure 10.5 The population of Dublin and other cities

Decentralisation

The government has tried to halt Dublin's growth with a policy of **decentralisation**. This meant moving some economic activities from the centre (Dublin) to other parts of the country in order to promote economic activity nationwide.

Some government offices have been relocated in towns in other parts of the country. For example, the Examinations branch of the Department of Education and Skills has been in Athlone for many years. However, in 2008 the government decided to halt funding for decentralisation because of the economic downturn.

Figure 10.6 Dublin draws workers from the surrounding areas. This has created a 'commuter belt' around the city

Questions

1. Explain **one** reason why the Vikings built coastal settlements in Ireland.
2. What advances did the Normans bring to defensive settlements? Use the example of Roscommon Castle.
3. Explain **three** reasons for the primacy of Dublin in Ireland today.

Section 3 · Social Geography

10.3 Resources, terrain and the distribution of settlements

KEYWORDS
- altitude
- bridging point
- ford
- fertile land
- market centre
- peatland

The following resources and terrain factors influence the distribution of towns and cities:

- Altitude
- Rivers
- Land quality.

Altitude

Nucleated settlements in Ireland avoid high altitudes. Mountains and hills are exposed to high winds. They also attract relief rain. Temperatures are lower than at sea level.

Most nucleated settlements are confined to the **coast** and to **valleys** that cut through mountains. Coastal settlements may be fishing ports, such as Killybegs, Co. Donegal, or coastal resorts such as Tramore, Co. Waterford.

Carlingford, Co. Louth, is located on coastal lowlands with sheltering uplands in the background. The uplands are uninhabited. Can you explain why?

Rivers and river valleys

Rivers and river valleys have attracted settlement in Ireland since ancient times.

Many towns are located at **bridging points** on rivers. That is because bridging points become a focus for routes from one place to another. Towns grow to provide services for people at these bridging points.

Many towns in Ireland contain the Irish word **áth**, e.g. Baile Átha Luain – Athlone; Baile Átha Cliath – Dublin; Béal an Átha – Ballina. **Áth** means **ford**. This indicates that these settlements are located at bridging points.

Limerick is situated at the lowest crossing point of the Shannon

The **largest urban centres** on the island of Ireland are located at **river mouths** or on the **banks of river estuaries**. These include Dublin, Belfast, Sligo, Galway, Limerick, Cork and Waterford. These centres are at the lowest crossing point of the river on which they are located.

Land quality

Poor land that may be marshy, infertile or subject to flooding repels settlement. **Fertile land attracts settlement**. Much of the best land in the country is in the eastern half of Ireland. Towns that were located in the centre of rich agricultural land thrived. This was because they became **market centres** for the produce from the surrounding area. They also provided services for the local population.

The **Normans** settled mainly in Leinster and east Munster in **rich agricultural valleys**. Maynooth is surrounded by the fertile plains of Kildare. Kilkenny, on the River Nore, became a market centre for the farmers of the rich agricultural region.

Mitchelstown, Co. Cork, is surrounded by excellent land

Peatlands

Marshy land does not attract settlement, so people have avoided the large **peat bogs** in the centre of Ireland. Nevertheless, nucleated settlements have developed on the boundaries of the peatlands. They have grown because **Bord na Móna** provides employment in nearby peatlands. These settlements include Shannonbridge and Tyrellspass.

*Shannonbridge is located at an important bridging point on the River Shannon. Today, it is a resource-based settlement. The **peat resources** in the background are used for the power station. The power station is located in the foreground*

Section 3 · Social Geography

Questions

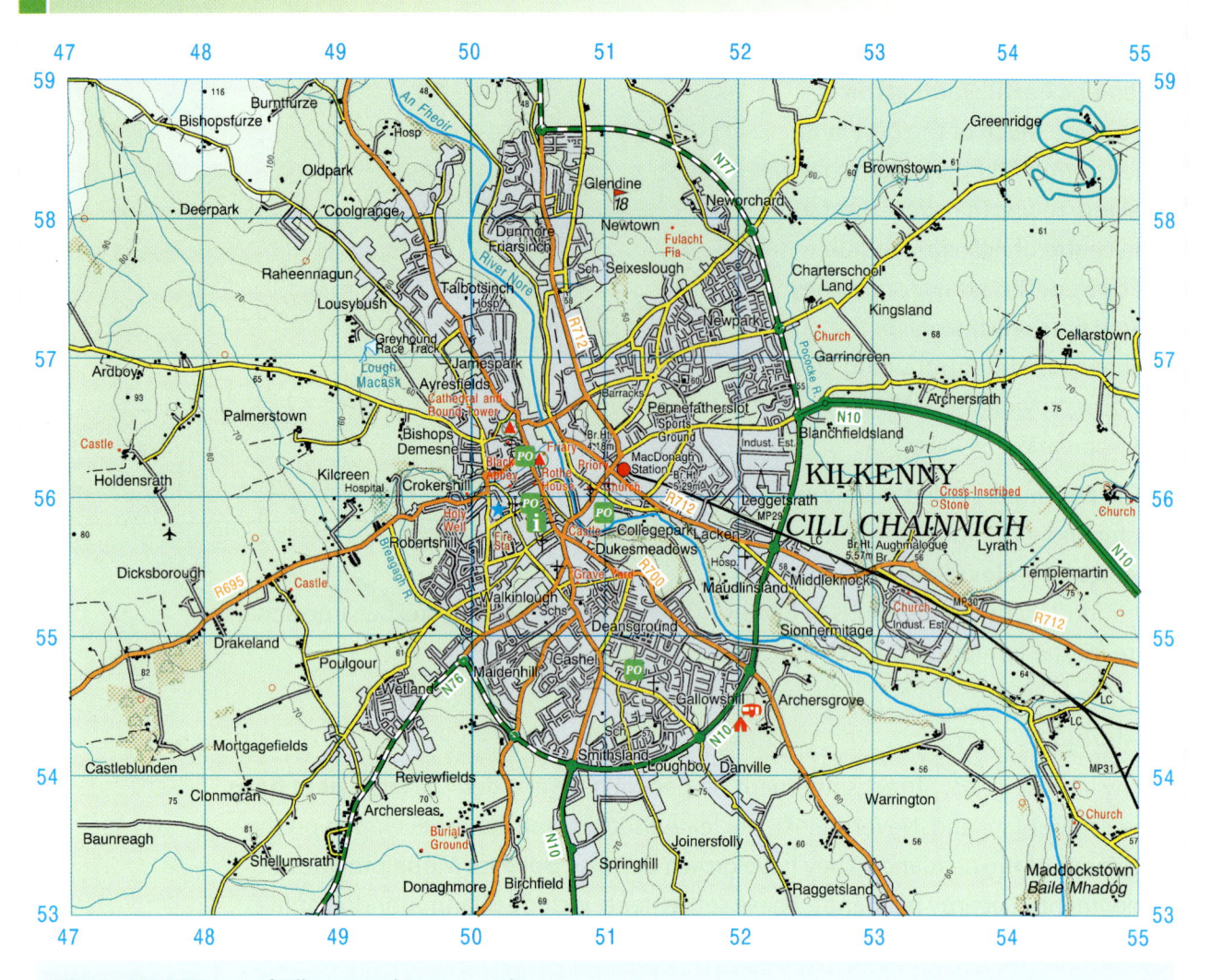

Figure 10.7 OS map of Kilkenny and its surroundings

Study the map of Kilkenny and answer the following questions:

1. Draw an outline of the OS map of Kilkenny and its surroundings and include the following:
   - The River Nore
   - The shaded area of Kilkenny city
   - The railway line and railway station
   - A national primary road.

2. What evidence in the OS map tells us that Kilkenny is an important bridging point?

3. Name **two** pieces of evidence that indicate that Kilkenny began as a settlement many hundreds of years ago. Give a grid reference for each.

4. What evidence tells us that the land around Kilkenny is well drained?

Chapter 10 · Settlement

10.4 Settlement in the new polders of the Netherlands

> **KEYWORDS**
> - polder
> - reclaimed land
> - Zuyder Zee project
> - barrier dam
> - radial pattern

In recent times, the creation of new settlements has continued on land newly reclaimed from the sea.

'God made the world but people made Holland.'

The Netherlands

The Netherlands is one of the most densely populated countries in the world. Much of the country is below high-tide level. For hundreds of years, the Dutch have built **dykes** to create new land below sea level. These areas of newly created (**reclaimed**) land are called **polders**.

Geo fact
Population density in the Netherlands is 498 per km² (Republic of Ireland: 67 per km²).

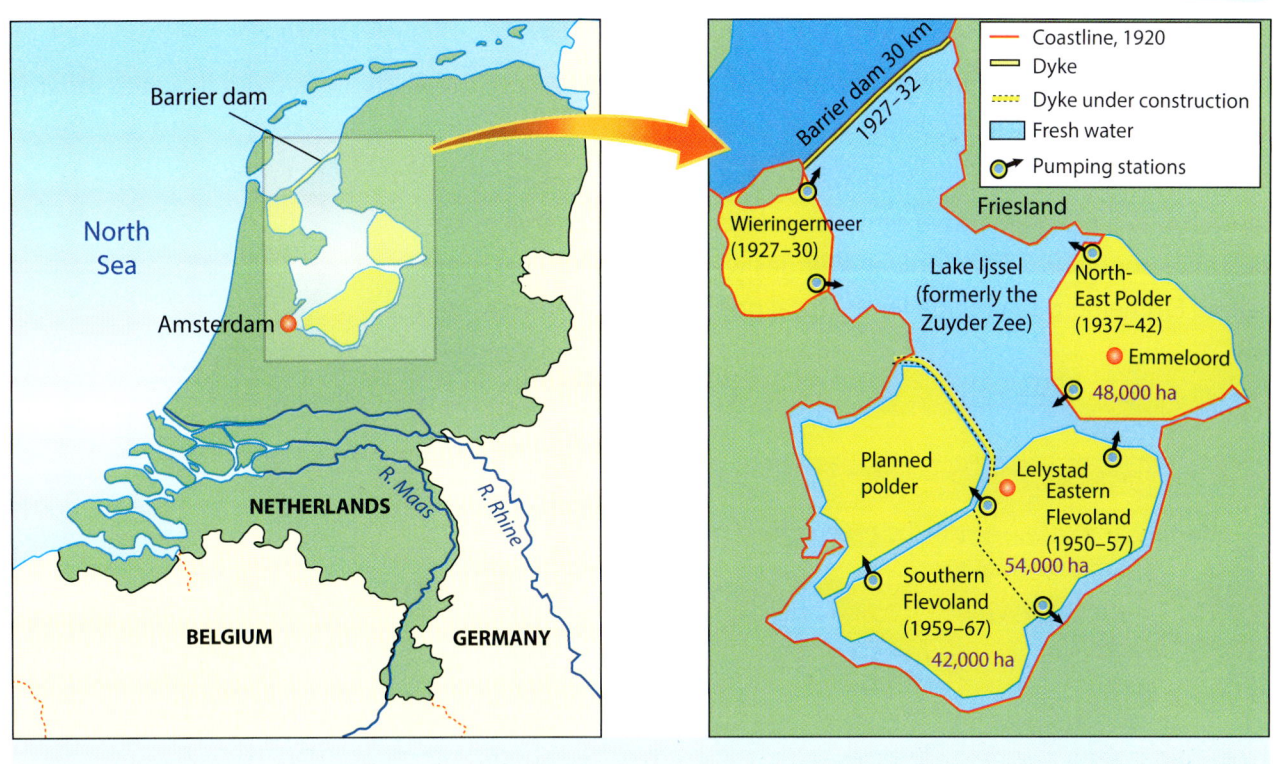

Figure 10.8 The Netherlands has reclaimed polders from the sea by building a barrier dam across the former Zuyder Zee, now Lake Ijssel

Figure 10.9 The new polders have added significantly to the land mass of the Netherlands

The Zuyder Zee project

Until the 1930s, the Zuyder Zee was open to the sea. Disastrous storms and loss of life over the years led the Dutch to enclose the Zuyder Zee with a **barrier dam**. They were then able to create new land for farming and turn the Zuyder Zee into a freshwater lake (Lake Ijssel) for domestic use.

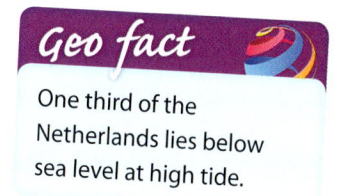

Geo fact
One third of the Netherlands lies below sea level at high tide.

277

Section 3 · Social Geography

How were the new polders of Lake Ijssel formed?

1 A barrier dam enclosed the newly named Lake Ijssel from the sea.
2 Saltwater was pumped out using oil-powered pumps.
3 New polders were created by building dykes of mud and stone around large areas.
4 Roads were laid out. Drainage channels were dug. Diesel and electric pumps controlled groundwater levels.
5 Roads, farms and villages were planned and laid out. New settlements grew throughout the twentieth century in each of the new polders.

The barrier dam enclosing Lake Ijssel

Settlement patterns in the North-East Polder

In the North-East Polder, farmers live on **family-run farms** where the fields are laid out in a chessboard pattern. **Farmhouses** are built in a **linear pattern** along a rural road.

The locations of nucleated settlements were carefully chosen. **Emmeloord** is the main urban centre to provide important services for the entire population of the polder. **Villages** were built in a **radial pattern** around Emmeloord to provide for the local population's day-to-day needs.

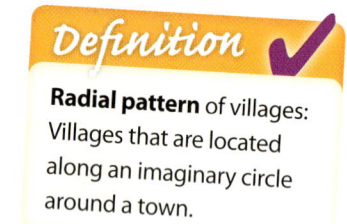

Definition ✓

Radial pattern of villages: Villages that are located along an imaginary circle around a town.

Settlement on the polders. Much of the land is used to grow crops

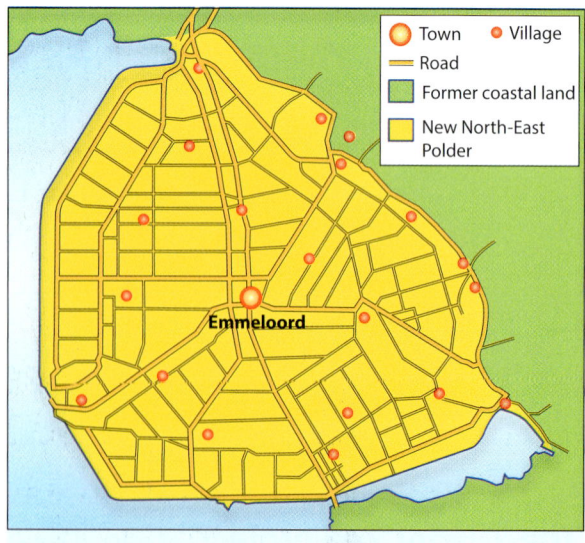

Figure 10.10 The North-East Polder

Settlement in Eastern and Southern Flevoland

The new polders of Eastern and Southern Flevoland are very near the **Randstad**, a ring of cities that includes Amsterdam. These cities are very overcrowded. The Dutch therefore decided that Flevoland would be used to relieve some of the population pressure in the Netherlands. **Lelystad** and **Almere** are now large urban centres. Almere has a population of 183,000.

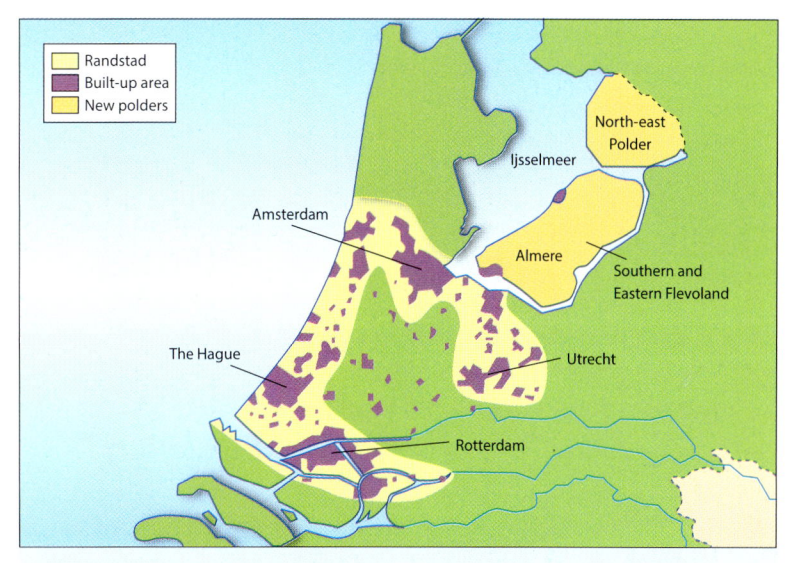

Figure 10.11 The Randstad contains almost 40 per cent of the population of the Netherlands

Questions

1 What does the term 'polder' mean?

2 Describe **one** way in which settlement in a polder is different from settlement in other areas.

3 Give **two** advantages that came about with the building of the polders in the Netherlands.

10.5 Functions of nucleated settlements

KEYWORDS
- market settlement
- defensive settlement
- resource-based settlement
- port settlement
- residential settlement
- recreational settlement
- ecclesiastical settlement
- multi-functional
- dormitory town
- oil terminal
- inland port
- route focus

Nucleated settlements may be classified by function:

- Village
- Market settlement
- Defensive settlement
- Resource-based settlement
- Port settlement
- Residential/dormitory settlement
- Recreational settlement
- Ecclesiastical settlement.

All urban centres have **functions**. Usually, urban settlements have more than one function. When we classify a settlement according to its function, we use its **most important function**.

For example, Killarney has a residential function because people live there. However, its most important function is **recreational**. It also has schools, shops, medical and personal services. Therefore, Killarney is **multi-functional**.

Section 3 · Social Geography

Activity
What evidence in the photograph of Kinsale shows that it is a recreational settlement? **Discuss** in pairs.

Kinsale, Co. Cork, is a recreational settlement

Table 10.2 Settlement classification

Settlement type	Functions	Examples
Village	Provides a small range of services to the people of the surrounding parish, e.g. primary school, church, shop, post office.	Ballinalee, Co. Longord; Doonbeg, Co. Clare
Market settlement	Provides a wide range of services, e.g. ● Supermarkets and other retail outlets ● Hotels and restaurants ● Dental and medical services ● Financial services – banks and building societies.	Mullingar, Co. Westmeath; Ennis, Co. Clare; Castlebar, Co. Mayo
Defensive settlement	Many settlements began with the building of a castle on a defensive site. The ruins of the castle are part of the heritage of the town today.	Trim, Co. Meath; Carrickfergus, Co. Antrim; Bunratty, Co. Clare
Resource-based settlement	Resource-based settlements grow because a resource, such as an important mineral ore or peat, exists nearby.	Navan, Co. Meath; Silvermines, Co. Tipperary
Port settlement	Ports are equipped to handle ships and their cargoes. They contain docks and cranes to load and unload ships. Ports provide a lot of employment. Ports also often have other functions.	Dublin, Co. Dublin; Waterford, Co. Waterford; Foynes, Co. Limerick
Residential/ dormitory settlement	A **dormitory town** is one where people live, but they commute to work daily in a town or city nearby.	Sixmilebridge, Co. Clare – dormitory town for Shannon and Limerick Towns surrounding Dublin, e.g. Malahide, Blanchardstown
Recreational settlement	People go on holidays to these settlements because of particular attractions such as beautiful scenery, beach facilities or golfing facilities.	Lahinch, Co. Clare; Bundoran, Co. Donegal; Killarney, Co. Kerry
Ecclesiastical settlement	Ecclesiastical settlements have a religious function. They provide for people's spiritual needs.	Knock, Co. Mayo; Maynooth, Co. Kildare

Chapter 10 · Settlement

Case study

Settlement in an Irish river basin: the Shannon basin

The **Shannon** is the longest river in Ireland and Britain. The Shannon has many urban centres along its course. **Limerick** is the largest centre by far, with Athlone taking second place in terms of population.

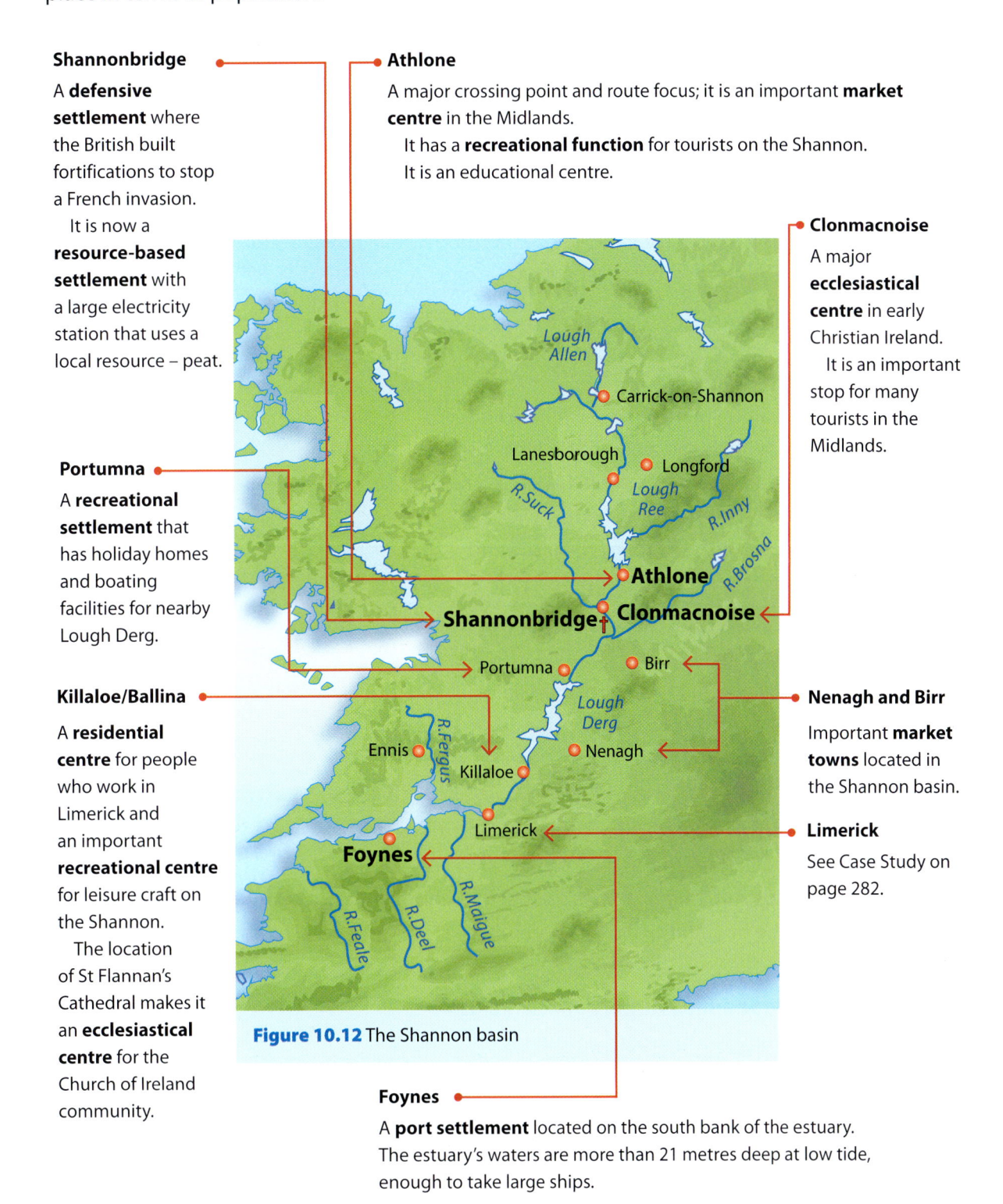

Shannonbridge
A **defensive settlement** where the British built fortifications to stop a French invasion.
It is now a **resource-based settlement** with a large electricity station that uses a local resource – peat.

Athlone
A major crossing point and route focus; it is an important **market centre** in the Midlands.
It has a **recreational function** for tourists on the Shannon.
It is an educational centre.

Clonmacnoise
A major **ecclesiastical centre** in early Christian Ireland.
It is an important stop for many tourists in the Midlands.

Portumna
A **recreational settlement** that has holiday homes and boating facilities for nearby Lough Derg.

Killaloe/Ballina
A **residential centre** for people who work in Limerick and an important **recreational centre** for leisure craft on the Shannon.
The location of St Flannan's Cathedral makes it an **ecclesiastical centre** for the Church of Ireland community.

Nenagh and Birr
Important **market towns** located in the Shannon basin.

Limerick
See Case Study on page 282.

Figure 10.12 The Shannon basin

Foynes
A **port settlement** located on the south bank of the estuary. The estuary's waters are more than 21 metres deep at low tide, enough to take large ships.

Section 3 · Social Geography

> # Case study

Limerick City: a multi-functional urban centre

Limerick is by far the largest urban centre in the **Shannon basin**. We will now examine three of its present functions.

1 Market function

Limerick is located at the lowest **bridging point** of the River Shannon. The city became a **route focus** in north Munster. Therefore, the city grew as a **market centre** over time. Limerick's port function also helped the city to grow.

Today, Limerick is a major shopping centre for the midwest of Ireland. The city has major department stores and suburban shopping centres.

A pedestrianised shopping street in Limerick city centre. What function is evident in this photo of Limerick?

2 Residential function

Limerick had a population of more than 57,000 in the 2011 Census. Many people who work at Shannon Airport and at Shannon's industrial estates live in Limerick. The city has expanded as an **educational centre** with the University of Limerick. It also has many hospitals and industrial estates.

Lecturers, medical staff and manufacturing workers require residential accommodation. Therefore, the city has expanded by building many new **residential areas** to house its growing population.

The University of Limerick has helped to make Limerick an important educational centre

3 Recreational function

Limerick is one of the most important **tourist centres** in the west of Ireland. Its attractions include the **Hunt Museum** and **St John's Castle**, which was built at the beginning of the thirteenth century.

Limerick is beside **Shannon Airport**, which brings visitors from Europe and North America. Limerick has many **hotels** to cater for them. Buses leave Limerick to visit sights in the surrounding region, including the Cliffs of Moher and Bunratty Folk Park in Co. Clare.

St John's Castle is now a major tourist attraction

Limerick is a major centre of **sport**. The Gaelic Grounds host many major GAA matches. **Thomond Park** is well known to rugby supporters as many European club teams have played there. Limerick also has a horse-racing track.

Questions

Figure 10.13 OS map of Limerick City

Study the OS map of Limerick and answer the following questions:

1 Draw a sketch map of the area shown in the OS map of Limerick city. Include the following:
   - The River Shannon
   - The railway station and railways
   - The castle at R 577 578
   - A named university at R 614 583
   - A hospital at R 571 575.

2 What evidence in the OS map shows the following?
   (a) Limerick had a defensive function.
   (b) Limerick has an educational function.
   (c) Limerick has a recreational function.
   (d) Limerick has a residential functional.
   (e) Limerick has an ecclesiastical function.

Section 3 · Social Geography

Settlement in the River Rhine basin

The Rhine is one of the great rivers of Western Europe. Millions of people live in cities along its course. Its cities are home to some of Europe's largest manufacturing industries.

The Rhine waterway is a great **trade route**. Barges carrying coal, sand, timber and mineral ores are a frequent sight on the Rhine and its tributaries. Therefore, many cities on the Rhine have a **port function**, as well as other functions.

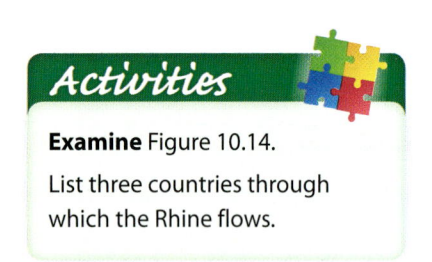

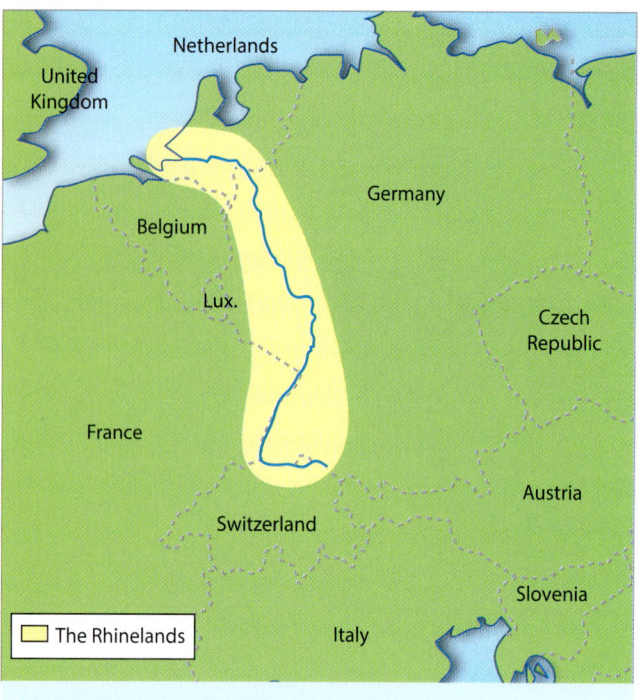

Activities

Examine Figure 10.14.
List three countries through which the Rhine flows.

Figure 10.14 The River Rhine in Europe

Rotterdam

Rotterdam is **Europe's largest port** and among the largest in the world. Docks, warehouses and oil terminals line each side of the river from Rotterdam to the mouth of the Rhine, a distance of 27 km. Cargoes are distributed by train, barge and pipeline to Rhineland cities.

Köln, see Case Study on page 285.

Recreational settlements

The Rhine supports a great **tourist industry**. Cruise boats carry tourists through the Rhinelands every day.

Rüdesheim is a recreational settlement on the Rhine with craft shops and art galleries.

Heidelberg has a famous castle that is very popular with tourists.

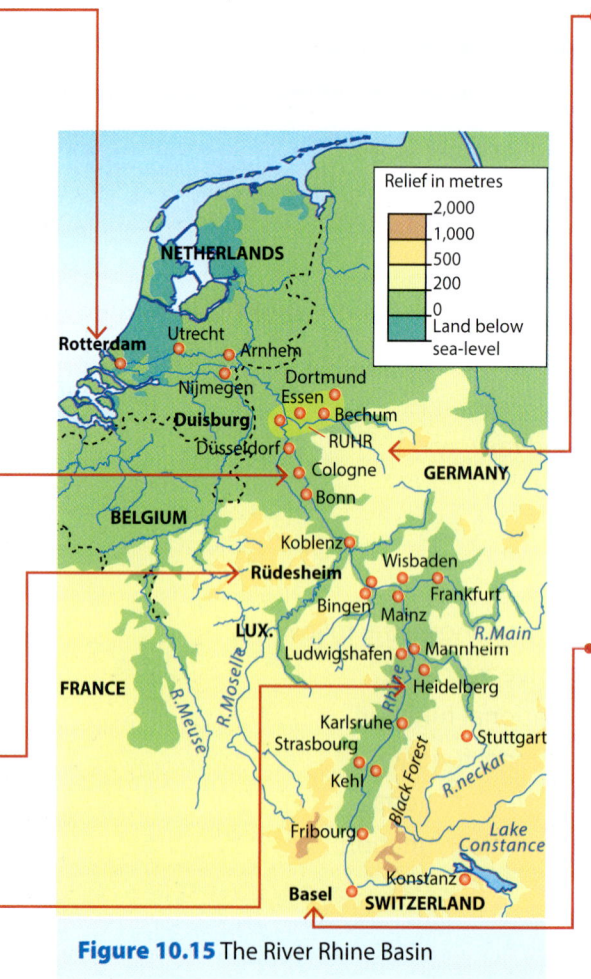

Cities of the Ruhr

The Ruhr is a group of cities that developed on the Ruhr coalfield. Therefore, these cities grew as **resource-based settlements**.

Ruhr cities were home to coalminers who worked the coal pits every day until the 1950s. By then, the best coal seams were exhausted. Thousands of workers became redundant.

Today, the Ruhr is a great **manufacturing region**.

Basel

Basel, Switzerland's port, is located hundreds of kilometres from the sea. Barges unload imports for the Swiss economy, including minerals, timber and oil.

Figure 10.15 The River Rhine Basin

Chapter 10 · Settlement

Case study

Köln (Cologne)

1 Market function

Köln is the largest city along the Rhine. It is one of the most important **bridging points** on the River Rhine in Germany. The city is a major **route focus** for rail and road transport routes. This is one of the key factors that led to Köln's development as a market centre. Its port is one of the most important on the Rhine. Its **trade fairs** attract companies and buyers from all over the world. The city is a very important shopping, banking and **business centre**. For instance, Ford's European headquarters are located in the city.

2 Port function

Köln is one of the most important **inland ports** on the Rhine. The docks are large enough to handle ocean-going vessels. As Köln is a **route focus**, cargo from barges is easily distributed to destinations along the river. Köln is also an important port of call for river cruises. Cruise vessels carry passengers upstream, where the Rhine passes through beautiful countryside and towns.

3 Recreational function

Köln has an important recreational function. It is one of Germany's most beautiful cities with belfries, cathedral spires and bridges. Köln has the largest historic town centre in Germany and has interesting **medieval architecture**.

Much of the historic centre near the city's famous cathedral has been pedestrianised. The area is lined with bookshops, art galleries, coffee shops and boutiques.

Definition

Route focus: A place where routes, e.g. roads from the surrounding area, come together.

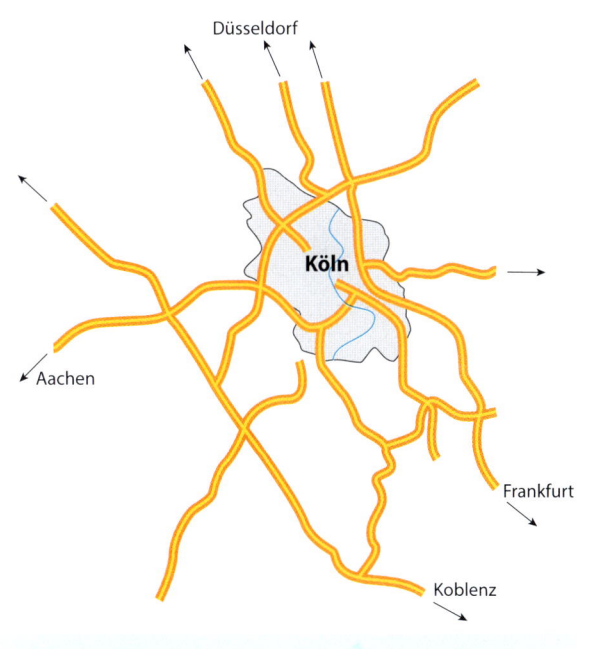

Figure 10.16 Köln is located at a major transport junction on the banks of the Rhine. Ten motorways connect the city with neighbouring regions

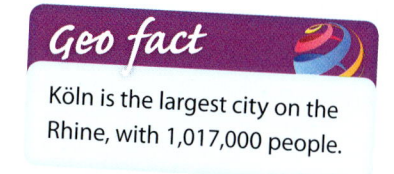

Geo fact

Köln is the largest city on the Rhine, with 1,017,000 people.

Köln city centre, with the twin spires of its medieval cathedral

285

Section 3 · Social Geography

Case study

Other functions

Köln has many other functions. It is a great **cultural centre** with theatres and concert halls.

The city also has a **residential function**. Many people in Köln live in apartments because Germany has a very high population density. Families are small, with one to two children in general, as is the case in all of Germany.

Köln has numerous parks and playgrounds where families spend many hours, especially during the summer months. It is a wealthy city and the standard of living is high. The residents of Köln have a very good quality of life.

Apartments and offices in Köln on the banks of the Rhine

Questions

1. (a) Name the urban settlement in which you live or where you attend school.
   (b) Name **three** functions of that settlement.
   (c) Did this settlement have a function in the past that no longer exists today, and if so, what was that function?

2. Draw a sketch map of the River Shannon. Mark in and name the following:
   - Limerick; Killaloe; Athlone; Carrick-on-Shannon.

3. Draw a sketch map of the River Rhine. Mark in and name:
   - Köln; Duisburg; Mannheim.

10.6 Change in the function of settlements

KEYWORDS
- barbican
- smelter
- commute
- tax incentive

Settlements often change in function over time.

Many Irish urban settlements began more than a thousand years ago. Some began as **defensive settlements** around a castle. Others began as **monastic settlements**.

As time passed, the original function of many towns changed. Towns gradually lost their defensive functions and monasteries were closed and fell into ruins. Towns then took on other functions, such as transport, market and tourism functions.

We will now examine Trim, Co. Meath, to see how its function has changed over time.

Case study

1 Trim: change in function over time

Trim Castle was founded by the Normans at the end of the twelfth century. It was located on the banks of the Boyne for **defensive reasons**. The river may also have been used for the transport of goods. It is surrounded by a **high defensive wall** and had a **barbican**. The de Lacy family lived in the keep and many knights and soldiers lived inside the walls. A **settlement grew around the castle**.

Trim, Co. Meath, with the River Boyne and Trim Castle

Augustinian friars established the **abbey**, the ruins of which can still be seen. The abbey attracted friars and a **school**.

Over time, the castle and abbey fell into ruins. Today, the town has a thriving **tourist industry**. This is a modern function which brings visitors to the town to see the largest Norman castle in the country.

The car parks are used by tourists and by **shoppers** who use Trim as a market town.

Therefore, Trim's function has changed over time.

> **Definition**
>
> **Barbican:** A defensive tower on a gate or drawbridge at the entrance to castle.

The function of a settlement can also change for a number of other reasons, including:
- When mining becomes important in the area
- When large-scale industrial development takes place.

We will now look at an example of each of these.

Section 3 · Social Geography

Case study

2 Navan: where mining has become important

Navan is the **county town** of Co. Meath. It is a **route focus** and, therefore, it has a market function for the people of Co. Meath.

The town has also been an **important manufacturing town**, with furniture and carpet manufacturers. Navan Carpets exported its products to many countries. However, in 2004 foreign competition brought an end to Navan Carpets.

In 1970 a large **lead and zinc deposit** was discovered within three kilometres of Navan. In 1977 **Tara Mines** began to mine the deposit. Since its opening, lead and zinc ores have been exported via Dublin port to **smelters,** mainly in Norway and Finland.

Figure 10.17 The location of Navan, the county town of Co. Meath

Definition

Smelter: In a smelter, a metal is extracted from a raw material called ore.

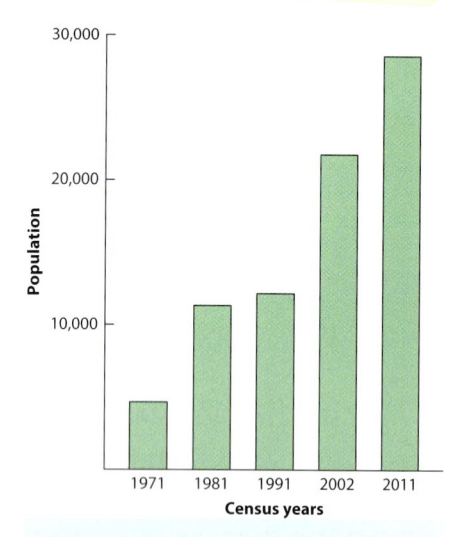

Impact of mining on Navan's economy

- Tara Mines employed about 650 people in 2015.
- The mine is a major **boost to the town's economy**. Housing sales, car sales, restaurants and shops have benefited from the presence of the mine since 1977.
- **Suppliers** of equipment to run the mine, both in Navan and further afield, also benefit. Explosives, drilling equipment and transport are major requirements.

Figure 10.18 Navan's population, 1991–2011

Navan: a dormitory town

Navan has also become a **dormitory town** for Dublin in recent years. After 1995, when the Celtic Tiger economy began, Dublin house prices soared. Many people bought cheaper homes in Navan and other towns surrounding Dublin. These workers **commute** to the capital every day. Because of this, Navan's population grew rapidly between 1991 and 2011.

Navan, Co. Meath, on the River Boyne, with the mine in the foreground

Questions

Figure 10.19 OS map of Navan

1. Draw a sketch of the area shown in the OS map above and show the following features:
   - A castle and motte
   - The railway line
   - An industrial estate
   - The mine area at N 851 678.

2. What evidence in the OS map tells us that Navan has a market function?

3. Navan is a resource-based settlement. What is the evidence for that in the OS map?

4. Explain why a rail line is running as far as the mine area at N 851 678.

5. What evidence in the OS map suggests that Navan has a residential function?
   Name **two** residential districts in Navan.

Section 3 · Social Geography

Case study

3 Leixlip becomes a manufacturing centre

For many decades, Irish governments have invited **major companies from abroad** to locate in Ireland. The government offered **tax incentives** to attract these companies to Ireland. These companies, mainly from the USA, have built factories in many towns and cities in Ireland. One example is Leixlip in Co. Kildare.

A market centre

Leixlip was a small town situated west of Dublin. It acted as a **market centre** for the people of the surrounding areas of counties Kildare and west Dublin. It provided many services such as schools, churches, banks and shops. It was **well served by the N4** to Dublin.

A manufacturing centre

Leixlip became the **location of two high-tech companies** in recent decades. Two manufacturing companies set up there:

- **Intel**, which manufactures microchips for computers and is **one of the largest employers in Ireland** with more than 4,500 workers
- **Hewlett Packard**, which manufactures ink cartridges and employs more than 1,000 workers.

Figure 10.20 Leixlip is situated west of Dublin in Co. Kildare

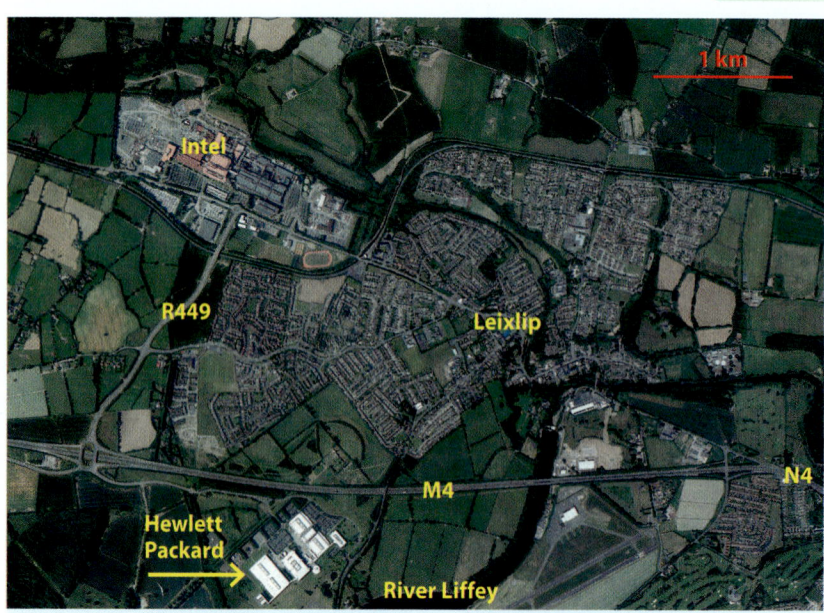

Definition
Tax incentives: Low tax rates to encourage business.

Activity
Have you seen the logo **Intel inside™** on laptops?

Intel and Hewlett Packard are located close to the town of Leixlip and to major transport routes

290

Case study

The presence of these manufacturers has changed Leixlip.

- Many well-paid workers live locally.
- Local services such as restaurants, banks and schools have expanded to meet the needs of workers and their families.

As in the case of Navan, Leixlip is also a **dormitory town** for Dublin.

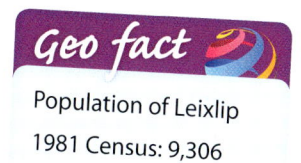

Geo fact

Population of Leixlip
1981 Census: 9,306
2011 Census: 15,543

Questions

1. Look at the photograph of Trim on page 287.
   (a) Give **one** past function that existed in Trim that no longer exists.
   (b) Using evidence from the photo, give **one** modern function of Trim at the present time.

2. How has Leixlip, Co. Kildare, changed in function in recent decades?

10.7 Communication links

All students must study the Irish road network. Higher Level students must study the EU airports **and** transport on the Rhine. Ordinary Level students must study **one** of the topics.

KEYWORDS

- communication links
- industrial estate
- access road
- commuter town
- ring road
- toll road
- hub
- aviation industries
- navigable river
- raw material

People and goods move between settlements, by road, rail, ship and air. Information too moves on telecommunications networks, by telephone and Internet. The paths along which they travel are **communication links**. The existence of such links aids the development of settlements.

In this section, we examine these important communication links:

- The Irish road network
- EU airports
- Transport on the River Rhine.

Section 3 · Social Geography

> # Case study
>
> ## The Irish road network

Figure 10.21 The national road network of the Republic of Ireland (Source: NRA)

Chapter 10 · Settlement

Case study

The **road network** that exists in Ireland today was laid out when Ireland was a colony of Britain. **Dublin** became the **political centre** of the colony. Ireland supplied Britain with cheap raw materials and Dublin grew to become the **main port** for the export of goods. Therefore, Ireland's road network is **radial**. Major roads **radiate** outwards **from Dublin to the provinces**.

Geo fact

Leinster has more motorways than any other province in Ireland.

Roads aid the development of settlements

- **Manufacturing towns** and **industrial estates** need good access for trucks that bring raw materials to factories. **Shannon Town** and industrial estate is served by the N18 and the N19. This has helped the town to grow.
- **Market towns** grow when they have good access to the surrounding area. People use **access roads** to go to town to do the shopping and for other personal and financial services, e.g. county towns such as **Navan** (see page 288–89).
- Towns grow as **dormitory towns**, especially around Dublin. Naas, Navan, Drogheda, Wicklow and many others are dormitory towns for people who work in Dublin. These **commuter towns** are all connected by road and, increasingly, by motorway (see Figure 10.21 page 292).
- The **M50** is a great **ring road** outside Dublin. It links together all the major routes as they approach Dublin. The M50 is a **toll road** and is the busiest motorway in the country.
- An **urban centre** that is located at an important **river crossing point** becomes the focus of several routes. This brings traffic and business to the urban centre and helps it to grow, e.g. Limerick (see page 282–83).
- **Tourist towns** need good road access, so that visitors can travel to these towns easily, e.g. the tourist centres of the south coast. The **Wild Atlantic Way** travels along the west coast of Ireland and has become a very popular tourist route. Urban centres such as Galway, Ballina and Sligo have benefited from tourist traffic.

Motorways bypass local towns and are safer than two-lane roads

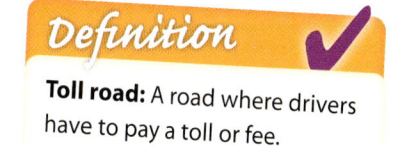

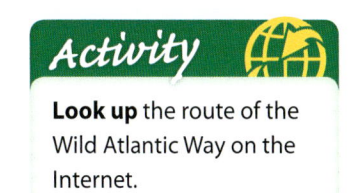

Definition

Toll road: A road where drivers have to pay a toll or fee.

Activity

Look up the route of the Wild Atlantic Way on the Internet.

Section 3 · Social Geography

Case study

EU airports

Busy **air routes link urban centres**. Air routes make urban centres in different countries and continents very accessible to each other.

Air transport is very popular today because:

- The population of Western Europe is **wealthy**.
- **Low-cost airlines** and competitive prices have greatly reduced air fares.

Europe's busiest airports include London (Heathrow), Paris, Frankfurt, Barcelona and Schiphol Airport in Amsterdam. **Stansted** Airport near London has grown because it is a Ryanair **hub**.

Many EU airports such as London Heathrow and Charles de Gaulle Airport in Paris have connections with international airports in every continent.

Tourism accounts for most of the passenger traffic in **Mediterranean airports**.

How do air links help to develop settlements?

To answer that question, we will briefly examine London and Shannon.

Airports serving London

London's five airports – Heathrow, Gatwick, Stansted, London City Airport and Luton – **employ great numbers of people**. This employment has helped London and its surrounding towns to grow.

- **Heathrow** has **76,000 employees** in the airport itself. About 40 flights an hour touch down at London Heathrow during peak hours.
- London is home to the **headquarters of some of the most important companies** in Europe and indeed in the world.

> **Geo fact**
> London Heathrow handles about 1,300 flights a day and has direct flights to 185 international airports.

Figure 10.22 The location of major airports in the EU

Table 10.3 Airport passengers in 2014

Heathrow	73 million
Charles de Gaulle	64 million
Frankfurt	60 million
Schiphol	55 million
Madrid	42 million
Dublin	22 million

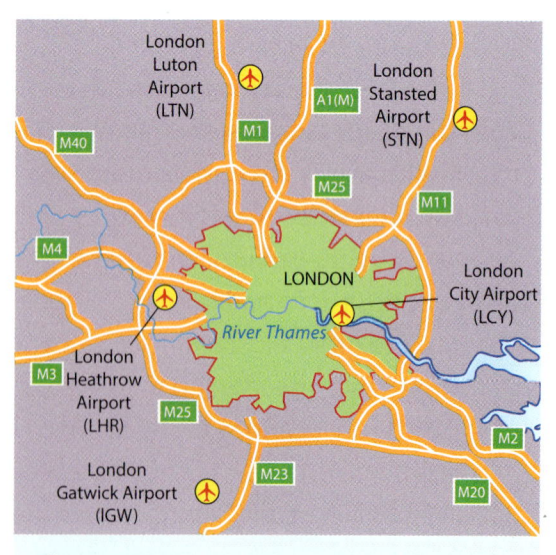

Figure 10.23 The locations of London's airports

Chapter 10 · Settlement

Case study

- Airlines bring passengers and **passengers bring business**. Many people travel to London for business reasons. It is a major **centre for international conferences** because it is so easy to reach by air.
- London is a great **tourist destination** for the same reason and because of its cultural attractions. Therefore, London is a **major hotel centre**.
- **While visitors are in London**, they stay in hotels, use taxis, eat out, do some shopping and take in a show. In other words, **they spend money**. This **creates employment** in London.

Heathrow Airport – one of the busiest airports in the world

Shannon Airport

Shannon Airport is very **important to nearby urban centres**. Many people working in the airport live in Limerick, Ennis, Newmarket-on-Fergus, Clarecastle and Sixmilebridge. These centres have a **dormitory function** for people working in Shannon.

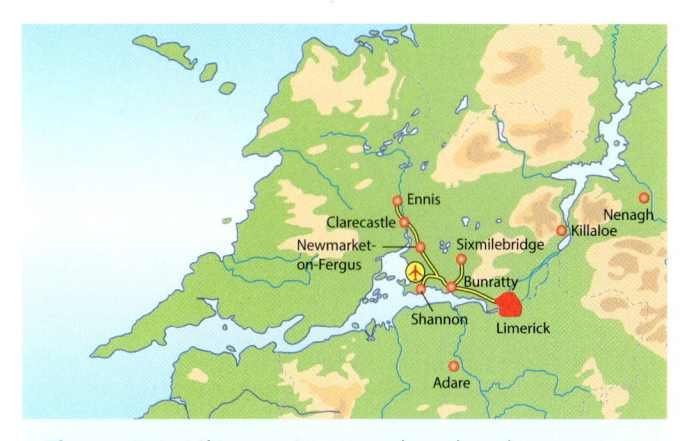

Figure 10.24 Shannon Airport and nearby urban centres

A new town

In 1962, a new town was begun near the airport called **Shannon Town**. Many people in the town work at the airport and nearby industrial estates. **Aviation industries** such as Shannon Aerospace are located beside the airport. This has **led to further growth** in Shannon Town. The population of Shannon Town was more than 9,500 in the 2011 Census.

Shannon Airport with the industrial estate

Definition ✓

Aviation industries: Industries that manufacture aeroplane parts and that service aeroplane engines and instruments.

Geo fact

Shannon Airport served 1.7 million passengers in 2015.

295

Section 3 · Social Geography

Questions

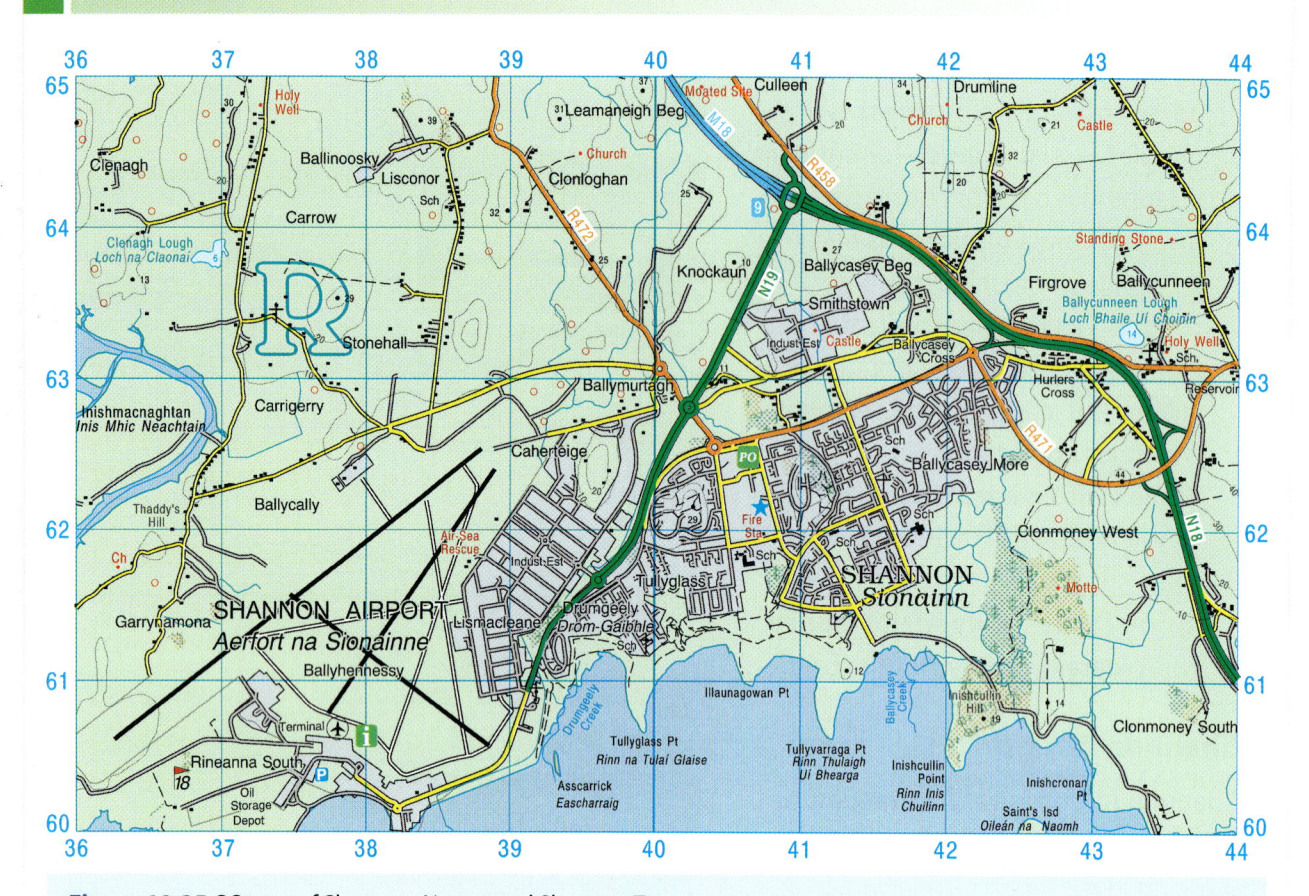

Figure 10.25 OS map of Shannon Airport and Shannon Town

Study the OS map of Shannon Airport and answer the following questions:

1 Name the features found at the following locations:
   - R 376 606
   - R 409 643
   - R 410 632
   - R 367 604.

2 Study the site on which the airport is built. Write down **two** reasons why the site is suitable for an airport.

3 Shannon has an industrial function. What evidence is provided in the OS map to support that?

4 Shannon Town has a residential function. Write down **two** pieces of evidence in the OS map that support that.

Case study

Transport on the River Rhine

Many large urban centres are located on the banks of the River Rhine and its tributaries. The Rhine is a **navigable river**. It reaches into the heart of Western Europe as far as Switzerland.

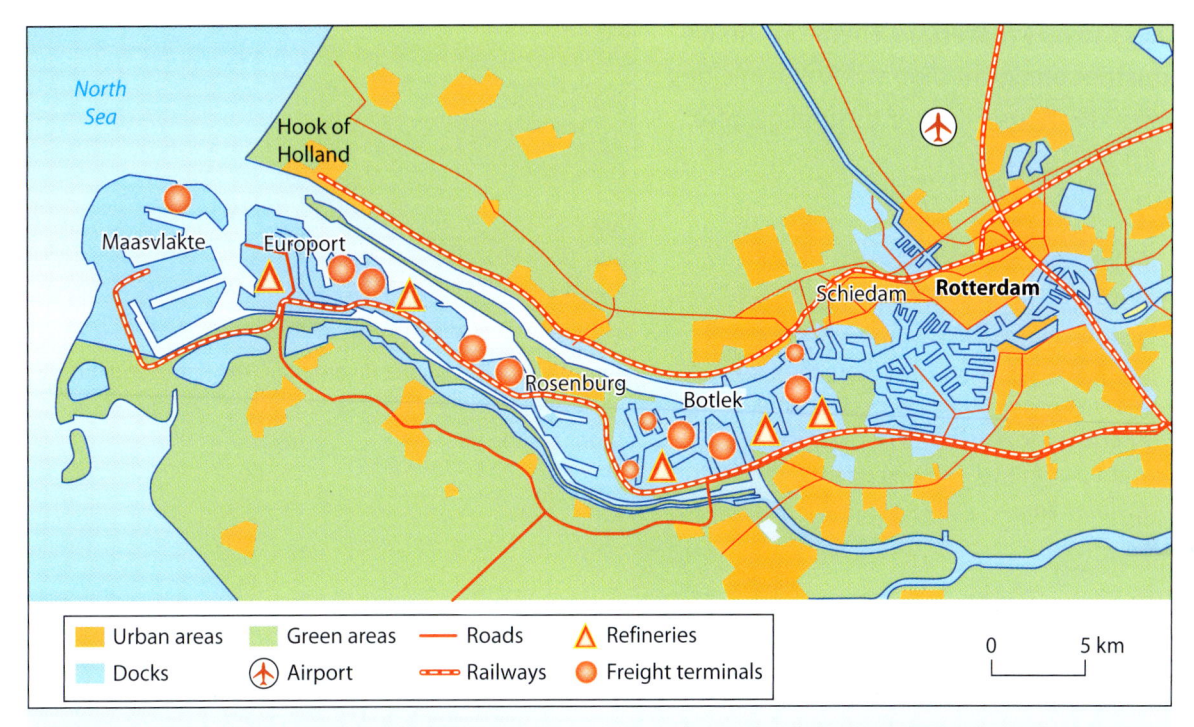

Figure 10.26 The location of the port of Rotterdam

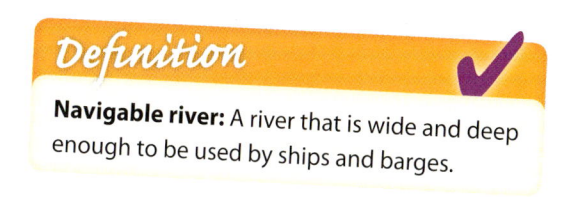

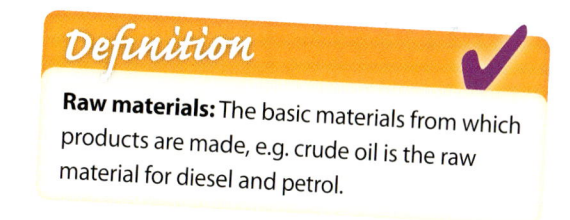

> **Definition**
> **Navigable river:** A river that is wide and deep enough to be used by ships and barges.

> **Definition**
> **Raw materials:** The basic materials from which products are made, e.g. crude oil is the raw material for diesel and petrol.

Rotterdam-Europoort

Rotterdam-Europoort is located at the mouth of the Rhine. As **one of the world's largest ports**, Rotterdam **imports raw materials** such as crude oil, metal ores, timber, chemical raw materials and much more. This material is then **transported by barge** to manufacturing centres as far as Switzerland.

> **Link**
> See also **Settlement in the River Rhine basin**, page 284.

continued on next page

Section 3 · Social Geography

Case study

Manufacturing cities on the banks of the Rhine

The Rhine waterway has **aided the growth of manufacturing cities** that are located on its banks. The Rhine gives industries **access to raw materials**. Therefore, heavy industries are located on the Rhine in cities such as Duisburg, Köln and Ludwigshafen.

Advantages of water transport

Water transport is a **cheap way of transporting bulky cargo**, e.g. mineral ores, timber, sand and coal. Even though river transport is **slow**, barges can carry **enormous loads**. Barges last a long time and, apart from the engine, need **very little maintenance**.

Barge transport on the River Rhine. The Rhineland has beautiful scenery and has many towns nestling on the banks of the river

A waterway network

Barges also travel on many of the **tributaries** of the Rhine that are navigable. The Rhine is connected to other inland waterways in Western Europe. Therefore, the Rhine is the **central artery** in a great river and canal network in Western Europe.

Tourists travel on **cruise boats** to many towns and cities located on the River Rhine.

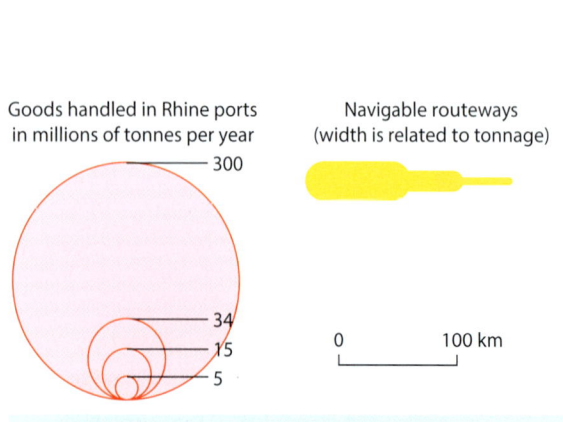

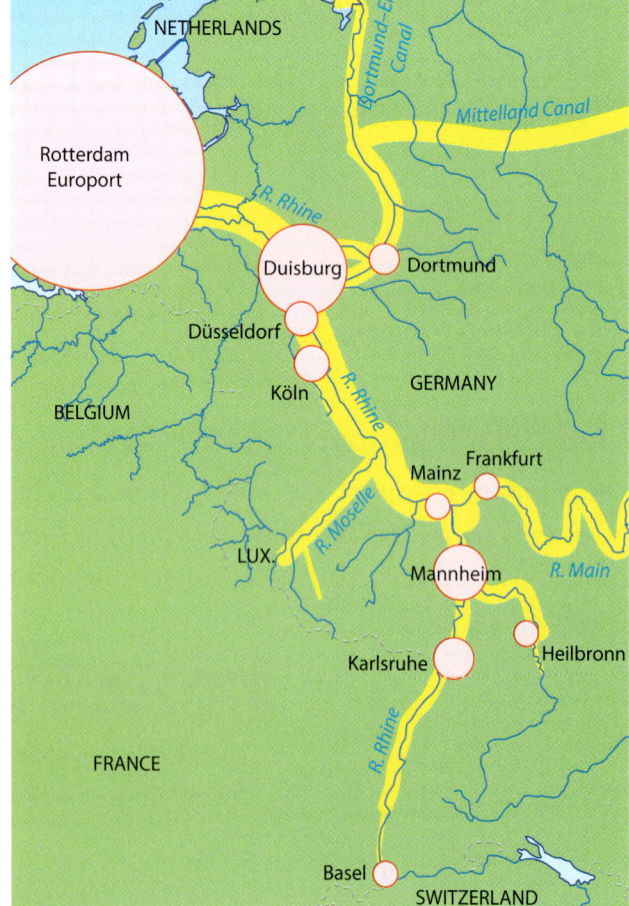

Goods handled in Rhine ports in millions of tonnes per year
- 300
- 34
- 15
- 5

Navigable routeways (width is related to tonnage)

Figure 10.27 Traffic on the Rhine and adjoining waterways

Chapter 10 · Settlement

Questions

1. Name the motorway between Dublin and the border with Northern Ireland.
2. Where would you find the M50?
3. What is the Wild Atlantic Way?
4. Draw a sketch map of the London area. Mark in and name **four** airports in the London area.
5. How has Shannon Airport helped Shannon Town to grow?
6. Give **two** reasons for the importance of the river Rhine as a transport route.

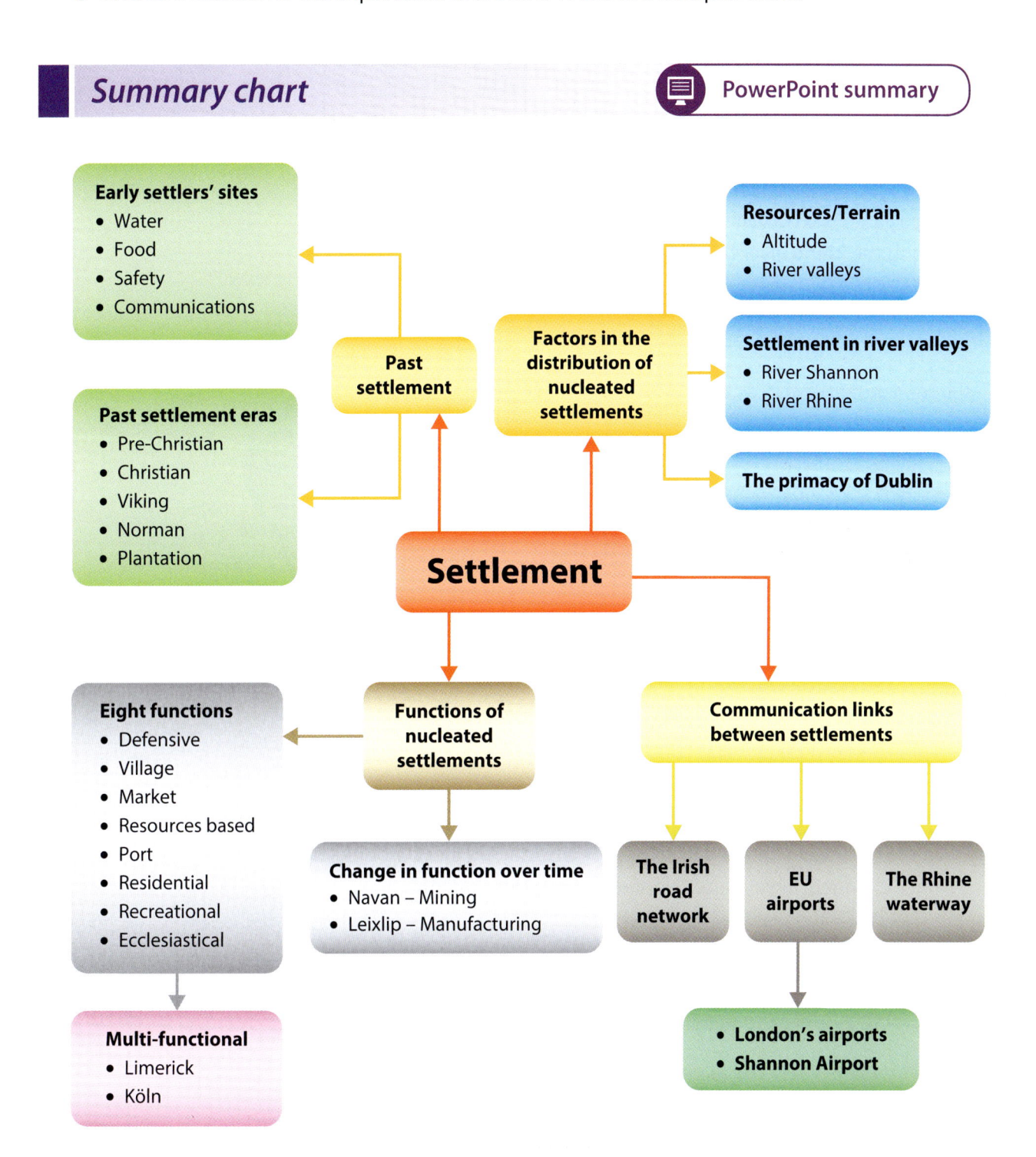

Summary chart

PowerPoint summary

Early settlers' sites
- Water
- Food
- Safety
- Communications

Past settlement eras
- Pre-Christian
- Christian
- Viking
- Norman
- Plantation

Past settlement

Factors in the distribution of nucleated settlements

Resources/Terrain
- Altitude
- River valleys

Settlement in river valleys
- River Shannon
- River Rhine

The primacy of Dublin

Settlement

Eight functions
- Defensive
- Village
- Market
- Resources based
- Port
- Residential
- Recreational
- Ecclesiastical

Functions of nucleated settlements

Change in function over time
- Navan – Mining
- Leixlip – Manufacturing

Communication links between settlements

- The Irish road network
- EU airports
- The Rhine waterway

Multi-functional
- Limerick
- Köln

- London's airports
- Shannon Airport

299

Section 3 · Social Geography

Exam questions

1. Circle the correct option in **each** of the following statements:
   (i) Polders refer to reclaimed land. ***True / False***
   (ii) Germany is famous for the polder landscape. ***True / False***
   (iii) Planned farms are evident in the polders. ***True / False***

   HL 2011

2. Describe any **three** different functions associated with urban settlement(s) along the Rhine River basin.

   HL 2013

3. The functions of many towns have changed over time.

   In the case of **one** named Irish town or city that you have studied, describe how its functions have changed. In your answer refer to **three** different functions.

   HL 2007

4. Explain the development of any transport network that you have studied.

   HL 2011

Chapter 11
Urbanisation

Learning outcomes

By the end of this chapter, you should be able to understand:

- How towns and cities grow over time
- That Dublin acquired many functions over time
- That cities have distinct functional zones
- That each city has a central business district
- That cities face challenges and problems
- That building new towns and urban renewal and redevelopment are efforts to solve urban problems
- That cities in the developing world suffer from different problems.

11.1 Changing patterns in where we live: cities

KEYWORDS
- urbanisation
- economic activities
- administrative activities
- social activities
- tenement
- suburb

Towns and cities have existed for thousands of years. Over time, they have grown in number and size all over the word. At the same time, the proportion of people living in cities has increased. This process is known as **urbanisation**.

The growth of towns has happened because of key activities:

- **Economic activities:** towns and cities developed as **market centres** where people bought and sold goods, **manufacturing centres** where goods were made and **ports** through which goods were exported and imported.
- **Administrative activities:** cities became the places from which rulers governed their territory by using law courts and civil servants.
- **Social activities:** people came to see plays and sporting activities, to meet friends and to enjoy themselves.

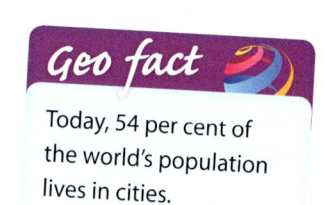

Geo fact
Today, 54 per cent of the world's population lives in cities.

Section 3 · Social Geography

The growth of Dublin

Viking Dublin

The **Vikings** built a fortified settlement on the south bank of the River Liffey in the early ninth century. This was the **birth of Dublin**. The Vikings used wood as a building material. Viking Dublin continued as a **trading post** after the Vikings were defeated at the Battle of Clontarf in 1014. We know this from coins that have been found dating back to that period.

The Normans

After the **Normans** invaded Ireland in 1169, Norman knights occupied Dublin. They were skilled builders with stone, so they built **city walls**.

Dublin became a medieval city of narrow streets and unhealthy conditions. The **Black Death** caused the death of many of its citizens in the fourteenth century. However, Dublin's trade with England increased. The port grew further.

Dublin Castle became the **administrative centre** of English power in Ireland, and remained so until Irish Independence in 1922. St Patrick's Cathedral and Christchurch were added over the years.

The sixteenth to the eighteenth centuries

Queen Elizabeth extended English rule over large parts of Ireland. As a result, Dublin became more important as an administrative centre. **Trinity College** was also built, adding to the city's importance.

Throughout the eighteenth century, Dublin was extended. Streets and squares were built on the north and south sides. St Stephen's Green and Merrion Square were laid out and surrounded by **Georgian houses**. These large houses were occupied by wealthy Irish gentry who came to Dublin from the provinces to attend parliament.

Dublin became a **distribution centre** as barges on the Royal and Grand Canals brought goods from Dublin port westwards towards the Shannon. Dublin's **docklands**, such as Grand Canal Docks, were extended.

Wealthy Dubliners had an excellent **social life**, and enjoyed plays and concerts.

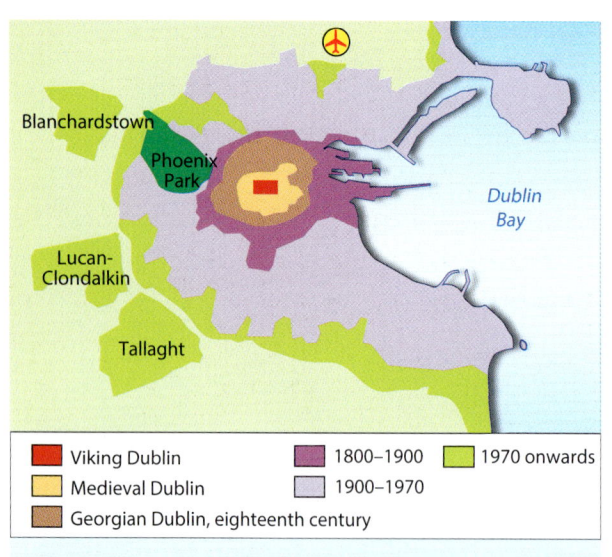

Figure 11.1 Since Viking times, Dublin has grown outwards from the centre

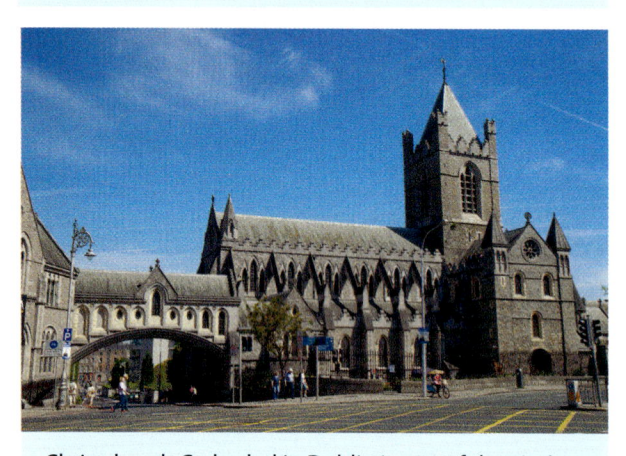

Christchurch Cathedral in Dublin is one of the city's most famous buildings

Trinity College in the heart of Dublin dates from 1592

Geo fact

Dublin was the second largest city in the British Empire at the end of the eighteenth century and this was reflected in its buildings and parks.

The nineteenth century

The **Act of Union** of 1800 abolished the Irish parliament in Dublin. Members of parliament moved to London and sold their Dublin homes to landlords. Dublin's social life collapsed. Dublin became a city of overcrowded **tenements**. Tenements often housed one family per room.

Economic activity centred around the port. Canals and later railways connected Dublin to the provinces. Goods from the port were distributed by canal and rail to urban centres all over Ireland.

Geo fact
20,000 Dublin families each lived in just one rented room, and many of them took in a lodger to help pay the rent.

Dublin families who lived in tenements during the strike and Lockout of 1913

The capital of the Irish state

Dublin has grown very rapidly since independence in 1922. The reasons for this include the following:

- The city had **high birth rates** for several decades after independence.
- **Inward migration** from the provinces increased the population.
- The city became **multi-functional**. Banking, insurance, radio and television media, hospitals and universities all expanded.
- As the capital city, it was also the **administrative centre** for an independent country. The **civil service** that helps to run the country was based there.
- Dublin's economy rapidly expanded in recent times. Many companies from abroad, such as Google and Microsoft, brought more jobs and people to the city.

Urban growth in recent decades

New **suburbs** have extended outwards into the countryside to house the growing population. From the 1970s onwards, satellite towns such as Tallaght were built.

The city of Dublin, its suburbs and surrounding **dormitory towns** are now home to more than 1.2 million people.

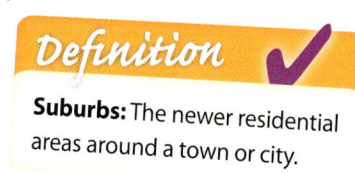

Definition
Suburbs: The newer residential areas around a town or city.

Link
For more on Dublin, see **The importance of Dublin**, page 272.

Questions

1. Describe the growth of Dublin with reference to the following:
   - The Viking period
   - Medieval buildings
   - Georgian buildings
   - The growth of Dublin port.

2. Explain **two** reasons why Dublin has grown since Ireland became independent in 1922.

Section 3 • Social Geography

11.2 Cities: functional zones

> **KEYWORDS**
> - functional zone
> - central business district (CBD)
> - satellite town
> - ring road
> - heavy industry
> - industrial estate
> - world city
> - technology park

If you look at any city, you can see that different areas are used for different purposes. These areas are known as **functional zones**.

These zones include:

- The CBD (central business district)
- Smaller shopping areas
- Shopping centres
- Industrial areas
- Residential areas
- Open space for recreation.

The CBD

The centre of every city has a **central business district (CBD)**. It is the main area for **business and shopping**. This is where banks, building societies, large department stores and company headquarters are found. **Land in the CBD is very expensive** so there are often high-rise office blocks.

Geo fact
The first skyscraper was built in Chicago in 1884.

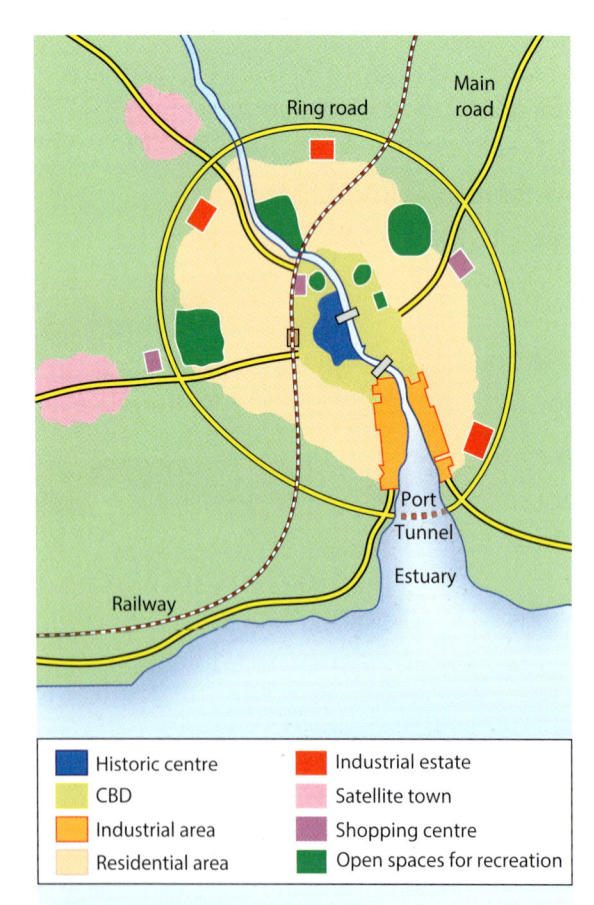

Part of the Manhattan skyline in New York. This is the CBD and competition for space is intense

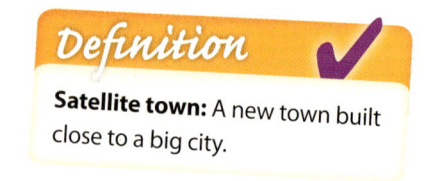

Historic centre	Industrial estate
CBD	Satellite town
Industrial area	Shopping centre
Residential area	Open spaces for recreation

Figure 11.2 Urban functional zones

Definition
Satellite town: A new town built close to a big city.

304

Small shopping areas

Most people who live in cities do not go into the CBD every day to do their shopping. They shop in smaller shopping areas **in the residential districts** where they live. Examples in Dublin include **Blackrock** and **Rathgar**. These former villages have been swallowed up by the growth of the city.

Large shopping centres

Large shopping centres exist **in the suburbs** of Irish cities. They are built **close to ring roads** so that shoppers have good access by car. Therefore, fewer people shop in the city centre. This sometimes leads to the closure of city centre stores.

Industrial areas

Cities are also **manufacturing centres**. Seaport cities have industries in the port area, e.g. oil refining, ship manufacturing and flour milling. **Heavy industries**, such as the manufacturing of train carriages and engines, are located near railway lines and canals.

A view of part of west Dublin, with ① an industrial estate, ② the M50, ③ Liffey Valley shopping centre, ④ a residential suburb and ⑤ a school

Industrial estates

Modern **industrial estates** with light industry are located on the outskirts of towns and cities. There are many reasons for this:

- **Land is cheaper** on the outskirts than in the city centre and therefore more space is available.
- **Workers** live in nearby suburbs.
- A **ring road** around the city makes factories very accessible to heavy lorries. Materials can enter and leave the factories easily.

Activity

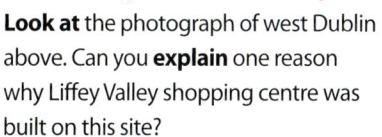

Look at the photograph of west Dublin above. Can you **explain** one reason why Liffey Valley shopping centre was built on this site?

Residential areas

Residential districts generally take up the **greater part of the built-up area** of a city.

- **Older houses** are close to the **city centre**.
- As cities grow into the countryside, **newer housing estates** and detached homes are added at the **city limits**.

Open space for recreation

Cities need **green spaces** where children can play and people can escape from the hustle and bustle of traffic. Green spaces bring the countryside into the city. **Phoenix Park** in Dublin is one of Europe's finest city parks.

Phoenix Park, Dublin

Section 3 · Social Geography

Case Study

Paris

Paris is the capital of France and is also a **primate city**. The population of Greater Paris is more than 12 million people. Lyon, the second city of France, has just over 2 million people.

Paris is a **world city**, ranking in importance with New York, Tokyo and London. Paris has a world influence in fashion and culture.

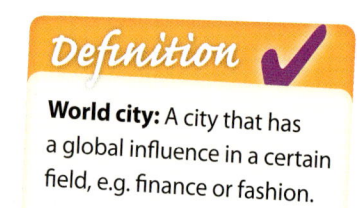

> **Definition**
>
> **World city:** A city that has a global influence in a certain field, e.g. finance or fashion.

Functional zones in Paris

The CBD

The CBD in Paris is a core area of business and shopping activity. It contains:

- The **headquarters** of many French banking and commercial companies
- The stock exchange, known as the **Paris Bourse**
- The political and administrative **offices of the government** of France.

The CBD is served by the underground rail system – the **Paris Métro**. Therefore, the area is very accessible. The CBD now reaches as far as **La Défense**, a new high-rise office district.

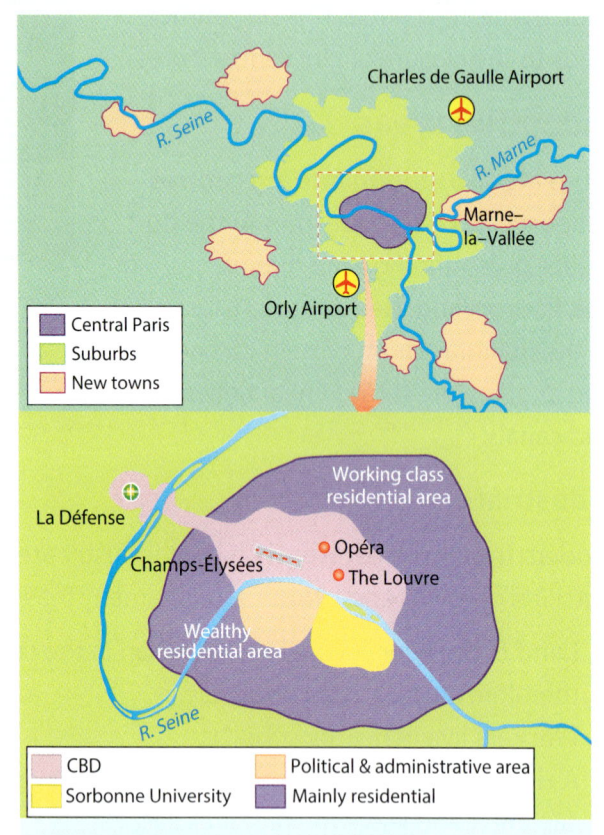

Shopping activity

Paris is a shoppers' paradise. As a world centre of fashion, for both men and women, the **CBD has large shopping areas**. Big department stores such as **Galeries Lafayette** and Printemps are found in many locations in central Paris. The streets around the **Champs-Élysées** and Boulevard Hausmann are major shopping areas.

Figure 11.3 Functional zones in Paris

Smaller shopping areas

Paris grew outwards from its centre over time. As it did so, it **absorbed nearby villages**. These villages became **suburbs** of Paris. Each of those suburbs has a smaller shopping area where locals do their shopping. Branches of supermarket chains such as **Intermarché** and **Carrefour** are found in many residential districts in Paris.

The Arc de Triomphe and the Champs-Élysées

306

Case Study

Residential areas

The greater portion of Paris is made up of **residential districts**. The city has affluent areas, middle-class areas and working-class areas.

- Most people live in **apartment blocks** that are up to ten storeys high. The city has high population densities. Many apartment blocks have a **concierge**, who acts as a door person and checks on the comings and goings in the building.
- Many people now live in the new **satellite towns** that have been built around Paris. The new towns have a variety of housing types, ranging from apartment blocks to attached and detached homes. Amenities in these new towns are very good; they have parks, artificial ponds and leisure areas. **Disneyland Resort**, **Paris**, is located in one of the new towns called **Marne-la-Vallée**.

Industrial areas

Paris is the **most important manufacturing region in France**.

- The **fashion industry** is located on the banks of the River Seine in central Paris where fashion products are designed and produced. **Jewellery** and **perfumes** are produced in the same parts of Paris.
- **Printing and publishing** firms are found near the Latin Quarter, where the Sorbonne University is located.
- **Modern industries**, such as aerospace, defence equipment, healthcare and optical equipment, are located in the **technology parks** on the urban fringe and in the new towns.
- The **car assembly industry** has been part of the Paris scene for more than a hundred years. However, car assembly factories are now moving to Eastern Europe where labour is cheaper.

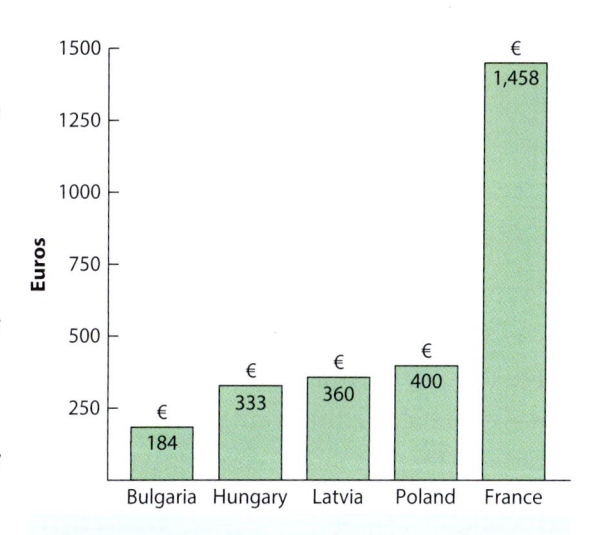

Figure 11.4 The minimum wage per month in France and some EU countries in Eastern Europe. High wages in France are making French factories uncompetitive

Open spaces in Paris

Paris has a wide variety of parks that are open to the public. The **Bois de Boulogne** is in the very centre of the city. Green spaces include the Jardin de Luxembourg and the Champs de Mars.

Thousands of people stroll along the tree-lined quays on the **banks of the Seine**, where artists display their work.

A view over Paris with the Champs de Mars in the foreground

Section 3 · Social Geography

> ## Questions
>
> 1. Explain the term 'functional zones' as applied to cities.
> 2. Give **two** examples of functional zones in cities.
> 3. Write down **three** commercial activities that are found in the CBD of cities.
> 4. Explain **two** reasons why industrial estates are found on the outskirts of towns.
> 5. Name **two** manufacturing activities that take place in Paris.

11.3 Land values and land use in cities

> **KEYWORDS**
> - city centre
> - demand and supply
> - land value
> - footfall
> - office block
> - multi-storey building

Land values tend to increase towards the city centre.

The city centre

Students will know from their business studies that when the demand for goods exceeds the supply, the price goes up. This is the case with **land values** in cities. The highest land values are in the city centre (the **CBD**). This is because there is a **high demand** for space as shops and other companies all compete for a foothold in an area with a **limited supply** of land.

> **Definition** ✓
>
> **Land value:** The cost of purchasing or renting land for a particular use.

Commerce in the city centre

- **Many shops locate in the city centre**, e.g. boutiques, jewellers, entertainment retailers and mobile phone shops. Cinemas, banks and some hotels also tend to be in the centre. The **footfall of customers** through these companies' doors is so high that companies can afford the high cost or rent of a city centre location.
- **Office blocks** are also found in the city centre. Companies that use these offices include law firms, accountancy firms, newspaper companies and advertising agencies.

> **Activity** 💡
>
> What do you think **footfall of customers** means?

The solution to limited supply of land in the CBD

In order to get the most out of a small site in the CBD, developers build **multi-storey buildings**. This greatly increases the supply of floor space. This is the case in most cities across the world today.

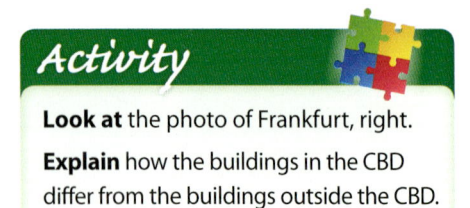

> **Activity**
>
> **Look at** the photo of Frankfurt, right.
> **Explain** how the buildings in the CBD differ from the buildings outside the CBD.

Frankfurt, Germany. Can you locate the CBD in the photo?

Outside the city centre

As one moves out from the city centre, land use is not as intensive as in the CBD because there is **less demand for, and a greater supply of land**. Land values decline as a result. This changes the intensity of land use away from the city centre.

- The **height of buildings is much lower** than in the city centre.
- Small **parks and playing fields** are evident.
- **Residential areas** take up most of the land.
- Terraced housing closer to the city centre gives way to **semi-detached homes** and detached homes.
- **Shopping centres**, filling stations and hotels are located here also.

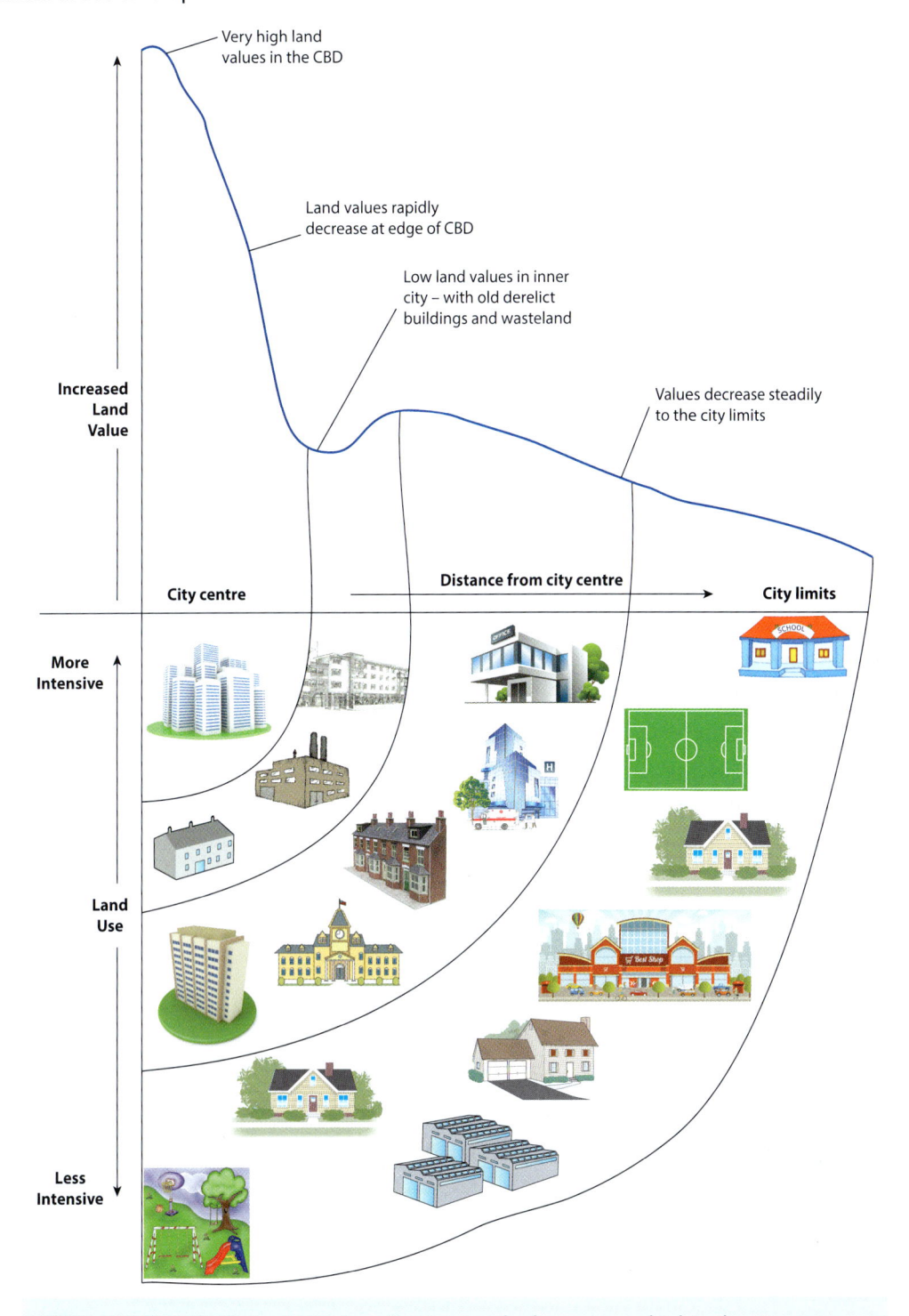

Figure 11.5 Land values and land use in cities. Land values are very high in the city centre

Section 3 · Social Geography

> **Questions**
>
> 1 Why are the tallest buildings found in the city centre?
> 2 Why can jewellers and hotels afford to locate in the city centre?
> 3 Why do land values decrease sharply away from the CBD?

11.4 Residential accommodation in Irish cities

KEYWORDS
- apartment block
- terraced house
- town house
- semi-detached house
- detached house
- two-up two-down
- home insulation
- superwarm

The quality, type and age of residential accommodation vary significantly within a city.

Age of residential accommodation

Ireland's cities have grown outwards from small town centres over hundreds of years. Therefore, **city centre residences are older** than recently built suburbs. Many city centre residences have housing styles that belong to earlier centuries. For example, **Georgian houses** were built more than 200 years ago. They can be found in many cities and towns in Ireland.

Types of residential accommodation

Many types of residential accommodation exist in cities today.

- **Council apartment blocks** have replaced poor quality housing in the inner city. They are four to five storeys high and have a high population density.
- **Streets of terraced housing** are close to the city centre. They have very small back yards and do not have front gardens. The front door often opens directly onto the pavement.
- **Expensive town houses** and high quality apartment blocks exist near the city centre. High earners, who may work in the nearby CBD, live in them.
- Large housing estates of **semi-detached houses** are found in the suburbs. They are modern family homes that have front and back gardens. Many front gardens have been paved over as parking spaces for two or three cars.
- **Luxury detached houses** are found in highly desirable locations, e.g. close to the sea or on elevated sites.
- Increasingly, high quality **apartment blocks** have been built in suburban centres in Irish cities. This is because land prices everywhere became very expensive during the Celtic Tiger years from 1995 to 2008.

Georgian houses in Merrion Square, Dublin. These are part of the cultural heritage of the city

Activity

Can you locate Georgian houses in your town or city? Name three features of these houses.

Terraced houses without front gardens are found close to the city centre where land is expensive

Semi-detached homes are found in the suburbs, where there is more land available than in the city centre

Detached homes are found on the outskirts of towns, where land is much cheaper than in the city centre

Quality of residential accommodation

The quality of residential accommodation has changed greatly over the years in several ways that include:

- Home size
- Materials used.

Home size

Many years ago, in poor times, much of the housing in the centres of towns and cities consisted of **brick-built terraced houses**. Most were small and called **two-up two-down** houses. They had two bedrooms upstairs and a kitchen and sitting room downstairs heated by a coal fire. The toilet was outside in the back yard. Many of these terraced houses have been **modernised** over the years.

In recent decades, as Ireland became wealthy, larger suburban homes with **three to four bedrooms** have become standard.

Modern materials

In recent times, fuel has become very expensive, so the cost of heating homes has risen. Therefore, **home insulation** is very important today. Modern homes – both apartments and houses – have double-glazing, attic and wall insulation, and efficient gas and oil boilers. Some housing estates have been built of **'superwarm'** materials that retain the heat so well that heating costs are much lower.

Questions

1. Explain the following terms:
   - Terraced houses
   - Apartment blocks
   - Town houses.

2. Explain **two** reasons why the houses close to the city centre are terraced.

3. Why are semi-detached and detached homes found towards the outskirts of cities?

Section 3 • Social Geography

11.5 Commuting to work in cities

KEYWORDS
- commuting
- rush hour
- congestion
- traffic management
- public transport
- quality bus corridor (QBC)
- DART
- Luas
- metro

Many people commute to work and back every day in a city. Others travel to college or school, to meet people or to go shopping. These journeys or movements of people fall into clear **patterns**.

Commuting

People **commute** to the CBD of Irish cities and towns for work every weekday. Some go by train and bus, but **most travel by car**. This can be a very stressful experience for motorists.

- **Rush hour** happens twice a day.
- The morning rush hour occurs because most **offices and schools open around 9.00 a.m**. As roads get busier and more dangerous, more parents bring their children to school by car.
- The evening rush hour is when the **commuters and shoppers return home**.
- Streets into the city centre are **congested** at rush hours. It is challenging for traffic planners and commuters alike.

Geo fact

In 2015, 580 long-distance commuters travelled daily by rail to and from Dublin from as far away as Thurles, Limerick Junction and Athlone.

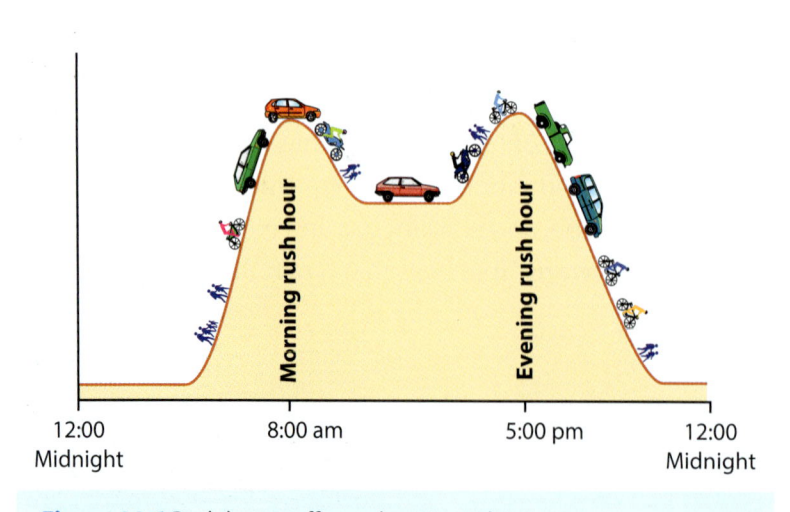

Figure 11.6 Rush hour traffic peaks twice a day

"Why is the time of day with the slowest traffic called rush hour?"

Rush hour is a feature of cities around the world

Solving the congestion problem

1 Restricting car use

Many measures are used to discourage car use in city centres:

- Expensive hourly **parking charges** put people off bringing their cars into the city.
- **Clamping** for illegal parking and heavy **on-the-spot fines** back up the parking charges.
- **Pedestrian-only streets** make cars less useful.
- Many cities use **congestion charges** to make motorists think twice about using the car during the day. In London, cars entering the Congestion Zone between **7.00 a.m. and 6.00 p.m.** are charged a fee.

2 Traffic management

The purpose of traffic management is to improve the **flow of traffic**. This can be attempted in many ways:

- One-way streets
- Traffic lights, roundabouts and yellow grids at junctions
- The use of double yellow lines to ban all parking on busy traffic routes
- Ring roads that keep traffic out of the city centre
- Tunnels, such as Dublin Port Tunnel, that take traffic off the streets
- Park-and-ride facilities that allow commuters to leave their cars in the suburbs and take public transport such as the Luas into the city centre.

Traffic management at a junction in Dublin's city centre. How is traffic managed here? Name three ways

3 Public transport

Is public transport the solution to rush-hour traffic congestion?

Two cars occupy the same space as a bus. Most cars carry just the driver, while **a bus can carry 75 passengers**. Therefore, persuading people to leave the car at home is one solution to rush-hour traffic congestion.

However, public transport must be **nearby**, **cheap**, **reliable** and **fast**. Public transport includes buses, trams, suburban rail and light rail.

Table 11.1 How people get to work in Dublin

Mode of transport	Percentage
On foot	12%
Bicycle	4%
Bus/minibus/coach	11%
Train/DART/Luas	7%
Car – driver	56%
Car – passenger	4%
Other, including lorry	6%

The Dublin bikes scheme is proving very popular in Dublin's city centre as cycle lanes continue to be developed

Section 3 · Social Geography

Public transport in Dublin

Great sums of money have been spent on public transport in the Dublin area in recent years.

- Dublin has a very good **bus network** with 1,600 buses. Quality bus corridors (**QBCs**) on bus lanes have made commuting by bus much faster.
- The **DART** (Dublin Area Rapid Transit) brings commuters from coastal towns and suburbs to Dublin's CBD.
- **Luas** (the tram) has two lines and is a major success. Work has begun to join the two lines with a new cross-city line.
- A **metro** (underground railway) from the city centre north to the airport and onwards to Swords is likely to be built in a few years' time.

Geo fact
In 2015, Luas carried 34.6 million passengers – a record number.

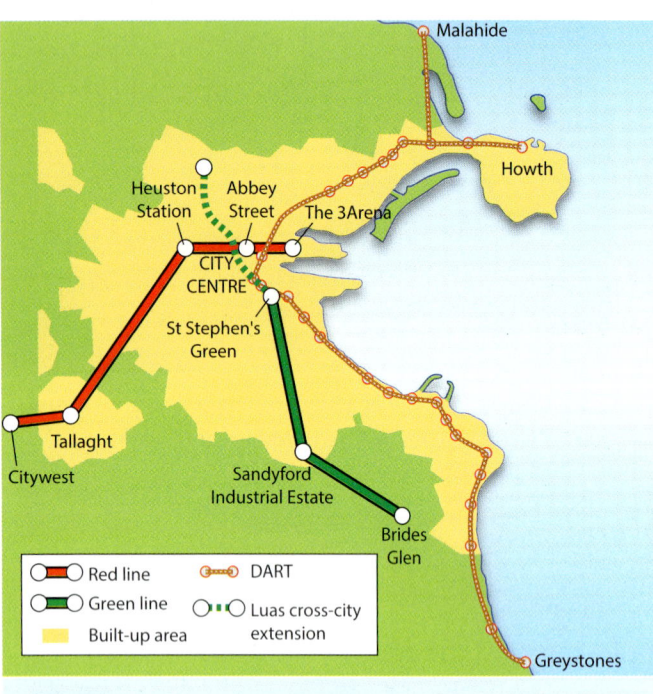

Figure 11.7 The DART and Luas lines in Dublin offer commuters an alternative to the car

Luas has been a great success since it opened in 2004

Buses now offer real-time schedules and have their own bus lanes in Ireland's main urban centres

Geo fact
Some people can now work from home using their PCs and thus avoid the rush hour. That would be unlikely to work for secondary school students!

Questions

1. Explain the term 'commuting'.
2. Explain **two** reasons why the car is a very popular mode of transport in Irish cities.
3. Explain the terms:
   - QBCs
   - Luas
   - DART.

11.6 Urban problems

KEYWORDS
- zone of decline
- inner city
- unemployment
- crime
- community disruption
- extended family
- infrastructure
- urban sprawl

The rapid pace of social and economic change within Western cities in the twentieth and twenty-first centuries has caused problems for those living in them:

- Zones of decline
- Unemployment
- Crime
- Community disruption
- Urban sprawl
- Poor infrastructure.

Higher Level students must select **two** of the problems listed for study. Ordinary Level course students must select **one** problem.

Urban decline

Many places in city centres are **zones of decline**.

- These are often found in an area known as the **inner city**.
- Many people who live in the inner city are poor and the housing in some places is old and in bad condition.
- A high proportion of people live in large blocks of **city council apartments**.
- There are often **derelict buildings** that have been abandoned and boarded up.

In recent years, city councils have invested a lot of money in improving zones of decline with **urban renewal** projects (see pages 318–19).

Definition
Derelict buildings: Buildings that are no longer used and are falling into disrepair.

Inner city decline in London. When this occurs, homes become deserted and streets are uninviting

Unemployment

Unemployment has been a problem for many decades in inner cities both in Ireland and abroad. In the past, many **small workshops and factories** employed people in the city centre. Today, most factories are located at the edge of cities, where space is available and ring roads have been built. This leads to **unemployment in the city centre**.

Many jobs in the CBD are skilled office jobs in banks and insurance companies. Third-level education is needed for those jobs. While many in the inner city are highly qualified, **some young people leave school early**. They are **more likely to be unemployed** than those who remain in education.

Geo fact
Homelessness has become a major issue in Dublin in recent times.

Section 3 · Social Geography

Crime

There is crime in all areas and the great majority of inner city residents do not turn to crime. However, **in inner cities crime is a serious social problem**. Much of the crime is **drug-related**. Many murders occur among rival drug gangs who supply drugs. Some young people are feeding a drug habit. They may turn to robbing vulnerable people to get money for their daily supply.

Many **community projects** have been set up to help people with drug problems in inner cities today.

Community disruption

What maintains a **sense of community**? Weddings, funerals, local sports teams and shared memories bind a community together. The **extended family** is one of the most important units in a community. Grandparents, uncles and aunts, cousins and in-laws are able to support and look out for each other.

However, in the 1960s, inner city Dublin faced a **housing crisis**. When housing was made available in **Ballymun** and **Tallaght**, young families moved out of the city centre. These families lost the support of the inner city community. They felt **cut off from their extended family**. Their sense of community had been disrupted.

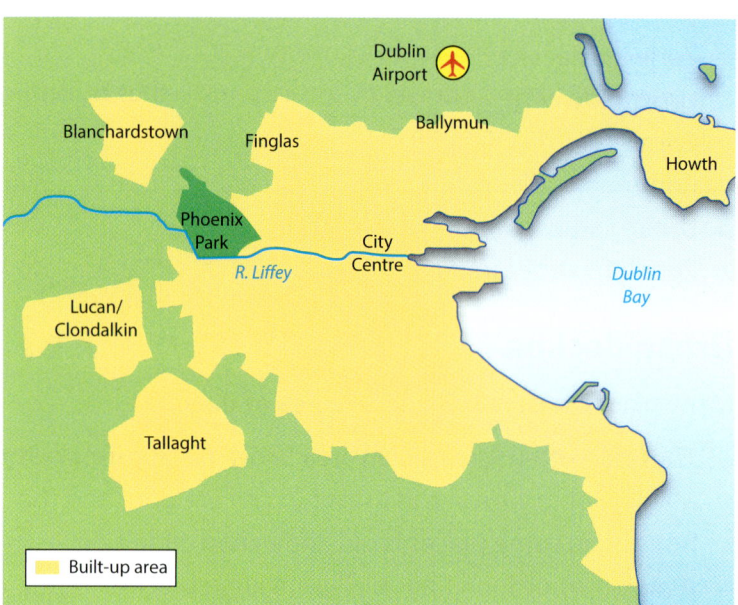

Figure 11.8 Ballymun is located on the northern fringe of Dublin

> **Definition** ✓
> **Infrastructure:** The basic facilities (roads, power, etc.) that are needed for a society to work.

Poor infrastructure

Many towns and cities in Ireland have a **road infrastructure** that cannot cope with modern traffic. There are several reasons for this:

- Many streets were laid out in medieval times and are narrow for modern traffic.
- Many urban centres, such as Waterford, Galway and Drogheda, are built beside rivers. They have too few bridge crossings and delays occur at all rush hours at bridge points.
- In Ireland, with very few exceptions such as Dublin Port Tunnel, the Jack Lynch Tunnel in Cork and the Shannon Tunnel in Limerick, all traffic travels on the surface. In European cities, underground rail systems reduce pressure on surface transport.
- Far too many people in Ireland continue to use the car in congested streets in spite of improvements in bus transport in cities.

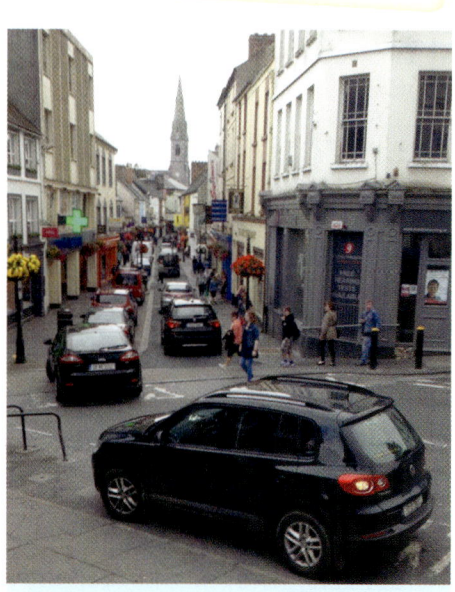

O'Connell St, Ennis, is typical of the narrow streets of many towns: very attractive but slow for traffic

Urban sprawl

Sprawl is the word used to describe the uncontrolled spread of the city into the countryside around it. This is happening in Irish cities. Large estates of semi-detached homes have been built on areas that were once farms. Population densities are low in these estates.

Parents like to have a front and back garden for children to play in. Urban sprawl has many **disadvantages**:

- Sprawl **invades the countryside** and leads to the cutting of hedges and a reduction in wildlife.
- Sprawl leads to **long daily commuter journeys** to the CBD.
- Sprawl causes the **spread of houses and other buildings** over a large area at the edge of the city.

Geo fact
More than 60 per cent of Irish people now live in towns and cities.

Urban sprawl in Rochestown, Cork

Urban sprawl disrupts the natural world

Questions

1 Explain the term 'inner city'.
2 Explain **two** social problems that are found in the inner city.
3 What is urban sprawl?
4 How does urban sprawl affect the natural world?

Section 3 · Social Geography

11.7 Urban improvements

KEYWORDS

- urban renewal
- urban redevelopment
- sheltered accommodation

Governments and city planners in Western cities have tried to tackle the problems of urban decline and urban sprawl in the following ways:

- Inner-city renewal and redevelopment
- Planning of new towns.

Inner-city renewal and redevelopment

For many years, urban authorities in Ireland have been **renewing** and **redeveloping** large areas of Ireland's inner cities.

During the Celtic Tiger years, a great deal of public and private money was available for these projects. However, when the economic recession hit in 2008 funds dried up very quickly. As a result, urban renewal and redevelopment ceased for several years.

Urban renewal

When urban renewal occurs:

- **Residents are moved out** of their old sub-standard homes and apartments in the inner city.
- They are given **temporary accommodation** by the city council.
- The **homes are then demolished and replaced** with new homes with modern facilities.
- The **residents then return** to live in their new homes.

In this way, **community disruption does not take place**.

Urban redevelopment

When urban redevelopment occurs:

- Derelict buildings and homes in an area of the inner city are **demolished**.
- Where there are residents, they are given **permanent accommodation elsewhere**.
- **Offices**, **hotels** and some **apartments** are then built to replace the derelict buildings.

As a result, **the function of the area changes**.

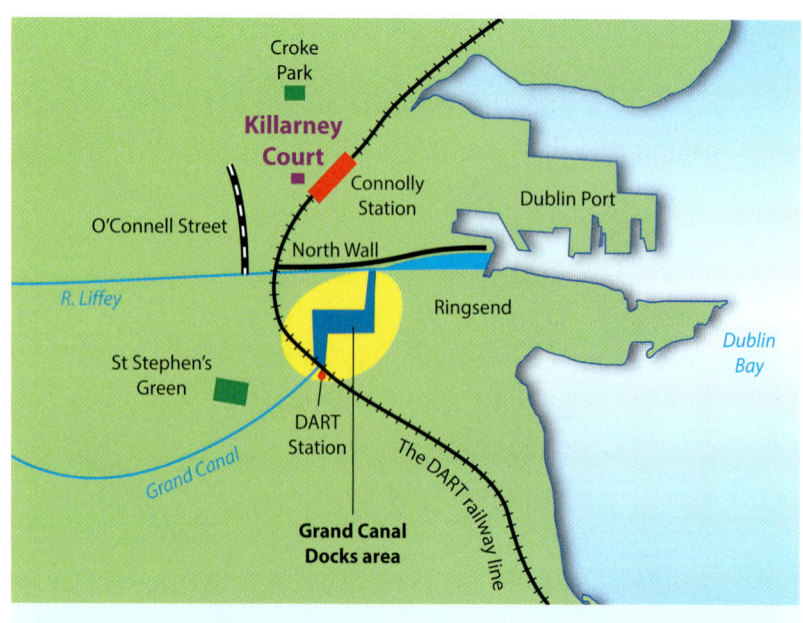

Figure 11.9 The Dublin Docklands area showing Killarney Court (urban renewal) and Grand Canal Dock (urban redevelopment)

Case study

Urban renewal: Killarney Court, Killarney St, Dublin

The problems

Killarney Court is located north of the Liffey and east of O'Connell St. It is a square four-storey block of apartments built around a central courtyard. Before renewal, it suffered from many **problems**:

- The **apartments were very small** and inadequate for the needs of families.
- Insulation was non-existent and the **apartments were very cold** and damp in winter with mould on many walls.
- Public stairwells were **dirty and damp**.
- There were **no lifts** and elderly people found the stairs very difficult.
- Some of the **apartments were abandoned** and became derelict over time.
- The Killarney Street area had **high levels of unemployment** and poverty.

Killarney Court before renewal

The solutions

Clearly, **urban renewal** was necessary in Killarney Court. It took place during the Celtic Tiger years.

- The shell of the old buildings was retained in the renewal scheme. Killarney Court has an **enclosed courtyard** and this brings a **sense of security** to those who live there.
- The number of apartments was reduced from 138 to 106. The new **apartments are bigger** and all fittings in the apartments were **modernised**.
- **Lifts** were installed.
- Killarney Court includes **sheltered accommodation**. This is aimed at the elderly and those who find themselves in difficulty. Purpose-built homes allow residents to live independently with some support.
- Killarney Court also has a **community centre**, a **mother and baby centre** and **shops**. These features encourage a sense of community.

Killarney Court after renewal

An exterior view of Killarney Court with street art on the pavement

319

Section 3 · Social Geography

Case study

Urban redevelopment: Grand Canal Dock

Grand Canal Dock was an **enclosed harbour** between the River Liffey and the Grand Canal. It was built in the eighteenth century. The docks and warehouses fell into disuse many decades ago because of the **decline of canal traffic** and because the dock area was **too small for modern cargo ships**. Much of the area became derelict.

Since 2000, the area has been greatly redeveloped.

- While some of the original buildings remain, several **new buildings** have totally changed the character of the area.
- Part of Grand Canal Dock has become known as **Silicon Docks** because many offices in the area are occupied by some world-famous companies that include Facebook, Twitter, LinkedIn and, of course, Google.
- Several **apartment buildings** are also located in the docks area.
- **Boland's Mills**, well known to history students for its role in the 1916 Rising, is now derelict, but there are plans to redevelop it.
- The Grand Canal Dock area is served by **Grand Canal Dock Station** on the DART line.

The redeveloped Grand Canal Dock has kept the waterfront and replaced old warehouses with offices, apartments and a theatre

Planning of new towns

We have seen that urban sprawl has many disadvantages. Planners have created **new towns in order to control urban sprawl**, e.g. Tallaght, Lucan-Clondalkin and Blanchardstown in the Dublin area. We will examine Tallaght.

Chapter 11 · Urbanisation

Case study

New towns: Tallaght

Tallaght is located south-west of the city of Dublin. In the 1960s, it was a village surrounded by farmland. Today its population is more than 71,000.

Much of Tallaght was built in the 1970s. The residents include people from Dublin's inner city and those who came to Dublin from other parts of Ireland.

Initial problems

To begin with there were a number of problems in the new town of Tallaght:

- As **housing densities were very low**, people without a car had a long walk to the bus stop.
- For many years, **services** such as leisure areas, shops and public transport were poor.
- A high percentage of the population was under 15 years of age.
- The community had high **unemployment** in the recession of the 1980s.

However, much has been done to change Tallaght since then.

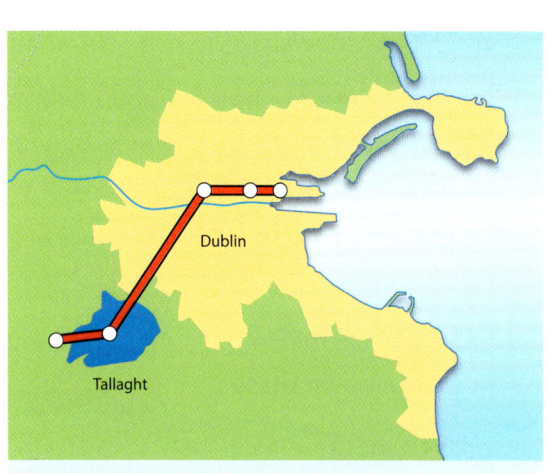

Figure 11.10 The location of Tallaght. Tallaght is connected to Dublin by the Luas Red Line

Population of Tallaght	
1961	4,634
2011	71,467

Tallaght today

Developments in Tallaght in recent years have brought great advances. **New developments** include:

- The **Square**, which is one of Ireland's best-known shopping centres
- A **regional hospital** serving south-west Dublin
- The terminal of the **Luas Red Line** that brings passengers into the city quickly
- **Industrial estates** and business parks that have many international companies

Tallaght centre showing recent developments

- The **Tallaght Institute of Technology** that caters for third-level students
- **Sporting facilities** that include the National Basketball Arena, GAA clubs and the home of Shamrock Rovers
- **Cultural projects** including two theatres.

Because of these investments, thousands of people now work in Tallaght itself. Tallaght may soon become a city in its own right.

321

Section 3 · Social Geography

Questions

1. Explain what is meant by the following terms:
   - Urban renewal
   - Urban redevelopment.

2. (a) Name **one** example of urban renewal.
   (b) Explain **three** reasons why urban renewal was necessary in that example.
   (c) Explain **three** improvements that were brought about because of urban renewal.

3. (a) Why were new towns built west of Dublin?
   (b) Name **two** of those towns.

4. Study the OS map of Tallaght below and answer the following questions:
   (a) Write down **three** pieces of evidence in the OS map that tell us that Kilnamanagh is a residential area.
   (b) Find the light rail line (Luas) that serves Tallaght. Write down the grid reference for the final stop in the centre of Tallaght.
   (c) Do you think that the light rail line is accessible to all of the population of Tallaght? Explain your answer.
   (d) Tallaght is unlikely to expand southwards in future years. Why is that the case?

Figure 11.11 OS map of the Tallaght area

11.8 Urbanisation in the developing world

> **KEYWORDS**
> - amenity
> - social inequality
> - economic inequality
> - infrastructural service
> - squatter settlement
> - bustee
> - waste disposal
> - favela

Urbanisation in the developing world has led to a different pattern of urban growth from that of Western cities. The problems are also different, and they are getting worse. They include:

- Sharper social and economic inequalities
- Greater degree of unplanned development
- Lack of infrastructural services
- Faster growth.

> Higher Level students must study **two** of the problems listed. Ordinary Level students must study **one** of the problems.

Westerners who visit or work in developing world cities often experience **culture shock**. They are struck by the **contrasts between rich and poor**. This is evident in how people dress, the transport they use and the homes in which they live. Many of the poor live under makeshift plastic shelters.

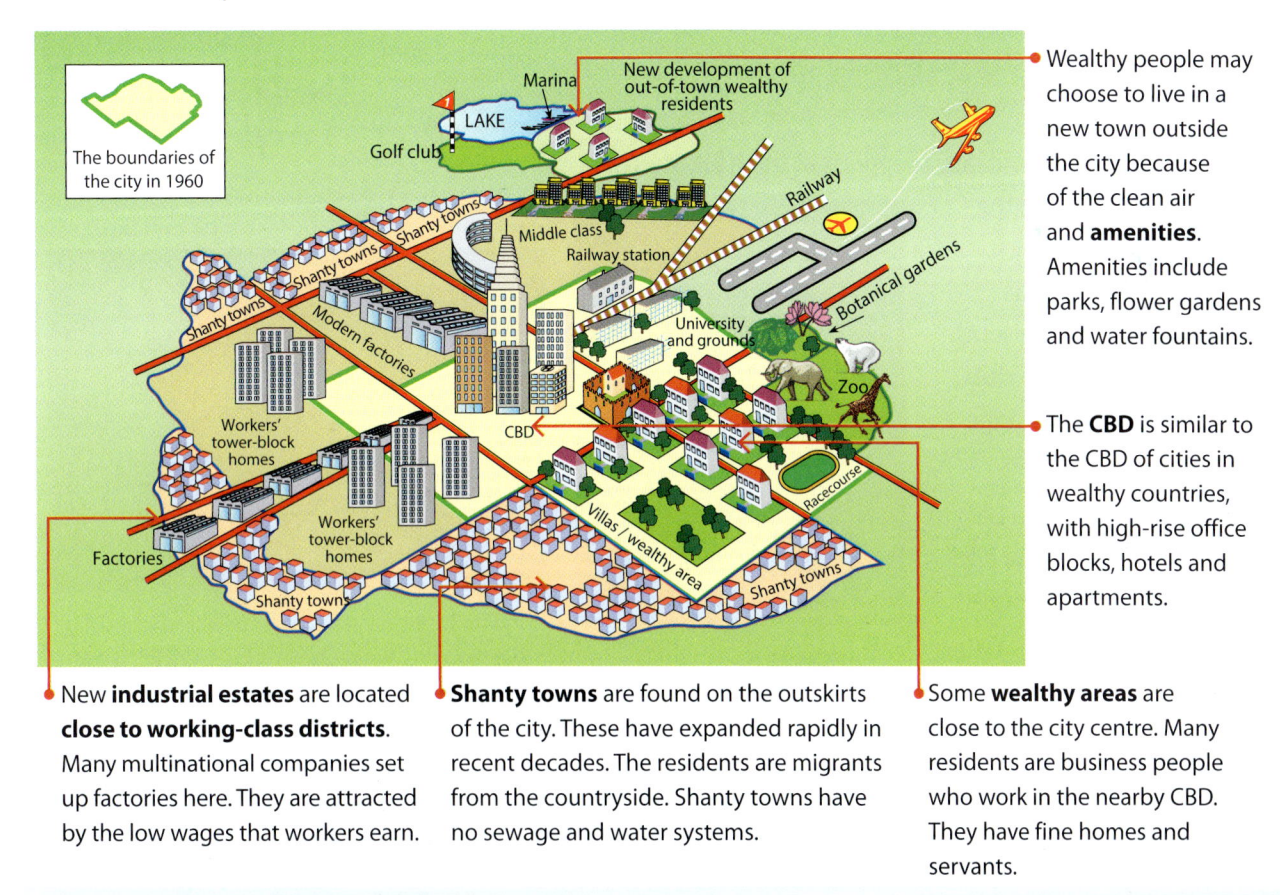

- Wealthy people may choose to live in a new town outside the city because of the clean air and **amenities**. Amenities include parks, flower gardens and water fountains.
- The **CBD** is similar to the CBD of cities in wealthy countries, with high-rise office blocks, hotels and apartments.
- New **industrial estates** are located **close to working-class districts**. Many multinational companies set up factories here. They are attracted by the low wages that workers earn.
- **Shanty towns** are found on the outskirts of the city. These have expanded rapidly in recent decades. The residents are migrants from the countryside. Shanty towns have no sewage and water systems.
- Some **wealthy areas** are close to the city centre. Many residents are business people who work in the nearby CBD. They have fine homes and servants.

Figure 11.12 Developing world cities share many characteristics

> **Link**
> For more on **shanty towns**, see Chapter 9, pages 227, 248–9.

Section 3 · Social Geography

Case study

Kolkata: a city of contrasts

We have already seen that **overcrowding, shortage of clean water and pollution** are problems that the people of Kolkata face. We will now examine further aspects of the city.

> **Link**
> See **High population densities** in Kolkata, pages 248–9.

Social and economic inequalities

Sharp social and economic inequalities are very evident in Kolkata.

Wealth

The **CBD is in the city centre**.

- It has some **luxurious air-conditioned hotels** and nice restaurants.
- There are **fine shops** in the Park Street area that wealthy people visit.
- Metered **taxis** are everywhere and are used by wealthy people.
- The **New Market** is a huge bazaar area that comes alive in the cool of the evening when locals do their shopping.

Wealthy locals attend race meetings at the **Kolkata Turf Club** racecourse in the Maidan. The very rich are members of the Tollygunge Club in south Kolkata, a **country club** that offers a wide range of sporting activities.

The city centre has several **nightclubs** and discos, mostly in hotels, for the young who can afford to visit them.

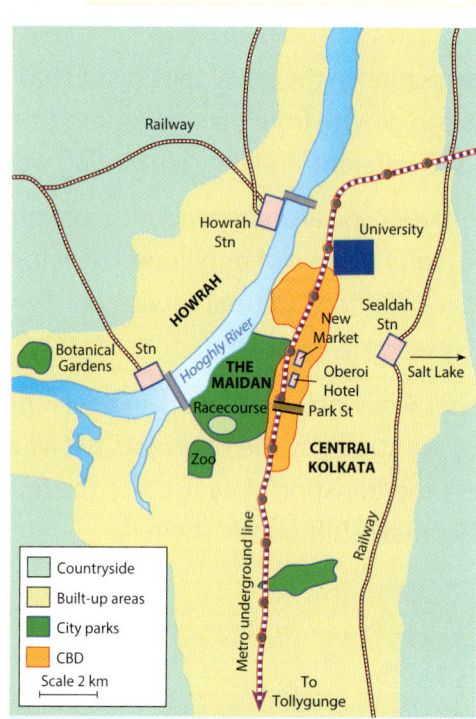

Figure 11.13 Central Kolkata

A shopping mall in south Kolkata

Indian supporters in Kolkata celebrating India winning the World Cup in cricket. Cricket is one of the passions that unites rich and poor

Poverty

The greater part of the city is made up of **poor neighbourhoods**.

- These have narrow streets and very small, low-rise homes.
- A family of three generations will often live in a tiny home.
- Some multi-storey rented apartments with basic facilities are being built in these areas now.
- The poorest people live in **squatter settlements**, these are examined below.

A family living on the street in Sudder St, Kolkata

Case study

Unplanned development: squatter settlements

Kolkata has very high **inward migration of rural poor** people. These people live in squatter settlements or **shanty towns**.

- These settlements are found close to railway stations, on rail sidings, on steep banks, on grass road margins, under flyovers, on waste land and on the **outskirts of the city**. The settlers have **no legal right to remain** there.
- Squatter settlements have **no sanitation or running water**. Disease is a constant hazard. Stomach and chest infections are a threat to children's health.

Heavy labour

People in squatter settlements are at the **bottom of the social ladder**.

- They work as rickshaw workers, as labourers in construction work and as pullers of heavy loads in two-wheel carts.
- Many squatters scrape a living from recycling cardboard, drink cans and waste timber.
- Men work as delivery men and carry heavy loads on their heads. Many of the very poor are severely underweight.

Geo fact
Shanty towns and squatter settlements are known as **bustees** in Kolkata.

Infrastructural services

The image that some people have of Kolkata is that nothing works. In fact, that is not the case.

- The **public telephone service** is very good. People can phone Ireland and any other countries cheaply from telephone kiosks that are rented out to the public.
- **Email** and **broadband infrastructure** are in place and are widely available in the CBD.
- The city has an excellent underground **metro service**. The bus service is frequent, but the buses are of poor quality and are heavy polluters.
- Electrified **trams** also carry passengers, and auto rickshaws are fast and cheap.

However, there are also **poor services**.

- **The electricity infrastructure:** Electricity power supplies fail, often on a daily basis. When it fails in the evenings the crowded streets are plunged into darkness.
- **Waste disposal:** In many districts, **trash** is gathered and stored for several days in rotting heaps before it is taken away by lorry.

Buses in Kolkata are old, overcrowded and heavy polluters

Kolkata people are very enterprising. Here a family with a street kitchen prepares chapatti for the passing trade

Section 3 · Social Geography

Case study

São Paulo

São Paulo is the **largest city in South America** and the most important city in Brazil. It is a city of enormous wealth and great poverty.

We will examine three aspects of the city:

1. Social and economic inequalities
2. Unplanned development
3. Infrastructural services.

Social and economic inequalities

São Paulo is a city of rich and poor. In the **richest districts:**

- People's incomes are close to the average income of Spain.
- Many wealthy people send their children to private schools in chauffeur-driven cars.
- Some business people go to work in helicopters.
- Servants do all the housework.

Figure 11.14 Major urban centres in Brazil

However, in the **poorest districts:**

- Incomes are as low as those in the poorest countries in Africa.
- It is a real struggle to survive, and some people are **malnourished**.
- Children are underweight and **child mortality** is much higher than it is in wealthier districts.
- People live in **shanty towns**.

> **Definition** ✓
>
> **Malnourished:** People who are in bad health because of a poor diet.

Unplanned development: favelas

Squatter settlements or shanty towns are known as **favelas** in Brazil.

- At least two million people live in favelas in São Paulo. **Heliopolis** is one of the largest favelas in São Paulo.
- Favelas are located in **difficult terrain**, such as hillsides, close to streams or beside factories and busy, noisy roads.
- In favelas, **poverty** is normal and many young male gangs turn to **drugs and crime**.
- Services such as **water and sewers** are coming to the favelas, but development is happening very slowly.

Chapter 11 · Urbanisation

Case study

The favelas at the edge of São Paulo are very evident in this picture

Infrastructural services

Transport services are a major concern in São Paulo. However, the city has five **metro lines** that carry three million passengers every day. This certainly eases the burden on the roads.

- Street traffic is very congested.
- The city has **seven million cars**, as well as trucks. There are no ring roads and this adds to the problem.
- Traffic flow is very slow for at least four hours of every day and urban speeds are among the slowest in the world during these times.
- Therefore, **traffic pollution** is a major health hazard for people. This is partly why some of the wealthiest people use helicopters to get around.

Questions

1. Briefly outline the lives of the wealthy in Kolkata. Refer to:
    - Where they live
    - How they spend their leisure hours.

2. Describe the daily lives of people who live in squatter settlements in Kolkata.
   Refer to:
    - Where squatter settlements are found
    - The daily work of the poor
    - Their living conditions.

3. Examine the photograph above showing the living conditions of the poor in São Paulo.
   (a) What are squatter settlements called in Brazil?
   (b) Describe **two** of the problems that exist in these squatter settlements in São Paulo.

327

Section 3 · Social Geography

Summary chart

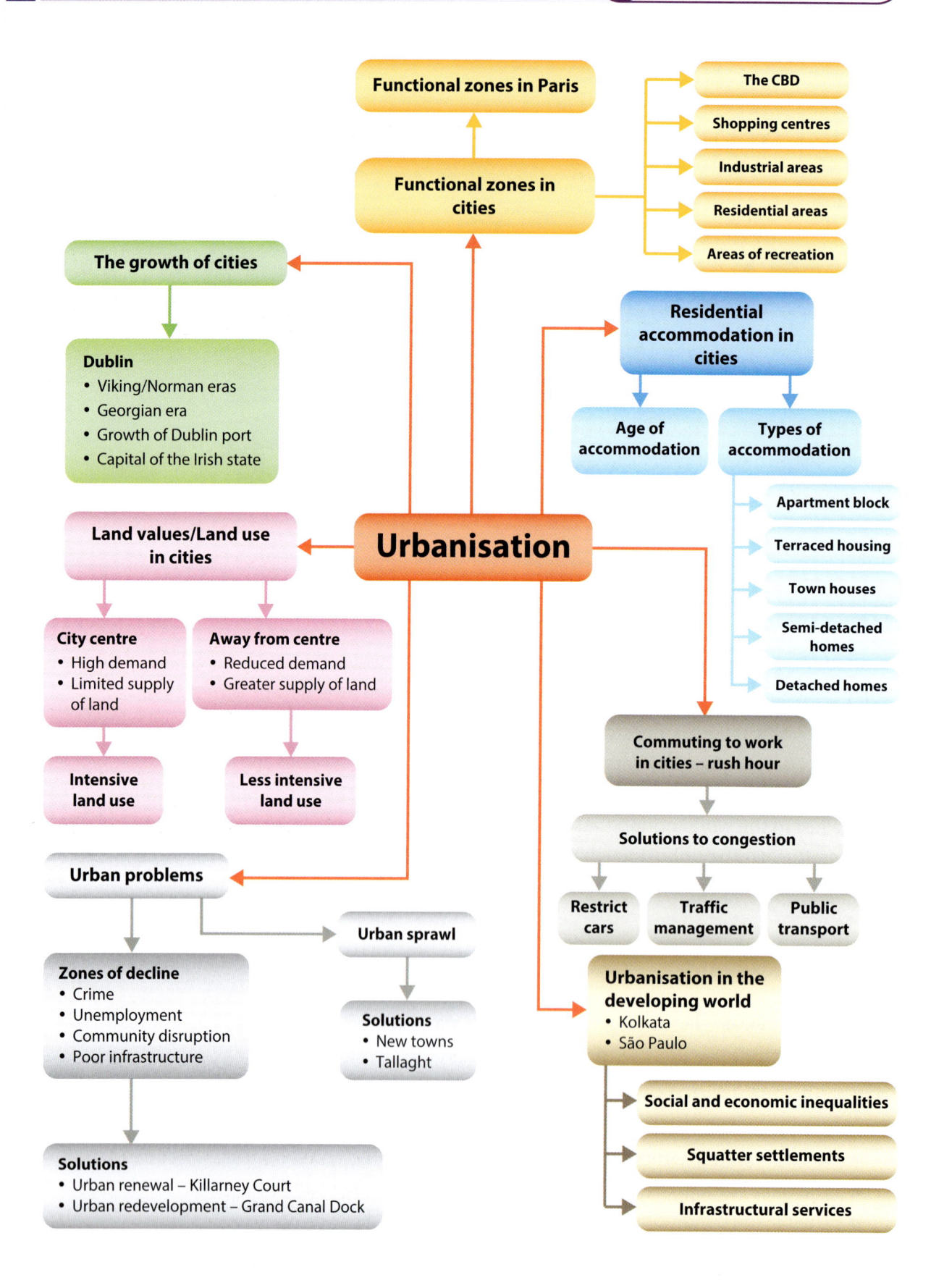

PowerPoint summary

Urbanisation

Functional zones in Paris

Functional zones in cities
- The CBD
- Shopping centres
- Industrial areas
- Residential areas
- Areas of recreation

The growth of cities

Dublin
- Viking/Norman eras
- Georgian era
- Growth of Dublin port
- Capital of the Irish state

Residential accommodation in cities
- Age of accommodation
- Types of accommodation
  - Apartment block
  - Terraced housing
  - Town houses
  - Semi-detached homes
  - Detached homes

Land values/Land use in cities

City centre
- High demand
- Limited supply of land

Away from centre
- Reduced demand
- Greater supply of land

Intensive land use

Less intensive land use

Commuting to work in cities – rush hour

Solutions to congestion
- Restrict cars
- Traffic management
- Public transport

Urban problems

Zones of decline
- Crime
- Unemployment
- Community disruption
- Poor infrastructure

Urban sprawl

Solutions
- New towns
- Tallaght

Solutions
- Urban renewal – Killarney Court
- Urban redevelopment – Grand Canal Dock

Urbanisation in the developing world
- Kolkata
- São Paulo

- Social and economic inequalities
- Squatter settlements
- Infrastructural services

328

Chapter 11 · Urbanisation

Exam questions

1. (i) In which of the city zones **A**, **B** or **C** would land values be highest?
   (ii) State **two** reasons why land values are highest in this zone.
   (iii) Describe **two** problems resulting from urban sprawl.

   HL 2013

2. Cities have different functional zones including:
   - The Central Business District (CBD)
   - Shopping areas
   - Industrial areas.
   - Residential (housing) areas
   - Open spaces

   Explain the location of any **two** functional zones in a city you have studied.

   HL 2010

3. (i) Describe **one** reason why traffic congestion occurs in Irish cities.
   (ii) Explain **two** methods that could be used to reduce traffic congestion in Irish cities.

   HL 2015

4. **Traffic in an Irish city**

Time Period	9 a.m. to 10 a.m.	11 a.m. to 12 noon	2 p.m. to 3 p.m.	5 p.m. to 6 p.m.
No. Bicycles	20	8	17	23
No. Cars	403	350	260	578
No. Trucks	79	58	35	89

The table above shows the results of a traffic survey carried out by a group of students.

(i) What was the number of trucks counted between 9 a.m. and 10 a.m.?
(ii) What was the total number of bicycles counted during the survey?
(iii) State **one** reason for the larger number of cars counted between 5 p.m. and 6 p.m.
(iv) Explain **two** solutions to traffic congestion.

OL 2013

Section 3 · Social Geography

Exam questions

5

(i) The photograph above shows an area in Cork city that has undergone urban renewal. Explain what is meant by the term *urban renewal*.

(ii) Name any *new town* in Ireland that you have studied.

(iii) Describe any **two** characteristics of this *new town*.

HL 2014

6 (i) Name **one** city in the developing world that you have studied.

(ii) Explain **two** problems associated with unplanned development in this city.

HL 2013

7 % of People Living in Urban Areas in Selected Countries in 1990 and 2010

Country	1990	2010
Bangladesh	19.8%	27.9%
Germany	73.1%	73.8%
Ireland	56.9%	61.9%
Sudan	28.6%	33.1%

(i) Which country had the highest percentage of people living in urban areas in 2010?

(ii) Calculate the increase in the percentage of people living in urban areas in Ireland between 1990 and 2010.

(iii) Explain **two** reasons why people move to live in urban areas (towns and cities).

OL 2015

Section 4
Economic Geography

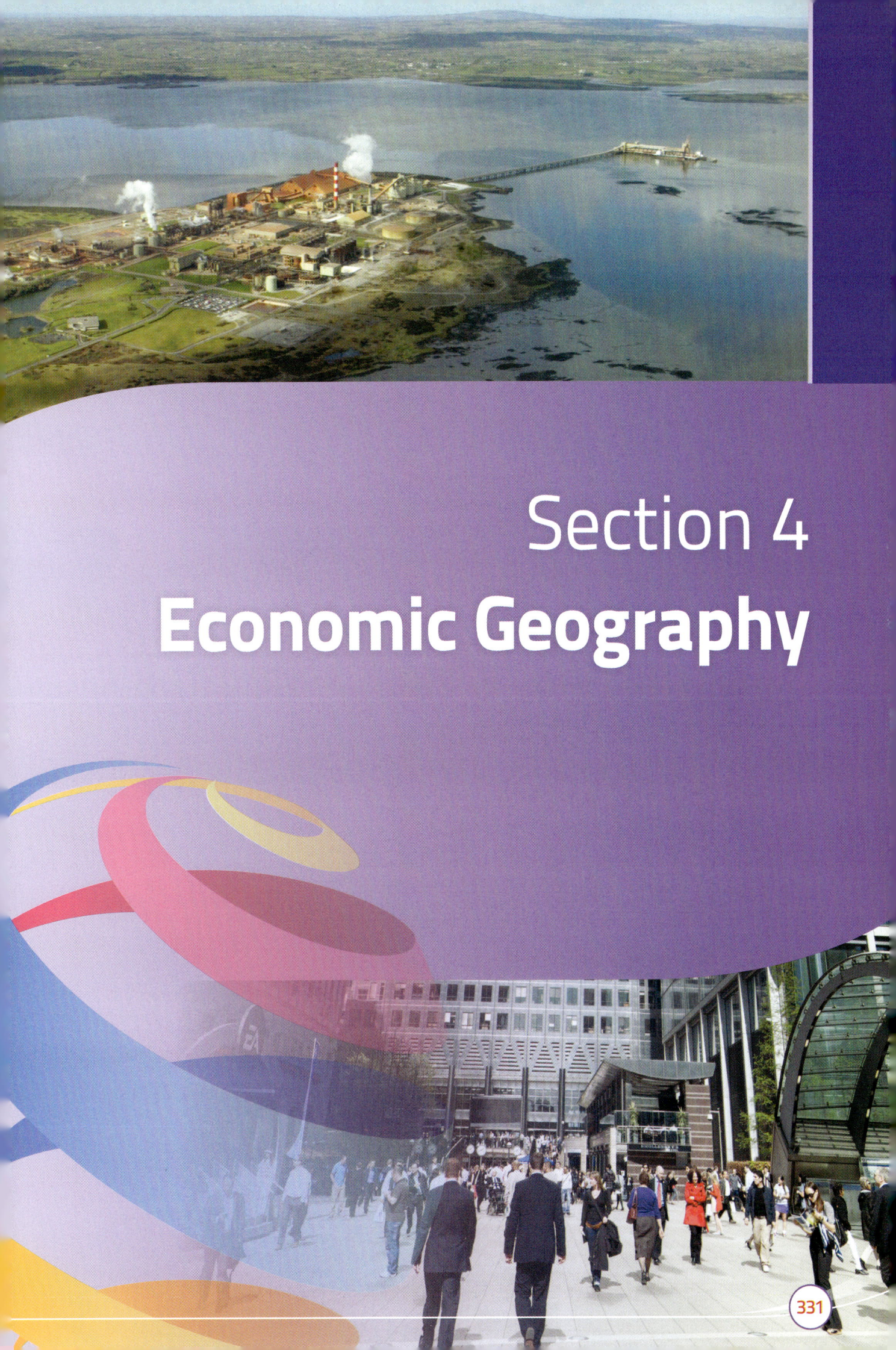

Chapter 12
Primary Economic Activities

Learning outcomes

By the end of this chapter, you should be able to understand:

- That primary economic activities involve the production of raw materials
- That resources are either renewable or non-renewable
- That water is vital to people and to agriculture
- That oil is a finite resource and is very important in today's world
- How modern technology can exploit resources
- That farming is a system of inputs, processes and outputs.

12.1 The Earth as a resource

KEYWORDS

- primary
- secondary
- tertiary
- services
- renewable
- non-renewable
- finite
- non-finite
- sustainable exploitation
- recycle

There are three types of economic activity: **primary**, **secondary** and **tertiary**.

- In **primary activities**, raw materials are produced from the Earth. Primary activities include farming, fishing, forestry (the three Fs) and mining.
- In **secondary activities**, workers in factories use raw materials to manufacture goods that people can buy, e.g. the manufacture of cars and computers.
- In **tertiary** or **service activities**, people provide **services** that other people require, e.g. teaching and hairdressing.

The **tertiary** sector is also known as the **services** sector.

Chapter 12 · Primary Economic Activities

In **poor countries**, most people are working in the **primary sector**, as farmers, fishermen/women and miners.

As the wealth of a country grows, more people work in manufacturing and in services. In very wealthy countries, most people work in services.

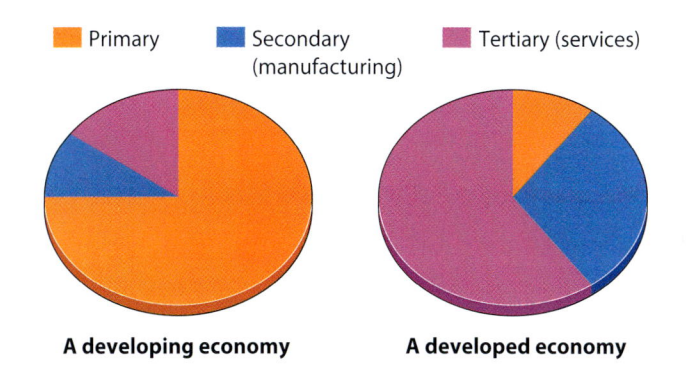

Primary | Secondary (manufacturing) | Tertiary (services)

A developing economy   A developed economy

Figure 12.1 The sectors where people work

Activity
Look at the pie charts in Figure 12.1. **Describe** the differences between the workforces of a developed and a developing economy.

Table 12.1 Jobs in each sector

Primary	Secondary	Tertiary
Fishermen/women	Bakers	Bank workers
Farmers	Tailors	Hotel staff
Quarry workers	Furniture makers	Newsreaders
Miners	Car assembly workers	DJs
Forestry workers	PC assembly workers	Shop assistants

To which economic sector does each of the above workers belong?

Earth's resources

There are two types of natural resource: **renewable** and **non-renewable**.

Activity
What other term describes a renewable resource?

Renewable resources

Renewable resources are **non-finite**. That means that **they do not run out**. If carefully managed, these resources will always exist.

Definition
Sustainable exploitation: A way for people to use resources without the resources running out.

Examples of renewable resources include **water**, **fish** and **timber**. If foresters cut down trees, they can replant them so that there will be more trees to cut down in the future. This is called **sustainable exploitation**.

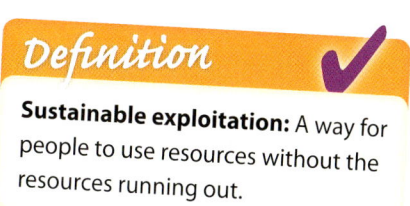

333

Section 4 · Economic Geography

Non-renewable resources

Non-renewable resources are also known as **finite** resources. **Minerals** are finite. Oil wells will run dry and coal seams are worked out.

Wealthy people use more resources than poor people. In recent years, we have become aware of the need to **recycle** our resources so that they will last longer.

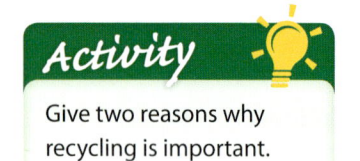

Forestry harvesting in Sweden. The Swedes replant harvested forests in Sweden to make sure that their children inherit the trees

Motorists recycling waste materials. People now understand the importance of recycling

Definitions

Finite resource: Something of which there is only a limited supply.

Recycle: Convert waste into something that can be used again.

Activity

Give two reasons why recycling is important.

Questions

1. Write the headings *primary*, *secondary* and *tertiary* in your copybook. Put the following list of workers under the appropriate headings:

   miner, bus driver, glass blower, hotel receptionist, farmer, pottery maker.

2. Write down the headings *renewable resource* and *non-renewable resource* in your copybook. Put the following under the appropriate headings:

   coal, water, natural gas, crude oil, timber, fish.

12.2 Water as a resource

KEYWORDS
- water treatment
- reservoir
- water conservation
- water pollution
- irrigation
- oasis

Water is a **basic natural resource**, needed to maintain human life and to grow food. It is a **renewable resource**.

You have already studied the **water cycle** (see Chapter 5, page 93). Water is vital to humans and animals. People die if they are deprived of water for more than four days. Therefore, it is a very precious resource.

People collecting water in rural India. Water is a very precious resource

Activity
In pairs, **describe** to each other what you see in Figure 12.2.

Activity
Find out where the water for your residential area is sourced and treated for use.

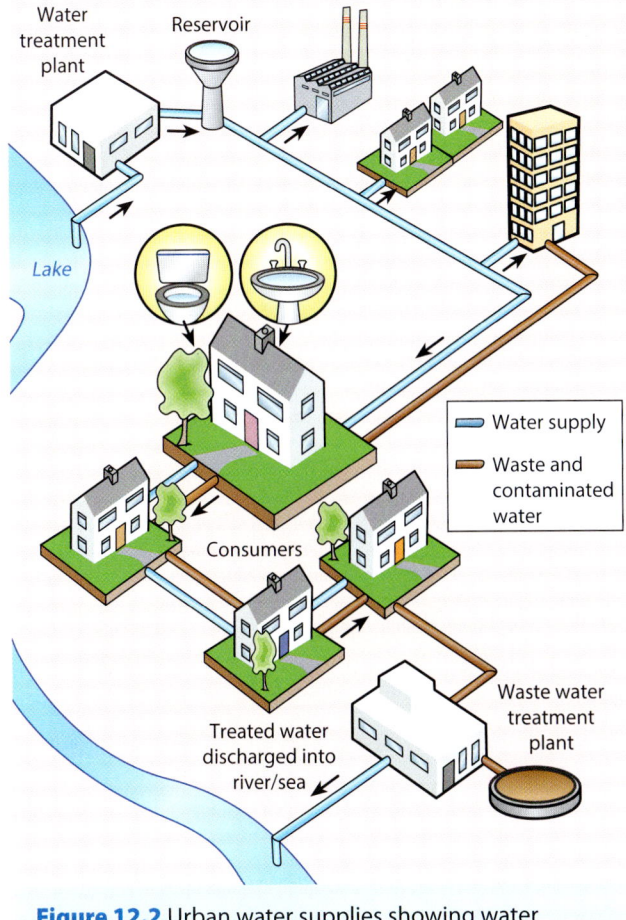

Figure 12.2 Urban water supplies showing water treatment to waste treatment

335

Section 4 · Economic Geography

Case study

Water supply for the Dublin region

The Dublin region has more than one million people, and thus has very high water demands.

Most of Dublin's water supply comes from **Co. Wicklow**. This is because:

- Wicklow has a **high annual rainfall** that is well distributed throughout the year.
- The **bedrock** of the Wicklow Mountains is composed of **granite**. Water does not seep downwards through granite because it is an **impermeable rock**.
- The mountains are thinly populated. Farming takes place in the lowlands. Therefore, the region has **low levels of pollution**.

Water from the Liffey

Liffey valley waters are collected in Blessington Lakes and in Leixlip Reservoir. Water is treated in modern **treatment plants** before it is fed into the urban supply system.

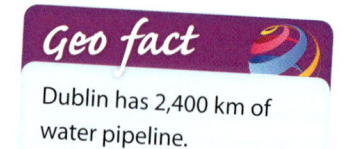

Figure 12.3 Dublin's water supply

The Blessington Lakes reservoir, with Poulaphouca power station in the right foreground

Activity
Find out what the population of the Dublin region is.

Geo fact
Dublin has 2,400 km of water pipeline.

Water conservation

Water is a **precious resource**. Ireland sometimes has long periods of low rainfall. Reservoirs can drop to very low levels. In dry periods, people are encouraged to **conserve** water. To learn how water can be conserved study Figure 12.4.

Geo fact

Denmark has the highest water charges in Europe – €6.33 per cubic metre.

Table 12.2 Water use per person per day in Ireland

Washing machine	15 litres
Showering & bathing	56 litres
Toilet flushing	40 litres
Dishwasher	10.5 litres
Cooking	4.5 litres
Drinking	4.5 litres
Other (car washing, garden watering, etc.)	18 litres

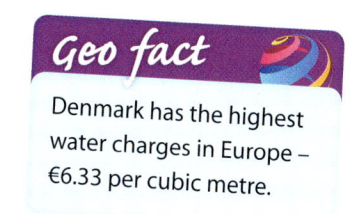

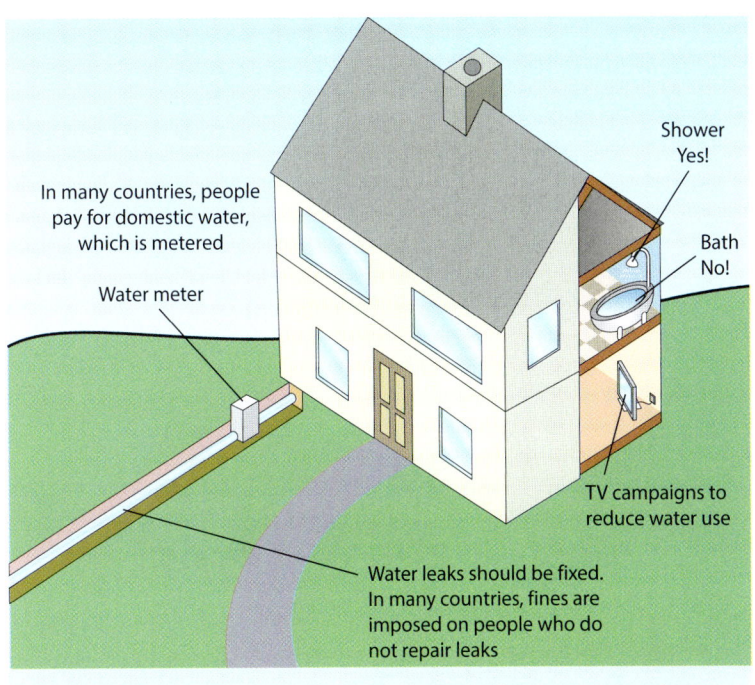

Figure 12.4 Households are becoming aware that water must be conserved

Labels: In many countries, people pay for domestic water, which is metered; Water meter; Shower Yes!; Bath No!; TV campaigns to reduce water use; Water leaks should be fixed. In many countries, fines are imposed on people who do not repair leaks

Water pollution

Water can be polluted by many things, including **industrial and agricultural wastes**. Indeed, the River Rhine has often been called **Europe's open sewer**. It takes a lot of time and money to clean polluted rivers.

Activity

Discuss why it is that Irish people use more water per person today than their grandparents did.

Activity

Examine the figures for water use per person in Table 12.2.
1. How many litres of water does each person in Ireland use per day?
2. Suggest one way that you personally can reduce your water use.

Irrigation

Food crops and grass will not grow without water. In many regions of the world, **rainfall amounts are small and uncertain**. In those regions, farmers have to use **irrigation** to help crops to grow.

Irrigation means **bringing water to crops that need it**, using **canals**, **ditches**, **piping** and **spraying** techniques. Irrigation helps to feed the world's increasing population.

Irrigation schemes

Large irrigation schemes are found in Australia, the Mediterranean region and in California. In South-East Asia rice is grown in irrigated **paddy fields**.

Section 4 · Economic Geography

Case study

Irrigation in the Nile valley, Egypt

The Nile is Africa's longest river. It rises in the highlands of East Africa and its total length is 6,671 km. It flows northwards through the **Sahara** to the Mediterranean. Without the Nile, Egypt and its ancient civilisation would not exist.

Almost all the population of Egypt – 85 million – is found in less than 5 per cent of the country. People live in the **floodplain** of the River Nile and in the **delta** region.

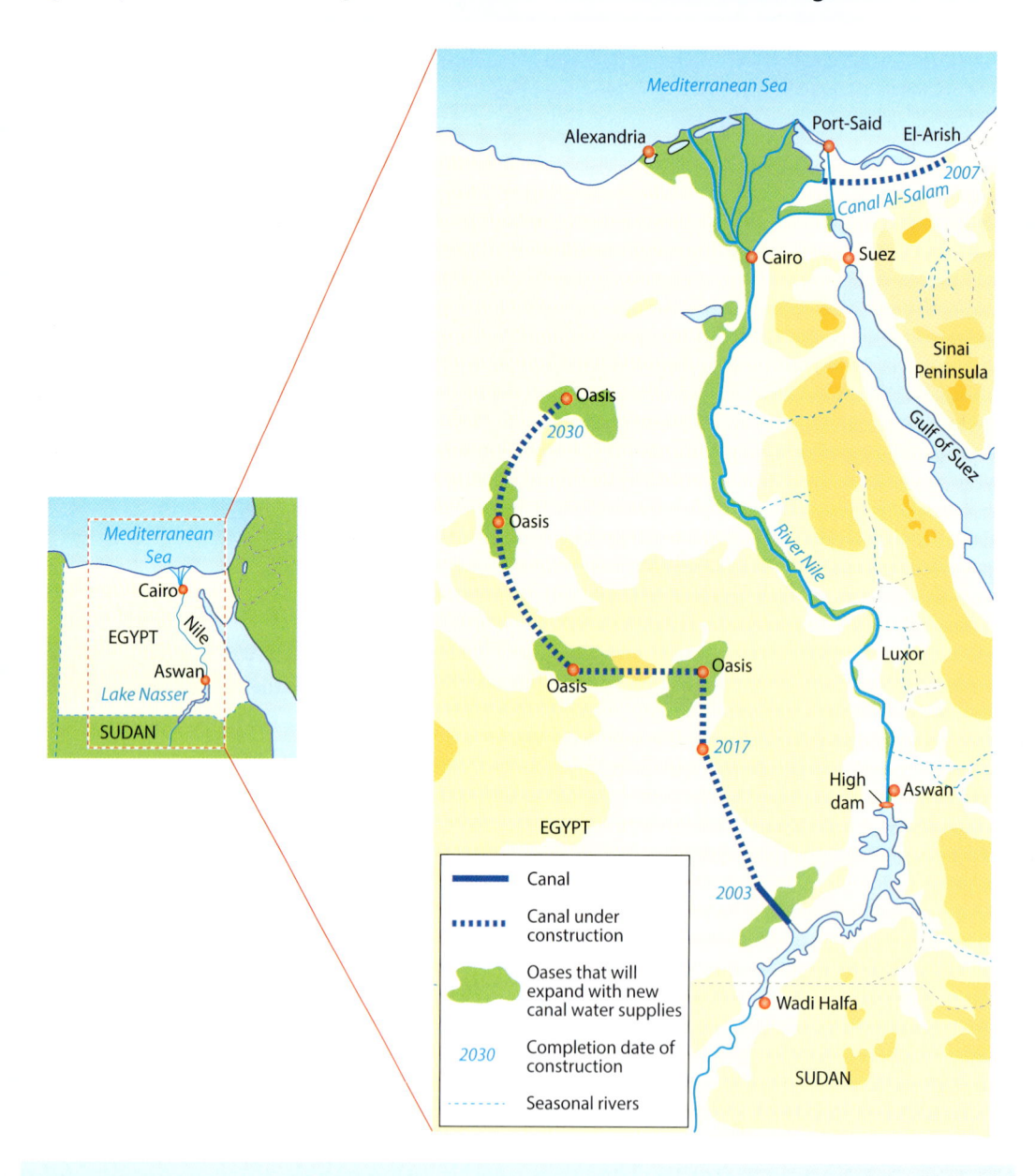

Figure 12.5 Egypt and the River Nile

Annual flooding

Since ancient times, the Nile floodplain in Egypt was under water for several weeks every year because of rains in East Africa. When the water level fell, people grew crops on the damp soil. The soil was **fertilised by sediments** carried by the floodwaters. In the 1960s, construction of a dam began in Aswan to control the flooding.

338

Chapter 12 · Primary Economic Activities

Case study

The Aswan High Dam

In 1975, the Aswan High Dam was completed. The dam stores millions of tonnes of water in **Lake Nasser**. The dam means that water can now be released throughout the year through **canals** and **plastic piping** along farmland in the Nile valley. Therefore, **farmers can grow several crops** in succession throughout the year. The farmland provides additional food for Egypt's growing population.

The disadvantages

There are disadvantages to the irrigation system in Egypt.

- The Nile floodplain no longer floods annually because the waters are stored in Lake Nasser. Therefore, fertile sediments that covered the valley floor remain at the bottom of Lake Nasser. Now **farmers have to buy expensive fertilisers**.
- The canals that distribute the irrigation waters in the valley are overrun with a **water snail** which carries an infection that affects humans.
- Much water is lost because of **evaporation** from Lake Nasser.

The Nile valley with irrigated crops. Irrigation has made the desert bloom in the Nile valley in Egypt for thousands of years

Activity
Can you **explain** why evaporation is high in Lake Nasser?

Future plans

Egypt is developing a major scheme to irrigate parts of the **Western Desert**. A canal will bring water from Lake Nasser to **oases** in the desert. Some people from the overcrowded Nile valley have migrated to these areas to begin a new life.

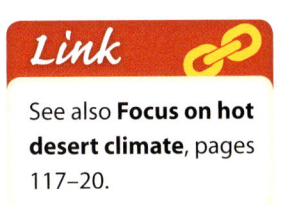

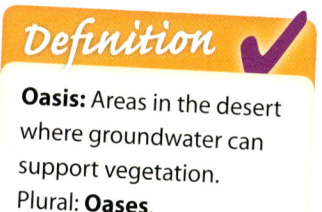

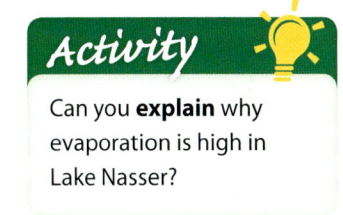

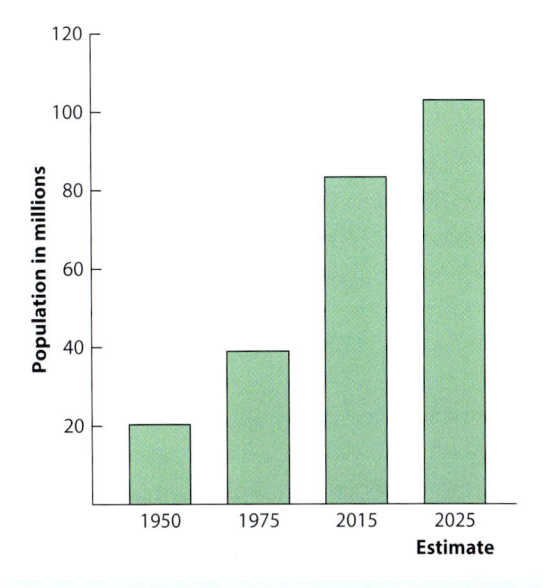

Link
See also **Focus on hot desert climate**, pages 117–20.

Definition
Oasis: Areas in the desert where groundwater can support vegetation. Plural: **Oases**.

Figure 12.6 Egypt's population growth

Section 4 · Economic Geography

Case study

Irrigation in the south of France

- The Mediterranean coast of France has **hot, dry summers**. This is good for tourism but limits agriculture. Without irrigation, farmers along the coast of Languedoc grew **vines only**. The wine was of poor quality and fetched very low prices. Therefore, the **farmers were poor**.
- In the **1960s**, an **irrigation scheme** was established. Water was pumped from the **Rhône** and other local rivers. Irrigation canals were built along the coastal plain. Diesel pumps helped to distribute the water to farms.
- Over the years, the region changed as farmers began to use irrigation water. Farmers began to grow a great **variety of crops and vegetables**.
- Farmers now grow **salad crops** such as lettuces, cucumbers and spring onions. They also produce potatoes, cauliflowers, sunflowers, aubergines and artichokes for sale in the cities and in the local tourist resorts.

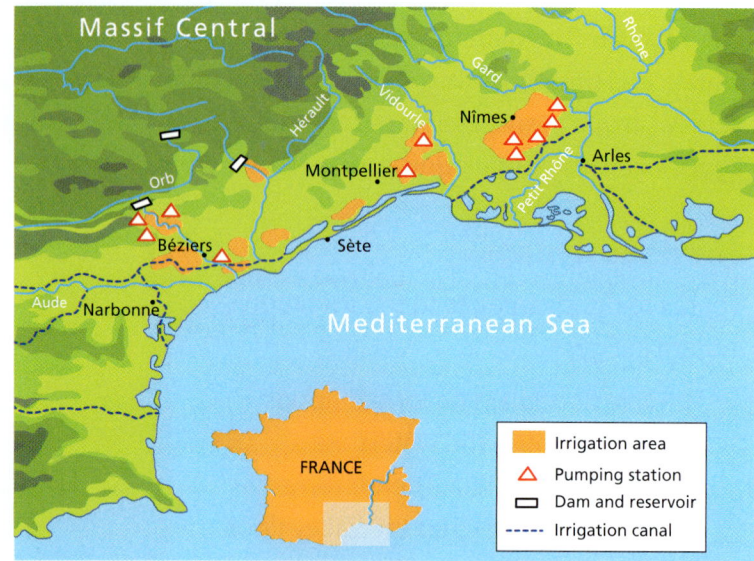

Figure 12.7 Irrigation projects in the south of France

An irrigation canal and intensive farmland in the South of France

- Because of irrigation, Languedoc is now **intensively farmed**. Farmers are well paid for their fresh produce. Their standard of living has improved greatly in recent decades.

Questions

1. Name the county from which Dublin receives much of its water.
2. Explain **one** reason why people should conserve water.
3. Explain **two** ways in which the Nile is vital to Egypt.
4. In what ways has irrigation been of benefit to farmers in southern France?

12.3 Oil: a finite resource

KEYWORDS
- finite resource
- energy consumption
- oil reserves
- urban lifestyle
- migrant worker
- absolute monarchy
- refinery
- renewable energy

Societies today use huge quantities of energy. **Oil** is a very important source of energy. Oil is an example of a **finite resource**.

In the nineteenth century, **coal** was a major source of energy. However, oil began to replace coal in the twentieth century.

- Oil powers cars and trucks.
- Oil is used to generate electricity and to heat homes.

However, like coal, oil is also a **source of greenhouse gases**.

A finite resource

Oil will eventually run out, and it will happen this century. For that reason, **we need to conserve the oil resources of the world**.

However, the rich world – the USA, Europe, Japan and now an increasing number of people in China – has a **love affair with cars**. This is because cars are very convenient. As long as people can afford petrol, it seems they will use their cars.

Geo fact
There are almost 2 million cars in the Republic of Ireland, i.e. just under one car for every two people.

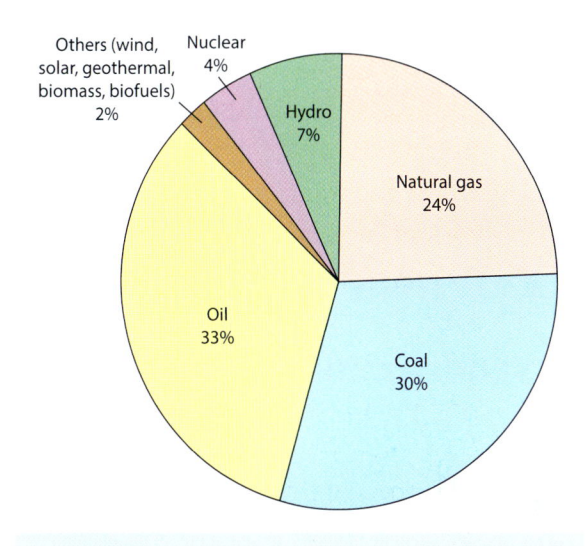

Activity
Class **discussion**: 'People have the right to use their cars as much as they wish.'

Figure 12.8 Sources of world energy consumption

- Others (wind, solar, geothermal, biomass, biofuels) 2%
- Nuclear 4%
- Hydro 7%
- Natural gas 24%
- Oil 33%
- Coal 30%

This busy junction outside Birmingham in the UK is commonly known as Spaghetti Junction

The location of oil deposits

Oil is found in the USA, Mexico, Venezuela, Russia and other countries. However, the bulk of the world's **oil reserves** are in the Persian Gulf region. Oil was found in this area in the 1930s. This region exports oil to the USA, the EU, Japan and other countries. However, it is a region that has seen many wars in recent times.

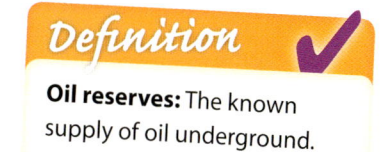

Definition
Oil reserves: The known supply of oil underground.

The Persian Gulf holds much of the world's oil reserves

Section 4 • Economic Geography

Table 12.3 World oil reserves by region

Persian Gulf region	49%
Central and South America	20%
North America	13%
Africa	8%
Russia	7%
Oceania	2%
Europe	1%

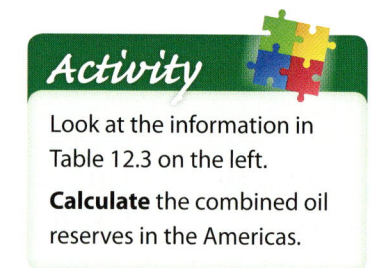

Activity

Look at the information in Table 12.3 on the left.

Calculate the combined oil reserves in the Americas.

Saudi Arabia is to be studied by Higher Level students only.

Case study

Saudi Arabia: an oil-producing country

Saudi Arabia is a country that is mostly desert. Until the 1930s, it was a little-known land of **nomadic herders**. The discovery of oil changed all of that.

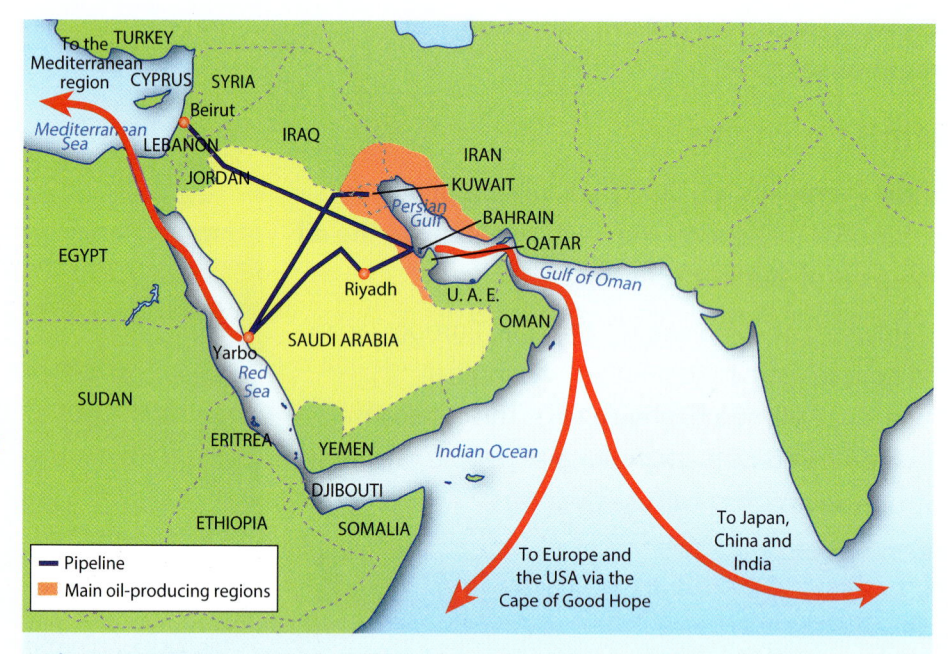

Modern lifestyles

With the export of oil, vast wealth flowed into Saudi Arabia.

- Oil production brought with it many **jobs**.
- People from the **nomadic tribes abandoned the desert** to work in the oil industry.
- Camels were replaced by **jeeps** and later by **SUVs**.
- Desert tents were replaced by urban homes and an **urban lifestyle**.
- **Incomes rose** rapidly.
- Expensive **consumer goods** from all over the world appeared in the shops.

Figure 12.9 Oil regions and oil pipelines in Saudi Arabia and the surrounding regions. Name three oil-producing countries in the Persian Gulf

An oil refinery in Saudi Arabia

Case study

Inward migration

The demand for workers brought many **migrant workers** to Saudi Arabia. Workers from Egypt, Pakistan, Bangladesh and many other countries work in Saudi Arabia today. Many people from Europe and the USA who work in Saudi Arabia experience **culture shock**.

Table 12.4 Saudi Arabia in figures

Population	30 million
Life expectancy	76 years
Births per mother	2.1
Urban population	82%
Access to clean water	89%
Adult literacy	87%

Politics

In spite of rapid changes, some aspects of life remain the same.

- Saudi Arabia is not a democracy, but an **absolute monarchy**. The king rules without political parties or elections.
- There are concerns about human rights, such as the rights of prisoners.
- It is also an **Islamic society**. Islam is the **official state religion**, and all citizens are required by law to be Muslims and to obey Sharia law.

Geo fact
There were nine million migrant workers in Saudi Arabia in 2014, most from South Asia.

Geo fact
Alcohol and pork are banned in Saudi Arabia.

The role of women

The role of women in Saudi Arabia has not changed in spite of the rapid increase in wealth.

- It is illegal for a man and a woman who are unmarried to be together in a **public place**.
- Women are **not allowed to drive**.
- They must be **completely covered** outside the home.
- Women have almost no opportunities to take part in any kind of **sport**.
- Very **few women work** outside the home.
- Many examples show that women are **discriminated against in the courts**.

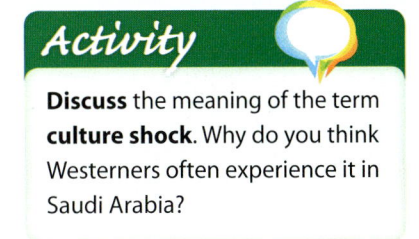

Saudi women dressed in the chador

Activity

Discuss the meaning of the term **culture shock**. Why do you think Westerners often experience it in Saudi Arabia?

Geo fact
In December 2015, some women were elected to urban councils for the first time in Saudi history.

Section 4 · Economic Geography

Case study

The search for oil in Irish waters

The demand for oil and natural gas in recent decades led many countries to search for oil in offshore waters. This search was successful, especially in the **North Sea** in Norwegian and British waters.

Irish coastal waters

The presence of oil and gas in the North Sea prompted oil companies to look in **Irish waters** for oil. The government granted **licences** to oil exploration companies to drill for oil off the Irish coast.

- **Oil** was found off the coast of Waterford and the coast of Cork (Barryroe field).
- **Gas** was found off the coast of Kinsale and later off the coast of Mayo.

Oil finds

These oil finds have not been developed so far. This is because the finds are small ones. The **cost** of bringing the oil ashore would be **greater than the value** of the oil. However, as **oil prices rise in the future**, oil wells may be drilled there.

The Kinsale Head gas field

The Kinsale Head gas field is an offshore field. It has been providing **natural gas** to the Irish economy for more than 30 years. It has been used to generate electricity in Aghada by the ESB on the coast of Co. Cork. The Kinsale gas field has also supplied natural gas to many Irish towns and cities. However, the Kinsale field will soon be exhausted.

The Corrib gas field

Natural gas has also been found **off the coast of Mayo**. This is known as the **Corrib gas field**.

Bringing the gas ashore from the Corrib gas field was delayed because of a dispute between Shell – the company involved – and some local people. People were concerned about the **safety of the gas pipeline** and an onshore refinery. Locals wanted the refinery to be located at sea.

However, in 2008 construction of the onshore pipeline started. The gas finally began to come ashore in **2015**.

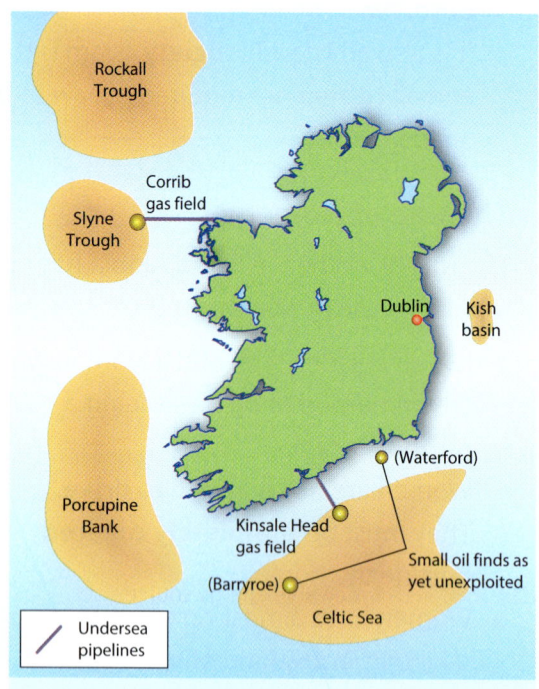

Figure 12.10 Oil and gas finds in Irish waters

The new refinery in Mayo that processes the gas from the Corrib gas field

Chapter 12 · Primary Economic Activities

Renewable energy

Everyone agrees that the **demand** for oil and natural gas will be **greater than supply** in the coming years. Therefore, people must develop other energy sources that are **renewable**.

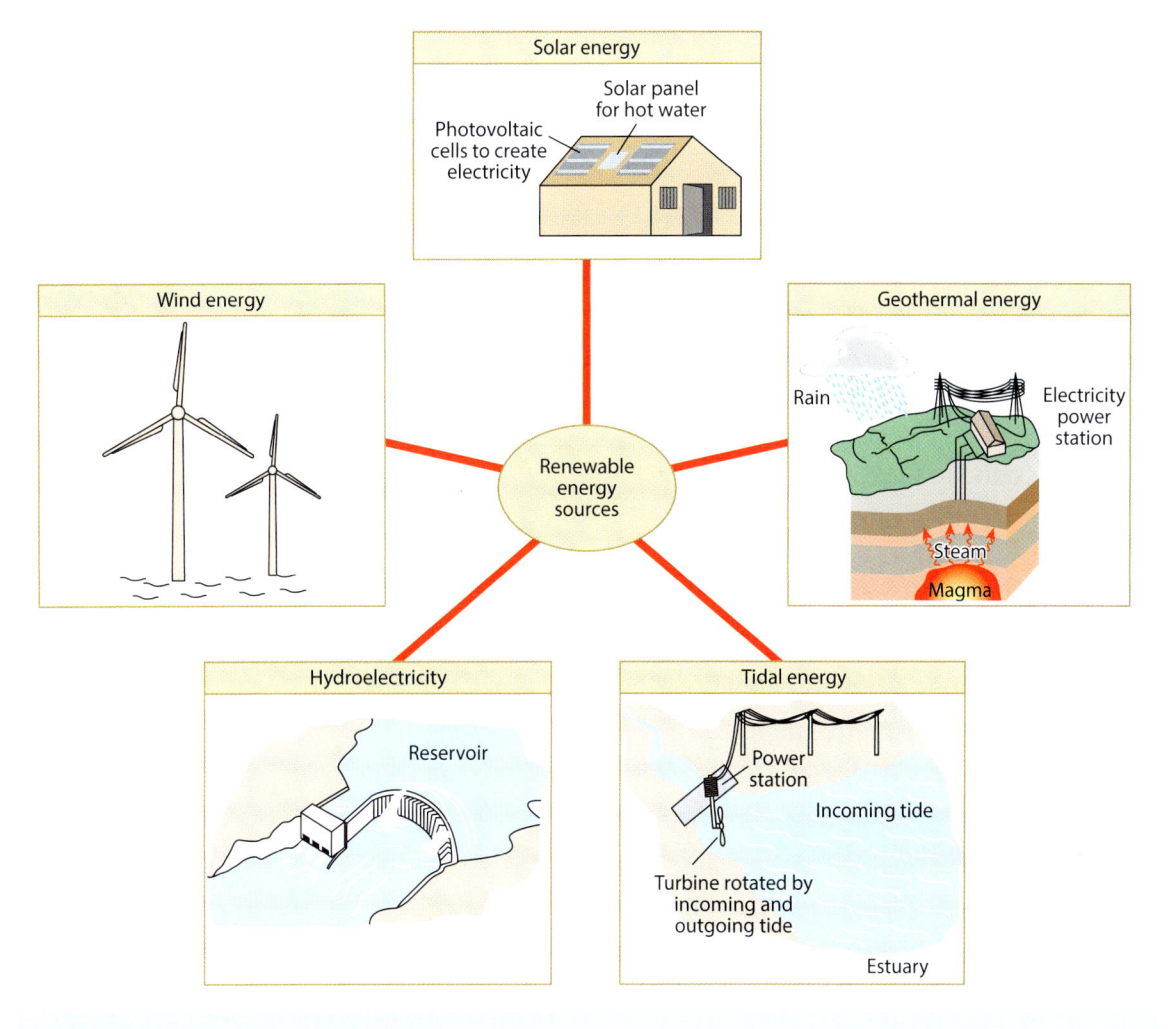

> **Geo fact**
>
> In 2015, there were 195 wind farms in the Republic of Ireland.

Figure 12.11 Renewable energy sources

Questions

1. Explain **two** reasons why oil is very important in the modern world.
2. Explain why demand for oil has increased in China in recent years.
3. Why is the Persian Gulf important in the oil industry?
4. Explain **two** changes that oil production has brought to Saudi Arabia.
5. Give **two** examples of renewable energy.
6. Explain **one** reason why we should increase our use of renewable energy.

Section 4 · Economic Geography

12.4 The exploitation of Ireland's peatlands

KEYWORDS
- raised bog
- blanket bog
- meitheal
- sleán
- self-sufficient
- Bord na Móna
- milled peat
- ditcher
- grader
- miller
- harrow
- ridger

Peat is another **non-renewable resource**. It is a natural resource that the people of Ireland have **exploited** for hundreds of years. We will look at the history of Ireland's peat, and how new **technology** has made it **easier to exploit it**, and **changed the ways in which it is used**.

Link
See also OS extract Figure 8.46, page 173.

Ireland's peat bogs

Bogs in Ireland began to develop about 10,000 years ago. There are two types of bogs in Ireland:

- **Raised bogs** are found in shallow depressions in some Midland counties. These bogs can be up to 12 metres deep in their natural state.
- **Blanket bogs** are found in upland regions and in lowlands in the western seaboard counties. These bogs are 1.5 metres deep on average.

Geo fact
Bogs in their natural state are dangerous places for people and animals, as they are composed of more than 90 per cent water.

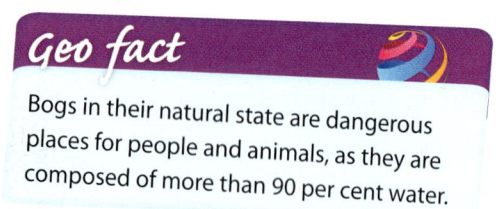

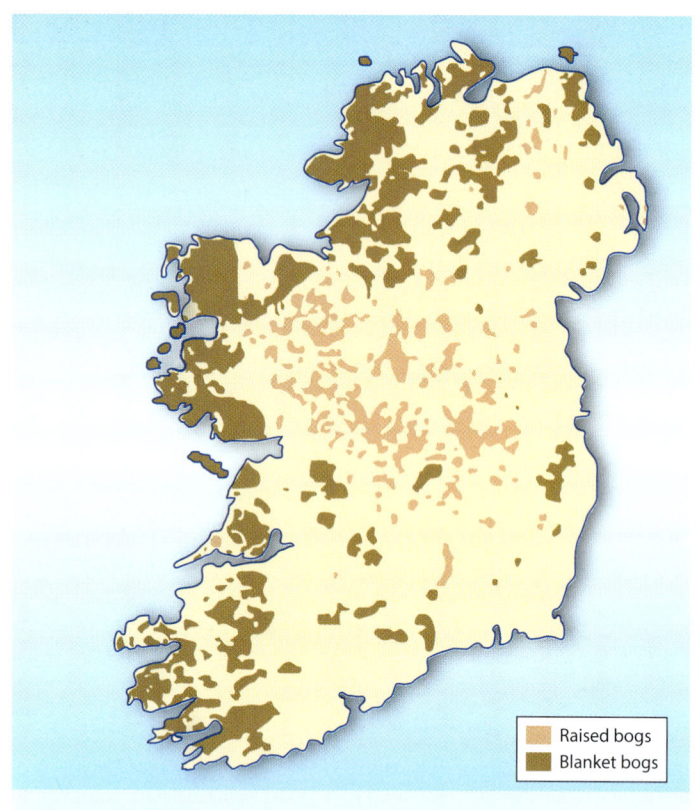

Figure 12.12 The distribution of Ireland's peat bogs

Traditional methods of peat cutting

For generations, Irish people harvested turf. **Meitheals** of workers cut turf for kitchen fires using a **sleán** – a type of spade. The sleán was an example of **traditional technology**. Output per worker was very low. Saved turf was brought home by pony and cart.

Definition
Meitheal: A group of neighbours and friends who worked together at a common task in rural Ireland.

Cutting turf by hand meant that the exploitation of peat was very slow

Bord na Móna

In 1946, the Irish government established Bord na Móna to exploit Ireland's bogs and to make the country more **self-sufficient** in energy resources.

> **Definition** ✓
> **Self-sufficient:** Reliant on a country's own resources.

Modern peat production

Bord na Móna developed **modern machinery** to exploit the bogs of the Midlands. Bogs here covered thousands of hectares and were on **level ground**. Bogs were **drained** so that water ran off, allowing the peat to compress. Machinery could then travel over the bogs.

> **Geo fact**
> Tractors used in bogs have very wide tyres so that they do not sink.

Phase 1 The bog is drained → **Phase 2** The peat is harvested → **Phase 3** The peat is transported → **Phase 4** The peat is marketed

> **Geo fact**
> Bord na Móna has 1,000 km of narrow gauge railway network in its bogs – the longest in the world.

Figure 12.13 The stages in the exploitation of a bog

The stages in the production of milled peat

A ditcher

A miller

A harrow

A **ditcher** is used to drain the bog. A **grader** levels the surface of the bog. → A shallow layer of peat is scraped loose by a **miller** on the peat's surface. → This layer is later harrowed using a **harrow** pulled by a tractor to dry it.

A ridger

A train takes peat to the power station

Peat is gathered in long ridges using a **ridger** and covered in plastic to protect it from rain. → The ridges of peat are brought to the power station or factory on **light railways**. The peat is either used to generate electricity or manufactured into products (see next page).

Section 4 · Economic Geography

Peat products

Peat products include the following:

- **Horticultural products** such as moss peat, seed and potting compost are sold to gardeners.
- **Peat briquettes** are sold to domestic consumers for home heating.
- **Milled peat** is sold to ESB power stations in the Midlands to generate electricity.

> **Definition**
>
> **Milled peat:** Peat that has been scraped off the surface of the bog and dried.

The life cycle of a bog

Bogs have developed over thousands of years. However, a bog can be worked out in **fifty years**. Peatlands are a unique habitat that is home to rare plants and insect life.

Bord na Móna's change of direction

In 2015, Bord na Móna announced that it would end the exploitation of bogs for peat production by 2030. By then, peat briquettes will be a thing of the past. However, some peat will continue to be harvested for horticultural use.

In the future, Bord na Móna will use the peat lands for **wind farms**, **solar energy** and **willow plantations**. Willow plantations will be harvested as **biomass** for the ESB power stations that currently burn peat.

Some of the boglands will be slowly restored to their natural state by closing drains and allowing water levels to rise. They will be used for **ecotourism**.

The ending of the large-scale exploitation of Ireland's peatlands will be the largest change in land use in the history of the Irish state.

Bog cotton in a bog in the west of Ireland. Bog flora adds to the diversity of plant life and needs to be preserved

Harvesting a willow plantation in England. The willow regrows very quickly. This will become a common sight in Ireland's peatlands in the coming decades

> **Definitions**
>
> **Biomass:** Material from plants, such as willow timber, which is burned to make energy.
>
> **Ecotourism:** Tourism to places with unspoiled natural resources where tourists can observe and enjoy plant and animal diversity.

> **Activity**
>
> Building wind farms in bogs in the Midlands has become controversial. **Discuss** this issue in class.

Questions

1. Why was the exploitation of bogs very slow when turf was cut by hand?
2. Are peat resources renewable or non-renewable?
3. Explain **three** reasons why peat reserves have been rapidly exploited in recent decades.
4. Explain **one** way in which Midland counties have benefited from peat exploitation.

12.5 Fishing

> **KEYWORDS**
> - sustainable fishing
> - overexploitation
> - depletion
> - continental shelf
> - radar/sonar
> - hydraulic winch
> - trawling
> - purse seining
> - drift netting
> - pelagic fish
> - demersal fish
> - spawning ground
> - quota

Fish is a very important food. It is prized as part of a healthy diet because it is **low in fat** and contains **healthy oils**.

Sustainable fishing

Fish are a **renewable resource**. Although some are caught, others can breed and replace their numbers. If fishing is carried out sensibly there will always be enough fish to catch. This is known as **sustainable fishing**.

Overexploitation

However, in many places trawlers take more fish than are replaced by breeding. This is called **overexploitation** (overuse) of a resource – in this case, overfishing.

As a result of overfishing, **fish stocks get smaller and smaller** until there are too few fish to be worth catching. We call this **depletion** of a resource.

Ireland's continental shelf

Irish waters have traditionally been rich in fish. The seas off the Irish coast form a **continental shelf**. This is an area of sea close to land in which large shoals of fish can thrive.

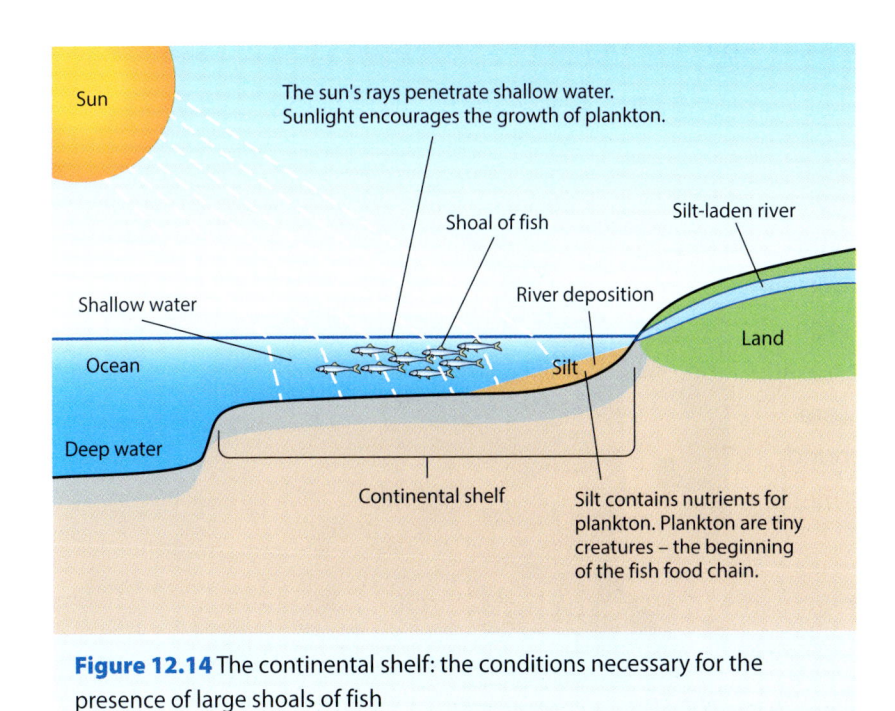

Figure 12.14 The continental shelf: the conditions necessary for the presence of large shoals of fish

> **Activity**
> **Research** 'plankton' on the Internet. Click on images to see what these creatures look like.

Section 4 · Economic Geography

The Irish fishing industry

The Irish fishing industry was small in scale until recent decades. Many fishermen fished in-shore for generations in **currachs**. Most trawlers were small and had small nets. Therefore, **catches were small**. This all changed when Ireland joined the EEC – now the EU – in 1973.

Men putting to sea in a currach. Currachs were incapable of depleting the fish of the seas. Can you explain why?

Table 12.5 Top ten fish-landing ports, 2012

Port name	Tonnes
Killybegs	197,523
Castletownbere	32,566
Dunmore East	13,489
An Daingean/ Dingle	11,927
Cork Harbour ports	9,387
Greencastle	7,155
Rossaveal	6,019
Duncannon	5,658
Kilmore Quay	5,128
Howth	4,590

Figure 12.15 Irish fishing ports

EEC membership

EEC (EU) membership meant that Ireland gave up control of its fisheries. **Ireland had to share its fisheries** with other members of the EU. Therefore, the amount of fish taken from waters around Ireland greatly increased, especially after Spain joined in 1985. More than half the fish taken from waters around Ireland today are caught by foreign trawlers.

Geo fact

The 28 EU member states have 87,000 trawlers in total – a number that is far too high for the available fish stocks.

Unloading a catch from the deck of a trawler in Howth, Co. Dublin

Chapter 12 · Primary Economic Activities

Modern fishing technology

The modern trawler is well equipped to catch fish.

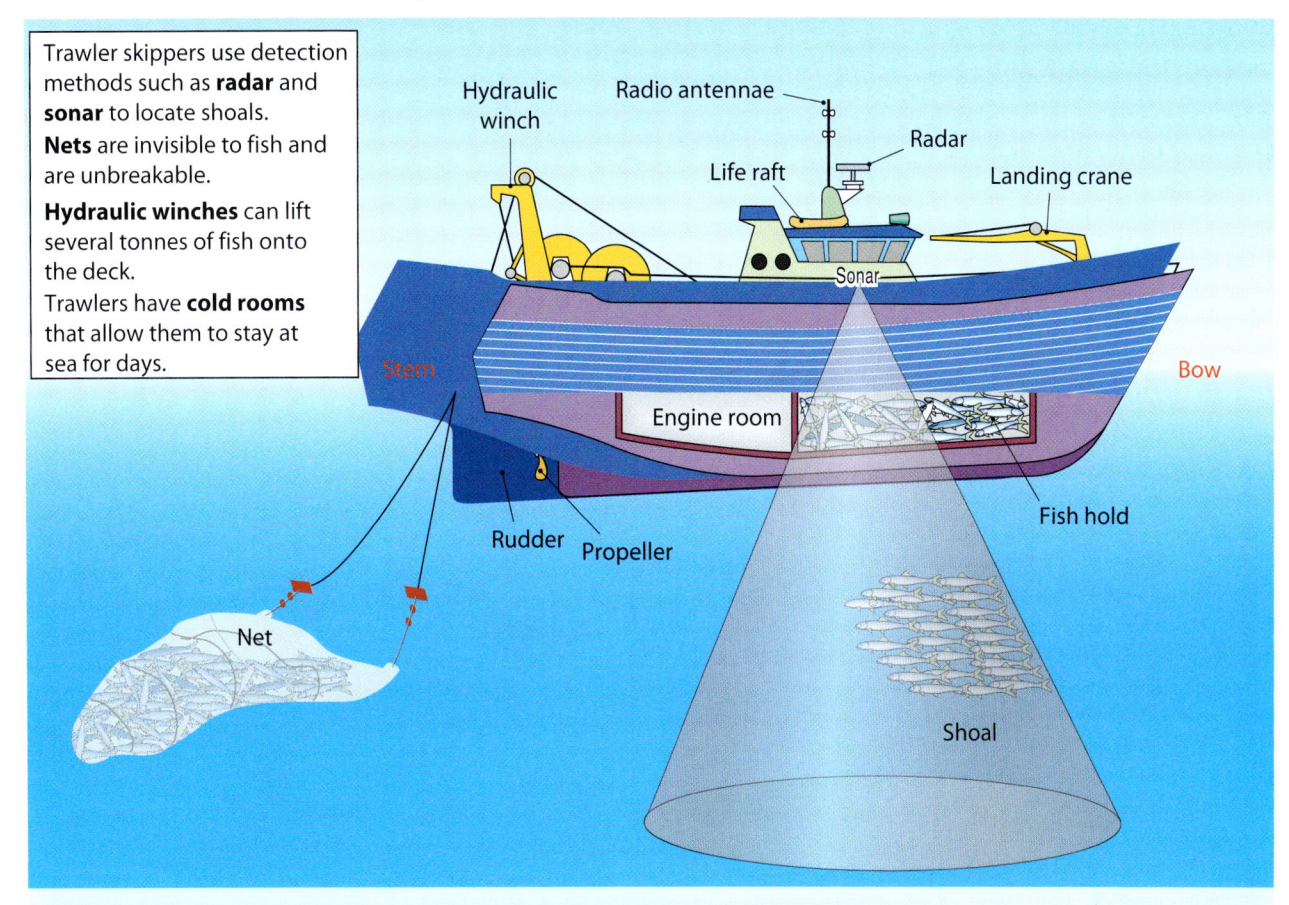

Trawler skippers use detection methods such as **radar** and **sonar** to locate shoals.
Nets are invisible to fish and are unbreakable.
Hydraulic winches can lift several tonnes of fish onto the deck.
Trawlers have **cold rooms** that allow them to stay at sea for days.

Figure 12.16 Trawlers have very modern equipment to help them find and catch fish

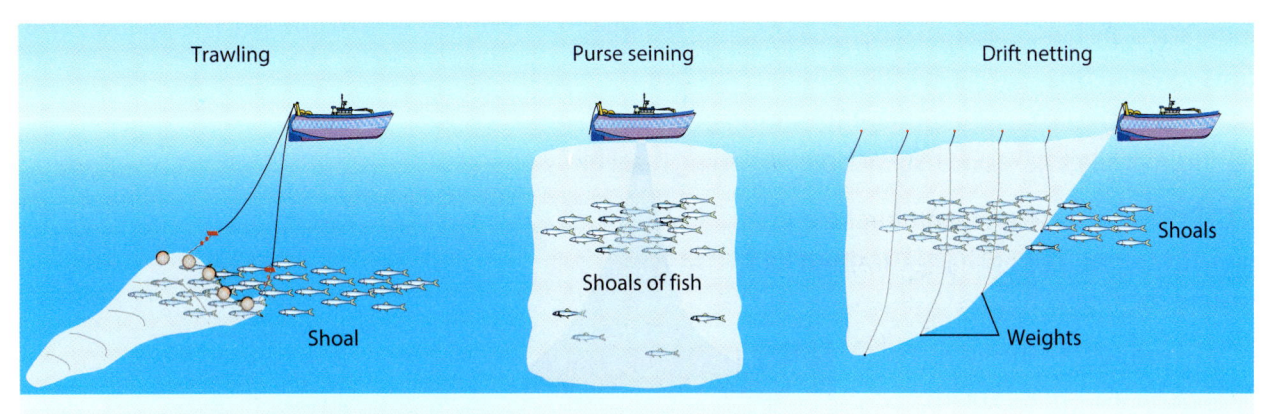

Figure 12.17 Ocean fishing methods. Fishing nets are enormous today

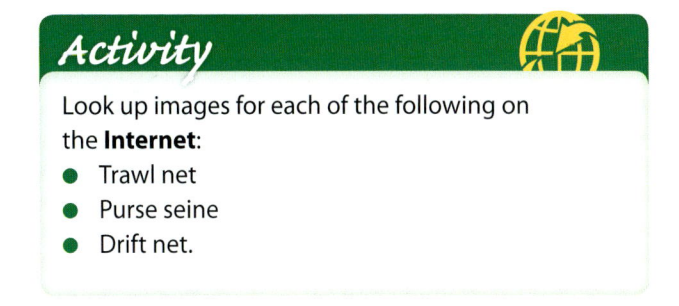

Activity

Look up images for each of the following on the **Internet**:
- Trawl net
- Purse seine
- Drift net.

351

Section 4 · Economic Geography

Endangered species of fish

Due to overfishing many species of fish caught in Irish waters are **in decline**. These include **herring**, **cod**, **hake**, **haddock**, **plaice** and **sole**.

The reasons for overfishing include the following:

- Too many **well-equipped trawlers** are chasing too few fish.
- The seas around Ireland cover a wide area. It is impossible to stop **illegal fishing**.
- Many juvenile fish are being caught because some fishing trawlers use **nets with a small mesh**. This reduces the next year's catch.

Geo fact
Very large trawlers are known as **supertrawlers**.

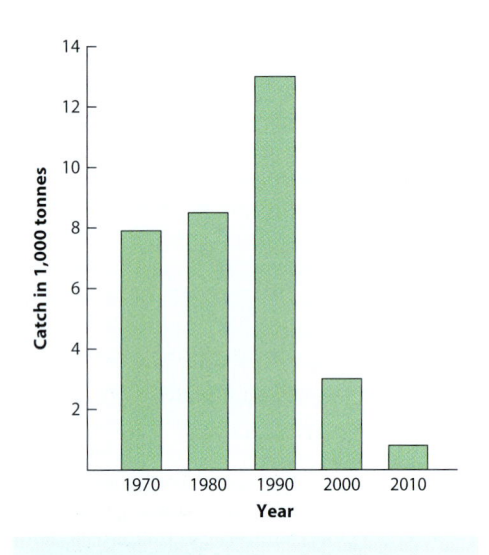

Figure 12.18 The cod catch in the Irish Sea over time. There has been a severe decline since the peak of 1990

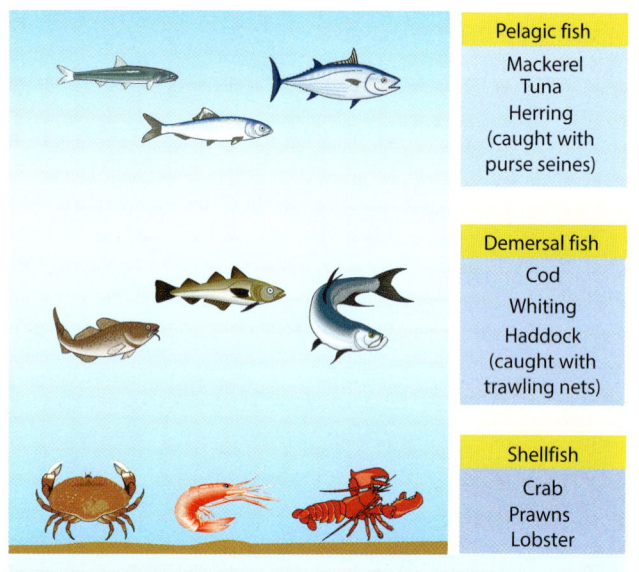

Pelagic fish
Mackerel
Tuna
Herring
(caught with purse seines)

Demersal fish
Cod
Whiting
Haddock
(caught with trawling nets)

Shellfish
Crab
Prawns
Lobster

Figure 12.19 The main types of ocean fish

Conserving fish stocks

Some steps are being taken to reduce overfishing. The **Irish Conservation Box** – an area of 100,000 km² – has been established. The Box is an important **spawning ground**, where herring, mackerel, hake and haddock breed. Fishing is **severely restricted** in this area.

Other steps that are used to **conserve fish stocks** include the following:

- Scientists check the numbers of particular species of fish in the seas. **Quotas** are then placed on the amount of each species that can be caught.

Definition
Quota: A limit on the amount of fish that can be caught annually.

- The **number of trawlers** is being reduced. Fishermen can retire with an EU pension.
- The **mesh size of nets** is fixed so that juvenile fish can escape.
- The **fishing season** for some species is shortened.
- Trawlers from **countries outside the EU**, such as Russia, are not allowed to fish in EU waters.

Figure 12.20 A conservation zone has been created in the seas around Ireland in order to protect fish for future generations

Questions

1. Explain the meaning of the following: overexploitation of a resource.
2. Explain **three** ways in which modern fishing methods are very efficient at catching fish.
3. Explain the terms: pelagic fish, demersal fish.

12.6 Farming

KEYWORDS
- system
- input
- process
- output
- fertiliser
- mixed farm
- weanling
- traceability

Many primary economic activities may be examined as **systems**, with **inputs**, **processes** and **outputs**.

> **Geo fact**
> In cattle farms, slurry is an output. It is also an input because it is spread on the land as an organic fertiliser.

The system of farming

Farming is a primary economic activity. It is also a **system** that works in a structured way.

- Farmers use many **inputs** in their farms. These are the things that they need to make the system work. They include seeds, fertilisers and machinery.
- The **processes** of farming include the tasks that farmers perform throughout the year. Examples of processes are milking cows, spreading fertiliser and cutting silage.
- The **outputs** are the produce from the farm. These outputs may be vegetables, milk, beef cattle or sheep. Some farmers grow crops for cereal production; these include wheat and barley.

Mixed farms

Most farmers today specialise in one type of farming. There are dairy farmers, beef producers, market gardeners and cereal producers. However, some are **mixed farmers**. They are involved in more than one type of activity, e.g. dairy **and** beef producers, or barley **and** beef farmers.

> **Geo fact**
> The average age of Irish farmers in 2015 was 57 years.

Section 4 · Economic Geography

Case study

A mixed farm

We will now examine a 70-hectare mixed farm in the mid-Clare area. Up to 20 hectares are flooded under a seasonal lake in winter. The farm is a **beef and sheep farm**.

The farmer is called Pat. As a mixed farmer, he engages in two farming activities. His farm is under grass. The soil is too heavy for growing crops on a large scale, but he grows potatoes, onions and lettuce for the family in a kitchen garden.

The inputs in Pat's farm

Labour
- Pat works full time on the farm.
- His wife works as an office worker in Ennis. She keeps the farm accounts.
- Their son and daughter – both now in university – help out with herding and feeding animals during the holidays and at weekends.

Animals
- **Cattle**: Pat has a herd of **suckler cattle**. Each cow produces a calf every year. The calves suckle the cows for many months after they are born. They put on weight quickly.
- **Sheep**: Pat also keeps sheep, partly because it is a tradition and partly to have another source of income when the **price of beef** drops. Sheep produce lambs in early spring, a very busy time.

> **Definition**
> **Suckler cattle:** Cows that suckle (give milk to) their calves for several months.

Machinery and other inputs
- Pat has two tractors and several pieces of equipment including a fertiliser spreader, a trailer, a front loader and a tractor box.
- Other inputs include fertiliser, concentrated animal feed, seeds for reseeding grassland and electric fences.

A tractor spreading fertiliser on grassland. A tractor is a vital machine on a farm

Specialist inputs
- The vet is called to attend to sick animals.
- The **Teagasc** representative advises Pat on farm management.
- Pat also attends **IFA** meetings and has gone abroad on farming tours to Germany and Denmark.
- He reads the *Farmers Journal*.

> **Definition**
> **Teagasc:** The Irish farm body whose instructors provide courses and advice to farmers.
>
> **IFA:** The Irish Farmers' Association, which promotes the interests of Irish farmers.

354

Chapter 12 · Primary Economic Activities

Case study

Processes

Figure 12.21 Farm processes throughout the year

Outputs

- The major outputs of Pat's farm are **cattle** and **lambs**.
- Pat sells the young cattle as **weanlings** in Ennis and Sixmilebridge Marts in the autumn. Buyers come from cattle factories. Pat's name and address appears on meat products in Irish supermarkets because of the EU policy of meat **traceability**.
- **Lambs** are bought by local butchers. These are slaughtered and sold in butcher shops and to hotels in Co. Clare.
- **Slurry** from the winter sheds is spread on the fields as an **organic fertiliser**.

The scene at a sheep sale in the west of Ireland. A visit to the mart is an important day in Pat's life because he gets paid for his livestock

Definitions

Weanlings: Young cattle that have been weaned from cows' milk.

Traceability: Beef and sheep can be traced back to the farms where the animals were raised.

Activity

Pat has two enterprises: cattle and sheep. Can you think of one advantage in doing this? **Discuss** in groups or as a class.

Section 4 · Economic Geography

Questions

1. Write the headings *inputs*, *processes* and *outputs* in your copybook. Put the following farming words into the correct column: harvesting silage, weanling cattle, diesel fuel, milking the cows, lambs for slaughter, animal feed.
2. Pat's farming activities change with the seasons. Explain that statement.

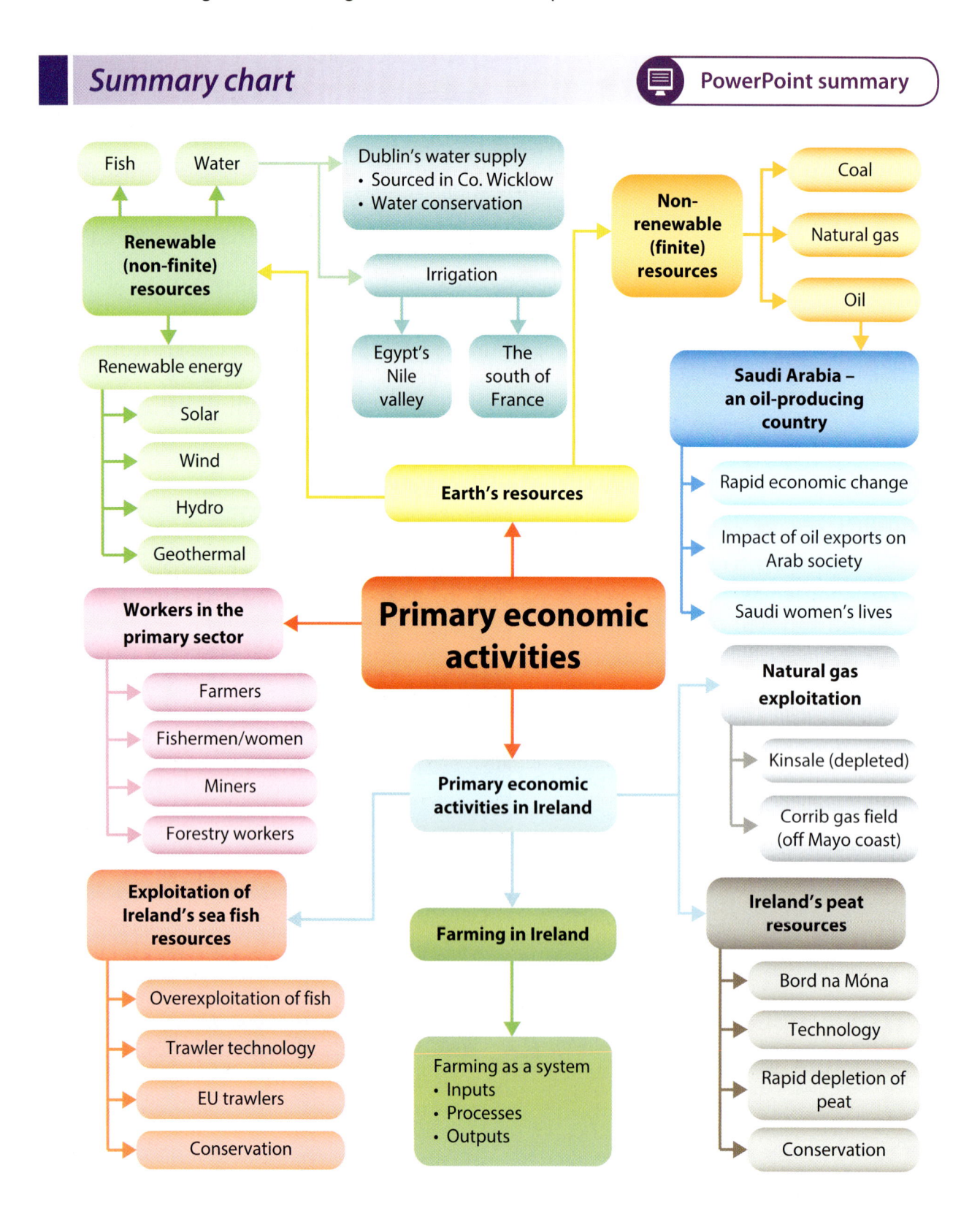

Summary chart

PowerPoint summary

Primary economic activities

- Renewable (non-finite) resources
  - Fish
  - Water
    - Dublin's water supply
      - Sourced in Co. Wicklow
      - Water conservation
    - Irrigation
      - Egypt's Nile valley
      - The south of France
  - Renewable energy
    - Solar
    - Wind
    - Hydro
    - Geothermal

- Non-renewable (finite) resources
  - Coal
  - Natural gas
  - Oil
    - Saudi Arabia – an oil-producing country
      - Rapid economic change
      - Impact of oil exports on Arab society
      - Saudi women's lives

- Earth's resources

- Workers in the primary sector
  - Farmers
  - Fishermen/women
  - Miners
  - Forestry workers

- Primary economic activities in Ireland
  - Natural gas exploitation
    - Kinsale (depleted)
    - Corrib gas field (off Mayo coast)
  - Farming in Ireland
    - Farming as a system
      - Inputs
      - Processes
      - Outputs
  - Ireland's peat resources
    - Bord na Móna
    - Technology
    - Rapid depletion of peat
    - Conservation

- Exploitation of Ireland's sea fish resources
  - Overexploitation of fish
  - Trawler technology
  - EU trawlers
  - Conservation

356

Chapter 12 • Primary Economic Activities

Exam questions

1. (i) What is the term given to the artificial watering of crops as shown (on the right)?
   (ii) Name **one** such scheme that you have studied.
   (iii) Explain **one** advantage of this scheme.
   (iv) Explain **one** disadvantage of this scheme.

   HL 2012

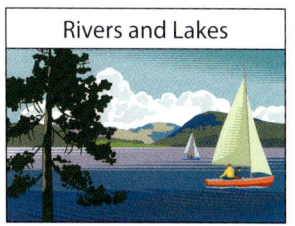

2. | Water Treatment Plant | Houses, Schools, Shops | Reservoir | Rivers and Lakes |

   The pictures above show different stages in providing a local water supply. The pictures are not in the correct order.
   (i) Describe the stages involved in providing a local water supply.
   (ii) Explain how a water supply can become polluted.

   OL 2015

3. (i) Name **one** example of renewable energy.
   (ii) Explain any **two** physical (natural) factors that are required for the generation of energy using the renewable energy source named in part (i) above.
   (iii) Explain **one** advantage of renewable energy.

   HL 2012

4. (i) Name **one** area off the Irish coast where oil/natural gas has been found.
   (ii) Explain **one** positive effect and **one** negative effect of such a discovery for an area.
   (iii) State **one** reason why it is important to reduce the amount of fossil fuels being used.

   OL 2015

5. (i) Describe **two** ways in which technology has aided in the exploitation of peat.
   (ii) Explain **two** reasons why the majority of Bord na Móna's commercial peat production takes place at the raised bogs in the Midlands.

   HL 2013

357

Section 4 · Economic Geography

Exam questions

6 (i) Explain **two** reasons for the overexploitation of fish.

(ii) Describe **two** measures that could be used to prevent the overexploitation of fish.

HL 2015

7 A farm can be viewed as a system, involving inputs, processes and outputs. Answer each of the following questions with reference to any mixed farm that you have studied.

(i) Name **two** farm inputs.

(ii) Describe **two** processes that take place on the farm.

(iii) Name **two** outputs from the farm and state how each may be used.

HL 2015

8 Examine the sketch map of an Irish farm below and answer the questions which follow:

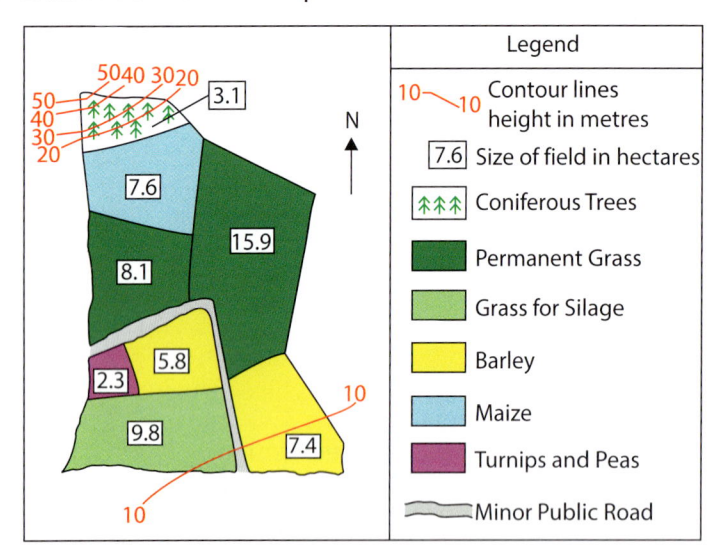

(i) What is the size in hectares of the largest field on the farm?

(ii) How many hectares in total are devoted to barley?

(iii) The total area of the farm is 60 hectares. Calculate the percentage of the land that is devoted to permanent grass.

(iv) Why is the growth of coniferous trees an appropriate land use for the 3.1 hectare field at the north of the farm?

HL 2009

Chapter 13
Secondary Economic Activities

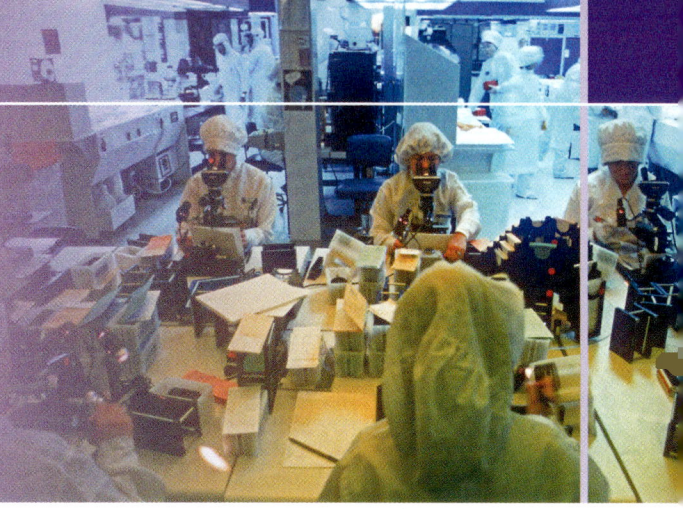

Learning outcomes

By the end of this chapter, you should be able to understand:

- That secondary economic activities are ones in which raw materials are turned into products
- Why different types of manufacturing industry locate in different places
- That modern industry is footloose
- Why the locations of the British iron and steel industry have changed over time
- That some regions of the world are more industrialised than others
- That industrial activity can damage the environment and can lead to local opposition.

13.1 Turning resources into products

KEYWORDS

- system
- input
- process
- output
- resource material
- product
- light industry
- information technology
- greenfield site

Secondary economic activities are those in which raw materials are **processed**. Any secondary activity may be viewed as a **system of inputs, processes and outputs**.

This chapter deals with manufacturing. Every factory has a system of **inputs**, **processes** and **outputs**.

- **Resource materials** enter the factory as **inputs**.
- These materials are **processed** into **products** in a factory.
- Finished products and waste are factory **outputs**.

The following two case studies look at factories/plants as systems of inputs, processes and outputs:

- Nutricia Infant Nutrition Ltd, Macroom, Co. Cork
- Intel, Leixlip, Co. Kildare.

> **Definitions**
>
> **Resource materials:** The raw materials or components that are used to make a product.
>
> **Products:** What a factory makes; the end result of the production process.

Section 4 · Economic Geography

Case study

1 Nutricia Infant Nutrition Ltd

This **food-processing plant** is located in Macroom, Co. Cork. It is owned by Danone, the French food company. Nutricia produces baby and toddler **formula foods**. These are foods with precise amounts of pure water and nutrients needed for children's development. Thus they are products that depend on scientific research. Therefore, many of the 120 workers are highly qualified graduates in **food science**. Nutricia is a **light industry**.

The formula food containers are sent by road to the Danone plant in Wexford. In Wexford, the powder is repackaged for consumers and exported to markets in 60 countries, including China. The exports are worth about €150 million a year to the Irish economy.

Definition

Light industry: The manufacture of goods that are easily transportable, e.g. clothes and healthcare products.

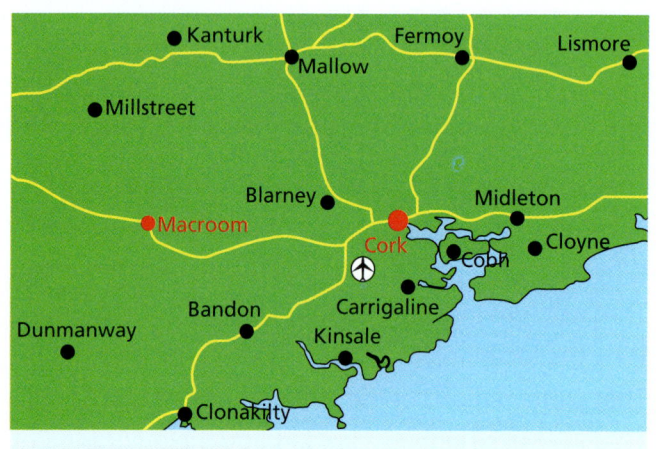

Figure 13.1 Macroom, Co. Cork

Inputs
- Milk and whey
- Skimmed milk powder
- Lactose
- Electricity and natural gas
- Workers
- Capital
- Water

Outputs
- Baby formula foods
- Toddler formula foods
- Plastic and packaging waste for recycling

Processes
- Materials are dissolved.
- Vitamins are added.
- The mix is dried to powder form.
- The product is tested for quality.
- Formula powder is packaged in bulk containers.

Geo fact

Milk for the Nutricia plant is supplied by dairy companies in Munster, where the cows graze on rich pasturelands.

Figure 13.2 Inputs, processes and outputs in Nutricia – a light industry

Chapter 13 · Secondary Economic Activities

Case study

2 Intel Ireland

Intel was one of the first big computer technology firms to come to Ireland, in 1989. Intel makes microprocessors, also known as **microchips**, in Leixlip, Co. Kildare. Microchips are the brains of computers. Microchip manufacture is very complex.

The Intel campus at Leixlip is built on a **greenfield site**. The Leixlip plant is Intel's largest plant outside the USA and employs 4,500 people. Intel is one of Ireland's flagship companies. Its exports are very important to the Irish economy.

Inputs, processes and outputs in Intel

Inputs

- **Electricity** – the power source
- **Water** – purified
- **Silicon wafers** – on which the microchips are created
- **Labour** – highly qualified graduates in engineering and science
- **Cleanrooms** – where the microchip manufacture takes place
- **Air purification systems** – to purify the air and eliminate dust in the cleanrooms
- **Capital** – financial investment in new techniques and manufacturing to stay ahead of the competition.

Processes

- In the cleanroom, workers wear special clothing to prevent dust from the body and clothes from reaching the silicon wafers.
- Microchips such as Intel Core and Celeron are created in rows on the surface of silicon wafers. This involves about 300 manufacturing steps.
- Huge numbers of **transistors** or switches are created on the microchips. The active switching part of the transistors is less that 1/400 of the thickness of human hair.
- The microchips are then tested and packaged for markets abroad.

Outputs

- **Microchips** on silicon wafers
- **Waste water**, that is treated and released
- **Solvent wastes**, carefully disposed of through a certified waste contractor
- Waste products such as paper and packaging are **recycled**. New technologies are used to reduce waste in the plant.

Geo fact

Ireland is the second largest exporter of computers and **information technology** services in the world because of the presence of Intel and many others.

Definitions ✓

Information technology: The use of technology, especially computers, for storing and sending information.

Greenfield site: A site located in a rural area which had not been built on previously.

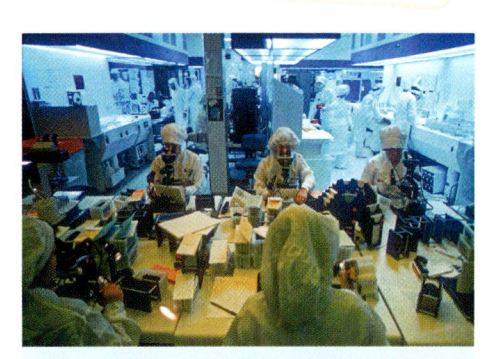

Intel workers oversee the industrial process in a cleanroom. The air in the Intel cleanroom is a thousand times cleaner than in a typical operating theatre in a hospital because all dust has to be removed

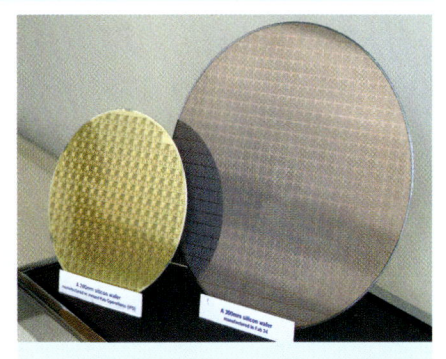

Silicon chips are manufactured on silicon wafers

361

Section 4 · Economic Geography

> ## Questions
>
> 1 Macroom is in which county?
> 2 What is the meaning of the expression 'light industry'?
> 3 Which of the following is **not** an input in Nutricia?
>   *Labour, baby formula foods, milk and whey, water*
> 4 Leixlip is in which Irish county?
> 5 What products are manufactured by Intel in Leixlip?

13.2 Factory location

> **KEYWORDS**
> - resource material
> - transport facilities
> - labour force
> - high-tech manufacturer
> - market location
> - multinational company
> - capital
> - the IDA
> - entrepreneurs
> - heavy industry
> - refinery

The location of a factory is based on a number of factors.

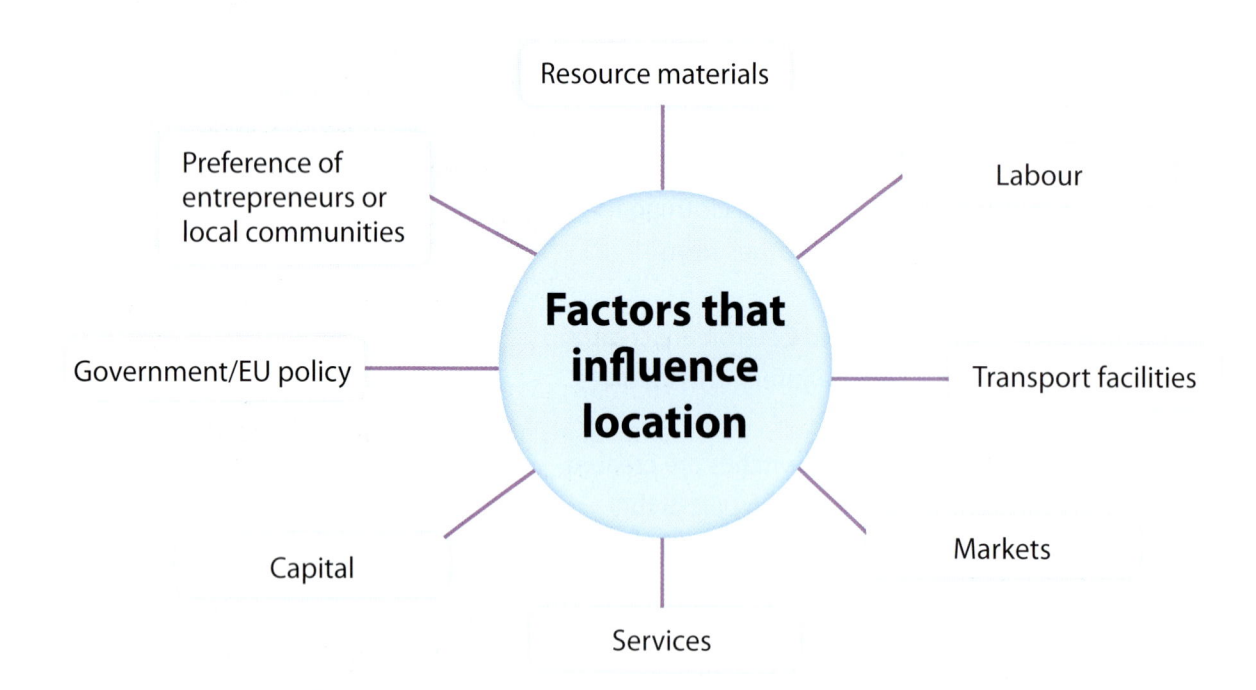

Factors that influence location:
- Resource materials
- Labour
- Transport facilities
- Markets
- Services
- Capital
- Government/EU policy
- Preference of entrepreneurs or local communities

We will now examine the **factors that influence location** in the case of two of Ireland's largest plants:

- **Intel Ireland** – a light industry – in Leixlip
- **RUSAL** – a heavy industry – in Aughinish Island in the Shannon Estuary.

Chapter 13 · Secondary Economic Activities

Case study

Intel Ireland, Leixlip – a light industry

Resource materials
- When resource materials are **small and light**, as in Intel, factories are **not tied to a resource location** because transport costs are low.

Intel is a **light industry** using light resource materials that include silicon wafers. These are mainly imported by air through Dublin Airport.

The Intel plant in Leixlip

Labour
- Every factory requires a **labour force:** the people who work there. Factories employ people with the **skills they need**.
- Large factories need a **pool of workers** who live reasonably close. Workers are more mobile today because most can afford cars.

Intel is a **high-tech manufacturer**. Therefore, it **needs highly educated workers**. Many Intel workers are graduates of universities in Dublin, Maynooth and elsewhere.

Intel is located in the residential town of **Leixlip**, which is close to Maynooth and Dublin's western suburbs. These areas provide the pool of workers the factory needs.

Transport facilities
- **Roads, rail, ports and airports** are vital to manufacturing plants for the transport of raw materials and finished products.
- Many manufacturing plants are built near **motorways**, dual carriageways and **ring roads** for easy access.

Intel is well served by transport networks. The **M4 motorway** is only two kilometres to the south. This is evident on the OS map on page 365. The M4 connects with the M50 and **Dublin Airport** – ideal for importing and exporting light materials.

Markets
- This is **where the goods are sold**.
- Some factories, such as bakeries, are located **close to the market** because the goods are perishable.
- However, where a product has a high value and low bulk, the factory can be **far from the market**.

Intel is a major **multinational company**. Its **market is global**: it supplies microchips to companies all over the world. Because microchips are high value and low bulk (very small), they can be made far from where they are sold.

Definition

Multinational company: A company that produces goods or services in one or more countries other than its home country.

continued on next page

363

Section 4 · Economic Geography

Case study

Services
- Factories need services, including **water**, high-voltage **electricity** and **telecommunications**.
- Telecommunications include telephone and high-speed **broadband** services. Ireland's telecom services meet international standards.

→ Water is taken from the nearby **Liffey** and purified for the Intel plant. Electricity is supplied to Intel by **Electric Ireland**.
Telecommunications are vital to the success of Intel. Intel managers can hold video-conferences with customers across the world using Ireland's telecom services.

Capital
- **Companies need capital** – the cash to buy land, build and equip a factory and get established.
- **Banks provide loans** to companies that have good prospects for growth.

→ Intel is a highly profitable global company. It invests huge sums in researching and developing next-generation microchips. The Leixlip plant has been upgraded and expanded over the years at huge capital cost by Intel itself.

Government/EU policy
- Governments use **tax incentives** on company profits to attract companies.
- Ireland's **low corporation tax** on company profits is meant to attract foreign companies to the country.
- The **IDA** is the agency that encourages companies to invest in Ireland.

→ Government policy was a **key reason** for the location of Intel's Leixlip plant. The Irish government, through the IDA, actively supported the establishment of Intel in Leixlip in 1989 with **grants** and **tax incentives**.

Definition
IDA: The Industrial Development Authority.

Preferences of entrepreneurs and local communities
- Local communities welcome companies that do not pollute the **environment**.
- However, they may object to plants that present **health and safety risks**, e.g. incineration plants.

Figure 13.3 Leixlip, Co. Kildare

→ The Leixlip plant is located on a pleasant **greenfield site**, a former stud farm. Intel was welcomed by local communities as the plant is a modern, clean facility without emissions into the atmosphere. It is also a very large employer.

Geo fact
A microchip plant must be built in an area where the rock is stable. Ireland is an ideal location as it is free from earthquakes.

Chapter 13 · Secondary Economic Activities

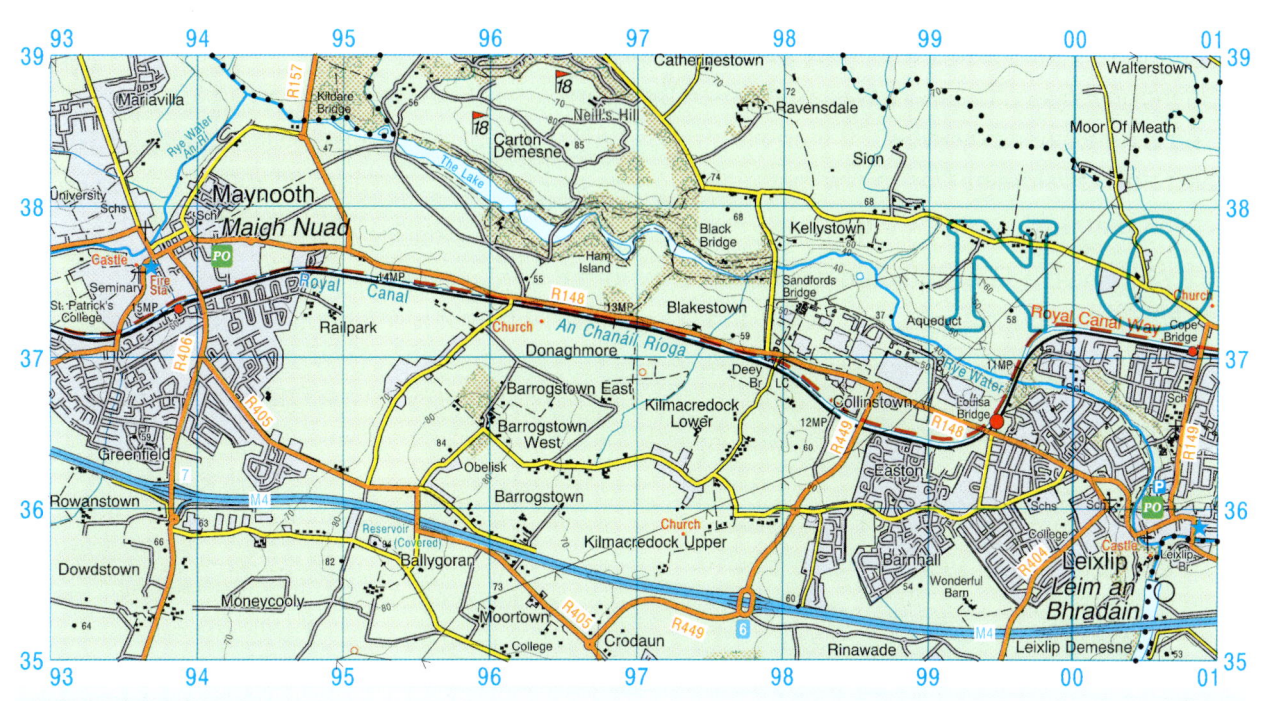

Case study

Figure 13.4 OS map of Leixlip and Maynooth, Co. Kildare

Questions

Study the OS map above and answer the following questions:

1. The Intel plant is well served by road and rail. What evidence on the OS map supports this statement?

2. What evidence in the OS map suggests that many of Intel's workers may live in Maynooth and Leixlip?

3. An energy source, visible on the OS map, runs close to the Intel plant. What is it?

4. Draw a sketch map of the area shown in the OS map, and include the following:
   - The M4 and the R148
   - The Intel plant
   - The ESB power line
   - The built-up area of the town of Leixlip.

365

Section 4 · Economic Geography

Case study

RUSAL Aughinish – a heavy industry

RUSAL Aughinish is located on Aughinish Island, in the Shannon Estuary. The plant was established by Alcan and is now owned by RUSAL. It is an **alumina refinery** and extracts alumina from a raw material called **bauxite**.

> **Definition**
> **Heavy industry:** Manufacturing that is heavy both in the raw material used and the product that it makes. Examples include iron and steel smelting and cement manufacture.

Alumina is a **semi-finished product**. It is exported to European countries such as the UK and Scandinavia, where it is smelted into **aluminium**.

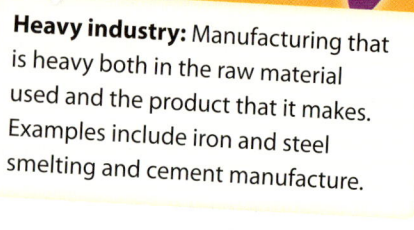

Figure 13.5 The Shannon Estuary

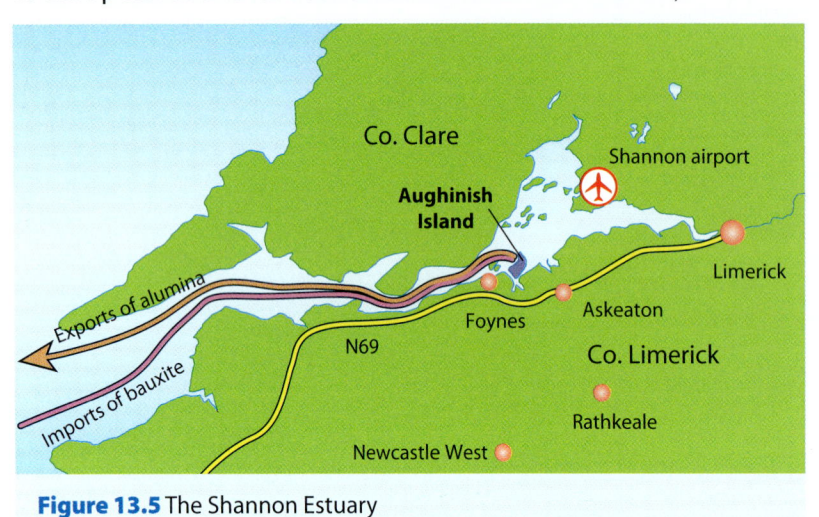

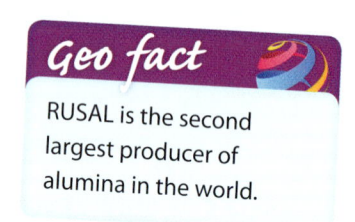

> **Geo fact**
> RUSAL is the second largest producer of alumina in the world.

Why is the refinery located in Aughinish?

The most important factors for the location of Aughinish are:

1. **The source of raw material:** Bauxite comes mainly from Guinea in West Africa and from Brazil by ship. Therefore, the refinery needs to be located on the coast.

2. **Transport:** The Shannon Estuary is a deep-water estuary. Large ships, known as **bulk carriers**, can bring the bauxite ore to the jetty, where it is unloaded. The end product – alumina – is re-exported.

3. **The site of Aughinish Island:** This is a very large site of almost 4 km². The site is large enough to store the waste material – an inert mud – on the western side of the island.

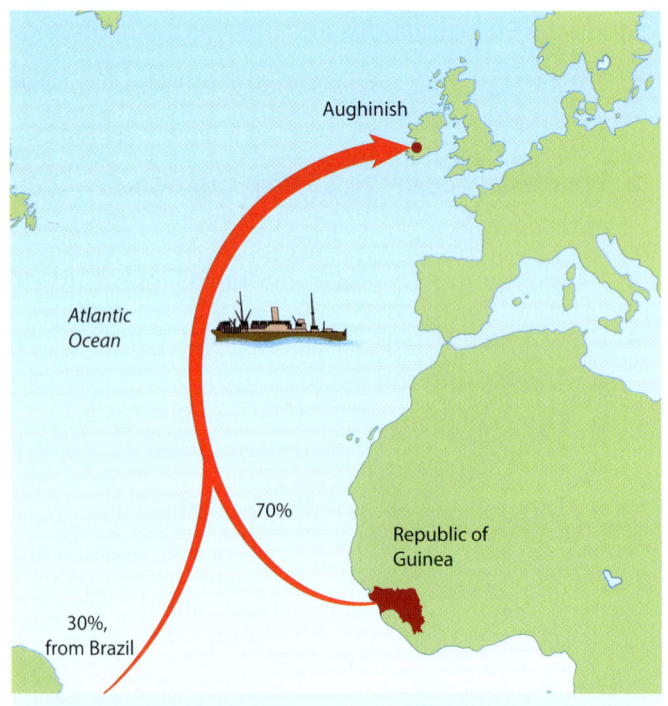

Figure 13.6 Transport of bauxite from the Republic of Guinea, West Africa, and from Brazil, to Aughinish, Co. Limerick

Chapter 13 · Secondary Economic Activities

Case study

4 **Government policy:** The Irish government sees the Shannon Estuary as a great resource. **Shannon Development** actively worked to encourage heavy industry to the estuary. The alumina refinery is one of the results of government policy for the estuary.

5 **Labour force:** The company employs 450 workers directly. This is a huge boost to the local economy. Workers come from Foynes, Askeaton, Newcastle West and elsewhere. Several sub-contractors also work for RUSAL.

Geo fact

RUSAL Aughinish is the largest manufacturing site in the Republic of Ireland.

Bauxite

The RUSAL refinery plant in Aughinish, Co. Limerick

Table 13.1 RUSAL Aughinish as a system

Inputs	Processes	Outputs
Bauxite + soda + lime Labour Electricity Water	The alumina is extracted from the bauxite by: • Crushing the ore • Mixing the raw materials • Digesting the materials • Drying the alumina.	Alumina Mud waste

367

Section 4 · Economic Geography

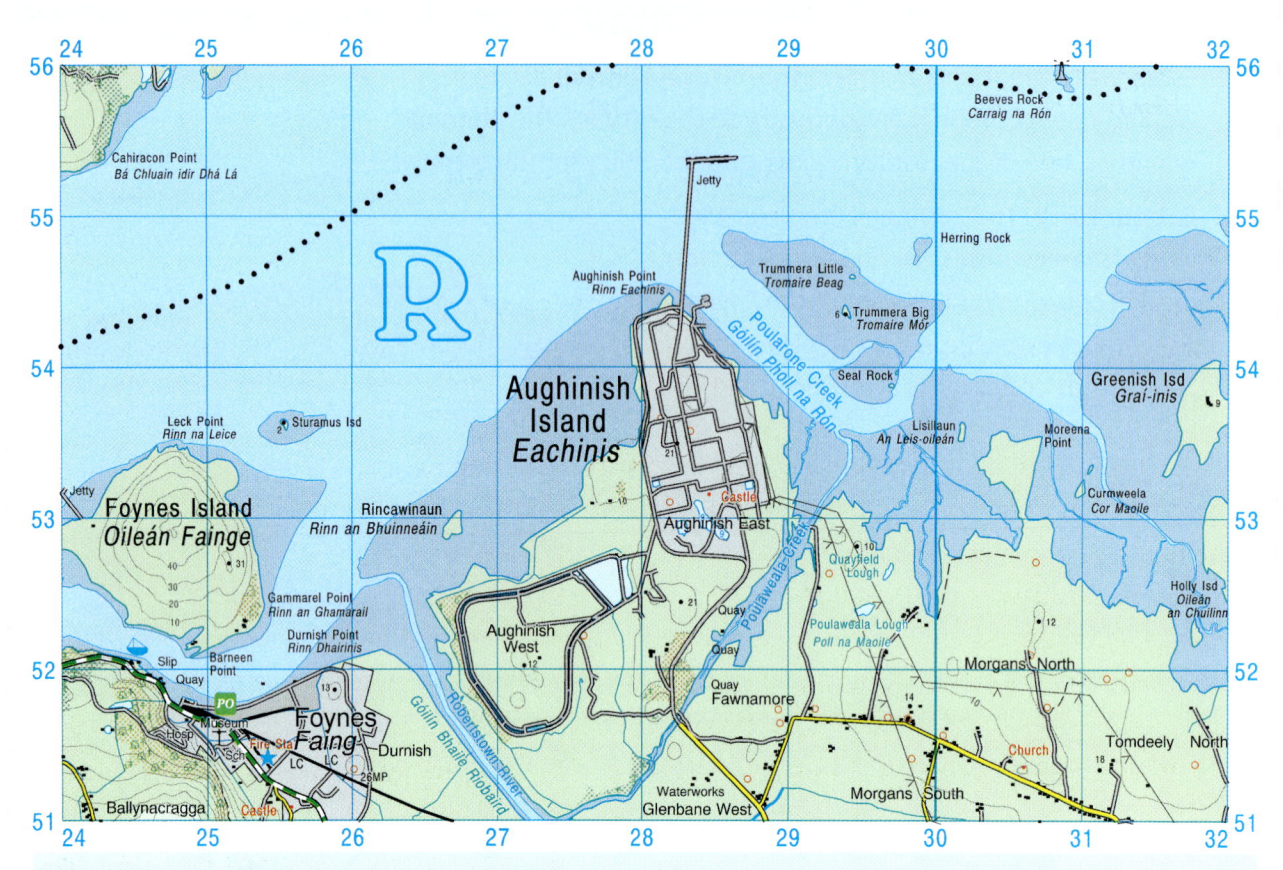

Case study

Figure 13.7 OS map of Auginish, Co. Limerick

Questions

Study the OS map of Aughinish and answer the following questions:

1. What is the approximate size of Aughinish island in km^2?
2. Why, do you think, does the jetty extend northwards from the island?
3. Name the power source that enters the island at R 290 531?
4. Aughinish Island is low-lying. What evidence on the map supports that statement?
5. On a sketch map of the area shown on the map, include the following:
   - The mainland coast
   - Aughinish Island and the jetty
   - Foynes
   - The site of the industrial plant on the island.

13.3 Footloose industry

KEYWORDS
- footloose industry
- Industrial Revolution
- coalfield site
- industrial estate

Modern industry, unlike industry in the past, tends to be '**footloose**'.

Definition ✓
Footloose industry: Manufacturing business that is not tied to one location.

Industry in the past

The **Industrial Revolution** began in the 1780s in Britain. The major industries of the Industrial Revolution were iron and steel, textiles and heavy engineering.

Coalfield sites

- **Heavy industries**, such as the iron and steel industry, were **tied to coalfield sites** in Britain, Belgium, France and Germany. This was because **coal was the energy source** for smelting iron and steel.
- The **textile industry** was also tied to coalfields because textile machinery used **steam power**. Water was turned into steam by burning coal.
- Manufacturing in Britain, Belgium, France and Germany has not been tied to coalfields for many decades. This is because **coal is no longer the only source of energy** that powers factories.

Earlier manufacturing sites in Ireland

Ireland had little or no coal. Therefore, **water power** on rivers was used to power small flour and textile mills along rivers throughout the country.

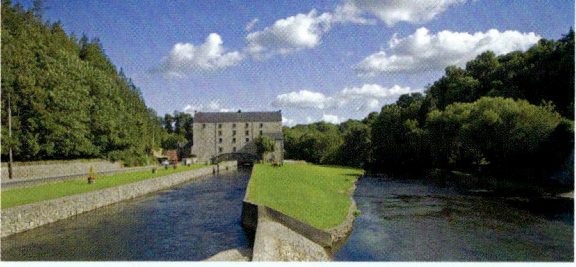

A water mill in Castletownroche, Co. Cork – a relic of manufacturing in nineteenth-century Ireland

Modern footloose industry

Many manufacturing industries are footloose today. Why is this?

Why are modern industries footloose?

Industrial estates are widely dispersed both in Ireland and abroad. In Ireland, the IDA has encouraged many companies to set up light industry in small towns.

Ring roads around cities such as Dublin, Cork, Limerick and Galway attract footloose manufacturing industry.

The workforce today is generally car-owning. This allows factories in small towns to draw its workforce from rural areas.

Electricity is widely available. Electricity is the main source of energy for manufacturing today.

Excellent transport on national road and rail routes allows the transport of resource materials to factories in many locations.

Light industry products – high in value and low in weight – can be distributed cheaply to markets.

Section 4 · Economic Geography

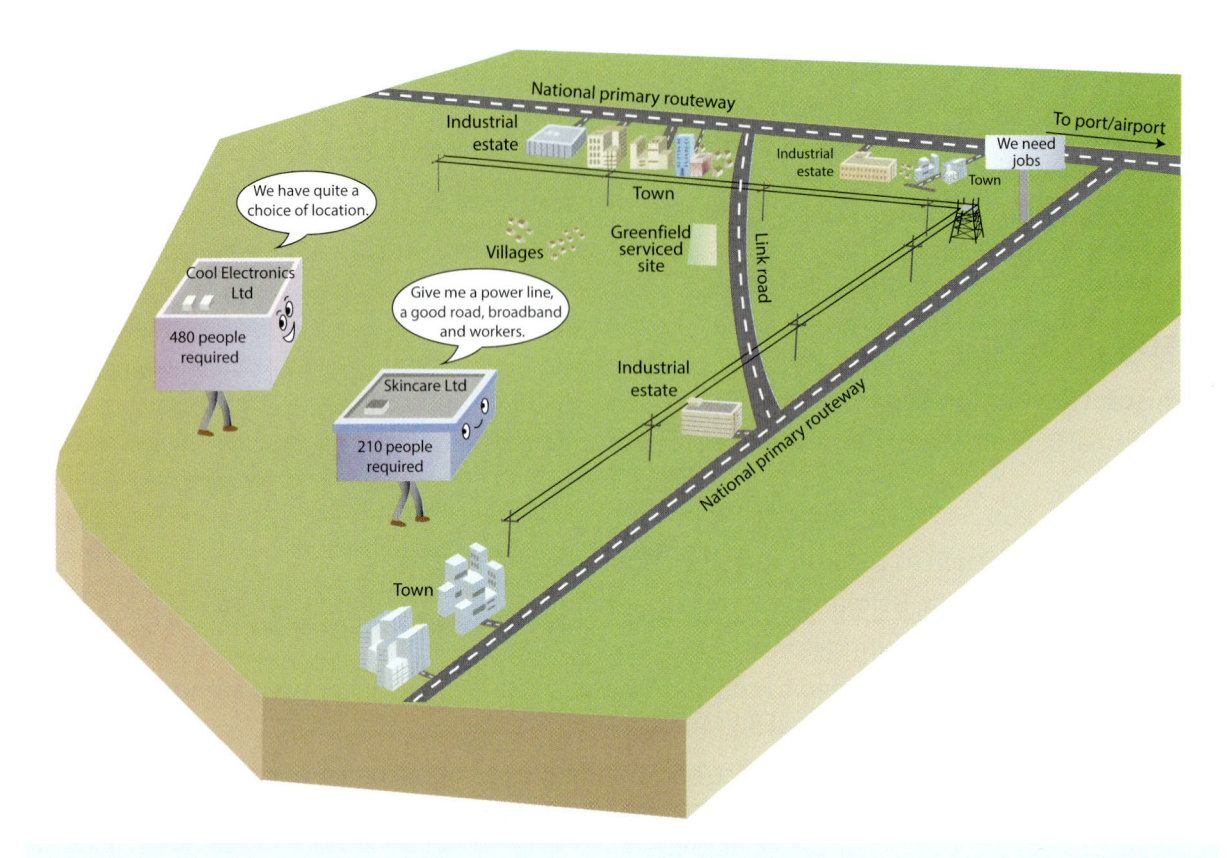

Figure 13.8 The needs of footloose industry can be met in many different locations

Industrial estates

Industrial estates attract footloose industries and offer many advantages to industrialists:

- Industrial estates are on land zoned for manufacturing, usually at the edge of towns and cities where **large and cheaper sites** are available.
- **Transport facilities** into the industrial estate are very good.
- **Services** – electricity, water and telecommunications – are laid on by service providers.
- Manufacturers can often purchase inputs and components from **other manufacturers in the same estate**.

Shannon Industrial Estate, Shannon, Co. Clare

> ### Questions
>
> 1. Why was manufacturing industry tied to coalfields in the past?
> 2. Explain the term 'footloose industry'.
> 3. Explain **two** reasons why many modern manufacturing industries are footloose.
> 4. RUSAL Aughinish is **not** a footloose industry. Can you explain why it is not?

13.4 Industrial location: change over time

> **KEYWORDS**
> - industrial decline
> - industrialisation
> - industrial inertia
> - charcoal
> - iron ore
> - coal
> - coalfield
> - relocate
> - niche product

Over the course of time, the **factors that influence the location of factories change in importance**.

- This can change the **distribution** of manufacturing industry.
- Some areas may suffer from **industrial decline**.
- Other areas may see the growth of industry, or **industrialisation**.
- However, in some cases an industry does not relocate, even though there are good economic reasons to do so. This is called **industrial inertia**.

The history of the **British iron and steel industry** shows how some of these changes can work themselves out.

The British iron and steel industry is to be studied by Higher Level students only.

The British iron and steel industry

Early eighteenth century

Iron-making furnaces used **charcoal from forests** to smelt **iron ore**. As transport was very poor, ironworks were located where the **resources** – iron ore and forests – were found. But forests were quickly cut down. Therefore, the industry **relocated** to take advantage of a new energy source – **coal**.

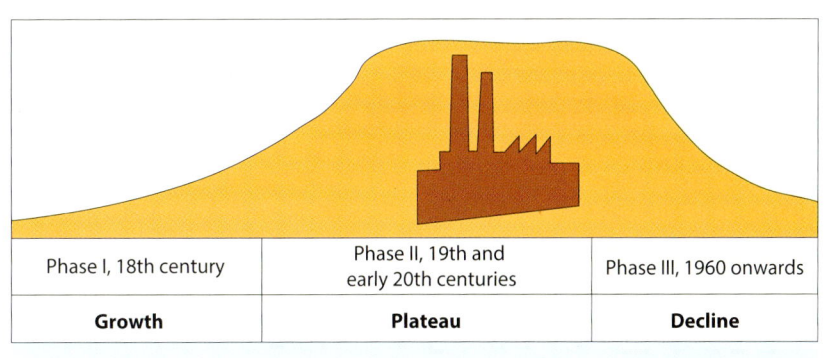

Phase I, 18th century	Phase II, 19th and early 20th centuries	Phase III, 1960 onwards
Growth	Plateau	Decline

Figure 13.9 Growth, plateau and decline in the British iron and steel industry

> **Link**
>
> You learn about the growth of the British iron and steel industry in your **Junior Cert. History course**. You also learn about the terrible conditions in the coal mines, where women and children worked as well as men.

371

Section 4 · Economic Geography

The nineteenth century

At the end of the eighteenth century, during the Industrial Revolution, the **demand for iron and steel** was very high.

- Ironworks were located **on or close to coalfields**.
- **Canals**, and later **railways**, carried iron ore to the iron and steel works.

The coalfields remained the main location for iron and steel smelting until the second half of the twentieth century.

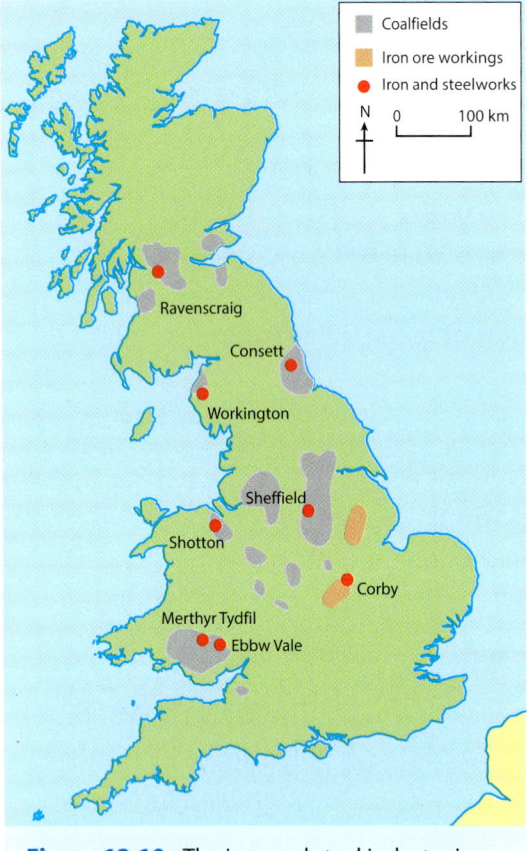

Figure 13.10a The iron and steel industry in Britain in the 1950s

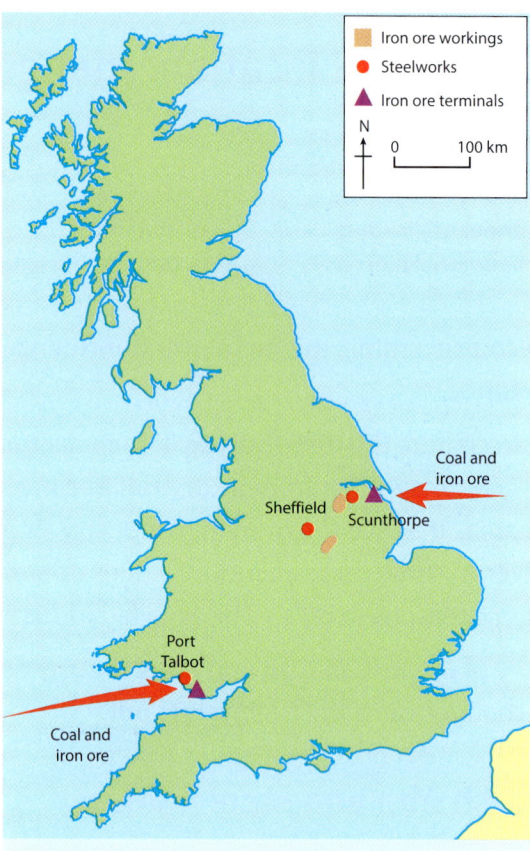

Figure 13.10b The iron and steel industry in Britain today

Decline: 1960 onwards

The British iron and steel industry declined after 1960 for the following reasons:

- **Coalfields were exhausted** after generations of mining.
- **New processes** required far less coal to smelt iron and steel. Therefore, coalfields lost their importance as locations of iron and steel works.
- **Foreign steelmakers** in Germany and Japan were producing cheaper steel than British producers. Demand for British-made steel declined. British steel companies began to lose money.

The **coast** of Britain became a more attractive location for steel plants. Iron ore and cheap Polish coal could be imported to coastal steel plants.

As a result, **inland steel plants closed** with great job losses. For instance, the **Corby** steel plant closed in 1980 with the loss of 5,000 jobs in a single day.

Geo fact
The steel plant at Redcar in north-east England was closed in October 2015 because of the decline in the global demand for steel.

Geo fact
Employment in the British steel industry has declined by more than 80 per cent in fifty years.

Industrial inertia in Sheffield

Most of the inland iron and steel plants in Britain have closed down. The iron and steel industry has **relocated** to the coast. However, Sheffield has continued as a steel producer.

As a result of all these factors, Sheffield steel has survived into the twenty-first century.

Steelmaking in Sheffield in 2015. Here we see heavy equipment being used to lift a freshly made cylinder of steel

Why is there industrial inertia in Sheffield?

- The steel smelters of Sheffield have been **modernised** to make them more efficient. In this way, they can **compete in price** with imported steel.
- Sheffield cutlery is famous for its **good quality**. Today, it also specialises in **niche products** such as surgical instruments.
- Sheffield has a **highly skilled workforce** that has a long and proud tradition of steelmaking.
- Sheffield has excellent **road and rail connections** to its customers.

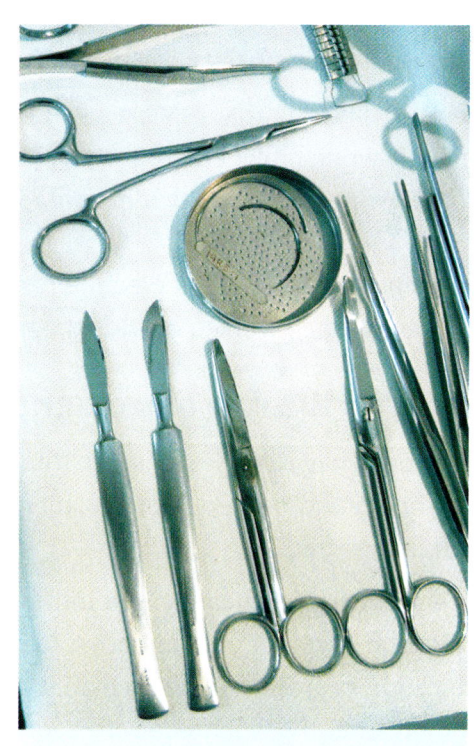

Surgical instruments are manufactured in Sheffield

> **Definition** ✓
>
> **Niche product:** A good manufactured for a particular use, e.g. surgical instruments used in hospitals.

Questions

1. Why was heavy industry such as iron and steel smelting anchored to coalfields during the Industrial Revolution?
2. Explain **two** reasons for the sharp decline in the British iron and steel industry after 1960.
3. Explain the term 'industrial inertia'.
4. Give **three** reasons for the survival of the steel industry in Sheffield.

Section 4 · Economic Geography

13.5 The role of women in industry

> **KEYWORDS**
> - traditional role
> - gender equality
> - Women's Liberation movement
> - career break
> - Export Processing Zone

The **role of women** within industry has changed in both developed and developing countries.

Women in the workforce in Ireland: a developed country

One hundred years ago, women's roles in Ireland were very different from those of today. At that time, Ireland, apart from north-east Ulster, was an **agricultural society**.

- Many women's marriages were arranged.
- Very few women owned property.
- Women were tied to the **traditional roles** of wife and mother.
- Women in general did not plan their families.
- Very few women worked outside the home.

Women in a traditional role in Ireland in the past

Changes in the role of women

Women today have lifestyles that are totally different from the lives of their grandmothers. Many women work outside the home.
What has changed?

- **Free secondary education** was introduced in 1967. This increased education levels for girls and boys. Today, women enter third-level education in greater numbers than men. Many women enter the workforce with degrees in law, business and architecture.
- **The Women's Liberation movement** of the 1970s – an international movement – led to many changes in the status of women.
- **Gender equality laws** gave women equal pay and equal status for equal work in the job market.
- **Crèches** allow mothers to go to work.

Geo fact
In 1918, women of 30 years and upwards were given the vote in Ireland for the first time.

A crèche worker doing a jigsaw with two children. Crèches are very important for mothers who work outside the home

Chapter 13 · Secondary Economic Activities

- Many women choose to work outside the home for **personal** and **economic reasons**.
- The great increase in the **cost of homes** means that in many homes both partners have to work to pay the mortgage.
- Mothers today have, on average, two children each. Therefore, women are **less tied to motherhood** and home-making.

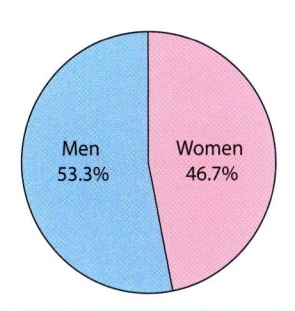

Figure 13.11 Ireland's workforce in 2015

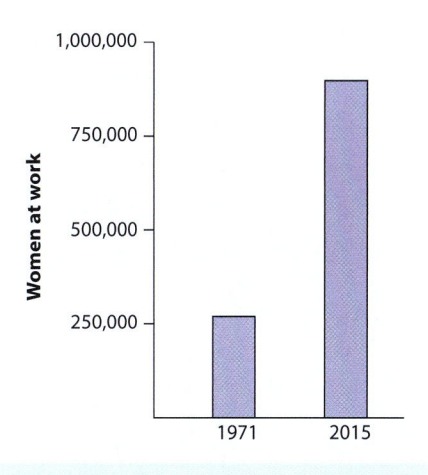

Men 53.3% | Women 46.7%

Figure 13.12 The number of women at work in Ireland has increased enormously in recent decades

Geo fact
Women in Ireland were paid almost 14 per cent less than men in 2014, even though women do better at school and university than men.

The work/life balance

Many women find it difficult to balance the demands of work and home. Therefore, some women do not seek promotion to senior positions. Some also choose to work **part time** or to take **career breaks** to raise their families.

Family-friendly policies are essential for workers today

Geo fact
Women made up 22 per cent of TDs in the Dáil after the February 2016 election, compared to 15 per cent after the 2011 election.

Women find promotion in the workforce difficult. Explain two obstacles to women's promotion

375

Section 4 · Economic Geography

Women in the labour market in China: a developing country

When the Communist Party took over China in 1949, the **economy was agricultural**. In rural areas women's lives were very difficult. As well as being wives and mothers they also worked in the fields. They had **large families** before the one-child policy was introduced in 1979.

> Women in the labour market in China is for Higher Level students only.

Industrialisation

China has experienced great change in recent years. Since 1980, the country has industrialised very rapidly. Companies from abroad have established factories in **Export Processing Zones** along the east coast. Many other companies, including American companies, hire Chinese sub-contractors in China to produce goods to order.

China: the workshop of the world today

China has now become the **workshop of the world**, producing many of the goods that teenagers in wealthy countries buy. Millions of Chinese women work in these factories. They often fill orders for Western companies.

> **Geo fact**
> 45 per cent of Chinese workers are female.

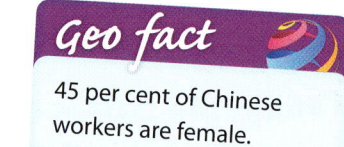

Figure 13.13 Chinese-made goods are worn by teenagers in Ireland today. Check the labels on your own clothes

Women at work in a garment factory. Describe what you see in this picture

Women's working conditions

China is a very big country and work practices vary throughout the country. However, the following statements can be made:

- Millions of female workers are **recent migrants from the countryside** who have come to the coastal cities to seek work.
- Women do **not belong to independent trade unions**. These do not exist in China.
- Millions of women work at **dull, monotonous and repetitive tasks** all day every day, sewing garments, stitching handbags and making shoes for Western companies.
- Women have 90 days' paid **maternity leave**.
- **Wages** are rising in China, but they are **very low** by Western standards.
- As in many countries, **women's wages are lower** than men's.
- Women are often obliged to do **overtime** to fill orders.
- Millions of women workers live far from home with little privacy in **crowded dormitories** that are attached to the factories.

Apartment blocks in Shenzhen, China, an industrial city that has grown hugely in recent decades. This is an example of a concrete jungle. What do you think is the meaning of the term 'concrete jungle'?

Geo fact

The minimum wage in Shanghai in 2014 rose to €293 per month – the highest in mainland China.

Life in China

Life in China has its challenges:

- The east coast is very crowded.
- Air quality in cities is poor.
- Rivers are very polluted.
- People do not enjoy the freedoms that we in the West take for granted.

A classroom in China. Girls receive the same schooling as boys

Nevertheless, since 1949 women's lives have changed greatly. Almost all girls in China are enrolled at school. Life expectancy for women has more than doubled to 77 years, which is very close to European levels.

Questions

1. 'Women were tied to traditional roles in Ireland in the early decades of the twentieth century.' Explain that statement.
2. Explain **three** reasons for the great increase in the number of women who work outside the home in recent decades.
3. Explain **two** challenges that face women who work outside the home in Ireland today.
4. Can you suggest **two** reasons for the great increase in life expectancy for women in China in recent decades. (You may need to look at pages 253–55.)
5. Explain **two** challenges that female workers in Chinese factories face.

Section 4 · Economic Geography

13.6 Manufacturing on a world scale

KEYWORDS
- newly industrialised country
- industrially emergent region
- Latin America
- labour costs

Across the world, countries and regions can be classified as **industrialised**, **newly industrialised** or **industrially emergent**.

Industrialised regions

The industrialised regions are the **wealthy, developed countries** of the North (see pages 251–52). The Industrial Revolution began in Britain about 1780 and spread to other European countries. By 1900, the USA and Japan were rapidly industrialising.

Today, Western Europe, the USA, Japan and, in recent years, China, dominate world manufacturing. However, other regions are catching up. This is partly because multinationals are transferring their factories to Asia and **Latin America**. **Labour costs** are cheaper in those regions.

Silicon Valley, California, where high-tech manufacturing companies develop new technologies for worldwide sales

Definition

Latin America: The region spreading from Mexico south to Chile and Argentina.

Newly industrialised countries

Newly industrialised countries are countries in the South (the developing world) that have been manufacturing goods for export to the North for several decades. They include Asian countries such as Taiwan, Singapore and China.

Some Latin American countries, such as **Mexico, Brazil and Argentina**, are industrialising quickly also.

Geo fact

South Africa is Africa's most industrialised country.

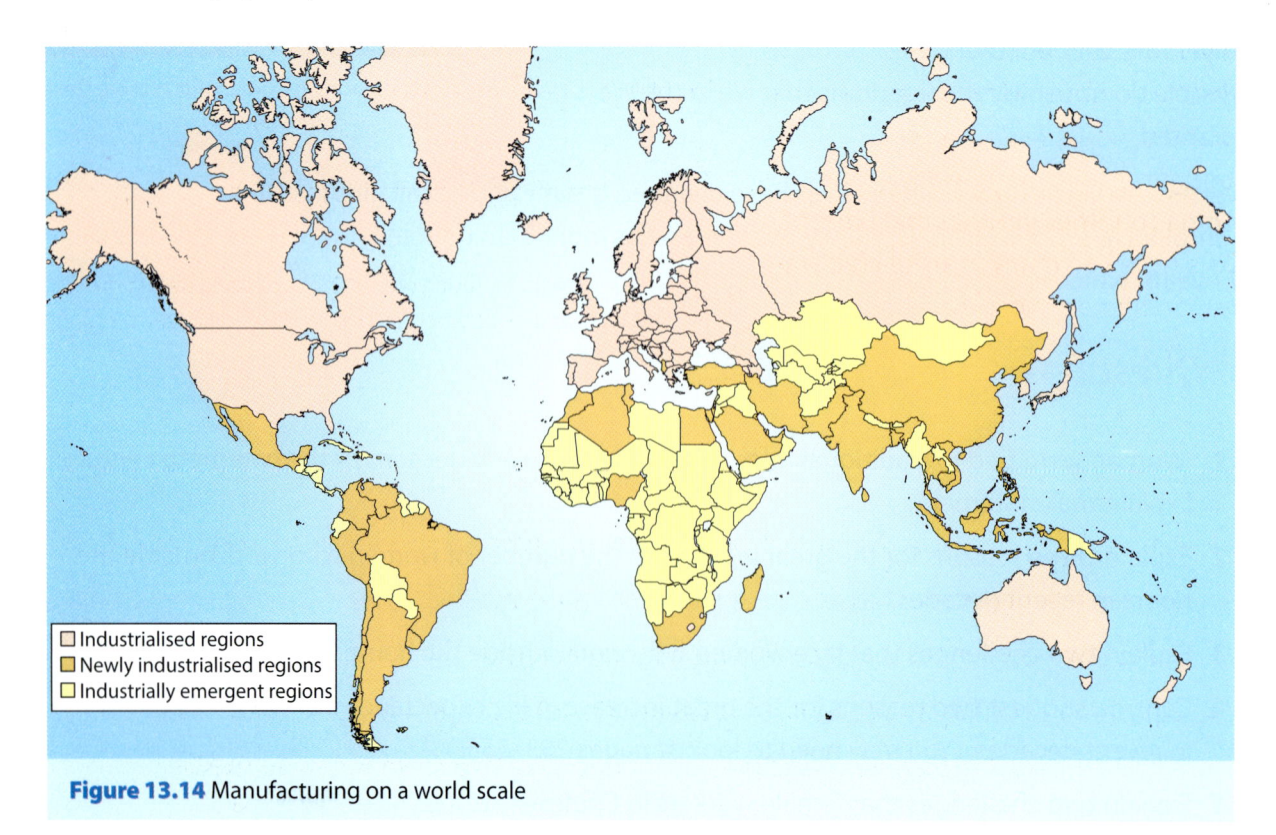

- Industrialised regions
- Newly industrialised regions
- Industrially emergent regions

Figure 13.14 Manufacturing on a world scale

378

Low labour costs

Asia's newly industrialised countries are attractive to multinationals from the USA and Japan because of their **low labour costs**. Manufacturing brings jobs and a rising standard of living to these countries.

Vietnam, Indonesia and Bangladesh are now targets of multinationals because their labour costs are lower than China's.

Geo fact

In 2010, 75 per cent of the skyscrapers being built in the world were in China.

Algae on a beach in Qingdao, north-eastern China. The Chinese people and the environment are paying a heavy price for their rapid development

Industrially emergent regions

Industrially emergent regions have little or no modern manufacturing. **Most of Africa, parts of Asia and parts of South America** are in this position.

Reasons for this include the following:

- **Poor services** such as a lack of electricity and water supplies
- **Badly developed transport systems** such as poor-quality roads and bridges
- Some countries in Africa and parts of Asia have had many years of **civil war**. Multinationals avoid these regions as a result.

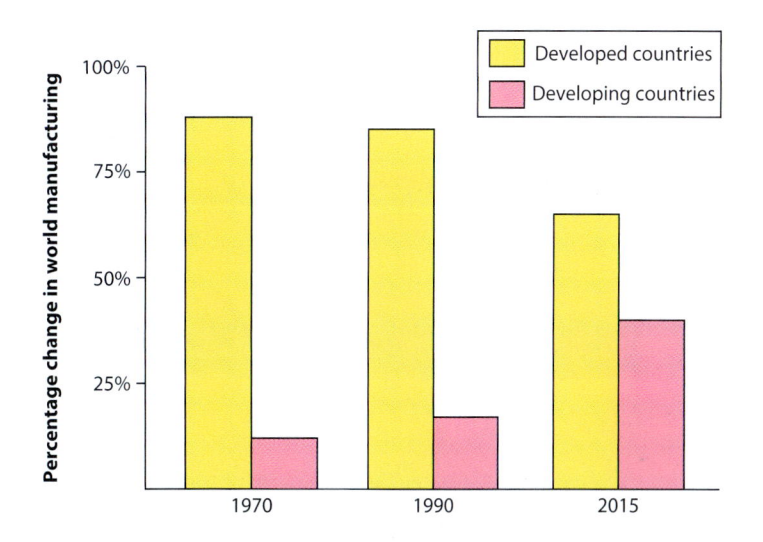

Figure 13.15 Manufacturing output in the developed and the developing world for selected years. Output in the developing world is increasing

Questions

1. Can you name **three** of the most important manufacturing countries in the world today?
2. Describe clearly where the Latin American region is located.
3. Name **two** newly industrialised countries in Latin America.
4. Explain **one** positive and **one** negative result of rapid industrialisation in China.
5. What is the least industrially developed continent? Give **two** reasons for your answer.

Section 4 · Economic Geography

13.7 The impact of industrial activity on the environment

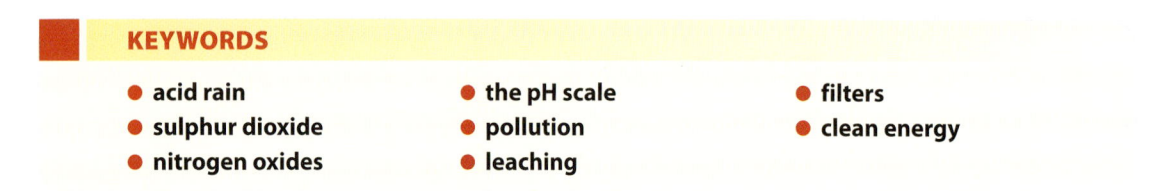

KEYWORDS
- acid rain
- sulphur dioxide
- nitrogen oxides
- the pH scale
- pollution
- leaching
- filters
- clean energy

Industrial activity may have important impacts on **agriculture**, **forestry**, **tourism** and the **quality of life**.

Acid rain

Acid rain is a mixture of water and gases such as **sulphur dioxide** and **nitrogen oxides**. Water in the atmosphere that is not contaminated has a pH of about 5.6. Acid rain has a **pH below 4.3**. Acid rain can be as acidic as lemon juice or vinegar.

The sources of acid rain

Power stations that burn fossil fuels, along with **smelters**, are major sources of acid rain. **Coal** and vehicle engines release harmful gases into the atmosphere. These gases include sulphur dioxide and nitrogen oxides. They combine with water vapour to fall to earth as acid rain.

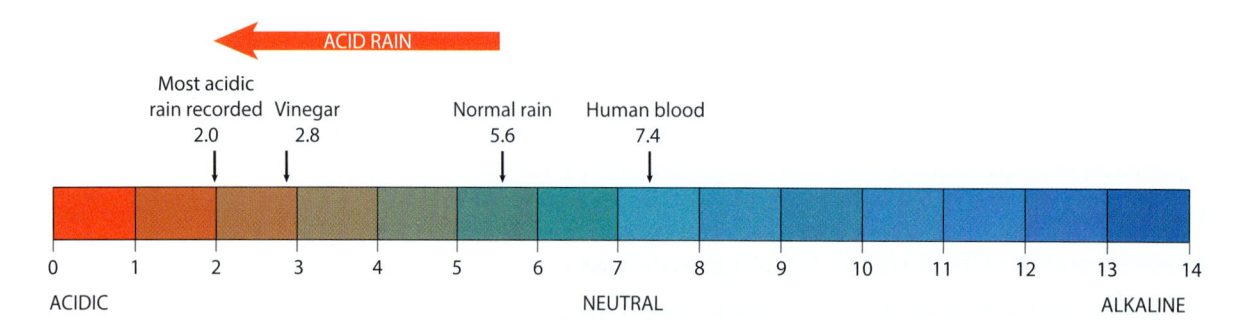

ACID RAIN

Most acidic rain recorded 2.0
Vinegar 2.8
Normal rain 5.6
Human blood 7.4

0 1 2 3 4 5 6 7 8 9 10 11 12 13 14
ACIDIC   NEUTRAL   ALKALINE

Figure 13.16 Acid rain on the pH scale

The role of the wind

Since the 1970s, power stations have had tall **smokestacks** to release gases high into the air. This was because it was believed that **dilution** was the **solution to pollution**. It was thought that if gases were dispersed by the wind over a wide area, they would be less harmful.

Unfortunately, diluting harmful gases was **not** the solution to pollution. Europe has so many power stations that millions of tonnes of gases are carried from one country to another. Thus, Swedish lakes and forests are damaged by acid rain from Britain and Central Europe.

Traffic on the motorway in the Rhinelands, Germany

380

Chapter 13 · Secondary Economic Activities

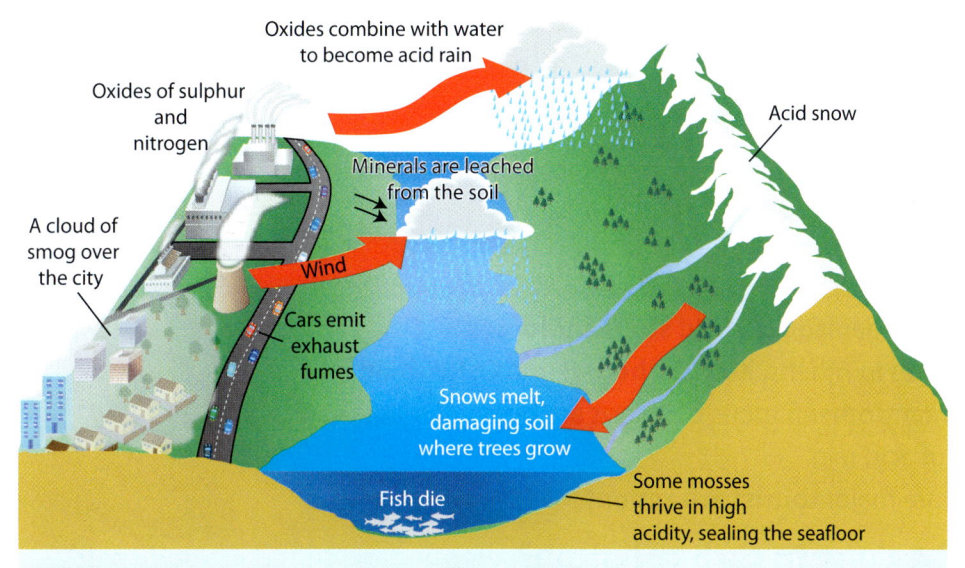

Figure 13.17 Acid rain falls over forests, lakes and farms and damages the natural world

The damage caused by acid rain

Forests

- Acid rain **leaches** or washes away **nutrients** from the soil.
- **Trees weaken** because of a lack of nutrients.
- Acid rain also **damages the foliage** of trees. Damaged and weakened trees die from **diseases** and attacks by **parasites**.

Fish life in lakes

- Rivers carry acidic rainwater and meltwaters from **acid snow** into lakes.
- **Fish eggs are damaged** when the pH falls below 4.3 in lakes.
- Fish no longer hatch and **fish life disappears** from lakes.
- Many lakes, especially in Sweden, are **biologically dead**.

Trees in many parts of Europe are ill and dying

Quality of life

- Acid rain also affects the **quality of water supplies** that come from lakes.
- The concentration of **metals** in lakes rises because they are washed out of the soil by acid rain.
- The polluted water can affect **human health**, especially the health of infants.

Activity

Examine Figure 13.18.
Name three countries in Europe where forests are severely damaged.

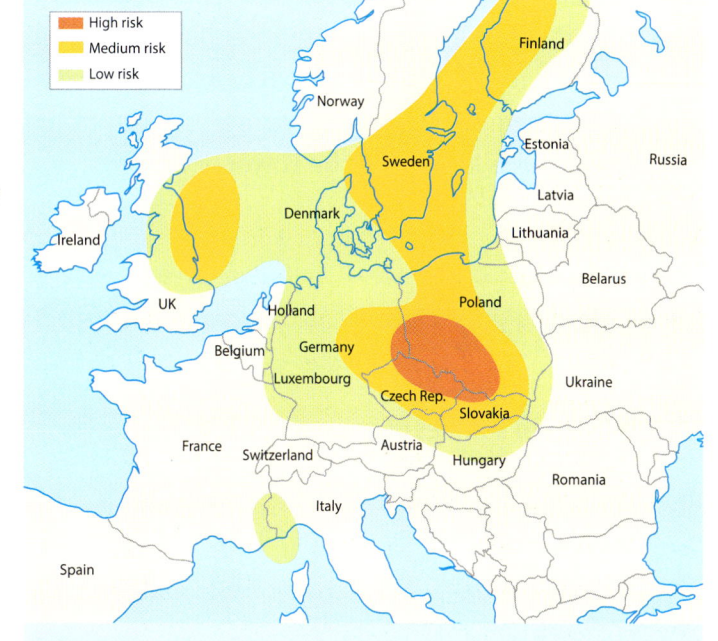

Figure 13.18 The effects of acid rain on forested areas of Europe

381

Section 4 • Economic Geography

Agriculture
- **Minerals** and **trace elements** in soil, such as copper and calcium, are **washed out** of soil by acid rain.
- Soil loses its fertility. Farmers have to replace these lost minerals with expensive **fertiliser**.

Historic buildings
- Acid rain is very damaging to **old stone buildings**.
- The **Parthenon** in Athens, **Köln Cathedral**, the **Colosseum** in Rome and many other famous buildings are being damaged by the effects of acid rain.
- These sites are major **tourist attractions**.

What can be done to curb pollution?
- Coal-fired power stations are gradually being replaced by modern power stations that use **natural gas**. Natural gas releases carbon dioxide only.
- Smokestacks in existing coal-fired power stations are being fitted with **filters** to reduce emissions of sulphur dioxide.
- **Car engines** release far fewer toxic emissions today than in 1990. However, the continued increase in car numbers means that nitrogen oxide levels are still rising.
- **Clean energy** sources, such as **solar and wind energy**, need to be developed. Denmark is a leader in wind energy. Spain and Germany lead the way in solar energy.
- People must be persuaded to **use cars less**. Efficient public transport can help people to reduce their acid rain footprint.
- People can reduce their **personal use of electricity** in the home to decrease the output of harmful gases from power stations. This is known as 'The Power of One'.

Reims Cathedral in France – badly damaged by acid rain

Solar panels on the roof of farm buildings in Bavaria, Germany. These panels generate electricity

Geo fact
On 9 June 2014, a very sunny day, Germany produced 50.6 per cent of its total electricity needs from solar power.

Geo fact
France produces more than 75 per cent of its electricity from **nuclear power**, an energy source that releases no acid rain.

Questions

1. Give **two** sources of acid rain.
2. How can polluting gases from one country lead to acid rain in a neighbouring country?
3. Explain how fish life declines in lakes that are affected by acid rain and acid snow.
4. Explain **three** changes that you can make in your daily life to reduce your personal use of energy.

13.8 Conflicts of interest

KEYWORDS

- wind turbine
- wind farm
- incineration
- throw-away society
- waste-to-energy
- landfill

Conflicts of interest may arise between industrialists and others. We will look at two conflict areas that can arise between industrialists and others:

1 The wind turbine controversy   2 The incineration controversy.

Case study

1 The wind turbine controversy in Ireland

Everyone who travels by car across the countryside today is aware that the number of **wind turbines** in Ireland is growing quickly. However, **wind farms** have aroused a lot of controversy. Many people find the idea of wind farms difficult to cope with, especially if wind farms are located near their homes.

Some of the arguments on both sides of the debate are presented below in Table 13.2.

A wind turbine farm in Co. Kerry

Geo fact
During the first three months of 2015, wind energy generated 27 per cent of the Republic of Ireland's electricity needs.

Geo fact
There were 195 wind farms in Ireland in 2015.

Activity
Can you think of any arguments that are not mentioned here?

Table 13.2 Arguments for and against wind farms

In favour of wind farms	Against wind farms
• The **wind comes free**. Wind is a natural resource because it is blowing in many parts of Ireland most of the time. It is a **renewable resource**. • Wind farms will **reduce our dependence on imported energy** such as oil from the Persian Gulf and Russia's gas fields. • Wind energy is completely **clean**, unlike fossil fuels which produce gases that damage our health and contribute to global warming. • Most advanced countries in the EU are developing wind energy. Wind is the way to go. • Building and maintaining wind farms provides **employment**, especially in poorer rural areas. • We are going to run out of oil and gas in time. **We must develop new sources of energy**. Wind is a far better option than nuclear energy.	• Wind turbines today are far too big. They cause **visual pollution**. They change the landscape. • The **whirring noise** of the blades and the shadows that they cast upset some people. An area loses its peace and quiet. • We are constantly finding new oil and gas supplies all over the world. We will not run out of fossil fuels any time soon. • Wind is **unreliable**. There are calm days and nights. Electricity stations running on oil and gas are needed as a back-up at those times. • Wind turbines should be built **offshore** if they are to be built at all. • Wind turbines may reduce the **value of property** in the area.

The arguments continue on both sides. However, the number of turbines continues to grow in Ireland.

Section 4 · Economic Geography

Case study

2 Incineration in Poolbeg, Dublin Bay

Because of our **throw-away society**, we are waste-makers. Each of us produces three quarters of a tonne of municipal **waste** every year. This waste has to be managed. **Incineration** is one option.

Incineration has caused huge controversy in Ireland, especially in Dublin, where the controversy concerning the Poolbeg **waste-to-energy** project has gone on for many years. The Poolbeg plant will burn household and other waste in an **incinerator** to **generate electricity**.

Geo fact

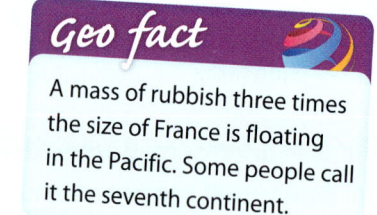

A mass of rubbish three times the size of France is floating in the Pacific. Some people call it the seventh continent.

Definition

Landfill: When waste material is buried and covered with soil.

Table 13.3 Arguments for and against the incinerator in Poolbeg

In favour of the incinerator	Against the incinerator
● **Landfill is unsustainable**. We are running out of landfill sites, so we have to build incinerators to take some of our waste. ● Landfill has to be reduced under **EU guidelines**. Many EU countries, such as Germany and Denmark, are far ahead of Ireland in their use of incinerators. ● **Dublin** should take care of its own waste. ● The Poolbeg waste-to-energy plant will provide **power and heating** for tens of thousand of homes nearby. ● Modern incinerators do not damage the environment because they have very **high health and safety standards**.	● **Incinerators are not needed**. If we reduce, reuse and recycle waste as much as possible, landfill will take the rest. ● Incineration reduces the amount of waste that can be recycled. ● Incinerators may release **deadly toxins** if they do not work properly. These could damage people's health. ● **Lorry traffic** bringing waste to Poolbeg day after day will increase **pollution** in the area. ● The Poolbeg plant will be an **eyesore**. It will be a huge building – the size of Croke Park.

A computer-generated image of the Poolbeg incinerator

Figure 13.19 Location of the Poolbeg incinerator

After many years of delay due to the controversy, construction of the plant began at the end of 2014. It is expected to open at the end of 2017.

Chapter 13 · Secondary Economic Activities

Questions

1. Explain **two** reasons why some people object to wind turbines.
2. Explain why some locations are more acceptable than others for wind farms.
3. Do you have a personal position on the incineration controversy? If so, explain your answer.

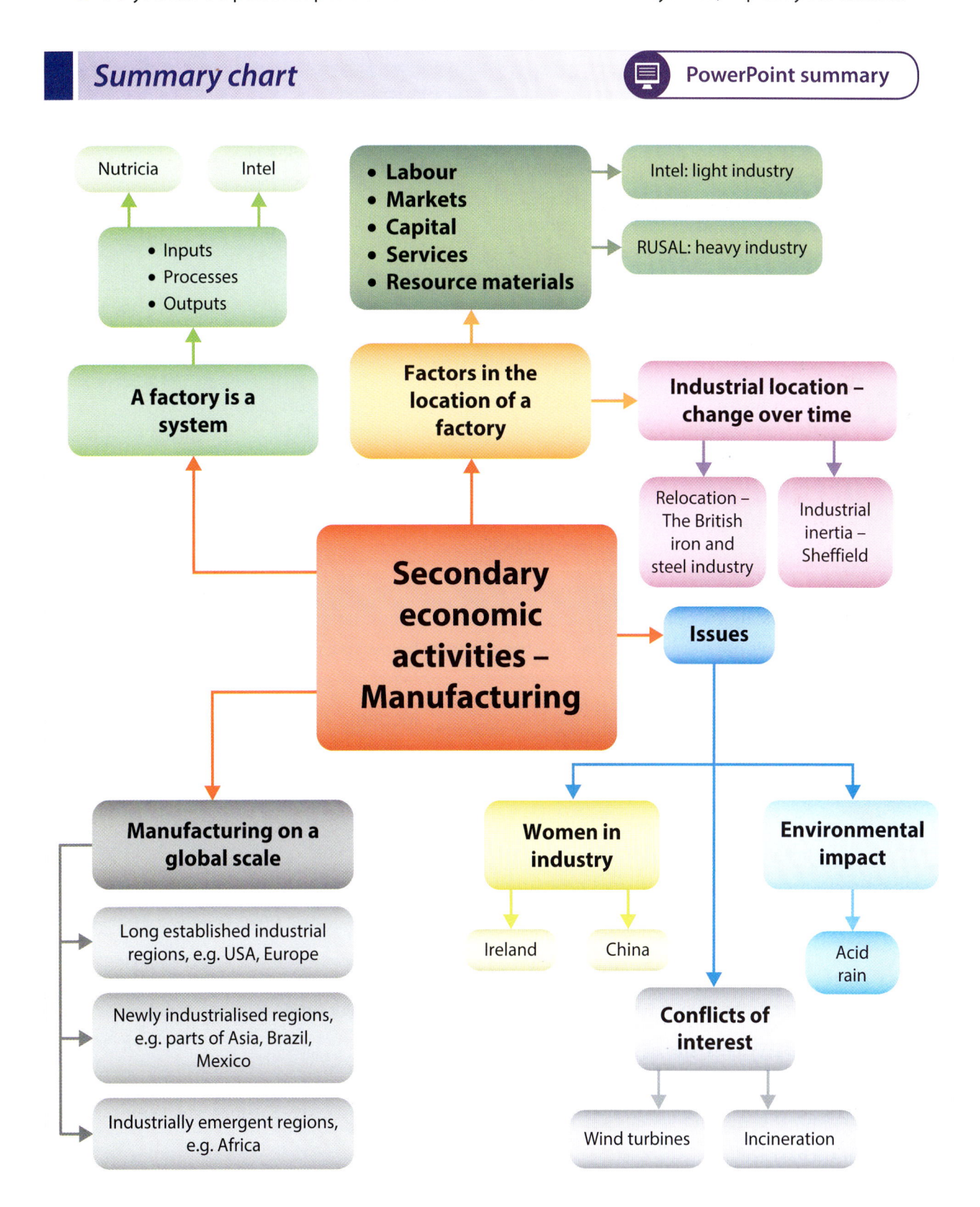

Summary chart

PowerPoint summary

- Nutricia
- Intel

- Inputs
- Processes
- Outputs

A factory is a system

- Labour
- Markets
- Capital
- Services
- Resource materials

→ Intel: light industry

→ RUSAL: heavy industry

Factors in the location of a factory

Industrial location – change over time

- Relocation – The British iron and steel industry
- Industrial inertia – Sheffield

Secondary economic activities – Manufacturing

Issues

Manufacturing on a global scale
- Long established industrial regions, e.g. USA, Europe
- Newly industrialised regions, e.g. parts of Asia, Brazil, Mexico
- Industrially emergent regions, e.g. Africa

Women in industry
- Ireland
- China

Environmental impact
- Acid rain

Conflicts of interest
- Wind turbines
- Incineration

385

Section 4 · Economic Geography

Exam questions

1. (i) Name **one** manufacturing industry you have studied.
   (ii) Describe this industry referring to its inputs, processes and outputs.

   HL 2010

2. The diagram shows that a factory is a system with inputs, processes and outputs.

   INPUTS → PROCESSES → OUTPUTS

   In the box below, circle three items, which may be factory inputs.

   | Labour | Capital | Waste material |
   | By-products | Transport | Manufactured products |

   HL 2010

3. The location of manufacturing industries is influenced by many factors including:
   - Raw Materials
   - Capital
   - Labour
   - Services
   - Markets
   - Government Policies
   - Transport.

   Explain how any **three** of the factors listed above influence the location of **one** manufacturing industry that you have studied.

   HL 2014

4. The general location of Britain's iron and steel industry has changed over time. Explain why this happened. You may use the diagram below to assist you.

   Ancient forest sites → Industrial Revolution coalfield sites → Modern coastal sites

   HL 2007

5. (i) Explain **two** effects of acid rain.
   (ii) Describe **two** ways of reducing acid rain.

   HL 2015

6. (i) Explain **one** impact of industrial activity on the environment.
   (ii) Explain how the role of women in industry has changed over time.

   HL 2012

7. (i) Explain **two** factors which influence the location of industry.
   (ii) Economic activities can give rise to local conflicts. Name and explain an example of such a conflict.

   HL 2011

Chapter 14
Tertiary Economic Activities

Learning outcomes

By the end of this chapter, you should be able to understand:

- That in developed countries, most people work in services
- That tourism is an example of a service industry
- Why tourism is an important industry in Ireland
- Why Spain has a major tourist industry
- That road, rail and air links were modernised to support tourism in Spain
- That there are some disadvantages to tourism.

14.1 Services

KEYWORDS

- tertiary economic activities
- services
- facilities

Tertiary economic activities are ones that provide **services** and facilities.

- In **poor countries**, very few people work in services. This is because people are too poor to be able to buy services that others provide.
- As a **country becomes wealthy**, people demand personal services such as hairdressing, financial services such as banking, and educational services for their children.
- A **developed economy** provides a very wide range of services.

Link

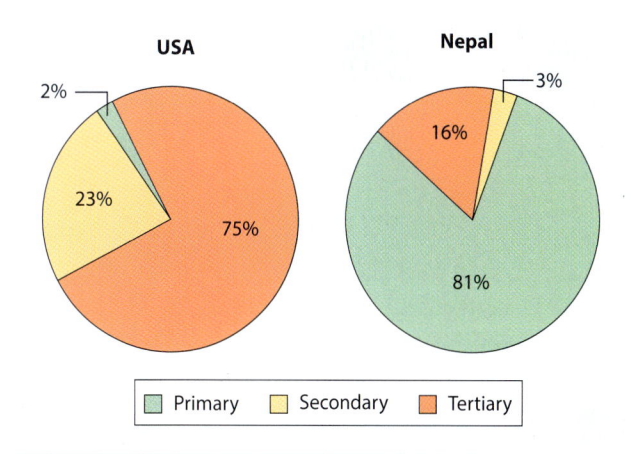

For more about **Nepal**, see Chapter 1, page 14.

Figure 14.1 As the economy of a country develops, the tertiary or service sector grows. Nepal is one of the poorest countries in the world, while the USA has the wealthiest economy in the world

Section 4 · Economic Geography

Business services: Advertising workers, accountants, tax consultants

Distribution services: Bus and lorry drivers, couriers

Communication services: TV, radio and newspaper editors and journalists

Financial services: Bank and building society managers

Legal services: Court workers, solicitors, barristers

Services

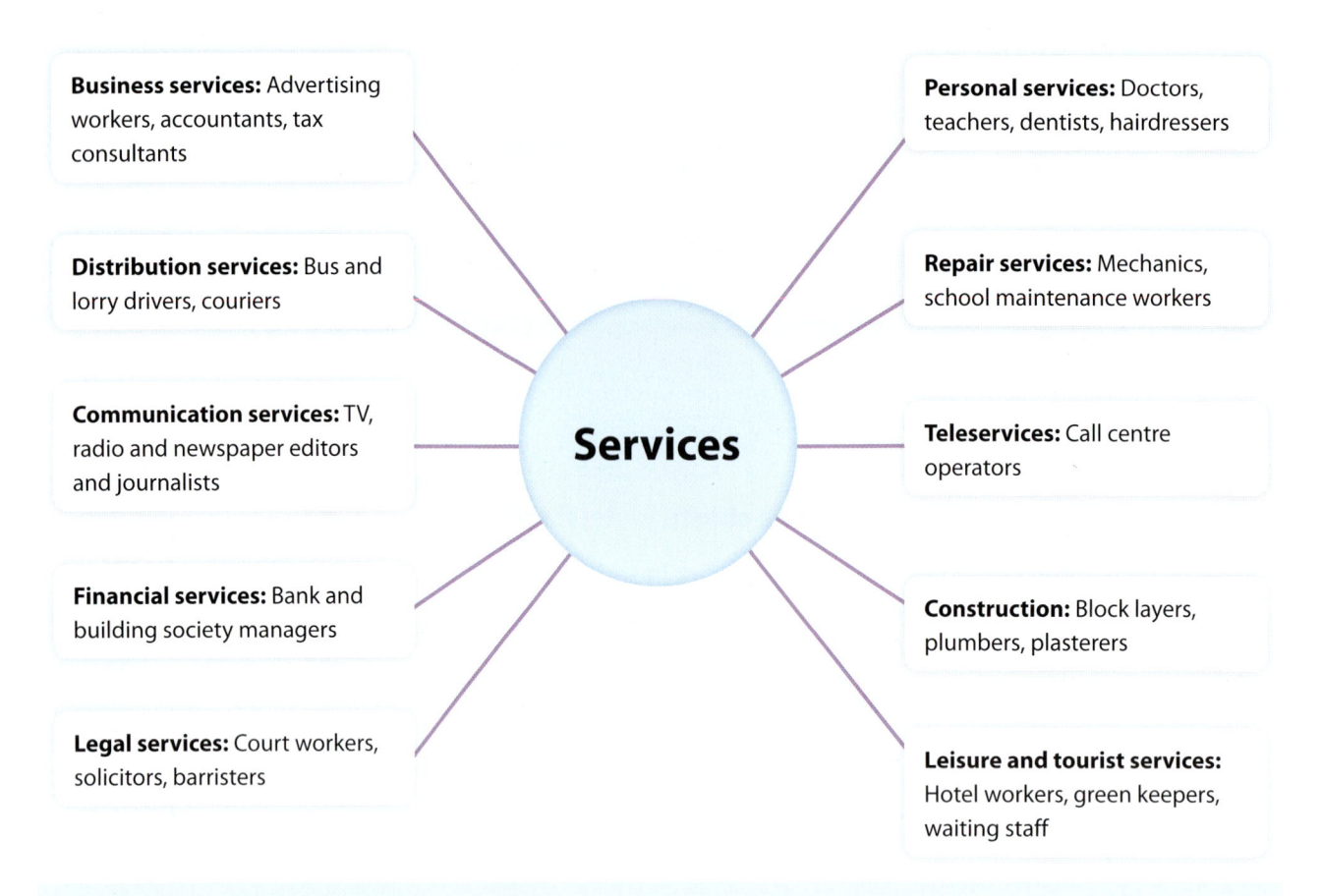

Personal services: Doctors, teachers, dentists, hairdressers

Repair services: Mechanics, school maintenance workers

Teleservices: Call centre operators

Construction: Block layers, plumbers, plasterers

Leisure and tourist services: Hotel workers, green keepers, waiting staff

Figure 14.2 The range of services

CBDs in wealthy cities have very large office buildings where thousands of services staff spend their working day. This office block in Manchester partly powers itself with solar panels on one south-facing wall

Questions

1. Look at Figure 14.1 and answer the following questions.
   (a) What percentage of people in Nepal work in secondary and tertiary services combined?
   (b) What percentage of people work in the tertiary sector in the USA?
   (c) The great majority of the people of Nepal live in rural areas. How does the information in the Nepali pie chart show that?

2. In your town or city, name **four** different services that are available. Name the part of the town in which most of these services are available.

3. Explain **two** reasons why Dublin has large numbers of administrative staff.

Link

For more on **Renewable energy**, see pages 345 and 382.

Chapter 14 · Tertiary Economic Activities

14.2 Tourism

KEYWORDS

- area of natural beauty
- tourist attraction
- tourist industry

Tourist services and facilities are usually in regions that offer certain **attractions**. These regions include:

- Areas of natural beauty
- Beaches and coastlines
- Regions with recreational and sporting facilities
- Cities.

Tourism in Ireland

Ireland is an important tourist destination with up to **8 million visitors** each year. Ireland is not a mass tourist destination, unlike countries such as France and Spain. Nevertheless, the **tourist industry** is very important to the Irish economy in terms of jobs and income.

Tourists visit Ireland for a variety of reasons.

Areas of natural beauty

Ireland is a beautiful country and offers the tourist great contrasts in scenery.

- The Ice Age carved out many spectacular valleys in the mountains of Ireland, e.g. the Lakes of Killarney in Co. Kerry and Glendalough in Co. Wicklow.
- Many regions of Ireland are havens of peace and calm, e.g. Gougane Barra in West Cork and the Glen of Aherlow in Co. Tipperary.

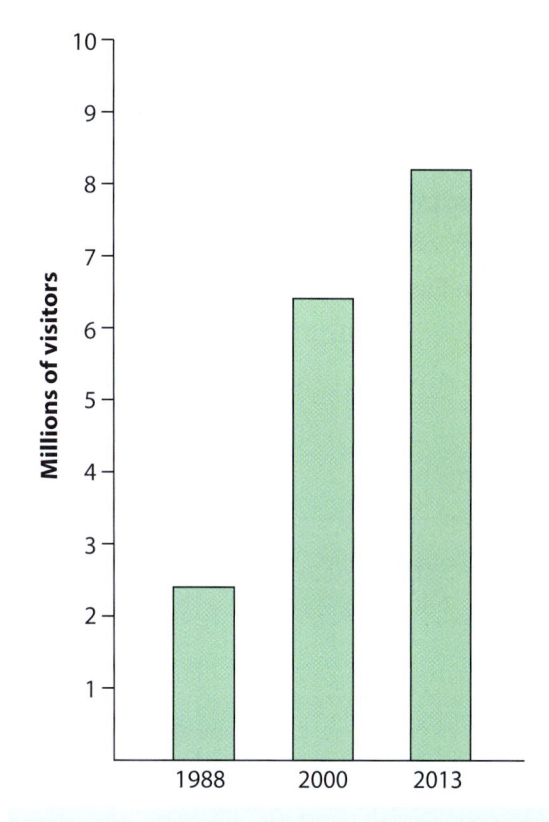

Figure 14.3 The growth in the number of visitors to the Republic of Ireland for selected years

Geo fact

Including part-time workers, 205,000 people are employed in the tourist industry in Ireland.

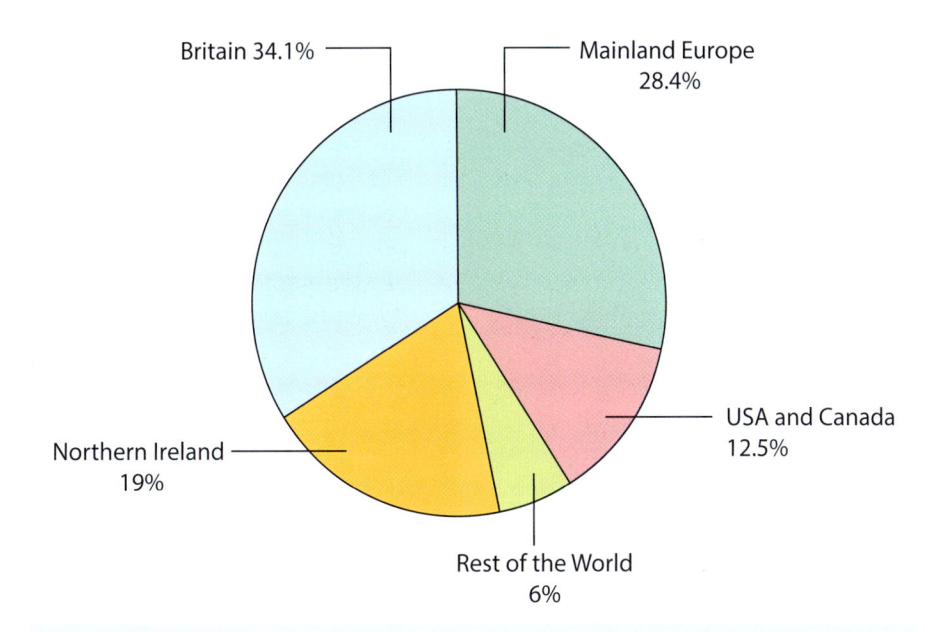

Pie chart: Britain 34.1%, Mainland Europe 28.4%, Northern Ireland 19%, USA and Canada 12.5%, Rest of the World 6%

Figure 14.4 Where visitors to the Republic of Ireland came from in 2013

389

Section 4 · Economic Geography

Beaches and coastlines

Coastal **erosion and deposition** have created a coastline of great beauty. The west coast of Ireland is very spectacular.

- The Cliffs of Moher in Co. Clare rise to 200 metres. The cliffs now have a visitors' centre, which is one of the most popular tourist destinations in the country.
- The peninsulas of the coast of West Cork and Kerry have spectacular cliffs and much bird life. Islands off the coast, such as Skellig Michael, are very dramatic.
- The east and south coasts are more noted for coastal deposition. **Longshore drift** has produced excellent beaches such as Tramore in Co. Waterford. Long stretches of beach are found from Wexford to Bray, and north of Dublin city.
- **Blue Flags** were awarded to 81 beaches and five marinas around the state's coastline in 2015.

> **Activity**
> Use the Internet to find out what a Blue Flag beach is.

> **Activity**
> Find out about the Wild Atlantic Way on the Internet.

The Cliffs of Moher, Co. Clare. The cliffs can be reached via the Wild Atlantic Way

Skellig Michael, off the coast of Kerry, where the latest *Star Wars* movie was filmed in 2015

Skellig Michael lies 12 km off the coast of Co. Kerry. A monastery was founded there some time between the sixth and the eighth centuries, and the remains of the beehive huts the monks lived in can still be visited. Skellig Michael was added to the World Heritage List by UNESCO in 1996 because of its historical importance and its wonderful setting. Its towering cliffs are a very important site for breeding seabirds. In 2015 it was used as a location for filming the final scene of *Star Wars: The Force Awakens*.

Chapter 14 · Tertiary Economic Activities

Figure 14.5 The coast of Co. Kerry offers many attractions to tourists

Questions

Study the OS map of Banna Strand and answer the following questions:

1 If you want a good walk, what is the distance in kilometres along Banna Strand between the following two grid references Q 740 200 and Q 750 280.

2 Write down **three** attractions that can be enjoyed by visitors who use the caravan park at Q 755 230.

3 Name **three** services that are available at Ballyheige – Q 751 280.

4 Link each grid reference below with one of the following features of deposition:
   - Beach
   - Sand dunes
   - Lagoon
   - Sand spit.

   (a) Q 757 265
   (b) Q 735 187
   (c) Q 750 255
   (d) Q 741 191

5 Link each grid reference below with one of the following features of erosion:
   - Cave
   - Headland
   - Cliff
   - Sea stack.

   (a) Q 740 282
   (b) Q 746 247
   (c) Q 744 281
   (d) Q 736 283

391

Section 4 · Economic Geography

Regions with recreational and sporting facilities

Ireland is a playground for people who enjoy active holidays.

- Ireland has many parkland and **links** golf courses. Links are playable for most of the year because of good drainage.
- **Angling** is an important holiday activity, with fishing in freshwater lakes and rivers, as well as offshore. Many European lakes are no longer healthy enough to support fish life because of pollution. European anglers come to Ireland because of its **unpolluted waters**.
- **Waterways** such as the Shannon are used by people who enjoy boating holidays. Tourists bring business to small towns along the Shannon from Killaloe to Carrick-on-Shannon.
- International **sporting fixtures** draw many tourists to the country, e.g. international rugby and soccer matches.
- **Horse racing** in Ireland, including the Irish Derby in the Curragh, and events like the Dublin Horse Show attract foreign visitors.

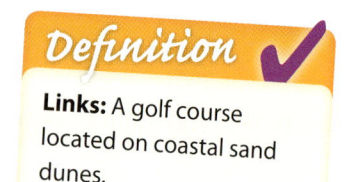

> **Definition**
> **Links:** A golf course located on coastal sand dunes.

The Curragh racecourse on Irish Derby Day

Cities

- **Dublin** is the country's most visited city. This is partly because of its status as a **historic capital**. Dublin Airport has better flight connections with British and European airports than other Irish airports.
- Dublin has many **attractions**, including the treasures of the National Museum, the Book of Kells in Trinity College, Grafton Street, the National Gallery and Georgian architecture.
- **Cork** is an excellent centre for exploring the surrounding region. Blarney Castle is just outside the city. Kinsale is famous for its seafood restaurants. The Queenstown Story in Cobh pays tribute to the great numbers of people who emigrated to the USA in the generations after the Famine.

The entrance to the library in Trinity College Dublin in which the Book of Kells is stored

Table 14.1 Ireland's top five fee-charging attractions in 2013

Attraction	Number of visitors
1) Guinness Storehouse, Dublin	1,157,090
2) Dublin Zoo	1,026,611
3) Cliffs of Moher Visitor Experience, Co. Clare	960,134
4) National Aquatic Centre, Dublin	858,031
5) Book of Kells, Dublin	588,723

Fáilte Ireland

> **Activity**
> **Search** the Internet to find out why great numbers of tourists visit the Book of Kells.

Notice that four of the top five attractions in the table above are in Dublin.

> ### Questions
>
> 1. (a) Name the county in which you live.
>   (b) Name an area of attractive scenery in your county.
>   (c) Name **one** historic feature of interest to tourists in your county.
>   (d) Name an urban centre that provides tourist facilities in your county and list **three** of these facilities.
> 2. Why, do you think, is Dublin Ireland's most visited city? Give **three** reasons.

14.3 Tourism in Europe

KEYWORDS

- Mediterranean
- package holiday
- tourist resort
- marina
- niche holiday

Climate is an important factor in making some regions attractive for tourists.

- The **snow in the Alps** attracts skiers and snowboarders in the winter.
- The **sunshine and warmth of Mediterranean countries** like Spain and Portugal has made them very popular with tourists all year round.

Tourism is the **world's largest industry** today. Millions of people from northern Europe have been holidaying in the Mediterranean countries since the 1950s. There are many reasons for this:

- Europeans could afford annual holidays when the **economic boom** of the 1950s started.
- The travel industry provided cheap **package holidays** for tourists.
- The introduction of **large aeroplanes**, such as the Boeing 707, made it possible to transfer millions of passengers quickly and safely to Mediterranean resorts.
- Mediterranean countries such as Spain, Italy and Greece developed **tourist resorts** in order to cater for large numbers of tourists.
- Sporting a **tan** was fashionable.

The result was that the **Mediterranean** became the largest tourist destination in the world.

Passengers in London Stansted Airport. Air transport is vital to the tourist industry

Geo fact

The Costa del Sol in southern Spain receives 3,000 hours of sunshine during the year. Ireland receives between 1,100 and 1,200 hours.

Section 4 · Economic Geography

Case study

Tourism in Spain

Spain developed its tourist industry very rapidly after 1955. It is the second most important tourist destination in Europe, with more than 65 million tourists in 2014. The **Balearic Islands** in the Mediterranean, and the **Canaries** off the coast of southern Morocco – both Spanish territories – are major tourist destinations.

Sun, sand and sea

For the pale-skinned tourists from northern Europe, Spain has the **sunshine** and **high temperatures** for many months of the year that they want.

- **Hotels** and **apartments** are built along the coast, close to the beaches where the tourists want to be.
- **Restaurants** and **discos** are located along the seafront of every resort.
- Resorts welcome **family groups**.
- Almost every resort has a **marina** where boating enthusiasts can spend their days messing about in boats.

Activity

Examine Table 14.2 and answer these questions:
1. What is the midday temperature in August?
2. The midday temperature is at 25°C or higher for how many months?
3. What month has the fewest hours of sunshine?
4. The average daily hours of sunshine are seven or more for how many months?

Table 14.2 Temperature and hours of sunshine per month in the Costa del Sol

Months	Jan	Feb	Mar	Apr	May	Jun	Jul	Aug	Sep	Oct	Nov	Dec
Average midday temperature (°C)	16.0	17.2	19.5	21.2	24.7	27.5	31.1	32.3	28.1	25.0	18.4	16.4
Average daily hours of sunshine	6.0	7.1	7.2	9.3	9.9	11.0	12.0	11.0	8.9	7.1	5.9	5.7

Millions of tourists

- Germany 9.9
- France 9.5
- Scandinavia 4.9
- Italy 3.3
- Netherlands 2.6
- Ireland 1.3
- Rest of Europe 8.0
- USA 1.2
- Rest of Americas 1.9
- Rest of world 3.9
- UK 14.3

Source: Spanish Tourism Institute

Activity

Examine the pie chart and answer the following questions:
1. From which country did the greatest number of tourists come to Spain?
2. What was the total number of tourists from Germany and France combined?
3. From which country did the greater number of tourists travel to Spain, the USA or Ireland?

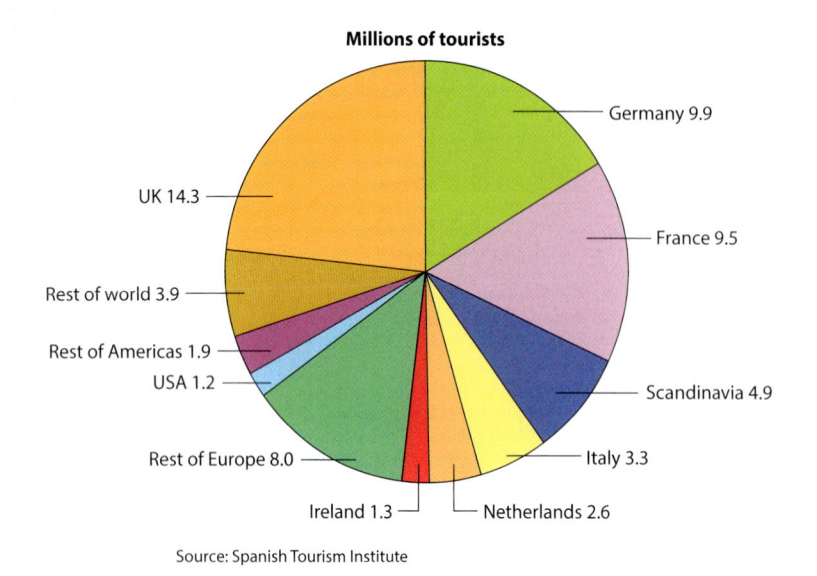

Figure 14.6 Tourist arrivals in Spain 2013 by home country in millions

Chapter 14 · Tertiary Economic Activities

Case study

Winter sunshine

Many people from northern Europe, including Ireland, have bought apartments and **holiday homes** in Spain. Some retired people from northern Europe spend part of the winter months in southern Spain or in the Canaries because of the mild winter temperatures. Even in January, the Costa del Sol has an average of six hours of sunshine a day. **Niche holidays** such as golfing holidays are popular in autumn, winter and spring.

Inland tourist centres

Spain is marketing its **inland attractions** so that those regions can share in the tourist boom. Inland attractions include Seville, Cordoba and Granada in the south. As well as Madrid itself, historic cities such as Toledo, Segovia and Avila are well worth a visit.

Definition

Niche holidays: Holidays that cater for special interests, such as golfing, trekking and angling.

Geo fact

The flight time from Dublin Airport to Malaga is three hours.

The beach in Torremolinos, Costa del Sol, Spain

Figure 14.7 The coastal and inland tourist centres of Spain

The interior of the mosque in Cordoba dates from the Middle Ages. This mosque is one of the great cultural sights of Spain's interior

Section 4 · Economic Geography

Case study

Benefits of tourism to the Spanish economy

Many regions of Spain have greatly benefited from tourism:

- Tourism provides **employment** in hotels, restaurants, golf clubs and other tourist services. One in eight workers in Spain works in the tourist industry.
- Tourism also supports a major **construction industry** with the building of hotels, apartment blocks and other facilities.
- Farmers along the coast have a large **market for fresh produce** such as salad crops that are sold to nearby supermarkets.
- **Airports** have greatly expanded in eastern Spain and in the islands. These airports also provide employment.
- Local **landowners** have been well paid for land sold for tourist development.

However, as we will learn later, tourism has brought some disadvantages to Spain.

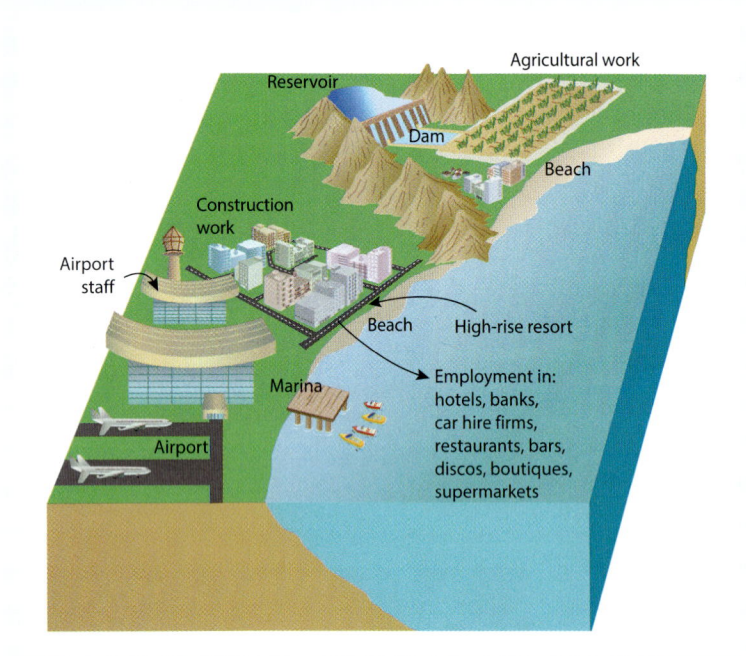

Polytunnels in eastern Spain. These are filled with vegetable crops that need vast quantities of water

Figure 14.8 Beach resorts in Spain provide a great deal of employment

Questions

1. Explain **three** reasons for the popularity of Spain among Irish holidaymakers.
2. Explain **two** ways in which the Spanish economy benefits from the tourist industry.
3. Draw a sketch map of Spain and Portugal and include the following:
   - The border between Spain and Portugal
   - The Costa del Sol and the Costa Brava
   - The cities of Barcelona and Malaga
   - The Balearic Islands.

Chapter 14 · Tertiary Economic Activities

14.4 Tourism and transport links

KEYWORDS

- transport links
- motorway
- road network
- E15
- toll road
- high-speed train

Tourism can lead to **transport links** being improved.

The road and rail network in Spain existed before mass tourism began in the 1950s. However, these networks have been **modernised** to cope with tourist traffic, especially in coastal regions. **New motorways** have been built, especially along the Mediterranean coast.

The Spanish road network

Many tourists, especially the French, Swiss and Dutch, enter Spain **by road**. The **E15** is a great motorway along the east coast of Spain, which speeds French tourists on their way south. The E15 is a **toll road** because it was so expensive to build. The E15 is also used by truck traffic to supply the needs of the tourist industry.

Madrid has excellent road connections with all the provinces of mainland Spain.

Figure 14.9 The Spanish road system radiates outwards from Madrid. The coastal routes are well served by roads

Spanish rail

The Spanish rail system is also used by tourists. The rail network connects all major cities.

High-speed trains

High-speed trains, running at speeds up to **310 km per hour**, operate in many parts of Spain. Madrid has high-speed rail connections with the south and east coasts.

Many tourists use trains to take a trip to other tourist centres in Spain. Tourists staying in Malaga can travel to Seville, Cordoba and Madrid on a high-speed train. Tourists on the Mediterranean coast take day trips to Barcelona on high-speed trains.

Figure 14.10 On Spain's high-speed train network it takes less than three hours to travel from Madrid to Malaga

Section 4 · Economic Geography

A high-speed train in Spain's interior. High-speed trains are used by Spaniards and foreign tourists alike

Geo fact
The Spanish high-speed train systems is known as the AVE. It is a play on the Spanish word *ave*, which means *bird*.

Airports

Great numbers of tourists from Ireland, Britain and Scandinavia travel to Spain **by air**. Therefore, most of Spain's airports are linked to the tourist industry. Apart from Madrid, most of Spain's international airports are **close to coastal tourist resorts**.

Airports are vital to the success of tourism in the Canaries and the Balearic islands. Irish tourists can reach the Canaries in less than four hours from Dublin, Shannon and Cork.

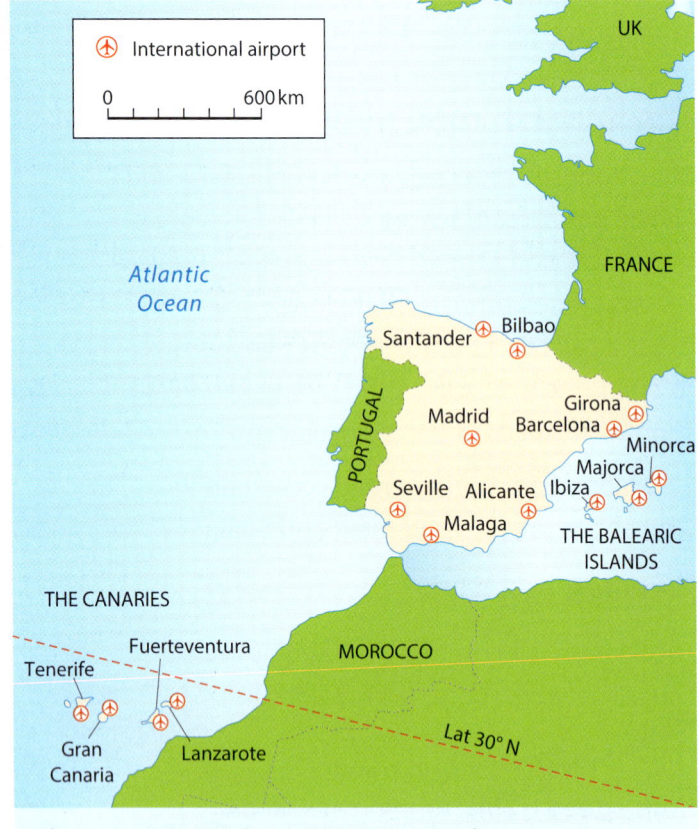

Figure 14.11 Spain has many international airports as tourists travel by air to Spain and its islands

Questions

1. What is the E15 and where in Spain is it located?
2. Explain **two** ways in which the E15 benefits the tourist industry.
3. What is the AVE?
4. Airports are vital to the success of the tourist industry in mainland Spain and in the Spanish islands. Explain that statement.

14.5 The impact of tourism

KEYWORDS

- mass tourism
- social impact
- environmental impact
- speculator

Tourism can have an **unwelcome impact** on society and the environment.

Mass tourism

Mass tourism – where great numbers of tourists gather in the same resort – can bring some **disadvantages**. These disadvantages are evident in the Spanish resorts located along the Mediterranean coast.

The social impact of tourism

Resorts on the coast of Spain have seen many social changes.

- **Spanish culture is being swamped** by the cultures of northern Europe. British entertainers and DJs work in the club scene. English-language pop songs are played in discos. There are many American fast-food outlets. Irish pubs are also found in Spanish resorts.
- Many tourists do not learn any Spanish. Spanish tourist workers speak English and German. The resorts are **losing their Spanish identity**.
- Some **holidaymakers behave badly**.
- Petty **crime and drug taking** are problems in some resorts.
- The **cost of land** has risen along the coast. It is now too expensive for most locals. Young Spanish couples have to live in inland villages where property is cheaper.

Tourism and the environment

Tourism, as one of the largest industries in the world, has a great impact on the environment.

- Much of the Spanish **coast is built up**. A quarter of the land along the coast of the Costa del Sol is now covered in high-rise apartments and hotels.
- Modern **high-rise buildings** have swamped the traditional architecture found in local fishing villages.

High-rise buildings spread along the coast in Benidorm. These developments form part of the 'Great Wall of Spain'

Section 4 · Economic Geography

- Agricultural land along the coast from Barcelona to Gibraltar is bought up by **speculators**. Some large holiday schemes have been built without planning permission.
- **Pollution** is a problem along the coast of Spain. Some partly treated sewage enters the Mediterranean Sea. This a shallow sea, with a very narrow entrance at Gibraltar. Therefore, it takes decades for the Mediterranean to renew itself through the Straits of Gibraltar.
- **Water is scarce** in eastern Spain because of very low rainfall during the summer. Meeting the water needs of tourism and irrigated farming is a major challenge.

> **Definition**
> **Speculators:** People who buy land or other property in the hope of making a large profit when they sell it.

How should mass tourism be managed?

There are no easy answers to how mass tourism should be controlled. In Lanzarote, mass tourism is being managed in the following ways:

- **Only low-rise buildings** using traditional designs and materials are permitted.
- **Advertising signs are forbidden** on road margins.
- **Discreet shop fronts** do not use plastic or gaudy colours.
- Gardens and parks use **local plants** and do not disturb the natural landscape.
- **Planning laws** are very strict and have wide public support among the 79,000 local people.

A beach resort in Lanzarote, one of the Canary Islands. The people of Lanzarote opted for low-rise buildings instead of the high-rise resorts of the Spanish mainland

Questions

1. Resorts are losing their Spanish identity. Explain **two** ways in which this is happening.
2. Why are some young Spanish couples unable to afford to live on the coast of Spain?
3. Explain **two** ways in which the Spanish coastal environment is under pressure as a result of mass tourism.
4. Explain **two** ways in which the people of Lanzarote have chosen to control large-scale tourism.

Chapter 14 · Tertiary Economic Activities

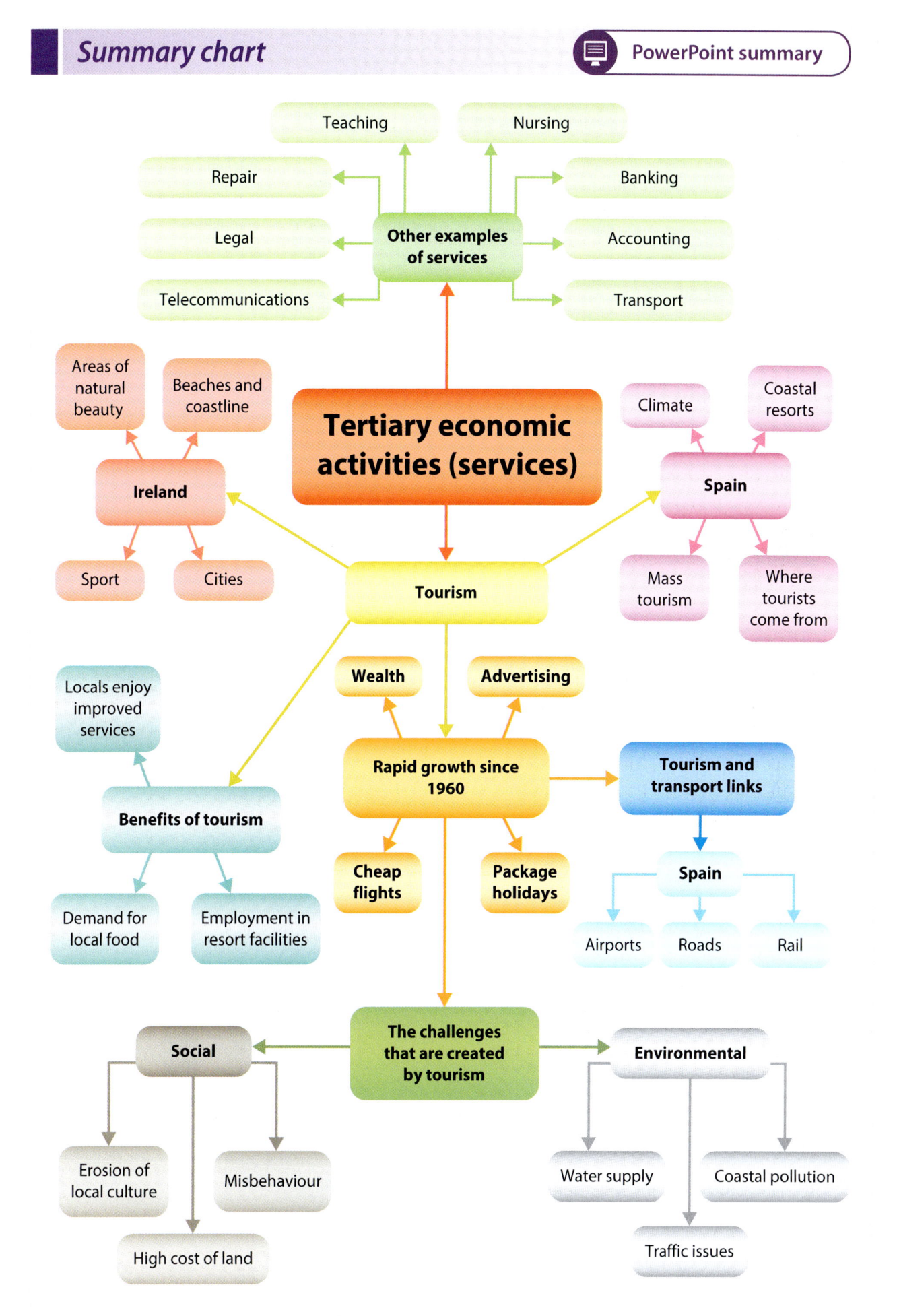

Summary chart

PowerPoint summary

Tertiary economic activities (services)

- **Other examples of services**
  - Teaching
  - Nursing
  - Repair
  - Banking
  - Legal
  - Accounting
  - Telecommunications
  - Transport

- **Ireland**
  - Areas of natural beauty
  - Beaches and coastline
  - Sport
  - Cities

- **Spain**
  - Climate
  - Coastal resorts
  - Mass tourism
  - Where tourists come from

- **Tourism**

- **Rapid growth since 1960**
  - Wealth
  - Advertising
  - Cheap flights
  - Package holidays

- **Tourism and transport links**
  - **Spain**
    - Airports
    - Roads
    - Rail

- **Benefits of tourism**
  - Locals enjoy improved services
  - Demand for local food
  - Employment in resort facilities

- **The challenges that are created by tourism**
  - **Social**
    - Erosion of local culture
    - Misbehaviour
    - High cost of land
  - **Environmental**
    - Water supply
    - Coastal pollution
    - Traffic issues

401

Section 4 · Economic Geography

Exam questions

1 Climate data for Dublin and the Costa del Sol (Spain)

Month	June		July		August	
	Hours of sunshine	Mean temp °C	Hours of sunshine	Mean temp °C	Hours of sunshine	Mean temp °C
Dublin	6.5	17.0	5.0	18.0	5.0	18.0
Costa del Sol	9.0	27.0	10.0	30.0	9.0	31.0

With reference to the information given in the table above, explain **two** reasons why the Costa del Sol would be a better location than Dublin for a sun holiday.

HL 2015

2

(i) Name **four** reasons why tourists come to Ireland.

(ii) Large-scale tourism may have **unwelcome impacts** on some tourist areas.

Describe **two** such impacts.

HL 2009

Exam questions

3 Coastlines and beaches   Sporting and recreational    Cities    Natural beauty

(i) Choose any **two** of the types of tourist regions illustrated above and name an example of each.

(ii) Explain why tourists are attracted to **each** of your named examples.

HL 2013

4 (i) Name **two** types of tourist regions.

(ii) Explain **one** positive effect of tourism, referring to an example you have studied.

(iii) Explain **one** negative effect of tourism, referring to an example you have studied.

HL 2011

Chapter 15
Economic Inequality

Learning outcomes

By the end of this chapter, you should be able to understand:

- That the world is composed of developed, quickly developing and slowly developing economies
- That rich and powerful states have taken advantage of the resources of weaker states in the past and continue to do so today
- Why development assistance – aid – is sometimes effective and sometimes not
- That climate change, population growth and war make the development of poor states, such as Sudan, difficult
- That in many European countries, including Ireland, some regions are wealthier than others
- Why trying to solve economic inequalities is a major challenge.

15.1 The Earth's resources: who benefits?

KEYWORDS

- inequality
- developed world
- quickly developing
- slowly developing
- foreign debt
- HIV/AIDS
- civil war
- corruption
- GNP

The world can be divided into the **developed world**, the **quickly developing world** and the **slowly developing world**.

Geo fact

196: The number of internationally recognised countries in the world in 2015.

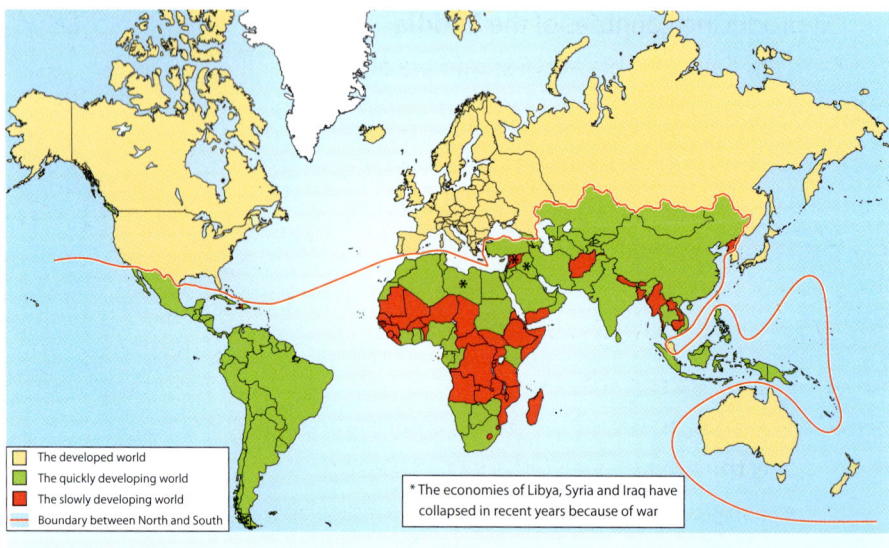

Map legend:
- The developed world
- The quickly developing world
- The slowly developing world
- Boundary between North and South

* The economies of Libya, Syria and Iraq have collapsed in recent years because of war

Figure 15.1 The developed world, the quickly developing world and the slowly developing world

The developed world

The **developed world** is made up of wealthy countries. Almost all of these are in the northern hemisphere, so the developed world is also known as **the North** (see Chapter 9, page 251). However, the developed world also includes **Australia and New Zealand**, which are in the southern hemisphere.

In **East Asia**, the countries of Japan, South Korea, Taiwan and Singapore are also in the developed world. These East Asian countries are major exporters of manufactured goods, such as computer parts, televisions and camcorders.

In the developed world, the **majority of people work in services**. People have high average incomes. The **Infrastructure** of roads, electricity and water supplies is of a high standard.

Why is the developed world represented by office workers?

Geo fact
Income per head in France was 61 times greater than in Rwanda in 2014.
Source: *The Economist*

Canary Wharf in London – one of the world's wealthiest cities

Quickly developing countries

Countries that have **quickly developing economies** are found in the **developing world**.

Most countries in **Latin America** are quickly developing. Many countries in **Asia** are also rapidly developing through the manufacturing of export goods. Indonesia, Malaysia, Vietnam and parts of India are in this group. And China has grown so rapidly in recent decades that it is now the second-largest economy on earth.

Oil-producing countries of the **Middle East** such as Saudi Arabia and Bahrain are also developing rapidly.

A few decades ago, these regions were very poor, but living standards are rising for many people in quickly developing countries.

Slowly developing economies

At least fifty countries are very poor. **Sub-Saharan Africa** is the world's **poorest region**. It is the area south of the Sahara Desert. Africa has more poor countries than any other continent.

In Asia, Afghanistan, Bhutan, Nepal, Bangladesh and Laos are also very poor.

Cyclists on their way to work in Shanghai, China. China's vast workforce has helped the country to become an economic superpower

Section 4 · Economic Geography

Some characteristics of the poorest countries

- Some of the world's poorest countries are **landlocked**, e.g. Mali.
- Many have experienced **civil wars**. These include Liberia and the Democratic Republic of Congo (DRC) – both in Africa.
- Many countries have crippling **foreign debts**. Repaying these debts forces countries to cut back on education and health spending.
- **Corrupt political leadership** is a problem. Some countries are ruled by criminals who steal from their own people.
- Slowly developing economies have **high population growth**.
- **HIV/AIDS** is a major problem in Sub-Saharan Africa and robs the region of many young adults as so many die as a result of the condition.

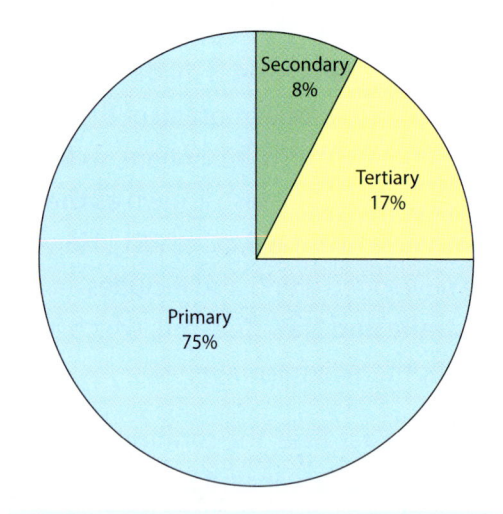

Figure 15.2 The workforce in Ethiopia has a high percentage of primary workers. This is typical of slowly developing countries

Primary 75%
Secondary 8%
Tertiary 17%

A village in Laos, one of the poorest countries in the world

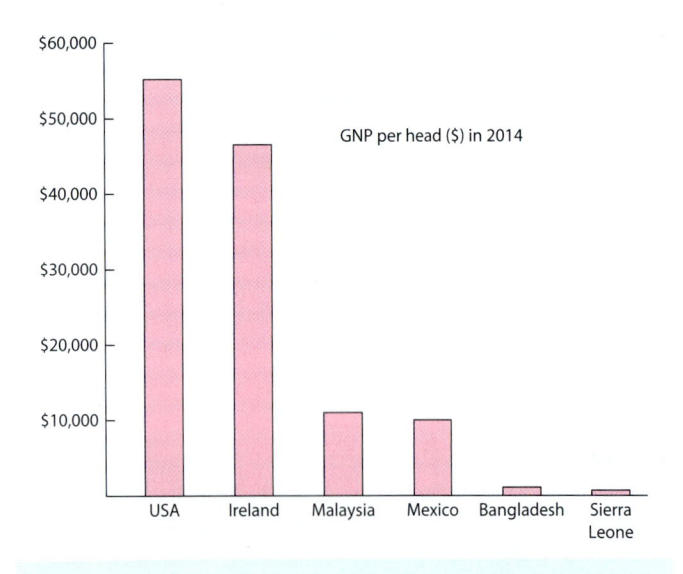

Figure 15.3 GNP per head in selected countries in 2014. Two countries are developed, two are quickly developing and two are slowly developing

Definition

GNP per head: Gross national product (GNP) per head is the total value of goods and services produced by a country in a year, divided by its population.

Questions

Study Figure 15.1 on page 404 and answer the following questions:

1. Name the continent with the greatest number of slowly developing countries.
2. Name **three** countries in South America that are quickly developing.
3. One small country in the Caribbean is slowly developing. Find it in Figure 15.1 and find out the name of that country in the world map on pages 218–19.

Chapter 15 · Economic Inequality

15.2 Exploitation of poor countries by wealthy countries

KEYWORDS
- exploit
- colonisation
- scramble for Africa
- agricultural raw materials
- foreign debt
- coffee plantation
- tariff barrier

Throughout history, rich and powerful developed states have **exploited** less developed states. Even today richer countries dominate world markets. This makes it difficult for poorer states to develop economically.

Definition ✓
Exploit: Take advantage of.

Wealthy countries with superior technology have always taken advantage of poor countries. European countries did this in the past by a policy of **colonisation**.

European colonisation

European countries began to colonise the American continents after Christopher Columbus discovered the New World in 1492. **Spain** and **Portugal** colonised Latin America.

- Spain exploited the **gold and silver mines** of their colonies for generations.
- Spanish and Portuguese colonists stole land from native people.

The scramble for Africa

Britain, France and other European countries rushed to divide Africa between them after 1875.

- The wealth of Africa – gold, diamonds, copper, cotton, mahogany and palm oil – was **exploited** for the benefit of Europeans.
- Colonies were used as sources of **cheap raw materials** for the benefit of the colonial powers.
- European countries became wealthy while colonies remained poor.

We will now examine how Ireland was exploited in the past by Britain.

What do you think this cartoon tells you about colonialism?

407

Section 4 · Economic Geography

Britain's exploitation of Ireland

Britain **colonised** Ireland over many centuries. Ireland remained a colony until the twenty-six counties gained independence in 1922. During colonial times, Ireland was exploited by Britain as a **source of raw materials and food**.

Britain's exploitation of Ireland is for Higher Level students only.

- Centuries ago, Ireland had great oak **forests**. British colonists cleared the land of forest and exported timber to Britain. This **timber was used to make ships** in Britain.
- Most of the **land** of Ireland was taken over by colonists during the plantations of the sixteenth and seventeenth centuries. Land was wealth at that time and Irish people were reduced to working the land for the landlords. Landlords became wealthy while the Irish became very poor tenants.

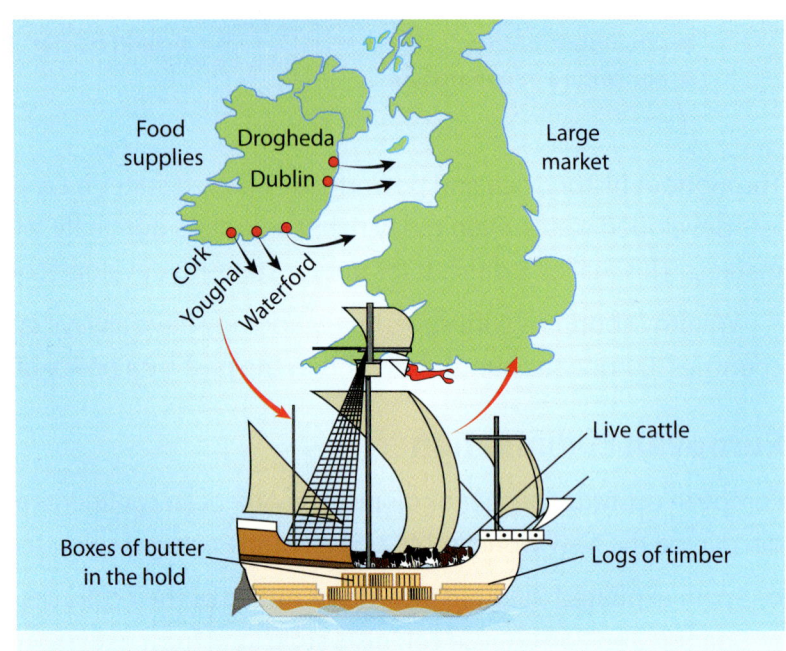

Figure 15.4 Britain used Ireland as a source of cheap food and cheap raw materials for centuries

- The Irish colony supplied Britain with live **cattle and butter** as well as wheat and barley. Live cattle were slaughtered in Britain. British butchers and shopkeepers took the lion's share of the profits in the meat business.
- Even during the **Great Famine** of the 1840s, food continued to be exported while over 800,000 Irish people died of hunger and disease.

The ruins of Moore Hall in Co. Mayo where the wealthy Moore family lived

The Famine Memorial in Dublin's Docklands to the victims of the Great Famine

408

World trade today

Even though former colonies in Africa have been independent for decades, most are still extremely poor. This is partly because countries of the developed world **exploit** poor countries **through world trade**.

Many countries in the South still export unprocessed **minerals** and **agricultural raw materials** to the North. Prices of many raw materials have declined in recent decades. So the South must produce more to earn the same amount. The result is that Africa's exports were valued at only 3 per cent of world trade in 2015.

Geo fact

Agricultural raw materials include: cotton fibre, cocoa beans, coffee beans, raw rubber and palm oil.

What do you think the message is here?

Dependence on one export

Today, the poorest countries in the world, many of them in Africa, are dependent on the export of one or two unprocessed raw materials whose prices fluctuate or decline.

Some of these countries also have large **foreign debts**. They find it very difficult to repay debt because of the poor prices they receive for their exports.

We will now examine the **coffee trade** to show how world trade works to the advantage of wealthy countries rather than the countries that grow coffee.

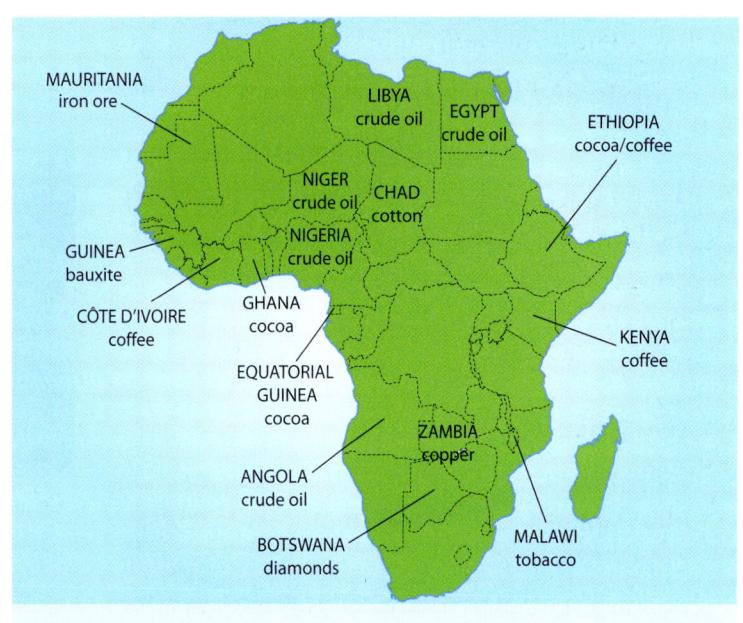

Figure 15.5 Many countries in Africa are heavily dependent on the export of one agricultural or mineral raw material

Section 4 · Economic Geography

Case study

The story of coffee

Growing coffee plants

Coffee plants are very demanding in terms of climate:

- They cannot tolerate frost.
- Annual average temperatures must be above 21°C.

Therefore, coffee growing is confined to the tropics.

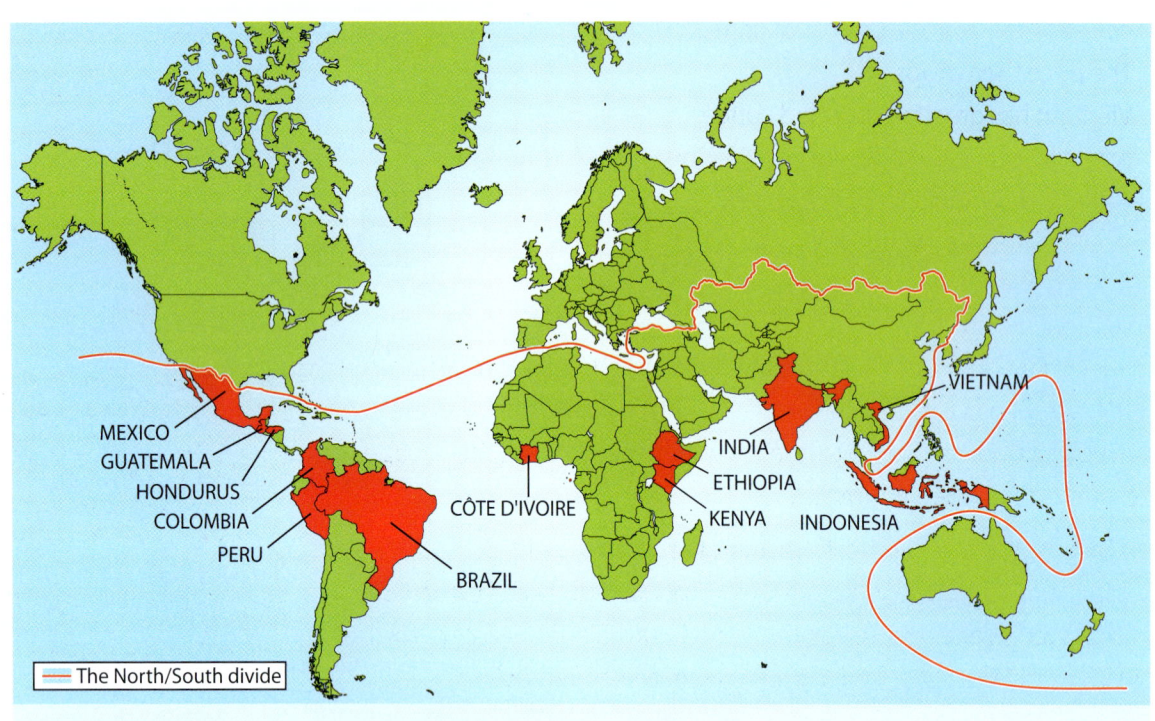

Figure 15.6 Coffee is grown in many tropical countries

Coffee-growing countries

Coffee is an important export crop for many developing countries. Some coffee is grown on big farms called **plantations**. Small farmers also grow coffee as a cash crop. More than 25 million farmers and their families depend on coffee for their income.

The price of coffee

Coffee beans are picked, dried and bagged. Most coffee is exported as unprocessed coffee beans. The growers have no control over coffee prices. The price of coffee beans **fluctuates** from year to year. A decline in price is disastrous for coffee growers and for countries that depend on coffee exports.

Coffee workers in Côte D'Ivoire, West Africa. The harvesting of coffee requires much manual labour

Geo fact

Brazil and Vietnam between them account for 51 per cent of the global production of coffee beans.

Chapter 15 · Economic Inequality

Case study

Supply and demand

The supply of coffee is often greater than demand. The reasons for this include the following:

- Many countries have large **foreign debts**. To repay these debts they have to increase exports. Therefore, farmers grow more coffee. This leads to a surplus of coffee. The price then drops.
- Vietnam has greatly expanded coffee production in recent decades and is now the second largest producer of coffee after Brazil.

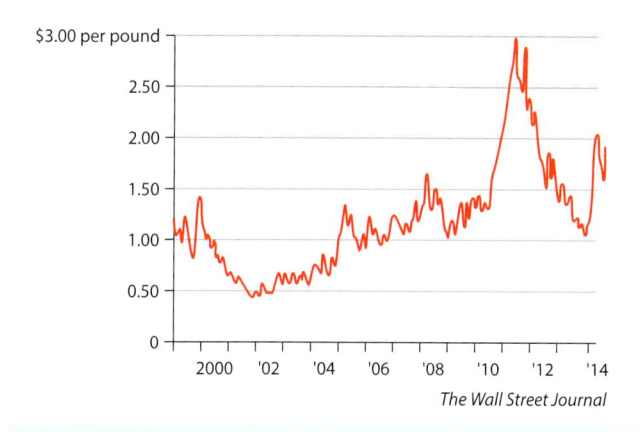

Figure 15.7 World coffee prices, 2000–2014

Tariff barriers in the North

A small number of **multinational companies**, including Kraft and Nestlé, dominate the international coffee trade. Coffee beans are roasted, ground and packaged in their factories in the USA, Europe and other developed countries.

Governments in the North protect the interests of the multinationals and the jobs that they provide with **tariff barriers** on imported processed coffee from the South. Therefore, the North continues to take most of the profits from the coffee business.

Definition

Tariff barriers: Taxes on imported goods, which make them more expensive.

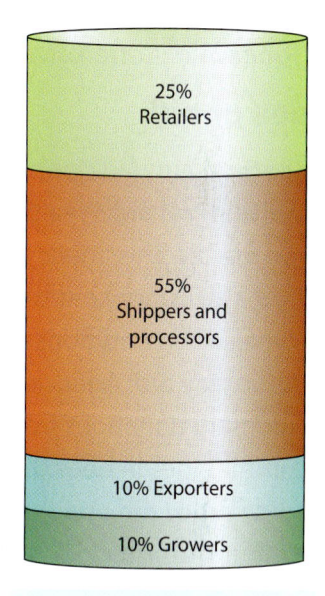

- 25% Retailers
- 55% Shippers and processors
- 10% Exporters
- 10% Growers

Figure 15.8 The division of money in the coffee business. Growers get a very small slice, which explains why they are poor

Questions

1. Name **two** European countries which had colonies in Africa at one time.
2. Explain **two** ways in which Britain exploited Ireland during colonial times.
3. Name the **two** largest producers of coffee beans.
4. Explain what happens to the price of coffee if there is a global surplus of coffee beans.
5. Examine Figure 15.8. What percentage of the money in the coffee business goes to the growers?

Section 4 • Economic Geography

15.3 Aid to the South

KEYWORDS
- bilateral aid
- multilateral aid
- tied aid
- voluntary aid
- emergency aid
- appropriate aid
- donor country
- recipient country
- sustainable solution
- self-reliance
- good government
- accountable
- NGOs
- people-to-people aid
- Ebola

For many decades, rich countries have given aid to poorer countries. Aid can take many forms:

- **Cash**: Money is given to build roads, hospitals, schools and water-filtering systems.
- **Skills**: Skilled people, such as engineers, teachers and doctors, from developed countries work for a time in projects in the South.
- **Goods**: Aid is often given as goods, such as food, hospital equipment and weapons.

Geo fact
Globally, governments spend 13 times more on armies and weapons than they spend on official aid.

Types of aid

- **Bilateral aid**: Aid donated by one country to another, e.g. Ireland to Ethiopia.
- **Multilateral aid**: Wealthy countries donate money to an agency, e.g. the UN. This agency then distributes it to countries in need.
- **Tied aid**: Donor countries give aid to poor countries. But, this aid comes with conditions attached that benefit the **donor country**.
- **Voluntary aid**: Agencies such as GOAL, Hope and Concern receive voluntary donations from the public and use them to provide aid to communities in poor countries.
- **Emergency aid**: Aid that is provided to a region that has suffered a natural disaster, e.g. after the Nepal earthquake in 2015.

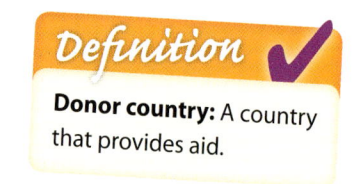

Definition
Donor country: A country that provides aid.

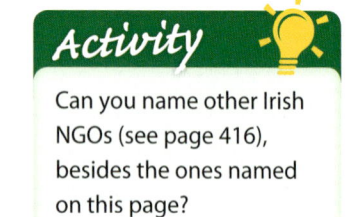

Activity
Can you name other Irish NGOs (see page 416), besides the ones named on this page?

Emergency aid at work – a family who lost their home in the Nepali earthquake of 2015 living in a tent donated by emergency aid

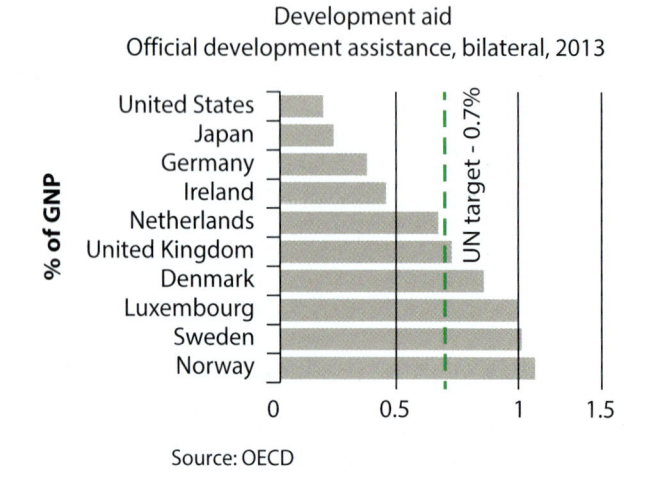

Development aid
Official development assistance, bilateral, 2013

% of GNP
- United States
- Japan
- Germany
- Ireland
- Netherlands
- United Kingdom
- Denmark
- Luxembourg
- Sweden
- Norway

UN target – 0.7%

0   0.5   1   1.5

Source: OECD

Figure 15.9 The aid donated by selected donor countries as a percentage of their GNP in 2013

Does aid work?

People often ask whether the money they give to good causes helps those in need in the way they want it to. Below we look at both sides of that question.

Advantages of aid

- **Emergency aid saves lives**. Refugees, fleeing from war or famine, are fed, clothed and given shelter.
- Aid can contribute to people's **quality of life**. Aid used to bore wells, to filter drinking water, or to establish blood banks, improves local people's health.
- Aid that is targeted at certain groups can be very effective. Women who are trained in sewing skills can make items of clothing that they can sell in the market. This gives them **independence**.
- Some aid creates local **employment**, e.g. local building workers are paid by aid organisers to build schools and clinics.
- Aid can teach people **self-reliance**. Farmers are taught techniques such as crop rotation, fertiliser use and food storage. They can provide for their families and sell what they don't need for themselves in the market.

Refugees register for food aid in the Democratic Republic of Congo, one of the world's poorest countries

'Give people a fish and they eat for a day. Teach them to fish and they eat for the rest of their lives.'

Mahatma Gandhi

Disadvantages of aid

- Aid can create a **dependent mentality** among those who receive it. In other words, people can get used to relying on help, and stop doing anything to help themselves.
- Many developing countries are led by **corrupt politicians and officials**. Dishonest people steal some aid given by donor governments.
- **Tied aid favours the donor country**. In tied aid, the donor country takes back much of what it gives in aid.
- **A lot of aid misses its target** – the poorest people. This is because the poorest are also the weakest and the least demanding. Many of the very poor live in remote rural areas.
- Some aid is not **appropriate** to local needs, e.g. lorries sent to parts of Ethiopia that have no roads or diesel filling stations.

Definition

Appropriate: Suited to people's needs.

Conclusion

After sixty years of aid, there are still 805 million people going to bed hungry every night. There is plenty of food in the world. The problem is that the poor cannot afford it. Therefore, **aid has not eliminated poverty or hunger**.

Activity

Find out where the Democratic Republic of Congo is located on the world map, pages 218–19.

Corruption among politicians and officials often reduces the amount of aid that the poor receive because leaders steal from their own citizens

Chapter 15 · Economic Inequality

413

Section 4 · Economic Geography

Irish Aid programmes

Irish Aid is the official name for the support supplied by the Republic of Ireland to developing countries. The Department of Foreign Affairs sends the aid to **recipient countries**. The aim of Irish Aid is 'to help developing countries to find **sustainable solutions** to the problems of poverty that confront them'. The Irish taxpayer contributes a lot of money to Ireland's bilateral aid programmes. It is important that the money is well spent.

Figure 15.10 Eight countries in Africa receive bilateral aid from Ireland. Ireland also gives bilateral aid to Vietnam

Irish Aid's activities in Ethiopia

Ethiopia is a very poor country with more than 94 million people. It is 17 times the size of Ireland and suffers from **severe water shortages** because of long periods of drought. The average temperature of the country has been increasing due to climate change.

Ethiopia has been one of Ireland's partner countries for more than 20 years. Irish Aid provides **bilateral aid** to Ethiopia, working with the Ethiopian government to attain these goals:

- That poor rural households are better able to cope in times of food shortages
- That mothers and children live healthier lives.

Geo fact
80 per cent of Irish Aid's budget is directed to Africa, where the need is greatest.

Ethiopian children benefit from Irish Aid funds in this rural school

414

Irish Aid works in many ways to attain these goals, including the following projects:

Water projects and food security

Irish Aid funds the **boring of deep wells** in rural Ethiopia so that villages have a continuous water supply.

- These wells provide **water for the village**.
- Water is also used for cattle and for local **irrigation projects**. Irrigation is used to grow fruit crops, vegetables and potatoes. Irrigated land can grow three crops a year.
- Farmers can sell their **food surplus** in the towns and can afford to send their children to school. Farmers can build up some cash savings for periods of drought so that they do not have to sell their livestock to buy food.
- Irish Aid also supports farming families where the household is headed by women.

Cattle on good grazing land in Ethiopia. Irish Aid has helped to improve the quality of cattle there

Geo fact
In 2014, 35 per cent of the people of Ethiopia were undernourished.
Source: World Bank

Health projects

The **health of mothers and children** in Ethiopia is targeted by Irish Aid. Irish Aid works with local health workers to improve the health of women and children.

- **Midwives** are trained to ensure that mothers do not die in childbirth.
- **Children are vaccinated** in village clinics.
- Irish Aid helps to provide essential drugs, vaccinations and **bed nets** to prevent malaria in children.
- Mothers are educated in **children's nutrition** so that children can have a balanced diet.
- Health workers are trained to assist patients who suffer from **HIV/AIDS**.
- Irish Aid puts great effort into **training local people** in basic nutrition, hygiene and sanitation.

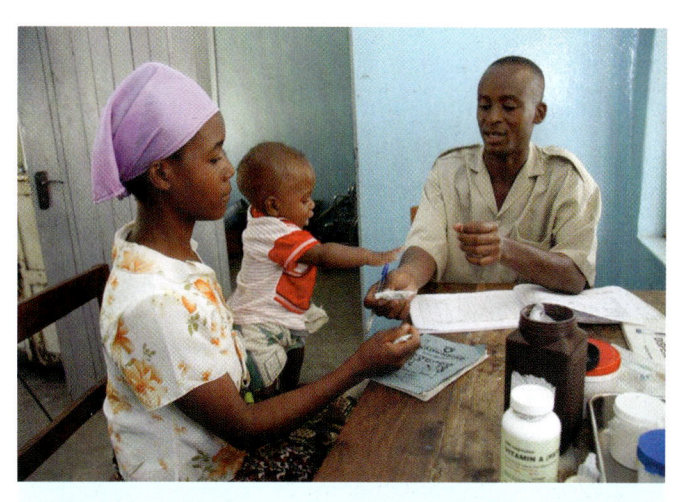

Irish Aid provides the resources for this village clinic in Ethiopia

Geo fact
An Ethiopian woman has a 1 in 52 risk of dying in childbirth during the course of her child-bearing years. (In Denmark it is 1 in 12,000.)

The promotion of good government practices

Irish Aid works with local community organisations to identify village needs such as schools, clinics, bridges and water pipes. Communities can then demand that the Ethiopian government provide these needs. In this way people are **empowered** to put pressure on their government to provide services. This helps to make local politicians and officials more **accountable** and helps to **reduce corruption**.

By giving Ethiopians **a hand up rather than a hand out**, Irish Aid is helping villagers to help themselves. That is the purpose of Ireland's **long-term development aid** to Ethiopia.

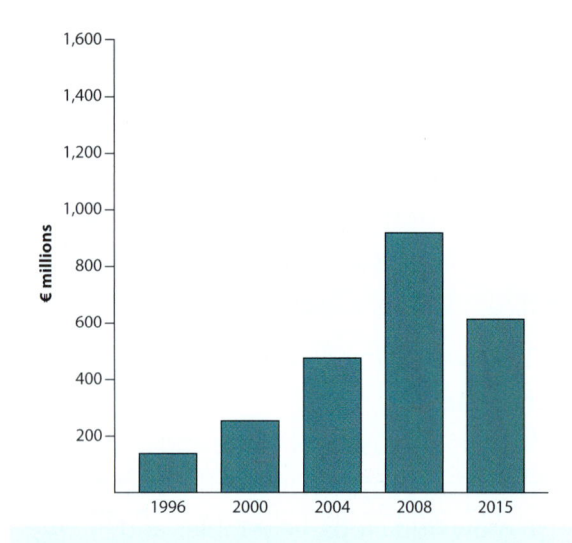

Figure 15.11 Irish overseas development assistance

> **Definition**
> **Accountable:** Politicians are accountable when they have to explain and justify their actions.

The work of Irish NGOs

Irish **NGOs (non-governmental organisations)** are voluntary organisations. They are independent of the Irish government. They collect money from the general public and spend it on projects in many countries in the South.

People-to-people aid

NGOs get permission from governments to provide assistance to communities in poor countries. Their funds go directly into community projects. Therefore, this is called **people-to-people aid**.

NGOs work on small-scale projects such as village clinics and women's classes in literacy, dressmaking, nutrition and household budgeting.

Niamh Sweeney, a volunteer with Nurture Africa, an Irish NGO, teaching pupils in Uganda in 2015

Education of the Irish public by NGOs

Many NGOs also **raise awareness** of development issues among the Irish public. For example, **Concern**, the Irish NGO, has conducted debates on development issues among pupils of secondary schools for many years. In this way, young people and their parents learn about issues such as poverty, debt, international trade and the arms industry.

This may help to explain why many Irish people spend time abroad on development projects.

Chapter 15 · Economic Inequality

Case study

Emergency aid: the Ebola outbreak in West Africa

Ebola virus disease is a severe, often fatal illness in humans. The virus is transmitted to people from wild animals and spreads in the human population through human-to-human transmission.

(World Health Organization)

The most recent outbreak of Ebola began in West Africa in 2013, mainly in Liberia, Sierra Leone and Guinea, and continued into 2015. More than 10,000 people died of Ebola in those three countries.

The three countries are **among the poorest in the world** and are poorly equipped to deal with the outbreak, as we can see from the **indicators of poverty** for Sierra Leone.

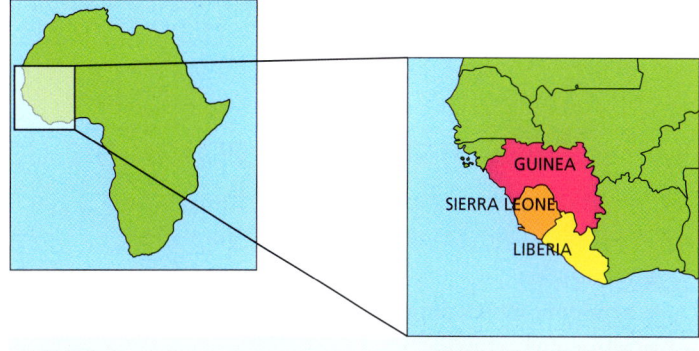

Figure 15.12 The countries of West Africa affected by the Ebola virus

Table 15.1 Sierra Leone: indicators of poverty

Population	Life expectancy	Adult literacy	Under-nourished	Access to clean water	Income per head
6 million	49 years	41%	35%	55%	$820

Many people were undernourished to start with, so when a life-threatening virus broke out, people were at great risk. The Ebola outbreak caused disruption of normal daily lives. Schools were closed, traffic into and out of villages that were affected ceased, and there was terrible fear. Movement to neighbouring countries was halted.

The health services of the countries affected were overwhelmed by the Ebola outbreak. **Medical aid** from abroad was urgently required. The response from abroad included the following:

- Irish **NGOs** such as **Plan Ireland** helped with funding and with aid workers.
- The **Irish government** provided direct funding of almost €17 million up to spring 2015 to organisations working on the Ebola response in Sierra Leone and Liberia.
- The Irish government also dispatched 42 tonnes of **practical equipment** to be distributed to affected communities, including blankets, tents, mosquito nets, water cans and soap.
- In addition, Ireland's embassy in Freetown, Sierra Leone played a key role in the local **co-ordination of medical aid**.
- The French organisation **Doctors without Borders – *Médecins Sans Frontières* (MSF)** – was actively involved at the front line, working with local medical workers to contain the virus.
- Most importantly, **research in medical labs in the USA** led to the development of a treatment that may offer hope for the future.

Section 4 · Economic Geography

Questions

1. What is the type of country-to-country aid that is given by the Irish government to Ethiopia called?
2. Define the term 'multilateral aid'.
3. Describe briefly **two** ways in which Irish aid in Ethiopia is spent.
4. Explain the term NGO and give **two** Irish examples.
5. Give **one** recent example of emergency aid.
6. Name **three** countries in West Africa that were affected by the Ebola crisis in 2014–15.

15.4 Factors that hinder economic development

KEYWORDS
- failed state
- economic development
- population growth
- climate change
- oil revenue

Many factors, such as climate change, population growth, arms expenditure and war, slow down **economic development.**

We have already seen that some countries are classified as slowly developing countries and that most of these are in Africa. Many are failing or **failed states**. These countries face very great challenges. We will now examine the challenges facing South Sudan.

Definition

Failed states: Countries – mainly in Africa – that are badly ruled and where most of the people are trapped in poverty.

Case study

South Sudan

Introduction

South Sudan became the world's newest country in 2011. In that year, it became independent from Sudan after many years of civil war. South Sudan is bigger than Spain and Portugal combined. It is one of the world's poorest countries. The country faces very difficult challenges.

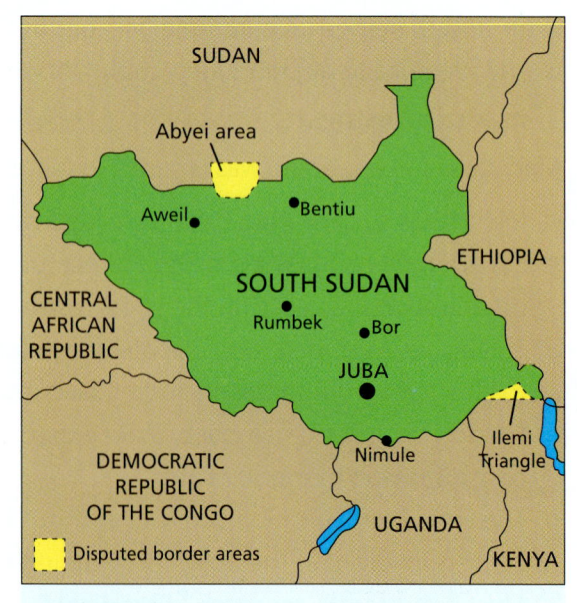

Figure 15.13 South Sudan, Africa's newest country

Chapter 15 · Economic Inequality

Case study

Population growth in South Sudan

South Sudan has one of the highest **population growth rates** in the world. The country is at stage 2 of the population cycle (see page 224). Population growth is **more than 4 per cent annually**. That means that the population of 11.5 million people will double in about 17 years!

Forty-two per cent of the population is aged 14 years or under. The task of educating huge numbers of children is proving to be beyond the capacity of the government.

Climate change

Part of South Sudan lies in the **Sahel**, an area of semi-desert just south of the Sahara (see pages 119–20). Much of the country is experiencing a change in rainfall patterns and longer periods of **drought**.

Figure 15.14 The population pyramid for South Sudan

- This leads to **desertification** and the death of the cattle and goats on which many tribes depend. Climate change leads to a decline in local food supplies. Many people are **short of food**.
- Many pastoral farmers whose animals have died have become **refugees** and fled to the cities. Towns and cities are not able to cope with the people coming in from the countryside.
- South Sudan is **landlocked** and has **very poor roads**. This makes it difficult to bring in food aid or to encourage **inward investment**.

Arms spending and civil war in South Sudan

After South Sudan became independent, **tribal rivalries** came to the fore. A **civil war** broke out in 2013. The conflict has led to the deaths of thousands of people, and more than one million people fled the conflict in fear of their lives and have become **refugees**.

Boy soldiers in South Sudan in February 2015. Here they are handing in their weapons and are about to return to ordinary life

South Sudan is also in conflict with Sudan over its borders.

The government of South Sudan is spending **more than 38 per cent of its oil revenue** on arms and the military. This is more than double the amount that the government is spending on health and education combined.

The country is awash with arms. The UN has **7,500 peacekeepers** in South Sudan trying to keep warring tribes apart. An uneasy truce was put in place in 2014. The civil war has given a very bad start to one of the world's poorest countries.

Section 4 · Economic Geography

> # Questions
>
> 1. Draw a sketch map of Africa and show the following countries:
>   - Sudan
>   - South Sudan.
>
> 2. Explain why the population of South Sudan is at stage 2 of the population cycle.
>
> 3. Describe **two** consequences of climate change that are affecting the people of South Sudan.
>
> 4. Name **one** way in which armed conflict has affected the people of South Sudan.

15.5 Economic inequalities within the EU

KEYWORDS
- the BMW
- peripheral location
- inward investment
- infrastructure
- the Mezzogiorno
- organised crime
- the *Cassa*

Some regions of the EU are much poorer than other regions. The new member states of Eastern Europe are much poorer than older member states in Western Europe. However, over time, the wealth of many countries increases. For example, Ireland was the poorest of the members when it joined in 1973. By 2007, it was among the wealthiest.

Even within each country, some regions are poorer than others. We will look at examples in the Republic of Ireland and Italy.

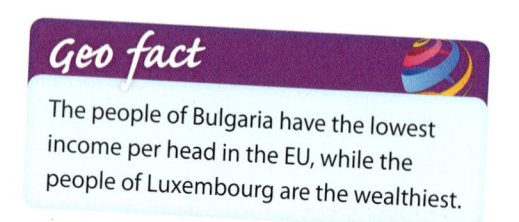

Geo fact

The people of Bulgaria have the lowest income per head in the EU, while the people of Luxembourg are the wealthiest.

Figure 15.15 Economic inequality in the EU

Economic inequality in the Republic of Ireland

The Republic of Ireland can be broken into two economic regions:

- The more prosperous Southern and Eastern region
- The less prosperous Border, Midlands and Western region, called the **BMW**.

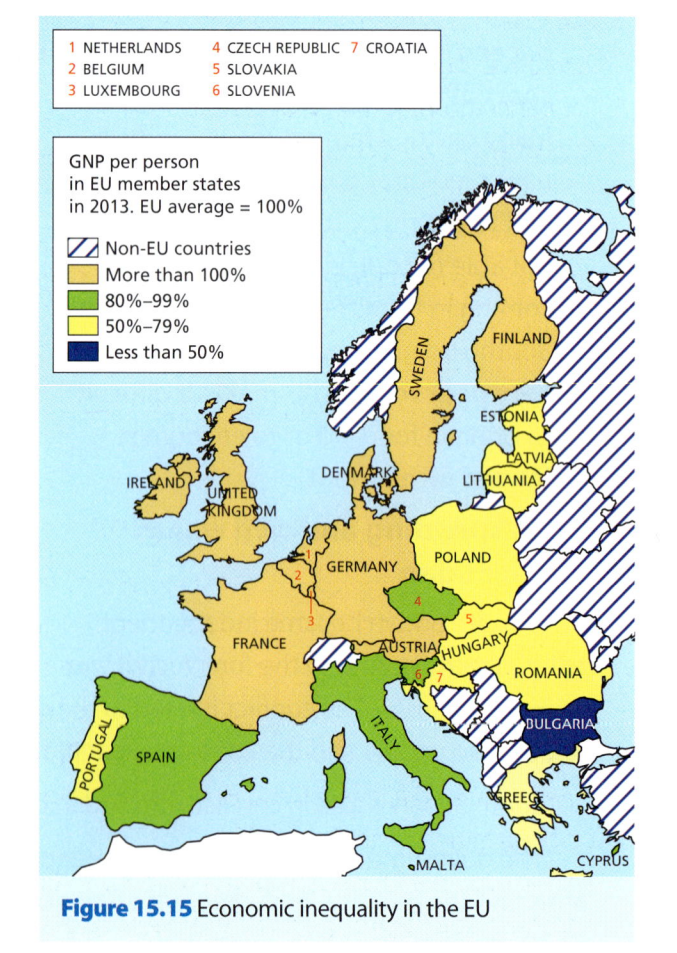

The BMW

The BMW has a **peripheral location**. That means that it is far away from the centre of things. It is some distance from Dublin, which is the centre of political power and influence.

> **Link**
> See **Low population densities: the west of Ireland**, pages 243–44.

- The BMW contains much **mountainous land**, especially in Galway, Mayo and Donegal. Mountainous land gives farmers a poor income.
- Because of soils, mountainous terrain and climate, farmers in most BMW counties concentrate on **sheep and cattle farming**. This is less profitable than wheat and barley.
- Many **farms are small** and there is a high percentage of elderly farmers.
- The BMW is composed of thirteen counties. It contained only 1.25 million people in the census of 2011. The BMW has a **low population density**.
- Apart from Galway, Sligo, Dundalk and Drogheda, the **urban centres of the BMW are small**. This makes the BMW region less attractive for major companies to invest in.
- For generations, young people have **migrated** outwards from the BMW to find employment. The population has grown since 1995, but many young people continue to move to other regions to work.
- **Infrastructure** in the BMW is not as good as in the south and east. The BMW has only one international airport: Knock, Co. Mayo.

Figure 15.16 The Republic of Ireland's two economic regions: the BMW and Southern and Eastern Region

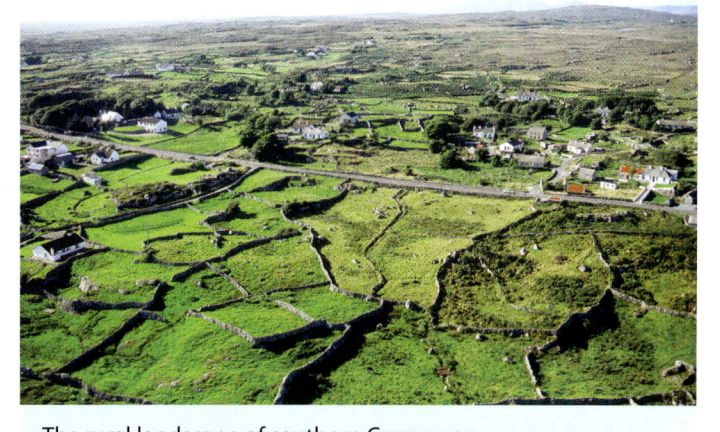

The rural landscape of southern Connemara

The Southern and Eastern region

- The south and east contain some **excellent soils** in river valleys such as the Barrow and the Munster Blackwater. The east has less rainfall. The south-east has more sunshine than western counties.
- Many farmers in the south and east are engaged in **tillage farming** because the soil is suitable for ploughing. **Profitable crops** such as wheat and barley are grown. Farmers have very good incomes from dairy farming in the Golden Vale.
- The Southern and Eastern region had 3.3 million people in 2011. This gives it a **higher population density** than the BMW. The region benefits from the **inward migration** of young people from the BMW.
- Apart from Dublin, **large urban centres** such as Cork, Limerick and Waterford are located in the south and east. These centres have attracted a lot of **inward investment** from foreign companies.

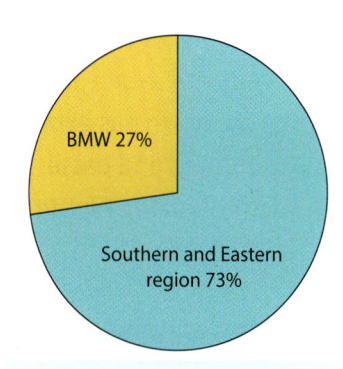

Figure 15.17 The population of the Republic of Ireland is unevenly divided between the BMW region and the Southern and Eastern region

Source: 2011 Census

Section 4 · Economic Geography

- The **infrastructure** of the Southern and Eastern region is good. Three international airports and the largest seaports in the state are all located there. The main roads from Dublin have long stretches of motorway.
- Most of all, **Dublin** is the centre of the Republic's economy.

Economic inequalities in Italy is for Higher Level students only.

The lush farmlands of Garrettstown, Co. Cork have large fields under tillage crops

Case study

Economic inequalities in Italy

There are sharp differences in income between the north and south of Italy.

The north of Italy

- Northern Italy has a **favourable climate**. It has a long growing season with summer showers.
- Agriculture in the **Po valley** is very productive. The valley contains **rich alluvial soils**, which are ideal for cereal production. The region produces excellent crops of wheat, rice, sunflowers, maize and vegetables.
- The north of Italy is **one of Europe's greatest manufacturing centres**. Companies such as FIAT (cars), Benetton (clothing), Gucci (leather goods) and Zanussi (electrical appliances) are located there. Milan and Turin are major economic centres.
- The **hydroelectric power** resources of the Alps are a major source of power for manufacturing.
- The north has **excellent roads and railways**. Tunnels and passes connect northern Italy through the Alps to markets in France, Switzerland and Austria. Genoa is one of Europe's leading ports.
- The north has benefited from **inward migration** of young people from the south.
- The north has a **great tourist industry** with winter sports in the Alps, lake resorts, the coastal resorts of the Italian Riviera, and the jewel of the Adriatic – Venice.

Figure 15.18 Italy's major cities; the red line indicates the north–south divide in Italy

Milan Cathedral and piazza (square). Milan is Italy's wealthiest city

Chapter 15 · Economic Inequality

Case study

The south of Italy: the Mezzogiorno

The south of Italy is called the **Mezzogiorno**. This region includes the southern portion of the Italian peninsula, as well as the islands of Sardinia and Sicily. The south of Italy is a **peripheral region**. The region is much poorer than the north of Italy for many reasons:

- Much of the south has a **mountainous landscape**. This makes farming difficult.
- The south suffers from a **lack of rainfall during the summer months**. This severely limits agriculture.

The town of Matera in southern Italy

- **Agricultural output** per hectare is much lower than in the north because of the terrain and summer drought. Many farms are too small to support a family. Irrigation is confined to small areas on narrow coastal plains.
- The south has suffered from **outward migration** for generations. This has drained it of many young people.
- Companies, both Italian and foreign, are less willing to invest in the south than in the north. The south is **far from the markets of the EU**.
- The south is infamous for **organised crime**, e.g. the Mafia in Sicily. This does not help inward investment.
- The south has many **tourist attractions** such as Vesuvius, Pompeii, the Isle of Capri and Sorrento. However, these have not been marketed abroad as successfully as the Spanish Tourist Board has done for Spain.

The *Cassa* (1950–1984)

Southern Italy has benefited from a government agency called *Cassa* and from EU funds. The *Cassa* invested funds in irrigation schemes to help farmers.

In the last fifty years, southern Italy has been connected by **motorway** to northern Italy. This has helped agriculture, tourism and manufacturing. Farmers can now market their fruit and vegetables in the cities of the north, while tourists can reach the south quickly.

Farmers are educated in modern farming methods.

Definition ✓

Cassa: An Italian word meaning fund.

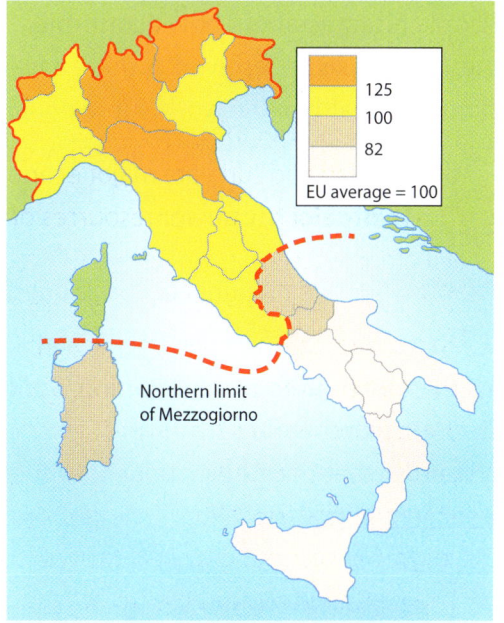

125
100
82
EU average = 100

Northern limit of Mezzogiorno

Figure 15.19 Income difference in Italy, in comparison with average income in the EU. What does this map tell you?

423

Section 4 · Economic Geography

> ## Questions
>
> 1. There are two major economic regions in the Republic of Ireland: the BMW is one. What is the name of the other region?
> 2. How many counties are in the BMW?
> 3. Draw a sketch map of Italy.
>   - Draw the division between the north and the south of Italy.
>   - Mark in and name the cities: Milan, Rome, Naples.
>   - Mark in and name **two** islands in the Mediterranean that are part of Italy.
> 4. What is the other Italian name for the south of Italy?
> 5. Explain **two** reasons why the south of Italy is poorer than the north.

15.6 Ending economic inequality

> **KEYWORDS**
> - economic inequality
> - appropriate aid
> - democracy
> - free press
> - world's trading system
> - trade justice
> - Fairtrade

The total wealth of the world is greater than ever, but it is not distributed equally. According to Oxfam, the poorest half of the world's population owns the same amount of wealth as the richest 85 people in the world.

People disagree about how **economic inequality** should be resolved. Is there a way of dividing the wealth of the world more equally, so that all people on the planet can enjoy clean water, a healthy diet, education and decent homes?

People who have thought about this question suggest that the answer lies in two areas:

- **Appropriate aid** to the developing world
- **Changing the world's trading system** so that trade helps poor countries to break free of poverty.

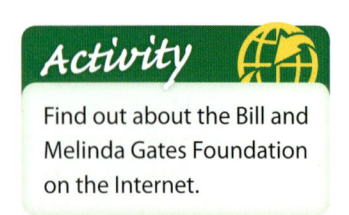

What is the message here?

Bill Gates, co-founder of Microsoft and one of the world's wealthiest people. He is making a difference to the lives of people in the South

> **Activity**
> Find out about the Bill and Melinda Gates Foundation on the Internet.

Appropriate aid

- Aid to the South must reach its target – the poorest people. **Aid funds must be carefully supervised** in recipient countries to prevent corruption.
- **Democracy** must be nurtured in the South by donor countries. Too many states are governed by corrupt rulers who steal from their own people. Democracy transfers power to the people.
- When a **free press** exists, an educated public can hold their leaders accountable for their actions. A free press can demand to see where the government is spending its money. Donor countries must insist on a free press as part of an aid package.
- **Military aid** and **tied aid** to the South should **cease**.
- Aid must be **appropriate** to the South. People in the South are entitled to be consulted as to what their needs are. Aid organisations must **listen to what local people have to say**.
- **Women's welfare** must also be targeted by aid donors because, in general, they do not possess anything like their fair share of the world's wealth.

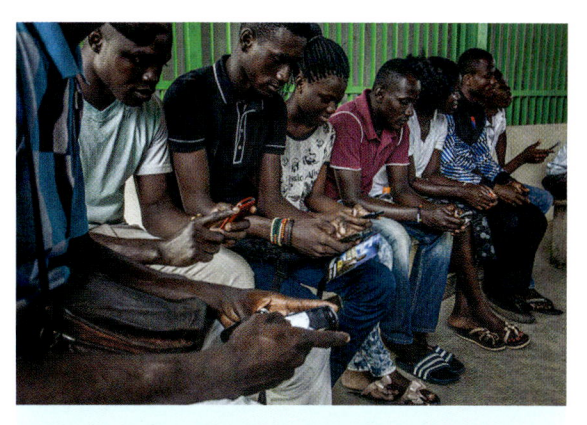

People in Côte D'Ivoire in West Africa using their mobile phones. The mobile phone gives citizens in Africa access to information, especially in countries where media blackouts by dictators are the order of the day. People can use the mobile to access social media such as Facebook and Twitter. This gives ordinary people more political power because they can report when people in authority act unjustly

Activity

In pairs or small groups, **discuss** why ordinary people are powerless in a country ruled by a dictator. Your study of Hitler and Stalin in your history class will help you here.

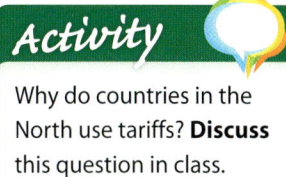

Changing the world's trading system

The world's **trading system** is unfair. The North imposes **tariffs** on many processed goods from the South. This must change and, to an extent, that is happening. The North has opened its markets to manufactured clothing, sports shoes, mobile phones and countless other goods from China, Vietnam and elsewhere. As a result, hundreds of millions of people have been lifted out of poverty in East Asia. China and other countries in Asia have proved that international trade greatly improves people's standard of living.

However, the North **continues to place tariffs** on processed coffee, cocoa and cotton from the South. This deprives many countries, especially in Africa, of billions of dollars in extra income. Until this changes, countries dependent on the export of unprocessed goods will remain poor. These are **mainly African countries.**

Trade justice for the South

The countries of the South regularly make their case for **trade justice** at World Trade Organization meetings. However, trade justice for the South is resisted by the North because the North fears that **lifting tariffs** on imported goods such as processed coffee and tea bags will cause unemployment in the North.

Cocoa, coffee and tea are not essential commodities. This weakens the bargaining power of the countries in the South that produce them. They are not at all as important as oil is to the North. The South faces an uphill battle in its struggle for trade justice.

Activity

Why do countries in the North use tariffs? **Discuss** this question in class.

Section 4 · Economic Geography

The Fairtrade movement

Fairtrade is designed to make the world trading system fairer to producers in the South. Fairtrade works on the following principles:

- Decent and healthy **working conditions for workers** in the South
- A **fair price for producers**. Fairtrade puts people before profits.

Fairtrade bananas, tea, coffee, chocolate and other products are for sale in many Irish shops.

Fairtrade is changing the lives of co-op farmers in the South. Because they receive more for their produce, co-ops can build clinics, schools and water treatment plants. These facilities improve the lives of local people.

When people buy Fairtrade coffee and other Fairtrade products, they make a difference to the lives of producers in the South

Questions

1. Explain **two** ways in which aid to the South can be more effective.
2. Explain **one** way by which people in the South may demand more effective leadership from politicians.
3. Give **one** reason why international trade is of little benefit to many African countries.
4. What does trade justice mean?
5. What is the Fairtrade movement and how does it benefit poor people in the South?

Chapter 15 · Economic Inequality

Summary chart

PowerPoint summary

An unequal world

Aid
- **Types of aid**
  - Bilateral
  - Multilateral
  - Emergency
  - Tied
  - Voluntary (NGOs)
- **Irish Aid**
  - Ethiopia
- Official aid
- Advantages and disadvantages of aid

The South
- **The quickly developing world**
  - Much of Asia
  - Brazil, Mexico
- **The slowly developing world**
  - Sub-Saharan Africa

The North (The developed world)
- **Economic inequality**
  - In Ireland
  - In the EU
  - In Italy

Exploitation of poor countries
- Ireland in the past
- The coffee business

Factors hindering economic development
- **South Sudan**
  - Rapid population growth
  - War
  - Climate change

Ending economic inequality
- Appropriate aid
- Changing the global trading system

427

Section 4 · Economic Geography

Exam questions

1 The graph shows who makes the profits in coffee production.

   Explain how unfair trading may be a cause of poverty in the developing world.

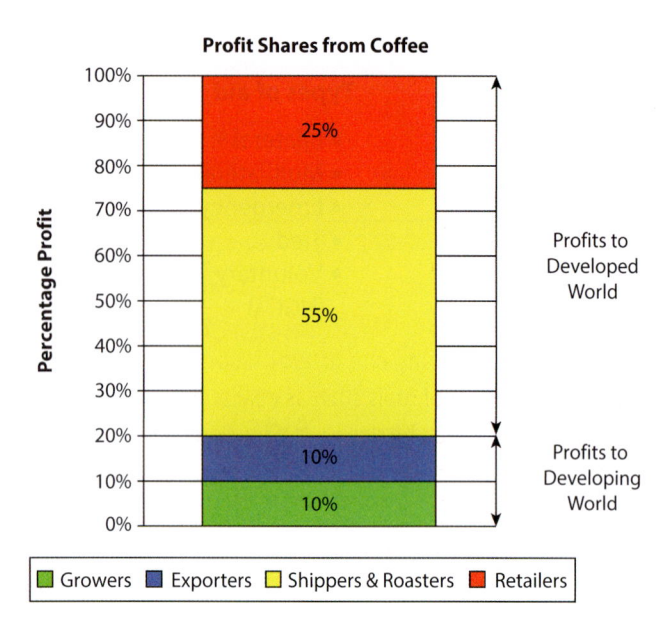

   Profit Shares from Coffee
   - Growers: 10%
   - Exporters: 10%
   - Shippers & Roasters: 55%
   - Retailers: 25%

   Profits to Developed World: 80%
   Profits to Developing World: 20%

   HL 2008

2 | Tied aid | Multilateral aid | Bilateral aid | Emergency aid | Development aid |

   (i) Choose any **one** type of aid named in the box above. Describe the advantages **and** the disadvantages of this type of aid.

   (ii) Name **one** place in the world where this type of aid is used or was used.

   OL 2015

3 (i) Name a developing country that you have studied.

   (ii) Explain how any three of these factors have slowed the development of this country:
   - Unfair trade
   - War
   - Population growth
   - Climate change.

   OL 2013

4 'Levels of economic development are unequal throughout the world.'

   (i) Explain **three** reasons why the level of economic development is lower in the 'south'.

   (ii) Name **two** ways in which this can be addressed.

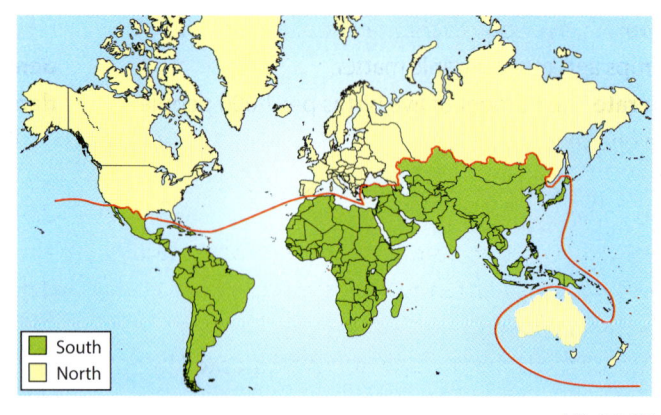

   HL 2012

5 (i) Name a developing region you have studied.

   (ii) Explain **three** reasons why this region is not as economically developed as other regions.

   HL 2011

Glossary

abrasion Erosion caused by the load carried by rivers, waves and glaciers.
acid rain Rainwater containing chemicals that occurs as a result of the burning of fuels such as coal and oil.
aid Development assistance by rich countries and other organisations to projects in the developing world.
air mass Large body of air that has similar temperature, pressure and moisture throughout.
alluvium Material transported and deposited by a river when it floods.
anemometer Instrument used to measure the speed of wind.
anticyclone An area of high atmospheric pressure (HP), usually associated with fine, settled weather.
aspect The direction in which a slope faces.
atmosphere The layer of gases, including nitrogen and oxygen, surrounding the Earth.
attrition Erosion caused when the particles in the load carried by rivers and waves bump off one another.
backwash Water returning to the sea after a wave has broken.
bauxite The mineral ore from which alumina is refined.
bedrock Solid rock that makes up the lowest layer of a soil profile.
biofuels Energy sources that can be extracted from crops and other organic matter.
birth rate The number of live births per 1,000 people in one year.
BMW The Border, Midland and Western region in the Republic of Ireland.
boreal Climate belt in northern latitudes that has long, cold winters and short summers; associated with coniferous forests.
boulder clay Mixture of clay and rocks deposited by a glacier.
bridging point A place where a river has been forded or bridged, at which a settlement often develops.
brown earth soil Fertile, well-drained soil that developed where deciduous forests grow.
carbonation Chemical weathering where rocks such as limestone are broken down by acid in rainwater.
CBD The central business district of a city.

chemical weathering When rocks decay or are dissolved by a chemical change.
child mortality The average number of deaths of children under five years of age per 1,000 live births.
cholera A potentially fatal infection caused by consuming contaminated food or water.
climate The average weather conditions of a region over a long period of time.
cloud A visible body of very fine water droplets or ice particles suspended in the atmosphere.
colonisation One country taking political control over another country.
commuters People who travel some distance from their homes to their places of work.
conservation The care, protection and careful use of resources and of the environment.
convection currents Currents in the mantle that move the heated molten magma upwards from the core towards the crust and cause the plates to move.
crust The thin, solid outer layer of the Earth.
DART Dublin Area Rapid Transit is a commuter railway line along the Dublin coast linking Malahide with Greystones
death rate The number of deaths per 1,000 people in one year.
demography The study of the structure of populations.
denudation Breaking up and removing rocks on the Earth's surface by weathering, mass movement and erosion.
deposition The laying down of the load transported by rivers, waves and ice.
depression An area of low atmospheric pressure (LP), usually associated with wet, cloudy and windy weather.
desertification The gradual spread of desert conditions into surrounding areas.
developed countries Countries that are wealthy, have good services and a high standard of living; also known as the North or the First World.
developing countries Countries that are poor, with few services and a low standard of living; also known as the South or the Third World.

Glossary

development The use of resources and technology to improve people's standard of living and quality of life.

doldrums Areas of low pressure and slack winds near the equator.

dormitory town A town to which people return home after their day's work.

drainage basin The area of land drained by a single river and its tributaries.

earthquake A sudden movement within the Earth's crust, usually close to a plate boundary.

economic migrant A person who has moved in search of work.

emigrant A person who leaves a country to live elsewhere.

environment The living conditions in which people, animals and plants exist.

erosion The breaking down of rocks and the removal of the resulting particles by rivers, waves and ice.

export processing zones Industrial estates, mainly in developing countries such as China, where goods are manufactured for export.

fertiliser Manure or a mixture of nitrates used to make soil more fertile.

fold mountains Mountains formed when rocks buckled and folded as two plates collided.

food processing The conversion of food resources, such as meat and milk, along with other ingredients into products such as sausages and cheese.

footloose industry An industry that is not tied to raw materials and has a wide choice of location.

fossil fuels Fuels such as coal, oil and natural gas that developed over time from the remains of plants and animals.

freeze-thaw Mechanical weathering where rocks are broken down due to water in cracks repeatedly freezing and thawing.

front The dividing line (cold front or warm front) between two air masses that have different temperatures and pressures.

glacier A large, slow-moving mass of ice flowing down a valley.

greenhouse effect The way that gases in the atmosphere trap an increasing amount of energy from the sun.

heavy industry The manufacture of goods in which heavy or bulky raw materials are used, such as smelting and oil refining.

horizon One of the layers that make up a soil profile.

horse latitudes Areas of high pressure and rising air, about 30°N and 30°S of the equator.

hydraulic action Erosion caused by the power of moving water in rivers or waves.

Ice Age A time when vast areas of the Earth were covered by ice sheets.

ice sheet Moving mass of ice that covers a large land area.

igneous rock A rock that formed from the cooling of molten magma or lava.

immigrant A person who enters a country with the intention of living there.

impermeable rock Rock that does not allow water to pass through it.

industrial estates An area where several manufacturing companies are located, often on the edge of a town or city.

industrial inertia When an industry does not relocate even though the original reasons for its location no longer exist.

industrially emergent regions Regions and countries that have little or no modern manufacturing, e.g. Africa and central Asia.

infrastructure Networks such as road, rail, electricity, water, telephone and broadband.

inner city The area of the city with older housing and industries that is located next to the city centre.

Irish Aid Development assistance given by the Irish government to some countries in the developing world.

irrigation Supplying dry agricultural land with water in order to grow crops.

karst An area of limestone with surface and underground features that result from chemical weathering.

landslide The very rapid movement of earth and rock (regolith) down a steep slope.

latitude The angular distance north or south of the equator.

life expectancy The average number of years that a person in a given country is expected to live.

light industry Manufacturing activity, such as fashion and hi-fi equipment, that uses moderate amounts of raw materials.

longshore drift The zigzag movement of material along a coastline by waves.

Luas A light rail system linking Dublin city centre with Tallaght and Bride's Glen.

magma The molten or semi-molten material that makes up the Earth's mantle.

mantle The layer of molten rock between the Earth's crust and core.

Glossary

market A place where goods are bought and sold, or a group of people who buy goods.

mass movement The movement down-slope of loose material under the influence of gravity.

mechanical weathering When rock is broken down into small pieces by freeze-thaw and plant roots.

metamorphic rock A rock that has been changed by extremes of heat and pressure.

meteorology The study of weather.

Mezzogiorno The south of Italy including the islands of Sardinia and Sicily.

migration The movement of people from one area to another to live and often to work.

mudflow Moving rivers of rock, soil and water.

multinational companies Companies with a base in more than one country.

navigable river A river that can be used for barge traffic.

newly industrialised countries Countries that have become rapidly industrialised in recent decades, e.g. in South-East Asia.

NGOs Non-governmental organisations, e.g. voluntary agencies that provide assistance to projects in the developing world.

nomadic herders Farmers who move according to the seasons from place to place in search of food, water, and grazing land with their animals.

non-renewable resource A finite resource that will eventually run out or be depleted, such as oil.

North Atlantic Drift Warm ocean current that begins as the Gulf Stream and warms the waters off Ireland's coast.

nucleated settlement A cluster of buildings and inhabitants in a particular location.

ocean current Regular patterns of water flowing like giant rivers through the oceans.

Pangaea The single land mass (supercontinent) that later broke up to form the continents.

permeable rock Rock that allows water to pass through it.

plate boundary The place where two plates meet. It is associated with volcanoes, fold mountains and earthquakes.

plate tectonics The theory that the crust of the Earth is divided into a number of moving plates, leading to folding, volcanic and earthquake activity.

plates The separate sections into which the crust of the Earth is broken.

plucking Erosion where blocks of rock are torn out by moving ice.

podzol Soil that formed in cold, wet areas that had a cover of coniferous forest.

polder An area of land that has been reclaimed from the sea.

pollution Noise, harmful substances and dirt produced by people and machines.

population cycle (the demographic transition model) Shows how changes in birth and death rates over time are related to a country's development.

population density The average number of people living in an area, usually per km^2.

population distribution The spread of people over an area.

population explosion A sudden rapid increase in the population of a region.

population pyramid A bar chart displaying the population structure of an area.

population structure The composition of a country's population by age and sex.

precipitation All forms of moisture from the atmosphere, including rainfall, snow, hail and fog.

prevailing wind The direction from which the wind blows most frequently.

primary activities Economic activities where resource materials are extracted from the land and the sea.

pull factors Things that attract people to live in an area.

push factors Things that make people decide to leave an area.

QBCs Quality bus corridors in cities and suburbs that are reserved for buses and taxis.

regolith Loose material (rocks and soil) that covers the surface of the Earth.

relief The shape and height of the land.

renewable resource A non-finite resource such as wind power or solar energy that can be used over and over again.

resource Any material or product that people find useful.

Richter scale A scale by which the strength of an earthquake is described.

Sahel A region at the southern edge of the Sahara Desert that is affected by desertification.

scree Loose pieces of rock with sharp edges. They are broken off by freeze-thaw and gather at the foot of a slope.

secondary activities Economic activities where raw materials are processed into products.

sedimentary rock A rock formed from sediments that were laid down and compressed over millions of years.

Glossary

seismometer (seismograph) An instrument used to measure (and record) the strength of an earthquake.
settlement The manner in which an area is settled by people, either as rural dwellers or in towns and cities.
shanty town A group of shacks or huts in an area of a city, usually lacking electricity, water supply and a sewage system.
soil The thin layer of loose material on the Earth's surface.
soil creep The slow, down-slope movement of soil under the influence of gravity.
soil erosion The removal of fertile topsoil by wind, rain and running water.
soil profile A cross-section of a soil that is made up of a number of layers (horizons).
solar energy Energy from the sun, giving heat and light to the Earth.
solution When a substance (rock) is dissolved in water.
Sub-Saharan Africa The region of Africa that lies south of the Sahara Desert.
suburb A mainly residential area on the edge of a city.
sustainable development A way of improving people's standards of living and quality of life without damaging the environment or putting the wellbeing of future generations at risk.
swash The movement of water up a beach after a wave breaks.
tariffs Taxes placed on goods when they are imported.
terrain The physical features of a land area.
tertiary activities Activities that provide a service to people, such as health and tourism.
trade The movement and sale of goods and services between countries.
tremors Series of shock waves that run through the rocks of the crust after an earthquake.
tsunami A huge wave that is caused by an underwater earthquake.
urban functional zones Areas of a city where different types of activity take place, e.g. manufacturing, residential and retail.
urban redevelopment The demolition of old derelict buildings and homes in the inner city and their replacement with offices, hotels and apartments.
urban renewal The demolition of old sub-standard homes in the inner city and the construction of modern homes for the residents in the same location.
urban sprawl The expansion of a city into the countryside in an unplanned and uncontrolled way.
volcano A cone-shaped mountain formed by the eruption of magma from inside the Earth to the surface.
water cycle The continual recycling of water as it passes between the atmosphere, the oceans and the land.
weather The day-to-day condition of the atmosphere, including temperature, precipitation, sunshine and wind.
weathering The breakdown and decay of rocks by mechanical (freeze-thaw) and chemical (carbonation) processes.
Women's Liberation movement A women's pressure group from the 1970s aimed at equal rights for women.

Index

A

abrasion
    by glaciers 67, 68, 69, 76
    by rivers 46, 56
    by the sea 57, 60, 66
acid rain 32, 380–82
aerial photography 181–96, 210
Africa
    aid to 414–17
    barriers to development 418–19
    child mortality 253
    exploitation of 262, 407, 409, 425
    life expectancy 254
    manufacturing in 378, 379
    population 223, 228, 230, 231, 235, 245–7, 419
    slowly developing economy 405–6
    trade with 366, 409, 425
aftershocks 13, 14
agriculture
    global warming and 105, 106, 120
    impact of industry on 382
    in Africa 245–6
    in Ireland 122, 243–4, 275
    Mediterranean 124, 241, 340, 422–3
aid to the South 412–17, 425
air masses 88–92, 108, 113
airports 164, 294–5, 398
alluvium 50, 51
Alpine folding 8
altitude 114, 154, 166, 196, 274
Amazon basin 35, 52, 237–9
anemometers 98, 101, 102, 108
anticyclones 91–2, 108
arêtes 68, 70
Armorican folding 8
aspect 113, 166
Aswan High Dam 338–9
atmosphere, the 78–9, 88, 108
atmospheric pressure 82, 83, 84, 90–92, 97, 98, 100, 108
attrition
    by rivers 46, 56
    by the sea 57, 66

Aughinish 366–8
avalanches 14

B

backwash 57, 60, 61
barometers 98, 100, 108
basalt 20, 21, 25
bays 58, 62
beaches 58, 61–2, 63, 65, 390
Beaufort scale 102
bedding planes 23, 32, 33, 34
bedrock 73, 136, 336
biofuel/biomass 238, 341, 348
birth rates 223–5
Black Death 222, 302
blowholes 59, 60
BMW region 420–21
bogbursts 30, 39
bogs 173, 275, 346–8
Bord na Móna 275, 347, 348
boreal climates 126, 127–9, 130
boulder clay 71, 72, 74, 138
Brazil
    coffee trade and 410, 411
    colonisation of 261, 262
    education in 229
    industry in 366, 378
    population of 226, 232, 237–9
    tropical red soils in 35
    urbanisation in 326–7
    water in 227
bridging points 168, 169, 274, 275, 285
brown earth soils 138
Burren, the 22, 33, 36

C

Calcutta 247
Campbell-Stokes sunshine recorder 98, 103, 108
Canaries Current 86, 87
carbonation 32–5, 42
cardinal points 153
caverns 34, 35
caves 34, 35, 59–60

CBD (central business district) 304, 306, 308, 309, 323, 324
Celtic Tiger 233, 237, 258, 259, 273, 288, 310, 318, 319
Celts 268
CFCs (chlorofluorocarbons) 105
child mortality 252–3, 326
China
    Hong Kong and 249–51
    industry in 378–9, 425
    life expectancy 255
    population of 224, 229, 230, 235
    quickly developing economy 405
    women in 376–7
cirques 68, 70
cities 328
    activities in 301
    functional zones in 304–7, 323
    housing in 310–11
    in the developing world 323–7
    land values in 308–9
    location of 168, 274–5
    population of Irish 273
    primate 272, 306
    problems in 315–17
    redevelopment in 318–20
    tourism and 392
    transport in 312–14
    world 306
clean energy 107, 345, 382
cliffs 58–60, 154, 268, 390
climates 111, 130
    altitude and 114
    aspect and 113
    boreal 126–9
    change 75, 106, 119, 414, 419
    cold 115, 126–9
    continental 112
    cool temperate oceanic 121–2
    currents and 86–7
    desert 116, 117–20
    distance from the sea and 112
    equatorial 116–17, 140
    hot 115, 116–20

433

Index

latitude and 112
local 113–14
Mediterranean 123–5
population and 235, 237, 238, 241, 242, 246, 256
prevailing winds and 113
savanna 116–17
soils and 135, 136
temperate 112, 115, 121–5
tourism and 393–5
tundra 126
warm temperate oceanic 121, 123–5
world 115–29
clints 33, 34
Clonmacnoise 166, 271, 281
clouds 79, 89, 91, 93, 94, 95, 96
coal 23, 25, 341, 369, 371, 372
    pollution 105, 380, 382
coalfield sites 369, 372
coastal protection 64–5
coffee 410–11, 425, 426
cold climates 115, 126–9, 130
Cologne 285–6, 298
colonisation 226, 237, 246, 260–62, 407–9
communications 291–8, 299
    and industry 362–8, 370
    in Ireland 244
    on OS maps 164
    pre-Christian 268
commuter belts 273
commuting 280, 288, 293, 312–14
compass points 153
compressed air 57, 59, 66
condensation 93, 94, 95, 119
coniferous forests 127, 139, 141, 172
constructive plate boundaries 4, 17
continental drift 6
continental shelf 349
contours, map 154, 155
convection currents 5, 17
convectional rainfall 96
core, the Earth's 2–3, 5
Coriolis effect 84, 108
Corrib gas field 25, 27, 344
crime 316, 399, 423
crop rotation 226, 413
cross-sections of maps 156
crust, the Earth's 2–5, 11, 13, 17, 19–20
currents, ocean 85–7, 108, 116–17
cyclonic (frontal) rainfall 95

D

dams 54, 277–8, 338–9
DART 313, 314
death rates 223–5
decentralisation 273
deciduous forests 122, 138, 141, 172
deforestation 105, 107, 140
deltas, river 52–3
denudation 30, 42
demographic transition model 223–4
deposition
    by glaciers 71–3, 76
    by rivers 47, 49–50, 51, 52, 56
    by the sea 61–3, 66
depressions 90–91, 123
desert climates, hot 116, 117–20, 130
desertification 119–20, 246, 419
destructive plate boundaries 4, 7, 17
developed world 251–4, 333, 374–5, 378, 379, 387, 404–5, 407–9, 411, 420–23, 425, 427
developing world 251–5, 323–7, 333, 376–7, 378–9, 404–6, 409–11, 412–17, 418–19, 425, 427
Discovery Series (OS maps) 147
distributaries 52
doldrums 84
dormitory towns 280, 288, 291, 293, 295
drainage 45, 141, 163, 166
drilling 26
droughts 105, 106, 117, 119–20, 242, 246, 414, 419
drumlins 72
Dublin
    growth of 302–3
    importance of 272–3
    population of 239–40, 273
    public transport 313–14
    resources and terrain 239–40
    water supply 74, 336
    tourism 392
    urban improvements 318–21

E

earthquakes 4, 12, 13–16, 39
eastings 150–52
Ebola outbreak 417
economic activities
    primary 332–3, 356
    sea and 64
    secondary 332–3, 359, 385
    tertiary 332–3, 387–8, 401

economic inequality 251–5, 404–7, 409–11, 427
    ending 424–6
    factors in 418–19
    in the EU 420–23
    in Ireland 408, 420–22
economic migrants 258, 259
economies 404–6, 427
emergency aid 412, 413, 417
emigration 236, 256–8, 259
energy
    consumption 341
    geothermal 10, 345
    renewable 54, 107, 345, 382
    solar 79–81, 345, 382
    sources of 25–7, 238, 341–8, 384
    wind 345, 382, 383
equatorial climate 116–17, 140
erosion 28, 30, 33, 44
    by glaciers 67–76
    by rivers 45–56
    by the sea 57–66, 106
erratics 71
eskers 73, 74, 268
Ethiopia 406, 414–16
European Union (EU)
    economic inequality in 420–23
    fishing in 350, 352
evaporation 93, 119, 339
export crops 244, 409, 410

F

factory locations 362–8
factory systems 359–61
failed states 418
Fairtrade 426
family planning 228, 233
famine 120, 226, 236
farming 186, 226, 353
    in the developing world 245, 337–9, 410–11
    in Europe 241–2, 340, 423
    in Ireland 240, 243–4, 354–5, 421
fault lines 7, 13, 16
fertilisers 105, 119, 225, 226, 339, 353
fertility rates 231, 232
finite resources 334, 341
fiords 70
fishing 64, 349–52
flooding 55, 106, 338
floodplains 50, 53
fold mountains 7–8

Index

food supply 226, 408, 413, 415, 419
forestry 172, 334, 380–81
fossil fuels 105, 383
fossils 22
freeze-thaw 31–2, 42
fronts 89, 90, 91

G

gabions 65
gas, natural 25–7, 105, 341, 344
Giant's Causeway 11, 21, 94
glaciated valleys 69, 70
glaciation 74–6
   deposition 71–3
   erosion 67–70
glaciers 67–70, 71–3, 75
gley soils 138, 139
global warming 104–7, 119
GNP (gross national product) 406, 420
gorges 49
gradient on maps 154–5
granite 20–21, 25, 26, 135, 336
greenfield sites 361, 364
greenhouse effect 80, 104–7
grid referencing 150–52
grikes 33–4, 36
ground moraines 71, 72
groynes 64, 65
Gulf Stream 86, 87

H

hanging valleys 69, 70
hardpan 137, 139
headlands 58, 59, 60, 268
high pressure 82–5, 91–2, 100, 123
Hong Kong 249–51
horizons, soil 136–9
hot climates 115, 116–20, 130
housing 192, 305, 310–11, 315, 316, 318–19
humus 133–41
hydraulic action 46, 56, 57, 59, 66
hydroelectric power (HEP) 54, 74, 241, 341, 345
hygrometers 101, 108

I

Ice Age 26, 67, 138, 267, 389
Iceland 9, 10
IDA (Industrial Development Authority) 364, 369
IFA (Irish Farmers' Association) 354

igneous rocks 20–21, 25, 28
immigration 233, 256, 258, 259
incineration 384
India, population of 229, 231, 235, 248–9, 255
industrial inertia 371, 373
industrial regions 378–9
industry
   British iron and steel 371–3
   environmental impact of 380–84
   footloose 369–70
   heavy 305, 366–7
   light 360–61, 363–4
   location of 305, 307, 323, 369–70, 371–3
   on a world scale 378–9
   women in 374–7
inner cities 309, 315–16, 318–20
Intel Ireland 290, 361, 363–5
interlocking spurs 48
Irish Aid programmes 414–16
Irish Conservation Box 352
irrigation 120, 124, 226, 245, 337–40, 415, 423
Italy 240–42, 422–3

J

Japan 11, 16, 230, 378

K

karst landscape s 33–5
Kinsale gas field 25, 27, 344
Kolkata 247, 248–9, 324–5
Köln 285–6, 298

L

Labrador Current 86, 87
lagoons 62, 63
lahars 39–40
land bridges 267
land use 172–4, 180, 186, 275, 308–9, 328
land value 308–9, 328
landfill 105, 384
landlords' towns 272
landslides 14, 30, 38–9
lateral moraines 71, 72
latitude 80, 108, 112
latosols 140
lava 11, 12, 21
leaching 136–7, 141, 381
levees 51, 52

life expectancy 232, 233, 253–5, 377
Limerick 274, 281, 282–3
limestone 22, 24, 25, 26, 32, 33–6, 135
limestone pavements 33–6
literacy 229, 230
local climates 113–14, 130
London airports 294–5
longshore drift 60–61, 62, 63, 64, 65, 390
low pressure 82–4, 90–91, 100
Luas 313, 314, 321

M

magma 3–5, 9–11, 21, 24, 28, 345
Mali 245–7
malnutrition 254
mantle, the Earth's 2–5, 17
manufacturing 385
maps 146
   antiquities on 165
   area, calculating 149–50
   colour coding 154
   cross-sections of 156
   direction on 153
   Discovery Series 147
   distances, measuring 148–9
   drainage on 163
   Europe 214, 215
   gradient on 154–5
   grid references 150–52
   height on 154
   human landscape on 163–80
   Ireland 212, 213
   land use on 172–4
   legends for 147, 211
   Ordnance Survey 146–80, 196
   physical landscape on 162–3
   relief on 162
   scale of 146–7
   settlements on 165–9
   sketch 157
   slope on 154–5
   symbols on 147, 163, 164, 165, 168, 172, 173, 211
   tourist facilities on 173–4
   transport on 164
   urban functions on 170–71
   weather 89, 90, 91, 100
   World 216–17, 218–19
marble 24, 25
marram grass 61, 62
mass movement 30, 37–40, 42
meanders 49–50, 53

Index

meat traceability 355
medial moraines 71, 72
Mediterranean climate 123–5, 130
Met Éireann 97, 98
metamorphic rocks 23–5, 28
meteorology 97
Mezzogiorno 240, 242, 423
micro-organisms 134, 135
Mid-Atlantic Ridge 4, 9, 10
migration 255–62, 263
mineral matter 133, 134
mining 26, 287–8
monastic settlements 75, 166, 271
moraines 71, 72
Mount St Helens 11, 12
mudflows 12, 30, 39–40
multinational companies 237, 323, 363, 378–9, 411

N

National Grid (OS maps) 150
natural gas 25–7, 105, 341, 344
natural increase 225
natural regions 115
natural resources 25–7, 133, 241, 333–4, 356
natural vegetation 115, 117, 121, 122, 124, 126, 127, 141, 172, 238
Navan 26, 288–9
Nepal 14, 387, 412
Netherlands, the 277–9
Nevado del Ruiz 40
NGOs (non-governmental organisations) 416
Nile valley 338–9
nomadic peoples 129, 245, 342
non-renewable resources 334, 341
Normans, the 165, 271, 275, 287, 302
North, the 251; see also developed world
North Atlantic Drift 86, 87, 106
North/South divide 251–5, 404–7, 409–11, 427
northings 150–52
Nutricia Infant Nutrition Ltd 360

O

oases 118, 338–9
oil 25–6, 341–4, 383
Ordnance Survey (OS) maps 146–80, 196, 211; see also maps
outwash plains 73

oxbow lakes 50–51
ozone layer 79, 105, 108

P

Pacific Ring of Fire 11
Pangaea 6
Paris 294, 306–7
paternoster lakes 69, 70
peatlands 25, 275, 346–8
peaty soils 138, 139
permafrost 128
pillars 35
placenames 175, 268, 270
plant litter 136, 138, 139, 140, 141
Plantation of Ulster 260–61
plantation settlements 271–2
plates, tectonic 3–6, 7–16, 17
plucking (glaciers) 67–8, 76
plunge pools 49
podzol soils 138, 139, 141, 142
polders 277–9
polygamy 246
population 263
   causes of change 225–9
   cycle 223–4
   density 234–51
   distribution 234–42, 301
   growth 222–5, 229, 230–31, 419
   pyramids 232–4, 419
precipitation 93, 94–6, 97, 98, 102, 108
prevailing winds 83, 85, 86, 87, 113, 123
primate cities 272, 306
production systems 359
public transport 313–14
pyramidal peaks 68, 70

Q

QBCs (quality bus corridors) 314
quarrying 24, 26
quartzite 24, 25
quickly developing economies 404–6, 427

R

rain gauges 98, 102, 108
rainfall 94–6, 106
reclaimed land 277–9
recycling 107, 334, 384
refugees 120, 413, 419
regolith 30, 37
relative humidity 101, 108

relief (physical landscape) 162, 168, 188
renewable resources 54, 107, 333, 335, 345, 349, 383
Rhine, River 284–6, 297–8, 337
ribbon lakes 69
Richter scale 14, 15, 16
rivers 45–56
road networks 272, 292–3, 312, 316, 397
rock armour 64, 65
Rosslare 65
Rotterdam 284, 297, 298
route focus 168, 169
rural settlements 166–7, 180, 186, 210
RUSAL Aughinish 366–8

S

Sahara Desert 87, 116, 118, 119, 130
Sahel 119–20, 245–6, 419
sand bars 63
sand dunes 61, 62, 63
sand spits 62, 63
sandstone 23, 24, 25, 26, 135
São Paulo 326–7
satellite towns 303, 304, 307, 316, 320–21
Saudi Arabia 342–3, 405
savanna climate 116–17, 130
scale (maps/photos) 146–7, 196
scree 31
scramble for Africa 407
sea, the 57–66
sea arches 59
sea stacks 59, 60
sea walls 64, 65
seasons 81, 183
sedimentary rocks 22–3, 25, 28
seismographs/seismometers 15
settlements 180, 210, 299
   ancient 165, 186, 266–8
   dispersed 167, 186
   distribution of 238, 274–9, 281, 284
   functions of 165, 170–71, 189, 210, 279–80, 286–91, 304–7
   linear 167, 186
   nucleated/clustered 167, 186–7, 270–73, 279–91
   on OS maps 165–9
   patterns 167, 278
   rural 166–7, 186
   urban 168–9, 187–8, 272–3, 282, 285–6, 301–28
shales 25

Index

Shannon, River 54–5, 275, 281, 366–7, 392
Shannon Airport 282, 295–6
Shannon Town 293, 295–6, 370
shanty towns 227, 249, 323, 325, 326–7
Sheffield 372, 373
shopping zones 304, 305, 306, 308
sketch maps, drawing 157, 183–4
slate 24
slope on maps 154–5
slowly developing economies 404–6, 427
soil 133–5, 142
   creep 30, 38
   Irish 138–9
   profiles 136–7
   tropical red 35, 140
   vegetation and 141
solar energy 79–81, 341, 345, 382, 388
solution (by rivers) 46–7, 56
South, the 251; *see also* developing world
South America, colonisation of 261–2
South Sudan 418–19
Southern and Eastern region 421–2
Spain, tourism in 125, 393, 394–400
spot heights 154
sprawl, urban 303, 317
stalactites 35
stalagmites 35
steel industry 369, 371–3
Stevenson screens 98
storm beaches 61–2
striae 68
Sub-Saharan Africa 405–6
sun, the 79–81, 104, 108
sunshine 97, 98, 103, 393–5
sustainable exploitation 333, 349
swallow holes 33–5
swash 57, 60–62
synoptic charts 97, 98, 100
systems of production 353–4, 359–61, 367

T
taiga 127–8
Tallaght 240, 321
tariff barriers 411, 425
tarns 68, 70, 74
Teagasc 354
tectonics, plate 3–6
temperate climates 112, 115, 121–5, 130
temperature 97–9, 104–7, 108
tenements 303
terminal moraines 72
terracettes 38
thermometers 98–9, 101, 108
tidal energy 345
tombolos 62, 63
tourism 65, 389, 401
   in Europe 10, 125, 284, 393–400, 422, 423
   in Ireland 36, 74, 281, 282, 287, 293, 389–92
trade justice 425–6
trade winds 84, 116
traffic 191, 312–13, 316, 327
transform plate boundaries 4, 17
transport
   air 294–5, 398
   on maps 164, 169, 180
   public 313–14
   road 272, 292–3, 312, 313, 316, 397
   rail 272, 313, 397–8
   river 297–8
transportation of load
   by glaciers 71, 76
   by rivers 47, 56
   by the sea 60–61, 66
tremors 13, 15, 16
triangulation pillars 154
Trim 188, 287
tropical red soils 35, 140, 142
troposphere 79, 108
tsunami in Japan 16, 17
tundra climates 126, 130

U
urban decline 315
urban functions 170–71, 180, 189, 210, 304–7
urban planning 193
urban redevelopment 318–21
urban settlements 168–9, 180, 187–8, 210, 272–3
U-shaped valleys 69

V
Viking settlements 270, 302
volcanic activity 9–12, 17
V-shaped valleys 48

W
wars 228, 254, 418–19
water 335
   clean/safe 227, 248, 252–3
   conservation 337
   cycle 93–6
   pollution 248, 251, 254, 325, 337
   supply 74, 226, 248, 250, 336
   transport 297–8
   usage 337
waterfalls 49, 69
wave-cut platforms 58
waves 57, 58, 60–62, 66
weather 88–92, 94–5, 97–103, 108
weathering 30–35, 42
weirs 54
west of Ireland 236–7, 243–4, 256–7, 421
Wicklow and glaciation 74–5
wind 82–5, 86, 91, 97, 108, 113
   energy 107, 345, 382, 383
   measuring 98, 101–2
   vanes 98, 101, 102, 108
women
   and work 371–7
   status of 228, 343, 425
world climates 111, 115–30
world trade 409, 425–6

Acknowledgements

The authors and publisher would like to thank the following for permission to reproduce photos and other material:

Alamy, Bord Iascaigh Mhara, Bord na Móna (page 347), Bridgeman Images (page 272), Clúid Housing (page 319), Collins Bartholomew (pages 212–19), Colm Ashe, Conor McCarthy, Copernicus Emergency Management Service (page 55), Corbis, CSO, Covanta (page 384), Darko/Columbia Tribune (page 424), Discover Ireland (page 402), Donal Murphy Photography (page 319), Electric Ireland, Elisabetta Ravaioli (pages 324, 325, 412), ESB (pages 44, 54, 74), Fáilte Ireland, Frances Ashe, Getty Images, Graham Waters/Jantoo (page 312), Intel, Intel Ireland Photos (page 361), Irish Aid (pages 404, 414, 415), iStock, NASA, National Road Network (page 292), Nilsson-Maki, Kjell/Cartoon Stock (page 413), Nurture Africa (page 416), Nutricia Infant Nutricia Ltd. – Macroom, REUTERS/Amit Dave (page 335), Science Photo Library, Shell E & P Ireland (pages 27 and 344), Shutterstock, The Connacht Tribune Group (page 39), The Irish Times (page 320), The Royal Society of Antiquaries of Ireland (page 303), Ria Flanagan (page 316), Rose McCarthy, RUSAL Aughinish (pages 331, 367), USGS

Aerial photography

European Photo Services Ltd (Peter Barrow Photographer): Blessington, page 74; Knockrobin, page 75; Trim, page 188; Expanding Dublin, page 239; Carlingford, page 274; Shannonbridge, page 275; Trim, page 287; Navan, page 288; Shannon, pages 295 and 370; Tallaght, page 321; Intel, page 363

irelandaerialphotography.com (John Herriott Photographer): Cashel, pages 145 and 205; Charleville, page 182; Wexford, pages 182 and 203; Kilfinane, page 184; Blarney, page 185; Ardmore, page 186; Ballyduff, pages 146 and 187; Cahir, page 189; Ballybunion, page 190; Kilkenny, page 192; Blackpool, page 193; Drogheda, page 194; Nenagh, page 195; Kilmallock, page 197; Listowel, page 199; Galway, page 209; Limerick, page 274; Mitchelstown, page 275; Limerick University, page 282; Trinity, page 302; M50, page 305; Rochestown, page 317; Blessington, page 336; Danone (Macroom), page 360

Ordnance Survey Ireland: Rosslare, page 65; Wexford, page 182; Charleville, page 182; Leixlip, page 290

While every care has been taken to trace and acknowledge copyright, the publishers tender their apologies for any accidental infringement where copyright has proved untraceable. They would be pleased to come to a suitable arrangement with the rightful owner in each case